The Italian Reformers and the Zurich Church, c. 1540–1620

For my parents

The Italian Reformers and the Zurich Church, c. 1540–1620

MARK TAPLIN

ASHGATE

Published by
Ashgate Publishing Limited
Gower House
Croft Road
Aldershot
Hants GU11 3HR
England

Ashgate Publishing Company
Suite 420
101 Cherry Street
Burlington, VT 05401-4405
USA

Ashgate website: http://www.ashgate.com

British Library Cataloguing in Publication Data

Taplin, Mark
    The Italian Reformers and the Zurich Church, c. 1540–1620. –
    (St Andrews studies in Reformation history)
    1. Reformed Church (Zurich, Switzerland) – History – 16th
    century 2. Reformation – Italy 3. Italians – Switzerland –
    Zurich – History – 16th century 4. Reformation – Switzerland
    5. Protestantism – Italy – Influence
    I. Title
    274.9'457'06

Library of Congress Cataloging-in-Publication Data

Taplin, Mark, 1972–
    The Italian Reformers and the Zurich Church, c. 1540–1620 / Mark Taplin.
        p. cm. – (St. Andrews studies in Reformation history)
    Includes bibliographical references (p.).
    ISBN 0–7546–0978–2 (alk. paper)
    1. Reformation – Switzerland – Zurich. 2. Zurich (Switzerland) – Church history. 3. Italians
– Switzerland – Zurich – History. I. Title. II. Series.

BR410.T36 2003
274.94'5706'08951–dc21   2002043961

ISBN 0 7546 0978 2

Printed on acid-free paper

Typeset in Sabon by Bournemouth Colour Press, Parkstone, Poole
Printed and bound in Great Britain by MPG Books Ltd, Bodmin, Cornwall.

Contents

St Andrews Studies in Reformation History

Belief and Practice in Reformation England: A Tribute to
Patrick Collinson by his Students
edited by Susan Wabuda and Caroline Litzenberger

Frontiers of the Reformation: Dissidence and Orthodoxy
in Sixteenth-Century Europe
Auke Jelsma

The Jacobean Kirk, 1567–1625:
Sovereignty, Polity and Liturgy
Alan R. MacDonald

John Knox and the British Reformations
edited by Roger A. Mason

The Education of a Christian Society:
Humanism and the Reformation in Britain and the Netherlands
edited by N. Scott Amos, Andrew Pettegree and Henk van Nierop

Tudor Histories of the English Reformations, 1530–83
Thomas Betteridge

Poor Relief and Protestantism:
The Evolution of Social Welfare in Sixteenth-Century Emden
Timothy G. Fehler

Radical Reformation Studies:
Essays presented to James M. Stayer
edited by Werner O. Packull and Geoffrey L. Dipple

Clerical Marriage and the English Reformation:
Precedent Policy and Practice
Helen L. Parish

Penitence in the Age of Reformations
edited by Katharine Jackson Lualdi and Anne T. Thayer

The Faith and Fortunes of France's Huguenots, 1600–85
Philip Benedict

Christianity and Community in the West:
Essays for John Bossy
edited by Simon Ditchfield

Reformation, Politics and Polemics:
The Growth of Protestantism in East Anglian Market Towns, 1500–1610
John Craig

The Sixteenth-Century French Religious Book
edited by Andrew Pettegree, Paul Nelles and Philip Conner

Music as Propaganda in the German Reformation
Rebecca Wagner Oettinger

John Foxe and his World
edited by Christopher Highley and John N. King

Confessional Identity in East-Central Europe
edited by Maria Craciun, Ovidiu Ghitta and Graeme Murdock

The Bible in the Renaissance:
Essays on Biblical Commentary and Translation
in the Fifteenth and Sixteenth Centuries
edited by Richard Griffiths

Obedient Heretics:
Mennonite Identities in Lutheran Hamburg
and Altona During the Confessional Age
Michael D. Driedger

Acknowledgements

This book, and the thesis on which it is based, would not have been possible without the support of many people. Particular thanks are due to my supervisor, Dr Bruce Gordon, who first kindled my interest in early modern Zurich, and who acted as a sure and knowledgeable guide to the intellectual world of the Swiss Reformation. In Switzerland, I wish to thank Dr Heinzpeter Stucki of the Institut für schweizerische Reformationsgeschichte, Zurich, for introducing me to the Zurich archives and for helping me to locate some of the sources used in this study; Dr Hans Ulrich Bächtold, Rainer Henrich and Kurt Rüetschi, the current editors of Bullinger's correspondence, for placing their superb resources at my disposal and responding generously to requests for material; Frau Annaluisa Bonorand, for her kind hospitality during my stay in Chur in May 1997; Professor Emidio Campi and his research student, Emanuele Fiume, for sharing insights gained from their work on Bernardino Ochino and Scipione Lentolo; and the von Orelli family, for supplying me with microfilm copies of some of their unique holdings. I am grateful to the British Academy for funding me throughout my time in St Andrews; to the Friends of the St Andrews Reformation Studies Institute and the Royal Historical Society for contributing towards the cost of research trips; to Stephen Colvin and Claudia Nocentini, for assistance with some trickier passages of Latin and Italian; and to Ian Johnston, for supplying such beautifully drawn maps. I also thank the staff of all the libraries and archives that I have used in the course of my research, especially the Staatsarchiv and Zentralbibliothek Zürich; the Staatsarchiv Graubünden in Chur; the Bodleian Library, Oxford; the British Library; and St Andrews University Library. In St Andrews, thanks go to all my colleagues, past and present, at the Reformation Studies Institute, whose research in a variety of fields has enriched my own. Finally, I owe a special debt of gratitude to Sarah Colvin, whose comments on successive drafts of the text have proved invaluable, and whose presence has sustained me throughout.

Abbreviations

ADB	*Allgemeine deutsche Biographie* (56 vols, Leipzig, 1875–1912)
AERSG	Archiv der Evangelisch-Rhätischen Synode Graubündens
ARG	*Archiv für Reformationsgeschichte*
Basel UB	Universitätsbibliothek Basel
BHR	*Bibliothèque d'Humanisme et Renaissance*
BM	*Bündner Monatsblatt*
BSSV	*Bollettino della società di studi valdesi*
CCSL	*Corpus Christianorum: Series Latina* (Turnhout, 1954–)
CO	*Ioannis Calvini opera quae supersunt omnia*, ed. G. Baum, E. Cunitz, E. Reuss et al. (Braunschweig, 1834–60)
Correspondance	*Correspondance de Théodore de Bèze*, ed. F. Aubert et al. (Geneva, 1960–)
CTJ	*Calvin Theological Journal*
DBI	*Dizionario biografico degli italiani* (Rome, 1960–)
EA	*Amtliche Sammlung der ältern eidgenössischen Abschiede, 1245–1798*, ed. A.P. von Segesser et al. (8 pts, Lucerne and Berne, 1839–78)
ET	*Epistolae Tigurinae de rebus potissimum ad ecclesiae Anglicanae Reformationem pertinentibus* (Cambridge, 1848)
FA Orelli	*Familienarchiv von Orelli*
HBBibl	Staedtke, Joachim, *Heinrich Bullinger Bibliographie: Beschreibendes Verzeichnis der gedruckten Werke von Heinrich Bullinger* (Zurich, 1972)
JHGG	*Jahresbericht der Historisch-antiquarischen Gesellschaft von Graubünden*
NRS	*Nuova rivista storica*
PG	*Patrologiae cursus completus ... Series Graeca ...*, ed. J.P. Migne (Paris, 1857–87)

PL	*Patrologiae cursus completus [Series Latina] ...*, ed. J.P. Migne (Paris, 1844–55)
RCP	*Registre de la Compagnie des Pasteurs de Genève*, ed. R.M. Kingdon, J.-F. Bergier et al. (Geneva, 1964–)
RSI	*Rivista storica italiana*
Schiess	*Bullingers Korrespondenz mit den Graubündnern*, ed. T. Schiess (3 vols, Basle, 1904–06)
SCJ	*Sixteenth Century Journal*
StAG	Staatsarchiv Graubünden
StAZ	Staatsarchiv Zürich
Wotschke	*Der Briefwechsel der Schweizer mit den Polen*, ed. T. Wotschke (Leipzig, 1908)
Z	*Huldreich Zwinglis sämtliche Werke*, ed. W. Köhler et al. (Leipzig, 1905–)
ZB	Zentralbibliothek Zürich
ZL	*The Zurich Letters*, ed. H. Robinson (2 vols, Cambridge, 1842/5)

Maps

Introduction

Over the past 30 years, our understanding of the reception of Protestantism in 16th-century Italy has been transformed. What was previously regarded as merely a sideshow to the main drama of religious change that was being played out north of the Alps has begun to be recognized as a significant movement for reform in its own right. Work on the archives of the Roman Inquisition – in Venice, Modena and elsewhere – has shed new light on the popular dimension of Italian 'evangelism', revealing the existence of a network of conventicles across the peninsula which met to read the Bible, to exchange Protestant literature and even to celebrate the reformed Lord's Supper.[1] Eva-Maria Jung's definition of the Italian movement for religious reform as undogmatic, aristocratic and transitory is simply no longer tenable: rather, Italy was home to a vociferous minority of genuine Protestants, committed to the northern reformers' understanding of salvation and drawn from a reasonably broad section of society, until concerted repression began to take its toll in the 1560s.[2] The work of Massimo Firpo and Dario Marcatto on the trial of Cardinal Giovanni Morone has shown that even the 'spirituali', that group of reform-minded senior clerics which has been seen to stand for a middle way between schismatic Protestantism and the harshly defined orthodoxy of the Tridentine Counter-Reformation, were more directly implicated in introducing reformist ideas to the Italian reading public than is traditionally assumed.[3] Now, following the appearance of several excellent local studies – particularly for the north Italian cities, where evangelical ideas had the greatest appeal – a comprehensive picture of the Italian response to Protestantism is emerging.[4] General surveys of

---

[1] The formal opening to scholars of the archives of the Congregation for the Doctrine of the Faith in 1998 has provided a welcome boost to research in this field, even though the records of most Inquisition trials were destroyed in the 19th century. See F. Beretta, 'L'archivio della Congregazione del Sant'Ufficio: bilancio provvisorio della storia e natura dei fondi d'antico regime', *Rivista di Storia e Letteratura Religiosa*, 37 (2001), pp. 29–58.

[2] E.-M. Jung, 'On the Nature of Evangelism in Sixteenth-Century Italy', *Journal of the History of Ideas*, 14 (1953), pp. 511–27.

[3] M. Firpo and D. Marcatto (eds), *Il processo inquisitoriale del cardinal Giovanni Morone*, 6 vols (Rome, 1981–95).

[4] The most significant are V. Marchetti, *Gruppi ereticali senesi del Cinquecento* (Florence, 1975); S. Peyronel Rambaldi, *Speranze e crisi nel Cinquecento modenese:*

what we must now call 'the Italian Reformation' have been published by Manfred Welti, Salvatore Caponetto and Massimo Firpo,[5] while the work of future scholars has been made a great deal easier by John Tedeschi's long-awaited bibliography of secondary literature on the subject.[6]

Protestant or crypto-Protestant ideas may have attracted more popular support in Italy than was previously realized, but Italian magistrates remained committed to the Catholic status quo (despite occasional wavering that raised evangelical sympathizers' hopes for a state-sponsored Reformation along German or English lines). Emigration was the only option for those Italian evangelicals unwilling to conform outwardly, but fearful of persecution. From the early 1540s, Italian exile communities emerged in the Swiss Reformed cities, in Geneva, in the Rhaetian Freestate and in London. Like their French, Dutch and English equivalents, the Italian evangelical exiles – who included virtually the entire intellectual leadership of the movement – helped sustain the cause of reform in their homeland, producing Protestant devotional and polemical literature for Italian consumption. As one might expect, their contribution has come to figure prominently in the study of the Italian Reformation. Of the various Italian exile communities, that of Geneva – which at its height boasted around 1,000 members, 5 per cent of the city's total population – has received most attention from scholars, although a definitive modern study is still lacking.[7] Some work has also been done on the much smaller Italian

---

Tensioni religiosi e vita cittadina ai tempi di Giovanni Morone (Milan, 1979); A. Olivieri, *Riforma ed eresia a Vicenza nel Cinquecento* (Rome, 1992); J. Martin, *Venice's Hidden Enemies: Italian Heretics in a Renaissance City* (Berkeley, 1993); S. Adorni-Braccesi, *<<Una città infetta>>: La repubblica di Lucca nella crisi religiosa del Cinquecento* (Florence, 1994); and G. Dall'Olio, *Eretici e Inquisitori nella Bologna del Cinquecento* (Bologna, 1999).

[5] M. Welti, *Kleine Geschichte der italienischen Reformation* (Gütersloh, 1985); S. Caponetto, *La Riforma protestante nell'Italia del Cinquecento* (Turin, 1992); M. Firpo, *Riforma protestante ed eresie nell'Italia del Cinquecento: Un profilo storico* (Rome, 1993). Firpo's work is reviewed at length in E. Campi, 'Remarques sur l'histoire de la Réforme en Italie', *BHR*, 56 (1994), pp. 495–507.

[6] J. Tedeschi, *The Italian Reformation of the Sixteenth Century and the Diffusion of Renaissance Culture: A Bibliography of the Secondary Literature (Ca. 1750–1997)* (Ferrara, 2000). See also the bibliographical essays in Firpo, *Riforma protestante*, pp. 181–94; and Martin, *Venice's Hidden Enemies*, pp. 249–71.

[7] See A. Pascal, 'La colonia piemontese a Ginevra nel secolo XVI', in D. Cantimori et al., *Ginevra e l'Italia* (Florence, 1959), pp. 65–133; E.W. Monter, 'The Italians in Geneva, 1550–1600: A New Look', in L. Monnier (ed.), *Genève et l'Italie: Etudes publiées à l'occasion du 50e anniversaire de la Société genevoise d'études italiennes* (Geneva, 1969), pp. 53–77; and S. Adorni-Braccesi (ed.), *Vincenzo Burlamacchi: Libro di ricordi degnissimi delle nostre famiglie* (Rome, 1993).

church in London.[8] More abundant still is the literature on individual exiles, which extends not only to such celebrated emigrés as Bernardino Ochino, Celio Secundo Curione and Pier Paolo Vergerio, but to a host of minor figures. Over recent years there has been a huge expansion of interest in Peter Martyr studies.[9]

This book offers a new assessment of the activities of early modern Italian religious exiles through an investigation of their relationship with the Reformed church of Zurich. The Zurich church has long been recognized, along with Geneva, as one of the two mainsprings of the Reformed tradition within Protestantism, but historians' attention has tended to be concentrated on the early years of the Zurich Reformation, before Huldrych Zwingli's death at Kappel in October 1531. More recently, there has been a welcome revival of interest in Zwingli's successor as *Antistes* (senior minister), Heinrich Bullinger. Although a full-length modern biography of Bullinger has yet to appear, thanks to historians such as Hans Ulrich Bächtold, Pamela Biel and Bruce Gordon we now know far more about the institutional development of the Zurich church under his leadership.[10] This work has been complemented by the ongoing publication in Zurich of Bullinger's voluminous correspondence.[11] Bullinger's international role has also been brought more sharply into focus: although, for obvious reasons, events in the Swiss Confederation were uppermost in his mind, there can now be no doubt that the *Antistes* saw his pastoral office as extending far beyond Zurich and its immediate neighbours.[12] Correspondents from across

---

[8] L. Firpo, 'La chiesa italiana di Londra nel Cinquecento e i suoi rapporti con Ginevra', in *Ginevra e l'Italia*, pp. 307–412; O. Boersma, *Vluchtig Voorbeeld: de nederlandse, franse en italiaanse vluchtelingenkerken in Londen, 1568–1585* (n.p. [Kampen], 1994); and O. Boersma and A.J. Jelsma (eds), *Unity in Multiformity: The minutes of the coetus of London, 1575 and the consistory minutes of the Italian Church of London, 1570–1591* (Amsterdam, 1997).

[9] See J.P. Donnelly and R. Kingdon, *A Bibliography of the Works of Peter Martyr Vermigli* (Kirksville, Mo., 1990).

[10] H.U. Bächtold, *Heinrich Bullinger vor dem Rat: Zur Gestaltung und Verwaltung des Zürcher Staatswesens in den Jahren 1531 bis 1575* (Berne, 1982); P. Biel, *Doorkeepers at the House of Righteousness: Heinrich Bullinger and the Zurich Clergy 1535–1575* (Berne, 1991); and B. Gordon, *Clerical Discipline and the Rural Reformation: The Synod in Zürich, 1532–1580* (Berne, 1992).

[11] U. Gäbler et al. (eds), *Heinrich Bullinger Briefwechsel* (Zurich, 1973–), henceforth cited as *HBBW*. In total some 12,000 letters to and from Bullinger survive, compared with around 10,000 for Melanchthon, and just over 4,000 each for Luther and Calvin (F. Büsser, 'Die Überlieferung von Heinrich Bullingers Briefwechsel', in Büsser, *Wurzeln der Reformation in Zürich: Zum 500. Geburtstag des Reformators Huldrych Zwingli* (Leiden, 1985), pp. 125–42 [126]).

[12] See A. Mühling, *Heinrich Bullingers europäische Kirchenpolitik* (Berne, 2001) (especially for the Empire); A. Schindler and H. Stickelberger (eds), *Die Zürcher*

Europe sought his advice, commendation and support, and translations of works such as the *Decades* appeared in most major European vernaculars.[13] Bullinger's crowning theological achievement, the Second Helvetic Confession (1566), was adopted by Reformed believers throughout the continent alongside their own national statements of faith.[14]

In his classic study *Eretici italiani del Cinquecento* – still an essential point of reference for students of the Italian Reformation – Delio Cantimori suggested that the theology of the Zurich church exercised a special hold over the imaginations of Italy's evangelicals.[15] Although one ought not to exaggerate the extent to which the latter had imbibed Zwinglian doctrine prior to their emigration – the Italian evangelical movement was subject to a wide array of theological influences, as we shall see – there can be no doubt that Bullinger's special concern for fellow believers who had suffered persecution or hardship for the sake of the faith provided a basis for close relations between the Zurich church and those Italian-speaking exiles who settled in the Swiss Confederation and Graubünden. Bullinger's correspondence contains around 500 letters to and from Italian-speaking evangelicals, many of which have yet to be published. Besides this correspondence, I draw on a variety of materials from Swiss sources, including theological works – both published and unpublished – by the Zurich divines and their Italian associates; council and synodal records; and the records of Zurich's own Italian-speaking community.

A central concern of this study is the role of the so-called 'heretics', that group of doctrinally heterodox exiles whom Cantimori describes as 'rebels against every form of organized and ecclesiastical religious

---

Reformation: Ausstrahlungen und Rückwirkungen (Berne, 2001). The key source for relations between Zurich and England remains the correspondence published by the Parker Society in the 19th century. On Bullinger's contacts with the French Reformed, see A. Bouvier, *Henri Bullinger, réformateur et conseiller oecuménique, le successeur de Zwingli, d'après sa correspondance avec les réformés et les humanistes de langue française* (Neuchâtel, 1940).

[13] See J. Staedtke, *Heinrich Bullinger Bibliographie: Beschreibendes Verzeichnis der gedruckten Werke von Heinrich Bullinger* (Zurich, 1972).

[14] J. Staedtke (ed.), *Glauben und Bekennen: Vierhundert Jahre Confessio Helvetica Posterior: Beiträge zu ihrer Geschichte und Theologie* (Zurich, 1966).

[15] D. Cantimori, *Eretici italiani del Cinquecento e altri scritti*, ed. A. Prosperi (Turin, 1992), p. 98: 'I zurighesi dovevano avere agli occhi di quegli italiani ... il pregio di aver per primi posto in atto la <<libertà christiana>> com'essi la intendevano, osando porre la verità al di sopra dell'unità, e resistendo all'autorevolezza e alla violenza di un Lutero. E i libri del Bullinger, con la loro dottrina, con le loro argomentazioni umanistiche che risentivano la preparazione erasmiana, con la loro preoccupazione di chiarezza e semplicità, dovevano attrarre particolarmente gli intelletti italiani.'

community'.[16] Cantimori took the heretics as his principal subject, identifying their radicalism, which reached its apogee in Socinianism, as Italy's unique and original contribution to the Reformation: a contribution that owed more to the legacy of Quattrocento humanism than to the ideas of the northern reformers. Subsequent scholarship has made clear that heresy of the kind emphasized by Cantimori – whose approach was much influenced by his own ideological development towards Marxism during the 1930s – was a minority tendency.[17] The religious landscape of 16th-century Italy was not dominated by Anabaptists or antitrinitarians, although the largely informal structure of the Italian evangelical conventicles did create space for a diversity of theological viewpoints unseen in those countries whose Protestant communities were subject to a process of 'confession-building' from an early stage. At least as many Italian exiles distinguished themselves by their commitment to Reformed orthodoxy as did by the profession of heretical ideas, and the majority of emigrants swiftly accommodated themselves to the doctrinal and disciplinary regimes prevalent in the northern Protestant churches. However, the impact of the heretics' activities, both on the exile communities which harboured them, and on relations between the exiles and their Swiss, German or English hosts, was out of all proportion to their numbers. Their criticisms of Reformed orthodoxy – and the Zurich church's response – form the centrepiece of this study, because they influenced how Italian evangelicals as a whole came to be perceived by the Protestant establishment: as intellectually restless, quarrelsome, and resistant to discipline.

The characterization is one associated particularly with Calvin, whose 'dogmatism' is sometimes played off against the 'free thinking' of the heretics.[18] It was accepted less readily by the Zurich church, whose definition of orthodoxy was comparatively flexible in some areas – notably predestination – up until the early 1560s. Bullinger was averse to doctrinal hair-splitting and the acrimonious disagreements between theologians to which it often led: as we shall see, he was prepared to make concessions to tender consciences in private, in the interests of preserving the public unity of the church. Such moderation goes some way towards explaining why Bullinger and the church over

---

[16] Cantimori, *Eretici*, p. 5. I use the term 'heretic' in this specific Cantimorian sense throughout.

[17] See *Eretici*, pp. xi–lxii; and Massimo Firpo's historiographical introduction to Tedeschi, *Italian Reformation*, especially pp. xliv–xlvi.

[18] But see the criticisms of this approach by V. Subilia, 'Libertà e dogma secondo Calvino e secondo i riformatori italiani', in Cantimori et al., *Ginevra e l'Italia*, pp. 191–214.

which he presided continued to be held in high regard by some Italian radicals long after they had become alienated from other Reformed leaders. However, it should not be confused with modern conceptions of religious tolerance: Bullinger's record of fighting Anabaptism, and his unabashed support for the execution of Michael Servetus, provide evidence of his determination to combat heresy wherever it manifested itself openly. His initial reluctance to move swiftly from correction to condemnation when dealing with the Italian radicals seems to have stemmed from a basic misunderstanding of the heretics' intentions – often articulated as a desire for clarification rather than as open criticism of Reformed doctrine – and from a failure to comprehend the extent to which their radical reconception of the Reformation enterprise differed from his own, essentially conservative, vision. Once the incorrigibility of the heretics had become apparent, Bullinger and his colleagues were as vigorous as any in their efforts to combat dissenting activity. This book is an attempt to explain how they moved towards that position.

The study is divided into six chapters. After a brief examination of the Zurich church's contribution to the spread of Protestant ideas in Italy itself, Chapter 1 summarizes the initial contacts between the Zurichers and Italian evangelical exiles, beginning with the arrival in Switzerland of the first significant wave of religious refugees in the early 1540s. In the final part of the chapter, I discuss the Zurich divines' early clashes over doctrine with such heterodox exiles as Camillo Renato, Celio Secundo Curione and Lelio Sozzini, and assess the implications of these exchanges for future relations between the two groups.

Chapter 2 opens with an account of the events which led to the formation of an Italian-speaking church in Zurich, made up primarily of evangelical refugees from the Swiss-ruled territory of Locarno. Consideration is given to the role of Bullinger and his fellow ministers in persuading the Zurich authorities first to receive the Locarnese exiles, and then to fund the establishment of a semi-autonomous Italian congregation in the city, led by Bernardino Ochino; this episode offers one of the most graphic examples of the Zurich church's commitment to the international Reformed cause in general, and to the plight of its Italian-speaking co-religionists in particular. Building on the work of earlier historians of the Zurich Locarnesi, such as Ferdinand Meyer,[19] I examine the make-up and organization of Zurich's Italian church, its contacts with other Italian exile communities (in Geneva, Graubünden

---

[19] F. Meyer, *Die evangelische Gemeinde von Locarno, ihre Auswanderung und ihre weitern Schicksale: Ein Beitrag zur Geschichte der Schweiz im sechszehnten Jahrhundert* (2 vols, Zurich, 1836).

and Basle), and its relations with the Zurich authorities and population during the eight years of its separate existence (1555–63).

Chapter 3 offers a reassessment of what I term the 'Ochino affair': the controversy triggered by the unauthorized publication in spring 1563 of Bernardino Ochino's *Dialogi XXX*, which resulted in Ochino's dismissal and the end of formal Italian-language worship in Zurich. Particular emphasis is given to this traumatic episode because it provides clear evidence for the Zurich church's adoption, from around 1560, of a much less indulgent attitude towards those Italian exiles who refused to give unqualified assent to Reformed teaching on matters such as soteriology and the Trinity.

The 'treachery' of Ochino, who had been lionized by the Reformed following his conversion to Protestantism in August 1542, and who had since earned himself a considerable reputation as a preacher and propagandist, was not easily forgotten by Bullinger and his colleagues. It influenced the stance that they took in other doctrinal disputes generated by Italian exiles in eastern Europe and Graubünden during the 1560s and early 1570s. Those disputes are the subject of Chapters 4 and 5, which provide a counterweight to the traditional perception of the Zurich theological tradition as eirenic and undogmatic by highlighting the increasing 'confessionalism' of Bullinger and younger Zurich divines such as Josias Simler. Both Simler and the later Bullinger emphasized the need for an explicit and comprehensive definition of orthodoxy, which would safeguard the doctrinal integrity of the church against subversion by the sort of queries and veiled criticisms that the Zurichers had previously been prepared to tolerate from some of their Italian associates. This stance was endorsed by a vociferous group of clerics drawn from among the exiles themselves (for example, Agostino Mainardi, Scipione Lentolo and Giulio da Milano). In the Reformed churches of Italian-speaking Graubünden those ministers were able, with the active support of the Zurichers, to ensure that dissenting elements were either eliminated or silenced.

The defeat of the heretics did not end the Zurich church's association with the Italian exiles: rather, the alliance forged between the Zurichers and orthodox ministers in Graubünden during the struggle against religious radicalism became the basis for renewed co-operation over subsequent decades. Because of scholars' understandable fascination with the dramatic confrontations of the earlier period, this later phase of the relationship has not been adequately explored in the existing literature, leaving the impression that doctrinal conflict was a consistent feature of the Zurich church's relations with those Italian evangelicals with whom it had contact. However, that was true only for the years prior to 1570, and even then only in part (the close working relationship which developed between Bullinger and Peter Martyr Vermigli is a case in point).[20] Chapter 6 identifies ways in which Bullinger's successors in the Zurich church continued to offer the Italian congregations of Graubünden practical assistance and encouragement, through an examination of their correspondence with exiles based in Chiavenna and the Valtellina (principally Scipione Lentolo, Scipione Calandrini and Ulisse Martinengo). The relationship was interrupted only by the 'sacro macello' of July 1620, which destroyed the once thriving Reformed communities of the Valtellina.

Through this study, I aim to contribute to the ongoing reassessment of Zurich's role in the wider European Reformation, which is itself testimony to scholars' increasing awareness of the multicentredness of 16th-century Reformed Protestantism. Thus far, interest has been focused on Bullinger but many of the *Antistes*' colleagues and successors were also significant figures within the international Reformed movement. It is to be hoped that in future years some of the churchmen who feature prominently in the pages of this book – Rudolf Gwalther, Johannes Wolf, Josias Simler, Johann Wilhelm Stucki and Kaspar Waser – will become objects of study in their own right. There is still a chronic shortage of secondary literature on the history of the Zurich church after Bullinger, which is only now beginning to be addressed.[21]

The book also feeds into the wider literature devoted to the phenomenon of exile *religionis causa* during the 16th century,[22] which historians such as Ole Peter Grell have deemed 'of paramount importance in providing Calvinism with an international character'.[23] More generally, it offers insights into the process by which a distinctive and precisely articulated Reformed 'confession' became established around the middle part of the century. The case of Bernardino Ochino, which is pivotal to the entire study, is particularly instructive in this

---

[20] Michael Baumann of the University of Zurich is currently preparing a doctoral thesis on Vermigli in Zurich. In the meantime, see M. Anderson, *Peter Martyr: A Reformer in Exile (1542–1562): A chronology of biblical writings in England and Europe* (Nieuwkoop, 1975); '*Vista Tigurina*: Peter Martyr and European Reform (1556–1562)', *Harvard Theological Review*, 83 (1990), pp. 181–206.

[21] A number of useful articles are available on Gwalther. See K. Rüetschi, 'Rudolf Gwalthers Kontakte zu Engländern und Schotten', in Schindler and Stickelberger, *Zürcher Reformation*, pp. 351–73, with further bibliographical references.

[22] This is best exemplified by A. Pettegree, *Foreign Protestant Communities in Sixteenth-Century London* (Oxford, 1986).

[23] O.P. Grell, 'Merchants and ministers: the foundations of international Calvinism', in A. Pettegree, A. Duke and G. Lewis (eds), *Calvinism in Europe, 1540–1620* (Cambridge, 1994), pp. 254–73.

regard. During the 1540s and early 1550s, Ochino's eclectic brand of Protestantism, anchored in justification by faith but not easily reducible to a single confessional system (hence, perhaps, his ability to move between such different contexts as Geneva, Basle, Augsburg and England) had proved broadly acceptable in Reformed circles. By 1563 that was no longer the case: the trend within Reformed theology was towards systematization, towards reconstructing a precise doctrinal framework into which the exegetical achievements of Reformed biblical scholarship could be incorporated. Ochino, and the other heterodox Italian exiles whose relations with Zurich are considered here, were casualties of that process. To that extent, their fate illuminates a crucial phase in the development of Reformed orthodoxy.

Note on Orthography, Translations and Some Terms Used

Most of the quotations in this study are taken from sources in one of three languages: Latin, German and Italian. The use of u/v has been adjusted throughout to conform to modern usage. In Latin quotations, i/j has usually been rendered as i. In quotations from Swiss German, certain forms of the vowel have been simplified, with superscript 'e' being rendered as an umlaut. Original punctuation has been retained where possible, but occasionally changes have been made for the sake of clarity.

Longer quotations appear in translation in the main body of the text, and in the source language in the footnotes (except where the passage cited is available in a modern edition). Translations are my own, unless otherwise stated.

Following established practice, I have used the term *Antistes* to designate the senior minister of the Zurich and other Swiss Reformed churches. The 16th-century federation – and modern Swiss canton – often known in English as the Grisons is here referred to as either Graubünden, the Rhaetian Freestate, or simply Rhaetia.

CHAPTER ONE

Zurich and the Italian Reformers to 1555

During the late medieval period, Zurich's contacts with the Italian peninsula were comparatively limited in scope. Some economic ties are documented: Zurich exported basic commodities such as cattle, hides and tallow to northern Italy, and was in turn supplied with iron and steel (from Como) and wine (from the Valtellina).[1] The city's geographical position, along the vital north–south axis linking the commercial centre of Nuremberg with Como, Milan and Genoa, also provided some Zurich merchants with an opportunity to engage in transalpine trade; between 1479 and 1517, for example, the important Ravensburg-based trading company known as the *Humpisgesellschaft* was represented in Genoa by Zurichers (Hans Kloter the Elder and Younger).[2] However, activities of this sort were confined to a handful of individuals and did not contribute greatly to what was, by the late 15th century, a more or less self-contained economy.

In strategic terms, too, Italy was of peripheral interest to Zurich's ruling elite, whose expansionist ambitions had historically been directed eastwards, towards the shores of Lake Constance and such territories as the Thurgau, Toggenburg and St Gallen. Although the Swiss Confederation emerged as a major player on the Italian political and military scene in the mid-1490s, the driving force behind the Swiss Italian campaigns of the early 16th century was not Zurich, but the inner states of Uri, Schwyz and Unterwalden, which were eager to secure control of the southern approaches to the Gotthard. In any case, military involvement in the affairs of Italy does not in the first instance seem to have been accompanied by enhanced intellectual or cultural ties. During the 15th and early 16th centuries, Italian universities ceased to attract Swiss students in large numbers, as they flocked to the newer centres of higher education springing up across the Empire (Basle, Vienna, Heidelberg and Erfurt were among the more popular choices).[3]

---

[1] H. Peyer, *Vom Handel und Bank im alten Zürich* (Zurich, 1968), p. 11; W. Schnyder, *Handel und Verkehr über die Bündner Pässe im Mittelalter zwischen Deutschland, der Schweiz und Oberitalien* (2 vols, Zurich, 1973/5), I, pp. 55, 59.

[2] Schnyder, *Handel*, I, pp. 96–7.

[3] S. Stelling-Michaud, 'La Suisse et les universités européennes du 13ème au 16ème

Throughout this period Zurichers continued to study in Italy, sometimes with the assistance of papal scholarships,[4] but Zurich itself was largely untouched by the new learning of the Italian Renaissance.[5] Culturally, the city remained in the shadow of Basle, with its flourishing printing industry, and Berne, which had succeeded in attracting the humanists Heinrich Wölfli, Valerius Anselm and Melchior Volmar to teach at its Latin school.[6] Even printing was slow to take root in Zurich: only two printers, Sigmund Rot and Hans Rüegger, were active in the city before 1517, and their (modest) production consisted in the main of papal bulls of indulgence and other traditional material.[7]

With the onset of the Reformation in the early 1520s, new opportunities for contact between Zurich and Italy manifested themselves. The establishment in June 1525 of the Zurich *Prophezei*, which served as the prototype for Reformed academies across Europe, provided a huge impetus for the development in Zurich of a humanist intellectual culture which appropriated many of the ideals and philological techniques of Italian Renaissance scholarship. Significantly, two of the early lecturers at the *Prophezei*, Jakob Ammann (1500–73) and Rudolf Collin (1499–1578), had studied in Milan prior to their conversions.[8] Zwingli himself owned an impressive collection of Italian humanist texts, among them works by Sabellicus, Poliziano, Ficino, and Giovanni and Gianfrancesco Pico;[9] one scholar has even been tempted to draw comparisons between elements of his mature theology and

siècle: Essai d'une statistique de fréquentation', *Revue universitaire suisse* (September 1938), pp. 148–60.

[4] M. Sieber, *Die Universität Basel und die Eidgenossenschaft 1460 bis 1529* (Basle, 1960), p. 69.

[5] P. Bänziger, *Beiträge zur Geschichte der Spätscholastik und des Frühhumanismus in der Schweiz* (Zurich, 1945), p. 85. According to Potter, 'the three Regular Orders represented in Zurich – Dominicans, Franciscans and Augustinians – did almost nothing for scholarship' (G.R. Potter, 'The Renaissance in Switzerland', *Journal of Medieval History*, 2 (1976), pp. 365–82 [371]).

[6] U.M. Zahnd, 'Lateinschule-Universität-Prophezey: Zu den Wandlungen im Schulwesen eidgenössischer Städte in der ersten Hälfte des 16. Jahrhunderts', in H. Dickerhof (ed.), *Bildungs- und schulgeschichtliche Studien zu Spätmittelalter, Reformation und konfessionellem Zeitalter* (Wiesbaden, 1994), pp. 91–115 (95–6).

[7] M. Vischer, *Bibliographie der Zürcher Druckschriften des 15. und 16. Jahrhunderts* (Baden-Baden, 1991), pp. 27–31.

[8] C. Bonorand, 'Mitteleuropäische Studenten in Pavia zur Zeit der Kriege in Italien (ca.1500 bis ca.1550)', *Pluteus*, 4–5 (1986–87), pp. 295–357 (326–7).

[9] Some of these works contain extensive marginal annotations dating from Zwingli's time in Glarus, on which see A. Schindler, 'Zwinglis Randbemerkungen in den Büchern seiner Bibliothek: Ein Zwischenbericht über editorische Probleme', *Zwa*, 18/1 (1989/1), pp. 1–11; and I. Backus, 'Randbemerkungen Zwinglis in den Werken von Giovanni Pico della Mirandola', *Zwa*, 18/4 (1990/2), pp. 291–309.

Florentine Neoplatonism.[10] Zwingli's successor as leader of the Zurich church, Heinrich Bullinger, had less direct exposure to Italian Renaissance thought – the formative influences on his theology were Netherlandish (the *devotio moderna*) and north German – but that did not prevent him from placing a high value on the intellectual achievements of figures such as Manuel Chrysoloras, Lorenzo Valla and Angelo Poliziano. In particular, he commended the Florentine revival of Greek studies, which had made possible Erasmus' recovery of the original text of the New Testament.[11]

More importantly for our purposes, Italy provided the Zurich reformers with a potential mission-field. From as early as 1518, when Luther's *Appellatio ad Concilium* was reprinted in Venice,[12] there is evidence that evangelical ideas were attracting support from sections of the Italian reading public; the works of northern reformers were relatively easy to come by in both Latin and (often disguised) vernacular translations. In the first part of this chapter, I shall offer a brief assessment of the Zurich church's contribution to the spread of Protestantism in Italy, and attempt to piece together what is known of its relations with the nascent Italian evangelical movement. Those contacts formed the backdrop to the relationship between the Zurich divines and the increasing number of Italian evangelicals who, from around 1540, began to settle in the Swiss Confederation, Geneva and the Rhaetian Freestate. As will become clear, this was a relationship which, almost from its inception, oscillated between co-operation and conflict: co-operation based on a shared commitment to the principle of reform, conflict as a minority of exiles struggled to come to terms with Protestantism as it had been institutionalized north of the Alps.

i. The Zurich church and the Reformation in Italy

The first reference to contacts between the Zurich reformers and evangelical sympathizers in Italy is tantalizingly vague. In the prefatory

---

[10] Schindler detects echoes of Giovanni Pico's *Oratio de dignitate hominis* in the opening to Zwingli's *De providentia*, although the anthropology of the work as a whole is pessimistic and unmistakably 'Reformed'. He also notes Zwingli's openness to the possibility of extra-biblical revelation in the pre-Christian dispensation, reminiscent to some degree of Pico's syncretistic approach. See A. Schindler, 'Huldrych Zwingli e Giovanni Pico della Mirandola', in *Dall'accademia neoplatonica fiorentina alla Riforma: Celebrazione del V centenario della morte di Lorenzo il Magnifico* (Florence, 1996), pp. 51–65 (60–63).

[11] J. Staedtke, *Die Theologie des jungen Bullinger* (Zurich, 1962), pp. 29–34.

[12] U. Rozzo and S. Seidel Menchi, 'The book and the Reformation in Italy', in J.-F. Gilmont (ed.), *The Reformation and the Book* (Aldershot, 1998), pp. 319–67 (321).

epistle to his *Commentarius de vera et falsa religione* of 1525, Zwingli describes the work as a response to requests for a concise summary of Christian doctrine from fellow-believers in Italy and France, but offers no clue as to the identity of these Italian 'brethren'.[13] Soon after the publication of the *Commentarius*, however, Zwingli received a letter from an Augustinian monk based in Como, Egidio da Porta, in which the latter made clear his disenchantment with Catholicism and requested instruction in the Reformed faith.[14] Zwingli's reply has not survived, but one can assume that it was encouraging, because in December 1526 Da Porta again wrote to the Zurich reformer, this time with the news that he and his colleagues had set to work on a vernacular translation of the New Testament. Da Porta also asked that Zwingli write to his superiors in the order, to request a relaxation of discipline, and to the duke of Milan, to press the case for religious and social reform.[15]

Little is known about the subsequent fate of Da Porta's evangelical circle,[16] but there is every reason to believe that his enthusiasm for Zwinglian reform was shared by other members of the Augustinian order, which in Italy (as elsewhere) produced numerous converts to Protestantism.[17] Of particular interest in this connection is a letter addressed to Zwingli in August 1529 from Sondrio in the Valtellina. Its author, who went under the pseudonym 'Augustinus Saturnius' (Augustine the Italian), sought Zwingli's help in publishing a (Latin?) grammar that he had written; he also made no secret of his evangelical sympathies, praising the reformer for his 'supercelestial gifts in Christ'. According to the editors of Zwingli's correspondence, 'Saturnius' was none other than Agostino Mainardi, who held a series of senior positions within the Lombard province of the Augustinian Hermits before coming under suspicion of heresy towards the end of the 1530s.[18] Later we shall encounter him as minister to the Reformed congregation

---

[13] See the editors' comments in Z, III, 591, n. 1.

[14] Z, VIII, no. 421.

[15] Ibid., no. 558. These letters are discussed at length in W. Köhler, 'Zwingli und Italien', in *Aus fünf Jahrhunderten Schweizerischer Kirchengeschichte: Festschrift zum 60. Geburtstag von Paul Wernle* (Basle, 1932), pp. 21–38 (30–32).

[16] Da Porta himself was later reconciled to the church, eventually serving as vicar general to the Mantuan chapter of the Augustinian Hermits (S. Peyronel Rambaldi, *Dai Paesi Bassi all'Italia: <<Il sommario della sacra scrittura>>: Un libro proibito nella società italiana del Cinquecento* (Florence, 1997), p. 79).

[17] On the Reformation and the Italian Augustinians more generally, see ibid., pp. 73–109; Caponetto, *Riforma*, pp. 24–8.

[18] Z, X, no. 884. See also P. Ricca, 'Zwingli tra i Valdesi', *Zwa*, 16/3 (1984/1), pp. 247–62 (254–6); and Köhler, 'Zwingli und Italien', p. 33. The standard biography of Mainardi is still A. Armand Hugon, *Agostino Mainardo: Contributo alla storia della Riforma in Italia* (Torre Pellice, n.d. [1943]).

of Chiavenna. In his letter, Mainardi refers Zwingli for further information to a certain 'presbyter Bartolomeus', probably the former Dominican Bartolomeo Maturo, who is credited with having introduced the Reformation to the Valtellina.[19]

These first tentative exchanges were nipped in the bud by Zurich's disastrous defeat in the Second Kappel War (October 1531). The defeat forced a reassessment of priorities in Zurich. Under pressure from a rural population that laid the blame for Kappel squarely at the door of meddling foreign clerics, the city's rulers – who had never been comfortable with Zwingli's vision of Zurich as the fulcrum of an anti-papal alliance stretching from the Adriatic to the Baltic – returned to a more conservative foreign policy. This change in direction was reflected in the Zurich church, which as the price for continued magisterial commitment to the Reformation was forced to accept a more limited political role and restrictions on its 'prophetic' office.[20] Under the leadership of Heinrich Bullinger, the Zurich church remained an important player in the ecclesiastical politics of Reformed Switzerland and of the Empire more generally, but before 1540 Bullinger and his colleagues do not appear to have given much thought to the progress of the Reformation further afield, especially in Italy; indeed, news of any kind from Italy barely features in Bullinger's correspondence for this period.[21] Superficially at least, this lack of interest appears to have been reciprocated from the Italian side. During the 1520s and early 1530s, Italian responses to the Reformation, whether hostile or sympathetic, centred for the most part on the figure of Luther, the 'monster of Saxony'.[22] Whereas 14 Italian editions of Luther's works have been identified for the period 1525 to 1566, Italian translations of works by Zwingli are conspicuous by their absence. This lacuna is difficult to account for, though Salvatore Caponetto has suggested that the violent circumstances of Zwingli's death caused the many Italian Erasmians who might otherwise have found his theology attractive to distance themselves from it.[23]

---

[19] See E. Arbenz and H. Wartmann (eds), *Der Vadianische Briefwechsel der Stadtbibliothek St. Gallen* (7 vols, St Gallen, 1890–1913), IV, no. 571.

[20] Bächtold, *Bullinger*, pp. 15–24.

[21] For a rare example, see Bullinger to Oswald Myconius, 1 September 1537 (*HBBW*, VII, no. 1037), in which the *Antistes* reports rumours of an imminent Turkish invasion of southern Italy.

[22] O. Niccoli, 'Il mostro di Sassonia: Conoscenza e non conoscenza di Lutero in Italia nel Cinquecento (1520–1530 ca.)', in L. Perrone (ed.), *Lutero in Italia: Studi storici nel V centenario della nascita* (Casale Monferrato, 1983), pp. 3–25.

[23] Caponetto, *Riforma*, pp. 53–4. A list of known Italian editions of the works of northern reformers published between 1525 to 1566 appears in Rozzo and Seidel

On the other hand, there is plenty of evidence to suggest that the works of Zwingli, Bullinger and other Zurich writers were available in Italy in Latin editions. In April 1533 Johannes Comander, the reformer of Chur, informed Joachim Vadian that he had responded to requests for Protestant literature from evangelical sympathizers in Italy by sending copies of works by Zwingli, Oecolampadius and Bucer (although not by Luther, for fear of stirring up controversy over the interpretation of the Eucharist).[24] Some years later Comander's colleague, Philipp Gallicius, reported that he was sending a copy of Bullinger's *Decades* to the Rhaetian magnate Anton Travers to be bound and presented to 'a certain good man' in Italy.[25] In addition, various Italian evangelical exiles are recorded as having read works by the Zurich reformers prior to their conversions. Girolamo Zanchi, for example, claimed to have bought and annotated a copy of Bullinger's *De origine erroris*, after the work was recommended to him by a certain Montalcinus;[26] similarly, Zwingli's *Commentarius de vera et falsa religione* and *De providentia* were among the Protestant works that Peter Martyr Vermigli read during his time as abbot to the Augustinian house of San Pietro ad Aram in Naples.[27] The *Commentarius* was in circulation among the Waldenses of Piedmont (who may have been introduced to Zwingli's doctrine of the Eucharist by Guillaume Farel) as early as 1535.[28]

Zurich-based writers also featured prominently on the Indices of prohibited books which began to be issued by the Italian states from the mid-1540s.[29] Of the 47 authors whose *opera omnia* were proscribed in the 1549 Venetian Index, four were or had been based in Zurich

---

Menchi, 'The book and the Reformation', pp. 346–54. On the reception of Luther's works in Italy, see also S. Seidel Menchi, 'Le traduzioni italiane di Lutero nella prima metà del Cinquecento', *Rinascimento*, 17 (1977), pp. 31–108.

[24]   *Vadian BW*, V, no. 732; compare ibid., no. 798.

[25]   Schiess, I, no. 265.

[26]   Zanchi to Bullinger, 24 June 1568 (*Epistolarum libri duo*, II, 128–9, in *Clarissimi viri D. Hieronymi Zanchii omnium operum theologicorum tomi octo* (Geneva, 1619); StAZ E II 356a, 833–5). 'Montalcinus' is to be identified with the Franciscan Conventual Giovanni Buzio da Montalcino, who was executed for heresy in Rome on 4 September 1553 (*DBI*, XV, 632–4; Caponetto, *Riforma*, p. 76).

[27]   J. Simler, *Oratio de vita et obitu Petri Martyris Vermilii, Sacrarum literarum in Schola Tigurina Professoris* (Zurich, 1563), fol. 7ʳ; P. McNair, *Peter Martyr in Italy: An Anatomy of Apostasy* (Oxford, 1967), p. 149. Vermigli later praised the *De providentia*, but J.P. Donnelly doubts whether the Florentine's understanding of predestination was influenced by his reading of this work (Donnelly, *Calvinism and Scholasticism in Vermigli's Doctrine of Man and Grace* (Leiden, 1976), pp. 128–9).

[28]   Ricca, 'Zwingli tra i Valdesi', pp. 249–51.

[29]   The Indices are analysed fully in P. Grendler, *The Roman Inquisition and the Venetian Press, 1540–1605* (Princeton, 1977), pp. 71–127.

(Zwingli, Bullinger, Konrad Pellikan and Theodor Bibliander).[30] Titles deemed worthy of specific censure included Zwingli's *Commentarius* and *Religionis antiquae capita* (in an edition published under the pseudonym of Charieus Cogelius); Rudolf Gwalther's *Antichristus*; and Bibliander's *Ad omnium ordinum reipublicae Christianae principes viros populumque Christianum relatio*.[31] The 1554 Index added Gwalther, Konrad Gesner, Leo Jud, Johannes Fries and Otto Werdmüller to the list of condemned authors.[32] New to appear among the proscribed works were Zwingli's *Supplicatio ad Hugonem Episcopum Constantiensem* and *Ad Matthaeum Alberum epistola*, the Zurich Latin Bible of 1539, Leo Jud's large and small catechisms, Gwalther's *Apology for Zwingli*, Bullinger's *Utriusque in Christo naturae assertio orthodoxa*, and an unspecified *Confessio ecclesiae Tigurinae de coena domini*. The Indices do not in themselves provide an accurate guide to what Italian evangelicals were reading,[33] but inventories of books seized by the Inquisition from suspected heretics confirm that works by Zurich churchmen were the subject of interest in Italian philo-Protestant circles. Among the texts owned by the Augustinian preacher Giulio da Milano at the time of his arrest in Venice in late 1540, for instance, were Bullinger's commentaries on the Pauline epistles and Acts, and Pellikan's *Repertorium Bibliae*.[34] The leading Venetian evangelical Francesco Stella also owned exegetical works by the Zurich divines, in this case Bullinger and Bibliander.[35]

Assessing the theological impact that such works may have had on their readers is no easy task. The Italian evangelical movement lacked a precise confessional identity, and its adherents did not obviously discriminate between 'Reformed' and 'Lutheran' writers in their choice of reading. Ugo Rozzo and Silvana Seidel Menchi have described the movement as tending towards 'an evangelical syncretism' – that is to say, an eirenical outlook that emphasized fundamental areas of doctrinal

---

[30] Grendler, *Roman Inquisition*, p. 86; J.M. De Bujanda (ed.), *Index des livres interdits III: Index de Venise 1549; Venise et Milan 1554* (Geneva, 1987), with an introduction by P. Grendler.

[31] For details, see De Bujanda, *Index*.

[32] Grendler, *Roman Inquisition*, p. 95.

[33] Bibliander, for instance, was one of 14 authors incorporated into the 1549 Venetian Index en bloc from the Paris Indices of 1544 and 1547 (De Bujanda, *Index*, p. 75). Konrad Gesner's *Bibliotheca universalis* was the source for many of the new titles included on the Index of 1554 (ibid., pp. 94–8).

[34] Rozzo and Seidel Menchi, 'The book and the Reformation', p. 339.

[35] See the inventory published in L. Perini, 'Ancora sul libraio-tipografo Pietro Perna e su alcune figure di eretici italiani in rapporto con lui negli anni 1549–1555', *NRS*, 51 (1967), pp. 363–404 (387–94).

agreement over divisions.[36] The popularity in Italy of works by the Augsburg reformer Urbanus Rhegius has been attributed precisely to the fact that his theology spanned the Lutheran–Reformed divide.[37]

The influence of views associated specifically with the Zurich church is most easily discerned in relation to the controversial topic of the Eucharist. By the early 1540s, it is clear that Zwingli's alleged 'sacramentarianism' had become a subject of debate (and a source of disagreement) within the north Italian conventicles. In the aftermath of the colloquy of Regensburg, the Strasbourg reformer Martin Bucer tackled the issue in a series of letters to certain 'Italian brethren', first in Bologna and Modena, and subsequently also in Venice and Ferrara.[38] In these letters, Bucer warned his correspondents against emulating the example of Germany's Protestants, now hopelessly divided over the sacrament. He argued that the incompatibility of the Lutheran and Zwinglian positions was more apparent than real, although both sides were guilty of using inappropriate language (with opposing results) when discussing the mode of Christ's presence in the Eucharist. Thus 'when [Luther] says that the bread is the body of Christ, or that the body of Christ is really present in the bread, it seems to me at any rate that – even if he himself does not understand this in a corporeal sense exactly – he is using language that might induce others to think that the Lord's body is in some crude sense united with or enclosed in the bread'. Zwingli, by contrast, while correctly teaching a form of spiritual presence in the sacrament, 'often spoke in such a watered-down fashion of the Lord's presence ... that he seemed to many to acknowledge in the Lord's Supper only a symbol of something absent'.[39] In place of the 'extremes' of Wittenberg and Zurich, Bucer offered his own mediating interpretation of the sacrament: any suggestion of a fleshly presence or of the *manducatio impiorum* was refuted (against Luther), but the true communion of believers with the body and blood of Christ, dispensed with the elements, was firmly upheld.[40]

---

36 Rozzo and Seidel Menchi, 'The book and the Reformation', p. 343.

37 S. Cavazza, 'Libri in volgare e propaganda eterodossa: Venezia 1543–1547', in A. Prosperi and A. Biondi (eds), *Libri, idee e sentimenti religiosi nel Cinquecento italiano* (Modena, 1987), pp. 9–28 (20–21).

38 For the first two letters, dated 17 August and 10 September 1541, see *Martini Buceri Scripta Anglicana fere omnia ...* (Basle, 1577), pp. 685–9. The complete text of the third letter, dated 23 December, is published in P. Simoncelli, 'Inquisizione romana e Riforma in Italia', *RSI*, 100 (1988), pp. 5–125 (107–12).

39 Simoncelli, 'Inquisizione romana', p. 111.

40 *Scripta Anglicana*, p. 687: 'Panem ... quem frangimus, non panis tantum: sed etiam corporis sui esse communicationem, et calicem gratiarum actionis sanguinis sui, non vini tantum.'

Bucer's appeal to his Italian co-religionists to avoid 'a spirit of curiosity and contention' appears to have fallen on deaf ears. The following year, the Venetian evangelical Baldassare Altieri informed Luther that, to his dismay, the German Eucharistic schism had now infected the Italian philo-Protestant movement.[41] In the first instance, Venice's evangelicals appear to have conformed to Luther's understanding of the sacrament. In August 1543, Altieri assured the Wittenberg reformer: 'We love, respect and are joined in the same spirit with those who, like you, hold the correct opinions [on this matter], and refuse to have any dealings with others who profane the word of God.'[42] Elsewhere in northern Italy, however, there was more sympathy for the Eucharistic teachings of Zwingli and other Swiss reformers. This was certainly the case in early 1540s Lucca where, under the leadership of Peter Martyr Vermigli, the Lateran convent of San Frediano had become a centre for the discussion and dissemination of evangelical ideas. Some of Vermigli's more enthusiastic followers made no secret of their 'sacramentarian' views. One, Girolamo da Pluvio, is reported to have celebrated the Lord's Supper after the Reformed fashion and to have instructed those involved 'that they must receive it solely in memory of Christ's passion'; another, Ottaviano da Verona, described the Eucharist as no more than a 'commemoration of the passion and death of Jesus Christ'.[43] Evidence for the spread of 'Zwinglianism' can also be cited for Cremona, where in November 1537 one Filippo Nicola made public his denial of the real presence by attacking the host.[44] That Nicola's act was more than simply an expression of popular materialism is suggested by the fact that a priest from the same area, Girolamo di Serafino Teggia, later confessed to having preached that the Eucharist was 'a memorial of the benefits that we have received from Jesus Christ'.[45]

---

[41] Evangelicals of Venice, Vicenza and Treviso to Luther, 26 November 1542 (*D. Martin Luthers Briefwechsel* (11 vols, Weimar, 1930–48), X, no. 3817): 'Quaestio illa de Coena Domini, in Germania primum orta, deinde ad nos quoque delata, proh dolor! quot turbas excitavit! quot dissidia peperit! quantum offendiculorum dedit infirmis! quantum iacturae ecclesiae Dei! quantum impedimenti gloriae Christi propagandae!'

[42] Ibid., no. 3907. For evidence that Altieri's views were not shared by all Venetian evangelicals, see F. Ambrosini, *Storie di patrizi e di eresia nella Venezia del '500* (Milan, 1999), p. 216.

[43] Adorni-Braccesi, <<*Una città infetta*>>, pp. 130; 262.

[44] F. Chabod, *Per la storia religiosa dello stato di Milano durante il dominio di Carlo V: Note e documenti* (Rome, 1962), pp. 115–16.

[45] Teggia revealed this in conversation with Domenico Morando, formerly chaplain to Cardinal Giovanni Morone (Firpo and Marcatto, *Morone*, II, pp. 904–8). See also the letter from Giovanni Domenico Sigibaldi to Morone dated 4 April 1541: 'El nostro don Domenico Morando ha ritrovato de la setta zuingliana circa la santissima eucharistia, et quello bravo, nepote de messer Baptista, lo perseguita e li guarda per obliquo: anchor lui ha la sua croce' (ibid., p. 971).

During the first half of the 1540s, opinions such as these rapidly gained ground in the Italian evangelical movement. In a letter to Konrad Pellikan dated 28 January 1545, the Polish student Samuel Micanus noted the popularity of Zwingli's works and Eucharistic theology among the evangelicals of Bologna:

> All the Italian brethren approve of [Zwingli's] writings and freely assent to them. In the matter of the Eucharist many are Lutherans, but far more, if not almost all, of them think along the lines of Zwingli and ourselves. Your works are available here and are highly prized (as God is my witness, I am not lying). But if the truth be told, they [the Italians] value above all other recent authors Huldrych Zwingli, who wrote most divinely and sincerely.[46]

As others have pointed out, Micanus' testimony needs to be treated with caution, given his pro-Zwinglian bias and understandable desire to flatter his Zurich mentors. However, there is plenty of independent evidence for the 'sacramentarian' orientation of the evangelical community of Bologna, as well as of its counterpart in nearby Modena.[47] The merchant Giovanni Battista Scotti, who played a key role in disseminating Protestant literature (including works by Zwingli) in Bologna, is said to have taught 'that the sacrament of the Eucharist is nothing but an example, constituted of bread, water and wine' and that the words 'Hoc est corpus meum' referred not to the host, but to 'the actual body and blood of our redeemer Jesus Christ'.[48] One of Scotti's associates, Angelo Ruggeri, took the view 'that the body of Christ was not in the consecrated host, but that it was like a sign'.[49] Some Modenese evangelicals showed a detailed grasp of Zwingli's symbolical interpretation of the words of institution: in 1544, the Franciscan Bartolomeo della Pergola, himself facing charges of heresy, argued in his defence that he had always sought to demonstrate the real presence of Christ in the sacrament against those who contended that the word 'est' was to be understood as '"significat", "repraesentat" vel

---

[46] The full text of the letter is published in A. Rotondò, 'Anticristo e Chiesa romana: Diffusione e metamorfosi d'un libello antiromano del Cinquecento', in Rotondò, *Aspetti della propaganda religiosa del Cinquecento* (Florence, 1991), pp. 19–164 (161–3). In May 1546, another of Pellikan's correspondents in Bologna, Thomas Erastus, reported that when preaching on predestination a local Dominican had seemed 'ipsissima Huldrici Zwinglii verba recitare' (ibid., pp. 72–4).

[47] In his important recent study of the Reformation in Bologna, Guido Dall'Olio notes that 'diversi indizi … fanno pensare a una netta e precoce predominanza di dottrine zwingliane e sacramentarie' in the 'churches' of Bologna and Modena (Dall'Olio, *Eretici e Inquisitori*, p. 116).

[48] Ibid., pp. 111–12.

[49] Ibid., p. 119.

"demonstrat".[50] Confirmation of Micanus' claim that the Bolognese evangelicals had direct access to the works of Zwingli and other Zurich reformers comes from Benedetto Accolti, who testified to having read 'some works of Zwingli addressed to the king of France' (probably the *Commentary on True and False Religion* and the *Fidei expositio*) while studying in Bologna during the early 1540s, and from the Franciscan Giovanni Antonio da Cerva, who admitted to buying a copy of Pellikan's commentaries on the Pauline epistles from a local bookseller.[51]

Micanus' letter was one of several from foreign visitors to Italy commenting on the emergence of an evangelical movement in the Italian cities that the Zurichers received during the 1540s. Early in the summer of 1543, Hans Ratgeb, a Zuricher in the service of the Duke of Ferrara, wrote to Bullinger about the difficulties which local Protestants faced. In the current climate, Ratgeb observed, anyone who dared speak of Christ, Paul or scripture risked being branded a 'luterano'. Various evangelical books had also been banned, notably Celio Secundo Curione's *Pasquino in estasi* and the sermons of Bernardino Ochino. Nevertheless, many continued to profess the Gospel 'here and in Bologna and in Venice and in all of Lombardy, but secretly, out of fear of the Antichrist'.[52] A rather more optimistic assessment of the Reformation's prospects in Italy was offered by the English bookseller Thomas Knight who, writing to Bullinger in January 1547, reported a steady growth in the number of believers in Venice. Not only that, the Venetian authorities had ordered a daily sermon to be preached 'in palatio maiore' during the forthcoming Lenten season, 'something not seen since the foundation of the city'. Knight remarked that Bullinger's commentaries were also increasingly popular in Italy and would be easier to sell were they not so large and expensive.[53]

---

[50] Firpo and Marcatto, *Morone*, III, p. 255. Even more striking is the testimony of the Modenese weaver Geminiano Callegari, who reproduced faithfully Zwingli's comparison of the sacrament to the ring given by a husband to his wife (Peyronel Rambaldi, *Dai Paesi Bassi all'Italia*, p. 248).

[51] Dall'Olio, *Eretici e Inquisitori*, pp. 123–4. For further evidence of the availability of Pellikan's works in Bologna, see Firpo and Marcatto, *Morone*, II, p. 430.

[52] StAZ E II 355, 104v–5r; published in *Zwa*, 2/2, pp. 60–3: 'Allso bald das ein von kristus, oder von paullus redt, oder von der hellgen schrifft, so sprechen sy, er sey ein luterano. Doch sind yren fil, hie und zů bolognia und zů vinedig und ym ganzen lombadia, aber haimlich vor vorcht des anticrists.'

[53] StAZ E II 343, 358: 'Evangelium in dies multo sincerius hic quam alibi in Italia praedicatur, Senatusque consulto decretum est concionem habere cotidie in palatio maiore futura quadragesima: quod nunquam ab urbe condita visum est. Crescit numerus fidelium magis ac magis. Tua commentaria indies pluris fiunt apud italos et nisi essent tam magna et chara nulla essent magis vendibilia.' Knight is perhaps to be identified with the 'Thomas Anglus' whose activities are alluded to in Rotondò, 'Anticristo', p. 75.

Some leading figures within the Zurich church were able to see for themselves the progress that the Reformation was making south of the Alps. In summer 1543, the Zurich professor of natural sciences, Konrad Gesner, visited Venice in order to collect information for his celebrated *Bibliotheca universalis*.[54] Two years later, the Zurich schoolmaster Johannes Fries made the same trip, with a view to purchasing books for his brother-in-law, Konrad Pellikan, and for Gesner. A brief account of Fries' itinerary (which took him to Milan, Pavia, Verona and Trent as well as Venice) survives.[55] It is likely that Gesner, at least, was in contact with local Protestant sympathizers during his visit; indeed, following his return to Zurich he appears to have assumed responsibility for supplying the Venetian evangelical community with prohibited books.[56] Similar links were forged by another Zuricher, Georg Keller, who spent part of the early 1550s in Padua studying medicine. In a letter to Rudolf Gwalther dated 7 June 1551, Keller commended the bearer, an evangelical from Naples who was planning to visit Switzerland to purchase Protestant works for distribution among his compatriots.[57]

Epistolary contacts between the Zurich church and philo-Protestant circles in Italy were also resumed around this time. In a letter to Joachim Vadian of September 1550, Bullinger gives a detailed account of the persecution to which Italian Protestants were subject, noting as the source of his information 'scriptum N. Itali ex Italia'.[58] Both Bullinger

---

[54] C. Bonorand, *Vadian und Graubünden: Aspekte der Personen- und Kommunikationsgeschichte im Zeitalter des Humanismus und der Reformation* (Chur, 1991), pp. 62–3. In Venice, Gesner was able to inspect the library of the imperial envoy Diego Hurtado de Mendoza (*Bibliotheca universalis, sive Catalogus omnium scriptorum locupletissimus* (Zurich, 1545), fol. *6ᵛ).

[55] Bonorand, *Vadian*, pp. 194–6; C. Zürcher, *Konrad Pellikans Wirken in Zürich 1526–1556* (Zurich, 1975), p. 235.

[56] In a letter to Bullinger dated 6 December 1543, Baldassare Altieri writes: 'De libris ... non est, cur tibi in ea re molesti simus, cum praestantissimus, et humanissimus Gesnerus noster, ut scribis, hanc provinciam pro nobis ultro obierit' (StAZ E II 369, 2). Gesner's *Bibliotheca* contains entries for a number of Italian evangelicals, including Francesco Porto, Antonio Brucioli, Aonio Paleario and Marcantonio Flaminio. He was also in communication with the Dutch printer Arnold van Egenhouts (Arnoldo Arlenio) who operated out of Bologna and acted as a conduit for the supply of prohibited literature to evangelical activists in the city (Bonorand, *Vadian*, p. 63; Dall'Olio, *Eretici e Inquisitori*, p. 126).

[57] ZB Ms. F 38, 52ʳ: 'Qui ad vos proficiscitur librorum sacrorum emendorum gratia quos Neapolim vehendos curabit, nam et ipse Neapolitanus est, inde cum quodam famosissimo ditissimo et Christianissimo viro nobili evangelii causa recessit propter suspiciones aliquot ...'. See T. Schiess, 'Briefe aus der Fremde von einem Zürcher Studenten der Medizin (Dr. Georg Keller) 1550–1558', *Neujahrsblatt herausgegeben von der Stadtbibliothek Zürich*, 262 (1906), pp. 1–38 (8–9).

[58] *Vadian BW*, VII, no. 98.

(one letter) and Pellikan (15 letters covering the period July 1540 to July 1548) were in correspondence with the evangelical secretary to the imperial chancery in Milan, Pietro Merbelio, who was able to provide them with an account of attempts by the local ecclesiastical and secular authorities to crack down on the spread of proscribed literature and on religious dissent more generally.[59] From Merbelio's letters, it would seem that the Zurich church was also in contact with the important Reformed conventicle in Cremona; on several occasions, Merbelio passes on greetings from one Petrus Manna, whom he describes as 'a Cremonese physician and a man with right opinions of Christ' ('phisico Cremonensi viro rectissime de Christo sentienti').[60] In February 1550 another Cremonese, Giacomo Susio, sent Gwalther a manuscript translation into Italian of the latter's *Antichristus*, with the request that he arrange for its publication.[61] Further evidence of the Zurich church's links with Cremona comes from the exile Paolo Gaddi, who on 28 October 1553 thanked Bullinger for sending a letter of support to the beleaguered evangelicals of his native city.[62]

Also documented is the relationship between the Zurichers and evangelical sympathizers in Venice. Although initially their spokesman Baldassare Altieri favoured a Lutheran interpretation of the Eucharist, this did not prevent him from seeking to establish good relations with Zwingli's successors in Zurich. In August 1543, for example, Altieri wrote to Bullinger outlining the difficulties faced by the local faithful, who lacked affordable Protestant literature and suitable pastors, and to request copies of the Zurich Latin Bible, Calvin's *Institutes*, and other works by the Genevan reformer.[63] Later he informed Bullinger of his plans for an alliance between Venice and the Schmalkaldic League, which he believed would pave the way for the triumph of the Gospel in Italy.[64] That prospect evaporated after the defeat of the German princes at Mühlberg in April 1547, which prompted the Venetian authorities to

---

[59] See Zürcher, *Pellikan*, pp. 74, 295–6; Merbelio to Bullinger, 18 May 1544 (StAZ E II 365, 36–7).

[60] Merbelio to Pellikan, 23 July 1540 (ZB Ms. F 47, 39) and 13 May 1543 (ibid., 72–3); Pellikan to Merbelio, 31 March 1545 (ibid., 111).

[61] The work appeared from the presses of Oporinus in Basle later that year as *L'Antichristo di M. Ridolfo Gualtero, ministro della Chiesa Tigurina*; Susio's letter is edited in Rotondò, 'Anticristo', pp. 163–4.

[62] Schiess, I, no. 231; A. Pastore, *Nella Valtellina del tardo Cinquecento: fede, cultura, società* (Milan, 1975), p. 98.

[63] StAZ E II 369, 3.

[64] Altieri to Bullinger, 13 November 1546 and 29 January 1547 (StAZ E II 365, 447; 449–50). On this scheme, see A. Stella, 'Utopie e velleità insurrezionali dei filoprotestanti italiani (1545–1547)', *BHR*, 27 (1965), pp. 133–82.

take steps to suppress Protestant proselytizing in the city. Faced with removal from his position as secretary to the English ambassador in Venice, Altieri visited Switzerland in an attempt to secure an alternative diplomatic post that would leave him free to continue his activity on behalf of the Reformation. Despite receiving support from Bullinger, he was unable to persuade the Swiss Diet to accede to this request, and on returning to Italy he was forced to seek sanctuary on the estates of Giovanni Andrea degli Ugoni near Bergamo. From there, Altieri continued to correspond with Bullinger until his death in August 1550.[65]

The Zurichers were keenly aware of the pressures to which evangelical believers in Italy were subject. Their pastoral concern for these embattled communities is perhaps most evident in two letters, from Gesner and Bullinger respectively, dated 6 January 1561. The first of these was prompted by news of the imprisonment of the Sienese evangelicals Dario and Cornelio Sozzini, while the second is addressed more generally to 'the faithful suffering persecution in Italy'.[66] Both Zurichers exhort their correspondents to remain steadfast in the faith and to draw comfort from the knowledge that their tribulations were foretold by Christ. According to Bullinger, persecution is to be understood as a sign of God's favour, even of election; citing Hebrews 12:5–6, he argues that it is to be expected that God, like any loving parent, will sometimes chastise his children.[67] In his letter, Gesner calls on the Sozzini to draw strength from the witness of the martyrs who have preceded them, so that they themselves may be an example to subsequent generations. He warns them against being tempted to abjure their faith, as to deny the Lord having once known him is either the sin against the Holy Spirit or something very close to it. Evangelicals may

---

[65] See *DBI*, II, 559. Degli Ugoni was also in correspondence with Bullinger; in a letter to the *Antistes* dated 13 January 1550, he defended Altieri against accusations of bigamy (StAZ E II 335, 2172). For further evidence of his evangelical leanings, see Ambrosini, *Storia di patrizi*, pp. 94–6.

[66] The text of Gesner's letter is published most recently in V. Marchetti and G. Zucchini (eds), *Aggiunte all'Epistolario di Fausto Sozzini 1561–1568* (Warsaw, 1982), pp. 106–10. For Bullinger's, see StAZ E II 342, 398–401.

[67] StAZ E II 342, 398ᵛ–99ʳ: '... non prohibet, imo permittit ut homines pravi (qui tamen non amplius quam ille velit possunt) nos divexent. At qui hoc facit, non modo Deus est omnipotens et omnia gubernans, sed Dominus quoque noster, qui nos condidit, cui nos obedire debemus: Quinimo pater est benignissimus, qui quae agit nobiscum, ad salutem nostram et in bonum nostrum agit, amans nos et nuspiam deterrens aut negligens. Licet itaque dura nobis videantur, quae nunc nos exercent in mundo cogitabimus tamen illa nobis imposita esse a patre, adeoque nos non hominum, sed Dei Patris benigna manu ita tractari, scriptura sancta hoc diserte testatur. An non Paulus Christi Apostolus manifeste clamat, Fili mi ne neglexeris correptionem Domini, neque deficias cum ab eo argueris. Quem enim diligit Deus corripit, flagellat autem omnem filium quem recipit.'

be called on to sacrifice family, wealth and status for Christ's sake, but their reward – eternal life – is something much more precious. Bullinger also makes an ecclesiological point: to be persecuted on account of the Gospel is to profess faith in the eternal Son of God and true 'supreme pontiff', who alone is the source of salvation, whereas to adhere to the church of Rome is to become a member of Antichrist, subscribing to invented human dogmas (purgatory, the veneration of the saints, the Mass) that in all respects contradict the teachings of Christ.[68]

The Zurich church did not mount anything approaching a sustained missionary campaign in Italy, but it did offer modest assistance, notably in the form of books, to the peninsula's emerging evangelical communities. The spread of 'memorialist' views of the Lord's Supper in many north Italian cities suggests that it also helped indirectly to shape their theology. In the confessionally fluid Italian context it is not always easy to disentangle specifically 'Zwinglian' from other evangelical currents of thought, so the Zurich church's contribution to the development of the Italian evangelical movement is difficult to assess with any precision. Nevertheless, from the evidence already cited it seems reasonable to assume that the high international profile of Bullinger and his colleagues made Zurich a natural pole of attraction for Italian evangelicals, alongside Geneva, Basle and Strasbourg. That was clearly true for those who came to constitute the public face of the Italian evangelical movement: the exiles.

---

[68] Ibid., 400[r–v]: 'Habent illi multos doctores, nos vero habemus unicum Christum loquentem nobis per prophetas et apostolos. Habent illi caput et pastorem universalem Pontificem Romanum. Nos abhorremus ab illo, ut Antichristo. Christus nobis est caput et pastor. Episcopi apud illos sunt principes: Nos scimus dixisse Dominum, Reges dominantur, vos autem non sic. Scimus inquam Christum instituisse ministros, qui sana doctrina et vita pura praeluceant populo Dei. Tribuunt illi operibus et meritis hominum iustitiam et vitam aeternam: Nos abhorremus ab hac doctrina, et gratiae Dei in Christo per fidem tribuimus. ... Purgatorium post sanguinem Christi nullum agnoscimus: illi ignem quendam finxerunt, quem aqua lustrali et indulgentiis rursus extinguunt, et mercatum ammirabile exercent. Ordinem monachorum isti miris modis commendant: Nos simpliciter dicimus, Frustra me colunt docentes doctrinas hominum. Isti multos hominibus peccatoribus obtrudunt mediatores et intercessores. Nos dicimus sanctos in caelis non usurpare sibi gloriam uni Dei filio debitam, neque homines in terris alium velle (qui modo fideles sint) intercessorem, quam Christum. Illi ipsi fideles coenam ut instituta est a Christo, celebrant: a Missa Papistica abhorrent. Christum ad dexteram patris, non in pane, adorant: sacrificium crucis, non Missae, venerantur. Idola omnia refugiunt. At Papistae contraria his obtrudunt hominibus, et reclamantes persequuntur.'

ii. The first generation of Italian exiles

Only limited contacts between the Zurich church and Italian evangelical refugees are attested from the 1520s and 1530s: buoyed up by the prospects for reform within the church and not yet subject to concerted repression, few Italian evangelicals felt compelled at this time to contemplate emigration. For those who did, the most popular destination was not Zurich, but the Strasbourg of Martin Bucer, who of all the northern reformers seems to have been keenest to exploit the possibilities that were opening up for the Reformation in Italy.[69] Among the earliest exiles were Francesco Negri, a former Benedictine from Bassano who converted to Protestantism around 1525, and the Venetian Bartolomeo Fonzio, who was resident in Strasbourg between July 1532 and October 1533.[70] Around the same time, Bucer established links with an Erasmian circle in Bologna, two of whose members, Giovan Angelo Odoni and Fileno Lunardi, spent the years 1534 to 1537 studying in Strasbourg.[71]

Through the good offices of Bucer and others, some of these Strasbourg exiles were able to make contact with the Zurich ministers. In early 1533, Fonzio (who is said to have been an avid reader of Zwingli's works) accompanied Bucer to Zurich on a mission aimed at healing the Eucharistic schism between the Lutherans and the Reformed.[72] Two years earlier, Francesco Negri had arrived in Zurich with a letter of introduction from Bucer's colleague Wolfgang Capito. In this letter, Capito asked Zwingli to commend the bearer, a man of great piety and learning who was hoping to find employment as a schoolmaster in Graubünden, to Johannes Comander and Anton Travers; he even nursed the hope that Negri's example might encourage further conversions in Italian-speaking lands.[73] Capito also wrote a letter

---

[69] As early as July 1526, Bucer dedicated his edition of the fourth volume of Luther's *Postillae* to 'gloriam domini Jesu Christi agnoscentibus fratribus per Italiam' (J. Rott (ed.), *Correspondance de Martin Bucer* (Leiden, 1979–), II, pp. 146–54). See also S. Seidel Menchi, 'Les relations de Martin Bucer avec l'Italie', in C. Krieger and M. Lienhard (eds), *Martin Bucer and Sixteenth-Century Europe* (2 vols, Leiden, 1993), pp. 557–69.

[70] Bucer's relations with Fonzio are discussed in J.V. Pollet, *Martin Bucer: Etudes sur la correspondance avec de nombreux textes inédits*, (2 vols, Paris, 1958/62), II, pp. 468–87; see further A. Olivieri, 'Il <<Catechismo>> e la <<Fidei et doctrinae ... ratio>> di Bartolomeo Fonzio, eretico veneziano del Cinquecento', *Studi veneziani*, 9 (1967), pp. 339–452, and the article by G. Fragnito in *DBI*, XLVIII, 769–73.

[71] Dall'Olio, *Eretici e Inquisitori*, pp. 75–6; Peyronel Rambaldi, *Dai Paesi Bassi all'Italia*, p. 71.

[72] *Vadian BW*, V, no. 736; *HBBW*, III, nos 212 and 214.

[73] *Z*, XI, no. 1220.

of introduction for Giovan Angelo Odoni on the occasion of a visit by Odoni to Zurich in April 1536.[74]

Traditionally, the year 1542 has been taken as a watershed in the history of the Reformation in Italy. Although recent historiography has played down the significance of this date – it has been pointed out that the reform-minded 'spirituali' continued to exercise influence at the highest levels of the Italian church long after the promulgation of the bull *Licet ab initio*, and that the 1540s saw the beginnings of a genuinely popular Protestant movement in cities such as Siena, Modena and Venice – in one respect its importance remains undiminished.[75] 1542 was a year of spectacular public defections from Catholicism: by Bernardino Ochino, Peter Martyr Vermigli and Celio Secundo Curione, to name only the most prominent of those involved. Like their French equivalents, the first Italian religious refugees acted as a magnet for others. Although some were uneasy about the repercussions of mass flight for the cause of the Gospel in Italy (in his *Esortatione al martirio*, Giulio da Milano argued that flight was only praiseworthy when undertaken at God's direct command and for the benefit of other believers) the reformers' almost unanimous opposition to the practice of dissimulation (Nicodemism) meant that, for the more committed among the faithful, exile offered the only theologically acceptable alternative to imprisonment or martyrdom.[76] As persecution intensified during the 1540s and early 1550s,[77] an Italian exile community (or more accurately, a series of communities with strong mutual ties) began to take shape.

---

[74] Capito to Bullinger, Pellikan and Bibliander, 18 April 1536 (*HBBW*, VI, no. 797). Konrad Gesner later claimed to have met both Odoni and Fileno Lunardi in Strasbourg (*Bibliotheca universalis*, fols 383r; 556v).

[75] See A. Schutte, 'Periodization of Sixteenth-Century Italian Religious History: The Post-Cantimori Paradigm Shift', *Journal of Modern History*, 61 (1989), pp. 269–84.

[76] Nicodemism has received considerable attention from historians of the Italian Reformation. Contributions include A. Rotondò, 'Atteggiamenti della vita morale italiana del Cinquecento: La pratica nicodemitica', *RSI*, 79 (1967), pp. 991–1030; C. Ginzburg, *Il Nicodemismo: Simulazione e dissimulazione religiosa nell'Europa del '500* (Turin, 1970); and Martin, *Venice's Hidden Enemies*, pp. 123–46. Ginzburg's description of Nicodemism as a coherent ideological standpoint, as opposed to a practical response to persecution, has come in for severe criticism from A. Biondi, 'La giustificazione della simulazione nel Cinquecento', in *Eresia e riforma nell'Italia del Cinquecento: Miscellanea I del Corpus Reformatorum Italicorum* (Chicago, 1974), pp. 7–68. On the *Esortatione al martirio*, see U. Rozzo, 'L'<<Esortazione al martirio>> di Giulio da Milano', in A. Pastore (ed.), *Riforma e società nei Grigioni: Valtellina e Valchiavenna tra '500 e '600* (Milan, 1991), pp. 63–88.

[77] This period saw the creation of a powerful Inquisition tribunal in Venice (1547), the martyrdoms of Fanino Fanini, Domenico Cabianca and Giorgio Siculo (1550–51), and major crackdowns against heresy in Lombardy, Tuscany and the Romagna. The situation for evangelicals worsened considerably following the election of the hardline Gian Pietro Carafa as Pope Paul IV in 1555.

The year 1542 also marks the beginning of intensive contacts between the Zurich church and Italian religious exiles. As we have seen, the latter were in many instances already familiar with the works of Zwingli, Bullinger and other Zurich writers. Geography also favoured such contacts: for those travelling north from Italy via the Bündner passes and Chur, Zurich was the first major port of call and Bullinger the first Protestant churchman of international stature they encountered. That was certainly true for the apostates of 1542, who passed through Zurich in rapid succession during the late summer and autumn of that year. In a letter to Joachim Vadian dated 19 December, Bullinger provides a detailed account of these events. In August, he notes, he received a Capuchin named Hieronymus, who claimed to have read his works in Naples. Shortly afterwards he was visited by Curione, whom he commended to the authorities in Berne. Next to arrive was Ochino, whose reputation as Vicar-General of the Capuchin order and the most acclaimed preacher of his day had, one assumes, gone before him: certainly Bullinger was impressed by the Sienese exile's demeanour. No sooner had Ochino departed to take up a preaching post in Geneva than Curione returned, with the intention of collecting his wife and children from Lucca. For the journey, Bullinger presented him with a copy of his commentary on Matthew's Gospel and a letter of recommendation addressed to the crypto-Protestant duchess of Ferrara, Renée de France.[78] Finally, the Zurichers received the former prior of San Frediano in Lucca, Peter Martyr Vermigli, along with his companion Paolo Lacizi. The procession of famous figures appears to have raised Bullinger's hopes for the breakthrough of the Reformation in Italy, causing him to remark, 'That Babylonian whore [the papacy] will be judged and is being judged, praise and glory be to God'.[79]

Some exiles chose to prolong their stay in Zurich, often enjoying the hospitality of Konrad Pellikan, whose high profile within the Italian evangelical movement has already been noted. Pellikan's house guests included Girolamo Mariano – perhaps the same Hieronymus mentioned in Bullinger's letter to Vadian – and, more famously, the young Sienese exile Lelio Sozzini, who lodged with Pellikan between October 1548 and June 1550 before returning to take up permanent residence in Zurich

---

[78] On his return to Zurich from Italy, Curione was supplied with a letter of introduction to the *Hofmeister* of the former monastery of Königsfelden describing his straitened circumstances and requesting help to cover his travel expenses to Berne (M. Kutter, *Celio Secundo Curione: Sein Leben und sein Werk (1503–1569)* (Basle, 1955), p. 55).

[79] *Vadian BW*, VI, no. 1271.

four years later.[80] But these were exceptional cases. The Zurich churchmen could offer the Italian exiles little in the way of long-term employment, and were not anxious to detain them: in a letter to Bonifacius Amerbach of 11 September 1542, Pellikan reported that he and his colleagues had advised some of the new arrivals to travel on to Geneva.[81] Basle, too, with its printing-houses and university, offered a more alluring prospect than Zurich. More than 30 Italians matriculated at the university of Basle between 1540 and 1555, including such prominent figures as Curione, Pietro Perna and Guglielmo Grataroli, who formed the core of an intellectually vibrant exile community in the city.[82] But even though only a handful of exiles actually settled in Zurich, many continued to look to its churchmen for spiritual leadership and practical assistance. Fleeting personal encounters developed into solid humanist friendships, articulated through and cemented by correspondence.

Probably the best known of the Zurichers' new Italian associates was the Florentine reformer Peter Martyr Vermigli, who after meeting Bullinger in September 1542 was invited to take up a professorship at the Strasbourg academy.[83] Over the next few years Vermigli was only sporadically in contact with the Zurich divines, but following his move to Oxford in December 1547 a flourishing correspondence developed between them. In letters to Bullinger and Gwalther, Vermigli provided a detailed account of his pedagogical activities at the university and of his confrontations with Catholic opponents such as Richard Smith. He was also able to offer the Zurichers an outsider's perspective on the faltering progress of the Edwardian Reformation (which he saw as being held back by a shortage of preachers outside London) and on episodes such

---

[80] B. Riggenbach (ed.), *Das Chronicon des Konrad Pellikan* (Basle, 1877), pp. 167–8, 177–8; Zürcher, *Pellikan*, p. 74. Mariano provided Pellikan with information on the activities of other Protestant-leaning Franciscans in Italy. He is mentioned in a letter from Celio Secundo Curione to Bullinger dated 29 July 1544 (StAZ E II 366, 87ʳ).

[81] F. Hartmann (ed.), *Die Amerbachkorrespondenz* (Basle, 1942–), V, no. 2495.

[82] G. Busino, 'Italiani all'Università di Basilea dal 1460 al 1601', *BHR*, 20 (1958), pp. 497–526. In April 1549 Pellikan received the Sardinian evangelical Sigismondo Arquer, whom he supplied with a letter of introduction to Bonifacius Amerbach in Basle (*Amerbachkorrespondenz*, VII, no. 3150; Caponetto, *Riforma*, p. 434).

[83] The best study of Vermigli's early career is still McNair, *Peter Martyr*, now to be supplemented by F.A. James III, *Peter Martyr Vermigli and Predestination: The Augustinian Inheritance of an Italian Reformer* (Oxford, 1998). See also E. Campi, 'Petrus Martyr Vermigli (1499–1562): Europäische Wirkungsfelder eines italienischen Reformators', *Zwa*, 27 (2000), pp. 29–46, and my forthcoming article for the new *Dictionary of National Biography*. An overview of Vermigli's correspondence with Bullinger is provided in M.W. Anderson, 'Peter Martyr, Reformed Theologian (1542–1562): His letters to Heinrich Bullinger and John Calvin', *SCJ*, 4 (1973), pp. 41–64.

as the first vestiarian controversy. The relationship was strengthened by the presence in Oxford of two Swiss students, Johannes ab Ulmis and Rudolf Stumpf, who formed part of Vermigli's inner circle in the mainly hostile university environment: in his letters home, Ab Ulmis remarked that Vermigli treated him not like a pupil, but like a son.[84] Doctrinally, and especially in the contentious matter of the Eucharist, Vermigli was also edging closer to the position of the Zurich church around this time, after initially aligning himself with Bucer.[85] In 1551, he had Gwalther arrange for the Zurich printer Christoph Froschauer to publish his commentary on 1 Corinthians, and there were plans for the Zurichers to publish his lectures on Genesis, Exodus and Romans as well.[86] For their part, Bullinger and his colleagues came to see in Peter Martyr a valuable theological ally. When Vermigli came into conflict with the Lutheran Johann Marbach during a second spell at the Strasbourg academy (1553–56), Bullinger took the opportunity to offer him the chair of Old Testament at the Zurich *Lectorium*, which had been left vacant by the death of Konrad Pellikan.[87]

Of equal significance was Bullinger's relationship with the Piedmontese exile Celio Secundo Curione. During the late 1530s, Curione emerged as a leading figure in north Italian evangelical circles, with links to the court of Renée de France in Ferrara as well as to the philo-Protestant wing of the Augustinian order. In November 1542, he was appointed lecturer in the liberal arts at the recently established Reformed academy in Lausanne, where he taught alongside Pierre Viret and Beat Comte. Curione's meeting with Bullinger earlier that year laid the basis for a flourishing correspondence between the two men: more than 20 letters from Curione to the Zurich *Antistes* survive from the 1540s alone.[88]

---

[84] *ET*, letter cxciv. Ab Ulmis, a native of the Thurgau, had close links with the Zurich church (see ibid., letter cxciii).

[85] S. Corda, *Veritas Sacramenti: A Study in Vermigli's Doctrine of the Lord's Supper* (Zurich, 1975), pp. 64–78.

[86] *ET*, letters ccxxx; ccxxxii; ccxxxiii; ccxxxv. In the event, only the Genesis commentary appeared in Zurich, and then not until 1569 (see Chapter 4:iii below).

[87] Bullinger to Vermigli, 1 May 1556 (StAZ E II 342, 323); Vermigli to Bullinger, 7 May 1556 (ZB Ms. F 60, 396). In an inaugural oration to the Zurich academy, Vermigli outlined the circumstances that had led to his departure from Strasbourg and emphasized his agreement with the Eucharistic teaching of the Zurich church. The text of the oration is published in *Loci communes D. Petri Martyris Vermilii, Florentini, Sacrarum literarum in Schola Tigurina Professoris* (London, 1583), 1062–5.

[88] The existing register of Curione's correspondence in Kutter, *Curione*, pp. 295–303, is in need of some correction. For a partial overview of the surviving letters, see S. Calvani, 'Note sul carteggio di Celio Secundo Curione dal 1535 al 1553', *BSSV*, 159 (1986), pp. 35–40.

The friendship between Bullinger and Curione was underpinned by a shared devotion to the memory of Zwingli. According to Curione's biographer and former student Nicholas Stupanus, the *Commentarius de vera et falsa religione* was among the first Protestant works that the Piedmontese humanist encountered in his youth.[89] More recently, Luca d'Ascia has suggested that Zwingli's symbolical interpretation of the words of consecration in the Eucharist may have provided Curione with a hermeneutical model when, in his most celebrated work, *De amplitudine beati regni Dei*, he came to grapple with those passages of scripture which suggested that the number of the elect was exceeded by that of the damned.[90] D'Ascia has also provided evidence for the dependence of one of Curione's early works, the *Aranei encomion* (first published in Venice in 1540), on Zwingli's own *De providentia*: one passage in which Curione defends Pythagoras from the charge of teaching the transmigration of souls is clearly derived from Zwingli's text.[91] After his departure from Italy, Curione continued to draw inspiration from the Zurich reformer, and in January 1545 he requested that Bullinger supply him with a copy of the soon-to-be-published complete edition of Zwingli's works.[92] In a subsequent letter he made plain his admiration for Zwingli's achievement, declaring: 'There are no theological books in existence today that I desire and covet so greatly, on account of the excellent teaching that they contain.'[93]

Curione's published works of this period provide plenty of evidence of his support for the Zurich church's teaching on the Eucharist. For example, in his *Institutione della Christiana religione*, a catechism for children, Curione offers a memorialist reading of the sacrament and describes the relationship between the elements and the spiritual realities that they signify in terms of analogy, much as Bullinger does in his *Decades*.[94] The

---

[89] Kutter, *Curione*, p. 13.

[90] L. d'Ascia, 'Celio Secundo Curione, erasmista o antierasmista?', in A. Olivieri (ed.), *Erasmo Venezia e la cultura padana nel '500* (Rovigo, 1995), pp. 209–23 (212, n. 16).

[91] Ibid., p. 216, n. 31. For a detailed comparison of the two works, see L. d'Ascia, 'Tra platonismo e riforma: Curione, Zwingli e Francesco Zorzi', *BHR*, 61 (1999), pp. 673–99 (677–90).

[92] Curione to Bullinger, 18 January 1545 (StAZ E II 346, 148–9). In the same letter Curione noted that Zwingli's writings were impossible to come by in Lausanne or Geneva – a reflection, perhaps, on Calvin's well-known disdain for the Zurich reformer (see Calvin's comments in *CO*, XI, no. 421, and ibid., XII, no. 657).

[93] Curione to Bullinger, 19 October 1545 (StAZ E II 366, 85r): 'Nulli hodie extant libri theologici, quos tantopere desiderem, et concupiscam, propter excellentem (quae in eis est) doctrinam.'

[94] *Una familiare et paterna institutione della Christiana religione* (Basle, n.d. [1550]), sigs D6v–7r. This was an amplified version of the Latin edition published the previous year (Kutter, *Curione*, p. 285).

Eucharistic theology of two other works published by Curione during the 1540s, the *Oration on the true and ancient authority of the Church of Christ against Antonio Fiordibello* and the *Pasquillus ecstaticus*, is also close to that of the Zurich church.[95] In Lausanne, however, Curione's Zwinglianism was something of liability, placing him in opposition to Pierre Viret and the rest of the city's Calvinist-leaning classis. These doctrinal differences may have been a factor in his dismissal from the academy of Lausanne towards the end of 1546, following a sexual scandal. Not long after the affair, Curione condemned Viret for his 'Bucerian' stance on the sacrament,[96] while later, as professor of rhetoric at the university of Basle, he opposed the drift towards Lutheranism of the Basle church under the leadership of Simon Sulzer.[97]

Although only one letter from Bullinger to Curione survives from the 1540s, there is no reason to suppose that the latter's warm feelings for the Zurich church were not reciprocated. If Curione is to be believed, it was Bullinger who first persuaded him to take up his pen on behalf of the Gospel; the selection of correspondence that Curione published in 1553 included a letter from the *Antistes* praising his work against Fiordibello.[98] The two men frequently exchanged books as well as letters. In March 1543, for instance, Curione requested a copy of the

---

[95] See *Pro vera et antiqua Ecclesiae Christi autoritate ad Antonium Florebellum Mutinensem oratio* (Basle, n.d.), pp. 181–3, for a figurative interpretation of the words of institution, and Peyronel Rambaldi, *Dai Paesi Bassi all'Italia*, pp. 207–8, on the Zwinglianism of the *Pasquillus*.

[96] Curione to Bullinger, 6 May 1548 (StAZ E II 346, 234; CO, XII, no. 1016). On hearing that his *Oration* had attracted criticism from Bucer for its statements on the sacrament, Curione remarked: 'Quid Bucerus de meis scriptis sentiat, modo sanioribus vere probentur, non valde moror. Neque enim me cum Calvino et Vireto volo coniungere in ea quaestione: quos audio Argentorati, Bucero subscripsisse, etiamsi domi aliter sapere videantur. Nam domi apud Lutheranos exagitant, quod apud Bucerum probant' (StAZ E II 346, 211; CO, XII, no. 943).

[97] Curione to Bullinger, 22 August 1569 (StAZ E II 377, 2461r): 'Discrucior cum video, quosdam homines eosque primas in ecclesia tenentes id unum studere, ut Zwinglii atque Oecolampadii sanctam memoriam, oblivione obruant sempiterna'. During the final years of his life, Curione acted as Bullinger's informant on the growing tensions between Lutherans and Zwinglians in Basle, although he was anxious to conceal this role from the Basle authorities. See his letters of 23 and 27 July 1569 (StAZ E II 377, 2463; 2462), and the discussion in Kutter, *Curione*, pp. 214–15. By this stage Bullinger and Sulzer were at loggerheads over the latter's pursuit of Lutheran-style reforms: see H.R. Guggisberg, 'Das lutheranisierende Basel: ein Diskussionsbeitrag', in H.-C. Rublack (ed.), *Die lutherische Konfessionalisierung in Deutschland* (Gütersloh, 1992), pp. 199–201; and A. Nelson Burnett, 'Simon Sulzer and the Consequences of the 1563 Strasbourg Consensus in Switzerland', *ARG*, 83 (1992), pp. 154–79.

[98] Curione to Bullinger, 29 July 1544 (StAZ E II 366, 87); *Caelii Secundi Curionis selectarum epistolarum Libri duo* (Basle, 1553), pp. 34–6.

new edition of the Zurich Latin Bible, along with some works by Konrad Gesner,[99] while later he received the Zurich *Confession* of 1545, portions of the *Decades*, and *De coena domini sermo* (1558).[100] In return, Bullinger and his sons were presented with several of Curione's own works.[101] Curione also took a special interest in the welfare of Zurich students in Basle, particularly Huldrych Zwingli the Younger.[102]

By virtue of his association with Curione, Bullinger was able to establish links with other members of Basle's growing Italian exile community, such as Girolamo Massari.[103] Massari, a former Augustinian from Vicenza who is best known as the author of the anti-papal work *Eusebius captivus, sive modus procedendi in curia romana contra evangelicos* (Basle, 1553), visited Zurich on at least three occasions: in May 1551, following his flight from Italy; in early 1553, as the bearer of a letter from Curione to Bullinger; and again around Christmas the same year.[104] During this period he also corresponded with Bullinger, usually to pass on news from England and Germany. More significant in terms of volume and frequency was Bullinger's correspondence with Guglielmo Grataroli, a physician from Bergamo; 15 letters from this Basle-based exile, covering the period August 1553 to February 1563, are held at the Zurich Staatsarchiv.[105] Grataroli also had contact with the Zurich printers Andreas Gesner and Rudolf Wyssenbach, who in 1553 published his *De memoria*, and with Konrad Gesner, to whose work *De*

---

[99] StAZ E II 366, 88ᵛ. The request for the Bible 'minore forma' was repeated in a letter of 30 November 1543 (ibid., 66ᵛ). Curione acknowledged receipt of the volume in May the following year (ibid., 62ʳ).

[100] Curione to Bullinger, 19 October 1545; 11 May 1549; 4 December 1550 (StAZ E II 366, 85; 74; 71). See also Curione to Bullinger, 21 March 1548; 15 April 1556; 18 May 1558 (StAZ E II 366, 79; 58; 54).

[101] Curione, *Epistolae*, p. 35; Curione to Bullinger, 30 November 1543, 18 January 1545, 24 August 1547, 20 January 1549, 11 May 1549, 25 November 1552, 15 October 1554 (StAZ E II 366, 66; StAZ E II 346, 148; StAZ E II 366, 211, 76, 74, 69, 61).

[102] Curione to Bullinger, 2 May 1547; 31 January 1548; 21 March 1548; 20 January 1549; 2 May 1550; 4 December 1550; 8 January 1551 (StAZ E II 366, 81; 77; 79; 76; 72; 71; 70). On returning to Zurich, Zwingli was appointed *Leutpriester* at the Grossmünster. He later served as professor of Hebrew at the Zurich academy and pastor at the Predigerkirche (E. Dejung and W. Wuhrmann (eds), *Zürcher Pfarrerbuch 1519–1952* (Zurich, 1953), p. 662).

[103] On Massari, see F. Church, *The Italian Reformers 1534–1564* (New York, 1932), pp. 45–6, 200–201; and Busino, 'Italiani', p. 517.

[104] Vergerio to Bullinger, 30 April 1551; Curione to Bullinger, 29 December 1553 (StAZ E II 366, 68); *ET*, letter clxvi.

[105] StAZ E II 366, 54–90; on Grataroli, see Church, *Italian Reformers*, pp. 194–201, and P. Bietenholz, *Der italienische Humanismus und die Blütezeit des Buchdrucks in Basel: Die Basler Drucke italienischer Autoren von 1530 bis zum Ende des 16. Jahrhunderts* (Basle, 1959), pp. 159–60.

Balneis, produced in collaboration with the Venetian printer Tomaso Giunta, he contributed a description of the spas of Graubünden.[106]

Another prominent figure in Basle's Italian-speaking community with links to the Zurich church was the Lucchese exile Pietro Perna, whose key role in the transmission of Italian Renaissance thought north of the Alps has been much emphasized in recent scholarship.[107] Perna settled in Basle in early 1543 and served his apprenticeship as a printer with Michael Isengrin, whom he assisted with the publication of Italian evangelical works such as *Le cento e dieci divine considerationi* of Juan de Valdés and Ochino's *Prediche*, four volumes of which appeared in Basle between 1549 and 1555.[108] As well as publishing works by a number of prominent Italian reformers (Ochino, Vermigli, Giacomo Aconcio, Mino Celsi), Perna was responsible for the first Latin edition of Machiavelli's *Il principe* and played an important part in the so-called 'Paracelsian revival' of the 1560s and 1570s. He was also involved in the clandestine traffic of evangelical literature to northern Italy, an activity that sometimes brought him to Zurich and, no doubt, into contact with Bullinger. At one point, he even planned to publish in Zurich an Italian translation of the New Testament, by the Benedictine Massimo Teofilo. Although this work ultimately appeared in Lyon from the presses of Jean Frellon, it has been shown to be heavily dependent on the Zurich Latin Bible, incorporating part of Bullinger's preface to the text, *De omnibus sacrae scripturae libris expositio*, together with material from the marginal glosses.[109]

Some Italian exiles were only sporadically in contact with the Zurich

---

106 M. Vischer, *Bibliographie der Zürcher Druckschriften des 15. und 16. Jahrhunderts* (Baden-Baden, 1991), p. 422 [I 47]); Bonorand, *Vadian*, pp. 36, 64; M. Bundi, *Frühe Beziehungen zwischen Graubünden und Venedig (15./16. Jahrhundert)* (Chur, 1988), pp. 86–7.

107 L. Perini, 'Note e documenti su Pietro Perna libraio-tipografo a Basilea', *NRS*, 50 (1966), pp. 145–200; 'Ancora sul libraio-tipografo Pietro Perna'; 'Gli eretici italiani del '500 e Machiavelli', *Studi storici*, 4 (1969), pp. 877–915; 'Note sulla famiglia di Pietro Perna e sul suo apprendistato tipografico', in *Magia, astrologia e religione nel Rinascimento* (Warsaw, 1974), pp. 163–209; 'Amoenitates Typographicae', in S. Rota Ghibaudi and F. Barcia (eds), *Studi politici in onore di Luigi Firpo* (2 vols, Milan, 1990), I, pp. 873–971; M. Welti, 'Le grand animateur de la Renaissance tardive a Bâle: Pierre Perna, éditeur, imprimeur et libraire', in *L'humanisme allemand* (Monaco, 1979), pp. 131–9.

108 Perini, 'Note sulla famiglia di Pietro Perna', pp. 183–5.

109 Compare *Il Nuovo ed eterno Testamento di Giesu Christo … per Massimo Teofilo Fiorentino* (Lyon, 1551), fols *7r–**r, and *Biblia sacra utriusque Testamenti* (Zurich, 1539), sigs Bv–B2r; B2v–3r. For further details, see Perini, 'Ancora sul libraio-tipografo Pietro Perna', pp. 379–82; and E. Barbieri, *Le Bibbie italiane del Quattocento e del Cinquecento: Storia e bibliografia ragionata delle edizioni in lingua italiana dal 1471 al 1600* (2 vols, Milan, 1992), I, pp. 144–9, 325–30.

divines. For example, we possess only two letters to Bullinger from Galeazzo Caracciolo, the founder of Geneva's Italian community, and one apiece from Pietro Bizzarri and Bernardino Ochino. A more regular correspondence was established between the Zurichers and two younger exiles whose very different theologies were to leave a lasting impression on Protestant Europe: Lelio Sozzini and Girolamo Zanchi. Sozzini's correspondence with Bullinger, Gwalther and Pellikan not only provides information on his European itinerary during the early 1550s, but reveals the extent of his connections with Zurich's tightly knit clerical elite (the letters include references to Gesner, Bibliander and Johannes Fries, as well as to the younger Zurich ministers Huldrych Zwingli, Ludwig Lavater and Josias Simler).[110] As we shall see, it also offers some fascinating insights into the Zurich church's approach to dealing with theological dissent. Zanchi's contacts with Zurich began somewhat later – following his appointment as professor of Old Testament and Hebrew in Strasbourg in March 1553 – and developed out of his links with both Vermigli (under whose influence he had first converted to Protestantism) and Curione, whose daughter Violanthis he married shortly after arriving in Strasbourg. Zanchi was also broadly sympathetic to the Zurich church in doctrinal terms: his early letters to Bullinger are dominated by news of his and Vermigli's resistance to pressure from their colleagues at the Strasbourg academy to conform to Lutheran teaching on the Eucharist.[111] With respect to Zurich, Zanchi played a role similar to that performed by his father-in-law Curione in Basle, providing assistance to young Zurichers during their studies at the Strasbourg academy and receiving gifts of books from Bullinger in return. He was also one of the few Italian exiles to give unqualified support to the stance adopted by the Swiss churches in the Servetus affair.

Another figure whose early contacts with the Zurich church should be mentioned at this point was the Mantuan exile Francesco Stancaro. Following his conversion to Protestantism around 1540, Stancaro settled first in Graubünden and then in Vienna, where he was appointed professor of Hebrew in 1544. Two years later, he moved to Augsburg, which was already home to a small Italian-speaking congregation headed by Bernardino Ochino. However, Stancaro's stay in Augsburg was cut short by the advancing armies of Charles V, which forced him to flee with Ochino to Basle. In a letter to Bullinger dated 8 February 1547, Curione reported that Stancaro was staying with him and thanked the *Antistes* for showing kindness to his fellow exile, whom he was keen

---

[110] See L. Sozzini, *Opere*, ed. A. Rotondò (Florence, 1986).

[111] See, for example, Zanchi to Bullinger, 28 December 1553 (StAZ E II 356, 740).

to see appointed to a lecturer's post in Lausanne.[112] Writing to Bullinger around the same time – and with the same end in mind – Stancaro expressed approbation for the Eucharistic stance of the Bernese church and repudiated Lutheranism.[113] Although, as we shall see, he soon developed a different understanding of the sacrament, several works that he published in Basle between May and August 1547 testify to the predominantly Zwinglian orientation of his theology at this time.[114] In the most important of these, the *Opera nuova della Riformatione*, Stancaro singled out the anti-Anabaptist works of Bullinger and Leo Jud for special praise, declaring that they should be read 'by all of Italy'.[115] Two subsequent works, the *Ispositione de la Epistola canonica di S. Giacobo* and the *Conciliationes quorundam locorum scripturae*, draw heavily on Bullinger's commentaries, although without acknowledgement; later, Josias Simler described the *Conciliationes* as incorporating 'nearly word for word' ('fere ad verbum') passages from Bullinger.[116]

In early 1548 Stancaro left Basle for Chiavenna, where he joined the growing band of religious exiles who had taken refuge in the Italian-speaking territories of the Rhaetian Freestate (Graubünden, the Grisons). These exiles, on whom a substantial body of literature now exists, have been credited with initiating a second wave of Reformed expansion in the three Rhaetian Leagues after 1540. Although the Second Ilanz Articles (1526) had in theory opened up the whole of Graubünden to the Reformation by investing individual communes with the *ius reformandi*, for most of the 1520s and 1530s Protestantism remained confined to the northern, German-speaking League of the Ten Jurisdictions and to the area around Chur. From 1537 onwards, a number of communities in the Romantsch-speaking Engadine also adopted the Reformation, but the establishment of Protestant congregations in the italophone communes of the Mesolcina,

---

[112] StAZ E II 366, 82.

[113] StAZ E II 335, 2087.

[114] See Bietenholz, *Der italienische Humanismus*, pp. 28–9.

[115] *Opera nuova di Francesco Stancaro Mantoano della Riformatione, si della dottrina Christiana, come della vera intelligentia de i sacramenti* (Basle, 1547), p. 549: 'Scrive Bullingero, et Leone Judah, il qual libro desiderai, che fosse letto da tutta la Italia.'

[116] J. Simler, *Bibliotheca instituta et collecta primum a Conrado Gesnero, deinde in Epitomen redacta et novorum librorum accessione locupletata … per Iosiam Simlerum Tigurinum* (Zurich, 1574), p. 207. Stancaro's dependence on Bullinger is most strikingly apparent in the 'Epistolae argumentum' that prefaces his commentary on James (*Ispositione de la Epistola canonica di S. Giacobo Vescovo di Gierusaleme* (Basle, 1547), pp. 20–1 (pp. 9–10 in the Latin edition); compare H. Bullinger, *In omnes apostolicas epistolas, divi videlicet Pauli xiii. et vii. canonicas, commentarii …* (Zurich, 1549) (*HBBibl*, no. 87), p. 109).

Valbregaglia and Poschiavo, and in the so-called 'subject lands' of Chiavenna, the Valtellina and Bormio, was the work of Italians attracted to Graubünden on account of its geographical proximity to their homeland and reputation for tolerance in religious matters.[117] Because the Rhaetian Reformed church was heavily dependent on Zurich, both for its theology and for its personnel, it was logical for the exiles to seek to initiate contacts with Bullinger and his fellow ministers, either directly or via the leadership of the Bündner church. The ensuing correspondence provided the Zurichers with a source of first-hand information on the progress of the Reformation in Italian-speaking Graubünden, as well as a means of exercising influence over the churches that were being set up there.

Graubünden's first Italian Reformed community was established in Chiavenna during the late 1530s, under the leadership first of Francesco Negri and then of Agostino Mainardi.[118] The cause of Protestantism in the region was given a significant boost by a decision of the Rhaetian Diet in 1544 to allow residents of the subject lands to maintain evangelical preachers and ministers at their own expense;[119] three years later, Giulio da Milano set up the first Protestant congregation in Poschiavo. But the crucial turning-point for Reformed fortunes was the arrival in Graubünden in early 1550 of Pier Paolo Vergerio, the former bishop of Capodistria.[120] During a ministry of three and a half years (1550–53), Vergerio achieved the conversion of the entire Valbregaglia

---

[117] The subject lands (*Untertanenländer, paesi sudditi*) had been conquered by the Leagues from Milan in 1512 and were administered by seven Bündner magistrates, each appointed for a period of two years by the Rhaetian Diet. The most powerful of these officials were the *commissario* of Chiavenna and the *podestà* of Sondrio, who also served as governor (*Landeshauptmann*) for the Valtellina as a whole. For further details of these arrangements, see A. Wendland, *Der Nutzen der Pässe und die Gefährdung der Seelen: Spanien, Mailand und der Kampf ums Veltlin (1620–1641)* (Zurich, 1995), pp. 37–46. On the constitution and government of the Freestate more generally, see R. Head, *Early Modern Democracy in the Grisons: Social Order and Political Language in a Swiss Mountain Canton, 1470–1620* (Cambridge, 1995), pp. 36–117.

[118] Until recently the standard account of the Reformation in Italian Graubünden was E. Camenisch, *Geschichte der Reformation und Gegenreformation in den italienischen Südtälern Graubündens und den ehemaligen Untertanenlanden Chiavenna, Veltlin und Bormio* (Chur, 1950). This work has now been superseded by C. Bonorand, *Reformatorische Emigration aus Italien in die Drei Bünde: Ihre Auswirkungen auf die kirchlichen, Verhältnisse – ein Literaturbericht* (Chur, 2000).

[119] U. Campell, *Historia Raetica*, ed. P. Plattner (Basle, 1890), p. 312.

[120] Important recent studies of Vergerio's career include A. Jacobson Schutte, *Pier Paolo Vergerio: The Making of an Italian Reformer* (Geneva, 1977), and R. Pierce, 'Pier Paolo Vergerio the Propagandist' (unpublished doctoral dissertation, University of Virginia, 1996). See also the essays published in U. Rozzo (ed.), *Pier Paolo Vergerio il Giovane, un polemista attraverso l'Europa del Cinquecento* (Udine, 2000).

and established a foothold for Protestantism around Sondrio in the Valtellina. He was also responsible for a vast outpouring of anti-Catholic propaganda, most of it destined for circulation in northern Italy.[121] Vergerio quickly reached the conclusion that Italian-speaking Rhaetia was ideally placed to act as a springboard for proselytizing activity in the Italian states themselves; he was even tempted to speculate that the region could play the same role for Italy as Geneva was playing for France. Although that ambition was never realized, through his collaboration with the Poschiavo printer Dolfin Landolfi, Vergerio was able to establish southern Graubünden as an important centre for the publication and distribution of Italian evangelical literature, on a par with Geneva and Basle.[122]

Throughout his sojourn in the Rhaetian Freestate, Vergerio kept up an intensive correspondence with the Zurichers. More than 70 letters from Vergerio to Bullinger survive from this period, to which may be added 17 addressed to Gwalther.[123] Vergerio also visited Zurich on as many as five occasions (August 1549, February 1550, August 1550, September 1551 and February 1552) in pursuit of various publishing projects.[124] His letters to Bullinger and Gwalther are dominated by news from the reconvened council of Trent, against which he was waging a fierce polemical campaign. Considerable attention is also given to the

---

[121] See Pierce, 'Vergerio', and S. Cavazza, 'Pier Paolo Vergerio nei Grigioni e in Valtellina (1549–1553): attività editoriale e polemica religiosa', in Pastore, *Riforma e società*, pp. 33–62. Of the approximately 150 titles that Vergerio published in his career, nearly a third appeared during the period 1549–51 (S. Cavazza, 'La censura ingannata: polemiche antiromane e usi della propaganda in Pier Paolo Vergerio', in U. Rozzo (ed.), *La censura libraria nell'Europa del secolo XVI* (Udine, 1997), pp. 273–95 [273]).

[122] On the Landolfi press, see C. Bonorand, 'Dolfin Landolfi von Poschiavo: Der erste Bündner Drucker der Reformationszeit', in M. Haas and R. Hauswirth (eds), *Festgabe Leonhard von Muralt* (Zurich, 1970), pp. 228–44; and U. Rozzo, 'Edizioni protestanti di Poschiavo alla metà del Cinquecento (e qualche aggiunta ginevrina)', in E. Campi and G. La Torre (eds), *Il protestantesimo di lingua italiana nella Svizzera: Figure e movimenti tra Cinquecento e Ottocento* (Turin, 2000), pp. 17–46.

[123] See E. Campi, 'Pier Paolo Vergerio e il suo epistolario con Heinrich Bullingero', in Rozzo, *Vergerio*, pp. 277–94. Unfortunately, I have not had an opportunity to consult the recent article by the same author on Vergerio's letters to Gwalther, which are in Italian. Gwalther's knowledge of Italian was shared by numerous other 16th-century Zurich churchmen, including Johannes Fries, Johannes Wolf and Konrad Gesner (see Vergerio to Gwalther, 13 September 1550 (ZB Ms. F 40, 563–4); and Curione to Bullinger, 22 June 1550 [ZB Ms. F 62, 182ᵛ]), although not by Bullinger (see Vergerio to Bullinger, 20 February 1551 (Schiess, I, no. 145); and Bullinger to Calvin, 21 April 1551 [CO, XIV, no. 1489]).

[124] Riggenbach, *Chronicon*, p. 178; E. Walder, 'Pier Paolo Vergerio und das Veltlin 1550', *Schweizer Beiträge zur allgemeinen Geschichte*, 3 (1945), pp. 229–46 (241); *Vadian BW*, VI, no. 1705; *Amerbachkorrespondenz*, VIII, nos 3460, 3463, 3495.

plight of evangelical believers in Italy, many of whom had sought refuge from persecution in Vergerio's home parish of Vicosoprano,[125] and to the role played by Vergerio himself in the Reformation of Italian Graubünden. Particularly noteworthy is a letter to Bullinger dated 7 May 1551, in which Vergerio recounts the destruction of the relics of St Gaudentius at Casaccia in the Valbregaglia.[126] Other letters note the abolition of the Mass in Bivio and Sils (Segl), and the emergence of a Reformed community in Sondrio.[127]

Like Curione, Vergerio offered the Zurichers copies of his publications (especially his polemics against Trent) in return for their own works.[128] In Curione's case, such exchanges served principally to oil the wheels of his developing friendship with Bullinger, but Vergerio saw them as having a wider propaganda function. In August 1551, for example, he requested that the Zurichers send him copies of Bullinger's *Decades* and other works for distribution in Italy, where he claimed they were popular.[129] Vergerio was also one of the few Italian reformers to show an interest in translating Bullinger's works into the vernacular (again for missionary purposes). In his letters, he claimed to have completed translations of several major works by the *Antistes*, including the *Perfectio christianorum*, the *Thorough demonstration that the evangelical churches are neither heretical nor schismatical* and *De sacrosancta coena*, and to have published an expanded version of an oration by Bullinger against the council of Trent; unfortunately, none of these works survives.[130] Vergerio also planned to make extensive use of Zurich's presses for the publication of some of his own writings, but because the city lacked anyone qualified to edit works in Italian he was forced to turn elsewhere.[131] In the event, only one work, the *Operetta*

---

[125] Vergerio to Bullinger, 17 September 1550 (Schiess, I, no. 133), 23 December 1550 (ibid., no. 140.2), 7 January 1551 (ibid., no. 142); Vergerio to Gwalther, 13 September 1550 (ZB Ms. F 40, 563–4), 21 January 1551 (ibid., 552), 8 March 1551 (ibid., 568–9), 24 March 1551 (ibid., 572).

[126] Schiess, I, no. 152.2. Writing to Gwalther shortly afterwards, Vergerio attempted to distance himself from the iconoclastic excesses of his supporters (ZB Ms. F 40, 557).

[127] Vergerio to Bullinger, 1 August 1552 (Schiess, I, no. 187.3); 23 January 1553 (ibid., no. 201).

[128] Schiess, I, nos 145, 158, 161, 191; ZB Ms. F 40, 553–4, 559, 568–9, 574, 561.

[129] Vergerio to Bullinger, 6 August 1551 (Schiess, I, no. 158); Vergerio to Gwalther, 6 August 1551 (ZB Ms. F 40, 561); Vergerio to Bullinger, September 1552 (Schiess, I, no. 191).

[130] Ibid., nos 189, 224.3, 229; Vergerio to Gwalther, 8 March and 24 April 1551 (ZB Ms. F 40, 568, 575). The publication of the oration was noted by Bullinger in his diary (see E. Egli (ed.), *Heinrich Bullinger Diarium (Annales vitae) der Jahre 1504–1574* (Basle, 1904), pp. 39–40). Josias Simler summarizes the work's contents in his *Narratio de ortu, vita, et obitu reverendi viri, D. Henrici Bullingeri ...* (Zurich, 1575), fols 25ᵛ–6ᵛ.

[131] Vergerio to Bullinger, 13 December [?] 1550 (Schiess, I, no. 138).

nuova ... nella quale si dimostrano le vere ragioni, che hanno mosso i Romani Pontefici ad instituir le belle ceremonie della Settimana santa, appeared in Zurich under his name, published by Andreas Gesner and Rudolf Wyssenbach in 1552.[132] Nor was Vergerio's experience unique: Zurich's output of Italian-language texts during the 16th century lags way behind that of Basle, Geneva or Poschiavo.[133] However, it should be noted that the Gesner–Wyssenbach partnership gave further, indirect support to Vergerio's polemical campaign, through the supply of type and other equipment to Dolfin Landolfi.[134]

Although Vergerio was by far the most prolific of Bullinger's Italian correspondents in the Rhaetian Freestate, more significant in the long term were the links forged between the Zurich church and the substantial Italian-speaking Reformed congregation in Chiavenna. Two senior figures within the town's evangelical community, Agostino Mainardi and Francesco Negri, entered into correspondence with Bullinger during the second half of the 1540s (although as early as 1542 Bullinger supplied a copy of his commentary on the New Testament epistles to Mainardi via Johannes Comander).[135] Negri was in correspondence not only with Bullinger, but with Bullinger's colleagues Johannes Wolf, pastor at the Fraumünster, and Johannes Fries; his son also attended one of the Zurich Latin schools. The Bassanese exile's humanist background, on show in his dedication of anti-papal distichs to Wolf and in his panegyric *Rhaetia* – a copy of which he sent to Bullinger – undoubtedly facilitated the development of this relationship.[136] Two of Negri's works, *Ovidianae metamorphoseos epitome* (1542) and *In dominicam precationem Meditatiuncula* (1560), were also printed in Zurich, by Christoph Froschauer. The fact that Konrad Gesner was able, in his *Bibliotheca universalis*, to signal in advance the publication of Negri's *Tragedia del libero arbitrio* (one of the most successful works of propaganda produced by the Italian

---

132 Vischer, *Bibliographie*, p. 419 (I 39). Recently Robert Pierce has argued for Vergerio's authorship of the *Annotomia della Messa*, traditionally ascribed to Agostino Mainardi. Pierce suggests that this work, too, was published by Gesner and Wyssenbach ('Agostino Mainardi, Pier Paolo Vergerio, and the *Anatomia missae*', BHR, 55 (1993), pp. 25–42). However, the attribution of the *Annotomia* both to Vergerio and to the Gesner-Wyssenbach press has been challenged by U. Rozzo ('Edizioni protestanti', pp. 29–33).

133 Robert Pierce lists only six editions for the period 1533–1609, out of a total of 269 books produced for an Italian readership (Pierce, 'Vergerio', appendix 1).

134 R. Bornatico, *L'arte tipografica nelle Tre Leghe (1549–1803)*, p. 43; Bonorand, 'Landolfi', p. 233; Pierce, 'Vergerio', p. 120.

135 Schiess, I, nos 31–2.

136 For the distichs and other verses dedicated by Negri to Wolf and Fries, see ZB Ms. D 75, fols 120ʳ, 266ʳ. The *Sylvula* appended to Negri's *Rhaetia* includes verses addressed to Gwalther and Fries.

evangelical movement) is a further indication of the closeness of Negri's ties with Zurich.[137]

During the early 1550s the Zurichers also forged links with other important centres of Protestantism in Italian Graubünden. In July 1553 Bullinger played host to Paolo Gaddi, a Cremonese evangelical who was later appointed minister to the Reformed church in Teglio. From there, Gaddi continued for a short while to correspond with the *Antistes*, although the principal influences on his theology seem to have been Calvinist rather than Zwinglian.[138] Better attested are Bullinger's contacts with the pastor of Samedan in the Engadine, Pietro Parisotto, to whom he supplied copies of some of his most important works;[139] with Giulio da Milano, the minister to Reformed congregations in Poschiavo and Tirano; and with Giovanni Beccaria, the reformer first of Locarno and then of the Mesolcina. Through Friedrich von Salis, Bullinger also had dealings with the Mantuan exile Alfonso Corradi, who in the preface to his commentary on the Apocalypse (1560) alludes to Bullinger's recently published sermons on the same text.[140]

Until now, my emphasis has been on those factors that united the Zurichers and their Italian correspondents: shared literary and cultural interests and, above all, a virulent anti-papalism. However, that was not the whole picture: by the end of the 1540s disagreements over doctrine, both within the Italian exile community, and between the more radical exiles and their Zurich correspondents, were threatening to turn this relationship sour. Increasingly, it was becoming clear that a significant

---

[137] Gesner, *Bibliotheca*, fol. 253ᵛ. On the *Tragedia* see E. Barbieri, 'Note sulla fortuna europea della "Tragedia del libero arbitrio" di Francesco Negri da Bassano', *BSSV*, 181 (1997), pp. 107–40.

[138] For biographical details and further references see Bonorand, *Reformatorische Emigration*, pp. 72–4.

[139] See Bundi, *Frühe Beziehungen*, p. 151; and Bonorand, *Reformatorische Emigration*, pp. 104–5.

[140] *In Apocalysim D. Ioan. Apostoli commentarius Alfonsi Conradi Mantuani* (Basle, 1560), fol. Aʳ: 'Sed cum ad finem huius mei laboris pervenissem contigit, ut magnus ille vir atque admodum de Christiana Republica benemeritus Henricus Bullingerus, suam in hunc librum praelectionem ediderit. Quae res effecit, ut videre videar, fratres mihi consulturos, ut meam potius supprimendam quam imprimendam procurem, quod omnem meam post ipsam lucubrationem facile iudicent supervacaneam esse, quicunque norint qualem se gesserit vir ille in totius novi Testamenti enarratione. Quod sane consilium, ut omnino a Christiana veritate proficisci confido, ita quam libenter admitterem, si huc in meis lucubrationibus spectassem, ut ex his aliquid nominis apud eruditos mihi accederet: sed cum nihil aliud inde quaeram, quam ut hi fratres qui meam ex me confessionem non audierunt, eam ex his meis petere possint, non video quid mihi obstet Bullingeri erudita in hunc librum enarratio.' In a letter dated 15 October 1557, von Salis informed Bullinger of Corradi's plans to publish a commentary on the Apocalypse and promised to pass on a copy of the work once it was complete (StAZ E II 365, 204; Schiess, II, no. 33).

number of the new arrivals brought with them expectations of reform that the Zurich church was unable or unwilling to meet. It is to those differences that I now wish to turn.

iii. Theologies in conflict: early encounters between the Zurich church and Italian 'heresy'

To understand why doctrinal controversy came to occupy such a central place in relations between the Zurichers and their Italian contacts, we need to consider the religious context from which the latter emerged. The Italian evangelical movement was shaped by an extraordinary mix of influences: Erasmianism (often understood as a form of 'Lutheranism'), northern Protestantism (of all complexions), and autochthonous reformist currents, such as the Cassinese Benedictine tradition explored by Carlo Ginzburg, Adriano Prosperi and Barry Collett.[141] During the 1520s and 1530s the spiritual climate in Italy was extremely fluid, inviting comparison with the 'magnificent religious anarchy' of France prior to the advent of Calvinism,[142] or the *Wildwuchs* of the early German Reformation. The establishment of the Roman Inquisition in July 1542 did not alter that situation fundamentally, at least in the first instance. As Massimo Firpo and others have demonstrated, for at least another decade senior clerics such as Giovanni Morone and Reginald Pole continued to juggle their loyalty to the hierarchical church with their adherence to an essentially Protestant understanding of justification.

What set the Italian evangelical movement apart was its inability to move beyond this 'Gärungsphase' (Seidel Menchi): to make the transition from conventicles to 'gathered' churches of the sort which took shape in France during the years immediately prior to the wars of religion.[143] Giulio da Milano drew attention to this in his *Esortatione al martirio*, observing: 'The Christians of Italy are like dead, dispersed limbs without a head, without direction, for the Italian churches are neither congregated nor regulated according to

---

141 C. Ginzburg and A. Prosperi, *Giochi di pazienza: Un seminario sul <<Beneficio di Cristo>>* (Turin, 1975); B. Collett, *Italian Benedictine Scholars and the Reformation: The Congregation of Santa Giustina of Padua* (Oxford, 1985). See, however, the criticisms of both works in S. Seidel Menchi, *Erasmus als Ketzer: Reformation und Inquisition im Italien des 16. Jahrhunderts* (Leiden, 1993), pp. 171–2, n. 12.

142 L. Febvre, 'Une question mal posée: Les origines de la réforme française et le problème des causes de la réforme', in Febvre, *Au coeur religieux du XVIᵉ siècle* (Paris, 1957), pp. 3–70 (66).

143 Seidel Menchi, *Erasmus*, pp. 13–14.

the Word of God'.[144] According to Giulio, the lack of formally constituted churches was responsible for the lukewarm faith of Italian believers and their readiness to abjure in the face of persecution. Without the public preaching of God's word and the proper administration of the sacraments (the 'soul' and 'nerves' of the church), how could Italy's evangelicals be expected to take up arms and fight for Christ?[145]

The organizational weakness of Italy's evangelical communities also hindered the establishment of mechanisms for the promotion and enforcement of doctrinal uniformity such as developed elsewhere.[146] To quote Silvana Seidel Menchi:

> Because in Italy the historical situation was not reached in which out of the Reformation of doubt could develop the Reformation of certainties, and because, therefore, the two were never able to come into conflict, the Reformation movement [in Italy] continued to be characterized by the habit of doubt and the theme of tolerance.[147]

In the absence of institutional restraints on belief, or of a normative authority (besides scripture) to replace that of the old church, there was little to prevent individuals slipping over into strikingly heterodox positions once the initial breach with Catholicism had been made. It is important to emphasize that Italy's evangelicals did not assimilate the ideas of the northern reformers uncritically, but selectively and as aids to their own, more or less independent, scrutiny of traditional religion. In Italy, 'The paradox of Erasmus – that "every person has the right to be a theologian" – was taken literally'.[148]

There is evidence that this process was under way even before the impact of the Reformation had begun to be felt in Italy. In 1519, for example, the Calabrian Tiberio Russiliano published a work in which he argued for the eternity of the universe and denied the divinity of Christ

---

[144] 'Gli christiani d'Italia son come membri dispersi, e morti, senza guida, e senza capo, non essendo le chiese Italiane congregate, ne regolate secondo la parola di Dio' (*Esortatione al martirio, di Giulio da Milano, riveduta, et ampliata* (n.p., 1552), p. 77; English translation from Martin, *Venice's Hidden Enemies*, p. 9).

[145] *Esortatione*, pp. 77–8: 'Il corpo non puo vivere senza l'anima, ne le membre possano star congionte senza i nervi. Però essendo le congregationi de li nostri Italiani senza nervo, e senza vita, come possono pigliar l'armi in mano, e combattere per Giesu Christo?'

[146] Exceptions to this pattern include Cremona (see Chabod, *Per la storia religiosa*, pp. 172–8) and Vicenza, where Alessandro Trissino attempted to impose a distinctively Calvinist brand of reform (see A. Olivieri, *Riforma ed eresia a Vicenza nel Cinquecento* (Rome, 1992), pp. 324–46).

[147] Seidel Menchi, *Erasmus*, p. 269.

[148] Ibid., p. 100.

– views that appear to have been widely held in Bologna at the time.[149] Home-grown radicalism of this sort continued to influence many of those drawn to the Italian evangelical movement, fuelling theological experimentation within its ranks. Recent work on perhaps the best-known philo-Protestant group – the circle of Juan de Valdés in Naples – provides a dramatic example of where such speculation could lead. Following Valdés' death in 1541, several of his former disciples came under the influence of another Spaniard, Juan de Villafranca, who taught them to question the doctrines of the Trinity and the divinity of Christ.[150] Radicalized Valdesians such as Girolamo Busale were subsequently responsible for transforming Venetian Anabaptism into an antitrinitarian movement with strong judaizing tendencies; some ended up rejecting the New Testament and revealed religion altogether.[151] The susceptibility of Italian evangelicals to ideas of this sort was a major preoccupation of orthodox Protestants such as Giulio da Milano, who warned his compatriots against heretics who 'with hidden cunning disturb the pious churches, and with a malicious fury make every effort to ensure that the ministers of the Gospel are accounted liars'.[152] Few adopted positions as extreme as that of the Venetian Anabaptists, but indifference towards the niceties of Protestant dogma, even a tendency towards universalism, was widespread.[153]

Such sentiments were unlikely to find favour with the representatives

---

[149] Dall'Olio, *Eretici e Inquisitori*, pp. 34–44.

[150] A. Stella, *Anabattismo e antitrinitarismo in Italia nel XVI secolo: Nuove ricerche storiche* (Padua, 1969), pp. 25–6; M. Firpo, '<<Ioanne Valdessio è stato heretico pessimo>>: forme, esiti e metamorfosi dell'<<heresia>> valdesiana', in *Tra alumbrados e <<spirituali>>: Studi su Juan de Valdés e il valdesianismo nella crisi religiosa del '500 italiano* (Florence, 1990), pp. 9–125 (92).

[151] On Venetian Anabaptism, see Stella, *Antitrinitarismo*, and *Dall'anabattismo al socinianesimo nel cinquecento Veneto: Ricerche storiche* (Padua, 1967); Martin, *Venice's Hidden Enemies*, pp. 99–112. The testimony of Pietro Manelfi, formerly our principal source of information on the movement (C. Ginzburg (ed.), *I costituti di don Pietro Manelfi* [Florence, 1970]), has now been shown to be unreliable (see Stella, *Antitrinitarismo*, pp. 64–72; U. Gastaldi, *Storia dell'anabattismo*, (2 vols, Turin, 1972/81), II, pp. 554–8).

[152] *Esortatione*, pp. 86–7: 'Gl'Anabatisti accompagnati da Georgiani, et da tutti gl'altri heretici, con una mascherata astutia disturbano le pie chiese, et con una velenosa rabbia fanno ogni sforzo, accioche li ministri de'l Vangelio siano tenuti bugiardi.' Giulio's detailed knowledge of Italian Anabaptism is evident from a tract appended to the second edition of the *Esortatione*, in which he names the areas where Anabaptists are active, identifies some of their leaders, and lists their distinctive doctrines. Those included denial of the virgin birth and large parts of the New Testament, and – in the case of the Anabaptists of Naples – a belief in the imminent re-establishment of the earthly Jerusalem.

[153] Silvana Seidel Menchi cites the example of the silk weaver Pietro Antonio Ungari, who argued that Muslims and Jews could be saved in their own faith (*Erasmus*, p. 179).

of the emerging Protestant orthodoxies which the Italian exiles would encounter north of the Alps. False perceptions of Protestant Europe current in Italy provided another potential source of friction. In Italian evangelical circles the 'Lutheran' states of Germany and Switzerland had the reputation of havens of religious liberty, where each was permitted to live and worship 'after their own fashion' ('a suo modo').[154] Many Italians suffered bitter disillusionment when, as exiles, they came face to face with the reality of the magisterial Reformation. The experience of Pietro di Casalmaggiore, a Lombard evangelical who spent time in Chiavenna during the late 1540s and early 1550s before returning to the Catholic church, is instructive. Pietro told the Milanese inquisitors that he had gone into exile 'thinking to find a paradise of manners and faith', but had been forced to leave Graubünden after daring to criticize the doctrines and lifestyles of the local Reformed.[155] Having repudiated the spiritual 'tyranny' of the papacy, many exiles were impatient of alternative, Protestant, attempts to constrain consciences. In his *De amplitudine beati regni Dei*, for example, Curione denounced the use of force in the service of religion:

> The Gospel ... of our Lord Jesus Christ is not to be propagated by violence or arms, but by preaching and the power of the spirit, and by clear demonstration, example, patience, charity, placability, justice, temperance, constancy, goodness, faith and gentleness, by which the strength of the holy spirit is made manifest. ... Nothing is so voluntary and so free as religious belief. That is why it is passed down by instruction and persuasion, rather than by threats or fear. We defend it not by killing, but by dying; not by rage, but by patience; not by fraud, but by faith. If you seek to protect religion by compulsion and violence, you will not defend it, but rather pollute and violate it.[156]

Neither was a readiness to resort to coercion the only similarity that

---

[154] Seidel Menchi, *Erasmus*, p. 135. This impression was encouraged by works such as Vergerio's *Epistola ... nella quale sono descritte molte cose della Città, e della Chiesa di Geneva* (Geneva, 1550), and *Del battesmo et de fiumi che nascono ne paesi de signori Grisoni* (n.p. , n.d. [Poschiavo, 1550]). See the analysis of the *Epistola* in Pierce, 'Vergerio', pp. 267–73.

[155] The confession is published in Chabod, *Per la storia religiosa*, pp. 240–47.

[156] *Coelii Secundi Curionis de amplitudine beati regni Dei, dialogi sive libri duo* (n. p. [Poschiavo], 1554), pp. 215-17: 'Evangelium ... IESU CHRISTI Domini nostri, non vi aut armis propagandum est, sed praedicatione, spiritus energia, et evidentia, moribus, patientia, charitate, placabilitate, iustitia, temperantia, constantia, bonitate, fide, lenitate, quibus vis illa sacri spiritus sese exerit, et ostendit. ... Nihil est tam voluntarium, nihil tam liberum quam religionis sententia. Idcirco illa instituendo ac persuadendo, non minis aut metu traditur: quam non occidendo, sed moriendo, non saevitia sed patientia, non fraude sed fide defendimus. Si enim imperiis, ac vi religionem tueri velis, iam non defendetur, sed polluetur ac violabitur potius.'

dissenting exiles noted between the papacy and the leaderships of the various Protestant churches. Some also accused the Reformed establishment of seeking to dilute the scripture principle in the interests of upholding a conservatively defined orthodoxy, thereby perpetuating many of Rome's most fundamental errors.

Evidence has already been adduced to show that the theology of the Zurich church found at least some echo among Italy's evangelicals. However, it would be a mistake to assume that the Italian manifestation of Zwinglianism was a faithful reproduction of its Zurich prototype. Significantly, where Zwingli's name was mentioned in the Italian context it was usually in connection with the most radical aspect of his theological programme, his doctrine of the Eucharist; Zwingli the gradualist reformer, the fierce opponent of Anabaptist sectarianism, hardly featured. The Zurich reformer's iconoclastic reputation, put about by his Lutheran and Catholic opponents, may well have left many Italian evangelicals with a one-sided view of the man and of the reforms for which he was responsible.[157] In fact, the emphasis of Zwingli's Reformation was on continuity with existing practice wherever possible; the legacy of medieval Christendom was not rejected out of hand. As has been demonstrated recently, the institutions of the remodelled Zurich church were firmly grounded in the reforming traditions of the 15th-century diocese of Constance, while canon law continued to inform its approach to such issues as the regulation of marriage.[158]

The Zurichers were similarly cautious in their handling of sensitive doctrinal questions, in particular the fundamentals of triadology and Christology. Zwingli had no wish to see the church's traditional stance on those matters altered. In his first Berne sermon of 1528, he drew on Augustine's analogy with the faculties of the human soul to illustrate the interrelationship of the three persons of the Godhead, while in the *Fidei ratio* he affirmed his belief in the Trinity as set out in the Nicene and Athanasian creeds.[159] On numerous occasions Zwingli endorsed the Chalcedonian understanding of Christ's person, against those who accused him of teaching Nestorianism.[160] In his final works he even sought to tone down the radicalism of his Eucharistic views, reappropriating much of the language traditionally applied to the

---

[157] Compare D'Ascia, 'Tra platonismo e riforma', p. 691.

[158] Gordon, *Clerical Discipline*, pp. 23–72; H. Stucki, <<Ergo legitima decernitur>>: Ein komplizierter Fall vor dem Zürcher Ehegericht, 1534', in H. Oberman et al. (eds), *Das Reformierte Erbe: Festschrift für Gottfried W. Locher* (2 vols, Zurich, 1993), I, pp. 419–26.

[159] Z, VI/1, 456–7; ibid., VI/2, 792.

[160] See, for example, ibid., VI/2, 792–4; VI/5, 66–8.

sacraments. Where he had earlier insisted on the radical duality of matter and spirit, and the corresponding ontological separateness of the sacraments and grace, he now began to explore ways in which the two might be linked – through analogy, or through the operation of the Holy Spirit as the mediator of Christ's presence (contemplatio fidei).[161]

This process of re-evaluation continued under Zwingli's successors, who were keen to rebut the charge of sacramentarianism commonly levelled against the Zurich church. From the mid-1530s onwards, Heinrich Bullinger presided over a concerted campaign to rehabilitate Zwingli's memory. That involved, among other things, bringing his more 'positive' late theology of the Eucharist to the attention of the reading public, notably through the publication of the Fidei expositio in 1536. In the Zurich Confession of 1545, Bullinger cites this last work as evidence for his predecessor's recognition of the benefits conferred by the sacrament on those who receive it with faith.[162] The same point is made in Rudolf Gwalther's Apology for Zwingli, published together with the first complete Latin edition of Zwingli's works, which also attempted more generally to underline his orthodoxy and in so doing, to put distance between Zwingli and those 'enthusiasts' (Schwärmer) with whom he had been associated by Luther.[163]

The very fact that Zwinglianism was historically tainted with heresy (although Bullinger strove to locate the origins of Anabaptism elsewhere, the prominence of Zwingli's early followers in the first sectarian community at Zollikon remained a source of embarrassment) lent added urgency to the Zurich theologians' efforts to demonstrate their orthodox credentials. The 'catholicity' of Reformed teaching, as opposed to that of the radicals, is therefore a recurring theme of Bullinger's works. In particular, Bullinger was anxious to show that the

---

[161] P. Sanders, 'Heinrich Bullinger et l'invention (1546–1551) avec Jean Calvin d'une théologie réformée de la cène: La gestion de l'héritage zwinglienne lors de l'élaboration du 'Consensus Tigurinus' (1549) et la rédaction des 'Decades' (1551)' (unpublished doctoral thesis, University of Lille, 1989). Summarized in Sanders, 'Heinrich Bullinger et le <<zwinglianisme tardif>> aux lendemains du <<Consensus Tigurinus>>', in Oberman, Das Reformierte Erbe, I, pp. 307–23.

[162] Warhaffte Bekanntnuß der dieneren der kilchen zu Zurych / was sy uß Gottes wort / mit der heyligen allgemeinen Christenlichen Kilchen gloubind und leerind ... (Zurich, 1545) (HBBibl, no. 161), fols 10ʳ–16ʳ.

[163] Rudolphi Gualtheri Tigurini ad Catholicam Ecclesiam omnemque posteritatem, pro D. Huld. Zuinglio et Operum eius aeditione Apologia (Zurich, 1545), fol. 49ᵛ: 'Licet enim signa et tesseras Sacramenta [Zuinglius] vocarit, non tamen ita extenuavit, ut illa nihil aliud, quam quod militaris aliqua tessera significat, continere sentiret. Quin potius talia agnovit quae et fidem provocarent, et nos de Dei promissionibus certiores redderent, adeoque ipsum Christum nobis praesentem ob oculos quasi statuerent, fidei contemplatione apprehendendum.'

teachings of the Reformed church did not constitute heresy as defined by imperial law.[164] To that end, his *Decades* (first published in 1549) were prefaced by a litany of confessional statements: the creeds of Nicaea, Constantinople, Ephesus, Chalcedon, and the first and fourth councils of Toledo; the declaration of faith of Irenaeus; Tertullian's rule of faith; the creeds of Athanasius and Pope Damasus; and, crucially, the anti-heresy edict of the Emperors Gratian, Valentinian II and Theodosius I (380).[165] Bullinger's reasons for including this material in his most important theological work were not simply tactical: the ancient creeds embodied for him the eternal truths of the Christian faith.[166] Although the *Antistes* stressed simplicity of exposition, this ought not to be confused with the desire of some Italian exiles for a simplified Christianity. When Bullinger chose not to probe the more abstruse articles of doctrine, it was because he believed that such speculation was unlikely to contribute to the edification of ordinary believers, rather than because he had ceased to regard those tenets as fundamental: Bullinger's preferred option was simply to take the doctrinal formularies of the early church as read. In a later work, the *Summa Christenlicher Religion* (1556), he warned his readers against pondering the doctrine of the Trinity too deeply, pointing out that for a thousand years Christian princes had forbidden such questioning 'on pain of death' ('by verlierung lybs und läbens').[167] From Bullinger's point of view, the execution of Michael Servetus – of which, as we shall see, many Italian exiles were critical – was entirely justifiable on the basis of imperial law.

Bullinger's traditionalism is further manifested in his attitude towards the early church councils and the Fathers. The Fathers had played a key role in Bullinger's initial conversion to Protestantism and in shaping his early theology: the *Antistes*' emphasis on the link between the full divinity and the saving work of Christ, for example, was derived from

---

[164] See H. Bullinger, *Das die Evangelischen Kilchen weder kätzerische noch abtrünnige / sunder gantz rechtglöubige und allgemeine Jesu Christi kilchen syend / grundtliche erwysung ...* (Zurich, 1552) (*HBBibl*, no. 259), fols 18ʳ–19ʳ. Bullinger's colleague Theodor Bibliander takes a similar line in his work *De summa trinitate et fide catholica* (Basle, 1555).

[165] *Sermonum decades quinque, de potissimis Christianae fidei religionis capitibus, in tres tomos digestae, authore Heinrycho Bullingero, ecclesiae Tigurinae ministro* (Zurich, 1577), sigs βʳ–β6ʳ. A critical edition of the *Decades* is currently in preparation.

[166] See W. Hollweg, *Heinrich Bullingers Hausbuch: Eine Untersuchung über die Anfänge der reformierten Predigtliteratur* (Neukirchen, 1956), p. 199: 'Die Übereinstimmung der reformatorischen Lehre mit der der Alten Kirche darzutun ist neben dem Schriftprinzip eine zweite wesentliche Grundeigentümlichkeit unseres Predigtbuches [the *Decades*].'

[167] *Summa Christenlicher Religion* (Zurich, 1556) (*HBBibl*, no. 283), fol. 26ʳ.

Athanasius.[168] Bullinger also identified closely with the orthodox heroes of the early church in their struggles against doctrinal opponents, consciously modelling his massive history and refutation of Anabaptism, *Der Widertöufferen ursprung*, on Irenaeus' *Against the heresies*.[169] Like other Protestant writers, Bullinger refused to accord the councils or Fathers any authority independent of scripture, and accepted that they had frequently erred.[170] However, this formal adherence to the scripture principle concealed a subtle retention of tradition, as an interpretative filter through which the biblical text was to be received. For Bullinger, only those readings of the Bible that conform to the 'rule of faith' ('regel des gloubens') – the church's 'universal, certain and definitive interpretation of scripture' – are to be credited.[171] The 'articles of faith' ('artickel des Gloubens') are not to be rejected along with false traditions, as they are by certain radical heretics.[172] So far as the doctrines of God and Christ are concerned, the rulings of the early church councils and statements of the Fathers remain binding on Christians, because they faithfully articulate the position of scripture.[173] Of course, the circularity of the argument led to a blurring, in practice, of the distinction between biblical and conciliar/patristic authority. It was on precisely that point that the Zurichers were to clash with some of the more radical Italian exiles.

---

168 Staedtke, *Bullinger*, p. 44.

169 *Der Widertöufferen ursprung / fürgang / Secten / wäsen / fürnemen und gemeine jrer leer Artickel / ouch jre gründ und warumm sy sich absünderind / unnd ein eigne kirchen anrichtend / ...* (Zurich, 1561) (*HBBibl*, no. 395), fol. 1ʳ: 'Diewyl ich mir fürgenommen hab / mit der hilff Gott deß allmächtigen / zů schryben wider die schwären irrthumm und schädlichen secten / trennungen oder rottungen der Widertöuffern / hat mich gůt und kömlich syn bedücht / etlicher maß nachzevolgen dem byspel deß alten getrüwen Bischoffs und säligen martyres Christi Jesu / Irenei / das wie der selb in sinem werck wider die Valentinianer geschriben / grad von anfang jre leer und wunderbare zertrennungen verzeichnet / welche er dann hernach widerfochten und verworffen hat: also wil ich ouch dises mines werck wider die Widertöuffer anheben vom ursprung / unnd demnach erzellen jr wunderbarliche spaltung in vilerley Secten: unnd die selben hernach / mit Gottes wort / so kurtz es ymmer gesyn mag / widerlegen und umbkeeren / und das zů eeren Gottes und siner warheit / zů hilff der Kirchen und jren dieneren / zů underrichtung der einfaltigen unberichten / zů trost / sterckung und warnung aller glöubigen.'

170 In his *De conciliis* (Zurich, 1561) (*HBBibl*, no. 402), Bullinger cites disapprovingly Gregory the Great's assertion that the rulings of the four ecumenical councils are to be accorded equal authority with the four Gospels (fol. 103ʳ⁻ᵛ).

171 *Grundtliche erwysung*, fol. 9ʳ: 'Es hat aber die allgemein Christlich kilch allweg gehebt / und hat noch hütt by tag / ein allgemeine gewüsse unnd bestimpte ußlegung der geschrifft (genommen uß der änlikeit des gloubens) welche sy allen glöubigen trüwlich angäben hat / ... .'

172 Ibid., fol. 27ᵛ.

173 *Decades*, fol. 10ʳ (1:3).

Many of the exiles with whom Bullinger had dealings were, it must be stressed, perfectly content with his conservative vision of reform; some, like Agostino Mainardi, Giulio da Milano and, later, Scipione Lentolo, emerged as valued allies in the struggle to defend it, often outstripping Bullinger himself in their zeal for the cause. Others found it difficult to accept the restrictions on doctrinal speculation that Bullinger's approach entailed. In strictly doctrinal terms, the *Antistes'* Italian critics were a diverse group, as one might expect given the eclecticism of the Italian evangelical movement that had produced them; certainly they did not offer anything so coherent as an alternative programme for reform. What they shared was an uneasiness with the increasing confessionalism of official Reformed theology, and with the determination of the Reformed leadership to punish deviation from an orthodoxy defined with reference to catholic tradition as well as scripture: both characteristics of the papacy that the exiles had so publicly repudiated.

The fundamental differences of outlook between the Zurich church and this section of the Italian exile community, termed 'heretics' by Cantimori, came to the surface on several occasions during the 1540s and early 1550s. The most famous of these early confrontations involved Bullinger and the Sicilian exile Paolo Ricci (also known under the alias of Lisia Fileno), who after fleeing Italy for Graubünden in summer 1542 assumed the name by which he is best known, Camillo Renato.[174] In Italy, Camillo appears to have been a leading proponent of the Zwinglian view of the Eucharist; recently, Paolo Simoncelli has made a compelling case for linking the spread of 'sacramentarian' ideas in Modena, Bologna, Venice and Ferrara to his preaching itinerary.[175] In a lengthy statement to the Inquisition in Ferrara, Renato attacked those (Catholics) who interpreted the Mass as a sacrifice in its own right, rather than as simply the recollection of Christ's once-for-all self-offering; his language suggests a degree of sympathy, cautiously expressed, with the primary Zwinglian understanding of the Eucharist as memorial.[176] Given his Zwinglian sympathies, it was natural for Renato, following his departure from Italy, to seek to establish direct

---

[174] A bibliography of the sizeable literature relating to Renato has been compiled by S. Calvani in A. Séguenny (ed.), *Bibliotheca Dissidentium: Répertoire des non-conformistes réligieux des seizième et dix-septième siècles*, IV (Baden-Baden, 1984), pp. 155–90. The most important studies to date are G. Williams, 'Camillo Renato (c.1500–?1570)', in J. Tedeschi (ed.), *Italian Reformation Studies in Honor of Laelius Socinus* (Florence, 1965), pp. 105–83; and C. Renato, *Opere, documenti e testimonianze*, ed. A. Rotondò (Florence, 1968); see also Cantimori, *Eretici*, pp. 82–97.

[175] Simoncelli, 'Inquisizione romana', p. 39.

[176] Renato, *Opere*, p. 72.

contact with the Zurichers. In his first letter to Bullinger, which dates from late 1542, he described his experiences at the hands of the Inquisition and urged Bullinger to throw his weight behind the cause of the Gospel in Italy.[177] Another two letters survive from 1544, suggesting the beginnings of a regular correspondence with Zurich.[178] Throughout this time Renato was busy organizing an evangelical congregation at Caspano in the Valtellina, where he was employed as a tutor by a local branch of the Paravicini family.

However, Renato's 'Zwinglianism' was not all that it appeared. The records of his trial in Ferrara give evidence of heterodox tendencies in respect of such doctrines as the immortality of the soul, which remained a central tenet of Reformed belief.[179] There are also grounds for believing that he was critical of the orthodox doctrine of the Trinity.[180] In exile, Renato showed a marked reluctance to defer to the authority of established Reformed leaders like Bullinger, or to be confined by the doctrinal parameters that they had set; rather, he insisted on offering independent contributions to what he saw as an ongoing process of purging Christ's church of abuses, especially with regard to the sacraments. It has been suggested that his assumption of the name Camillus was designed to be connotative of this role: just as the classical Camillus had restored the *signa* captured by the Gauls to Rome, so his modern equivalent was to claim that he had rediscovered the true meaning of the evangelical 'signs', baptism and the Eucharist.[181]

Renato's independent stance first became apparent in May 1545, when Bullinger sent him a copy of the Zurich church's *Confession* on the Lord's Supper. In his reply, Renato began by emphasizing his basic agreement with Bullinger's formulation of the doctrine of the Eucharist. However, he also insisted on the right of the Caspano congregation to work out its own position on the basis of scripture, rather than in response to confessions devised by others. In a statement that must have worried Bullinger – who was concerned, as we have seen, to rebut the charge that Zwingli's followers had reduced the Eucharist to a ceremony

---

[177] Ibid., pp. 135–7; Schiess, I, no. 37.

[178] Renato, *Opere*, pp. 138–9; Schiess, I, nos 54–5.

[179] Renato, *Opere*, pp. 64–5.

[180] In a statement to the Venetian Inquisition, the Valtellinese merchant Gianbattista Tabacchino claimed that he and Renato shared a faith in one God the Father and in the Son, Jesus Christ, who would return his kingdom to the Father at the last judgment. When pressed on whether he believed in the Trinity, Tabacchino replied that he regarded the Father and the Holy Spirit as identical and the Son as a being filled with the plenitude of God's Spirit. Like the Venetian Anabaptists, he also denied the virgin birth of Christ (Stella, *Anabattismo*, pp. 58–64).

[181] Williams, 'Renato', p. 140.

devoid of spiritual benefit – Renato declared that the evangelicals of Caspano acknowledged nothing in the Lord's Supper 'besides the memory of Christ's death'.[182]

When pressed to respond to the *Confession* in more detail, he delivered a searching critique of the Bullingerian doctrine of the sacrament, focusing particularly on the notion of 'spiritual eating' (the idea that, in the Eucharist, the elect feed on Christ by faith). Like the Zurichers, Renato interprets the 'eating' (*manducatio*) of Christ's flesh described in Chapter 6 of John's Gospel as a metaphor for faith. But unlike Bullinger and his colleagues, he understands this act as temporally limited to the moment of conversion, to the first reception of faith by God, and therefore as extraneous to the Supper, which merely commemorates the event that made salvation possible (Christ's death). Renato sets up a series of antitheses to demonstrate the utter separateness of spiritual and physical eating: spiritual eating is a single event, which takes place in the heart of individual believers and in the absence of outward signs, whereas the Eucharist is a repeatable, public rite, which requires the presence of material elements; in spiritual eating, the faithful receive the grace of God and forgiveness of sins, but in the Lord's Supper they merely testify, by their participation, to a spiritual transformation that has already taken place within them. According to Renato, the Eucharist was instituted not so that believers might thereby experience communion with Christ, but so that they might make outward profession of their membership of his mystical body. It is not even a re-enactment of the Last Supper: there Christ's intention was to strengthen the faith of his disciples, whereas the Eucharist is an act of thanksgiving by those who already believe. There can be no question – and this sets Renato in clear opposition to Bullinger – of the sacrament confirming, let alone bestowing faith. In a further twist to his argument, Renato maintains that the Protestant Eucharist as presently constituted is no more than partially reformed. According to Renato, the Eucharist as conceived of by Christ consisted of two parts, which he terms *epulum* and *libatio*. For full conformity to biblical practice to be established, the first of these (identified by Renato with the love-feasts of the New Testament and sub-apostolic church) must be restored as a prelude to the consecration of the bread and wine.[183]

---

[182] Renato to Bullinger, 15 May 1545 (Renato, *Opere*, pp. 140–41; Schiess, I, no. 58).

[183] Renato to Bullinger, 10 August 1545 (Renato, *Opere*, pp. 141–6; Schiess, I, no. 59). This proposal has parallels in the liturgical practice of some of the Italian evangelical communities with which Renato was associated. Thus the schoolmaster Antonio Bendinelli reported having attended suppers organized by the Modenese evangelicals which included a Eucharistic blessing and the distribution of bread 'sufficiente non solamente a satiare i nostri animi, ma anchora a pascere i corpi' (Adorni-Braccesi, <<*Una città infetta*>>, pp. 211–12).

Renato's suggestion that the process of recovering and reinstating true doctrine and worship had not been carried forward to completion by the first generation of reformers was one that Bullinger was to come across repeatedly in the course of his dealings with Italian religious radicals. Initially, the *Antistes'* response to Renato's criticisms was conciliatory. In a letter dated 18 September 1545, he was careful to note areas of agreement between himself and his correspondent, such as their shared opposition to any suggestion of a corporeal presence in the Eucharist. If Renato examined his explanations carefully, Bullinger maintained, he would find that the position of the Zurich church was broadly compatible with his own. However, the detailed arguments set out in Bullinger's letter revealed the extent of the gulf separating the two reformers. Against Renato, Bullinger emphasized the links between 'spiritual' and 'sacramental' eating. He defended the claim made in the Zurich *Confession* that the sacraments act as auxiliaries to faith, and criticized Renato's attempt to posit a complete temporal disjunction between faith and sacrament: there was no contradiction, Bullinger argued, between the simultaneous 'recollection' and 'perception' of Christ's sacrifice. Similarly, there was no qualitative difference between the church's Eucharist and the Last Supper: both served the same dual function, to proclaim Christ's death and to build up faith in the elect. Bullinger also dismissed Renato's call for the restoration of love-feasts, for fear that such rites would serve as an occasion for profanity and excess, as they had in the early church.[184]

Renato was unmoved by Bullinger's arguments. In his reply, dated 2 November, he reiterated most of the points that he had made previously, insisting once again that his stance was consistent with scripture.[185] In a subsequent letter he cautioned Bullinger against attempting to enforce adherence to an interpretation of the Eucharist which lacked biblical foundation: the Zurichers should avoid emulating the bad example set by the Latin Fathers, 'who continue to vex us even though dead'.[186] That negative judgment on the Fathers – and, by extension, on all non-scriptural authority – is symptomatic of the extreme biblicism that underpins Renato's theology. Similar sentiments are expressed in his most important surviving work, the *Trattato del Battesmo e della Santa Cena*, written in Chiavenna between September 1547 and December 1548.[187] The *Trattato* was Renato's response to a sermon on the Eucharist delivered by the local Reformed minister, Agostino Mainardi,

---

[184] Renato, *Opere*, pp. 146–50; Schiess, I, no. 61.

[185] Renato, *Opere*, pp. 151–4; Schiess, I, no. 63.

[186] Renato, *Opere*, pp. 156–7; Schiess, I, no. 73.

[187] Renato, *Opere*, pp. 91–108; for the dating of the work, see ibid., pp. 295–7.

in which Mainardi faithfully rehearsed the Bullingerian doctrine of the sacraments.[188] In his own work, Renato repudiates Mainardi's 'conjectures' and proposes that all terms foreign to scripture (including 'sacrament' itself) be abolished. 'Innovation in language', he claims, is at the root of all 'new opinions' and doctrinal errors; it is the product of a 'carnal wisdom' fundamentally opposed to the 'Christian spirit'. According to Renato, Mainardi's doctrine of baptism and the Eucharist has its origin in human discourse, which 'ruins the company of Christ', as opposed to scripture, which 'builds it up'. In an impressive piece of humanist philological criticism, Renato explores the origins of the word 'sacrament' and deconstructs its meaning. On the basis of his analysis, he concludes that Mainardi's continued use of the term for theological purposes is 'profane and scholastic and papal, not worthy to be received by those who understand what is meant by it, and certainly not by Christians'.[189]

Bullinger's exchange with Renato illustrated a basic disagreement between the Zurichers and some Italian exiles (Cantimori's 'heretics') concerning the interpretation of the scripture principle and its implications for the discourse and practice of Reformed theology. Whereas radicals such as Renato favoured an exclusive biblicism, Bullinger and his colleagues were anxious to preserve as far as possible the link between the post-Reformation church and the centuries of catholic tradition that had preceded it; whereas the Zurichers' emphasis was on continuity with past doctrine and practice, many exiles aspired to recreate the golden age of apostolic Christianity.

This underlying difference of approach manifested itself even in Bullinger's correspondence with Curione, threatening to undermine their

---

188 The work in question is probably the 'Sermone del sacramento della Eucaristia' that appears as an appendix to the *Annotomia della Messa* of 1552 (*Annotomia*, fols 103^v–41^v). The sermon is principally concerned with refuting Catholic and Lutheran teaching on the real presence, but Renato's attention may have been caught by passages in which Mainardi described the sacraments as signs and seals confirming God's promises (fol. 108^r), and referred to the elements of the Eucharist as instruments of the Spirit, 'utile alla manducatione e bevanda spirituale' (fol. 112^v).

189 Renato, *Opere*, pp. 94–8. Mainardi answered Renato's tract with a lengthy refutation, the last part of which survives in manuscript form (Bürgerbibliothek Bern A 93, 4; see A. Rotondò, 'Esuli italiani in Valtellina nel Cinquecento', *RSI*, 88 (1976), pp. 756–91 [787–8]). In it he takes Renato to task for dismissing ecclesiastical tradition, and confronts the Sicilian's objections to his use of non-biblical language. Scripture, Mainardi accepts, 'non ha bisogno di nuove voci, ne nuovi discorsi, essa in se', but we need them in order to expound its meaning (provided that they are 'cavati dalla scrittura e non dal proprio senso'). Mainardi's own teaching on baptism and the Eucharist is defensible because he has established 'per necessaria deduttione' from scripture that the sacraments confirm God's promises and strengthen believers in faith (fol. 7^v).

relationship. Unlike Renato, Curione refrained from challenging openly the doctrinal position of the Zurich church; his friends within the Italian exile community included theological conservatives (Giulio da Milano, Mainardi, Zanchi), as well as 'heretics'.[190] However, when asked by Bullinger to give his opinion on the *Consensus Tigurinus*, Curione responded in terms reminiscent of Renato. In a letter dated 15 August 1549, he expressed serious reservations about the use in the *Consensus* of extra-biblical terminology to describe the status and function of the sacraments, implying that the 'pure' Zwinglian doctrine of the Eucharist that he so admired had been watered down under Calvin's Lutheranizing influence:

> I noticed that [in the *Consensus*] a strange and foreign leaven had been added, not without great skill, to your customary frankness. They [the sacraments] are called additions to the Gospel, seals, implements; they are said to confirm, to take forward and to renew communion with Christ. Certain benefits are said to be conferred by them and they are said in some way to increase Christ's [presence] within us when we receive them. Next their fruits, which may not have been present at the time when they were received, are said to be distributed and subsequently revealed over an unspecified period. All those things may be justified on certain grounds but, unless I am mistaken, they are alien to the simple custom of the divine scriptures. Things of this sort are likely to lead even those who are on their guard into great confusion and disputes that are not merely unprofitable, but actually harmful to the church of God.[191]

When pressed, Curione withdrew his criticisms of the *Consensus*, but the episode had highlighted differences that could not easily be swept under the carpet. They resurfaced some years later, when Curione submitted a draft of his controversial *De amplitudine beati regni Dei* to Bullinger for comment in advance of its publication. In his response, the *Antistes* took issue not so much with the arguments advanced in the work (which were in line with his own moderate position on predestination), but with Curione's suggestion that the

---

[190] Curione had met Mainardi while teaching at the university of Pavia in the late 1530s, and continued in exile to regard him as a theological mentor (Kutter, *Curione*, p. 21; Peyronel Rambaldi, *Dai Paesi Bassi all'Italia*, p. 110). In *De amplitudine beati regni Dei*, a 'Mainardus' articulates Curione's critique of Calvin's doctrine of predestination, despite the fact that his real-life counterpart is known to have held views much more in line with those of the Genevan reformer. In a letter to Pellikan dated 3 March 1547, the Polish student Jan Mączyński described how in conversation with him Mainardi had offered a robust defence of the doctrine of double predestination. Mączyński was shocked by Mainardi's insistence that God had willed both the Fall and the damnation of the reprobate, citing his views as an example of the 'Stoicism' prevalent among Italians, 'etiam inter eos qui vere pietatis volunt videri sectatores' (ZB Ms. F 47, 148–51).

[191] CO, XIII, no. 1243; also cited in Cantimori, *Eretici*, pp. 104–6.

question of the relative number of the saved and the damned had not been adequately treated by earlier theologians. Bullinger observed: 'I am convinced that all things necessary for salvation have now been revealed, by the grace of God, and satisfactorily expounded by both ancient and more recent commentators on scripture.'[192] Such conservatism and deference to tradition was fundamentally at odds with the belief of many Italian exiles that the reformation of doctrine remained a work in progress, to which they themselves had much to contribute.

Particularly illuminating in this context are the Zurich theologians' replies to the questions and criticisms of Lelio Sozzini. Between 1552 and 1555, Sozzini bombarded Bullinger, Gwalther and Johannes Wolf with letters and short treatises on problems ranging from the exposition of Matthew 16:20 to the personality of the Holy Spirit.[193] Lelio's approach to such questions, like that of Renato and Curione, was grounded in hostility to the continued reliance by the Reformed on extra-biblical authorities and terminology. In his most substantial surviving work from this period, *De Sacramentis Dissertatio ad Tigurinos et Genevenses*, which he presented to Johannes Wolf in early 1555, Sozzini reiterated Renato's detailed critique of the Bullingerian doctrine of the Eucharist.[194] More fundamentally, he challenged the authors of the *Consensus Tigurinus* to produce scriptural support for their claims: where, he asked, did the Bible say that the sacraments nourished and strengthened faith, that they enabled the believer to feed on Christ, and that they served as 'organa' and 'adminicula' of grace? But in their responses to this work and to other questions put to them by Sozzini, the Zurichers refused to accept the biblicist assumptions on which his arguments were based, insisting on the fundamental unity of scriptural and patristic authority. When Lelio questioned the Reformed doctrine of the sacraments, Wolf replied with quotations from Augustine

---

[192] 'Mihi certe persuasum est omnia ea quae verae salutis sunt, iam dei gratia esse revelata, et quantum satis est exposita, cum a veteribus tum a neotericis scripturae divinae tractatoribus' (Bullinger to Curione, 20 September 1553 (Basel UB G I 66, 71ʳ); Kutter, *Curione*, p. 202).

[193] On this correspondence, see also Cantimori, *Eretici*, pp. 147–51.

[194] Sozzini, *Opere*, pp. 81–92. Like Renato, Sozzini defines the sacraments as acts of thanksgiving for benefits received and testimonies to an already present faith in Christ. He also makes the same distinction between the Last Supper and the Christian Eucharist. Antonio Rotondò is sceptical of the likelihood of direct contacts between Renato and Sozzini (ibid., pp. 337–9; Renato, *Opere*, pp. 328–9), but has uncovered evidence which suggests that Lelio was familiar with Renato's works prior to his exile ('Per la storia dell'eresia a Bologna nel secolo XVI', *Rinascimento*, 13 (1962), pp. 107–54 (145–52); Renato, *Opere*, pp. 224–7).

and Chrysostom, as well as the Bible;[195] when he asked for clarification on the doctrine of the Trinity, Wolf cited the Fathers (Tertullian, Basil, Gregory of Nazianzus, Augustine) and even some pagan authors (Hermes Trismegistus, Plato, Proclus) in support of the church's traditional line.[196] Bullinger's advice to Sozzini was unambiguous: 'Our religion is not infinite, but is set down in abbreviated form. Correctly understood, this is content with the simple sense of scripture, admitting nothing foreign to it, referring all things to piety and paying no attention to varied and complex questions'. The *Antistes* called on his correspondent to heed the dictum of the Latin Father Tertullian: 'It was your faith that saved you, not contemplation of the scriptures. Faith is founded in the rule [of faith] ... To know nothing against the rule [of faith] is to know everything.'[197]

Exchanges of this sort were bound to have some negative impact on relations between the Italian exiles and the Zurich church. They were symptomatic of a growing anxiety surrounding the activities of the former, who by the end of the 1540s were fast acquiring a reputation for contentiousness, ill-discipline and heresy – particularly in the Rhaetian Freestate. In September 1547, Johannes Blasius, minister at the church of St Regula in Chur and Comander's deputy, visited Chiavenna, where he found the local Reformed congregation hopelessly split between supporters of Renato and Mainardi. Writing to Bullinger shortly afterwards he observed, with some exasperation, 'truly Italian minds are at work here' ('es sind vere Italica ingenia').[198] In what was to become a familiar pattern in such situations, the leadership of the Rhaetian church sought Bullinger's intervention in the dispute, hoping that his authority would be sufficient to bring the warring factions to heel. The *Antistes'* initial response was to dispatch a manuscript copy of a work that he had just completed on the sacraments, in which Renato's suggestion that the *agape* meal be restored as an integral part of the Eucharist was firmly rejected.[199] However, this failed to settle the controversy; in December 1547, Renato's authority to teach was withdrawn by the Rhaetian synod, after Mainardi accused him not only of denying the efficacy of the sacraments, but of attributing original sin to Christ, questioning the

---

[195] Sozzini, *Opere*, pp. 218–30.

[196] Ibid., pp. 248–59.

[197] Ibid., pp. 189–91. Gwalther took a similar line: 'Poenitentiam agere passim nos iubet Dominus, non de illa subtiliter et argute disputare' (ibid., p. 208).

[198] Letter of 20 September 1547 (Schiess, I, no. 86; Renato, *Opere*, pp. 200–201).

[199] The work was first published in London in 1551 under the title *Absoluta de Christi domini nostri sacramentis et ecclesia eius tractatio* (*HBBibl*, no. 183). Modified in the wake of the *Consensus Tigurinus*, it was later incorporated into the *Decades* (Sanders, 'Henri Bullinger', p. 356).

use of the triune formula in baptism, and rejecting both the immortality of the soul and the resurrection of the flesh.[200] The situation was further complicated by the arrival in Chiavenna early the following year of Francesco Stancaro who, rejecting the solutions offered by both Mainardi and Renato, succeeded in winning over some members of the local Reformed church – most notably, Francesco Negri – to his own, third, position on the Eucharist (following Calvin, Stancaro emphasized the connection between the sacraments and grace.)[201]

Unable to resolve the dispute themselves, Comander and Blasius referred it back to the Zurichers, who in June 1548 issued a statement on the views of the three protagonists in the Chiavenna Eucharistic controversy.[202] As expected, their judgment was broadly favourable to Mainardi (who, with Stancaro, had travelled to Zurich to present his case). Indeed, the terms in which it is framed suggest that Bullinger's exchange with Renato, and subsequent events, had had the effect of pushing the Eucharistic theology of the Zurich church in a conservative direction, paving the way for the *Consensus Tigurinus* the following year.[203] In a personal letter to the church of Chiavenna, Bullinger also commended Mainardi for his pure doctrine, contrasting him explicitly with those who would 'sow among the simple new, curious and harmful dogmas'.[204] Yet even this failed to end the affair; by August the following year, Mainardi was facing such opposition from Renato and his supporters that he was forced to ask Bullinger to intervene to persuade the Chur ministers to send an official delegation to Chiavenna with the aim of bringing the dissidents to heel.[205] Under severe pressure from this

---

[200] This is to be surmised from the confession that Mainardi submitted to the synod anathematizing 22 doctrinal errors of the Anabaptists (see Renato, *Opere*, pp. 202–5). In a letter to Bullinger dated 10 December 1548, Mainardi attributed all but one of these errors to Renato (Schiess, I, no. 104; Renato, *Opere*, pp. 221–2).

[201] See Stancaro, *Opera nuova*, pp. 596–9.

[202] The statement (published in Renato, *Opere*, pp. 208–19) is divided into two sections: first, the views of Mainardi, Renato and Stancaro are analysed and compared; next, the Zurich church's own interpretation of the sacraments is set out.

[203] For example, the Zurichers indicated that they were prepared to countenance the use of the terms 'conferre' and 'exhibere' to express the relationship between the sacraments and grace, language that Bullinger had previously criticized in Calvin as 'instrumentalist' (*CO*, VII, 695). Some of the arguments used in the document resurface in a statement on the sacraments that Bullinger submitted to Calvin in March 1549, which laid the foundations for the *Consensus*. In both this statement and the Zurich judgment of the previous year the function of the sacrament in relation to grace is compared to that of Paul as an instrument and co-worker in the divine plan of salvation (Renato, *Opere*, p. 210; *CO*, VII, 712–13).

[204] Renato, *Opere*, pp. 219–20.

[205] Mainardi to Bullinger, 7 August 1549 (Schiess, I, no. 110; Renato, *Opere*, pp. 228–30).

delegation, which included Blasius and his eventual successor Philipp Gallicius, Renato put his name to 21 articles that on the question of the sacraments echoed language used by Bullinger in his statement of June 1548.[206] However, in subsequent months Renato continued to show signs of resisting Mainardi's authority, an attitude that resulted in his excommunication on 6 July 1550.[207] The following January, Vergerio persuaded him to abjure his errors again, but the leadership of the Rhaetian church in Chur remained doubtful about this apparent change of heart.[208] In fact, the dispute between Renato and Mainardi was only resolved definitively by the former's departure from Chiavenna towards the end of 1551.

The Chiavenna Eucharistic controversy provoked repeated complaints from Bullinger's correspondents in Graubünden about the unreliability, ignorance and disputatiousness of the Italian exiles who had settled in the region. When Mainardi visited Zurich in June 1548, Comander wrote to Bullinger commending him as 'a most worthy man of Christ's church'. But at the same time, he made clear his low opinion of Italians in general: 'These Italian intellects ('ingenia illa Italica') are prone to quarrelling and difficult to pacify. In the end their disputes and arguments may damage all of us and be to the detriment of the Gospel.'[209] The Chiavenna Eucharistic controversy left the leadership of the Rhaetian church with an abiding distrust of Italians – a feeling reinforced by the eruption in February 1552 of a new dispute involving Gianandrea Paravicini, the newly elected pastor of Caspano. Philipp Gallicius informed Bullinger that, under examination, Paravicini had revealed himself to be a follower of Renato, denying not only the survival of the soul after death but the distinction of persons within the Godhead and the perpetual virginity of Christ's mother.[210] Worse still, another Italian member of the synod, Celso Martinengo, had defended Paravicini's position, on the basis that the terms 'Trinity' and 'person' were not found in scripture.[211] At stake was more than a simple

---

[206] Campell, *Historia Raetica*, II, pp. 329–34; Renato, *Opere*, pp. 266–71.

[207] Mainardi to Bullinger, 4 August 1550 (Schiess, I, no. 130; Renato, *Opere*, pp. 230–31).

[208] Renato, *Opere*, pp. 235–42.

[209] Comander to Bullinger, 1 June 1548 (Schiess, I, no. 97; Renato, *Opere*, p. 206).

[210] Gallicius to Bullinger, 23 and 29 February 1552 (Schiess, I, nos. 177 and 179; Renato, *Opere*, pp. 243–5). For evidence that Renato held similar 'Sabellian' views, see n. 180 above.

[211] Martinengo was a former Augustinian canon who had worked alongside Vermigli, Zanchi and the converted Jew Emmanuele Tremellio at the convent of San Frediano in Lucca, where he taught Greek. See Pastore, *Valtellina*, pp. 106–7; Bonorand, *Reformatorische Emigration*, pp. 90–92.

difference in theology: the affair threatened to undermine the institutional unity of the Rhaetian church, feeding support for demands by Vergerio for the establishment of a separate synod for Italian Graubünden. Writing to Bullinger on 5 April, Comander railed against the 'argumentative' and 'restless' Italians, who were prepared to spark off a quarrel over the most trifling issue and who stubbornly refused to accept correction.[212] In his own letters to the *Antistes*, Vergerio indignantly rejected any suggestion that he or Martinengo harboured heretical opinions.[213] However, the episode caused a permanent breakdown in Vergerio's relationship with the ecclesiastical authorities in Chur, prompting him to accept a post in the service of Duke Christoph of Württemberg. Comander and Gallicius took advantage of Vergerio's departure to impose a detailed confession of faith on the Rhaetian pastorate in April 1553. As they explained when sending this confession to Bullinger for approval, its aim was specifically to combat the errors of the Italian members of the synod, who misused the scripture principle to conceal their adherence to the very worst forms of heresy: antitrinitarianism, libertinism and denial of Christ's role in salvation.[214]

The warnings of Comander and Gallicius appeared to be borne out later that year, following the execution of the Spanish antitrinitarian Michael Servetus in Geneva. Servetus' death caused widespread consternation among the Italian exiles; even Vergerio, who was appalled by the condemned man's teachings, expressed doubts about the use of the death penalty in his case.[215] Others were more outspoken. In Geneva, Basle and the French-speaking territories of Berne verses were circulated attacking Calvin and the orthodox doctrine of the Trinity.[216] The Paduan jurist Matteo Gribaldi, who had been present in Geneva during Servetus' trial and made no secret of his support for the Spaniard's ideas, composed an *Apologia pro Serveto* as well as a number of pseudo-Servetian tracts,[217] while from his refuge at Traona in the Valtellina

---

212 Schiess, I, no. 181.

213 Vergerio to Bullinger, 8 and 30 April 1552 (Schiess, I, no. 180). In his correspondence with Bullinger Vergerio regularly condemned the errors of his more radical compatriots: in a letter dated 15 March 1551, for example, he professed himself shocked by the appearance of an Anabaptist, 'Josephite' sect in Padua (ibid., no. 148.2).

214 Comander and Gallicius to Bullinger, 22 April 1553 (ibid., no. 209). For an analysis of the confession, see E. Camenisch, 'Die Confessio Raetica: Ein Beitrag zur bündnerischen Reformations-Geschichte', *JHGG* (1913), pp. 223–60; W. Graf, 'Evangelische Kirchenordnung im Freistaat Gemeiner Drei Bünde', *Zwa*, 11/10 (1963/2), pp. 624–48.

215 Vergerio to Bullinger, 3 October 1553 (Schiess, I, no. 229.2).

216 U. Plath, *Calvin und Basel in den Jahren 1552–1556* (Zurich, 1974), p. 153.

217 Ibid., pp. 156–9; C. Gilly, *Spanien und der Basler Buchdruck bis 1600: Ein*

Renato penned a lengthy poem condemning Calvin for his role in Servetus' death.[218] More alarming, from Bullinger's perspective, was the involvement of the Basle Italian community in these protests. Curione's eldest son, Orazio, had studied under Gribaldi in Padua and owned a manuscript copy of Servetus' *Christianismi Restitutio*.[219] Another son, Agostino, later served as Gribaldi's amanuensis; the surviving copy of the *Apologia pro Serveto* is in his hand.[220] The same manuscript contains corrections by Curione himself, whom the Genevans suspected of having contributed to perhaps the best-known of the protests against Servetus' execution, Sebastian Castellio's *De haereticis an sint persequendi*.[221] Also prominent in the opposition to Calvin was Pietro Perna, who disseminated anti-Calvinist texts by Castellio and another French exile, Guillaume Postel.[222] Bullinger himself was convinced that the *De haereticis* had been brought to Switzerland by Perna 'from Italy'.[223]

Despite the damage done by the Servetus affair, the Zurich church remained for the most part resistant to blanket condemnations of the Italian exile community; at this stage Bullinger exhibited none of Calvin's instinctive suspicion of the Italian mindset.[224] The activities of the 'heretics' had, he knew, to be set against the efforts of other Italians, such as Mainardi, to maintain orthodoxy and discipline among their compatriots. In particular, Bullinger could take comfort from the fact that a number of exiles, including Grataroli, Vermigli and Zanchi, had

---

Querschnitt durch die spanische Geistesgeschichte aus der Sicht einer europäischen Buchdruckerstadt (Basle, 1985), pp. 298–318.

218 Renato, *Opere*, pp. 117–31; see also the English translation of this poem in Tedeschi, *Italian Reformation Studies*, pp. 187–95.

219 Gilly, *Basler Buchdruck*, p. 293, n. 68; Kutter, *Curione*, pp. 263–4.

220 Gilly, *Basler Buchdruck*, p. 299; Kutter, *Curione*, pp. 265–7.

221 Beza to Bullinger, 14 June 1554 (*Correspondance*, I, no. 45); Plath, *Calvin und Basel*, p. 144. In a statement to the Inquisition dated 2 September 1550, Girolamo Allegretti, formerly a minister to evangelical congregations in Cremona and Gardone, gave further evidence of Curione's antitrinitarian sympathies. Allegretti claimed that during a visit to Basle 'io veni in diferentia con messer Celio Secundo perché lui negava la divinità di Christo, per il che io li disi in faccia che era heretico et non volevo parte con lui' (Renato, *Opere*, p. 234; on Allegretti, see Seidel Menchi, *Erasmus*, pp. 263–8). Curione was also closely associated with Giorgio Filalete, known as 'il Turchetto', the Italian translator of Servetus' *De Trinitatis erroribus* (S. Seidel Menchi, 'Chi fu Ortensio Lando?', *RSI*, 106 (1994), pp. 501–64 [521, n. 56]).

222 Plath, *Calvin und Basel*, pp. 160–63. Previously Perna had supplied copies of Servetus' works to sympathizers in both Basle and northern Italy (among them Gribaldi and Bullinger's correspondent Girolamo Massari). For further detail see ibid., pp. 45–7; Gilly, *Basler Buchdruck*, p. 294; Perini, 'Note e documenti', p. 162.

223 Bullinger to Calvin, 22 April 1554 (*CO*, XV, no. 1944); Cantimori, *Eretici*, p. 169.

224 On which see A. Rotondò, 'Calvino e gli antitrinitari italiani', *RSI*, 80 (1968), pp. 759–84 (768–9).

come out firmly in support of the line taken by the Swiss churches in the Servetus affair; both Vermigli and Zanchi planned works in defence of the right of the Christian magistrate to discipline heretics.[225]

Yet Bullinger's approach even to those exiles whose orthodoxy had been called into question was conciliatory. He accepted without demur Curione's indignant denial of suggestions that he was responsible for some of the 'carmina' that had circulated in the wake of Servetus' execution, and played down rumours that the Piedmontese exile had collaborated in the writing of Castellio's *De haereticis*.[226] As has already been noted, in his correspondence with Renato the *Antistes* sought repeatedly to emphasize common ground over disagreement; this tendency was evident again in the Zurich church's judgment on the Chiavenna sacramentarian dispute, which, while condemning Renato's Eucharistic views, did so in relatively restrained language.[227] Time and again in such situations, Bullinger and his colleagues opted for dialogue over confrontation, allowing their orthodoxy to be tempered by a strong awareness of their pastoral responsibilities and the demands of 'charity'. In the case of Lelio Sozzini, for example, they saw their task as being to offer guidance to an erring but talented younger colleague, to persuade him to divert his energies away from unprofitable doctrinal speculation back to what Bullinger describes as 'practical theology': acceptance of the church's historic teachings, and leading a Christian life. Bullinger summed up the Zurichers' approach in a letter to Vergerio dated 9 July 1557:

> I believe that in such cases we should act with reason and moderation, distinguishing between types of doctrine and articles,

---

225 Grataroli to Bullinger, 5 January 1554 (CO, XV, no. 1893); Zanchi to Bullinger, 10 June 1554 (StAZ E II 356, 745), 12 July 1554 (ibid., 747), 2 September 1554 (ibid., 748), 24 September 1554 (ibid., 749), 3 March 1555 (ibid., 751). Zanchi notes that he encountered opposition to the project from some brethren (including, perhaps, his father-in-law Curione), who argued that a work of this kind would only encourage Catholic rulers in countries such as England and France to intensify their persecution of evangelicals.

226 Curione to Bullinger, [March/April] 1554 (CO, XV, no. 1938); Bullinger to Curione, 9 April 1554 (ibid., no. 1942); Bullinger to Calvin, 22 April 1554 (ibid., no. 1944).

227 Renato, *Opere*, p. 213: 'Dominus Camillus et qui cum eo faciunt, non sunt tantum prophani aut imperiti rerum divinarum ut negent sacramenta prorsus nihil conferre utramque rem. Absit ut hoc suspicemur. Sed quia Deus per suum Spiritum confirmat corda, putabunt sacramenta confessioni deservire, quae non tantum verbis sed etiam actione fit, ut contra sunt qui ore confitentur se nosse Deum, factis autem negant. Itaque volunt esse tesseras et symbola promissionis quibus et consortibus fidei et exteris atque hostibus palam testamur nos e numero illorum esse qui Christum suum principem et servatorem unicum agnoscant eique solide universam salutem ascribant.'

and not immediately denouncing those who dissent from us as wolves, heretics and impious. When dealing with those in error, our aim should be to return them to the right path, or at least to test them in a friendly fashion, because in that way you may make progress. If they remain stubborn and obstinate, we should continue to proceed with moderation, so that, as much as possible, everything may serve the purpose of edification. Hatred and envy should be far from all dealings of this sort.[228]

Given the doctrinal conservatism of Bullinger and his colleagues, this readiness to countenance the questioning of fundamental Reformed teachings may seem puzzling. It is to be explained, at least in part, with reference to the distinction that Bullinger drew between 'private' and 'public' heresy. In his commentary on Titus (3:10), he argues that while the authorities in church and state are right to insist on outward conformity, consciences cannot be forced: 'private' unbelief remains a matter for God alone.[229] Similarly, in *Der Widertöufferen ursprung* he differentiates between heresy that remains concealed in the heart (and is not punishable by the magistrate) and that which 'breaks out and begins to devour everything around it, like cancer, poisoning and corrupting many people, and causing God and his word to be blasphemed and publicly torn apart'.[230] So long, therefore, as Lelio Sozzini showed no signs of openly dissenting from the teachings of the Zurich church, Bullinger was prepared to treat him as one of the faithful, regardless of his private doubts.[231]

In addition, Bullinger's personal attachment to many of his Italian

---

[228] The letter is published in Campi, 'Vergerio', p. 294. Vergerio had complained about the failure of the Zurich church to condemn publicly Curione's *De amplitudine beati regni Dei.*

[229] Bullinger, *Commentarii*, p. 633: 'Fides et incredulitas cordium sunt, fateor, ea nemo hominum iudicare potest. Ex dictis vero et factis, iisque manifestis debent fieri hominum iudicia.'

[230] *Der Widertöufferen ursprung*, fol. 166[r] : 'Diewyl falscher gloub oder kätzery verborgen blybt im hertzen / mag sy von niemant / dann von Gott allein gerichtet werden: wenn sy aber ußbricht / unnd umb sich frißt wie der kräbs / daß vil frommer lüt nit nur dardurch vergifft und verderbt werdend / sondern Gott und sin wort darzu gelesteret und offentlich zerrissen wirt / so sol unnd mag ein Oberkeit sömtliche ussere übeltheten wol straffen.'

[231] Bullinger's treatment of Sozzini may be contrasted with the stance that he adopted in some well-known cases of 'public' heresy. For example, he endorsed not only the execution of Servetus, but the Rhaetian Diet's decision to impose the death sentence on the notorious Anabaptist Il Tiziano, subsequently commuted to banishment (Bullinger to Calvin, 12 June 1554 [CO, XV, no. 1967]). On the public-private distinction in Bullinger's thought, see also A. Mühling, 'Lelio Sozzini: Bemerkungen zum Umgang Heinrich Bullingers mit >> Häretikern<<', in A. Lexutt and V. von Bülow (eds), *Kaum zu glauben: Von der Häresie und dem Umgang mit ihr* (Rheinbach, 1998), pp. 162–70.

correspondents made him reluctant to lend credence to suggestions that they harboured heretical views. This is again best illustrated by the case of Lelio Sozzini. In November 1554, Bullinger was informed by Celso Martinengo, now restored to orthodoxy as minister of the Italian church in Geneva, that he and other office-holders within the congregation had received letters from Sozzini accusing them of false teaching; according to Martinengo, Lelio had even succeeded in converting a young member of his flock to antitrinitarian views.[232] Early the following year, similar allegations were levelled against Sozzini by the Poschiavo minister Giulio da Milano, whose uncompromising attitude towards 'heresy' has already been noted.

When confronted with these charges by Bullinger, Lelio denied that he sympathized with Servetus' doctrine of the Trinity,[233] or that he opposed in principle the punishment of heretics by the Christian magistrate (although he did admit to having some reservations about the manner in which Servetus' punishment had been implemented). He also reaffirmed his acceptance of the teachings of scripture and of the Apostles' creed. On the other hand, when pressed by Bullinger to endorse the more explicitly trinitarian Nicene and Constantinopolitan creeds, and to denounce the early church heresies and Anabaptism, Sozzini refused to commit himself, preferring to emphasize his commitment to the Zurich church:

> I adhere to the doctrine that has always been taught in the catholic and orthodox church, and that is today taught simply and with agreement in the church of Zurich. It is for that reason that I participate with you in the mystical supper of Christ the Lord and that I live here among you. I never seek to cause differences or to instruct others in errors, but live quietly.[234]

Remarkably, Bullinger professed himself satisfied with this cagey response. He also approved a confession that Lelio later submitted to him, even though he recognized that its endorsement of the orthodox position on the Trinity was conditional at best.[235] In his reply to Giulio,

---

232 CO, XV, no. 2045.

233 Strictly speaking, this was true: for Sozzini, Servetus' critique of orthodoxy did not go far enough (see Chapter 3:ii below).

234 The interview is described by Bullinger in a letter to Giulio da Milano of July 1555 (Schiess, I, no. 290).

235 For the text of the confession, see Sozzini, *Opere*, pp. 93–100. In a letter to Sozzini dated 10 July 1555, Bullinger noted: 'Agnoscis voces trinitatis, unitatis, consubstantialitatis, unionis et distinctionis usurpatas esse ab annis mille trecentis; sed addis magis te probaturum, <<si adhuc verbis Christi et apostolorum fides mea explicaretur>>. Ex quibus quidem verbis quis poterat colligere voces istas te non agnoscere pro evangelicis et apostolicis' (Sozzini, *Opere*, p. 240). The deeply ambiguous nature of

Bullinger conceded that Sozzini had a 'curious mind', but insisted that that was no proof of underlying heresy. He accepted that the young man would continue to raise awkward questions, but was confident that those could be dealt with adequately in the context of discussions with himself and other senior Zurich colleagues. Put another way, the distinction between public and private dissent was upheld: Lelio was free to pursue his theological enquiries, provided that he did not seek to communicate his doubts to others.[236]

Not all contemporaries shared Bullinger's belief that the public and private spheres could be so easily closed off from each other. Giulio da Milano, for one, was sceptical of the Zurichers' chosen strategy of containment, which did not accord with his experience of radicals in Italy and the Valtellina. In a letter to Bullinger dated 4 November 1555 he warned: 'The artfulness of the heretic, and the ability of this snake by twisting and turning to get away, unless suppressed by strong measures, is scarcely to be believed. For all Anabaptists [here, a blanket term for radicals in general] are treacherous, not fearing to blow hot or cold depending on the situation.' According to Giulio, Reformed ministers are duty bound to 'tear off' the mask of heresy by demanding that those under suspicion make clear their acceptance of fundamental Christian teachings.[237] That was certainly Calvin's preferred approach: when confronted with evidence for the emergence of antitrinitarianism in the city's Italian church in early 1558, he and the hardline Italian minister Lattanzio Ragnoni acted swiftly to counter this threat, insisting that the church's entire membership subscribe to a confession of faith which set out the doctrines of the Trinity and the two natures of Christ in uncompromising terms.[238] The two men most responsible for

---

Sozzini's confession is highlighted in E. Hulme, 'Lelio Sozzini's Confession of Faith', in *Persecution and Liberty: Essays in Honor of George Lincoln Burr* (New York, 1931), pp. 211-25.

236 See Rotondò's comments in Sozzini, *Opere*, p. 67. This compromise was suggested to Lelio by Bullinger in the letter cited above: 'Nemo vero eripit tibi libertatem modeste quaerendi discendique; nemo rursus probat aut probare potest, si tu vel alius cogitationes aut tentationes potius suas et pravas et offensione plenas efferat ubivis temere, non observato delectu temporis, locorum et personarum, immo has tueatur usque ad clamores et rixas ... Proinde melius esse existimo huiusmodi cogitationes et aestus animi saucii apud eos duntaxat proferre, qui mederi queant; deinde et his, iunctis simul precibus ad Deum piis, obsequi bene monentibus et non perpetuo in eodem haerere luto et easdem semper volvere et revolvere quaestiones' (ibid., pp. 245–6). Interestingly, in *Der Widertöufferen ursprung* Bullinger distinguishes between those heresiarchs who refuse to abjure their errors but agree to cease proselytizing (like Lelio?) and those who remain obstinate on both counts (fol. 169r–v).

237 Schiess, I, no. 296.

238 CO, XVII, no. 2870; ibid., IX, 385–8. Calvin was also unconvinced by Bullinger's

introducing heretical views to the community, Giorgio Biandrata and Giovanni Paolo Alciati, were forced to flee Geneva in fear of their lives. Bullinger's more flexible stance allowed him to retain the esteem of heterodox exiles for longer, but also exposed him to greater disappointment when the degree of their alienation from Zurich-style reform became apparent. And with such divergent visions of the future of the Reformation at stake, open confrontation could not be postponed indefinitely.

Almost from its inception, the relationship between Zurich and the Italian exiles was characterized by two contradictory impulses. The first was towards co-operation, on the basis of shared intellectual interests and a common commitment to the struggle against the papal 'Antichrist'. Through their contacts with those exiles who had settled in the Rhaetian Freestate, the Zurichers were able to contribute to the partial reformation of an Italian-speaking region; they also provided indirect support for Vergerio's propagandizing activities in Italy proper. At the same time, exiles such as Vermigli and Curione established themselves as trusted and valued correspondents of the Zurich *Antistes* Heinrich Bullinger. However, in the case of Curione a second, more problematic, aspect of the relationship presented itself. The Italian exiles were products of an evangelical movement in the early stages of its formation, with underdeveloped organization and no defined confessional stance. Understandably, many of them found it difficult to make the transition from this climate of free and easy religious experimentation to one of increasing doctrinal uniformity, such as that which they encountered in Zurich and other Swiss Reformed states. Some, like Camillo Renato, who felt that their aspirations for continuing reform were blocked by the conservatism of the Zurich church establishment, gave vent to their frustration in open criticism of an increasingly inflexible Reformed orthodoxy that they saw as contravening the founding principles of the Reformation. For their part, Bullinger and his colleagues were faced with a dilemma: how to square their commitment to solidarity with the exiles – on whose shoulders hopes for a possible Protestant breakthrough in Italy rested – with the need to defend the doctrinal integrity of their church and of the wider Reformation. This was a problem that would confront them repeatedly over the next two decades.

---

claim to be able to neutralize the threat posed by Lelio Sozzini's 'curiositas' (Calvin to Bullinger, 23 November 1554 [CO, XV, no. 2050]).

CHAPTER TWO

The Locarnese Exiles and Zurich's Italian Church

By the mid-1550s, the Zurich church had built up an impressive network of Italian contacts, including most figures of significance within the Italian exile community. However, this was a relationship conducted primarily at arm's length, through correspondence of varying regularity. Unlike Basle or Geneva, Zurich did not in the first instance become home to a substantial Italian exile population, for reasons that have already been outlined.[1] The few individuals, like Lelio Sozzini, who chose to make the city their permanent base could not be said to constitute a genuine Italian 'community'.

That situation was transformed by the arrival in Zurich in spring 1555 of around 130 Protestant refugees from Locarno. Although in its scale the influx does not bear comparison with the better-known migrations of religious exiles to London, Geneva or Emden, in the context of a city like Zurich, whose population in the 16th century did not exceed 5,500, it was significant.[2] With the Locarnesi, Zurich acquired its own Italian-speaking church, which quickly forged links with other Italian 'diaspora' communities in Geneva, Basle and Graubünden.

In this chapter I examine the structure and organization of this congregation, as well as its relations with the authorities and citizens of Zurich. Welcomed initially in the name of international evangelical solidarity, the Locarnesi soon became the target of popular resentment, focused on their economic activities and articulated through Zurich's powerful guilds. Faced with such opposition, the long-term survival of the city's Italian church was, as we shall see, always in doubt.

i. Zurich and the failed Reformation in Locarno

During the second half of the 15th century, the Swiss Confederation entered a phase of rapid territorial expansion. Perhaps its most dramatic

---

[1] See Chapter 1:ii above.

[2] L. von Muralt, 'Renaissance und Reformation', in *Handbuch der Schweizer Geschichte: Band 1* (Zurich, 1980), pp. 389–570 (394).

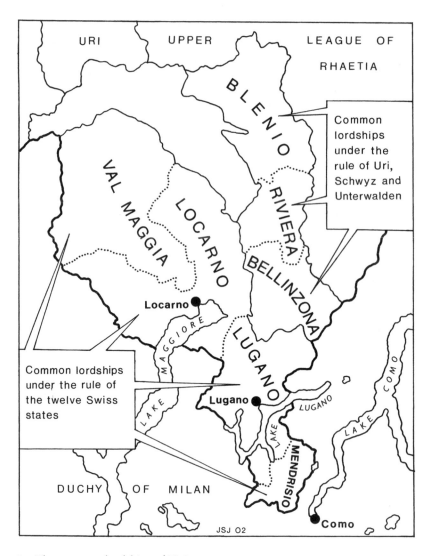

1   The common lordships of Ticino

success was the acquisition, between 1495 and 1513, of the Italian-speaking areas that make up the modern canton of Ticino. The drive southwards was spearheaded by the states of inner Switzerland, whose aim was to strengthen their grip on the vital trading corridor with Lombardy. In June 1503, Uri, Schwyz and Unterwalden secured French recognition of their sovereignty over Bellinzona and Blenio. Nine years later the Swiss, as part of the grand coalition assembled by Pope Julius II for the purpose of expelling the French from Italy, seized Lugano and Locarno, on the shores of the Lago Maggiore. Their possession of these territories was confirmed by the Eternal Peace signed with France in November 1516.[3]

From this point onwards Locarno, formerly part of the duchy of Milan, was subject to the joint rule of the 12 Swiss states that had participated in the campaign against Louis XII. Like the Confederation's other *Gemeine Herrschaften* (common lordships), Locarno was administered by a governor or *Landvogt*, appointed for a period of two years on a rotating basis from among the ruling states.[4] The *Landvogt's* authority was restricted, with policy decisions concerning the running of the territory reserved to the ruling states themselves at meetings of the Swiss Diet or at the annual *Jahrrechnung*. A good deal of power also remained in the hands of local elites, especially the noble corporation of the *capitanei*.[5] Many of the day-to-day functions of government were exercised by a territorial council of 21, consisting of 12 representatives from the town of Locarno, three from Ascona and six from the remaining communes.[6] In practice, the most powerful official in the territory was probably the secretary or *Landschreiber*, whose task was to liaise between the *Landvogt* and the native inhabitants. Whereas the *Landvogt* was an outsider, ignorant of the local language and legal system – deficiencies that could hardly be remedied during his brief term of office – the *Landschreiber* had the advantage of being a permanent

---

[3] G. Wielich, *Das Locarnese im Altertum und Mittelalter: Ein Beitrag zur Geschichte des Kantons Tessin* (Berne, 1970), pp. 439–93.

[4] For what follows, see Meyer, *Locarnergemeinde*, I, pp. 93–7, and R. Pfister, *Um des Glaubens willen: Die evangelische Gemeinde von Locarno und ihre Aufnahme in Zürich im Jahre 1555* (Zurich, 1955), pp. 17–18.

[5] The *capitanei* were divided into two 'parentele' or kinship groups, the Muralti (who included the Duni of Ascona) and the Orelli. The Magoria, a subgroup of the Orelli, were treated as a separate entity for some purposes (K. Meyer, *Die Capitanei von Locarno im Mittelalter* [Zurich, 1916]).

[6] The council was originally elected by the 'consilium generale dominorum capitaneorum', which met in December or January of each year. During the 1530s, the *capitanei* were required to surrender two to three seats on the council to non-noble 'terrieri', but that did not substantially undermine their dominant status in Locarno (Meyer, *Capitanei*, pp. 130–31; 265–6).

appointee, with long-standing and intimate knowledge of the area. Significantly, from 1540 to 1556 (the period with which we are principally concerned) Locarno's *Landschreiber* was a staunch Catholic, Walter Roll of Uri.[7]

Unlike the German-speaking *Gemeine Herrschaften* of eastern Switzerland, Locarno and its associated territories were substantially unaffected by the first wave of Zwinglian reform, prior to the Second Kappel War. The only direct evidence we possess for the spread of Protestantism in the area at this time are two letters from 1530–31. In the first of these the Zuricher Jakob Werdmüller, who had recently been appointed *Landvogt*, informed Zwingli that he had lent a copy of 'your little Latin book' (perhaps the *Fidei ratio*) to a local priest 'who is versed in the scriptures'.[8] That priest has been identified as the Carmelite Baldassare Fontana, who on 1 March 1531 wrote to the Swiss Reformed churches to request that they send him a selection of works by Protestant writers, specifically Zwingli, Luther, Melanchthon, Brenz, Bucer and Jud.[9]

Fontana's Protestant sympathies seem to have left little lasting impression on the population of Locarno. The same could not be said of the activities of another evangelical cleric, Giovanni Beccaria, who began work as a schoolmaster in the town around 1535. One of Beccaria's pupils was Taddeo Duno, who in his history of the Reformation in Locarno, *De persequutione adversus Locarnenses*, attributes to Beccaria a founding role in Locarno's evangelical community.[10] During the early phase of his activity, Beccaria trod an uneasy path between heterodoxy and conformity, preaching in an evangelical manner while continuing to say Mass. Among his first converts were Duno, the latter's fellow student Ludovico Ronco and the lawyer Martino Muralto, all of whom later emerged as important figures within the Locarnese evangelical community. Between 1542 and

---

7 On Roll, see E. Walder, *Der Condottiere Walter Roll von Uri und die Beziehungen zwischen der Innerschweiz und Italien in der Wende zur Gegenreformation 1551–1561* (Berne, 1948), especially pp. 129–81.

8 Werdmüller to Zwingli, 20 August 1530 (Z, XI, no. 1081).

9 The letter appears in J.H. Hottinger, *Historiae ecclesiasticae novi Testamenti*, 9 vols (Zurich, 1651–67), VI, pp. 618–20. For a summary of its contents, see R. Pfister, 'Die Reformationsgemeinde Locarno, 1540–1555', *Zwa*, 10/3 (1955/1), pp. 161–81 (162–4).

10 The autograph manuscript of the *De persequutione* (StAZ W 20.72 [Vertreibung aus Locarno, no. 2]), dated 1602, is edited in A. Chenou, 'Taddeo Duno et la Réforme à Locarno', *Archivio storico ticinese*, 12 (1971), pp. 237–94 (261–85). The text published in F. Ernst, 'Taddeo Dunos Bericht über die Auswanderung der protestantischen Locarner nach Zürich', *Zwa*, 9/2 (1949/2), pp. 89–104, is a 17th-century German translation of the *De persequutione*.

1544 the progress of the Reformation in Locarno was further assisted by the presence of a Protestant *Landvogt*, Joachim Bäldi of Glarus, who seems to have acted as a conduit for the supply of evangelical literature to the area. In January 1545, another Glarner, Fridolin Brunner, reported that he had recently dispatched works by Bullinger and Erasmus to the *Landvogt* for the use of a local Minorite friar, probably the well-known preacher Benedetto Locarno.[11] In the same year Taddeo Duno published a short work praising Bäldi for his equitable governance of Locarno.[12]

The fledgling Reformed community in Locarno established close relations with the Zurich church. From as early as July 1544, Beccaria was in correspondence with Konrad Pellikan, whose attention had been drawn to the schoolmaster's activities by his Italian house guest Girolamo Mariano.[13] In his letters to Pellikan, Beccaria speaks of the inroads being made by the Reformation in Locarno and expresses confidence in the eventual triumph of the Gospel. In April 1546 he informed his correspondent: 'The number of believers is increasing day by day, even though Antichrist does not cease through his false teachers to oppress those whom he knows to have pure and faithful opinions of Christ.'[14] In the same letter he noted that a reform-minded preacher – possibly the Franciscan Cornelio of Sicily – was active in Locarno and had succeeded in winning many converts.[15] Elsewhere he discussed the prospects for the Reformation in Italy as a whole, reporting that the evangelical sermons of Benedetto Locarno had been positively received in Genoa and Sicily, not least by the Spanish viceroy.[16]

---

[11] Brunner to Bullinger, 19 January 1545 (StAZ E II 335, 2079); Meyer, *Locarnergemeinde*, I, p. 168; Pfister, *Um des Glaubens willen*, p. 25. On Benedetto Locarno, see n. 16 below.

[12] *In laudem ornatissimi praesulis, viri praetorii doctissimi, Ioachym Beldi Glaronensis, Thaddaei Duni Locarniensis ἐγκώμιον* (Basle, 1545).

[13] See Beccaria to Pellikan, 12 April 1546 (ZB Ms. F 47, 140): 'Biennium abhinc hortatu Mariani Minoritae hospitis literas ad me dare dignatus sis'; Pfister, *Um des Glaubens willen*, pp. 28–9.

[14] ZB Ms. F 47, 140: 'Sed tamen augetur in dies credentium numerus, tametsi non desinat Antichristus per suos pseudodoctores, eos pessundare, quos noverit de Christo pure ac fideliter sentire.'

[15] Cornelio was subsequently convicted of 11 doctrinal errors by the Milanese Inquisition. Those included teaching predestination, denying free will, and attacking the invocation of the saints, auricular confession and monastic vows. Documents relevant to the case, including Cornelio's abjuration, are published in Meyer, *Locarnergemeinde*, I, pp. 479–84.

[16] Beccaria to Pellikan, 12 July 1546 (ZB Ms. F 47, 120–21). The little that is known about Benedetto's activities is summarized by S. Caponetto, 'Una sconosciuta predica fiorentina del minorita Benedetto Locarno', in Caponetto, *Studi sulla Riforma in Italia*

The Zurich church also had links with Beccaria's protégé, Taddeo Duno, and with two Lombard exiles who had settled in Locarno, Guarnerio Castiglione and Antonio Mario Besozzi. Castiglione may have been a former student of Pellikan's (in a letter dated 23 June 1542 he addresses the Zuricher as his 'praeceptor'),[17] while Besozzi had visited Zurich in 1544, as the tutor to Rodomonte, son of Count Filiberto of Masserano.[18] Duno's contacts with Zurich probably date to the mid-1540s when, as a student in Basle, he seems to have come under the influence of Konrad Gesner; much later, Duno recalled that Gesner had been the first to encourage him to pursue the study of medicine, which resulted in his obtaining a doctorate in the subject at the university of Pavia in 1550.[19] Pellikan's correspondence with Beccaria provides further evidence of the Zurich church's active patronage of the Locarnese evangelical community. At Beccaria's request, Pellikan agreed to act as tutor to a local boy, the nephew of Benedetto Locarno.[20] He also helped to channel Protestant literature to evangelicals in Locarno: in May 1548, Beccaria reported that his friend Castiglione was concealing various books and letters by the Zurichers, including Gwalther's *Apology*, adding that he himself was keen to acquire certain works by Brenz, Calvin and Zwingli.[21]

The support of the Zurich church was needed to counteract growing opposition from other quarters to the evangelical presence in Locarno. By the late 1540s, news of the spread of Protestantism in Locarno had come to the attention of the Swiss Catholic states, always alert to possible breaches of the terms of the Second Kappel Peace (the treaty ruled out any change of religion in those common

---

(Florence, 1987), pp. 205–18. During the late 1530s, Benedetto was part of an Erasmian circle at the convent of San Francesco di Brescia; later he became professor of metaphysics in Bologna and provincial head of the local Franciscan Conventuals (1541–43). Caponetto claims that he subsequently returned to Locarno, although there is no evidence that he played a part in the emergence of a Reformed community there. A copy of part of one of his sermons (probably from the Bologna period) has survived. Scholastic rather than popular in style, the sermon is described by Caponetto as 'un tentativo d'innestare la giustificazione per fede nella teologia di Niccolò Cusano' (ibid., p. 212).

17 ZB Ms. F 47, 54; Meyer, *Locarnergemeinde*, I, pp. 155–6. On Castiglione, see *DBI*, XXII, 94–6.

18 Meyer, *Locarnergemeinde*, I, pp. 173–5; *DBI*, IX, 672–5.

19 T. Duno, *Muliebrium morborum omnis generis remedia* (Strasbourg, 1565), sig. Aii[r].

20 Beccaria to Pellikan, 12 April and 12 July 1546 (ZB Ms. F 47, 140; 120–21).

21 ZB Ms. F 47, 159: 'D. Varnerius [Castiglione] tegit literas ac libellos a vestris sanctis viris conscriptos; inter quos delectatus est supremum D. Rodolphi Apologia. Salutat te officiosissime, ac precatur Domini gratiam vestrae ecclesiae. Cupio mihi comparari Joannis Brentii Homilias in Joannem, una cum Catechismis duobus Joannis Calvini, quibus addes Zuinglii psalmos latinitati donatos ...'; Pfister, 'Locarno', p. 166.

lordships that were still Catholic in 1531). At the *Jahrrechnung* of July 1548, the outgoing *Landvogt*, Jakob Feer of Lucerne, warned his masters that the new faith was making significant advances in Locarno and advised the banishment of Beccaria.[22] The Catholic states responded by dispatching to the town a Dominican from neighbouring Lugano, where an incipient evangelical movement had already been crushed.[23] When his preaching encountered resistance, this cleric proposed a disputation with the Locarnese evangelicals, led by Beccaria, in which 15 theses covering papal supremacy, good works, justification, auricular confession, purgatory and (as Taddeo Duno puts it) 'other similar vain, absurd and ridiculous dogmas of the Roman church' were offered for debate.[24] But the disputation, fixed for 5 August, ended in a fiasco.[25] Duno, who was present as a spokesman for the Protestant side, blamed this outcome on the unhelpful intervention of the *Landvogt*, Nikolaus Wirz of Unterwalden, who sought to cut through the complicated doctrinal issues under discussion by demanding that Beccaria simply state whether or not he accepted the teachings of the Roman church. When the schoolmaster failed to give a satisfactory answer, Wirz terminated the disputation and placed Beccaria under arrest.[26] A popular protest led to his rapid release, but only at the price of permanent exile from Locarno to Mesocco, in Graubünden.[27]

Further repressive measures followed. In October 1550, a delegation representing the inhabitants of Locarno submitted a statement to the Swiss Diet affirming their determination to remain 'at all times in the old, true and undoubted Christian faith and religion that has been adhered to and believed until now by the holy Christian and Roman church', and calling for dissidents to be brought into line.[28] At the same meeting the punishment of several Locarnesi who had eaten meat

---

[22] *EA*, IV:1d, p. 969.

[23] See Meyer, *Locarnergemeinde*, I, pp. 156–9. On 18 December 1545, Camillo Renato and Bartolomeo Maturo wrote to Bullinger requesting assistance for one Gabriele Benedetti, who had been expelled from Lugano for preaching the Gospel in his parish of Marcote (Renato, *Opere*, pp. 154–6).

[24] For the text of the articles, see *EA*, IV:1e, pp. 167–8.

[25] Duno provides an account of the disputation in a letter to Bullinger dated 9 August 1549 (StAZ E II 365, 67–70; edited in Chenou, 'Locarno', pp. 285–9), and in *De persequutione*, fols 2v–4r (Chenou, 'Locarno', pp. 265–8). See also Beccaria's subsequent representation to the Swiss Diet in *EA*, IV:1e, pp. 163–4.

[26] For Wirz's version of what occurred, see *EA*, IV:1e, pp. 137–8.

[27] The Diet later ordered an enquiry into the circumstances surrounding Beccaria's release (ibid., p. 206). For the resulting testimonies, see ibid., pp. 256–9.

[28] Copy in StAZ A 350.1: Locarner Acten 1549–53; published in Meyer, *Locarnergemeinde*, I, pp. 485–7. See also *EA*, IV:1e, pp. 443–4.

during Lent was noted.[29] Just over two years later Castiglione, Besozzi and Gianantonio Viscardi, an apostate priest from Domodossola who had sought refuge in Locarno, were expelled from the territory, to be followed by their wives and children.[30] In the absence of a Catholic *Landvogt* – the Basler Hans Jeuchdenhammer succeeded Wirz in July 1550, and he was followed by Kaspar Stierli of Schaffhausen and Esaias Röuchli of Zurich – Walter Roll co-ordinated the campaign against the Locarnese Reformed, urging the Catholic states to take steps 'to destroy this firmly rooted sect' ('um diese eingewurzelte Sekte auszurotten').[31] In February 1553 he proposed that all inhabitants of Locarno be ordered to attend confession and receive the sacrament over the coming Easter season.[32] That suggestion was taken up the following year, with the additional provision that anyone who died having failed to take communion should be excluded from burial in consecrated ground.[33]

The Locarnese evangelicals responded to these attempts to reimpose religious uniformity by seeking the support of the Swiss Reformed states. Their well-established ties with the Zurich church were of key importance in this regard. As early as September 1549, the community (reputedly 200 strong) wrote to Bullinger and his colleagues to assure the Zurichers of its constancy in the face of persecution and to request backing for its campaign to be allowed to organize publicly.[34] Throughout the crisis year of 1554, Bullinger was in correspondence with both Taddeo Duno, by now the leader of the community,[35] and Antonio Mario Besozzi, who from Chiavenna was able to act as an intermediary between the Locarnesi and the Zurich ministers. When

---

29   *EA*, IV:1e, p. 438.

30   Ibid., pp. 743; 807–8. The Reformed states subsequently registered a formal protest against these measures, on the grounds that they had been implemented by the Catholics without consultation (ibid., pp. 837; 873; 922–3).

31   Walder, *Roll*, p. 153.

32   Ibid., p. 154.

33   The Italian text of the mandate is published in Meyer, *Locarnergemeinde*, I, pp. 492–3, from the copy in Daniel Orelli von Gemsberg's *Locarnische Verfolgung* (ZB Ms. B 31, pp. 10–11). Another, contemporary, copy is located in FA Orelli, 8.7, with Latin translations in StAZ A 350.1: Locarner Acten 1554, and StAZ E II 371, 634[r–v]. See also Meyer, *Locarnergemeinde*, I, pp. 284–5, and *EA*, IV:1e, pp. 884–5.

34   ZB Ms. F 60, 311–12. The previous month Beccaria had appeared before the Zurich council to describe the plight of Locarno's evangelicals and to petition 'das jnen zügelassen, ein kilch zehan, das gotzwort zehören und zepredigen wie jn anderen gemeinen herschafften der Eidtgnoschafft'. The council instructed Bullinger to write back assuring the Locarnesi that Zurich would do its best to help them realize this goal (StAZ A 350.1: Locarner Acten 1549–53; Pfister, *Um des Glaubens willen*, p. 39).

35   After completing his studies at Pavia, Duno had settled in the small town of Asso, not far from Como. Three years later he returned to Locarno, following a brush with the Milanese Inquisition (*De persequutione*, fol. 4[r–v]; Chenou, 'Locarno', pp. 269–70).

the Catholic states alleged that the evangelicals of Locarno were not, as they claimed, mainstream Reformed Protestants, but Anabaptists and sectarians, Bullinger supported the community in its efforts to rebut these potentially damaging charges.[36] He may even have prompted the Zurich council's decision in July 1554 to order an investigation into the orthodoxy of the Locarnesi, which revealed their beliefs and practices to be entirely consonant with those of the Zurich church.[37] Bullinger's assistance was gratefully received by the Locarnese evangelicals, who thanked him for his efforts behind the scenes and urged him to continue to make representations to the Zurich authorities on their behalf.[38]

Support from the other Swiss Reformed states was rather less solid. At a meeting in Aarau on 22 August, the four Protestant *Orte* called for the consciences of the evangelical minority in Locarno to be respected, arguing that the inhabitants' declaration of October 1550 – to which the Catholic states habitually referred in support of their actions – had been issued without the approval of the Reformed and was therefore invalid. As a solution to the dispute, they suggested allowing the territory's inhabitants to hold a plebiscite on the religious question, as had happened in other *Gemeine Herrschaften*.[39] However, this apparent common front concealed fundamental differences between the two major Protestant states, Zurich and Berne. Berne had little strategic interest in the Ticinese common lordships; during the negotiations that led to the Eternal Peace of 1516, it had even expressed itself willing to

---

[36] At the beginning of June 1554, Besozzi visited Zurich with letters from the church of Locarno to Bullinger and the Zurich council countering the accusations of Anabaptism (StAZ E II 365a, 560–61; StAZ A 350.1: Locarner Acten 1554). On 8 June, Bullinger commended Besozzi to Zurich's delegates in Baden, *Bürgermeister* Johannes Haab and *Stadtschreiber* Johannes Escher, noting that he brought with him letters from ministers in Graubünden and the Valtellina which supported the Locarnese evangelicals' protestations of orthodoxy.

[37] StAZ A 350.1: Locarner Acten 1554 (*EA*, IV:1e, pp. 950; 959). The investigation was carried out by Zurich's delegate to the *Jahrrechnung*, Johannes Wegmann, in collaboration with Esaias Röuchli. Röuchli submitted his findings on 9 July, along with a list of Locarnese evangelicals and an orthodox Reformed confession of faith drawn up by the community (StAZ A 350.1: Locarner Acten 1554; StAZ E II 371, 642v–3r; published in Meyer, *Locarnergemeinde*, I, pp. 499–500). On possible sources for the confession, see J. Staedtke, 'Das Glaubensbekenntnis der christlichen Gemeinde zu Locarno vom 9. Juli 1554', *Zwa*, 10/3 (1955/1), pp. 181–93. In subsequent letters Besozzi, Duno and the Locarnese community as a whole continued vociferously to protest their orthodoxy. See Besozzi to Bullinger, 13 October 1554 (StAZ E II 365a, 544-6); Duno to Bullinger, 5 November 1554 (StAZ E II 365a, 562-3); and the church of Locarno to the four Swiss Reformed cities, 15 November 1554 (StAZ A 350.1: Locarner Acten 1554).

[38] Besozzi to Bullinger, 13 July 1554 (StAZ E II 365a, 542–3).

[39] *EA*, IV:1e, pp. 984–5; Pfister, *Um des Glaubens willen*, p. 81.

surrender them to France in exchange for financial compensation.[40] Berne's main concern was that instability within the Confederation might threaten its dominant position in western Switzerland, allowing Savoy to challenge its control of the Pays de Vaud and disrupting the delicate negotiations in which it was engaged to acquire the (Catholic) county of Greyerz.[41] The leadership of the Bernese Reformed church, while sympathetic to the cause of the Locarnese evangelicals, could do little to influence matters: whereas in Zurich the clergy, through Bullinger, remained an important political force, in Berne they were rigorously excluded from council decision making. The other two Reformed states, Basle and Schaffhausen, lacked both the resources and the political will to risk an armed confrontation with the Catholic Swiss.

Zurich's isolation first became apparent at a meeting of the Reformed cities on 25 October. There the representatives of Berne, Basle and Schaffhausen declared themselves ready to allow the will of the Confederation's Catholic majority to prevail in Locarno, so long as no attempt was made to proceed on similar lines in the other *Gemeine Herrschaften*. They also conceded that the presence of a Protestant community in Locarno could not be justified on the basis of the Second Kappel Peace, as the Catholic states had long maintained. Zurich, by contrast, continued to contest this interpretation of the *Landfrieden*, arguing that forcible recatholization was applicable only to those territories specifically excluded from its terms, such as the Freie Ämter and Bremgarten.[42]

By mid-November, when the Swiss Diet met in Baden to consider a compromise solution to the dispute brokered by Aegidius Tschudi of Glarus and Othmar Kunz of Appenzell, the Reformed states were hopelessly divided over the Locarno issue. At the Diet, they were asked to assent to a series of articles which, on the key issue of the future confessional status of Locarno, endorsed the position of their Catholic opponents. In their arbitration (*Schiedsmittel*), Tschudi and Kunz urged those inhabitants of Locarno who had accepted the Reformed faith to return to Catholicism; failing that, they were to leave the territory by 3 March the following year. Some concessions – notably in respect of the property rights of those evangelicals who chose not to abjure – were made to the Protestant side, but overall the *Schiedsmittel* could only be interpreted as a victory for the Catholic

---

[40] Wielich, *Locarnese*, pp. 477–83.

[41] V. Jacobi, *Bern und Zürich und die Vertreibung der Evangelischen aus Locarno* (Zurich, 1967), pp. 94, 101; L. von Muralt, 'Zum Gedächtnis an die Übersiedlung evangelischer Locarner nach Zürich 1555', *Zwa*, 10/3 (1955/1), pp. 145–60 (151–2).

[42] *EA*, IV:1e, pp. 1050–52.

states and for the majoritarian principle to which they had consistently appealed.[43]

Delegates to the Diet from Berne, Basle and Schaffhausen immediately accepted the proposals, but Zurich's representatives demurred, insisting that the matter be referred back to the Zurich council for a decision.[44] With the other Reformed states now ranged against it, Zurich accepted that the battle to gain formal recognition for Protestantism in Locarno had been lost and that it could do little in practical terms to prevent the expulsion of the Locarnese evangelicals. At the same time, the Zurich authorities were anxious not to be seen to collude in the punishment of fellow Reformed believers. The position that they eventually adopted can be seen as an attempt to balance the competing demands of pragmatism and confessional loyalty: Zurich would not intervene if the other Swiss states insisted on the implementation of the Baden articles, but neither would it assist or approve their actions in any way. The Zurich council also refused to accept the Catholic interpretation of the principle at stake (namely, that the introduction of Reformed worship in Locarno contravened the terms of the Second Kappel Peace).[45] Subsequent attempts by envoys from the other Protestant states, supported by Glarus, Appenzell and Graubünden, to persuade Zurich to soften its stance met with no success.[46] In their determination to resist the *Schiedsmittel*, the Zurich magistrates may to some extent have been reflecting popular feeling in the city. Even the inhabitants of Zurich's rural subject territories, who were usually most keen to avoid conflict with the Catholic Swiss, gave their backing to the council's position in a plebiscite in January 1555.[47]

There was never any real prospect that the Protestant states, or Zurich alone, would take up arms in order to secure toleration for Locarno's Protestant minority; the Locarnese themselves stated repeatedly that they would rather undergo the rigours of persecution and exile than permit such an outcome to the dispute.[48] Zurich did, however, make the strongest possible protest against the expulsion of its

---

[43] Ibid., pp. 1074–6.

[44] Ibid., pp. 1063–4.

[45] Ibid., p. 1064.

[46] *EA* IV:1e, pp. 1096–8. See also the council's letter to Röuchli of 26 December (copy in ZB Ms. A 70, fols 425ʳ–7ʳ).

[47] K. Dändliker, 'Zürcher Volksanfragen von 1521 bis 1798', *Jahrbuch für Schweizerische Geschichte*, 23 (1898), pp. 149–225 (190–94); Bullinger to Calvin, 18 January 1555 (CO, XV, no. 2090).

[48] The church of Locarno to the four Reformed cities, 7 November 1554 (StAZ E II 371, 635ʳ; StAZ A 350.1: Locarner Acten 1554; *EA*, IV:1e, pp. 1052–3). Compare Duno to Bullinger, 5 November 1554 (StAZ E II 365a, 562–3).

co-religionists, short of provoking a third religious war within the Confederation. The city's determination not to shift from its position, even in the face of pressure from its Reformed allies, may be attributed in no small measure to Bullinger's powers of persuasion.[49] The importance he attached to the Locarno dispute is evident from a memorandum that he prepared for the use of the Zurich clergy dated 5 January 1555.[50] In this document, Bullinger argues that the measures agreed at Baden are irreconcilable with the duty of the state, as well as of individual Christians, to act in defence of the Gospel. It would be hypocritical of the Zurich council, he continues, to demand that its own subjects adhere to the Reformed faith, while aiding the suppression of Protestantism in a territory over which it held partial jurisdiction. Bullinger contends that support for such measures would adversely affect the status of Protestantism not only in Locarno, but in the Confederation as a whole. It would strengthen Zurich's adversaries in their 'false religion', and present them with a massive propaganda victory: 'The main issue is that [the Catholics] might then say, "If you can punish this religion in others, you should it punish in yourselves".'[51] Bullinger goes so far as to argue that it would be better for Zurich to surrender its rights of jurisdiction in the *Gemeine Herrschaften* than to punish those 'who are of our religion'.[52]

The events of 1554–55 had, it would seem, reawakened Bullinger's doubts about the religious commitment of Zurich's Reformed allies and – more seriously – about the value of Zurich's participation in a political arrangement (the Swiss Confederation) in which Catholicism was accorded privileged status. Unlike the more hard-headed Bernese, Bullinger was not prepared to condone actions against fellow evangelicals for the sake of maintaining a united front with the Catholic Swiss. In his view, such actions were both unjust and unlikely to have the desired effect: the unity of the Confederation could not be preserved in the long term 'by undertaking things that are against God'.[53]

---

[49] Bullinger wrote to Besozzi on 30 November 1554 and again on 7 December to inform him of the Zurich council's response to events in Baden and to assure him that he was doing his utmost to promote the cause of the evangelical Locarnesi (FA Orelli, 8.7, nos 2 and 3).

[50] Draft in StAZ W 20.72 (Vertreibung aus Locarno, no. 1). Copy in ZB Ms. S 197, 12v–15v, published in Meyer, *Locarnergemeinde*, I, pp. 505–10.

[51] Meyer, *Locarnergemeinde*, I, p. 506.

[52] Ibid., p. 508.

[53] Ibid., p. 509. See also Bullinger's criticisms of Berne in his *Warhafter Verzeichnis, wie die frommen vnd rächtgläubigen Lüth von deß H. Evangelischen Glaubnus wägen ... von Luggarus vertriben sind* (ZB Ms. J 287, fols 133–90), fol. 190r. Following the city's defeat in the Second Kappel War, Bullinger had called for Zurich to withdraw from the

ii. The *Ecclesia Locarnensis reformata* in Zurich

On 12 January 1555, envoys of the seven Catholic states and of Glarus arrived in Locarno to oversee the implementation of the Baden articles. Three days later they summoned representatives of the rural communes of Locarno, together with the entire population of the town, to inform them of the terms of the *Schiedsmittel*. The inhabitants of the countryside, which had remained more or less untouched by the activities of Beccaria and his followers, immediately reaffirmed their commitment to Catholicism.[54] The town-dwellers, by contrast, requested time to formulate a response to the Diet's ultimatum. On 16 January, the entire Locarnese evangelical community of 211 persons appeared before the commissioners to declare that it had no intention of renouncing the Reformed faith.[55] Over the next two months, however, intense pressure from the Catholic authorities succeeded in reducing the size of this group substantially. According to the *Landvogt* of Lugano, Jost Pfyffer, by the prescribed deadline of 3 March 98 adult evangelicals had left Locarno for Roveredo, in the Mesolcina, although others followed later.[56]

The exiles' ultimate destination was not immediately clear. In a letter dated 14 December 1554, Besozzi had asked Bullinger whether they might be permitted to settle in either Zurich or Berne.[57] The following month a delegation led by Taddeo Duno arrived in Zurich to inform the council that 80 heads of family were contemplating emigration; now, however, their intention was to settle in Graubünden.[58] The Zurich council itself appears to have favoured this option, which would have relieved it of the burden of accommodating the exiles. To that end, it instructed two prominent citizens, Hans Edlibach and Bernhard von Cham, to accompany Duno to a meeting of the Rhaetian Diet in February, at which the Locarnese evangelicals' request to be allowed to settle on Bündner territory was due to be heard.[59] In a letter to the Rhaetian authorities, the

---

Confederation rather than be party to the suppression of the Reformed faith in the common lordships (H.U. Bächtold, 'Bullinger und die Krise der Zürcher Reformation im Jahre 1532', in U. Gäbler and E. Herkenrath (eds), *Heinrich Bullinger, 1502–1575: Gesammelte Aufsätze zum 400. Todestag* (2 vols, Zurich, 1975), I, pp. 269–89).

[54] *EA*, IV:1, pp. 1107–8. See also Röuchli's letter to the Zurich council of 25 January, in which the commissioners' activities are described (ZB Ms. E 15, fols 151r–6v; *EA*, IV:1, pp. 1110–13).

[55] StAZ A 350.1: Locarner Acten 1555; summarized in *EA*, IV:1e, p. 1113.

[56] *EA*, IV:1e, p. 1150; Pfister, *Um des Glaubens willen*, p. 99.

[57] StAZ E II 365a, 552; Meyer, *Locarnergemeinde*, I, p. 398.

[58] Bullinger to Calvin, 18 January 1555 (CO, XV, no. 2090); Meyer, *Locarnergemeinde*, I, p. 429.

[59] Instruction dated 12 January (StAZ A 350.1: Locarner Acten 1555; summarized in *EA*, IV:1e, p. 1105).

council called on them to 'offer these poor, good, exiled Christians protection, refuge and a place to live', while committing itself to receive the exiles in Zurich, should that prove necessary.[60]

The Reformed majority in Graubünden responded favourably to this proposition: several communes voted to take in the Locarnese evangelicals, while Philipp Gallicius in Chur made repeated representations to the Diet on their behalf.[61] However, the Catholic Upper League – and in particular the Mesolcina, home to Beccaria and Gianantonio Viscardi since their expulsions and the preferred destination of the Locarnesi – was bitterly opposed to any such move.[62] Pressure was also brought to bear on the Freestate by the Swiss Catholic states, at the bidding of the papal nuncio Ottaviano Raverta, bishop of Terracina.[63] The exact course of events is unclear, but it appears that an initial decision allowing the Locarnese evangelicals to settle anywhere in Graubünden was subsequently amended to make their reception dependent on the consent of the relevant commune. In an address to the Zurich council of 23 February, Bullinger reported that the attempts of the Locarnesi to secure a permanent haven in the Mesolcina had been blocked and that they now hoped to settle in either Zurich or the Valtellina.[64] For some time to come, however, many exiles continued to regard the Italian-speaking Mesolcina as a desirable alternative to Zurich: in March 1556, Gianantonio Viscardi suggested that the elders of the Locarnese community send a delegate to the forthcoming Rhaetian Diet in order to try to have the ban on settlement in the Mesolcina overturned.[65] Gallicius, too, remained active on the exiles' behalf in this matter, though with little success.[66]

---

[60] '... jr wellen nach uwer selbs erbieten, den gůten verwysten Armen Christen, under uch schutz, schirm, underschlof und wonung geben' (StAZ A 350.1: Locarner Acten 1555). In a subsequent letter, dated 23 February, Zurich asked that the Locarnese evangelicals be permitted to settle 'in uweren landen, oder andern gemaynen herrschafften, Veltlin ald anderschwo, uwern verleiten und bewilligen nach' (ibid.); Meyer, *Locarnergemeinde*, I, pp. 443–4.

[61] See the letter from the council of Chur to Zurich, 13 February 1555, in StAZ A 350.1: Locarner Acten 1555; and Schiess, I, nos 281–3.

[62] Meyer, *Locarnergemeinde*, I, pp. 434–7.

[63] Pfister, *Um des Glaubens willen*, pp. 95; 117.

[64] StAZ A 350.1: Locarner Acten 1555: 'Es schrybend die Luggarner die sich von wägen unser waren religion uß irem vatterland ze ziehen begäben / und begärend üwer wyßheyt radt und hilff. Zygend an wie sy wol erfröwt uß der gegäbnen antwort uff dem pundtstag ze Chur: so bald aber die 8 ort verytten / und sy gen Roffle und in das mosaxer taal botten geschickt / sye inen geantwort etc. Hieruff habind sy sich entschlossen in das Veltlin / oder allher gen Zürych ze ziehen'. Compare Meyer, *Locarnergemeinde*, I, p. 438.

[65] FA Orelli, 8.7, no. 28.

[66] Gallicius to the Locarnese church in Zurich, 30 March 1556 (FA Orelli, 8.7, no. 30);

With the Mesolcina closed to the Locarnese evangelicals, and few of them showing any inclination to take up the offer to settle elsewhere in Graubünden, Zurich was bound to honour its promise to receive the exiles. On 18 March the first group of Locarnesi, including the weaver Pariso Appiano and the fisherman Stefano Pebbia, arrived in the city and was given leave to remain.[67] Twelve days later a delegation made up of 'two doctors, two noblemen, two merchants and two artisans from Locarno' formally sought permission for the Locarnese evangelicals to settle in Zurich, a request that was granted 'until further notice' ('bis uff witeren bescheid').[68] The main body of exiles arrived in the city on 12 May.[69]

During the course of these transactions, the Locarnesi were again able to rely on the active support of Heinrich Bullinger, who acted throughout as their advocate with the Zurich authorities. In the speech of 23 February already cited, Bullinger presented the Zurich council with a list of the exiles' demands: that they be permitted to reside in Zurich, that they be allowed to continue practising their current professions, and that they be free to trade with Milan.[70] In early June, he drafted a further petition from the Locarnesi to the council, in which they requested its help both in securing commercial access to Milan and in overturning convictions for blasphemy that had been issued against three Locarnese women (Barbara Muralto, Lucia Belò and Catarina Appiano) by the Catholic states.[71]

More importantly, Bullinger seems to have played a key role in persuading the Zurich magistrates – perhaps against their better judgment – to support the introduction of an Italian-language church

---

Gallicius to Bullinger, 29 April 1556 (Schiess, I, no. 312). In May the Catholic states wrote to the Rhaetian Leagues insisting that they block such moves (*EA*, IV:2, p. 8).

[67] Meyer, *Locarnergemeinde*, II, p. 3. See Röuchli's letters of recommendation for Filippo and Pariso Appiano, dated 8 and 9 March 1555, in StAZ A 350.1: Locarner Acten 1555.

[68] StAZ B II 90, 11; Meyer, *Locarnergemeinde*, II, p. 4.

[69] Meyer, *Locarnergemeinde*, II, p. 5.

[70] StAZ A 350.1: Locarner Acten 1555: 'So das mitt / ob sy hie möchtind in Statt oder uff dem Land hereberig haben? 2. Ob man inen vergonte ir gwerb und handtwerck ze tryben? 3. Ob sy die freyheit in Meyland etc. Oder ob man inen hulffe und riete das sy sich in der nähe möchtind nider lassen / und danachin hieuß besähen wo sy sich entlich setzen möchtind'. Compare Meyer, *Locarnergemeinde*, I, pp. 442–3.

[71] 'Supplication der vertribnen Luggarnern beträffend die Bussen und Meyland' (StAZ A 350.1: Locarner Acten 1555); Meyer, *Locarnergemeinde*, I, pp. 10–12. Muralto had been charged by the papal nuncio Raverta with speaking ill of the Virgin Mary and her property declared forfeit; her companions had received fines of 50 Kronen (*EA*, IV:1e, pp. 1108–9). See Muralto's later account of her conversation with the nuncio, published in Meyer, *Locarnergemeinde*, I, pp. 516–18.

service in the city, thereby fulfilling a long-cherished ambition of the Locarnese evangelicals.[72] As Bullinger indicated in his speech of 23 February, it was the wish of the Locarnesi that they remain together, and have their own church and Italian-speaking preacher.[73] Some of the exiles' own leaders were sceptical about the likelihood of the Zurich authorities' responding positively to such a request. While the Locarnesi were still in Roveredo, Beccaria advised them against settling in the Swiss cities for precisely this reason: 'You should know for certain,' he warned, 'that you will not be permitted in any of the cities of our illustrious Lords to have your own preacher, but will have to read [the scriptures] at home, or attend [preaching] in a language that you do not understand.'[74]

In the event, Beccaria's fears proved groundless, with the Zurich authorities showing themselves surprisingly well-disposed to the suggestion that, in the short term at least, separate pastoral provision should be made for the exiles. Bullinger's energetic support for the idea (which reflected his close relations both with the Locarnese evangelical community and with Italian Protestant exiles more generally) was probably an important factor in the council's decision, on 30 March, to instruct him to examine how the exiles' desire for a minister of their own might be satisfied.[75] On 22 May, the more concrete step was taken of asking the *Rechenrat*, the council's standing commission on financial matters,[76] and the clergy to draw up a 'constitution' for the proposed

---

[72] StAZ E II 365a, 560: 'obsecramus vos per Dei misericordiam (viri Piisimi) ut quantum in vobis est eripiatis nos misellos e tanta angustiarum profunditate, ac operam detis ut Ecclesia nostra sub aliquo tandem Pastore uniri possit, et cibum spiritualem accipere, ut relictis erroribus, et vitiis humanae carnis, spiritui pareat.' Compare n. 34 above, and the following letter from the church of Locarno to the Zurich council, dated 31 March 1554 (StAZ A 350.1: Locarner Acten 1554): 'Infantes nostros Christiano ritu baptizare non possumus iuxta voluntatem Domini, et conscientiam nostram nisi maximo cum periculo, neque sacramentum Corporis et Sanguinis Christi, administrare, quae omnia non minore dolore et angustia, animas nostras afficiunt … . Imo vix scimus quo nos vertamus, nam si clam baptizamus, Catabaptistas nos vocitant, sin palam nobis et ministris insidiantur, ac Haereticos et Lutheranos appellant, quia neque sal, neque oleum, neque sputem, neque exorcismos admittimus.'

[73] StAZ A 350.1: Locarner Acten 1555: 'Wohin sy noch kummen söltend were ir anmütung / daß sy [the Locarnesi] by einandern blyben möchtend / … und daß sy ein kylchen und wälschen predicanten gehaben möchtend'.

[74] FA Orelli, 8.7, no. 11: 'Dovete saper di certo che in niuna delle Città de nostri signori Illustrissimi vi serà concesso haver particolar predicante: ma vi bisognerà legger in casa, o andar ad udire lingua non intesa.' The letter, though anonymous, is in Beccaria's hand. It is undersigned 'manum nosti', a formulation which appears in other letters from Beccaria to Taddeo Duno.

[75] StAZ B II 90, 11.

[76] On the composition of the *Rechenrat*, see N. Flüeler and M. Flüeler-Grauwiler (eds), *Geschichte des Kantons Zürich: Band 2: Frühe Neuzeit – 16. bis 18. Jahrhundert* (Zurich, 1996), p. 26.

Italian church.[77] The *Rechenrat*'s report, which the council approved the following week, suggested that Zurich's third church, St Peter, be made available to the Locarnese community for Italian-language services, and outlined arrangements for the appointment, accommodation and remuneration of the new Italian minister. The *Rechenrat* proposed that nominees for the post should be required to submit to a theological examination by ministers and council members prior to appointment, a provision which it is tempting to link to the Italian exiles' reputation for 'heresy'; in fact, such examinations were routine for candidates seeking admission to the ministry in Zurich.[78] Of greater significance was the report's assertion that, once the Locarnesi had acquired an adequate knowledge of German, the maintenance of an Italian preacher should cease to be necessary.[79] Although mindful of its evangelical obligations, the Zurich council never envisaged the Italian church as anything more than a stop-gap; it certainly had no intention of allowing Zurich to become a multi-ethnic 'refuge' like Geneva or London. That needs to be borne in mind when considering the church's subsequent fate.

Following the adoption of the *Rechenrat*'s recommendations by the council on 29 May, it remained only to find a suitable candidate for the post of Italian minister. The obvious choice seemed to be Beccaria, who following his banishment from Locarno in August 1549 had retained strong links with members of the town's evangelical community; some of the Locarnese Reformed even sent their children to be educated by him in Mesocco.[80] The *Rechenrat* itself recognized the connection, noting in its report to the council that Beccaria was 'known and liked by the exiles' and proposing his election, subject to examination.[81] Beccaria's candidacy also had the backing of the church of Graubünden, which was grateful for his efforts on behalf of the Reformation in the Mesolcina: when Beccaria arrived in Zurich in early June, he brought with him a letter of recommendation from Philipp Gallicius, who argued that, as the 'apostle' to the Locarnesi, Beccaria was best equipped to serve as their minister.[82] However, not everyone shared Gallicius' view.

---

[77] StAZ B II 90, 28.

[78] Gordon, *Clerical Discipline*, pp. 93–4.

[79] StAZ A 350.1: Locarner Acten 1555; published in Meyer, *Locarnergemeinde*, II, pp. 359–61. The same recommendations are contained in the Latin 'Constitutio facta in Senatu Tigurino Ecclesiastico de Locarnensibus', also dated 23 May and published in Meyer, *Locarnergemeinde*, II, pp. 301–3 (copies in FA Orelli, 8.3; ZB Ms. E 15, fols 157r–8r; ZB Ms. S 197, fols 18v, 6r; Orelli, *Verfolgung*, pp. 107–9).

[80] *EA*, IV:1e, p. 808; Beccaria to Duno, 23 November 1554 (FA Orelli, 8.2, fol. 7av; Meyer, *Locarnergemeinde*, I, p. 249, n. 236).

[81] Meyer, *Locarnergemeinde*, II, p. 360.

[82] Schiess, I, no. 286: 'Hic eorum apostolus fuit et propter eos unaque cum ipsis passus

Opposition to Beccaria's appointment was expressed most vocally by Vergerio, who in letters to Bullinger sought to convince him of the schoolmaster's unsuitability for the post.[83] Vergerio's attitude is somewhat puzzling, given that he also claimed to hold Beccaria in high regard, but it appears to have reflected a desire to see the new congregation entrusted to someone with more established intellectual credentials, who could offer leadership to the wider Italian evangelical community in Swiss exile. Such considerations may have played a role in Beccaria's decision, shortly after arriving in Zurich, to turn down the council's offer of employment, on the basis that he lacked the qualifications needed for the post.[84]

The same could not be said of Bernardino Ochino, who quickly emerged as Beccaria's preferred replacement.[85] Ochino had already served as minister to Italian exile congregations in Geneva, Augsburg and London, and had an impressive publishing record (including several volumes of sermons and commentaries on Romans and Galatians). Although not one of Bullinger's regular correspondents,[86] he had long-

---

est multa ac diu, ut ipsi pro eo rogare deberent et gratulari ei aliquam propiciorem fortunam.' Cited in Meyer, *Locarnergemeinde*, II, pp. 7–8, n. 18.

83 Vergerio to Bullinger, 12 June 1555 (StAZ E II 365a, 661); see also Campi, 'Vergerio', pp. 284–5. Vergerio took a close interest in the fate of the Locarnese evangelicals. In July 1553, he asked Josias Simler to send six copies of a work against the Mass – perhaps the *Annotomia della Messa* – to Ludovico Ronco in Locarno (StAZ E II 356, 527; Meyer, *Locarnergemeinde*, I, p. 266; Pfister, *Um des Glaubens willen*, p. 53), while some months later he presented Bullinger with a manuscript copy of the preface to his Italian version of the *Antistes' De sacrosancta coena*, translated into Latin by Besozzi (Vergerio to Bullinger, 25 September 1553 [Schiess, I, no. 229]). For this preface, see StAZ E II 365, 173–4.

84 StAZ A 350.1: 'Uff üwer unser gnädigen herren erkanntnus / habend wir herren Johansen Beccaria von Luggaris berüfft / und imm fürgehallten wie uwer wyßheit inn habe geordnet zů einem predicanten der kylchen der vertribnen Luggarneren / mitt anderem was uwer wyßheit ordnung dann vermag. Daruff er uwer wyßheit uffs aller höchst und flissigst danket der fürträfflichen geoffen gnad / deren er in gůtem und gägen Gott nimmermer vergässen wölle. Zeygt aber darnäben das ouch an / dass er uwer wyßheit in allem dem das im möglich gern wöllte gehorsamm sin: aber in disem handel befinde er sich dermassen schwach unbericht und ungeüpt / das er sömlich ampt nitt annemmen / ouch nitt anders befinden könne / dann das es weder für die kylch noch für inn selbs gůt sye. Wölle den platz einem lassen der mitt mee frucht vorstande. Was er aber dem oder in ander wäg gedienen könne / wölle er gern thůn.'

85 There are two full-length biographies of Ochino in existence: K. Benrath, *Bernardino Ochino von Siena* (Braunschweig, 1892); and R. Bainton, *Bernardino Ochino, esule e riformatore senese del Cinquecento* (Florence, 1940). See also my forthcoming article in the new *Dictionary of National Biography*, with further references.

86 Only one short letter from Ochino to Bullinger survives, dated 4 January 1546 and published in Benrath, *Ochino*, p. 302. In this letter, written on behalf of an unnamed evangelical travelling to Zurich, Ochino asks Bullinger to pass on greetings to his colleagues, especially Pellikan.

standing ties with the Zurich church, having visited Zurich in September 1542 and again following his expulsion from Augsburg in early 1547.[87] One of his early works, the *Imagine del Antechristo*, was translated into Latin by Johannes Wolf.[88] Ochino was also the favoured candidate of the Locarnesi themselves, having forged links with the community during a visit to Chiavenna in July 1554.[89] All of these points were noted by Bullinger in an address to the Zurich council on 11 June, in which he formally proposed Ochino's appointment.[90] From this point, events moved swiftly. Letters were dispatched to the council in Basle, where Ochino was currently residing, to request his release, and to Ochino himself, setting out his conditions of employment.[91] Within days, the Sienese exile had arrived in Zurich to take up his new post; he preached his first sermon on 23 June.[92]

The community that had been placed in Ochino's charge consisted, at the time of his appointment, of more than 100 persons. For information on its early development, we are reliant on two main sources: the church's own records, which will be considered shortly, and a series of surveys commissioned by the Zurich council during the late 1550s, through which it sought to monitor the activities of Zurich's newly acquired foreign population.[93]

At the most basic level, the surveys provide details of the size of the

---

[87] On the latter occasion, attempts were made by the Spanish exile Francisco de Enzinas (Dryander) to secure Ochino a permanent post in Zurich (see F. de Enzinas, *Epistolario*, ed. I. García Pineda (Geneva, 1995), nos 21 and 25–7).

[88] Rotondò, 'Anticristo', p. 151. Compare Wotschke, no. 217.

[89] Besozzi to Bullinger, 13 July 1554 (StAZ E II 365a, 543); Meyer, *Locarnergemeinde*, I, pp. 296–7, n. 79; T. von Liebenau, 'Della chiamata a Locarno di Bernardino Ochino', *Bollettino storico della Svizzera italiana*, 12 (1890), p. 30.

[90] StAZ A 350.1: '... zeigend wir an / das ein doctor und gelerter man h. Bernhardin Ochin von Senen / ietzund zů Basel whonhafft ist / der kein ampt noch stand hat / vorhin aber zů Augspurg und ouch in Engelland geprediget / darzů in Italischer sprach vil geschriben hat / ein allter und verrümpter man / zů dem die Luggarner ein besonderbare anmůtung habend / und hoffend so der uwer wyßheit / gefallen möchte / were er zů bewegen dass er zů inen zuge. Sölichs alles habend wir uwer wyßheit uff das kürzist berichten wöllen / mitt underthäniger pitt uwer wyßheit wölle die vilgedacht der Luggarnern kylch in gnad bevolhen haben / und fürderlich verhälffen das sy mitt einem gottsfürchtigen trüwen diener oder prediger versähen werdint. Daran Gott ein gfallen haben / und uwer wyßheit lob und eer erlangen wirt.'

[91] StAZ A 350.1: Locarner Acten 1555.

[92] Bullinger, *Verzeichnis*, fol. 188[v]. Compare FA Orelli, 8.2, fol. 9[v]; ZB Ms. B 251, fol. 45[r].

[93] Originals in StAZ A 350.1; published in Meyer, *Locarnergemeinde*, II, pp. 375–87. On the background to these reports, see section iv below. They are analysed in detail in L. Weisz, 'Die wirtschaftliche Bedeutung der Tessiner Glaubensflüchtlinge für die deutsche Schweiz', part 1, *Zwa*, 10/4 (1955/2), pp. 228–48 (239–47).

exile community, allowing us to track quite precisely its growth over the period concerned. Among the documents submitted with the first survey (September 1556) is a list, in Taddeo Duno's hand, of the community's members, from which it can be deduced that the number of Locarnesi resident in Zurich stood at 125.[94] This total included some recent arrivals from Locarno, such as the cobblers Filippo di Campo and Francesco Albertino, whose wives had taken part in the initial emigration without them. Nor was the exodus yet complete: Duno indicated that around 20 persons, including the families of Bartolomeo Cataneo, Giacomo Zareto, Stefano Pebbia, Gianambrosio Rosalino and Giovanni Muralto, were expected to arrive in Zurich shortly. Despite losing members to Basle, Geneva and other centres, over the next couple of years the community continued to register overall growth. The third survey, conducted in April 1558, revealed that the Locarnese population of Zurich had risen to over 130 – a total which included at least five children born since the community's expulsion from Locarno, as well as Antonio Mario Besozzi and his family, who had migrated to Zurich from Chiavenna.

The surveys also contain extensive information on the occupations and economic activities of members of the community. The authors of the September 1556 survey noted significant disparities in wealth among the exiles, describing around one-third of households as well-off, but another seven, including those of Beccaria and the fisherman Stefano Pebbia, as poor or very poor. As we shall see, this economic division was to remain a feature of the community for years to come, as well as a source of tension between its different component groups.[95]

Of the more prosperous exiles, few were economically active: in the September 1556 survey, 11 households (including that of Guarnerio Castiglione, who had accompanied the Locarnesi to Zurich) are described as living off income from existing property. However, this was not the case for long. In July 1555, representatives of the duchy of Milan had agreed to a request from the Zurich council to permit the Locarnesi to operate on their territory, on condition that the exiles confined their activities strictly to trade.[96] Although to begin with only a handful of

[94] StAZ A 350.1: Locarner Acten undatiert; published in Meyer, *Locarnergemeinde*, II, pp. 372–5.

[95] Further information on the wealth of individual exiles can be gleaned from surviving wills and wardship records of a later date. In November 1582, Chiara Verzasca (widow of the wealthy, but childless, Battista de' Baddi) left 424 lb. (212 Gulden) to her female relatives and 64 lb. to the Zurich *Spital*, plus an unspecified amount to her brothers Gianantonio and Bartolomeo (StAZ B VI 320, fols 63r–4r; B VI 321, fols 390r–91r). When she married Francesco Muralto in January 1568, Catarina Orelli brought with her a dowry of 800 Gulden (FA Orelli, 4.300).

[96] StAZ B II 92, 7 (17 July 1555); cited in Meyer, *Locarnergemeinde*, II, p. 24, n. 76.

Locarnesi took advantage of this concession – the survey of September 1556 lists only five individuals (Martino Muralto, Gianantonio Rosalino, Pariso Appiano, Giacomo Zareto and Filippo Appiano) as having trading interests – by the time of the second survey (August 1557) the picture had changed dramatically, with 14 heads of household now engaged in mercantile ventures. The most important of these was a company that Ludovico Ronco had formed with Besozzi, Castiglione and Andrea Cevio for the import of textiles and luxury articles from Milan and Venice; other Locarnesi, such as the brothers Gianantonio and Bartolomeo Verzasca, had begun to profit from flourishing trades in rice, tallow, leather and cloth.[97] By the time of the third survey, the number of heads of household deriving their income in whole or in part from trade had risen to 16 – almost half of the community's adult male members. Most scholars attribute this development to the rigidity of the Zurich guild system, which made it difficult for the Locarnesi to practise their original professions.[98] That certainly helps account for the speed of the transformation, but the Locarnese experience was replicated in other contemporary refugee communities, for example in England.[99] The suggestion is that by virtue of their continuing links with their former homelands exiles were ideally placed to carve out new livelihoods in long-distance trade.

The survey of April 1558 also revealed that members of the community were extending their activity from trade to manufacture, specifically of textiles. Pariso Appiano, one of the first Locarnesi to begin trading with Milan and a trained silk-weaver, took the lead in this regard. By April 1558 his business, financed with the help of another exile, Gianantonio Rosalino, was employing four apprentices and was about to take on another two, including a Catholic from Locarno.[100] Appiano was also underwriting the operations of a French Protestant immigrant from Geneva, who himself employed two apprentices. A second, smaller enterprise on the same lines was run by Evangelista Zanino, the son-in-law of Andrea Cevio, in conjunction with his brother Paolo and another Locarnese youth, Giovanni Maria Toma. Zanino,

---

[97] Meyer, *Locarnergemeinde*, II, pp. 377–8.

[98] See, for example, M. Körner, 'Profughi italiani in Svizzera durante il XVI secolo: aspetti sociali, economici, religiosi e culturali', in M. Berengo et al. (eds), *Città italiane del '500 tra Riforma e Controriforma: Atti del Convegno Internazionale di Studi Lucca, 13–15 ottobre 1983* (Lucca, 1988), pp. 1–22 (10).

[99] See O. Grell, 'A new home or a temporary abode? Dutch and Walloon exiles in England', in Grell, *Calvinist Exiles in Tudor and Stuart England* (Aldershot, 1996), pp. 1–32; A. Spicer, *The French-speaking Reformed Community and their Church in Southampton 1567–c.1620* (Stroud, 1997), pp. 35–70.

[100] Meyer, *Locarnergemeinde*, II, pp. 382–3.

who was also involved in the transalpine trade with Italy, later became the first to attempt to produce silk on a large scale in Zurich, with the assistance of imported Italian labour.[101]

Other aspects of the community's life are documented in its own records, which survive in the form of minutes of meetings and accounts, and are currently held by the von Orelli family.[102] Unfortunately these records, which have only rarely been accessible to scholars since Ferdinand Meyer wrote his classic history of the Locarnese community in the 1830s, are deficient in a number of respects. In the first place, they have suffered significant physical damage. When Daniel Orelli von Gemsberg rediscovered them in 1684, the volume in which they were contained was already rotting away in parts; by Orelli's own account, he was forced to cut out substantial sections to save what remained.[103] Thus, for example, records of donations made to members of the community from its funds survive, while records of loans (which we know from other sources to have been substantial) do not. Secondly, there is no reference in the accounts to income from the collection which the church instituted in November 1556, and which may eventually have become its primary source of revenue;[104] Ferdinand Meyer speculates that this was entered in a separate volume, now lost.[105] Finally, the minutes themselves are of only limited value, as no entries survive for the period March 1561 to June 1565, during which Zurich's Italian-speaking community experienced its most severe crisis. Whether this gap in the records reflects a real decay in the institutional fabric of the church, or merely scribal negligence, is difficult to ascertain.

Nevertheless, the minutes for the years 1555–58 remain a useful source, providing insights into how the Locarnese church functioned as an institution and highlighting some of the issues that animated its members. Leadership responsibilities were in the hands of a college of elders, four of whom – Giovanni Beccaria, Ludovico Ronco, Alberto

---

[101] L. Weisz, 'Die wirtschaftliche Bedeutung der Tessiner Glaubensflüchtlinge für die deutsche Schweiz: Erste Fortsetzung', *Zwa*, 10/5 (1956/1), pp. 297–339 (315–29); W. Bodmer, *Der Einfluß der Refugianteneinwanderung von 1550–1700 auf die schweizerische Wirtschaft: Ein Beitrag zur Geschichte des Frühkapitalismus und der Textilindustrie* (Zurich, 1946), pp. 28–32. But recently Ulrich Pfister has warned against exaggerating the Locarnese contribution to the long-term development of the textile industry in Zurich (*Die Zürcher Fabriques: Protoindustrielles Wachstum vom 16. zum 18. Jahrhundert* (Zurich, 1992), p. 39).

[102] FA Orelli, 8.2: Libro degli ordini, Receuti, spese, et altri negotii secondo li besogni occorrenti nella Chiesia di Locarnesi habitante in Zuricho. Copy in FA Orelli, 8.7, part of which is published in Meyer, *Locarnergemeinde*, II, pp. 363–9.

[103] FA Orelli, 8.7, fol. 1r.

[104] FA Orelli, 8.2, fol. 14v.

[105] Meyer, *Locarnergemeinde*, II, p. 35, n. 124.

Trevano and Martino Muralto – were elected at a meeting of adult male members of the church on 12 June 1555.[106] At a second meeting later that month the number of elders was increased to six, through the addition of Taddeo Duno and Guarnerio Castiglione.[107] The names of two other elders are known: Francesco Verzasca, who replaced Beccaria when the latter returned to Mesocco in March 1559, and Peter Martyr Vermigli, who was added to the college (on Ochino's recommendation) following his appointment as professor of Old Testament at the Zurich academy.[108] For the most part, the membership of the college was drawn from the wealthier and more aristocratic sections of the community; even the relatively low-profile Trevano and Verzasca fell into this category.[109] Through the election of Duno, Ronco and Beccaria, an element of continuity was also preserved with the church's past in Locarno.

The powers and duties of the elders were defined at the meeting of 12 June as, first, 'to preside over the morals, discipline and governance of our congregation'; secondly, to administer the church's funds and record its revenue; and thirdly, to distribute alms to the needy.[110] However, there is no evidence that the Locarnese elders exercised discipline formally, in the manner that their equivalents in other 'Calvinist' exile churches did. Such an arrangement would have been highly irregular in the context of Zurich, where the secular magistrate retained the power of excommunication and where the church leadership was itself opposed to the introduction of ecclesiastical discipline on Genevan lines. From the surviving minutes, it would appear that in practice the elders' duties were confined to financial matters. Some of those elected were assigned particular responsibilities in this regard: Martino Muralto, for instance, was placed in charge of the church's common chest, while Ronco, who had acted as a scribe to the community in Locarno, was appointed 'Canceller', with the task of keeping the accounts and minutes up to date.[111] After 1558 this function

---

[106] FA Orelli, 8.2, fol. 9ʳ; Meyer, *Locarnergemeinde*, II, p. 364.

[107] FA Orelli 8.2, fol. 10ʳ; Meyer, *Locarnergemeinde*, II, p. 365.

[108] FA Orelli 8.2, fol. 13ᵛ. For the background to Vermigli's appointment, see M. Baumann, 'Petrus Martyr Vermigli: Doctor, Lehrer der Heiligen Schrift und Zürcher', in E. Campi (ed.), *Peter Martyr Vermigli: Humanism, Republicanism, Reformation* (Geneva, 2002), pp. 214–24, and Chapter 1:ii above.

[109] In the September 1556 survey, Francesco Verzasca is described as 'zimlich wolhabend' (Meyer, *Locarnergemeinde*, II. p. 376). The same survey reports: 'Albertus Trevanus tribt kein gwerb hatt daß er und sin frauw wol mögend ußkommen.' On his death in 1573, Trevano left property in Locarno and Zurich, including 145 Kronen to his niece Maddalena Muralto (StAZ B VI 316, fols 212ᵛ–13ʳ; B VI 317, fol. 41ʳ⁻ᵛ).

[110] FA Orelli, 8.2, fol. 9ʳ; Meyer, *Locarnergemeinde*, II, p. 364.

[111] FA Orelli, 8.2, fol. 9ᵛ; Meyer, *Locarnergemeinde*, II, p. 364.

passed to Duno, which may explain why the minutes of the community begin to peter out around that time.

One of the church's most important early tasks was to establish an effective system of financial administration – an issue made more pressing by the fact that the Locarnese community quickly came into possession of a substantial capital. Taking advantage of the publicity surrounding their expulsion from Locarno, on 12 June 1555 the exiles decided, with the encouragement of Bullinger and the Zurich council, to send representatives to the Swiss Protestant cities to request financial assistance for the community.[112] In Berne, Lausanne and Neuchâtel, local Reformed churchmen had already begun to institute collections on behalf of the Locarnesi, which yielded the impressive sum of more than 2000 Gulden. Smaller contributions were later made by Basle and Biel.[113] At a meeting on 5 November, the elders took stock of the money received, recording the church's total assets at around 1200 scudi.[114]

The acquisition of these resources was in some respects a mixed blessing, as disputes quickly broke out within the community about how they should be used. Many of the wealthier and more enterprising Locarnesi saw in the common chest a potential source of funding for their private or co-operative business ventures, whereas the poorer exiles were concerned that it should be used primarily for the relief of their needs. On 18 August 1555, the community considered, and rejected, a proposal for the bulk of the funds to be loaned out at interest either to its own members or to Zurichers, resolving instead to retain the entire sum for charitable purposes. However, a revision of policy quickly became necessary: at a meeting on 2 September, the elders complained that they had been besieged by requests for loans of 25, 30 and even 100 scudi, and warned that if that situation continued 'the money may soon run out'. Henceforth, they decided, the maximum amount available as a single loan should be limited to 10 scudi, and then only with proper

---

[112] Ibid. See also the letter, dated 12 June, from the *Bürgermeister* and *Rat* of Zurich to Basle (StAZ A 350.1: Locarner Acten 1555).

[113] For Berne, see the letter to the Locarnesi of 19 June 1555 (FA Orelli, 8.7, no. 15; copy in Bullinger, *Verzeichnis*, fol. 189ʳ) and the latter's reply, dated 22 June (FA Orelli, 8.7, no. 16); for Lausanne, Viret's letter of 17 April 1555 and the Locarnese reply of 21 June (ibid., nos 12 and 13); for Biel, the letter of the Locarnese elders to Ambrosius Blarer dated 8 October (ibid., no. 22); for Basle, their letter to Sulzer of 22 April 1556 (ibid., no. 31). The amounts received were entered in the community's accounts for 1555 (FA Orelli, 8.2, fols 88ᵛ–9ᵛ). These also record a further small donation of 5 scudi from Berne in September 1561 (ibid., fol. 90ᵛ). For further detail, see Meyer, *Locarnergemeinde*, II, pp. 14–18. Collections of this sort were to become a standard Reformed response to refugee crises (for a later example, see Chapter 6:iii below).

[114] FA Orelli, 8.2, fol. 12ʳ⁻ᵛ.

guarantees for its repayment ('idonea segurta per restituirli').[115] The elders' control over community finances was strengthened at a full meeting of the church two weeks later, where the upper limit of 2 scudi which they were permitted to dispense on their own authority was abolished and they were given 'complete freedom and authority to dispose of all the money that the church possesses now or may possess in the future'. To allay any suspicions of financial misconduct on the part of the elders ('levar ogni mal pensier'), the community resolved to have the funds deposited in a chest to which three individuals (Ochino, Duno and Martino Muralto) would have access. It was further stipulated that none of them might remove money from the chest, except in the presence of the others.[116]

Despite these measures, tensions over the use of the fund continued to surface, leading Ochino in September the following year to propose a further reform of the church's finances.[117] This time, it was agreed to set aside the majority of the money for commercial loans at an interest rate of 5 per cent, with the profits to be used for the benefit of the needy. In addition, interest-free loans of up to 50 scudi were made available to those with no visible means of support ('quali senza arte et altro essercitio et che non si pono mantenere et sostentar'). These rather more generous terms may have satisfied the clamour for increased access to the church's resources, but problems of administration remained: following a review of accounts conducted in September the following year by Francesco Verzasca, Aloisio Orelli and Francesco Michele Appiano, the minister and elders were advised to be less generous in future when responding to requests for loans (the church's total assets had fallen to below 950 scudi by this time).[118] In March 1561 trouble flared up again, as a minority within the community charged the elders with maladministration of the fund. An investigation by the Zurich council found nothing to substantiate these allegations, but revealed a further significant reduction in the community's total resources to 777 scudi. The elders responded to the worsening financial situation by attempting to recall loans from wealthier members of the community, but apparently with little success.[119]

Although the existence of the common chest was occasionally a

115 Ibid., fol. 11ᵛ; Meyer, *Locarnergemeinde*, II, p. 36, n. 127.

116 FA Orelli, 8.2, fols 11ᵛ–12ʳ; Meyer, *Locarnergemeinde*, II, pp. 35–6, 366–7.

117 FA Orelli, 8.2, fol. 14ʳ; Meyer, *Locarnergemeinde*, II, pp. 36–7, 367–9. On this reform, see also Weisz, 'Tessiner', pp. 235–6.

118 FA Orelli, 8.2, fols 15ᵛ–16ʳ; Meyer, *Locarnergemeinde*, II, p. 37.

119 Copy of the minutes in FA Orelli, 8.7, pp. 17–18; Meyer, *Locarnergemeinde*, II, p. 164.

source of conflict within the community, in general it had a unifying function, as a focus for charitable giving and the basis for an autonomous welfare system that underpinned the church's distinct identity.[120] (The Locarnesi received very little in the way of assistance from Zurich's own *Almosenamt*.)[121] The office of deacon was exercised in the first instance by Beccaria, and later by Castiglione, who administered the collection money – of which (as has been mentioned) we unfortunately have no record – and purchased food, clothing and other items on behalf of the poor.[122] Trevano, Francesco Verzasca and Francesco Michele Appiano also made occasional contributions in this area.[123]

Understandably, the system was under greatest pressure during the months immediately following the arrival of the Locarnesi in Zurich. In July 1555 alone, a total of 53 scudi was dispensed in poor relief; money also had to be found to reimburse those who had previously lent money to the community and to cover the expenses of the delegations that had been sent to request aid from the Swiss Reformed cities.[124] In subsequent years, most grants went to a small number of individuals and families who remained excluded from the growing prosperity of the community as a whole, in particular the young, widows and the infirm. Prominent among these was Battista Roggiolo, an invalid resident in the Zurich *Spital* from the time of his arrival with the first group of Locarnesi in March 1555 until his death around 1570, who received an average of

---

[120] The independent administration of poor relief was an integral feature of many exile congregations. See H. Schilling, *Niederländische Exulanten im 16. Jahrhundert: Ihre Stellung im Sozialgefüge und im religiösen Leben deutscher und englischer Städte* (Gütersloh, 1972), p. 27; and A. Spicer, 'Poor relief and the exile communities', in B. Kümin (ed.), *Reformations Old and New: Essays on the Socio-Economic Impact of Religious Change c.1470–1630* (Aldershot, 1996), pp. 237–55 (on the French church in Southampton).

[121] A. Denzler, *Geschichte des Armenwesens im Kanton Zürich im 16. und 17. Jahrhundert* (Zurich, 1920), p. 78.

[122] In January 1556, for instance, Castiglione received more than 3 scudi from the common chest 'per panno qual lui compro per comissione nostro per Battista Roggiolo cioe per suo vestire avanti a Nadale' (FA Orelli, 8.2, fol. 96v). Compare the entries for 15 October 1556 (fol. 97v) and 19 March 1558 (fol. 99v). According to the survey of April 1558, Castiglione also allowed other exiles to make use of baking facilities that he had set up in his house, 'und das umb kein Nutzes, sonder fründtschafft willen' (Meyer, *Locarnergemeinde*, II, p. 381).

[123] For Trevano, see the entries for 12 November 1555 (FA Orelli, 8.2, fol. 95v); 6 February 1556 (fol. 96v); 12 September 1557 (fol. 99r); 12 February 1558 (fol. 99v); and 15 June 1559 (fol. 100v). On 11 January 1558 Appiano was reimbursed for expenses on behalf of Battista Roggiolo (fol. 99v), while in March 1561 Verzasca reclaimed 1 scudo that he had issued to Stefano Pebbia 'a nome della chiesa' (fol. 102v).

[124] Ibid., fols 93v–4r.

four grants a year between 1555 and 1563. In Roggiolo's case, the sums dispensed were small, rarely exceeding 2 scudi, and tended to be designated for a specific purpose, such as the purchase of shoes. Other regular recipients of poor relief were the cobblers Francesco Albertino and Filippo di Campo, who were described in the survey of September 1556 as extremely poor. Albertino and di Campo were able to claim larger amounts (of up to 4 scudi) from the common chest to assist them with paying their rent; the fisherman Stefano Pebbia and the widow Lucia Belò also regularly received grants for the same purpose.[125]

The common chest was used not only as a safety net for those unable to support themselves, but as a means of subsidising the economic activities of poorer church members. On 3 October 1555, for instance, Stefano Pebbia and his brother-in-law Francesco Albertino received around 10 scudi to purchase fishing-nets.[126] In November the following year, 8 scudi were granted to Bernardino Roggiolo, son of Battista, who 'requested this subsidy in order to purchase equipment that will allow him to maintain and support himself through the trade of book binding, promising the church that he will not bother it further in future',[127] while in April 1557 Filippo di Campo received 2 scudi 'to buy leather to enable him to work'.[128] The apprenticeship in Basle of Bartolomeo Orelli was also financed from the common chest.[129]

Community solidarity found expression through the fund in other ways. In April 1556, for example, the church set aside 150 scudi to redeem the property of Barbara Muralto, Lucia Belò and Catarina Appiano, the three Locarnese women who had been convicted by the

---

[125] The accounts for the period 1555–63 contain 42 entries for Roggiolo, 15 for Albertino and his wife Angelina Pebbia, 20 for Filippo di Campo and his wife Elisabetta Robasciotto, 13 for Pebbia and his family and eight for Lucia Belò.

[126] FA Orelli, 8.2, fol. 95ᵛ.

[127] Ibid., fol. 98ʳ: 'E piu alli 25 di novembre per commissione come di sopra s'è numerato a Bernardino roggiolo, qual ha domandato alla chiesa questo sussidio, per comprar Instromenti per poter da sua posta essercitar l'arte de ligar libri accio che per questa si potesse mantener et sostentare, promettendo poi alla Chiesa nel avenir di non esserli piu grave in modo alcuno, numerato dico in tutta summa sol. 8'.

[128] Ibid., fol. 98ᵛ: 'E piu al di sopradetto [15 April] ... s'è dato a Filipo di Campo qual ha domandato sussidio per compra [sic] corio per poter lavorare sol. 2'.

[129] Ibid., fol. 12ᵛ (9 December 1555): 'Essendo congregati insieme li seniori, e comparso Ms. Bertholomeo Orello, espli[cava] ch'l'animo suo saria stato d'applicarse a qualche Impresa, dove ne potesse cavar il vivere, et ch'haveva designato di metterse in casa d'un qualche Cramer in uno de quattro Cantoni, et per donzena per un anno, accio che per questa via pigliasse ... prattica, et imparasse la lingua Tedescha, et che finito, sperava d'acquistarse poi il vivere, ma essendo inhabil ... povero supplicava alla chiesia li volesse dar soccorso. Li sopradetti seniori intesa la sua petione hanno ... che ogni volta ch'l detto Ms. Bertholomeo vorra ... ha supplicato che li siano datti solini dodici.' See ibid., fol. 96ʳ, for the relevant entry in the accounts.

Catholic states of blasphemy against the Virgin.[130] Resources were also found from the common chest to assist various exiles (Bartolomeo Cataneo, Stefano Pebbia and Francesco Albertino) in arranging for members of their families to join them in Zurich,[131] and to provide regular payments to Rudolf Gwalther, minister at the church of St Peter used by the Locarnesi, to Ochino, and to others who served the exiles in an official capacity.[132] Duno, who had agreed to act as physician to the community, received a quarterly salary of 20 scudi for his services, while Beccaria was paid half that amount in return for providing the children of the community with catechetical instruction.[133] The elders also drew on the common chest to purchase pews and books for the use of the church and its minister – the *Loci communes* of Wolfgang Musculus and a 1557 Latin edition of the Genevan Bible are mentioned[134] – and to pay for copies of Ochino's *Dialogo del Purgatorio* and *Syncerae et verae doctrinae de Coena Domini defensio* to be bound and presented to those churches which had contributed to the fund in the first instance.[135]

In the main, the extant minutes and accounts for the period 1555–63 suggest a thriving and cohesive community. Despite ongoing tensions over the use of shared resources, the Italian church service and the common chest served as rallying points for the Locarnesi in an alien and sometimes hostile environment (see section iv below). The exiles' exclusion from the mainstream economic life of Zurich resulted in the emergence of Locarnese business enterprises such as the Ronco company, which reinforced the community's distinctiveness and brought its members a degree of prosperity.[136] At this early stage, there were few indications that the Locarnesi were becoming integrated into wider Zurich society: they remained very much a community in exile, with tenuous links to their host city.

---

[130] Ibid., fol. 13ʳ. After making representations to the *Landschreiber* Roll, the Locarnesi eventually succeeded in having these penalties commuted (ibid., fols 13ᵛ; 97ʳ). On the whole affair, see Meyer, *Locarnergemeinde*, I, pp. 26–8.

[131] FA Orelli, 8.2, fols 97ʳ⁻ᵛ; 98ᵛ.

[132] See the references in Meyer, *Locarnergemeinde*, II, pp. 29–30.

[133] FA Orelli, 8.2, fol. 11ʳ; Meyer, *Locarnergemeinde*, II, p. 365.

[134] Ibid., fol. 15ʳ (cited in Meyer, *Locarnergemeinde*, II, p. 30, n. 98); fols 96ᵛ, 99ʳ, 99ᵛ, 101ᵛ.

[135] FA Orelli, 8.2, fol. 96ᵛ. Duno and Beccaria also took out a loan from the church to pay for the publication of these works, security for which was put up by Bartolomeo Verzasca and Ludovico Ronco (see ibid., fol. 19ᵛ).

[136] This was reflected in a fall in the number of persons receiving assistance from the common chest, from between seven and 12 annually during the period 1555–61 to four in 1563.

iii. The Locarnesi and other Italian exile communities

Earlier studies of the Zurich Locarnesi have tended to examine the
community in isolation, rather than in the context of a wider Italian
Protestant 'diaspora'. To some extent this neglect is understandable, as
the sources documenting the exiles' relations with Italian-speaking
Reformed communities elsewhere are patchy, to say the least. However,
there is clear evidence that such ties did exist, and that the Locarnesi
considered themselves – and were considered by others – part of the
Italian 'nation' in exile. It should be noted that in his *De persequutione
adversus Locarnenses* Taddeo Duno linked the experience of the
Locarnesi to the fate of the Reformation in Italy as a whole: the work is
prefaced with a list of prominent Italian converts to Protestantism,
nearly all of whom Duno claimed to have known personally.[137] As we
have seen, prior even to its enforced departure from Locarno the
community had played host to refugees from the neighbouring duchy of
Milan, some of whom (Besozzi, Castiglione) went on to assume
positions of leadership in the Zurich Italian church. While studying in
Basle during the late 1540s, Duno himself had been closely associated
with the Mantuan exile Francesco Stancaro, whose commentary on the
epistle of James he translated into Latin 'for the benefit of those who do
not know Italian'.[138]

One interesting feature of the April 1558 survey is the addition of a
'description of the other foreign people living here [in Zurich]'('Beschrybung
des Anndern weltschen volks das hie ist').[139] The existence of this group,
comprising persons 'who are from places other than Locarno, but who are
looked on and decried as Locarnesi because they attend [their] services' ('so
nit von Luggarus sonnder anndern orthen har sind, unnd aber zu jnen jnn
jre Predigen gonnd unnd deßhalb für Luggarner gehalten unnd verschrüwen
werden'), suggests that the Locarnesi were not as 'closed' a community as is
sometimes implied. The compilers of the list distinguished between
foreigners resident in Zurich on a more or less continual basis, and
occasional visitors to the city. The latter comprised for the most part

---

[137] *De persequutione*, fols 1ᵛ–2ʳ (Chenou, 'Locarno', pp. 262–3). Those named are
Vermigli, Ochino, Aonio Paleario, Vergerio, Galeazzo Caracciolo, Ulisse Martinengo,
Zanchi, Curione, Scipione Lentolo, Scipione Calandrini, Francesco Betti, Francesco
Stancaro, Ludovico Castelvetro, Giacomo Aconcio and Giulio Cesare Pascali.

[138] *Explanatio Epistolae divi Iacobi* (Basle, 1547), pp. 6–7: 'Quia vero in Italiae
nostrae gratiam, Italice haec ille [Stancaro] conscripsit, sicque legendi copia omnibus data
non est, rem gratissimam quamplurimis facturum me existimavi, si enarrationes has (sunt
enim consummatissime) in eorum qui Italica lingua destituti sunt gratiam, Latinitate
donarem.'

[139] Published in Meyer, *Locarnergemeinde*, II, pp. 387–90.

merchants, such as the Tridi and Ciseri of Como, and their servants. The former were an extremely varied group, in terms of both nationality and occupation. They included four Poles, six Frenchmen (three of them students), the English exile John Parkhurst and his wife,[140] six boys from Locarno and two others from Milan and Mesocco respectively,[141] a maid from Rhaetia, and three sons of the Milanese secretary Ascanio Marso, who were in Zurich with Martino Muralto in order to learn German.[142] A recent arrival in the city was Isabella Bresegna Manrique, the widow of the Spanish governor of Piacenza and a former associate of Juan de Valdés in Naples, who brought with her a large entourage of servants. Other exiles were hosted by Ochino (the Roman evangelical Francesco Betti, a 'Ludwig' and a 'Cesar' from Bologna, and another 'Ludwig' from Parma, with his wife and sister) and Peter Martyr (a brother and nephew of Lelio Sozzini, possibly Camillo and Fausto).[143] Lelio Sozzini himself is recorded as lodging with the Zuricher Hans Wyss. Omitted from the list are Vermigli, who had been accorded Zurich citizenship and did not therefore count as a foreigner, and his amanuensis Giulio Santerenziano, who after Vermigli's death worked as a corrector for Froschauer.[144]

It is reasonable to assume that the growth in Zurich's foreign population since 1555 had much to do with the establishment of Italian-language worship in the city, under the charismatic leadership of Bernardino Ochino. In the survey of September 1556, Battista de' Baddi, a member of the Locarno community who had initially settled in Chiavenna, reported that he had moved to Zurich 'on hearing that there was preaching here in their language [Italian]'.[145] Similar considerations

---

[140] On the English exiles, see P. Boesch, 'Die englischen Flüchtlinge in Zürich unter Königin Elisabeth I', *Zwa* 9/9 (1953/1), pp. 531–5. In October 1559 the Locarnesi received a bequest of 10 scudi from an unnamed English exile, probably Edward Frensham (FA Orelli, 8.2, fol. 17ᵛ; Meyer, *Locarnergemeinde*, II, pp. 33–4; ZL, I, letters xxix–xxx).

[141] Two of the Locarnese boys were staying with Trevano. The others lodged with Martino Muralto, Battista de' Baddi, Giovanni Beccaria and Francesco Verzasca.

[142] Marso, an evangelical sympathizer and former correspondent of Pellikan, was instrumental in securing for the Locarnesi the right to trade with Milan and in helping to overcome subsequent obstacles to such activity (see Meyer, *Locarnergemeinde*, II, pp. 23–4, and FA Orelli, 8.7, no. 4).

[143] Marchetti, 'Sull'origine', p. 140.

[144] P. Boesch, 'Julius Terentianus: Faktotum des Petrus Martyr Vermilius und Korrektor der Offizin Froschauer', *Zwa* 8/10 (1948/2), pp. 587–601. One letter from Santerenziano to Bullinger survives, dated 15 June 1571 (see ibid., pp. 598–9). His son and grandson went on to serve as ministers in the Zurich church.

[145] Meyer, *Locarnergemeinde*, II, p. 386: 'Baptista Badius antwurt, Das er mit andern Luggarnern Daselbs abgeträtten, und sich ettwas Zyts zu Cläva enthalten. Als er aber verstanden, das man hie in jrer Sprach predige, wäre er alhar kommen, und jmme von üch minen Herren vergunt worden hie zu wonen.'

had previously led the Chur-based exile Vincenzo Maggi to request permission to reside in Zurich.[146] Bullinger himself was aware of the drawing power of Zurich's Italian church: in a letter to Vermigli dated 1 May 1556, he cited its existence as one reason for the Florentine to accept his offer of a position at the Zurich academy.[147] The church was attractive not least to those evangelicals who had remained in Locarno after March 1555, conforming outwardly but continuing to adhere in secret to the Reformed faith. Just as previously Locarnese evangelicals had sent their sons to Mesocco to be educated by Beccaria, now they sent them to Zurich to be brought up as Protestants and, if possible, to be taught a trade.[148] The Zurich Italian church encouraged such contacts through the provision of financial and other assistance to members of Locarno's evangelical community. For example, in September 1555 and again in August the following year grants were made from the common chest to the family of Niccolò Greco, who had been executed in January 1555 for supposedly uttering blasphemies against the Virgin.[149] Later an apprenticeship was arranged in Zurich for one of Greco's sons.[150]

Charitable giving was not restricted to present or former members of the community: as a congregation with first-hand experience of persecution, the Locarnesi felt themselves under an obligation to assist others in similar straits. Support was targeted at fellow exiles, many of them Italians passing through Zurich en route to the larger refugee centre of Geneva. On 3 February 1556, the Locarnese elders asked the church of Aarau to arrange for a group of Sicilian evangelicals who were

---

[146] StAZ B II 92, 15; Meyer, *Locarnergemeinde*, II, p. 151; Church, *Italian Reformers*, p. 226, n. 31. On Maggi, see most recently B.R. Jenny, 'Jakob Clausers unvollendetes Porträt des italienischen Refugianten Vincenzo Maggi (ca. 1488–1564) im Amerbach Kabinett: Veranlasst es eine Korrektur im Personenkommentar zum Opus epistolarum Erasmi?', *Basler Zeitschrift für Geschichte und Altertumskunde*, 91 (1991), pp. 59–68; *Amerbachkorrespondenz*, X/2, no. 4346. Maggi's interest in the Locarnese community is evident from a letter that he wrote to Besozzi's wife Chiara Orelli in February 1555, in which he urged the church of Chiavenna to show hospitality to the exiles, adding: 'Desiderarei bene che al passare di questi santi Confessori per Chiavena, se ritrovassi l'occhino, accio gli spezzassi con quel suo bel modo il pane, ch'ha per costume' (FA Orelli, 8.7, no. 8).

[147] StAZ E II 342, 323: 'Habebis hic et invenies veterem tuum amicum et fratrem Bernardinum, habebis et invenies Italicam ecclesiam, qualem te non puto ullam inventuram in Germania.'

[148] On the residual Protestant presence in Locarno, see Pfister, *Um des Glaubens willen*, pp. 103–8, and B. Schwarz, 'La diffusione della Riforma nei baliaggi italiani dei cantoni svizzeri nel Cinquecento', in Campi and La Torre, *Il protestantesimo*, pp. 53–66.

[149] FA Orelli, 8.2, fols 95r; 97v.

[150] FA Orelli, 8.2, fol. 16v; cited in Meyer, *Locarnergemeinde*, II, p. 32, n. 111.

travelling to Geneva to be conducted as far as Berne,[151] while a month later money from the common chest was dispensed to one Battista Milanese, who required help with his travel expenses to Tübingen.[152] In July the following year another grant was awarded, this time to 'two poor Christians, one from Rome and the other from Trent', who had arrived with letters of recommendation from the churches of Chiavenna and Caspano.[153] Later the Locarnesi contributed to a collection organized by the Zurich church on behalf of the Waldenses of Angrogna;[154] they even made provision for a bed to be made, at the congregation's expense, 'for the benefit of poor travelling brethren' ('per beneficio de Poveri fratelli viandanti').[155]

The Zurich Locarnesi were also in contact with Italian evangelical communities elsewhere, notably those of Geneva and the Rhaetian subject lands. On 29 May 1555, Celso Martinengo, minister to the Italian church in Geneva, wrote to commiserate with them on their exile. The obedient suffering of the Locarnese evangelicals, he declared, should serve as a reproach to those Nicodemites who 'while professing to be Christians, prefer their comfort to the glory of God' ('facendo professione de cristiani, amano più le sue commodità che la gloria di Dio'). Martinengo proposed that the two communities co-operate closely in future:

> As the Lord has joined us in so many ways, both spiritual and political, and especially by geography and a common exile, let us be linked by an indissoluble chain and bond, so that when we have need of you we can approach you with confidence and you may do the same with us. We also ask that you write to us often with advice, exhortation and consolation on matters that come to light, promising to do the same from our side.[156]

---

151 FA Orelli, 8.7, no. 25; published in Benrath, *Ochino*, pp. 305–6. See also the letter commending the exiles to the church of Berne (FA Orelli, 8.7, no. 26) and the entries in the accounts for 21 December 1555 (FA Orelli, 8.2, fol. 96r) and 10 February 1556 (ibid., fol. 96v: 'spese fatte si per il viver per giorni xi si per farli condure certi fratelli et sorelle Napolitani al numero de novi per il viaggio di Geneva').

152 FA Orelli, 8.2, fol. 96v.

153 Ibid., fol. 98v. The two were Francesco Betti and Giacomo Aconcio, both commended to Bullinger by Curione in a letter of 1 July 1557 (StAZ E II 366, 55; published in G. Aconcio, *De methodo e opuscoli religiosi e filosofici*, ed. G. Radetti (Florence, 1944), p. 398).

154 FA Orelli, 8.2, fol. 103r.

155 Ibid., fol. 100r; cited in Meyer, *Locarnergemeinde*, II, pp. 33–4, n. 119. Around 20 grants of this kind were made during the period 1555–63.

156 FA Orelli, 8.7, no. 14: 'Poi che'l Signore ci ha congiunti in tanti modi, et spirituali et politici, et spetialmente per la vicinità del luogo, et per l'essilio commune, abbracciamoci con indissolubile vincolo et legame, et dove noi haveremo bisogno di voi, con fiducia vi richiederemo, ricercandovi che facciate il simile con esso noi, et con lettere vi preghiamo

The suggestion was reiterated in a letter of 1 August from the elders of Geneva's Italian church, which explicitly acknowledged the Locarnesi as fellow members of the Italian 'nation' in exile.[157] As these letters are all we possess in the way of formal contacts between the two churches, it is difficult to establish to what extent Martinengo's hopes were realized. But other sources, notably the surviving business records of Ludovico Ronco, provide evidence of a thriving commercial relationship between certain Locarnesi and members of Geneva's Italian community, which continued well into the 17th century. Among Ronco's trading partners was the Genevan merchant Franco Taruffo, who in November 1575 organized a weaver's apprenticeship for Ronco's son Giovanni Battista.[158] Taruffo was also present as a witness when another Locarnese, Francesco Orelli, was received as a resident of Geneva on 23 October 1572.[159] During the 1590s, Taddeo Duno's brother Giacomo was involved in a joint venture between the Werdmüller family and the Lucchese exile Francesco Turrettini, who afterwards settled in Geneva.[160] A second-generation member of the Locarnese community, Felix Orelli, participated for more than two decades in Turrettini's powerful textile cartel, the 'Grande Boutique'.[161]

Of equal importance to the Zurich Locarnesi were their links with Reformed churches in Chiavenna and the Valtellina, which actually predated their exile from Locarno. During the early 1550s, the Reformed pastor of Chiavenna, Agostino Mainardi, emerged as one of the community's strongest defenders against Catholic accusations of Anabaptism, personally vouching for its members' orthodoxy in a

---

che spesso ci visitiate, avisandoci mutualmente, essortandoci et consolandoci di quanto averrà alla giornata sicome vi promettiamo noi di fare il medesimo del canto nostro.' Copy in Orelli, *Verfolgung*, pp. 119–25.

[157] FA Orelli, 8.7, no. 19: 'Ci parebbe mancare assai del nostro debito, carissimi et honorissimi fratelli nel Signor Jesu Christo, se noi non vi visitassimo almeno con questa nostra: si per rallegrarci e congratularci con essovoi de la commune gratia che il Signor n'ha fatte, *si ancora per far con la vostra santa Chiesa quel medesimo offitio che habbiam gia fatto con le altre de la nostra natione*, che sono in Chiavenna e in tutta la Valtellina' (my emphasis). Copy in Orelli, *Verfolgung*, pp. 140–45.

[158] FA Orelli, 8.4, fol. 4ᵛ. Transactions between Ronco and Taruffo are detailed in ibid., fols 19ʳ⁻ᵛ; 46ᵛ⁻7ᵛ. For a fuller description of Ronco's business records, see Peyer, *Handel und Bank*, pp. 62–5.

[159] P. -F. Geisendorf, *Livre des habitants de Genève*, 2 vols (Geneva, 1957/63), II, p. 45.

[160] L. Weisz, *Die Werdmüller: Schicksale eines alten Zürcher Geschlechtes* (Zurich, 1949), pp. 90–93. On Turrettini, see Burlamacchi, *Libro di ricordi*, pp. 46–7; 179–80; 263–89.

[161] L. Mottu-Weber, *Economie et refuge à Genève au siècle de la Réforme: la draperie et la soierie (1540–1620)* (Geneva, 1987), pp. 471–4.

letter to Bullinger dated 31 May 1554.[162] Italian-speaking ministers from Graubünden also provided the Locarnese evangelicals with a certain amount of pastoral care: in the same letter, Mainardi informed Bullinger that Guido Zonca ('a man of sound doctrine and a faithful minister of Christ, who does not depart by a hair's breadth from the faith that you confess') had recently visited Locarno to baptize an infant and to preach.[163] Further evidence of Mainardi's close association with the Locarnese Reformed at this time is provided by two letters dated January and February 1555, in which he consoled them on their impending exile and assured them of the support of their fellow Reformed believers.[164] Mainardi encouraged the Locarnesi to welcome their suffering as a sign of special divine favour, even of election, calling on them to follow in Abraham's footsteps by leaving their idolatrous homeland for a country that God would show them. He also stressed the impact that their constancy, which he compared to that of the martyrs of the primitive church, was having on Italian believers everywhere, 'nothing like it having happened in our day'.[165]

These contacts continued following the departure of the Locarnese evangelicals for Zurich, facilitated by the decision of several former members of the community to settle, at least temporarily, in the Rhaetian Freestate. The families of Antonio Mario Besozzi, Battista de' Baddi and Cristoforo Postacolona took up residence in Chiavenna,[166] while Leonardo Bodetto, a Cremonese exile who had converted to Protestantism in Locarno, was appointed a schoolmaster in Tirano alongside the illustrious Francesco Negri. When shortly afterwards the local Reformed church informed Bodetto that it could no longer afford his services, Bodetto turned for help to Zurich's Italian congregation,[167] which responded with several grants of money from the common

---

162 Schiess, I, no. 260.

163 The accounts for September 1555 record a grant of 3 scudi to Guido Zonca for 'consolationi spirituali hauti a Locarno' (FA Orelli, 8.2, fol. 95r). A further payment was made on 24 August 1556 (ibid., fol. 97v). Zonca later served as minister to the Reformed community of Mese near Chiavenna (for biographical details, see Bonorand, *Reformatorische Emigration*, pp. 56–7).

164 FA Orelli, 8.7, nos 5 and 7.

165 Ibid.: 'Vi consoli anchora et vi dia gaudio che questo vostro caso rarissimo ha in tutta l'Italia appresso di tutti far gran romore et gran frutto appresso degli eletti per non esser accaduto cosa simile alli giorni nostri.'

166 Bullinger claims that of 183 persons expelled from Locarno, 19 settled in Chiavenna (*Verzeichnis*, fol. 186r).

167 Bodetto to the Locarnese church, 8 October and 23 December 1555 (FA Orelli, 8.7, nos 23 and 24). Besozzi also wrote to the Locarnesi on the schoolmaster's behalf (ibid., no. 21). On the circumstances of Bodetto's conversion, see *EA*, IV:1e, p. 946.

chest.[168] The presence in Zurich of an Italian-speaking community may have had the effect of reinforcing existing ties between the Zurich church and its sister congregations in Chiavenna and the Valtellina, as the Locarnese exiles were ideally placed to add extra weight to requests by the latter for assistance from the Zurich authorities. One piece of evidence in support of this hypothesis is a letter from Pietro Guicciardi of Teglio to the Locarnese church dated 29 June 1556. In this letter, Guicciardi reported that Valtellinese Catholics were seeking the removal of the local Reformed minister, Paolo Gaddi, and asked that the Locarnese commend the church of Teglio to Bullinger and Gwalther, 'as in time we may be forced to make use of them to preserve the Gospel in this valley'.[169] Significantly, Guicciardi thanked Ochino for his intercession with Bullinger ('degli officii fatti col Bulingero') in this matter.

A third important point of contact for the Zurich Locarnesi was the Italian exile community of Basle, and especially its two leading members, Celio Secundo Curione and Pietro Perna. Shortly after the arrival of the Locarnesi in Zurich, Curione wrote to congratulate them on their new situation.[170] In their homeland, he claimed, the Locarnesi had been subjects, but in Zurich they had become free; in place of several masters, they had gained 'one benign and holy magistrate' ('un solo benigno e santo magistrato') whose attitude towards them would be not that of a master ('padrone'), but that of a father ('padre'). Curione may have been instrumental in securing Basle's donation to the Locarnese common chest: in the same letter he assured the exiles that on

---

[168] See the entries in the accounts for 16 February 1556 (FA Orelli, 8.2, fol. 96ᵛ); October 1559 (fol. 101ʳ); and 12 August 1560 (fol. 101ᵛ). The second of these grants is noted in the minutes for October 1559 (fol. 17ᵛ).

[169] FA Orelli, 8.7, no. 32: 'cosi fate vi preghiamo da parte et del nostro Ministro, et nostra le medesime raccomandationi con i Ministri della chiesa Tigurina, et particolarmente con i pii et Dotti Bullingero et Gualtero, de' quali forsi saremo sforzati al tempo suo di loro servirci, per sostentamento dello Evangelio in questa valle per lo favore de' suoi Magnifici, et potenti signori.' Guicciardi claims that the Catholics were acting in concert with a third party, possibly religious radicals, who refused to adhere either to the papacy or to the state-approved Reformed church ('tanto piu lo scandalo con gli infermi è pericoloso, perche il Diavolo usa hipocriti che fanno professione di intendere la verità, et che del Papato non participano ne della chiesa cristiana'). In a subsequent letter dated 2 September, he warned the Rhaetian magnate Friedrich von Salis against attempts to have Gaddi replaced by a more pliable individual (StAG D II b 3). For more on this affair, see the letter from Paolo Gazo (Gaddi?) to Tomaso della Chiesa, September 1556 (ibid.); and P.D.R. de Porta, *Historia Reformationis ecclesiarum Rhaeticarum*, 2 vols (Chur, 1771), II:3, p. 93.

[170] FA Orelli, 8.7, no. 17; copies in Orelli, *Verfolgung*, pp. 137–9. See also the church's reply of 9 July (FA Orelli, 8.7, no. 18).

Simon Sulzer's return to Basle he would 'raise with him and the other ministers that matter about which you have written to me, which I would have done even had you not brought it to my attention'.[171] Further evidence of Curione's links with the Locarnesi is lacking until 1564 when, following the death of his three daughters from the plague, he visited Zurich in the hope that his wife might derive comfort from 'conversations with Italian women' ('italarum mulierum colloquiis').[172] Three years later, his son Leo married Martino Muralto's daughter Flaminia.[173]

In Perna's case, these links were even more direct: both his first wife, Giovanna Verzasca, and his second, Aurelia Muralto, were Locarnesi.[174] During the late 1550s, Perna was a frequent visitor to Zurich, sometimes as a courier for letters from Curione to Bullinger.[175] He was also a long-standing devotee of Ochino, whose preaching may have been a decisive factor in his conversion to Protestantism during the late 1530s.[176] Later, while working as an apprentice to Michael Isengrin, Perna had helped publish the Basle edition of Ochino's sermons; it has even been suggested that he wrote the anonymous preface to part 2 of these *Prediche*.[177] Perna's working relationship with Ochino was renewed following the latter's move to Zurich. Of the seven works written by Ochino during this period, five were published by Perna, including the infamous *Dialogi XXX*.

Intellectual and family ties between the Locarnesi and Italians resident in Basle were supplemented by commercial contacts – for example, with Antonio Sonzini, an evangelical from Bellinzona who moved to Basle in 1555.[178] Those contacts, like the links between the Locarnesi and Geneva's Italian community, are documented to some extent in the business records of Ludovico Ronco, which describe how in 1570 Ronco set up a new company for the import of rice from Italy in conjunction with his relative Geronimo Orelli of Locarno and the

---

171 FA Orelli, 8.7, no. 17: 'E subito che sara gionto il nostro, Sulzero, faro con lui et con gli altri ministri l'officio del qual mi scrivete: il qual anco havea deliberato di fare se ben non mi haveste avisato.'

172 Curione to Bullinger, 22 August 1564 (StAZ E II 366, 52).

173 Kutter, *Curione*, p. 268.

174 Perini, 'Note sulla famiglia', pp. 180–81; 193–4. One was the sister of Francesco Verzasca, the other the daughter of Martino Muralto (both elders in Zurich's Italian church).

175 See, for example, Curione to Bullinger, 28 June 1557 (StAZ E II 366, 56): 'Petrus Perna, iam civis Basiliensis, aut Socinus, nostram primam ad Vergerii calumnias responsionem, ostendet'.

176 Perini, 'Note sulla famiglia', pp. 172–3.

177 Ibid., p. 185.

178 See StAZ B V 13, fol. 319r-v; Weisz, 'Tessiner', p. 381.

Genoese exile Francesco d'Isola, who operated out of Basle.[179] There was also a steady trickle of Locarnese emigrants from Zurich to Basle, who were able to serve as a bridge between the Italian-speaking communities in the two cities. Among the first was Bartolomeo Orelli, who became a citizen of Basle in 1559 and was closely associated with prominent members of the city's academic establishment such as Basilius Amerbach and Theodor Zwinger.[180] Another was Olinorio Rosalino, who served as a witness at the baptism of Perna's twins Lelio and Laura on 30 August 1563; Olinorio was probably the eldest son of Gianambrosio Rosalino, described in the survey of April 1558 as an apprentice to a Basle printer.[181] Many more Locarnesi were to tread this path over the coming years, as relations between the exiles and their Zurich hosts deteriorated.

iv. Opposition to the Locarnesi in Zurich

The success of the Locarnesi in establishing ties with other Italian exile communities was not replicated in their dealings with the indigenous population of Zurich. The most important Locarnese mercantile enterprises, the Ronco company and Appiano's silk-weaving business, have the appearance of exclusively exile concerns: nearly all of those listed in the April 1558 survey as employees of Appiano were Locarnesi (Giacomo Duno, Giangiacomo and Gianantonio Rosalino, and a son of Lucia Belò). Besides Bullinger and other clergymen, the exiles' closest Zurich associates appear to have been members of the Ziegler family. At the time of the 1558 survey, one of Aloisio Orelli's sons was in the service of Hans Ziegler the younger, probably the same 'Giovanni Zieglero' whose generosity towards a member of Zurich's Locarnese community is acknowledged in the accounts for December the following year.[182] This association is best explained by the fact that the Zieglers, like many of the Locarnesi, were active in transalpine trade.

Later generations of Zurich Locarnesi were inclined to gloss over any hostility their forebears had encountered on first arriving in Zurich, stressing rather the munificence of the city authorities and populace. In

179 FA Orelli 8.4, fol. 21ᵛ. The company was wound up in November 1573 (ibid., fol. 35ʳ). On D'Isola, see T. Geering, *Handel und Industrie der Stadt Basle: Zunftwesen und Wirtschaftsgeschichte bis zum Ende des XVI Jahrhunderts* (Basle, 1886), pp. 452–3.

180 Orelli was the channel for correspondence between the Milan-based evangelical Aonio Paleario and the Basle humanists (S. Caponetto, *Aonio Paleario (1503–1570) e la Riforma protestante in Toscana* (Turin, 1979), pp. 136; 227).

181 Perini, 'Note sulla famiglia', p. 181; Meyer, *Locarnergemeinde*, II, p. 385.

182 FA Orelli, 8.2, fol. 101ʳ.

a poem commissioned in 1592 by the descendants of the original exiles, Zurich appears as 'das gelobte land', offering deliverance from the tyranny of Egypt/Locarno.[183] Duno, in his *De persequutione*, suggests that many exiles found it difficult to come to terms with the alien customs and language of their new home, but does not refer explicitly to tensions with Zurich's native population.[184] Similarly, in his account of the reception of the Locarnesi in Zurich, Bullinger's emphasis is on the generosity with which ordinary Zurich citizens responded to the plight of the Locarnesi.[185]

But the minutes of the Zurich council present a rather different picture – one of widespread opposition to the exiles almost from the moment of their arrival in Zurich. Significantly, the commission charged with drafting proposals for the establishment of an Italian church towards the end of May 1555 had as one its tasks to investigate 'how the bad feeling towards the exiled Locarnesi that has arisen in certain guilds can be assuaged'.[186] Hostility towards the exiles was such that the *Rechenrat* felt it necessary to recommend steps to prevent disruption of the Italian service by the 'gmeyn volk': a guard was to be put in place around the church of St Peter during sermons, and citizens were to be warned against subjecting the exiles to physical or verbal abuse.[187] That some Zurichers should have responded to the presence of the Locarnesi in this way comes as no surprise: the Zurich populace was prone to bouts of xenophobia, as evidenced by the reaction against 'foreign' clerics that greeted Zurich's defeat in the Second Kappel War.

The most vociferous opposition to the Locarnesi came from the guilds. In that respect Zurich was no different from other cities where religious exiles had settled (London, Frankfurt, Cologne). But according to Heinz Schilling, the potential for conflict was always greater where, as in Zurich, the guilds played an important role in government.[188] The strength of the Zurich guilds should not be exaggerated – although 144

---

[183] L. Weisz, 'Ein Lehrgedicht über die Locarner aus dem Jahre 1592', *Zwa*, 10/3 (1955/1), pp. 193–8.

[184] *De persequutione*, fol. 8ᵛ (Chenou, 'Locarno', p. 278): 'Urbem incolentes Locarnenses lingua peregrina, vivendi et vestiendi modus, populi mores a patriis plurimum differentes initio terrebant non parum, quod mirandum non erat pauperum praecipue respectu, quanquam tempore illo rerum omnium vilitas erat magna ut parvo vivere liceret: constanter tamen atque fortiter perseverantes et in domino (qui eos quasi ex Ur Chaldaeorum, vel ex Aegypto in promissam terram eduxerat) sperantes, paulatim vivendi et vestiendi rationi assuefacti urbis leges et instituta servarunt, linguam autem didicerunt.' Cited in Meyer, *Locarnergemeinde*, II, p. 38, n. 133.

[185] *Verzeichnis*, fol. 186ʳ; Bullinger to Calvin, 14 June 1555 (CO, XV, no. 2228).

[186] StAZ B II 90, 28; cited in Meyer, *Locarnergemeinde*, II, p. 359.

[187] Meyer, *Locarnergemeinde*, II, p. 360. Compare Bullinger, *Verzeichnis*, fols 186ᵛ–7ᵛ.

[188] Schilling, *Niederländische Exulanten*, pp. 28–9.

out of the 212 members of the Large Council were guildsmen, most power resided with a relatively small number of officials – but they were still able to put considerable pressure on the magistracy to ensure that their privileges were safeguarded. In London, by contrast, guild-led protests against economic competition from Netherlandish migrants tended to fall on deaf ears.

The Zurich council's attitude towards the exiles strikes one as ambivalent. On the one hand, it recognized its responsibility to them as fellow evangelicals and residents of Zurich. In July 1555 it helped them secure the lifting of the trade ban with Milan, while the following year it made representations to the Swiss Diet on behalf of the three Locarnese women fined for blasphemy by the Catholic states.[189] Again, when Gianantonio Pairano was murdered while travelling through the canton of Zug in 1558, Zurich insisted that its Catholic neighbour take action against the perpetrators to ensure that the dead man's property was restored to his heirs;[190] the exiles also benefited from the Zurich council's support in a series of property disputes with relatives in Locarno.[191] Yet at the same time, the Zurich authorities continued to draw a clear distinction between their own citizens and the Locarnesi, whose presence they envisaged as strictly temporary. To discourage the exiles from settling permanently in Zurich, the Zurich council tightened its already rigid policy on citizenship. In December 1556, it confirmed an existing prohibition on the creation of new citizens from outside the Confederation and extended it to immigrants from the *Gemeine Herrschaften* and *Zugewandte Orte*, claiming that the city was already overburdened with foreigners and that its economic well-being was threatened as a result.[192] The council also seems to have been anxious to restrict the autonomy of Zurich's recently established Italian church, which from August 1555 was obliged to consult the two city treasurers (*Seckelmeister*) before taking decisions about the use of its assets.[193] When, in December that year, the council received reports that some Locarnesi were suffering from 'great hunger and want', four prominent Zurich citizens (Hans Edlibach, Melchior Wirz, Hans Konrad Escher and Bernhard Sprüngli) were instructed to investigate whether the funds in the Locarnese common chest were being used, as intended, to relieve

---

[189] Meyer, *Locarnergemeinde*, II, p. 25.

[190] StAZ B IV 21, fols 42ʳ, 164ʳ; Meyer, *Locarnergemeinde*, II, p. 158.

[191] StAZ B IV 21, fol. 64ʳ; StAZ B II 95, 55; StAZ A 350.1: Locarner Acten 1555 (Martino Muralto); StAZ B IV 21, fol. 152ᵛ (Lucia Belò); Meyer, *Locarnergemeinde*, II, pp. 159–60.

[192] StAZ A 71.1, no. 51.

[193] StAZ B II 93, 17; cited in Meyer, *Locarnergemeinde*, II, p. 22, n. 72.

the needs of the community's poor, or whether they were being retained by 'the rich' for their own purposes.[194]

From the end of 1555, the guilds began to put pressure on the council to intervene to regulate the economic activities of the Locarnesi. Guild-members were suspicious of the exiles' innovative business practices, and sensed a threat to their control of Zurich's commercial life; their insecurities were heightened by a downturn in the city's economy around this time, which produced a marked increase in poverty.[195] The first sign that the council was taking heed of the guilds' concerns came in August 1555, when an attempt was made to prevent the exiles profiting from the re-sale, in Locarno, of grain purchased cheaply in Zurich.[196] All three official surveys of the community were initiated in response to complaints of this sort. In September 1556, the Locarnesi were accused of showing contempt for the guilds,[197] while a year later several Zurichers, led by the cobbler Heini Ulrich, informed the council 'that the Locarnesi were encroaching on their crafts and trades' ('das jnen von den Luggarnern an jren hanndtwerck unnd gewerben jngriff beschäche').[198] The rapid expansion, over subsequent months, of such new enterprises as Appiano's silk-weaving business merely added to the guilds' sense of grievance (even though Appiano's activities had the official sanction of the Zurich authorities).[199] For its part, the Zurich council was concerned by reports that some wealthier exiles were taking steps to purchase property in Zurich, which did not sit well with its policy of treating the Locarnesi as temporary residents.[200] This new development was probably a factor in its decision, on 2 March 1558, to instruct the *Rechenrat* to carry out a fresh review of the situation.

The commission's proposals, which were issued as a council mandate on 18 March, amounted to a delicate balancing-act, attempting to honour Zurich's existing commitments to the Locarnesi while going some way towards meeting the guilds' demands for regulation of their

---

194 StAZ B II 93, 59; cited in Meyer, *Locarnergemeinde*, II, p. 31, n. 102.

195 Bächtold, *Bullinger*, pp. 236–41.

196 StAZ B II 93, 17; Weisz, 'Tessiner', pp. 237–8.

197 StAZ B II 96, 12 (9 September).

198 StAZ B II 101, 3 (7 July).

199 In August 1557 the council had permitted Appiano to place the arms of Zurich on his products (StAZ A 350.1).

200 See StAZ B VI 337, fol. 299r, where the purchase of the house 'Zum Mohrenkopf' by Martino Muralto is noted. According to the survey of April 1558, Guarnerio Castiglione and Gianambrosio Rosalino had also acquired property in Zurich. Opposition to exiles maintaining independent households was not confined to Zurich: the London strangers faced criticism on this score during the 1590s (O. Grell, *Dutch Calvinists in Early Stuart London: The Dutch Church in Austin Friars 1603–1642* (Leiden, 1989), p. 21).

commercial activities.[201] The right of the Locarnesi to remain in Zurich and to support themselves 'by their earnings and trades' ('mit jren gwün und gwerben') was confirmed, but they continued to be barred from citizenship. In addition, the exiles were forbidden to purchase property or to introduce 'new trades and shops' (although there was an exemption for those businesses that had already been set up). Finally, the Locarnesi were made subject to the regulatory system operated by the guilds. No exile was to practise more than a single trade, and all were to pay an annual fee to the relevant guild and to observe its 'trades ordinances and regulations' ('gwerbsordnungen und satzungen'). Those exiles not engaged in a recognized trade were instructed to join Zurich's noble corporation, the Constaffel. At the same time, the Locarnesi were excluded from the benefits of guild membership, such as eligibility for public office.

In its mandate, the council also expressed alarm at the recent influx into Zurich of foreigners who 'under the guise of Locarnesi have settled here without permission', declaring that henceforth no citizen or resident was to receive a foreigner in their house without its written consent. In order to ensure that this regulation was observed, Hans Konrad Escher and Hans Göldli were instructed to examine the Locarnesi and other foreigners every six months, 'or as often as they deem necessary', in order to ascertain whether any aliens had entered Zurich illegally; only students were exempted from this provision.[202] The mandate also contained the strongest sign yet of the council's determination not to allow Zurich to develop into an exile centre along the lines of Geneva or London. It stated that Zurich, which could barely support its own citizens, was becoming overburdened by the Locarnesi and their increasing numbers of offspring. For this reason the exiles should be urged 'to seek ways and means whereby in the future they or their sons [sic] may be taken in by other evangelical cities or states, so that the burden [of accommodating them] does not rest solely on the citizenry here'.[203]

---

[201] StAZ A 350.1, published in Meyer, *Locarnergemeinde*, II, pp. 390–92. Draft in StAZ B V 15, fols 284r–6v; copy in StAZ W 20.72: Aufnahme in Zürich, no. 2. Compare W. Schnyder, *Quellen zur Zürcher Zunftgeschichte* (2 vols, Zurich, 1936), I, p. 296.

[202] The third survey, which was carried out the following month and included other foreigners resident in Zurich as well as the Locarnesi, was probably an attempt to obtain reliable information on the scope of this problem. The number of foreigners in Zurich may well have been exaggerated in the popular imagination. That was certainly the case in other centres with large immigrant populations, such as London. There the authorities, less hostile to the exile presence than their Zurich counterparts, compiled registers of aliens as a way of counteracting speculation about the size of the city's foreign community (Grell, *Dutch Calvinists*, p. 22).

[203] Meyer, *Locarnergemeinde*, II, p. 392.

The mandate of March 1558 exposed the precariousness of the exiles' situation in Zurich. As we have seen, some Locarnesi had already migrated from Zurich to Basle; the survey of 1558 mentions others resident in Geneva, Neuchâtel and Constance. The Zurich magistrates had now given a clear indication that this was their preferred solution to the Locarnese 'problem', and many exiles were quick to take the hint. The years 1558–63 saw the departures of Pariso Appiano, Filippo Orelli (brother of Bartolomeo),[204] Giananbrosio and Bartolomeo Rosalino, and the Verzasca brothers, all of whom settled in Basle. On the surface there was plenty of opposition towards the 'Welschen' in Basle, as in Zurich. In April 1550, for instance, the Basle council issued an edict forbidding the publication of any works in languages apart from Latin, Greek, Hebrew and German, following the appearance of Giacomo Susio's Italian translation of Gwalther's *Antichristus*.[205] The Basle authorities also refused repeatedly to sanction the establishment of a French or Italian church service in the city.[206] However, unlike their counterparts in Zurich, they operated a flexible, if selective, citizenship policy, aimed at attracting new capital and skills to the city: between 1565 and 1601, Basle saw an average of 35 new citizens created each year.[207] As mere 'residents' (*Hintersassen*) of Zurich, the Locarnesi did not enjoy the trading privileges and immunities open to full citizens: those disadvantages could be overcome by moving to Basle.

In Zurich, meanwhile, the exiles remained the target of popular and guild hostility. In June 1558, Antonio Mario Besozzi was excluded from membership of the merchants guild, Saffran, after breaching trading regulations;[208] shortly afterwards certain Locarnesi were accused of hoarding supplies of tallow for export, thereby inflating the price of that commodity.[209] In August 1560 the council again received complaints from some citizens, this time about competition for places in recognized trades

---

204 See the testimonial issued to Filippo by the Zurich council on 14 August 1559 (ZB Ms. S 95, 118).

205 Gilly, *Basler Buchdruck*, p. 339. The ban seems to have been enforced for only a short time, however.

206 P. Denis, *Les églises d'étrangers en pays rhénans (1538–1564)* (Paris, 1984), pp. 241–55.

207 Geering, *Handel und Industrie*, pp. 446–8. Of around 1,500 new citizens created between 1550 and 1599, 34 were Italian speakers (Denis, *Les églises d'étrangers*, p. 242).

208 StAZ B II, 102, 31. Besozzi's business practices were also the subject of criticism within the Italian community itself. Several years later, Bartolomeo Verzasca testified that he had at one point been ordered to appear before Ochino and the Locarnese elders 'seins handtels und wechsells halb' (StAZ A 350.1; Meyer, *Locarnergemeinde*, II, p. 156).

209 StAZ B V 15, fols 274ʳ; 306ʳ: 'Es ist angezogen, wie etlich Luggarner, so alhie wonend, das unschlitt zů hůffen ůfkouffind, hinweg fürind und damit treffenlich verthürind.'

from the growing number of younger Locarnesi in Zurich.[210] In this climate, the continued existence of the Italian church was bound to come into question. In spring 1559, Giovanni Beccaria and Isabella Bresegna left Zurich for Mesocco and Chiavenna respectively, depriving the community of its founding father and of a potential patron.[211] Even Bullinger doubted that the church could be sustained over the longer term. In a letter to Johannes Fabricius dated 30 March 1562, he commented: 'When Ochino dies, I doubt that we will continue to maintain an Italian church here. More likely, we will send the honest Locarnesi to our other parishes.'[212]

In the midst of its difficulties, the Locarnese community had the comfort of knowing that it had powerful supporters in Bullinger and the other senior ministers of the Zurich church. The surviving sources offer only glimpses of this ongoing relationship, but enough to suggest its continued importance to the Locarnesi in the years following their arrival in Zurich. In June 1556, for example, Bullinger drafted a petition to the *Landammann* and council of Glarus on behalf of Lucia Belò, Barbaro Muralto and Catarina Appiano,[213] while the following year he presented the Italian church with a copy of his newly published *Sermons on the Apocalypse* (specifically dedicated to those exiled on account of religion).[214] Bullinger also composed a short history of the Locarnese evangelical community to celebrate its steadfastness in the face of persecution. Perhaps the highlight of this work is an account of the 'martyrdom' of Niccolò Greco which, despite its hagiographic tone, shows every sign of being based on eye-witness descriptions of the incident.[215] Further evidence of the close relations between the Locarnesi and the Zurich clergy may be found in Konrad Gesner's *liber amicorum*, which includes entries for several prominent members of the community (Beccaria, Duno, Castiglione and Martino Muralto).[216]

---

[210] StAZ B II 113, 13 (7 August 1560); Bodmer, *Refugianteneinwanderung*, p. 27.

[211] StAZ B II 106, 7 (23 February); FA Orelli, 8.2, fol. 17ᵛ. Beccaria served as minister to the Reformed congregation of Mesocco until November 1561, when pressure from local Catholics forced him to leave the area for Chiavenna. By 1570 he was again in the Mesolcina, but two years later he was expelled definitively from the region. He ended his life as pastor of Bondo, in the Valbregaglia. For further details, see Camenisch, *Reformation und Gegenreformation*, pp. 107–22.

[212] StAZ E II 373, 309 (Schiess, II, no. 426).

[213] ZB Ms. F 154, fol. 40ʳ⁻ᵛ; Meyer, *Locarnergemeinde*, II, pp. 28–9, n. 87.

[214] StAZ E II 346, 142ʳ; FA Orelli 8.2, fol. 99ʳ; Meyer, *Locarnergemeinde*, II, p. 30, n. 98. He was also involved in collecting information on the community for the Zurich authorities (see the list in his hand in StAZ E II 342, 360–61).

[215] *Verzeichnis*, fols 182ʳ⁻5ᵛ. Compare Duno, *De persequutione*, fols 6ʳ⁻7ʳ (Chenou, 'Locarno', pp. 273–5).

[216] Serrai, *Gesner*, pp. 363–6.

So long as the Locarnesi showed no signs of harbouring heterodox opinions, they could continue to rely on the support of the Zurich divines. Up until his death in November 1562, Peter Martyr Vermigli may have acted as a guarantor of the community's orthodoxy, in his dual role of Locarnese elder and professor at the *Carolinum*.[217] Bernardino Ochino, too, enjoyed the confidence of the Zurich church establishment, at least in public. However, that confidence was sorely tested by the publication of Ochino's *Dialogi XXX* in the spring of 1563. For the first time, the Zurich churchmen were confronted with what they took to be clear evidence of the spread of heresy in the city's Italian community. That discovery was to have momentous consequences both for the Locarnesi and for the future attitude of Bullinger and his colleagues towards the Italian exiles as a whole.

---

217 Vermigli's role within the Locarnese community is rather obscure, but he is known to have conducted the Italian church service at times when Ochino was ill (see Wolfgang Haller to Zanchi, 18 December 1562, in Zanchi, *Epistolae*, II, 131–2). Both his widow, Caterina Merenda, and his posthumous daughter Maria later married Locarnesi (Ludovico Ronco and Bernardo Zanino).

CHAPTER THREE

The Ochino Affair and its Aftermath

On 5 June 1563, Theodore Beza wrote to Bullinger with some alarming news concerning Zurich's Italian minister, Bernardino Ochino. Many good and learned persons, he reported, had taken offence at two volumes of Latin dialogues recently published by Ochino in Basle, in which 'arguments for the worst heresies are put forward clearly and plainly, to be rebutted not at all or with reasoning of the weakest sort'. According to Beza's anonymous informants, Ochino was guilty in many places of allowing himself 'curious and vain speculations' and of distorting the meaning of passages from scripture. Although Beza himself had not had an opportunity to examine the suspect volumes in detail, he was keen that the Zurich church should investigate the matter further, to damp down any potential scandal.[1]

Initially Bullinger was dismissive of his Genevan colleague's fears. He was, of course, aware of the Italian exiles' reputation for doctrinal unreliability and, in particular, for antitrinitarianism. To ensure that Zurich's Locarnese community was not 'contaminated' by such ideas, in June 1555 the Zurich council and clergy had stipulated that its minister was not to believe or teach anything contrary to the doctrines or rituals of the Zurich church 'whether privately or publicly', that he was to use the Zurich liturgy in translation, and that he was to submit to the discipline of the Zurich synod.[2] In his reply to Beza, Bullinger indicated that he had no reason to believe that Ochino had contravened those terms. Like Beza, he had not had time to read the work that had given such cause for concern, but he was convinced that Ochino had nothing in common with the antitrinitarian followers of Michael Servetus, Matteo Gribaldi and Giorgio Biandrata. Indeed, in conversation with the Polish Protestant Christopher Thretius, Ochino had dissociated himself utterly from those Italian exiles who opposed the orthodox doctrine of the Trinity, promising to refute their ideas in writing. Bullinger was inclined to view any weaknesses in the arguments presented by Ochino in his dialogues charitably, as the product of ignorance and old age rather than of malice. As a further mitigating

---

[1] *Correspondance*, IV, no. 271.
[2] Meyer, *Locarnergemeinde*, II, p. 362.

factor, the *Antistes* pointed to the recent accidental death of Ochino's wife, which had left him solely responsible for the care of several young children and seemed likely to hasten his own demise.[3]

Yet within a few months, Bullinger had revised his judgment radically. With the approval of the *Antistes* and other senior Zurich churchmen, Ochino had been convicted of teaching false doctrine, removed from his post and summarily banished from Zurich, to end his days in a small Italian-led Anabaptist community in eastern Europe. I shall argue that the Ochino affair highlighted – and set the seal on – an important shift in the Zurich church's attitude towards the Italian exiles. First, however, it is necessary to place the work at the centre of the controversy, the *Dialogi XXX*, in the context of Ochino's overall theological development.

i. The emergence of a radical reformer: heterodox tendencies in Ochino's Zurich works

Scholars' interpretations of Ochino's later works have inevitably been coloured by the circumstances of his departure from Zurich, and by his subsequent vilification by the Reformed establishment and canonization by their radical opponents.[4] Cantimori, for instance, did not hesitate to include Ochino among his 'eretici', although he qualified this with the statement that Ochino's heresy consisted more in indifference than in outright opposition to such doctrines as the Trinity.[5] Roland Bainton, Ochino's most recent biographer, doubts whether the Sienese exile ought to be regarded as an antitrinitarian, but argues nevertheless that his understanding of justification directly influenced Socinianism.[6] Conversely, there have been attempts to restore Ochino's reputation as a (relatively) orthodox Reformed theologian, notably by Erich Hassinger. While acknowledging the existence of 'spiritualist' elements

---

[3] Bullinger to Beza, 12 June 1563 (*Correspondance*, IV, no. 273).

[4] For the opposing 'orthodox' and 'radical' views of Ochino, see the exchange between Beza and Andreas Dudith-Sbardellati in *Correspondance*, XI, nos 796 and 780. Ochino was among those singled out by Giorgio Biandrata in the antitrinitarian manifesto *De falsa et vera unius Dei … cognitione* as having helped 'reclaim' the scriptural doctrine of a unipersonal God (A. Pirnát (ed.), *De falsa et vera unius Dei Patris, Filii et Spiritus Sancti cognitione libri duo* (Budapest, 1988), pp. 32–44). On Ochino's place in Socinian historiography, see C. Madonia, 'Bernardino Ochino e il radicalismo religioso europeo', *Bollettino senese di storia patria*, 98 (1991), pp. 110–29.

[5] Cantimori, *Eretici*, p. 258.

[6] R. Bainton, *Bernardino Ochino, esule e riformatore senese del Cinquecento* (Florence, 1940), p. 156.

in Ochino's theology (which he attributes to the influence of Juan de Valdés), Hassinger insists that Ochino remained faithful to the core teachings of the Helvetic reformers in all of his Protestant works, up to and including the *Dialogi XXX*.[7]

Here I do not hope to resolve the question of Ochino's orthodoxy. As Emidio Campi points out, attempting to classify individuals as 'orthodox' and 'heretical' at a time of considerable doctrinal fluidity – and before those terms had themselves been rigorously defined – is to some extent a misguided enterprise.[8] Judged by the standards of later Reformed orthodoxy, many first and second-generation Protestant thinkers do not fit neatly into either category, and that is certainly true of Ochino. But from the early 1550s – Servetus' execution is something of a watershed – the leaderships of the various Swiss Reformed churches became less willing to tolerate diversity within their ranks. A unified Reformed 'confession', derived from the convergence of existing doctrinal positions and defined in opposition to Catholicism, Lutheranism and the multifarious brands of religious radicalism, began to take shape. It is my belief that Ochino was out of sympathy with this trend, which ran counter to his own, increasingly anti-dogmatic, approach. Any apparent change in Ochino's position during his time in Zurich was as much one of perception as one of substance: what was acceptable in a Reformed theologian in the early 1550s had often come to be regarded with suspicion a decade later. However, I do not share Hassinger's view that all the movement was on the side of the Reformed establishment: there is much evidence to suggest that Ochino was attracted by heterodox solutions to some critical theological, especially soteriological, problems. Instead of following his compatriots Peter Martyr Vermigli and Girolamo Zanchi into Reformed orthodoxy, Ochino kept open the channels of communication with thinkers whose position was more unambiguously radical than his own. Under their influence, he came to question, if not to reject, certain aspects of received Protestant teaching.

For Ochino, as for most early Italian evangelicals, the initial appeal of the Reformation lay in its core teaching of justification by faith alone. In the *Epistola ai signori di Balìa della città di Siena*, published in the wake of his flight from Italy in August 1542, Ochino declared that it was for the sake of this doctrine that he had finally broken with the

[7] E. Hassinger, 'Exkurs: Über die Theologie Bernardino Ochino's vornehmlich in seiner Spätzeit', in Hassinger, *Studien zu Jacobus Acontius* (Berlin, 1934), pp. 97–109.

[8] E. Campi, *Michelangelo e Vittoria Colonna: Un dialogo artistico-teologico ispirato da Bernardino Ochino, e altri saggi di storia della Riforma* (Turin, 1994), pp. 188–9.

Roman church.[9] Repudiating the 'works righteousness' of Catholicism, he argued that only Christ's vicarious sacrifice could make satisfaction for sin:

> I believe and confess with Paul that, because of the sin of their first parents, men are sons of wrath and damnation, dead and incapable of lifting themselves up and reconciling themselves with God. For that reason, Christ our justice was sent by his eternal father to take on ['atribuirsi'] the sins of his elect and to offer himself up on the cross for them. He has atoned fully [for their sins] and has entirely placated God's anger, adopting them as sons of his eternal father and making them his heirs, rich in all divine treasures and graces.[10]

The same point is made forcefully in his Galatians commentary of 1546:

> After the sin of our first parents we cannot gain life through the observance of all the divine commandments, because of the contrary desires within us. Only Christ has observed the whole [of the law]. There has never been a saint who has observed even the least important commandment of the law, let alone the law in its entirety, not for the blink of an eye, let alone for their entire life. Thus there has never been a saint who in this present life has done a single good deed with that complete faith, spirit, love, zeal, humility and right intention and in the manner that was required of him by the supremely perfect law of God, and in accordance with God's infinite goodness.[11]

The function of the Law is not to save, but to bring humanity to an awareness of its own sinfulness and of its need for God's mercy, manifest in Christ.[12] Good works are the consequence, rather than the cause, of justification: just as only a good tree can yield good fruits, so only a person already justified can perform good works.[13] Even the regenerate

---

[9] This text is republished in Benrath, *Ochino*, pp. 294–302; B. Ochino, *I <<dialogi sette>> e altri scritti del tempo della fuga*, ed. U. Rozzo (Turin, 1985), pp. 136–45; and V. Marchetti, *Gruppi ereticali senesi del Cinquecento* (Florence, 1975), pp. 247–54. All references are to the last-mentioned edition.

[10] *Epistola*, pp. 247–8.

[11] *Espositione di Messer Bernardino Ochino sopra la Epistola di Paulo à i Galati* (n.p., 1546), fol. 78[r–v]: 'Doppo'l peccato de primi parenti non potiamo andare alla vita per la via della osservantia di tutti li divini precetti, per le nostre repugnanti concupiscentie, tal che sol Christo l'ha osservata tutta; ne è stato alcun santo, ilquale habbia osservato, non diro tutta la legge, ma ne il minimo suo precetto, non diro per sempre, ma ne per un batter d'occhio, impero che non fu mai santo nella presente vita, che facesse un sol bene, con quella somma fede, spirito, amore, zelo, humilita, retta intentione, et in quel modo che era obligato secondo la sommamente perfetta legge di Dio; et si come si conveniva alla infinita divina bonta.'

[12] Ibid., fol. 53[v]. Compare *Bernhardini Ochini Senensis expositio Epistolae divi Pauli ad Romanos* (Augsburg, 1545), fols 33[v]–4[v].

[13] *Galati*, fol. 38[r–v]. The image is a favourite of Protestant writers from Luther onwards.

remain subject to 'vicious and immoderate desires' ('le prave, et immoderate concupiscentie'), the effects of original sin, as a perpetual reminder of their dependence on God.[14] At this stage in his career, Ochino seems to have understood justification as a transaction involving the imputation of the sins of the elect to Christ and the corresponding ascription of his merits to them. In his commentary on Romans, for example, he writes:

> In those reborn through Christ, corrupt desires may remain so as to train them in virtue. Those desires may hold them held back and hinder them, making them unable to offer God the complete worship that they wish to give him. However, because not sin, but God's spirit reigns in them, they do not acquiesce in the cravings of the body and are not drawn into vices, as if they were slaves of sin; rather, they resist those desires and overcome them. Thus as long as they are joined with Christ by living faith, there is nothing damnable in them, not because they are not far from the perfect observance of the law, but because God does not view their failure in this regard as a vice – not because, without Christ, it is not sinful, but because, by virtue of their connection with Christ, their sins pass over to Christ, to whom God imputes them. Christ has ransomed and atoned for them.[15]

There is little in Ochino's doctrine of justification, as set out above, to which Bullinger or his Zurich colleagues could have taken exception. A clear distinction is made between justification, an extrinsic process accomplished on behalf of the elect by Christ, and sanctification, which reaches its conclusion only in the next life. That distinction formed the basis for Luther's understanding of the regenerate person as *semper peccator semper iustus*, which was also, needless to say, axiomatic for the Reformed. From Ochino's *Catechismo* of 1561, it would appear that his position on this issue changed little during his time in Zurich. The 'Illuminato' who replies to the questions of 'Ministro' in the catechism declares at one point, 'In the present life, there is no one who perfectly fulfils the law of God, because of the resistance of our flesh and our

---

[14] Ibid., fol. 85ᵛ. Compare *La seconda parte delle Prediche di Mess. Bernardino Ochino Senese* (n.p. [Basle], n.d.), sigs xx4ʳ–xx5ᵛ.

[15] *Expositio Epistolae ad Romanos*, fol. 58ʳ: 'Quamvis in renatis per Christum restent pravae cupiditates ad virtutis exercitationem, a quibus ita retardentur, atque impediantur, ut deum summa observantia colere nequeant, ut velint: tamen quia in eis non regnat peccatum, sed Dei spiritus, tantum abesse, ut corporis affectibus assentiantur, et ab eis, tanquam peccati mancipia, ad vitia traducantur, ut etiam eis resistant eosque superent. Itaque in eis, quandiu sunt viva fide cum Christo coniuncti, nihil quod damnandum sit inest, non quia ii non a perfecta legis functione absint: sed hac in re, quod a suo officio absunt, id eis a deo vitio non datur, non quia per se, semoto Christo, peccatum non sit, sed quia eorum peccata propter eam, qua cum Christo cohaerunt, coniunctionem, transeunt in Christum, cui deus ea imputat: Christus ea sibi vendicavit, et luit.'

imperfect knowledge of God.'[16] That view is reiterated during the discussion of the tenth commandment: 'while we are in the present life, [miserable desires] remain not only in carnal men, but also in regenerate and spiritual persons'.[17] It is impossible for the elect to free themselves from the effects of original sin, although they may control their inclination to evil with the help of God's Spirit. Illuminato compares human appetites to serpents curled up in the shade, which sometimes appear dead, but always reawaken to spew forth their venom.[18] We may not even legitimately ask God to eradicate our tendency to sin, because it is his will 'that until our deaths unruly desires should remain in us, to train us in virtue'.[19]

But elsewhere in Ochino's Zurich works there are signs of a growing tension in his thought between the doctrine of imputed righteousness and theories of 'essential' justification, as championed both by Catholic writers and by Protestant dissidents such as Servetus, Osiander and Sebastian Castellio (on whom see below).[20] This tension is most evident in the fifth volume of the *Prediche*, published in 1562. In sermon 8 of this collection, entitled 'Why Christ came, and why he was sent by the Father' ('Perche venne Christo, et perche fu mandato dal Padre'), Ochino proclaims that Christ did not die in order that we might remain in sin, but so that we might be free of it ('non morì, accio stessemo ne peccati, ma per liberarcene'). He continues: '[Christ] was crucified to make us free not to do evil, but to do good; nor did he wash us clean of sin so that we might soil ourselves with it, but so that we might be innocent and virtuous.'[21] Similarly, in his *Laberinti del libero arbitrio*,

---

[16] *Il catechismo, o vero institutione christiana di M. Bernardino Ochino da Siena, in forma di Dialogo* (Basle, 1561), p. 55: 'Nella presente vita, non è chi perfettamente adempia la legge di Dio, per la repugnante carne, et imperfetto lume che habbiamo di Dio.'

[17] Ibid., p. 129: 'mentre che siamo nella presente vita, [triste concupiscentie] sono non solamente ne gl'huomini carnali, ma et anco ne regenerati et spirituali.'

[18] Ibid., pp. 130–32. See also pp. 143; 147.

[19] Ibid., p. 209: 'Dio vuole che in fin a morte sieno in noi le sfrenate concupiscentie, a esercitio di virtù.'

[20] Ochino was not the only Italian evangelical attracted by the notion of essential justification. The Cassinese Benedictine tradition that influenced the celebrated *Beneficio di Cristo* was characterized by an emphasis on the sinlessness of the regenerate (Ginzburg and Prosperi, *Giochi di pazienza*, pp. 55–6). Similarly, Curione understood the infusion of virtue into the soul of the Christian as an integral part, rather than a secondary consequence, of justification (T. Balma, *Il pensiero religioso di C.S. Curione* (Rome, 1935), p. 27).

[21] *La quinta parte dell prediche di M. Bernardino Ochino, non mai prima stampate* (Basle, 1562), p. 58: '... non volse anco essere crocifisso, per farci liberi al male, ma al bene: ne anco ci lavò di peccati, accio c'imbrattassemo in essi, ma perche fussemo innocenti e virtuosi.'

Ochino argues that the regenerate person has regained the liberty proper to Adam and Eve. 'Truly free' ('veramente libero'), he or she is no longer a slave of sin, but capable of performing spiritual works. In both the *Prediche* and the *Laberinti*, Ochino stops short of asserting the sinlessness of the regenerate, pointing out that even those who have received the light of faith can fall (as the biblical examples of David and Peter demonstrate).[22] With that qualification added, none of the statements cited above are necessarily incompatible with Reformed orthodoxy: Zwingli and his successors in the Zurich church had always argued for the close intertwining of faith and works. However, the Zurichers were at pains not to blur the fundamental distinction between justification and its secondary consequence, sanctification. With Ochino, on the other hand, one senses an increasing disinclination to view the two as discrete processes.

This was coupled with an important shift in his understanding of Christ's role within the economy of salvation. In his sermons and commentaries of the 1540s, Ochino speaks of Jesus taking on and satisfying for the sins of humanity by his death: Christ, through his expiatory sacrifice, is the operative agent in salvation. Yet in some of his Zurich works Ochino offers a rather different reading of the atonement. In the *Dialogo del Purgatorio* of 1556, for example, he denies that Christ was capable, by his own merits, of reconciling God with humanity; the efficacy of his death lies solely in the fact that God has chosen to accept it as satisfaction for sin.[23] Increasingly, Ochino seems to have had difficulty integrating the orthodox doctrine of the merits of Christ into a soteriological scheme that envisaged salvation as the product of God's freely given grace, expressed through election.[24] Thus

---

[22] *Prediche di M. Bernardino Ochino Senese, nomate Laberinti del libero, o ver servo Arbitrio, Prescienza, Predestinatione, e Libertà divina, e del modo per uscirne* (Basle, n.d. [1560]), pp. 204–5. Compare ibid., pp. 131–2, 205; *Prediche*, V. p. 121.

[23] *Dialogo del Purgatorio di Messer Bernardino Occhino di Siena, Pastore della Chiesa de Locarnesi, in Zuricho* ([Zurich], 1556), pp. 41–2: 'Se Dio havesse voluto entrar in giudicio per pagarci, secondo che di giustitia ci era debitore, senza farci una minima gratia: et havesse pesato le opere di Christo, con le quali meritò, harebbe trovato che per se stesse, et per lor propria natura, semota ogni divina gratia de accettatione, non eran tali ch'havessero di giustitia obligato Dio à perdonarci li nostri peccati. L'obligorno adunque solamente per gratia, se come anco per gratia et non per lor propria natura, furno satisfattorie per li nostri peccati.' This statement did not pass unnoticed; in June 1558, Ochino was forced to write to Friedrich von Salis to defend himself against the charge that he had taught 'che Christo habbia meritato o soddisfatto è una bestemmia' (letter published in Benrath, *Ochino*, pp. 306–7).

[24] For Calvin there is no such contradiction between the doctrines of Christ's merit and God's grace. See J.T. McNeill (ed.), *Calvin: Institutes of the Christian Religion* (2 vols, Philadelphia, 1960), I, p. 529 (2:17): 'It is absurd to set Christ's merit against God's

in sermon 9 of the *Prediche*, volume 5, he describes Christ as neither the cause nor the means ('mezzo') of salvation, but merely as one charged with implementing the divine decree. At this point the notion of the substitutionary atonement retreats entirely into the background. Christ's death, Ochino argues, is not a form of expiation, but a demonstration of God's love for humanity: 'God wanted his son to die on the cross so that man would see that God was not angry, but loved him excessively, and so that he might therefore return to God.'[25] Here we may relate Ochino's changing understanding of the atonement to his statements on justification in the *Prediche* and the *Laberinti*. In the former work, Ochino argues that Christ's function is to effect a transformation of humanity's attitude to God, rather than vice versa:

> God did not need the death of Christ in order to love us, but we needed Christ's death in order to love God. Although Christ is the instrument through which we experience all the effects of God's love, it was not because of him that God loved us: he loved us out of pure grace, without any mediator. Just as God has given us his love directly ['senza mezzo'] – while communicating the effects of that love to us through Christ – so he has given us Christ directly, because although Christ could not act as a mediator between himself and God, he could act as a mediator between us and God.[26]

Again, this represents a subtle change of emphasis rather than a clear break with orthodox Reformed teaching. In sermon 8 of the *Prediche*, Ochino still speaks of Christ's death in terms of reparation ('He was sent

---

mercy. For it is a common rule that a thing subordinate to another is not in conflict with it. For this reason nothing hinders us from asserting that men are freely justified by God's mercy alone, and at the same time that Christ's merit, subordinate to God's mercy, also intervenes on our behalf. Both God's free favour and Christ's obedience, each in its degree, are fitly opposed to our works. Apart from God's good pleasure Christ could not merit anything: but did so because he had been appointed to appease God's wrath with his sacrifice, and to blot out our transgressions with his obedience.' These remarks flowed from an earlier discussion of the atonement between Calvin and Lelio Sozzini (for whose views see the article cited in n. 106 below).

25 *Prediche*, V, pp. 67–8: 'Dio vuolse che il suo figliuolo morisse in croce, accioche l'huomo vedesse che Dio non era irato, ma che l'amava eccessivamente, et cosi andasse a lui.'

26 Ibid., p. 17: 'Dio non haveva bisogno della morte di Christo per amarci, ma è ben vero, che noi havevamo bisogno della morte di Christo per amare Dio: però se bene Christo è stato quello, per mezzo del quale habbiamo havuti tutti gli effetti dell'amore di Dio, non però per mezzo suo ci ha Dio amati; imperoche egli ci ha amati per pura gratia, et senza mezzo alcuno. Anzi sicome Dio ci ha donato il suo amore, senza mezzo, benche gli effetti dell'amore ce gli habbia donati per mezzo di Christo, cosi anco ci ha donato Christo senza alcun mezzo, atteso che Christo non poteva esser mezzo tra se et Dio, ma si ben tra noi et Dio.' This passage appears in sermon 2, 'Nella quale si mostra quanto sia grande et magnifica la liberalità di Dio'.

by the Father, so that bearing our iniquities, as prophesied by Isaiah, and accepting them himself, and carrying them with him on to the cross, he might liberate us, taking away the sins of the world and saving us from them'),[27] although he is clearly more concerned with its transformative effect on humanity ('He came to remove our heart of stone and to give us one of flesh, ... to regenerate us, and of carnal persons to make us spiritual, of earthly persons to make us heavenly, of humans to make us angels, and of devils to make us divine').[28] Ochino's discussion of the atonement in the *Prediche* must also be set against the corresponding passages in the *Catechismo*. There he offers a much more traditional formulation of the doctrine: Christ offered himself up for the elect on the cross 'and this divine sacrifice pleased God so much, that his anger was assuaged' ('piacque tanto a Dio, quel divin sacrifitio, che placò l'ira sua').[29]

In the *Catechismo*, Ochino also articulates a clear doctrine of double predestination:

> Those who are elect in the mind of God are always elect, and those who are reprobate are always reprobate. Because those to whom God does not impute sins are elect, he never imputes sins to them, and because those to whom God imputes sins are reprobate, he always imputes sins to them. Christ died to free the elect from all of their sins, but he did not die to free the reprobate from a single sin.[30]

This is consistent with the position that Ochino had set out in his works of the 1540s, notably the series of sermons on predestination that appear in the second volume of the *Prediche*. There he describes election as the surest proof of the 'surpassing goodness of God' ('eccessiva bontà di Dio'), grounding this teaching in the immutability of the divine nature: 'to say that [God] can damn the elect is false, heretical and impossible ... because in God there can be neither change nor development.'[31] Even Christ, the mediator of salvation, cannot reverse

---

[27] Ibid., p. 61: 'Fu dal Padre mandato a cio, che ponendo in esso le nostre iniquità, sicome Isaia predisse, et esso accettandole, et portandole sopra il legno della croce, ce ne liberasse, tollendo i peccati del mondo, et salvandoci da essi.'

[28] Ibid., p. 62: 'Venne per tor da noi il cuor di pietra et darcelo di carne, ... per rigenerarci, et di carnali farci spirituali, di terreni celesti, di humani angelici, et di diabolici divini.'

[29] *Catechismo*, p. 155.

[30] Ibid., p. 282: 'Quelli i quali nella divina mente, sono eletti, son sempre eletti, et quelli che son reprovati, son per ogni tempo reprovati. Quelli a quali Dio non imputa i peccati, sicome sono gli eletti, non glieli imputa mai, et quelli a quali gli imputa, sicome sono i reprovati, gli imputa sempre. Christo morì per liberare gli eletti da tutti i lor peccati, et non morì per liberare i reprovati pur da un solo.'

[31] *Prediche*, II, sig. rr6ʳ: 'Che [Dio] l'eletto possi dannare, è cosa falsa, heretica, et impossibile, non si puo verificare in senso composto, ne anco in diviso, poi che in Dio, non puo essere mutatione, ne successione.'

the effects of these eternal decrees.[32] In this group of sermons, Ochino resists any attempt to link election to divine foreknowledge of good works; rather, it is an unmediated act of God's will. He also specifically defends the doctrine of reprobation against the charge that it offends against God's justice, alluding to a favourite predestinarian text, Romans 9:19–21:

> Even more than a potter with the vessels that he has made, [God] may dispose of us as he wishes and may do with us as he pleases, entirely justly. What obligations does God have towards us? Through the sin of Adam, we are all lost and he could justly have damned us all, but he saves many of us. Given that we are not worthy, why should we complain when he punishes us to illustrate his glory? It should therefore be preached that God has elected some but not others, to cast down the wisdom of man and to render him humble and subject to God.[33]

Ochino refuses to question the reasons for God's choice. It is enough to accept that God is just in whatever he wills, and therefore that his decision in this matter is also righteous, however incomprehensible it may seem to us.[34]

Ochino's statements on predestination in the years immediately subsequent to his conversion in fact place him closer to Calvin than to Bullinger, who was alarmed by the implications of the Genevan reformer's doctrine of reprobation.[35] In the second volume of the *Prediche*, Ochino's interpretation of the text most commonly adduced in support of universal salvation, 1 Timothy 2:3–4, is identical to that of

---

[32] Ibid., sig. rr7v–rr8r: 'voglio che sappi, che ben che Christo sia quello, per mezzo del quale si salvano tutti gl'eletti, nientedimeno (non per l'impotentia sua, essendogli data ogni potestà, ma per che la cosa non è in se possible) non potrebbe Christo salvare un reprobato, ne dannare un'eletto.'

[33] Ibid., sig. oo6r–v: 'Puo disporre di noi a modo suo, farne quello gli piace, piu ch'el figolo de vasi, et tutto giustamente. Et che oblighi ha Dio con noi? Di poi, per il peccato d'Adamo siamo tutti persi, et potrebbe tutti giustamente dannarci, et lui ne salva tanti, et ci lamentaremo, dove non siamo degni, che col punirci illustri la sua gloria? Imo debba predicarsi, che Dio alcuni ha eletti et alcuni no, per sbattere per terra la sapientia dell'huomo, et renderlo tutto humile et soggetto a Dio.'

[34] Ibid., sig. ss5v: 'Non si ha … a cercare causa alcuna della nostra eletione, fuor della divina volontà. De reprobati, non intendo disputare, per che Dio gli reproba, per non esserci necessario, ne utile il saperlo.'

[35] See, among others, P. Holtrop, *The Bolsec Controversy on Predestination, from 1551 to 1555: The statements of Jerome Bolsec, and the Responses of John Calvin, Theodore Beza, and Other Reformed Theologians* (2 vols, Lewiston, NY, 1993); W. Neuser, 'Calvins Kritik an den Basler, Berner und Zürcher Predigern in der Schrift <<De praedestinatione>> 1552', in Oberman, *Das Reformierte Erbe*, II, pp. 237–43; and C. Venema, 'Heinrich Bullinger's Correspondence on Calvin's Doctrine of Predestination, 1551–1553', *SCJ*, 17 (1986), pp. 435–50.

Calvin: both argue, with Augustine, that Paul's statement 'God wills all people to be saved' is to be understood as meaning that no class of persons is excluded from election.[36] In his commentary on this passage, by contrast, Bullinger prefers to emphasize the availability of salvation to all who believe in Christ.[37]

By the beginning of the 1560s, Calvin's explicit double predestinarianism had begun in most places to prevail over Bullinger's more moderate line. Ochino's affirmation of the double decree in the *Catechismo* would seem to align him with this emerging Reformed consensus. However, the *Catechismo*, as an example of a 'public' genre, is perhaps to be read more as a statement of the Zurich church's views on a particular issue than of Ochino's private opinions. The Zurich church's position on predestination had been clarified in January 1560 by the dismissal from his post at the *Carolinum* of Theodor Bibliander, who had taught a doctrine of predestination by classes (believers and unbelievers) against the double predestinarianism favoured by Peter Martyr Vermigli.[38] Unsurprisingly, it is Vermigli's position – now the official stance of the Zurich church – which is endorsed in the *Catechismo*. For Ochino's personal response to the debate between Vermigli and Bibliander, one must turn to the *Laberinti del libero arbitrio*.

The *Laberinti* signal a retreat from Ochino's earlier double predestinarianism, as articulated in the second volume of the *Prediche*. There is no evidence in the work of support for the disgraced Bibliander's opinions: Ochino continues to teach the election of individuals, rather than of classes, and to argue that the performance of good works is entirely dependent on the operation of grace within the

---

36 *Prediche*, II, sig. uu6ʳ: 'Et se bene è scritto, che Dio ha cura di tutti, chiama tutti, vuol salvare tutti, è morto per tutti, illumina tutti, et simili sententie, dico che s'intende, che ha cura di tutti generale, ma degl'eletti spetiale, et cosi chiama tutti con vocatione universale, ma gl'eletti con interna et singolare. Quando anco Paulo disse, che vuol salvare tutti, intese, ciò è d'ogni sorte di persone'. Compare *Institutes*, II, pp. 983–4 (3:24).

37 Bullinger, *Commentarii*, pp. 564–6.

38 J. Staedtke, 'Der Zürcher Prädestinationsstreit von 1560', *Zwa*, 9/10 (1953/2), pp. 536–46. Bibliander's views are summarized in E. Egli, 'Biblianders Leben und Schriften', in *Analecta Reformatoria II: Biographien* (Zurich, 1901), pp. 1–144, especially pp. 71–9. Vermigli interprets both reprobation and election as products of God's will, but seeks to counter the charge that this makes God the author of sin by arguing that the actual commission of evil acts leading to damnation is dependent on a secondary cause, the corruption of the human will (*In Samuelis prophetae libros duos D.D. Petri Martyris Vermilii Florentini, S. Theologiae in Schola Tigurina professoris, Commentarii doctissimi* (Zurich, 1595), fol. 275ʳ). For a fuller discussion, see Donnelly, *Calvinism and Scholasticism*, pp. 116–40, and James, *Vermigli*.

believer.[39] However, he appears to have modified his conception of predestination in response to the persistent criticism (voiced by Catholics and radical reformers alike) that the doctrine rendered God ultimately responsible for sin. In the *Laberinti*, Ochino distinguishes sharply between election, an act of the divine will, and reprobation, which belongs rather to the realm of God's foreknowledge. God knew, for instance, that Peter would be saved as he had already so determined. In the case of Judas, by contrast, '[God] did not see that he would sin, because he had so determined, but because [Judas'] sin was present to him' ('non vedde che peccherebbe, perche havesse così determinato, ma perche il suo peccato gl'era presente'). Ochino illustrates the link between damnation and foreknowledge by comparing God to a man who sees another fall from a high tower, but does nothing to prevent it. He concludes, 'God's seeing is not the cause of our sins; we do not sin because he sees them, but because we sin he sees them' ('il veder di Dio non è causa di nostri peccati; ne perche gli vede pecchiamo, ma perche pecchiamo gli vede').[40] (Vermigli, it should be noted, had explicitly rejected the idea that reprobation was consequent upon foreseen sin.[41]) Ochino also seems to have revised his understanding of 1 Timothy 2:3–4. In sermon 8, he dismisses the interpretation of this text offered by Calvin and Augustine (which, as we have seen, he had earlier shared).[42] Neither is he prepared to countenance the existence of competing 'revealed' and 'hidden' aspects of the divine will, as

---

[39] See, for instance, *Laberinti*, pp. 103; 233. Nevertheless, in a letter to the Basle schoolmaster Thomas Platter dated 16 August 1560, Bibliander noted the publication of 'Labyrinthum quendam Italicum de providentia, de praedestinatione, electione et eiusmodi' and requested a copy of 'tam sublime opus' as soon as a Latin edition was available. The letter provides no indication that Bibliander was aware of the identity of the work's author (published in Pollet, *Martin Bucer*, II, pp. 333–4).

[40] *Laberinti*, pp. 163–4.

[41] *Loci communes*, p. 994: 'Peccata non sunt causa reprobationis, quod videlicet aliqui a dilectione Dei praetereantur, et relinquantur, quamvis causae sint damnationis. Unde si Patres aliquando dicunt: Peccata esse causam reprobationis, id intelligunt quo ad extremam damnationem, quae prorsus ob peccata infligitur.' Vermigli's authorship of the tract in which this passage occurs is disputed, but a convincing case is made for it by P. Walser, *Die Prädestination bei Heinrich Bullinger im Zusammenhang mit seiner Gotteslehre* (Zurich, 1957) pp. 200–10; and J.P. Donnelly, 'Three disputed Vermigli tracts', in S. Bertelli and G. Ramakus (eds), *Essays presented to Myron P. Gilmore* (2 vols, Florence, 1978), I, pp. 37–46. See P.M. Vermigli, *Philosophical Works* (Kirksville, Mo., 1996), ed. J. McLelland, pp. 268–70, for a summary of this debate.

[42] *Laberinti*, p. 87: 'Ne anco appruovo la opinione di quelli, li quali disseno, che la mente di Paulo fu di dire, che vuole salvare d'ogni sorte persone, ... imperoche questo è dubbio, ne consta per la parola di Dio.'

postulated by Vermigli to explain God's simultaneous tolerance and condemnation of human sin.[43]

In the *Laberinti*, Ochino appears, on one level, to be calling for a return to the moderate single predestinarianism professed by the Zurich church prior to the Bibliander affair. If this had been the total extent of Ochino's differences with Reformed orthodoxy, it is likely that he would have been permitted to live out his days in Zurich undisturbed: in an address of 1536, Bullinger himself had argued that reprobation was the product of God's foreknowledge, rather than his will.[44] But as we have seen, Ochino's understanding of soteriology in general was taking on an increasingly heterodox hue. In addition, like many Italian exiles he was unsympathetic to the growing 'confessionalism' of the Reformed leadership, above all to its preoccupation with precise doctrinal definition. In the *Laberinti*, Ochino suggests that this quest for certainty is both destructive of Christian unity and, ultimately, futile. In form, the work anticipates the *Dialogi XXX*: problems are raised, alternative opinions are considered, but the reader is rarely presented with a firm conclusion. In the 19th and final sermon Ochino proposes 'learned ignorance' ('dotta ignoranza') as the 'way to escape from all the aforementioned labyrinths' ('via per uscire di tutti i sopra detti laberinti').[45] He compares salvation to a meal prepared for humanity by God, arguing that we ought to enjoy what is offered to us rather than speculating about the manner in which it was prepared: 'We can be saved, not only without knowing, but without thinking about, whether we are free or not.'[46] The same anti-dogmatic tendency is apparent in Ochino's *Disputa della Cena*, published in 1561. There, Ochino suggests that the controversy over the sacrament may be resolved 'by leaving to each faction its own opinion' ('con lassare a ciascuna delle parti la sua opinione'), since the mode of Christ's presence in the Eucharist is not among the articles necessary for salvation, as set out in scripture and the Apostles' creed.[47]

---

[43] Ibid., p. 88. Contrast Vermigli, *Samuel*, fol. 21ʳ.

[44] Walser, *Prädestination*, pp. 163–7.

[45] *Laberinti*, p. 246.

[46] Ibid., p. 248: 'Possiam salvarci, non solo senza sapere, ma et senza pensare, se siam liberi, ò nò.'

[47] *Disputa di M. Bernardino Ochino da Siena intorno alla presenza del corpo di Giesu Christo nel Sacramento della Cena* (Basle, 1561), p. 169: 'I sacramenti et le ceremonie sono accidentali, e non essentiali alla osservanza di precetti morali, cosi et alla viva fede.' See the recent analysis of this work by E. Campi, '<<Conciliatione de dispareri>>: Bernardino Ochino e la seconda disputa sacramentale', in Oberman, *Das Reformierte Erbe*, I, pp. 77–92. Like some of his compatriots (see Chapter 1:iii above), Ochino clung to a strongly Zwinglian view of the Eucharist that diverged in some respects from the

Nothing in the works published by Ochino prior to 1563 could be said to have placed him in open opposition to the Reformed establishment. The *Catechismo*, in particular, is in most respects a model of Reformed orthodoxy. From the *Laberinti* and the final volume of the *Prediche*, however, it would seem that in his later years Ochino was beginning to consider different approaches to the key problems of soteriology: justification, the atonement and predestination. In these works one finds a mix of views, some consistent with traditional Protestant teaching, others reminiscent of dissident figures like Sebastian Castellio and Lelio Sozzini. Ochino also hints at his growing dissatisfaction with the leadership of the Reformed churches. In the *Prediche*, he attacks those who, while claiming to be Reformed Christians, desire above all else to 'to be singled out, named and famous' ('d'esser additati, nominati, et famosi'), persecuting 'without end' ('senza fine') those whose talents threaten to put their own in the shade.[48] More fundamentally, Ochino suggests that the divisions among Protestants cast doubt on their claim to represent the true church of Christ: 'Spiritual union shows men to be evangelical and divine; in the same way, disunion shows them to be antichristian and diabolical. From that, one can only conclude that such partial churches are not truly Christian.'[49]

Similarly, when discussing the appropriate response to persecution in the *Disputa della Cena*, Ochino warns his compatriots that exile is no easy alternative to laying down one's life for the faith: often it is only the start of a longer and more bitter martyrdom among 'false brethren' ('falsi fratelli'). Again he criticizes the fissiparous tendency within Protestantism:

> You must know that for around 40 years many churches have been reformed and that all of them think of themselves as entirely perfect, especially when it comes to doctrine, in which they are so diverse and varied that each condemns as heretical all those that do not accept its teaching. And because there is only one Gospel and only one true doctrine, if they do not err by condemning the others either all of them must be in error, or only one of them must have the truth.[50]

Consensus Tigurinus. See, for instance, Ochino's comments on the use of the term 'exhibere' in his *Syncerae et verae doctrinae de Coena Domini defensio* (Zurich, 1556), pp. 126–7.

[48] *Prediche*, V, p. 305. Compare his later criticisms of Bullinger, cited in section ii below.

[49] Ibid., pp. 166–7: 'L'unione spirituale mostra gl'huomini essere evangelici et divini: cosi le disunioni mostrano che sieno Antichristiani et diabolici: però bisogna dire, che le Chiese cosi partiali non siano veramente christiani.'

[50] *Disputa*, pp. 258–9: 'devi sapere, che da circa quarant'anni in qua si son molte

Even if the exile should find sanctuary in a church that holds all that is necessary for salvation, 'you may also be required to believe things that it is not necessary for you to believe to be saved' ('forse vorrebbeno obligarti di piu, a credere di necessità quello, che non è necessario che creda per salvarti').[51] Here, one suspects, is an implied criticism of the increasing obsession with doctrinal minutiae on the part of Reformed theologians. Certainly the Zurich churchmen seem to have regarded Ochino's statement in that light: a manuscript copy of the passage is preserved in the Zurich Staatsarchiv among the documents relating to his banishment in November 1563.[52]

ii. The critique of Reformed orthodoxy in the *Dialogi XXX*

Ochino's last and most controversial publication, the *Dialogi XXX*, has proved resistant to interpretation by contemporaries and modern scholars alike. Commenting on dialogues 19 and 20 of the work, the Zurich theologian Josias Simler remarked that Ochino's mode of argument was so 'slippery' and 'obscure' as to make it virtually impossible to gauge his true intentions.[53] Simler's sentiments are echoed by Erich Hassinger, who observes:

> Very often one cannot tell which of the two participants in the *Dialogi XXX* represents his [Ochino's] deepest convictions. Even when both of them agree, the formulation of their agreement is from time to time so enigmatic and ambiguous that one is inclined to believe that something is being deliberately concealed.[54]

In rhetorical terms the *Dialogi XXX* are quite unlike, say, the evangelical dialogues of the early 1520s, or even Ochino's own earlier, anti-Catholic dialogues. The latter exploit the propagandistic potential of the dialogue, as a medium which allows for the demonstration of the clear supremacy of one viewpoint over another. The structural principle

---

chiese riformate, et tutte pensano d'esser sommamente perfette, spetialmente nella dottrina, nella quale son si diverse et varie, che ciascuna danna per heretiche tutte le altre, che non accettano le sua. Et perche non è senon un solo Evangelio, et una sola vera dottrina, se non errano in dannar le altre, bisogna, o che tutte sien in errore, o vero che una sola sia in verità.'

[51] Ibid., p. 260.

[52] StAZ E II 367, 375–7.

[53] Ibid., 304: 'De Bernardini Ochini dialogis duobus de Trinitate mihi iudicare est difficile, quod res alioqui ardua ita lubrice et obscure tractatur ut vix videre queas quid sibi velit.'

[54] Hassinger, *Acontius*, pp. 98–9. Compare the comments of F. Trechsel, *Die Protestantischen Antitrinitarier vor Faustus Socin* (2 vols, Heidelberg, 1939/44), II, p. 233.

of the *Dialogi XXX*, by contrast, is indeterminacy. Although in most of the dialogues an 'Ochinus' puts forward views consistent with the official teaching of the Zurich church, the opinions of his fictional interlocutors are given an equal, if not greater, airing. Dialogue becomes not simply a pedagogical or polemical device, but a means of exploring the contradictions of received theology and, more generally, of questioning the claims of the Reformed leadership to religious authority.

The *Dialogi XXX* is a lengthy work even by 16th-century standards, in its published form amounting to more than 950 octavo pages. Volume 1, entitled 'On the Messiah', contains 18 dialogues, in all but the last of which 'Ochinus' is opposed by one Jacobus Judaeus. In these dialogues, fresh consideration is given to the soteriological issues that had preoccupied Ochino in his earlier Zurich works: the nature of justification and sanctification, the role of Christ as redeemer, and the relationship between divine predestination and the human will. While Ochinus faithfully expounds the orthodox position on these questions, his interlocutor undertakes to expose the contradictions in the Reformed understanding of salvation, recapitulating – in intensified form – some of the statements made by Ochino himself in the later *Prediche* and in the *Laberinti*. In dialogue 3, for instance, Jacobus argues that one cannot logically designate both election and Christ's merits as the cause of salvation: the Messiah's mission is redemptive not in the sense of providing satisfaction for sin, but of liberating the elect from it and rendering them perfect.[55] In dialogue 6 – on how sins are forgiven by Christ's works – Jacobus makes clear his opposition to the doctrine of the substitutionary atonement:

> One cannot say that he [Christ] made satisfaction on our behalf, especially because his punishment and death would not in themselves constitute the satisfaction required for the injury and insult that the elect had committed against God. [Christ's death] would constitute satisfaction only because God in his goodness had

---

[55] *Bernardini Ochini Senensis Dialogi XXX. In duos libros divisi, quorum primus est de Messia, continetque dialogos xviii. Secundus est, cum de rebus variis, tum potissimum de Trinitate* (2 vols, Basle, 1563), I, pp. 88–9: 'nullius opera nos ad aeternam vitam amavit [Deus]. Sed cum peccata nostra videret, et nos servare immutabiliter decrevisset, non mutavit alioquin immutabile decretum suum, sed in aeterno et stabili suo in nos amore perseverans, cum videret nos sic impios, caecos, miseros non posse ad summam illam felicitatem perfectionemque cui ipse nos destinaverat, pervenire, statuit mittere Messiam, quo nos liberaret a peccatis omnibusque in quibus ob illa eramus miseriis, et perfectos beatosque reddere. Misit igitur eum ut essemus in eius conspectu sancti et intemerati, non ut nos eius opera amaret. Ita fiet ut sit Christus cusa [sic] nostrae salutis non praecipua, sed instrumentalis, quippe cuius opera executurus sit et reipsa praestiturus Deus, quicquid in seipso nullius adhibita opera facere irrevocabiliter decrevit.'

deigned to accept it in place of satisfaction, which is not really to satisfy at all.[56]

Like Ochino in the *Prediche*, Jacobus challenges as incompatible with the impassibility and immutability of the divine nature the orthodox claim that, through his death, Christ has assuaged God's anger towards sinful humanity:

> One cannot say that our sins are to be forgiven by the work of the Messiah, in the sense that God was angered and needed to be placated by the Messiah, and to be reconciled to us and pacified, as God in himself has never and will never be angered. Because he is most simple, he cannot be changed or troubled; because he is immutable, he cannot be disturbed; because he is most blessed, he cannot be made sad in the way that angry people can.[57]

Dialogues 11–13, meanwhile, contain a trenchant attack by Jacobus on the doctrine of justification by the imputation of Christ's merits. According to Jacobus, it is the office of the Messiah to redeem the elect from both actual and original sin; drawing on the Ignatian image of *Christus medicus* – Christ as healer of fallen human nature – he argues that a good physician seeks to eradicate the cause of a malady, rather than simply treating its symptoms, and that Christ would not have rendered his elect 'actors, outwardly good but inwardly evil'.[58] The failure of the Reformed to recognize that justification involves the radical transformation of the interior life of the believer, rather than merely the non-imputation of sin, is a sign that they, like the papists, possess only dead faith.[59] As a corollary of this, Jacobus takes issue with

---

56 Ibid., pp. 163–4: 'Dici non potest eum [Christum] pro nobis satisfecisse, praesertim cum eius supplicium atque mors non fuerit per sese idonea satisfactio pro iniuria et probro quo Deum affecerant electi: sed eo tantum fuerit satisfactio quod eam Deus pro sua benignitate satisfactionis loco haberi dignatus est: id quod non vere satisfacere est.'

57 Ibid., p. 162: 'Neque item dici illud potest, opera Messiae nobis ideo ignotum iri peccata, quia cum esset iratus Deus, placandus sit a Messia, et nobis reconciliandus atque pacificandus. Quandoquidem Deus in se nunquam vel iratus fuit vel irascetur: quippe qui cum sit simplicissimus, mutari conturbarive nequeat: cum sit immutabilis, commoveri: cum beatissimus, contristari non possit ut solent irati.'

58 Ibid., pp. 288–9: 'Non fuisset Christus vindex optimus, si nos tantum a poena liberasset debita peccatis, ac non a culpa. Non veniet Christus ut nos reddet histriones, foris bonos, intus malos: quin nequidem intus mali esse possumus, quin et foris simus, cum necesse sit ut si intus mala est arbor, fructus quoque malus sit. Quin veniet ut nos vere intus forisque lavet, ut mundet, ut peccata a nobis auferat, nosque intaminatos, puros, mundos reddat, sicuti passim traditur in sacris literis. ... Non est is bonus medicus, qui mali radicem non tollet: sic et Christus non fuisset bonus medicus spiritualis nisi a nobis originale peccatum abstulisset si modo, ut vos docetis, peccatum est, et aliorum omnium origo.'

59 Ibid., p. 290: 'Ita fit ut verear ne falso Evangelicorum nomine, vereque fide mortua

Ochinus over the interpretation of Romans 7:14–25, which Calvin and other Reformed commentators take to refer to the incomplete sanctification of the elect in this life. Jacobus, by contrast (following the younger Augustine), maintains that Paul is here describing not the justified person's continuing battle with sin, but the state of the unregenerate prior to grace.[60] According to Jacobus, the believer with 'living faith' will also possess the Christian virtues, above all charity. Justification is not by imputation, but by participation, through the indwelling of God, Christ and the Holy Spirit.[61] In support of this view, Jacobus cites the words of John the Baptist in John 1:29–30:

> Here, he says, is the lamb of God who takes away the sin of the world. He does not say, 'the one who ensures that sin is not imputed' but 'the one who takes away'. ... John says that Christ washed us with his blood, and elsewhere that his blood cleanses us of every sin: cleanses us, I say, not ensures that sins are not imputed to us even though we remain polluted.[62]

Whereas in the first volume of the *Dialogi XXX* Ochino concentrates almost exclusively on soteriology, the subject matter of part 2 of the work is much more diverse. Dialogues 19 and 20 tackle the thorny question of the Trinity, pitting the orthodox Ochinus against a 'Spiritus', who refuses to divulge his real name on the grounds that the Word of God is the sufficient and only authority for what he has to say.[63] This uncompromising restatement of the scripture principle – which recalls the attitudes of Camillo Renato, Lelio Sozzini and other Italian radicals – serves as the basis for Spiritus' critique of the orthodox doctrine of the Trinity (although he does also challenge it on philosophical grounds). Spiritus repeatedly lambasts the Reformed for having recourse to extra-biblical terminology and authorities in their efforts to shore up Nicene orthodoxy. When, for example, Ochinus seeks to place the Trinity

---

insigniti, caeteroquin peccatorum pleni, ac tales quales olim papani fuistis, et forsan aliquanto deteriores, sic ad mortem tendentes, ita dicentes: Hoc satis est quod nobis peccata nostra non imputentur.'

[60] Ibid., pp. 290–94. In his earlier Romans commentary, Ochino had himself suggested that Paul was speaking 'in hominis non renati persona' (*Expositio Epistolae ad Romanos*, fol. 55ᵛ). On the treatment of this text by 16th-century exegetes, including Ochino, see D. Steinmetz, 'Calvin and the Divided Self of Romans 7', in Steinmetz, *Calvin in Context* (Oxford, 1995), pp. 110–21.

[61] *Dialogi XXX*, I, p. 330: 'Itaque et iustus et sanctus est, postquam in eo deus et Christus et spiritus sanctus habitat, idque non imputatione, sed participatione.'

[62] Ibid., p. 336: 'Ecce inquit, agnus dei qui tollit peccatum mundi, tollit inquit, non facit ut non imputetur ... Dicit Johannes Christum lavisse nos suo sanguine, et alibi eius sanguinem mundare nos ab omni peccato: mundare inquam, non efficere, ut quamvis adhuc pollutis nobis peccata non imputentur.'

[63] Ibid., II, p. 9.

beyond debate, arguing that a settled position on the issue was arrived
at by the ancient councils, Spiritus retorts that the signal failure of those
same councils to follow scripture in other matters, such as the Eucharist,
makes it likely that they have erred in respect of the Trinity also.[64] The
fact that there is no record of Luther and Zwingli having repudiated the
doctrine is no proof of its validity; for Spiritus, the recovery of pristine
Christianity is a gradually unfolding process, rather than a revelation
made to one or more individuals at a particular point in history.[65] Even
if one concedes the existence of the Trinity, it does not follow that
Christians are duty-bound to believe in it, as to be saved one need assent
only to those doctrines that scripture designates as fundamental and
teaches without ambiguity.[66] In support of this view, Spiritus cites
biblical examples of individuals who were saved without knowledge of
the Trinity (the good thief, the Samaritan woman, the Ethiopian eunuch,
Cornelius);[67] even the Fathers, he notes, were inconsistent in their use of
the technical terms commonly employed to describe the interrelationship
between the persons of the Godhead, at times voicing support for
positions that the Reformed themselves would now consider heretical.[68]
According to Spiritus, the doctrine of the Trinity is to be regarded in
much the same light as the other 'errors' cultivated by the Roman church
(transubstantiation, the veneration of the saints and images, and
auricular confession). Had such doctrines been preached in the early
church, he contends, few people would ever have embraced the Gospel;
it is therefore hardly surprising that today Jews, Turks and pagans resist
conversion to Christianity.[69]

---

[64] Ibid., p. 49.

[65] Ibid., p. 50: 'Fieri potest ut quemadmodum cognitionem non habuit Martinus non
esse in pane corpus Christi, nec sanguinem in vino: et Zuinglius habuit: ita neuter
cognoverit non esse Trinitatem, si ea non est. Elargitur enim Deus dona sua et quando et
quibus ipsi placet.'

[66] Ibid., p. 146.

[67] Ibid., pp. 156–7. Compare *Laberinti*, p. 254: 'Si salvò il ladron buono, et non credo
che havesse un minimo pensiero della libertà, o servitù del suo arbitrio.'

[68] Ibid., p. 152: 'Vos Hylarium hominem doctum ac peritum esse existimatis,
praesertim in iis quae de Trinitate scripsit. Atqui is multis in locis dicit in Trinitate tres esse
substantias: quam sententiam Hieronymus ad Damasum sacrilegam esse censet. Vos vero
necessario credendum esse dicitis eas esse consubstantiales, eos haereticorum loco
habentes, qui non ita credunt. Rursum Hieronymus non vult vel dici vel credi tria esse
supposita: et nobis id caput est fidei. Ignatius in epistola septima de filio loquens, dicit eum
non esse Deum illum qui est supra omnia, sed illius esse filium. Irenaeus libro 2 c. 50 dicit
patrem esse filio scientia maiorem. Et Iustinus in secunda Apologia pro Christianis dicit
patrem esse filio potentia maiorem.'

[69] Ibid., p. 157: '... non est quod miremur si nostro tempore paucissimi Iudaei, aut
Turcae, aut Pagani, fiunt Christiani, quandoquidem ut Christiani fiant, credere iubentur
Christi corpus esse in pane, et sanguinem in vino, et unum esse Deum, et tres divinas

Other topics debated in the second volume of the *Dialogi* include polygamy (dialogue 21), divorce (dialogues 22 and 23), the appropriate punishment for adultery (dialogue 24), and the relative merits of contemplative and 'active' theology (dialogue 29). Dialogues 25 to 28 may conveniently be considered together, as all deal with aspects of Reformed ecclesiology: the nature of religious authority, the 'marks' of the true church, and the proper approach to combating heresy. Particularly striking in this connection is dialogue 27, 'on those things that enable one to know which church is truly sincere, pure and of Christ, and which is not'. According to Ochino, the purpose of this dialogue is to serve as a mirror to the churches in which they may discern their faults and vices, and thereby grow in virtue.[70] Ochinus' adversary in the dialogue is a Hungarian named Eusebius, who, having found in all existing reformed churches things that both please and displease him, is now returning to his native land with the intention of founding a church free of the errors that he has encountered elsewhere. Eusebius goes on to attack the Reformed for their retention of various papal 'superstitions', notably infant baptism (he has no time for the covenant theology on which Ochinus, following Bullinger, bases his defence of this practice), public prayer and bowing at the name of Jesus. At the end of the dialogue, he contrasts the kingdom of Christ, which is governed by charity and does not require 'the arms of the flesh' ('corporeis armis') in order to extend its dominion, with the church of Satan, which offers wealth and favour to some while leaving others to languish in poverty.[71] Implicit in this is the suggestion that the Reformed churches have lost touch with the morality of the Gospel, placing their trust not in God but in secular power. The same point is made more explicitly in dialogue 26, where Ochinus' interlocutor Christophorus denounces the French Huguenots for taking up arms in defence of the faith, arguing that the defeat of Catholicism can be brought about only by the preaching of God's word and that Christians should respond to persecution with charity and good will, rather than with force.[72] Similarly, in dialogue 28 ('on how heretics are to be treated, and when they are to be killed') Ochino sets up a fictional exchange between the current pope, Pius IV, and Cardinal Giovanni Morone, who – like

---

personas, et adoranda esse simulachra, et orandos sanctos, et omnia sua peccata sacerdoti esse confitenda, et huius generis alia ridicula, impia, stulta, quae si in prisca illa Ecclesia fuissent praedicata, nemo ad Christum conversum fuisset.' This argument was taken up by later antitrinitarians (see Chapter 4:iii).

70 *Dialogi XXX*, II, pp. 329–30.

71 Ibid., pp. 376–7.

72 Ibid., pp. 316–28.

Christophorus – maintains that the weapons of the flesh are powerless against error; according to Morone, persecution creates not converts, but hypocrites.[73]

In the first volume of the *Dialogi*, Jacobus Judaeus is presented as one hostile not merely to Reformed orthodoxy, but to Christianity in general. Dialogue 1, in particular, resembles a traditional Jewish–Christian disputation, with Jacobus raising objections to the Messiahship of Jesus – such as the fact that Jesus failed to realize the Old Testament prophecies of an earthly Messianic kingdom – that would not be out of place in Jewish anti-Christian polemic.[74] But in later dialogues, Jacobus resembles less a representative of Judaism than a mouthpiece for dissident elements within the Reformed churches; the same could be said of many of Ochinus' interlocutors in volume 2 of the *Dialogi*. As a result, Bullinger came to suspect that others – specifically, Lelio Sozzini and the Savoyard humanist Sebastian Castellio – had had a hand in the genesis of the work.[75] While not wishing to go that far, I would contend that there are indeed striking similarities between some of the ideas put forward by the participants in the *Dialogi* and the views of the two thinkers mentioned by Bullinger.

Castellio's relationship with Ochino dated back to at least 1545, when he translated the Sienese exile's commentary on Romans into Latin.[76] In his *Contra libellum Calvini* (written around June 1554, but not published until the 17th century), Castellio listed Ochino among those who, like himself, had criticized the execution of Servetus.[77] As is well known, Castellio was also responsible for the Latin translation of the *Dialogi XXX* eventually published by Pietro Perna (whose links with Ochino and the Zurich Locarnesi have already been noted).[78] Apart from this, there is little evidence of direct contact between the two men after 1555, though Castellio may well have visited Zurich during

---

[73] Ibid., pp. 379–429. Ochino's choice of Morone to front this dialogue is interesting; it is perhaps to be linked to the publication, by Vergerio in 1558, of the Inquisition's 'Articuli contra Moronum', which highlighted the cardinal's opposition in principle to the punishment of heretics (Firpo and Marcatto, *Morone*, V, pp. 366–79).

[74] *Dialogi XXX*, I, pp. 7–58.

[75] Bullinger to Johannes Fabricius, 20 April 1565 (StAZ E II 373, 593; Schiess, I, no. 690; Bainton, *Ochino*, p. 203). Compare ZB Ms. F 15, 445, where Bullinger makes a similar suggestion ('diewyl er h. Bernhardin, als zů besorgen sich von anderen, unruwigen, verireten lüthen laßen anstifftenn').

[76] F. Buisson, *Sébastien Castellion. Sa vie et son oeuvre: Etude sur les origines du Protestantisme libéral français* (2 vols, Paris, 1892), I, pp. 226–7; Simler, *Bibliotheca*, p. 97.

[77] *Contra libellum Calvini* (n.p. , 1612), sig. A6ʳ.

[78] See Chapter 2:iii above. Josias Simler claims that Castellio also produced the Latin editions of the *Laberinti* and the *Disputa* (*Bibliotheca*, p. 97).

Ochino's time there.[79] An undated letter from Ochino to Castellio also survives.[80] This appears to form part of an exchange concerning the definition of faith, as either an act of the intellect or of the will; certainly, Castellio takes up specific points raised by Ochino in the letter in his unpublished *De arte dubitandi*.[81]

Many of the arguments deployed by Jacobus Judaeus in the *Dialogi XXX* recall statements made by Castellio in part 2 of *De arte dubitandi*, which dates from 1563, and in the *Dialogi quatuor*, written before 1558 and revised in March 1562.[82] In dialogue 4, for instance, Jacobus attacks the Reformed for making God the author of sin by their doctrine of double predestination,[83] while in dialogue 6 he adopts a universalist stance: all are comprehended within God's decree of election, 'because he gave them what they required, and what is necessary for them to be saved' ('omnibus ea dedit quibus opus est, et quae sunt ipsis ad salutem necessaria').[84] Election is therefore to be understood as conditional, with each individual free to accept or reject the offer of salvation. In the *Dialogi quatuor* Castellio, too, repudiates the orthodox Reformed concept of the perseverance of the elect, arguing instead that Christians are to work out their salvation in fear and trembling.[85] Jacobus Judaeus'

---

79 See the entry in Gesner's *liber amicorum* for 10 November 1561 (Serrai, *Gesner*, p. 367).

80 Published in Buisson, *Castellio*, I, pp. 228–9, n. 1; and Benrath, *Ochino*, pp. 307–8.

81 *De arte dubitandi et confidendi ignorandi et sciendi* (Leiden, 1981), ed. E. Feist Hirsch, part 2:IV. At times Castellio appears to quote directly from Ochino's letter:

[Ochino]: La fede è atto del intelletto, e l'intelletto non ha altri atti senon di conoscere, et però la fede è cognitione.

[*De arte dubitandi*, p. 90, ll. 46–7]: Contra haec sic docent quidam. Fides est actio intellectus. Intellectus autem nullas habet actiones nisi cognoscere: ergo fides est cognitio

...

[Ochino]: L'intelletto è potenza naturale et però di necessità assentisce, dissentisce, o dubita, secondo la evidenza delle cose che gli son presentate. Senza evidenza adunque non assentisce et però ne anchor crede.

[*De arte dubitandi*, p. 91, ll. 12–14]: Addunt haec. Intellectus est facultas naturalis ideoque necessario assentitur aut dissentit aut dubitat, prout est evidentia rerum, quae ei obiiciuntur. Proinde sine evidentia non assentitur et porro neque credit.

See also ibid., p. 93, ll. 1–3; p. 94, ll. 46–8.

82 I have used the 1613 Gouda edition of the *Dialogi quatuor*, which includes material additional to that published in the original Basle edition of 1578. On the dating of this work, see C. Gilly, 'Die Zensur von Castellios *Dialogi quatuor* durch die Basler Theologen (1578)', in M. Erbe et al. (eds), *Querdenken: Dissens und Toleranz im Wandel der Geschichte* (Mannheim, 1996), pp. 169–92 (169). According to Fausto Sozzini, the *Dialogi quatuor* were Castellio's riposte to the predestinarian propositions of the Basle professor of Old Testament, Martin Borrhaus (*Dialogi quatuor*, fol. *4ᵛ).

83 *Dialogi XXX*, I. p. 114.

84 Ibid., p. 175.

85 *Dialogi quatuor*, pp. 71–3; 85–6; 183. Compare *De arte dubitandi*, p. 163.

violent antipathy to the Protestant doctrine of the imperfect sanctification of the elect has already been noted. Similarly, in the tract 'On whether it is possible for a man through the holy spirit to obey the law of God perfectly', dated 11 February 1562, Castellio argues that it is not merely possible to overcome sin in this life, but that doing so is a precondition for salvation: one cannot at the same time serve both God and sin, Christ and Belial.[86] In part 2 of *De arte dubitandi*, meanwhile, he pours scorn on the Reformed doctrine of extrinsic justification. Just as during his earthly mission Christ truly healed the physical ailments of the sick, Castellio contends, so he now truly purges believers of sin, the malady of the soul.[87] Reformed orthodoxy has fallen into the trap of confusing justification with Christ's other 'beneficium', the forgiveness of sins.[88] Significantly, both Castellio and Jacobus Judaeus cite John the Baptist's parents Elizabeth and Zacharias as scriptural examples of the 'true' (that is to say, intrinsic) righteousness that they advocate.[89] Their interpretation of Romans 7 – as a statement of the condition of the unregenerate, rather than an affirmation of the continuing presence of sin and the 'old Adam' in the elect – is also identical.[90]

Agreement between Castellio and Ochino was by no means total. For example, in the section of *De arte dubitandi* entitled 'On the benefit of Christ', Castellio takes issue with those, like Ochino in the *Prediche*, who argue that Christ's role is not to assuage God's anger against humanity, but rather to persuade human beings of the constancy of God's love and thereby to effect their conversion.[91] Castellio's universalist understanding of election also seems to be at odds with that of Ochino, who in the *Laberinti* continues to posit the election to salvation of individuals from eternity, without reference to foreseen good works. Overriding those differences, however, was the two theologians' shared concern about the implications of double predestination for human behaviour and God's justice. In the final sermon of the *Laberinti*, Ochino argues that the doctrine of the servitude of the will discourages the performance of good works, just as the

---

86 *Dialogi quatuor*, p. 239.

87 *De arte dubitandi*, p. 99; see also *Dialogi quatuor*, pp. 232–3: 'Vides frater in quae monstra, et se, et alios coniiciant, qui sic docent, et qualem medicum Christum faciunt, qui morbos non sanet, sed quasi emplastro tegat, et postea sanasse dicat.' Compare the statement by Jacobus Judaeus cited in n. 58 above.

88 *De arte dubitandi*, pp. 100–102; 104.

89 Ibid., pp. 120–21; *Dialogi XXX*, I, pp. 318, 339.

90 S. Castellio, *Defensio suarum translationum Bibliorum, et maxime Novi foederis* (Basle, 1562), pp. 192–8. Castellio makes an approving reference to Ochino's understanding of this text on p. 197.

91 *De arte dubitandi*, pp. 157–62.

doctrine of free will can lead to excessive pride in one's own abilities.[92] Elsewhere in the work he insists that the punishment of sinners must be related to actual faults committed: 'I do not deny that God could punish us without guilt and determine that we should be consigned to eternal fire without foreseeing any sin in us, but I do say that God has never done this and will never do it'.[93] Similarly, Castellio maintains that the doctrine of reprobation cannot be reconciled with the biblical teaching of a merciful God: to say that God created some for damnation is to make him worse than wolves or tigers, who do not devour their own offspring, as well as to undermine religion and the 'praxis pietatis', encouraging a fatalism that leads to licentious living.[94]

The parallels between Ochino's later theology and Castellio's thought are not limited to technical points of doctrine. From dialogues 26 and 28, it would seem that Ochino shared the Savoyard's well-known reservations about the secular punishment of heresy and the use of force by Christians.[95] More broadly, both Castellio and Ochino distinguish between the fundamentals of Christianity, spelled out clearly in scripture and comprehensible to all, and other, non-essential, dogmas. Castellio places questions such as baptism, the Lord's Supper, justification, predestination and the Trinity in this second category,[96] while in dialogue 20 Spiritus argues that only those doctrines explicitly taught in scripture and the Apostles' creed are necessary for salvation.[97] In dialogue 25, Ochinus makes much the same point:

---

[92] *Laberinti*, pp. 251–3. The potentially destructive consequences of belief in reprobation had been illustrated for Italian evangelicals by the well-publicized case of Francesco Spiera. This drama is replayed in dialogue 18 of the *Dialogi XXX*, on the sin against the Holy Spirit, in which 'Paracletus' attempts to soothe the fears of one 'Philautus' who, like Spiera, is convinced that his damnation has been foreordained.

[93] Ibid., p. 119: 'Non niego che Dio non potesse punirci senza colpa, et cosi anco determinare che stessemo nel fuoco eterno, senza prevedere in noi peccato alcuno; ma dico bene, che Dio questo non l'ha fatto mai, ne anco lo farà.'

[94] *Dialogi quatuor*, pp. 59–63.

[95] The arguments used by Christophorus in dialogue 26 anticipate Castellio's *Conseil à la France désolée*, published some months after the Savoyard had received Ochino's manuscript of the *Dialogi* (on the *Conseil*, see H. Guggisberg, 'Castellio und der Ausbruch der Religionskriege in Frankreich: Einige Betrachtungen zum *Conseil à la France désolée*', *ARG*, 68 (1977), pp. 253–67). In dialogue 28, Morone rejects attempts to apply the Mosaic penalties for blasphemy and idolatry to contemporary heresy (including antitrinitarianism), just as Castellio had done at the time of the Servetus affair. He also cites some of Castellio's favourite proof texts, including the parable of the wheat and the tares, and Gamaliel's counsel in Acts 5:34–9.

[96] *De arte dubitandi*, pp. 57–9.

[97] *Dialogi XXX*, II, p. 179: 'Credo ego Deum non frustra, sed ad hominum utilitatem dedisse mundo thesaurum sacrarum literarum, ut eis esset externa regula, cuius opera cognoscerent quid vel sibi discendum, vel alios docendum esset: necnon quo pacto resistere

If ... God has established that the first principles of the human sciences (which do not affect our salvation) should be in themselves so clear, explicit and manifest that they do not need to be preceded by anything clearer, it is easy for anyone to see that he would go to much greater lengths to ensure that the principles of the Christian faith, which are the first principles of true theology and are necessary for man to be saved, are in themselves clear, explicit and manifest, without the addition of human explanations.[98]

Ochino's biblicism links him with other Italian critics of Reformed orthodoxy, not least Lelio Sozzini. The relationship between Ochino and Sozzini is not particularly well documented, but Antonio Rotondò has uncovered evidence for contacts dating back to 1547.[99] In a letter to Bullinger of 18 July 1549, Curione noted that Sozzini and Ochino were in regular correspondence,[100] and the two men appear to have visited the Rhaetian Freestate together in summer 1554.[101] The following year, Sozzini was one of two envoys charged with conveying the Zurich council's offer of the position of minister to the Locarnesi to Ochino in Basle.[102] In addition, Rotondò has gone some way towards establishing that Ochino was familiar with the advanced critique of the doctrines of the Trinity and pre-existence of Christ that Lelio Sozzini developed during his final years in Zurich.[103] Some of the arguments put forward by 'Spiritus' in dialogue 19 of the *Dialogi XXX* have close parallels in

---

et convincere possent eos, qui veritatem oppugnarent. Easdem et ita perspicuas esse credo, ut quod ad veritatem attinet rerum ad salutem necessariarum, nihil egeant humanis commentationibus. Si enim iis egerent cum ab hominibus diversis modis exponantur nemo esset qui veritatem compertam haberet, pateretque omnibus erroribus ianua. Quare si nec in sacris literis, nec in Apostolorum Symbolo esset expressa veritas, penderetque eius expressio ab hominibus, fatendum esset eam [the Trinity] non esse creditu necessariam, ut pote cum de ea Dei sermonem non haberemus, in quo fidem nostram fundare possemus: sed tantum hominum verba, commentaria, expositiones.'

[98] Ibid., p. 292: 'Si ... statuit Deus ut humanarum scientiarum (quae ad salutem nostram non pertinent) prima principia sint per sese ita clara, expressa, manifesta, ut nihil egeant aliis antecedentibus, quae clariora sint ipsis, facile est cuivis cogitare eum multo magis statuisse ut Christianae fidei capita, quae prima sunt verae theologiae capita, et homini ad salutem necessaria, sint per sese clara, expressa, manifesta, nullis adhibitis humanis consequentiis.'

[99] Sozzini, *Opere*, p. 33.

[100] ZB Ms. F 62, 185r.

[101] Sozzini, *Opere*, p. 213, n. 6.

[102] The other was Martino Muralto. Sozzini's contacts with the Locarnesi predated their exile: see his letter to the community dated 13 January 1555 (original in FA Orelli, 8.7, no. 6; published in Sozzini, *Opere*, pp. 217–18).

[103] Rotondò, 'Calvino', p. 766; 'Sulla diffusione clandestina delle dottrine di Lelio Sozzini 1560–1568 (Risposta a Jerome Friedman)', in Rotondò, *Studi e ricerche di storia ereticale italiana del Cinquecento 1* (Turin, 1974), pp. 87–116 (98–100); and especially Sozzini, *Opere*, p. 344, n. 82.

Lelio's as yet unpublished commentary on the prologue to John's Gospel;[104] more generally, Spiritus' insistence on the invalidity of credal formulations which depart from the letter of scripture recalls Sozzini's rejection of extra-biblical terminology.[105] Ochino's increasing difficulties with the classic Anselmian doctrine of the atonement may also owe something to Sozzini who, like Jacobus Judaeus in volume 1 of the *Dialogi*, questioned whether the teaching of salvation by grace alone was compatible with the doctrine of Christ's merits.[106]

As we shall see, the Zurich churchmen came to regard the *Dialogi XXX* as an elaborate subterfuge in which Ochino, under cover of orthodoxy, offered the critics of the Reformed establishment a platform for their views. Some modern scholars have more or less endorsed that reading, while others have found it unconvincing.[107] A rather more subtle interpretation of the *Dialogi* has been proposed by Antonio Rotondò, who notes the similarities between Ochino's mode of argument here (and, one might add, in the *Laberinti*) and the stance adopted by Lelio Sozzini, Giorgio Biandrata and other Italian exiles when putting forward matters of doctrine for discussion with the Reformed leadership.[108] This 'modo accademico' (Rotondò) was characterized by questioning rather than direct statement; the aim of its proponents was to identify inconsistencies in the current position of the church on a particular issue, rather than to propound a fully worked-out alternative.[109] It was an approach fundamentally at odds with that

---

104 Compare Spiritus' comments on John 1:3, 'through him all things came to be', in *Dialogi XXX*, II, pp. 75–6, with Sozzini, *Opere*, p. 112.

105 See Chapter 1:iii above.

106 See D. Willis, 'The influence of Laelius Socinus on Calvin's Doctrines of the Merits of Christ and the Assurance of Faith', in Tedeschi, *Italian Reformation Studies*, pp. 231–41.

107 Contrast the positions of P. McNair, 'Ochino's Apology: Three Gods or Three Wives', *History*, 60 (1975), pp. 353–73, and G.G. Williams, 'The Theology of Bernardino Ochino' (unpublished doctoral thesis, Tübingen, 1955), pp. 106–7.

108 Sozzini, *Opere*, p. 71.

109 Silvana Seidel Menchi suggests that the method was born out of the medieval scholastic disputation, and that it became established among evangelical sympathizers in Italy as a means of self-defence against the Inquisition. When the Dominican Damiano of Brescia was accused of 'Lutheranism' in 1546, for example, he replied that he had put forward heretical tenets 'non assertive neque dogmatizando, sed disputative vel quaestiones proponendo' (Seidel Menchi, *Erasmus*, p. 250). According to Seidel Menchi, the 'modo accademico' evolved from a practical stratagem for the covert communication of heterodox opinions into a *habitus mentis* for Italian evangelicals (ibid., p. 241). Practitioners of the method were also able to draw on the Quattrocento humanist tradition of the 'dialogic' dialogue, which emphasized not the communication of predetermined truths but the role of discussion as *provocatio*, 'spurring the learned reader on to join the continuing quest [for truth]' (V. Cox, *The Renaissance dialogue: Literary dialogue in its social and political contexts, Castiglione to Galileo* (Cambridge, 1992), p. 62).

preferred by Bullinger and other Zurich ministers, who stressed clarity and simplicity of exposition, and, where possible, conformity with the historic position of the church catholic.

In my view, the *Dialogi XXX* represent Ochino's attempt to confront Reformed orthodoxy with the criticisms made of it by Castellio, Sozzini and other radicals. It is unlikely that at the time of writing Ochino identified with all aspects of the radical programme (if one can use such a term with reference to a group of dissenters united only in its opposition to Reformed doctrine and discipline as currently constituted). In dialogue 19, for instance, both Ochinus and Spiritus condemn the 'tritheism' of Biandrata, Matteo Gribaldi and Valentino Gentile;[110] Ochinus also denounces in unequivocal terms Lelio Sozzini's interpretation of the prologue to John's Gospel, while Spiritus gradually drops his objections to the pre-existence of the Logos in favour of a more conservative Arianism.[111] Ochinus' defence of orthodox soteriology is a good deal less robust, however. At several points in volume 1 of the *Dialogi*, he actually concedes ground in this area to Jacobus Judaeus – something which did not escape the notice of the Zurich divines. Thus in dialogue 6, he appears to modify his language

---

[110] *Dialogi XXX*, II, pp. 46–7.

[111] After his death Ochino came to be regarded as a pioneer of antitrinitarianism, but this was a judgement made very much in the light of his dismissal by the Zurich authorities. Ochino's published works prior to the *Dialogi XXX* contain few references to the Trinity, but that does not mean he was a closet antitrinitarian: Reformed theologians in general fought shy of the question until forced to address it by the Servetus affair. Furthermore, Ochino was examined by Calvin shortly after leaving Italy and found to be orthodox so far as the Trinity was concerned (*CO*, XI, no. 462). On the other hand, during the early 1560s the anti-Nicene faction among the Polish Reformed claimed to have Ochino's support for their views (see Stanisław Sarnicki to Christopher Thretius, 24 April 1563 [*CO*, XX, no. 3938]). In his preface to dialogues 19 and 20 – dedicated to the Lithuanian magnate Mikołaj Radziwiłł, who was himself sympathetic to antitrinitarianism – Ochino attempted to scotch such rumours: 'Nonnulli nulla a me data occasione, incipiebant non solum suspectum habere me, verumetiam a me eam [the Trinity] non credi dictitare, quae me res coegit eorum errorem ostendere' (*Dialogi XXX*, II, p. 6). For that reason, Rotondò is probably right to caution against attributing antitrinitarian views to Ochino prior to his expulsion from Zurich (see 'Atteggiamenti', p. 1006; 'Sulla diffusione', p. 100; Sozzini, *Opere*, p. 152, n. 13). At the same time, it is clear from the contents of the *Dialogi* that Ochino had taken note of the criticisms directed against Nicene orthodoxy by some of his fellow exiles. Bitterness at his treatment by the Reformed establishment may then have pushed him into a closer association with the nascent antitrinitarian movement during the final months of his life. In a letter to Bullinger dated 7 October 1566, Girolamo Zanchi reported that in Poland Ochino had come out openly as a 'Servetian', citing as his source the former minister to the Italian conventicle in Pińczów, Giorgio Negri (StAZ E II 356, 814; Schiess, III, no. 1). Ochino died at the home of the antitrinitarian Anabaptist Niccolò Paruta in Moravia in late 1564 or early 1565 (D. Caccamo, *Eretici italiani in Moravia, Polonia, Transilvania (1558–1611)* (Florence, 1970), p. 213).

on the atonement in order to accommodate some of the points made by his adversary:

> Christ did not come in order to change him [God], but in order to ensure that the divine decrees would be fulfilled. He did this by taking away the sins that prevented us from being saved and revealing the divine goodness to us, so that, caught up in God's love, we would be sorry for having offended him. Jesus therefore came to bring about the change in us that was needed, rather than to change God, who never ceased to love us and to desire that we should enjoy eternal life. Christ did not come so that by his death he might move God to show mercy to us; because God is the very essence of clemency, mercy and love, he had no need to be so moved. Rather, he came to move us to take possession of the mercy that was offered us.[112]

Elsewhere he accepts that Christ's death was not a precondition for the forgiveness of sins, arguing instead that it was designed to demonstrate God's love for humanity.[113]

On occasion Ochino also slips over into open criticism of the Reformed churches, and in particular of the Reformed clergy. In the preface to dialogue 25, he warns magistrates to be on their guard lest a 'new papacy' arise in Reformed lands from the ruins of the old;[114] in the dialogue itself, Ochinus condemns those who, while ostensibly teaching

---

[112] *Dialogi XXX*, I, pp. 165–6: 'Non venit ... Christus ut eum [Deum] mutaret, sed ut efficeret ut divina decreta reipsa sortirentur eventum, tollendo peccata, quae nos saluti prohibebant, nobisque divinam bonitatem aperiendo, ut Dei amore captus poeniteret eum offendisse. Venit igitur Iesus ut nos mutaret, quibus id opus erat: non Deum, qui nos ad aeternam vitam amare nunquam intermisit. Quinimo non adeo venit Christus, ut morte sua Deum ad tribuendam nobis misericordiam commoveret: quandoquidem cum sit Deus ipsa clementia, misericordia, charitas, nihil opus erat ut commoveretur. Sed ideo venit ut nosipsos ad capiendam nostri misericordiam commoveret.' Compare ibid., p. 208: 'Fatendum ... est Messiam placaturum esse iram Dei, non quia sit eum mutaturus, et ex irato placatum redditurus: sed quia sit nos mutaturus, ita ut ex improbis Deique inimicis bonis [sic] sit et eius amicos effecturus.'

[113] Ibid., p. 191: '[Jacobus]: ... si pendebat Christi satisfactio, qua pro peccatis nostris functus est, a gratuita acceptione Dei, non fuit necessaria mors Christi, quippe cum posset Deus vel unam Christi precationem pro sua benignitate loco idoneae pro peccatis nostris satisfactionis accipere.

Ochinus: Est ita, sed Christi mortem nominatim elegit, ut is moriendo maiorem charitatem exereret: fueruntque fructus maiores amoris.'

[114] Ibid., II, pp. 283–4: 'Et quoniam temporibus nostris vidimus et videmus divinam quandam miramque Ecclesiarum Christi reformationem, et ego ne in eis novi Papae existant timeo, exhortor cum omnes, tum in primis magnos et potentes, ut sapiant, et oculos apertos habeant, neve novum Papatum surgere permittant. Nam si parvulum illud cornu, quod vidit Daniel, videlicet Episcopus Romanus ecclesiam Christi demoliri, omnesque principes Christianos sibi subiicere potuit, idem posset et aliquis ministrorum nostrorum facere.'

the all-sufficiency of scripture, insist that it still requires explanation and commentary.[115] According to Ochinus, the inevitable consequence of such claims is the corruption of the church by false doctrine and the exaltation of human authorities, such as the Fathers, over the word of God.[116] Similarly, in his preface to dialogue 26, Ochino voices the fear that the Reformed churches, like the papacy before them, may succumb to the blandishments of Satan. Noting that some Reformed ministers may be tempted to usurp Christ's dominion, causing 'a new Antichrist' to arise, he urges the remainder to resist their ambitions, 'in the knowledge that we are all earthly men, not heavenly gods, and that our words, insofar as they are ours, are not oracles, but lies'.[117] The implication of Ochino's comments is clear: the Reformed have begun to reproduce within their churches the structures of authority which, in Catholicism, have led to the most grotesque distortions of biblical teaching. Elsewhere in the Dialogi XXX, Ochinus' interlocutors redirect charges that were the staple fare of anti-Catholic polemic – the abandonment of scripture for tradition, and the exclusion of the laity from effective participation in the life of the church – against the Reformed themselves. In dialogue 22, for example, Meschinus accuses the Reformed of acting in direct contradiction to the teaching of Paul, who in 1 Corinthians 14 recommends that contentious issues be settled in 'spiritual colloquies' in which all members of the church are given an opportunity to have their say. Instead, he claims, religious authority has been concentrated in the hands of a learned, clerical elite, with dire consequences:

> What the minister judges to be true and teaches, he thinks all others should believe as an article of faith. If anyone contradicts him, or does not subscribe unconditionally to what he teaches, that person is a heretic. [Ministers] write down and have published what they

---

[115] Ibid., p. 287.

[116] Ochinus dismisses appeals to the Fathers on the grounds that all of them erred in their interpretation of scripture and that many works are falsely attributed to them (ibid., p. 301).

[117] Ibid., p. 316: 'Iam quia Christi Ecclesiam video nonnisi ab Antichristiana eversam fuisse et ne idem nostris quoque ecclesiis usuveniat timeo, videlicet ne dum evertendo Antichristi regno incumbimus, existat ex nostris aliquis, qui erepto Christi sceptro et corona, eius dominatum sibi vendicet, occupatoque solio ecclesias nostras evertat, earumque novus Antichristus evadat, exhortor cum Paulo [Acts 20:18–35] et meipsum et caeteros omnes ut arrecti vigilesque operam diligenter navemus, ut Christum, unicum caput nostrum defendamus, eiusque solius verbis fidem sine ulla dubitatione praestemus: ac quisquis se caput facere, et Christi locum invadere conetur, huic resistamus, repugnemus, et audenter confidenterque contradicamus, scientes nos omnes esse homines terrenos, non deos caelestes: nostraque verba, ut nostra sunt, esse non oracula, sed mendacia.'

have dreamed up at night, and believe that their writings and words are to be taken as oracles. Neither is there any hope that they will recant or submit to the authority of their church. They want the church to believe what they say, rather than to believe what the church says, which is nothing other than to want to be popes and earthly gods, and to exercise a tyranny over the consciences of men, and to be lords of the faith of those who belong to the church, and to want what they say to be believed ... .[118]

According to Jacobus Judaeus, those who dare to question the clergy's decisions are likely to find themselves the targets of slander, invective or worse.[119] As Papanus notes towards the end of dialogue 25: 'Truly you will soon be bigger scholastics than us and will have more earthly gods than there ever were popes among the papists – and more wicked and cruel ones than ours were.'[120]

These criticisms are reiterated, with specific reference to the Zurich church, in Ochino's last known work, the *Dialogo della prudenza humana*, written in Nuremberg in early 1564.[121] Here Ochino denounces

---

118 Ibid., p. 269: 'Quod minister verum esse iudicat, docetque, id censet omnibus aliis credendum esse tanquam caput fidei. Quod si quis contradicit, neque illa citra ullam conditionem fidem adhibet, is haereticus est. Denique quod noctu somniarunt, id cartis mandant, excudique curant, suaque scripta et verba pro oraculis haberi volunt. Neque est quod eos speres unquam recantaturos, aut sese ecclesiae suae subiecturos. Volunt ut ecclesia, ipsorum, non ipsi ecclesiae arbitrio credant: id quod non est nihil aliud quam se quosdam Papas terrenosque deos esse velle, et in hominum conscientias tyrannidem exercere, ac dominos esse fidei eorum qui sunt in ecclesia, velleque ut ipsorum arbitratu credant.' Eusebius makes a similar point in dialogue 27 (ibid., pp. 374–5).

119 Ibid., I, p. 114: 'Si quis fraudem detegere, verumque aperire conatur, protinus sophistam esse dictitant, et scholasticum quendam, imperitum, indoctum, curiosum, et rerum novarum inventorem, ut sibi famem honoremque conciliet, dum se plus caeteris sapere vult. Postremo dicent esse et stultum et haereticum, atque ita vice responsionis ad argumenta quibus oppugnaveris eorum errores, evoment tota plaustra conviciorum, unde deinde calumniae et persecutiones existant.'

120 Ibid., p. 303: 'Verum brevi magis scholastici eritis quam nos, et plures terrenos deos habebitis quam unquam Papae fuerunt apud Papanos, eosque nostris sceleratores et crudeliores.' Ochino's anti-clericalism and anti-intellectualism are again reminiscent of Castellio. See C. Gilly, 'Das Sprichwort <<Die Gelehrten die Verkehrten>> oder der Verrat der Intellektuellen im Zeitalter der Glaubensspaltung', in Rotondò, *Forme e destinazione*, pp. 229–375; summarized in Gilly, 'Das Sprichwort << Die Gelehrten, die Verkehrten>> in der Toleranzliteratur des 16. Jahrhunderts', in J.-G. Roth and S. Verheus (eds), *Anabaptistes et dissidents au XVIe siècle* (Baden-Baden, 1984), pp. 159–72. Gilly maintains that anti-intellectualism, prominent in the early evangelical *Flugschriften*, was subsequently repudiated by mainstream Protestants (among them Bullinger), to become instead a feature of radical polemic against the Reformed establishment.

121 A copy of this text, dated 1572, was published by the 18th-century antiquary J.G. Schelhorn in his *Ergötzlichkeiten aus der Kirchenhistorie und Literatur* (3 vols, Ulm, 1764), III, pp. 2009–35. Philip McNair claims to have identified an autograph manuscript of the *Dialogo* in British Library Additional Ms. 28568, fols 13ʳ–22ʳ; a Latin translation

Bullinger as the 'pope' of Zurich, accusing the *Antistes* ('no friend of foreigners and especially of Italians') of engineering his dismissal.[122] According to Ochino, his treatment at the hands of his former colleagues belies their claim to represent the true church and identifies them rather with the 'synagogues of Satan' which 'being full of errors, do not want to be shaken up, lest they be unmasked'.[123] When his interlocutor Human Wisdom ('prudenza humana') criticizes him for failing in the *Dialogi XXX* to be sufficiently vocal in his support for the orthodox interpretation of the issues debated, Ochino responds with what amounts to a defence of the 'modo accademico'; truth, he claims, is strong enough in itself to prevail over error and does not require the assistance of 'many words' to do so.[124] According to Ochino, the real reason the Reformed wish to silence him is that they fear that his criticisms, though expressed 'discreetly' ('destramente'), will undermine their comfortable worldly positions ('turbar la lor pace mondana').[125]

On a doctrinal level, Ochino hints more openly than ever before at his opposition to the doctrines of double predestination and imputed righteousness, coming close to endorsing views articulated by Jacobus Judaeus in the first volume of the *Dialogi XXX*.[126] He now even seems

---

of the work (in the hand of Samuel, son of Konrad Pellikan) is held in StAZ E II 367, 333–48. After examining these two contemporary manuscripts, I no longer accept that the differences between the British Library text and the version published by Schelhorn are as significant as McNair would have us believe ('Apology', pp. 370–72).

[122] BL Additional Ms. 28568, fol. 20[r]: 'Ne debba dicio alcun maravigliarsi [that Bullinger urged the Zurich council to banish Ochino], in pero che glie poco amico de forestieri et spetialmente degl' italiani ... Et perch[e] fui eletto a esser ministro de lucarnesi, per la grande instantia che feceno, ma contra'l suo volere, mi ha sempre perseguitato, et non per altro, seno perche io non l'ho adorato per un Dio se ben l'ho sempre honorato et reverito quanto era giusto et conveniente.'

[123] Ibid., fol. 16[r]: '... le sinagoghe di satan come quelle che sono piene di errori, non voglian esser agitate, acio non sien scuperte. Si difendan con le armi col fuoco, con le persequutioni, esilii et false calunnie.' There are echoes here of language used by Ochino in his earlier anti-papal works. Compare *Galati*, fol. 21[r]: 'Si come Maumeth non vuol che la sua dottrina sia disputata, accio non sieno scoperti li suoi inganni; cosí Antichristo non vuol che si predichi la verita dello evangelio accio non sieno scoperti li suoi tradimenti.'

[124] BL Additional Ms. 28568, fol. 16[r]: 'La verita non ha bisogno di molte parole si come'l mendacio, in pero che la verita per se stessa si sostenta, si difende, resiste, supera et trionfa.' Compare *La terza parte delle prediche di M. Bernardino Occhino* (n.p, n.d.), sig. Ccc6[r], where Ochino argues that even those who are secure in the true faith should seek to 'chiarirsi et di crescere sempre in lume, certeza et chiarezza'. This path presents no dangers 'perche la verità quanto è piu discussa, tanto piu resplende.'

[125] BL Additional Ms. 28568, fol. 20[r].

[126] He envisages his opponents deliberating as follows: '[Ochino] dice anco che Dio non ha determinato di dannar i reprovati, sensa preveder i lor peccati si come noi diciamo. Et adduce ragioni si potenti, che lui proprio non le puo solvere, si che puo ognun pensar come le solveremo noi. Mostra chiaramente contra la nostra pia et santa opinione, che

ready to accept the Zurichers' interpretation of the *Dialogi*, as a covert assault on orthodox teaching. Some might say, he concedes, that he ought to have confronted his opponents' 'false opinions' openly, rather than posing as their defender. However, it was God's will that he should adopt the approach that he chose, in order that the pride and intolerance of the Reformed leadership might be demonstrated with greater force. If the doctrines espoused by the Reformed are true, Ochino maintains, he can have done them no harm in criticizing them. If, on the other hand, they are false, his opponents should be grateful to him for uncovering their errors. He himself is not to be blamed if the arguments that he cites in defence of orthodoxy fail to stand up to scrutiny; rather, the fault lies with those who insist that 'errors be defended as if they were the truth'.[127] In hindsight, Ochino views his expulsion from Zurich as a work of God, as it has allowed him to make public his disillusionment with the mainstream Reformed

---

nissun sara cruciato nel inferno sensa sua colpa. Dice esser una bestemia el dir, si come diciam noi, che l'huomo pechi di necessita et continuamente, etiam quando fa delle opere buone: et mostra cio con ragioni si efficaci, che noi per aiutarci non haviamo altro rimedio, se non dir mal di lui. Dice, che noi faciamo li huomini peggio che bestie, inpero che dove le bestie per non haver liberta non peccano, noi voliamo, che gl'huomini sien sensa liberta, et con tutto questo pechino.

Mostra et con ragioni potentissime, che noi faciamo Dio autor di tutti peccati che si son fatti, si fanno et faranno, se ben ci vergognamo di dir apertamente una si enorme bestemmia.

Non vuol consentir alla nostra santissima chiesa, laqual fa profession di creder che li huomini pechin sensa lor colpa.

Dice, che'l dir, si come diciam noi, che Christo sia venuto, non per liberarci da peccati, ma per far [che restando noi] in essi, non ci sieno impu[tati, è una pessima et diabolica dottrina et her]esia. Et cosi anco dice che'l [credere quel] che [crediamo] noi, cioe, che Christo sia venuto, morto in croce, et risuscitato, non per farci in verita giusti, ma lassandoci nelle nostre ingiustitie, per far che le non ci sieno imputate, ma ci sia imputata la sua giustitia, e un altra horrenda bestemmia.

Dice anco esser pessima heresia, el dir quel che diciamo, cioe che'l peccato originale accompagni li eletti infin a morte' (ibid., fol. 21r-v).

127 Ibid., fols 16v–17r: 'E ben vero, che qualcun potrebbe dire, che io non dovevo in modo alcuno favorir le lor false opinioni, ma liberamente alla scuperta danarle. Ma Dio ha voluto cosi, acio che ognun veda, che son si superbi, che non possan tollerar di esser ripresi de lor errori: etiam che'l si usi somma desterita, artificio, rispetto et gentileza si che puo ciascun considerar, quel che harebben fatto, se rigidamente alla scuperta, io havesse dannata la lor falsa et heretica dottrina. Non possan anco dannarmi, perche ho impugnate le lor opinioni, imperoche se le son vere, per impugnarle non ho lor nociuto ma giovato, et se le son false, doverebben ringratiarmi, se amassen la verita, poi che ho scuperti i lor errori. Ma essi in luogo della verita, aman le lor commodita, et in luogo del cercar l'honor d'iddio, cercan la gloria del mondo. Et se le ragioni che io adduco, contra le lor opinioni, son potenti, et le risposte invalide, questo non e per mio defetto, imperoche le ragioni sono insolubili, ma tutto e per lor colpa poiche voglian che li errori sien defesi per verita.'

churches in a way that would have been impossible had he remained in his post.[128]

Statements of this sort have led one scholar to describe the *Dialogo della prudenza humana* as an 'interpretative key' to Ochino's Zurich works.[129] That is perhaps to overstate the case: it is likely that to some extent Ochino was rationalizing his earlier conduct in the light of his present situation, as he had done following his apostasy from Catholicism.[130] On the other hand, the fact that in this final work Ochino makes specific, and supportive, reference to the criticisms directed at the Zurich church by disputants in the *Dialogi XXX* would seem to rule out any interpretation of the *Dialogi* as merely a well-intentioned, if at times poorly executed, defence of Reformed orthodoxy. Rather, the work suggests a theologian ill at ease with many aspects of orthodox teaching and with what he perceived to be the autocratic style of the Reformed leadership. At the same time, Ochino remained a member of the Zurich clerical establishment, with both the privileges and the responsibilities that that status carried with it. The ambiguity of his position – as both official defender and private critic of Reformed orthodoxy – is reflected in the structure and content of the *Dialogi XXX*. It was the Zurich authorities' response to the work that determined which of those roles he would ultimately adopt.

iii. The wider context of 'heresy' in Zurich's Italian community

Ochino's case acquired special importance in the eyes of Bullinger and his colleagues because it was seen not in isolation, but against the backdrop of growing unease about the spread of heterodox ideas in Zurich's Italian-speaking community as a whole. The presence of Lelio Sozzini in Zurich gave rise to fears that the Locarnesi – whom Bullinger had defended so vigorously from the charge of Anabaptism – might be exposed to views at variance with Reformed orthodoxy, especially antitrinitarianism. Such fears may explain the timing of Giulio da

---

[128] Ibid., fols 21ᵛ–2ʳ.

[129] B. Nicolini, *Il pensiero di Bernardino Ochino*, in *Atti della Reale Accademia Pontaniana di scienze morali e politiche*, 95 (1938), pp. 171–268 (207). Contrast Hassinger, *Acontius*, pp. 100; 109.

[130] See his *Responsio ad Mutium Justinopolitanum*, published in Benrath, *Ochino*, pp. 289–94, and Ochino, *Dialogi sette*, pp. 130–36. Here Ochino claims that he refrained from preaching openly against the papacy in Italy in order to protect himself and to avoid giving offence to his hearers. In private, however, 'esplicai el vero a molti' (*Dialogi sette*, p. 132). In a letter to Pellikan written following Ochino's flight from Italy, Pietro Merbelio provides confirmation of the latter's 'Nicodemism' (see ZB Ms. F 47, 64ᵛ).

Milano's denunciation of Sozzini to Bullinger in spring 1555: certainly, in his letter to the *Antistes* of 4 November that year Giulio urged Bullinger to take steps to protect Zurich's newly established Italian church from Lelio's harmful influence.[131] Three months earlier, the minister, elders and deacons of the Italian church in Geneva had written to their Locarnese counterparts in similar vein, to enjoin them to follow the example of the other churches 'of the nation' in repelling heresy. In their letter, the Genevans suggested that the two congregations form 'a firm confederation and alliance, so that united we may resist the strength of such an enemy, which like a roaring lion roams around seeking to devour Christ's flock and to rob it of the true and highest good, and of its eternal heavenly inheritance'.[132]

Replying on 1 September 1555, the Locarnese elders expressed the pious hope that membership of the Zurich church would protect them from exposure to evil and scandalous doctrines, adding that if problems should arise 'we will with confidence have recourse to you as elder and sincere brothers and members of the same body'.[133] However, of the Italian exiles who were attracted to Zurich over the coming years, a significant number are known to have held views at variance with Zwinglian orthodoxy. Some of the new arrivals were closely linked to

---

131 Schiess, I, no. 296.

132 FA Orelli, 8.7, no. 19: 'Noi vediamo, fratelli, che Satana nostro perpetuo avversario è hoggi piu che mai arrabbiato et infuriato contra le sante Chiese di Christo, ne cessa punto d'usare ogni arte, e tentar per tutte le vie e modi, ch'ei sa e puo, d'impedire, interrompere, o almen ritardare il corso del santo Evangelio, et oscurar la gloria del nostro Iddio, e la sua verità. Onde à noi tutti dal canto nostro s'appartiene opporsigli quanto per noi si puo, e procurare con ogni maggior diligentia che non gli riesca il disegno. E dove egli è padre et autor di sette et heresie, ne cerca altro che confondere e turbare ogni cosa: noi à l'incontro debbiamo con l'unirci, ristrignerci, et intenderci insieme, e con lo star d'un comune accordo vigilanti, aiutandoci, consigliandoci, avvertendoci, et inanimandoci l'un l'altro, fargli tal resistenza, che i suoi malvagii consiglii e macchinamenti riescano vani e senza effetto. Noi abbiamo l'esempio de le republiche e comunità mondane, lequali si collegano e confederano insieme per mantenere i loro stati caduchi e mutabili contra chiunque volesse occuparli, ò volesse privarle di qualche lor bene ò commodità terrene e temporale. Con quanto maggior cura dunque debbiamo ingegnarci noi altri d'haver tra noi una salda confederatione e collegamento, per opporci unitamente a la forza d'un tale e tanto nemico, che come ruggente leone va continuamente à torno, cercando di devorare il gregge di Christo, e spogliarlo del vero e sommo bene, e de la celeste eterna heredita?'

133 Ibid., no. 20: 'In fin'a hora per gratia de Dio (come anche speriamo ch'habbi a esser nel avenire) la chiesa nostra quanto alla dottrina, e sincera, se bene quanto alla vita e imperfetta. Speriamo anche che'l Demonio non hara forza di seminar tra noi dottrina trista, ne scandalosa, massime essendo membra di questa tanto sincera, pura, santa et in Christo stabil chiesa Tigurina. Et quando (il che Dio non permette) occoresse qualche spiritual besogno, confidentamente haremo refugio a voi come a maggiori et sinceri fratelli et membra d'un istesso corpo.'

Lelio Sozzini. They included his brother Camillo, who was obliged to leave Zurich in the wake of Ochino's expulsion,[134] and his nephew Fausto, who visited the city in 1558 and again following Lelio's death in May 1562.[135] Ochino was probably familiar with Fausto Sozzini's *Explicatio primae partis primi capitis Iohannis* (first published in 1568, but circulating in manuscript form some years before that), as Spiritus appears to allude to it in dialogue 19 of the *Dialogi XXX*.[136] In turn, he may have influenced Fausto's understanding of the atonement; decades later, Sozzini noted approvingly that in his dialogues Ochino had challenged the received notion that Christ made satisfaction for sins through his blood, teaching rather the freely bestowed forgiveness of transgressions by God.[137]

Another exile with close links to the Sozzini family was the Sienese merchant Dario Scala, whose presence in Zurich is attested as early as September 1555, when he stood godfather to the son of Hans Ziegler.[138] Scala's heterodoxy is beyond dispute: around 1560 he made an antitrinitarian confession of faith before the church of Chiavenna which, according to Rotondò, bears the clear imprint of Lelio Sozzini's ideas.[139] Word of his radical leanings had reached even Bullinger, who in

---

[134] See section iv below.

[135] Rotondò, 'Atteggiamenti', p. 1000.

[136] Sozzini, *Opere*, p. 344, n. 82.

[137] See Fausto Sozzini to Martin Vadovita, 14 June 1598: 'certe in dialogis illis [the *Dialogi XXX*], quorum non pauca exempla iam diu in ipsa Polonia mihi videre contigit, est sententia ista aperte expressa et inculcata: quae breviter est, Christum quidem sanguine suo delevisse atque expiasse peccata nostra, sed alia tamen ratione, quam ea quae vulgo recepta est, ut scilicet divinae iustitiae sanguinis sui fusione id persolverit, quod ei propter nostra peccata debebamus, seu pro nobis peccatisque nostris satisfecerit; quippe cum nec id ullo modo opus esset, nec nostrorum peccatorum poenas Deus a quoquam repetere, seu (ut sic loquar) debita cum ipso nostra exigere voluerit, sed ea tamen liberaliter remittere ac condonare, quemadmodum universae Sacrae Literae apertissime testantur' (*Fausti Socini Senensis opera omnia in Duos Tomos distincta* (2 vols, Amsterdam, 1656), I, p. 475). Compare Fausto's comments on the atonement in *De Jesu Christo servatore* (1578) with the analysis of Ochino's views given in sections I and II above: 'Tantum abesse ut in reconciliatione hac peragenda Christus nobis Deum placaverit; ut potius eum iam placatum ostenderit, et ab eo iam placato ad nos, qui adhuc illius inimici eramus, sibi reconciliandos missus fuerit' (*Opera*, I, p. 137).

[138] Stadtarchiv Zürich VIII, C.19, Taufbuch St Peter 1553–1690 (10 September 1555). Following the death of Lelio's father Mariano in 1556, the Ziegler family helped organize credit for the Sozzini in Switzerland, using Mariano's legacy as security (see G. Zucchini, *Celso e Camillo Sozzini nel gruppo ereticale familiare: Nuovi documenti in Svizzera (1561–1570)* (Bologna, 1981), p. 20).

[139] Sozzini, *Opere*, pp. 364–70 (with the text of Scala's confession). See the analysis of the confession in Rotondò, 'Sulla diffusione', pp. 95–8. Scala was the bearer of letters dated 10 and 17 July 1558 from Lelio Sozzini (currently in Tübingen) to Bullinger (Sozzini, *Opere*, nos 44 and 45).

a letter to Johannes Fabricius dated 27 September 1560 asked his Rhaetian colleague to confirm whether (as was rumoured) Scala had been expelled from Chiavenna the previous year as a follower of Servetus.[140] Fabricius' reply suggests a further intriguing connection: the Chur minister denied any knowledge of Scala's antitrinitarianism, but noted that a certain Ludovicus, long resident in Zurich, was an ardent Servetian.[141] The Ludovicus mentioned was probably the same 'Ludwig' of Bologna whose name appears in the 1558 survey of Zurich's foreign population and whom I am inclined to identify with the notorious radical Ludovico Fieri (known from other sources to have spent ten months in Zurich after fleeing Italy in late 1557).[142] Fieri, who prior to his exile had developed strong ties with the Sozzini family and who was censured by the Rhaetian synod in June 1561 for ridiculing the orthodox doctrine of the Trinity,[143] visited Zurich again in March 1562, in an apparently successful attempt to convince Bullinger of his return to orthodoxy.[144] Any such change of heart proved shortlived, however: by the end of the 1560s, Fieri had emerged as a key figure within the nexus of Italian exiles that was responsible for introducing advanced antitrinitarian ideas to Moravia and Transylvania at this time.[145]

Among those Italians who visited Zurich during the late 1550s were several other figures of dubious orthodoxy. They included Filippo Valentini, who later fell foul of the church of Chiavenna,[146] and Isabella Bresegna, to whom Ochino dedicated his *Disputa della Cena* in 1561.

---

[140] StAZ E II 373, 203 (Schiess, II, no. 276).

[141] Fabricius to Bullinger, 30 September 1560 (StAZ E II 376, 22; Schiess, II, no. 277).

[142] The 'Cesar' also mentioned in the 1558 survey may be Fieri's brother-in-law Cesare Cevenini, who accompanied him into exile. The main problem with both identifications is that the survey describes Ludwig of Bologna as unmarried (Meyer, *Locarnergemeinde*, II, p. 388). For further details of Fieri's early career, see Dall'Olio, *Eretici e Inquisitori*, pp. 356–61.

[143] Fieri was among the witnesses to the division of Mariano Sozzini's estate in Siena on 19 December 1556 (Zucchini, *Celso*, pp. 11; 20). On his difficulties with the Reformed church of Graubünden, see Trechsel, *Antitrinitarier*, II, p. 429; and Cantimori, *Eretici*, pp. 282–3.

[144] StAZ E II 375, 707; StAZ E II 378, 1767 (Schiess, II, nos 422 and 430).

[145] M. Firpo, *Antitrinitari nell'Europa orientale del '500: Nuovi testi di Szymon Budny, Niccolò Paruta e Iacopo Paleologo* (Florence, 1977), pp. 9–10; 212–14.

[146] Serrai, *Gesner*, p. 366. In September 1561 the papal nuncio in Switzerland, Giovanni Antonio Volpe, noted that Valentini had been staying with Martino Muralto in Zurich for the past eight months (Karl Fry (ed.), *Giovanni Antonio Volpe Nunzius in der Schweiz: Dokumente. Band 1: Die erste Nunziatur 1560–1565* (Florence, 1935), p. 145 [no. 286]). On Valentini's troubled relations with the church of Chiavenna, see S. Lentolo, *Commentarii conventus synodalis convocati mense Iulii 1571 in oppido Chiavenna de excommunicatione Hieronymi Turriani, Pluriensis ministri, Nicolai Camulii et Camilli Sozzini* (Bürgerbibliothek Bern, A 93, 7), fol. 25ᵛ.

Although described by Benedetto Nicolini as a 'Calvinist', prior to her exile Bresegna had been linked with the radical Valdesian Juan de Villafranca and with the antitrinitarian Anabaptists Girolamo Busale and Giovanni Laureto, to whom she gave refuge in her house in Piacenza during the late 1540s.[147]

The same ambiguity surrounds the Roman exile Francesco Betti, who was periodically resident in Zurich during the late 1550s and early 1560s.[148] Betti enjoyed close relations with the Zurich divines (especially Johannes Wolf) and his published works are impeccably orthodox in tone, as even Cantimori acknowledges.[149] In his *Lettera al Marchese di Pescara*, written in Zurich in October 1557 in defence of his recent apostasy from Catholicism, Betti praised the doctrine, form of worship and discipline of the Swiss Reformed churches, and presented an entirely conventional account of justification by faith and the atonement in which the sins of the elect were described as being washed away and God's anger as being placated by Christ's saving death.[150] Recently, however, it has been shown that he had strong ties with the Sozzini family: Betti took charge of Lelio Sozzini's papers following Fausto Sozzini's return to Italy towards the end of 1563, and was subsequently in correspondence with both Fausto and the latter's uncle Camillo.[151] During the 1570s he worked as a corrector for Perna in Basle, assisting with the publication of Castellio's *Dialogi quatuor* and forging links with the spiritualist radical Francesco Pucci.[152]

Betti was accompanied to Zurich in July 1557 by Giacomo Aconcio, an exile from Trent and former secretary to Cardinal Cristoforo Madruzzo, the governor of Milan. Like Betti's *Lettera*, Aconcio's early

---

[147] Stella, *Anabattismo*, pp. 30–35; Firpo, '<<Ioanne Valdessio>>', pp. 92, 98.

[148] Betti appears in the April 1558 survey of foreigners in Zurich as Ochino's house-guest (see Chapter 2:iv above). He seems to have left Zurich later that year, returning some time in 1563 (*DBI*, IX, 717–18).

[149] Cantimori, *Eretici*, pp. 287–91.

[150] *Lettera di Francesco Betti Romano, all'Illustrissimo et Eccelentissimo S. Marchese di Pescara suo padrone, ne la quale da conte à sua Eccellenza de la cagione perche licentiato si sia dal suo servigio* (n.p. [Basle], 1557), p. 31. The copy of this work in the Zurich Zentralbibliothek contains the handwritten dedication, 'A M. Rodolpho Gualthero suo cariss. Fratello Giovan Vuolphio d.'

[151] See the letter from Betti to Camillo Sozzini of 30 June 1570 (V. Marchetti and G. Zucchini (eds), *Aggiunte all'Epistolario di Fausto Sozzini 1561–1568* (Warsaw, 1982), pp. 150–52).

[152] A. Rotondò, 'Pietro Perna e la vita ereticale e religiosa di Basilea fra il 1570 e il 1580', in *Studi e ricerche*, pp. 273–391 (316–17); H. Guggisberg, 'Pietro Perna, Fausto Sozzini und die *Dialogi quatuor* Sebastian Castellios', in *Studia bibliographica in honorem Herman de la Fontaine Verwey* (Amsterdam, 1967), pp. 171–201 (193); Gilly, 'Zensur', p. 180.

Somma brevissima della dottrina christiana (published in 1558, but probably written some time before its author's public conversion to Protestantism) is entirely consonant with Reformed orthodoxy, particularly in its understanding of the function of the law, salvation and the sacraments. Thus (following Bullinger) Aconcio describes the sacraments as confirming and 'exercising' the faith of the elect,[153] and endorses wholeheartedly the doctrine of imputed justification, repudiating any suggestion of perfectionism: 'It is a thing certain that the regeneration preached by the papists, according to which man recovers the ability to fulfil the law of God and to earn eternal life, is not to be found in any man on earth'.[154]

After moving to England in 1559, however, Aconcio defended the dissident Dutch minister Adrian van Haemstede for pursuing a policy of conciliation with Mennonite Anabaptists, a stance which brought him into conflict with Nicolas des Gallars and the other leaders of the London stranger churches.[155] Aconcio reflected on these experiences in his best-known work, the *Stratagematum Satanae libri VIII*, which was published in Basle by Perna in 1564. In the *Stratagematum*, Aconcio elaborated Ochino's critique of Reformed confessionalism, identifying this as the root cause of the divisions which had afflicted the church since the Reformation and had left it vulnerable to Catholic attack.[156] As an alternative to current practice, he suggested that church members be required to assent only to those articles which scripture clearly specifies as necessary for salvation: the oneness of God; the distinction between Christ and the Father; the last judgment; the salvific mission of Christ; salvation by faith in Christ; the denial of salvation through another mediator or by means of good works; and the oneness of baptism.[157] He also argued for strict fidelity to the word of scripture as the only safeguard against error and a return to the corruptions of the papacy, rebuking Protestant writers for their reliance on the Fathers and other non-biblical authorities.[158] Like Ochino in the *Dialogi*, Aconcio condemned the Reformed clerical

---

153 Aconcio, *De methodo*, pp. 223–5; 250–51.

154 Ibid., p. 244. Compare Aconcio's comments on Romans 7 (ibid., pp. 227–8; 245–6).

155 Hassinger, *Acontius*, pp. 12–14.

156 Thus the Catholics may ask: 'Si unus Deus est, unus Christus, unum baptisma, una fides, quid sibi volunt ... haec tot confessionum nomina? Si est inter vos sententiarum consensio, si una fides, qui fit, ut non una sit vestrae omnium fidei confessio?' (*Stratagematum Satanae libri VIII* (Florence, 1946), ed. G. Radetti, p. 508).

157 Ibid., pp. 522–6.

158 Ibid., p. 256: '... optima nobis illa cautio videtur, ut quicquid ponatur tanquam cum divinis literis consentiens, eisdem etiam verbis ac loquendi formis, quibus Dei spiritus iis in literis est usus, exprimatur; alioqui fieri vix possit, quin aliquid de suo humanum

establishment for its high-handedness, intolerance and pride, and proposed that its will to dominate be offset by transferring control over doctrine, hitherto confined to the clergy, to the Christian community as a whole.[159] In conclusion, Aconcio warned his readers against assuming that the spirit of Antichrist was to found in the Roman church alone, arguing that it was inherent in fallen human nature:

> The papacy was not born in Rome, but has its origin from our first parents. There is none of us who does not nurse the papacy within their breast, from which it will certainly proceed at the earliest opportunity unless with great prudence we examine ourselves and exercise self-control – let this be understood by all who have ears![160]

It is usually assumed that the radical theological opinions of men like Lelio Sozzini, and even the more moderate criticisms of Ochino or Aconcio, were confined to a limited circle, with the bulk of Zurich's Italian-speaking community – the Locarnesi – remaining unaffected. That would certainly accord with what is known about the proselytizing methods of Sozzini and other Italian radicals, who were accustomed to concealing their adherence to advanced doctrinal positions in order to avoid both confrontation with the orthodox authorities and giving offence to 'weaker brethren'.[161] The suggestion that in Zurich dissident views were the property of a theological elite of 'adepti' is also supported by the fact that, following Ochino's dismissal, leading figures within the Locarnese community (specifically Taddeo Duno and Martino Muralto) went out of their way to distance themselves from the views expressed by Ochino in the *Dialogi XXX*, disclaiming any knowledge of their pastor's intention to publish the work and insisting that his preaching to date had been entirely orthodox in character.[162]

---

intrudet ingenium. Quod si accidat, propemodum immedicabilis sit error.' Elsewhere Aconcio insists that any confession to which church members are required to subscribe should, as far as possible, consist only of words and formulas 'quibus ipse Dei spiritus est usus', arguing (in terms reminiscent of Camillo Renato) that such a ban on extra-biblical language will act as a necessary check on 'hominis ingenium' (ibid., p. 518).

[159] Ibid., pp. 292–300; compare section ii above. Contact between Aconcio and Ochino did not end with the former's departure from Zurich in early 1558: in England, Aconcio supported Ochino's efforts to recover the income from his English benefices (see Ochino to Cecil, 25 August 1561 (*Calendar of State Papers, Foreign*, 23 vols (London, 1862–1950), 1561/2, no. 454); ZL, I, letters xvi, xxiv and xxxiii; Hassinger, *Acontius*, pp. 7–8 and 58–9).

[160] Aconcio, *Stratagematum*, p. 596. This passage recalls Curione's famous dictum, 'Non in sola Italia est Antichristus' (*Francisci Spierae, qui quod susceptam semel Evangelicae veritatis professionem abnegasset, damnassetque, in horrendam incidit desperationem historia* ... (Basle, 1550), sig. α2ᵛ).

[161] Rotondò, 'Atteggiamenti', pp. 1010–11; Sozzini, *Opere*, pp. 67–8.

[162] StAZ B II 125, 65; StAZ B VI 259, fol. 122ʳ.

On the other hand, all the indications are that Ochino and the exile community to which he ministered had formed a very close bond. It was to 'his' Locarnesi that Ochino dedicated the *Catechismo* in 1561, while in the *Dialogo della prudenza humana* he claimed that members of the congregation had rallied around him during the difficult days following his condemnation.[163] Despite the circumstances of Ochino's departure from Zurich, the Locarnesi continued to hold him in high esteem: as late as January 1566, Ochino is referred to as 'Ms. Bernardino di buona memoria' in the congregation's minutes.[164] In addition, two prominent members of the community, albeit originally foreigners – Guarnerio Castiglione and Antonio Mario Besozzi – have been identified as likely radical sympathizers. Castiglione, like Betti, had close connections with the Sozzini family, witnessed by the fact that he took charge of Camillo Sozzini's papers following the latter's departure from Zurich towards the end of 1563. Besozzi, meanwhile, was ordered to leave Zurich in December 1564 after an investigation into heretical remarks that he was alleged to have made at the fair of Zurzach earlier that year.[165] In conversation with a Florentine exile, Michele Pulliano, and a Genevan, Nicolas Denis (known as Le Fex), Besozzi was said to have denied the existence of original sin and to have claimed that it was possible to fulfil the demands of the Mosaic Law. Significantly, Pulliano claimed that Besozzi had cited John the Baptist's father Zacharias as a scriptural example of righteousness before the Law, just as Ochino (in the person of Jacobus Judaeus) and Castellio had done.[166]

Of particular interest are a series of statements taken up in the course of Besozzi's trial from Locarnesi who had been present at the incident in Zurzach (Lorenzo Pebbia, Evangelista Zanino, Bartolomeo Orelli and Bartolomeo Verzasca), as their testimonies are characterized by a marked reluctance to divulge any evidence that might serve to incriminate Besozzi. According to Pebbia, Besozzi would not concede that Christ died for all men, insisting, in line with orthodox teaching, that he died only for 'the believers' ('die gloübigen'). Similarly, in the accounts of Orelli and Zanino it is the Genevan Le Fex who presents the heterodox universalist view, and Besozzi who takes issue with it from an

---

163 BL Additional Ms. 28568, fol. 18ʳ.

164 FA Orelli, 8.2, fol. 19ᵛ; cited in Meyer, *Locarnergemeinde*, II, p. 182, n. 215.

165 Most of the documentation relevant to the case is located in StAZ A 350.1; see also StAZ B II 129, 26 (9 September 1564); StAZ B VI 259 (16 December 1564 / 15 January 1565), fols 166ᵛ–7ʳ. Detailed accounts of the Besozzi affair are to be found in Meyer, *Locarnergemeinde*, II, pp. 184–97; and Cantimori, *Eretici*, pp. 272–9. According to Socinian tradition, after Lelio Sozzini's death Besozzi held his papers in safe-keeping until Lelio's nephew Fausto was able to collect them (F. Sozzini, *Opere*, fol. **1ᵛ).

166 Cantimori, *Eretici*, pp. 275–6, n. 10.

orthodox standpoint.[167] Zanino also puts a positive gloss on Besozzi's supposed Pelagianism, which in his testimony resembles less an assertion of the possibility of righteousness under the law than an attempt to preserve human responsibility for sin against an extreme predestinarianism that would locate the ultimate cause of evil in the divine will.[168] Three of the Locarnesi interviewed – Zanino, Orelli and Pebbia – denied that Besozzi had ever spoken out in favour of the Dutch Anabaptist David Joris, as had been alleged.[169] The fourth, Bartolomeo Verzasca, acknowledged that Besozzi might have discussed religion with him in the past, but claimed (rather implausibly) not to recall what had been said in these conversations.[170]

From the testimonies cited above, it would seem that most Locarnesi were prepared at least to turn a blind eye to the presence of heterodox individuals within or on the fringes of their community. Significant in this context is the testimony of the incipient antitrinitarian Giorgio Biandrata, who following his flight from Geneva in May 1558 sought refuge in Zurich, only to have his overtures rebuffed first by Peter Martyr and then by Bullinger himself. Biandrata later claimed to have protested formally about his treatment by the Zurich authorities to Zurich's Italian church, implying that at least some of its members were sympathetic to his case.[171] Even Vermigli – who in respect of Biandrata adopted a hardline approach, insisting that he demonstrate his orthodoxy by subscribing to the strongly trinitarian confession of Geneva's Italian church – seems to have been prepared to offer dissenters attached to Zurich's Italian-speaking community a certain amount of leeway. In May 1558, he commended Lelio Sozzini to Calvin in glowing terms, although – according to one source at least – he had plenty of

---

[167] Zanino reports: 'Als der von Genff gsagt, Christus syge für jedermann gstorben, Anthwurt Marius, Es ist waar, er ist für alle gstorben, aber syn tod nützt allein die, so jnn jm glouben' (StAZ A 350.1).

[168] Ibid.: 'Evangelist Zanin von Luggaruß und allhie seßhafft seit, das under anderem Marius zů dem von Genff gsagt, Was wir menschen böses thůnd, das möchtend wir wol underlaßen, dann das böß von unns kompt, und heiße Gott uns nüdt böses thůn.'

[169] Ibid.: 'Hienebent sy all dryg einmündig, uff befragen hin der geordneten herren, gsagt, Das Jeörg Daviden halb, so zů Basel verbrendt worden, inn sollich reden nie gedacht worden. Und jnen nit witers, dann wie eins jedeß sag hievor stadt, hierumb zewüßen syge.'

[170] Cantimori, *Eretici*, p. 276, n. 11. Verzasca only agreed to testify in the case 'also, daß er sich aller verdachtlichey erledigt'.

[171] When Bullinger and Wolf confronted Ochino regarding these allegations, he informed them that the Locarnese church had received no correspondence from Biandrata and had not, to his knowledge, met to discuss the matter (Bullinger to Mikołaj Radziwiłł, 30 September 1561 [CO, XVIII, no. 3539]). In a letter dated 11 July 1558, Vermigli provided Calvin with a detailed account of his dealings with the Saluzzese exile (ibid., XVII, no. 2916); see also Cantimori, *Eretici*, p. 218.

reason to suspect that Lelio harboured antitrinitarian views.[172] Up to 1563, Zurich remained a relatively congenial environment for Italian dissidents, so long as they refrained from publicizing their opinions outside the exile community. Membership of the Zurich church was defined by outward conformity, not intellectual assent to its doctrines; as we have seen in the case of Lelio Sozzini, Bullinger was prepared to go to some lengths to ensure that tender consciences were accommodated. It took a public scandal, of the sort that accompanied the publication of the *Dialogi XXX*, to force him to rethink his approach.

iv. 'Latrina quam luce digniores':[173] the Zurich church's verdict on the *Dialogi XXX*

Initially, Bullinger was reluctant to accept that Ochino could be guilty of the errors attributed to him by critics of the *Dialogi XXX*. His response to Beza's denunciation of Ochino was consistent with the stance that he had adopted on previous occasions when confronted with evidence of deviation from orthodoxy by Italian exiles within his circle, such as Lelio Sozzini; his initial instinct was to interpret any apparent heretical lapse as a sign of weakness or misunderstanding, rather than malign intent. It was also hardly to be expected that Bullinger would rush to judgment in a sensitive case of this sort, which, handled wrongly, could do grave damage to the international reputation of the Zurich church.

In the *Dialogo della prudenza humana*, Ochino claimed that Bullinger had consistently opposed his presence in Zurich and had sought to block his appointment as the city's Italian minister,[174] but there is little evidence to substantiate either accusation; it was after all Bullinger, acting on behalf of the Locarnese exiles, who proposed that the Zurich council offer Ochino a preaching post in June 1555. Ochino's relations with his Zurich colleagues are poorly documented, but the few surviving references suggest that he was an esteemed and active member

---

[172] Sozzini, *Opere*, pp. 68–71. In a statement dated 1590, the judaizing antitrinitarian Matthias Vehe recalled hearing from Girolamo Zanchi that Lelio Sozzini had once criticized Vermigli's *Dialogus de utraque in Christo natura* (Zurich, 1561) in his presence, asserting that Christ possessed a single, human, nature. In Vehe's account, Zanchi claimed that Vermigli had overheard their conversation, but had failed to reprimand Sozzini for his remarks ('Matthias Vehe Glirius' Apology', published in R. Dán, *Matthias Vehe-Glirius: Life and Work of a radical antitrinitarian with his collected writings* (Budapest, 1982), pp. 284–5).

[173] The expression is Bullinger's (*Correspondance*, V, no. 370).

[174] BL Additional Ms. 28568, fol. 20r.

of the city's pastorate. It was with the full authority of the Zurich church that Ochino entered the lists against Joachim Westphal with his *Syncerae et verae doctrinae de Coena Domini defensio* in 1556 (Bullinger signalled the work's publication in a letter to Johann Travers dated 23 August).[175] His name also appears alongside those of Bullinger and Vermigli on a judgement issued by the Zurich church three years later in the divorce case of Galeazzo Caracciolo.[176] When the *Defensio* came in for criticism from Guillaume Farel, Pierre Viret and the Bernese *Antistes* Johannes Haller,[177] Bullinger made no effort (at least in public) to distance himself from the work.[178] Similarly, concerns about Ochino's *Dialogo del Purgatorio* related not so much to its doctrinal content as to the failure of Huldrych Zwingli the Younger, deacon at the Grossmünster, to secure authorization for his own German translation of the dialogue, which the Zurich council feared might be interpreted as defamatory by the Catholic Swiss.[179] Following Ochino's dismissal, it emerged that Bullinger had received complaints from outside Zurich about statements contained in the *Laberinti, Disputa* and *Catechismo*, but his reaction to those was again restrained: Ochino was simply warned not to publish any further works, either in Zurich or elsewhere, without the approval of the Zurich censor.[180] In later years the Zurich divines insisted that, prior to the publication of the *Dialogi*, they had been given no cause to suspect that Ochino was anything other than a loyal servant of their church.

In Chapter 1, I highlighted the patient manner in which the Zurichers responded to the problems put to them by the more radical Italian exiles, and related it to their inclusive vision of the church. It was that approach to dealing with dissent which enabled Bullinger and his colleagues to maintain good relations with heterodox members of Zurich's Italian community into the late 1550s and early 1560s. For evidence of these continuing links, one need look no further than Gesner's letter of

---

[175] Schiess, I, no. 319.

[176] The statement, dated 18 May 1559, is published in G. Zanchi, *De divortio* (*Opera*, VIII, 333).

[177] See CO, XVI, nos 2427; 2450; 2468.

[178] In his *Historia de origine et progressu Controversiae Sacramentariae de Coena Domini* ... (Zurich, 1563), Bullinger's colleague Ludwig Lavater mentions both of Ochino's Eucharistic works without adverse comment.

[179] See Bächtold, *Bullinger*, pp. 108–9, for references; also ZB Ms. J 287, fols 193r–5v.

[180] *Spongia adversus aspergines Bernardini Ochini, qua verae causae exponuntur, ob quas ille ab Urbe Tigurina est relegatus*, published in Hottinger, *Historia ecclesiastica*, IX, pp. 475–510 (410) and Schelhorn, *Ergötzlichkeiten*, III, pp. 2157–94. A manuscript copy of the *Spongia* is also to be found in StAZ E II 367, 349–74. All references are to Hottinger's text.

consolation to Dario and Cornelio Sozzini, which was written at the specific request of their brother Lelio,[181] or the ongoing contacts between Aconcio, Betti and Johannes Wolf following the two exiles' departure from Zurich.[182] Publicly, Bullinger also continued to have full confidence in Lelio Sozzini, to the extent of entrusting him with a delicate diplomatic mission to the colloquy of Worms in November–December 1557.[183] On a subsequent visit to Poland, Sozzini was received more or less as an official representative of the Zurich church.[184]

In the background, however, there were signs that attitudes were hardening, partly in response to a renewed spate of doctrinal disputes involving Italian exiles during the mid to late 1550s. In June 1557, Matteo Gribaldi was forced to flee from Tübingen after evidence of his continuing antitrinitarian sympathies came to light. The episode would have been particularly galling for Bullinger, because 18 months earlier he had approved as orthodox a confession submitted to him by the former Paduan professor.[185] Worse still, among Gribaldi's papers was discovered a heretical work, *De vera cognitione Dei*, which contained incriminating annotations by Curione; the latter was forced to make a public profession of faith in the Trinity in order to forestall further investigation.[186] Hard on the heels of this controversy came the confrontation between Calvin and dissidents in Geneva's Italian church, which culminated in the public abjuration of the 'tritheist' Valentino Gentile.[187] Even more disturbing for Bullinger were events in eastern Europe, where first Francesco Stancaro, and then Giorgio Biandrata, threatened to split the Polish Reformed church with their criticisms of orthodox Christology and triadology. In their letters to the Polish Reformed from 1561 (discussed in Chapter 4:ii below), both Bullinger and Johannes Wolf stress the value of explicit confessional statements as weapons in the fight against heresy; like Giulio da Milano earlier, they argue that clarity is the only defence against Satan's wiles. Whereas, in the case of Lelio Sozzini, Bullinger was inclined to overlook ambiguity and equivocation, by the early 1560s he had come to regard it as part of

---

181 See Chapter 1:i above.

182 Aconcio, *De methodo*, pp. 406–9. Wolf also enjoyed good relations with Fausto Sozzini (Wotschke, p. 432).

183 Sozzini, *Opere*, pp. 265–6; Cantimori, *Eretici*, p. 235.

184 Mühling, *Bullinger*, pp. 241–2.

185 Trechsel, *Antitrinitarier*, II, p. 287.

186 Cantimori, *Eretici*, pp. 260–62; G. Williams, *The Radical Reformation*, 3rd edition (Kirksville, Mo., 1992), p. 953.

187 T.R. Castiglione, 'Valentino contro Calvino: Il processo del <<secondo Serveto>> nel 1558, a Ginevra', in L. Chmaj (ed.), *Studia nad arianizmem* (Warsaw, 1959), pp. 49–71.

a conscious strategy to insinuate heretical teachings into the church and to neutralize its mechanisms of self-defence.

In this climate it was natural that the orthodoxy of Italians living in Zurich itself should come under increasing scrutiny. From around 1560, all new residents of the city were required to subscribe to a detailed confession of faith which included articles on the unity and distinction of the three persons of the Godhead, the dual procession of the Holy Spirit, and the eternal generation of the Son.[188] Bullinger's assessment of Lelio Sozzini had also changed radically by the time of the latter's death in May 1562: in his *Totenbuch*, the *Antistes* described his erstwhile pupil as a 'versipellis horribilis' and a follower of the Arian heresy.[189] Bullinger's choice of language is significant, as it shows that the 'academic method' of dissecting theological problems had been exposed in his eyes as mere trickery – as an attempt to pull the wool over the eyes of the Reformed establishment while subverting the faith of others. This new-found insight surely informed his reading of the *Dialogi XXX* when he finally came to examine the text.

For several months following Beza's denunciation of Ochino, Bullinger refrained from initiating proceedings against his elderly colleague. From his initial response to the Genevan churchman's complaint, it is clear that Bullinger was not yet prepared to bracket Ochino with the 'heretics' whose activities in Poland and Graubünden were causing so much concern. He may also have believed that the controversy surrounding the publication of the *Dialogi* would quickly blow over, and that any official enquiry by the Zurich church was only likely to prolong the affair. Beza saw matters differently. In a letter dated 1 July 1563, he dismissed Bullinger's attempts to explain away any errors contained in the *Dialogi* with reference to Ochino's age and mental frailty, insisting that the Zurichers take steps to distance themselves from the work 'so that all churches may understand that you do not approve of it'.[190]

Any hopes that Bullinger may have had of restricting the scope of the

---

[188] This confession is mentioned in the *Tigurinorum Consilium ad Synodum Curiae* of May 1561 (see Chapter 5:i below) and in a letter of October 1562 from the Polish minister Stanisław Sarnicki to his compatriot Christopher Thretius. Sarnicki notes that it had been adopted (on Bullinger's recommendation) by the orthodox faction of the Polish Reformed church at a recent synod in Cracow (*CO*, XIX, no. 3875). For the text of the confession, see the copy in ZB Ms. S 130, 14.

[189] Stadtarchiv VIII, C.48 (18 May 1562): 'Laelius Soccinus Senensis ist gestorben aber nitt verkündt worden / dass er in die Luggarner kylchen gehort, und verergehrnt Arianismi. Versipellis Horribilis erat [?]'. Cited in Rotondò, 'Calvino', p. 767, n. 18.

[190] *Correspondance*, IV, no. 274.

controversy were ended by an incident in early November that year. At the annual fair of Basle, a dispute over religion flared up between some Zurich merchants and Gorius Kraft, a nobleman from Baden, who pointed to the *Dialogi* as an example of the Zurich authorities' failure to ensure the teaching of correct doctrine.[191] On returning to Zurich the merchants' leader, Johannes Wegmann, informed the *Bürgermeister* and the three city ministers Bullinger, Gwalther and Wolf of what had taken place; they, in turn, alerted the Zurich council. Because Ochino held an official position within the Zurich church and could therefore be regarded as speaking on its behalf, the council was duty-bound to treat Kraft's allegations with extreme seriousness once they had been brought to its attention. With Zurich's good name at stake, there was no question of the issue being handled in the same low-key manner as the case of Lelio Sozzini, a private citizen, eight years earlier. Moreover, by publishing the *Dialogi XXX* without the knowledge of the Zurich censors, Ochino could be seen to have challenged magisterial control of religion in the city and to have breached his oath of loyalty to the council and synod.[192]

Initially the Zurich council's concerns related primarily to dialogue 21, 'on polygamy'.[193] Following the Münster affair and the bigamous marriage of Philip of Hesse, polygamy had become a question of extreme sensitivity to the Reformed, and indeed to Protestants in general. Any suggestion that Zurich condoned deviation from the Christian standard of monogamous marriage would lend support to the long-standing Catholic charge that the Reformation undermined traditional behavioural norms, with evangelical liberty taken to mean moral, especially sexual, licence. Both Zwingli and Bullinger flatly opposed the plurality of wives, which Luther and Bucer had been prepared to countenance in some situations on the basis of Old Testament precedent. In his commentary on Matthew's Gospel of 1542, for instance, Bullinger denies that there was any 'general' dispensation for polygamy under the old covenant, only 'permissiones' granted by God to individual figures, such as the patriarchs Abraham and Jacob, in

---

[191] A vivid description of the encounter is given in Meyer, *Locarnergemeinde*, II, pp. 168–70.

[192] The unauthorized publication of religious works was an extremely sensitive issue in Zurich because of its implications for relations with the Catholic Swiss. The appearance of Gwalther's *Endchrist* in 1546, for example, was met with vocal opposition from the *Fünf Orte*, who described the work as a 'Schändbüchlein' (Bächtold, *Bullinger*, pp. 95–103). A censorship committee had been established by the Zurich council in 1523, and its powers over printers in the city were progressively extended during the course of the 1550s (ibid., p. 108).

[193] *Dialogi XXX*, II, pp. 186–227.

exceptional circumstances.[194] In dialogue 21, by contrast, Ochinus' antagonist Telipolygamus, who has expressed a desire to take a second wife, maintains that polygamy was both sanctioned by the Mosaic Law and permitted by Christ and the apostles;[195] the legitimation of polygamy, Telipolygamus implies, is the logical consequence of the Protestant emphasis on the dignity of the married state.[196] (Many of Telipolygamus's arguments seem to have been derived from Johannes Lening's notorious *Dialogus Neobuli*, written in support of the bigamous marriage of Philip of Hesse.[197]) As usual, Ochinus defends the orthodox position, but fails to dissuade Telipolygamus from his resolution. In his final statement, he actually undermines the Reformed churches' absolute prohibition of polygamy by appearing to allow an exception for those men who are convinced that they have been called by God to take a second wife.[198]

After receiving word of the incident in Basle, the Zurich council ordered Bullinger and his colleagues to examine the dialogue on polygamy. A German translation of the dialogue was produced and considered at a meeting of Zurich ministers and professors on 21 November, which had no hesitation in condemning the work.[199] The

---

[194] *In sacrosanctum Iesu Christi Domini nostri Evangelium secundum Matthaeum commentariorum libri XII* (Zurich, 1542), fol. 179r-v; compare *Decades*, 2:10. For a fuller account of the polygamy debate among Protestants prior to the Ochino affair, see M. Taplin, 'Bernardino Ochino and the Zurich Polygamy Controversy of 1563' (unpublished M.Litt. thesis, University of St Andrews, 1995), Chapter 1.

[195] For a detailed analysis of the dialogue, see Taplin, 'Polygamy Controversy', Chapter 2:II.

[196] *Dialogi XXX*, II, pp. 226–7. In the *Dialogo della prudenza humana*, Ochino comes close to equating the relaxation of the prohibition on plural marriage with the abolition of obligatory clerical celibacy (BL Additional Ms. 28568, fol. 15v).

[197] The first to note the similarities in structure and content between the two texts was Johann Schelhorn (*Ergötzlichkeiten*, III, p. 2140). See the comparative analysis in Williams, 'Ochino', pp. 132–43, and the footnotes to chapter 2:II of Taplin, 'Polygamy Controversy'.

[198] *Dialogi XXX*, II, pp. 225–6: 'Si id feceris ad quod te Deus impellit, dummodo divinum esse instinctum exploratum habeas, non peccabis. Siquidem in obediendo Deo errari non potest.' Various explanations have been offered for Ochino's interest in the question of polygamy. Bainton, for example, suggests that the dialogue was written in response to the plight of Sigismund II of Poland, who was having difficulty obtaining an annulment of his third marriage and to whom dialogue 28 is dedicated (Bainton, *Ochino*, pp. 133–4). As pastor to the Locarnese community, Ochino would have been aware of the problems faced by those with 'unbelieving' spouses who refused to follow them into exile. I have already noted that he was party to the discussions surrounding the case of Galeazzo Caracciolo, which centred on precisely this issue; in July 1557, a member of Ochino's own congregation, Francesco Michele Appiano, was granted a divorce by the Zurich *Ehegericht* on similar grounds (StAZ YY 1.21, fol. 65r).

[199] *Spongia*, p. 478. The translation referred to may be the extended summary of dialogue 21, in Bullinger's hand, in StAZ E II 367, 281–8.

following day Bullinger, Gwalther and Wolf appeared before the council to inform it of the clergy's collective judgment. In their address, drafted by Bullinger, the ministers attacked Ochino on three counts: first, for ignoring the previous warning he had received not to publish anything without prior authorization; secondly, for raising such a contentious issue as polygamy at all; and thirdly, for failing to offer a cogent defence of the Zurich church's stance on the matter.[200] They did not call directly for Ochino's dismissal, but advised that appropriate measures be taken to protect the reputation of Zurich and its church, and to ensure that unity, along with 'healthy, simple and honourable doctrine', was at all times maintained.[201] The council's response was swift and decisive: Ochino was removed from his position and instructed to leave Zurich,[202] while a letter was sent to Basle requesting that the authorities there take steps to recall existing copies and stop further distribution of the *Dialogi XXX*.[203] Two days later, Ochino was presented with a formal letter of dismissal, but his request to be allowed to remain in Zurich until the spring was turned down.[204] In Basle, meanwhile, an investigation was launched into the circumstances surrounding the publication of the *Dialogi*, although punitive action against the work's translator, Castellio, was forestalled by his death on 29 December.[205] The Basle

---

200 StAZ E II 367, 261–4. Published in Benrath, *Ochino*, pp. 308–10.

201 Benrath, *Ochino*, p. 310: '[Wir] bittend ... uwer Wyßheit sy wölle dise sachen Christlich und wol beradtschlagen und verhälffen, das diser Kylchen kein verwysen darus entstande, sunderen ir guten namen behalte, einigkeit sampt gesunder einfalter und eerbarer leer aller zyt erhallten werde.'

202 StAZ B II 123, 57–8: 'Als mine herren von jren predicanten berichtet, das Gorius Crafft uß der Marggrafschafft Rötelen, burger zů Basel, unnsren koufflüthen Hannsen Wegman unnd andren, als sy jnn nechst verschiner Mäß zů Basel zum Ochsen gwesen, ufgehept, unnd gsagt, das uß Zürich secten ußgangen die schelmisch unnd kätzerisch sigen, und namlich Bernhardin Ochin, ein söllich bůch ußgen laßen, unnd sy daruf, als unnser burger das angezeigt, gheißen worden, disem bůch nachfragen, habind sy funden das er Ochin der Ehe unnd anderer sachen halb ein bůch geschriben, das zů Basel durch Petrum Bernam getruckt, das mer zů Ergernuß unser Religion, dann zu ufnung derselben reiche, unnd das sy von söllich bůch nit gwüßt. Habent min herren darab ein treffenlich beduren empfangen, unnd deshalb jnne Ochin angentz geurloubet unnd uß jr Statt unnd Land verweisen, unnd darneben hern Burgermeister Müller, J. Andares Schmiden Pannerher, J. Hanns Cunrath Äscher, unnd J. Hansen Göldli bevolch jme Ochino des antzůzeigen'.

Darnebent sölle söllichs angentz gen Basel geschriben, unnd sy dabj peten werden, sölliche bücher alle by dem Trucker, und jren burgern so die kouft, zů jren handen zebringen und dermaß zů behalten, das die nit mer ußgangind noch under den gmeinen man komind.' See also StAZ B VI 259 (22 November 1563), fols 121v–2r.

203 StAZ E I 4.1 (22 November); ZB Ms. F 15, 442r–3v; published in Benrath, *Ochino*, pp. 310–12.

204 StAZ E I 4.1 (24 November); Benrath, *Ochino*, pp. 312–13.

205 The *Dialogi* had already been denounced to the Basle authorities by Andreas von

council also rejected a petition by Ochino to be allowed to resume residence in the city, insisting that he first make his peace with the ecclesiastical and secular authorities in Zurich.[206]

By this time, Bullinger had moved a long way from the stance that he had adopted when first advised by Beza of the threat to orthodoxy posed by the *Dialogi XXX*. His change of attitude can be accounted for as follows. First, the increasingly public nature of the controversy over the work made it necessary for Zurich, as the senior Swiss Reformed state, to be seen to dissociate itself from Ochino's actions. Next, even the suggestion that Ochino had advocated polygamy, forever linked in the Protestant mind with the social and moral disorder of the Münster episode, was always likely to cause Bullinger to view his case in an unfavourable light: in their pronouncements on dialogue 21, both Bullinger and the council stress the work's potentially destabilizing effects on the 'gemeinen Mann'.[207] Finally, Bullinger would have been mindful of the controversy's implications not just for Ochino, but for the position of the Zurich clergy as a whole. Memories of the anticlerical backlash that had followed Zurich's defeat in the Second Kappel War were still fresh, and relations between church and state in Zurich remained on a knife-edge throughout Bullinger's period as *Antistes*. The controversy surrounding the *Dialogi* placed Bullinger and his colleagues in a vulnerable situation, because of their perceived close relationship with Zurich's Italian community. In a letter to Johannes Fabricius of 20 November, Bullinger predicted that xenophobic elements would seek to make capital out of the Ochino affair, which would be interpreted as the inevitable consequence of the clergy's policy of openness towards evangelical refugees: 'Now many will shout, "You are always taking in foreigners, and this is how they repay you".'[208] For this reason, in their address to the council two days later, Bullinger,

---

Bodenstein (see the letter published in Buisson, *Castellion*, II, pp. 483–93). In his defence, Castellio argued that he bore no responsibility for the subject matter of the dialogues, and that he was under the impression that the work had been endorsed by the Basle censors (CO, XX, no. 4046). Subsequently it became clear that Perna had submitted the manuscript of the *Dialogi* to Basilius Amerbach for examination. Because the work was written in Italian, Amerbach had passed it on to his colleague Curione, who testified to having inspected it but denied having formally approved it. Castellio's Latin translation of the *Dialogi* was seen by none of the relevant authorities prior to its publication (Bainton, *Ochino*, pp. 182; 190–91).

[206] Bainton, *Ochino*, p. 193.

[207] A sea change in Bullinger's attitude towards Ochino is evident almost from the moment at which he became aware that the *Dialogi* addressed the issue of polygamy. In a letter to Beza dated 15 November he observed: 'Senex et silicernium si saperet, scriberet potius de morte, cui jam vicinus est, quam de polygamia. Prodit hoc facto qualis sit ejus animus' (*Correspondance*, IV, no. 296).

[208] StAZ E II 373, 387 (Schiess, II, no. 556; Bainton, *Ochino*, p. 181).

Gwalther and Wolf were at pains to point out that Ochino had acted entirely without the knowledge or assistance of other members of the Zurich pastorate.[209] By endorsing the harsh measures resolved on by the magistracy, Bullinger was able to deflect any further criticism away from the clergy as a whole and to make Ochino the sole focus of investigation.

The decision to expel Ochino from Zurich appears to have been made following an examination of dialogue 21 alone. Only after the initial sentence had been passed were Bullinger and the other senior Zurich churchmen instructed to produce a report on the remaining dialogues, which was submitted to the council between 26 and 28 November.[210] Portions of this text were later incorporated into the Zurich church's official account of the affair, the *Spongia adversus aspergines Bernardini Ochini* of March 1564.[211] Both the completed report, and the preliminary notes of those theologians who were assigned the task of examining the *Dialogi XXX*, have survived.[212] In the course of their

---

209 Benrath, *Ochino*, p. 310: 'Und wie uns sin handlung leyd von seinem wegen, also ist ouch sy uns noch vil leyder von der kylchen wegen, die hiemit beleydiget und verergeret. Des wir doch nit vermögend und doran weder gemeinschaft noch gefallen habend und so wir darumb gewüsst, und es erweren mögen, hätend wirs erwert.' Compare the account in *Spongia*, p. 479: 'Testabantur [the three city ministers] apud amplissimum Senatum, ipsis quidem insciis, haec a Bernardino esse edita, neque antea a quocunque ipsorum lecta, tantum abesse, ut hac in causa ipsum suis iuverint conciliis. Proinde orare ne quid sinistri hac in re suspicari velint de ministris qui sancte sentiant, doceantque de sancto coniugio.'

210 See StAZ E II 367, 264; *Spongia*, p. 482; Bullinger to Fabricius, 26 November 1563 (StAZ E II 373, 383; Schiess, II, no. 557; Bainton, *Ochino*, p. 182); and Bullinger to Beza, 28 November 1563 (*Correspondance*, IV, no. 297): 'Bernardini Ochini Dialogos illos 30 inspeximus, capita quaedam perversarum doctrinarum (totus liber nil aliud est quam impia perversitas) annotavimus, ad Senatum retulimus, qui vehementer ista commotus hominis audacia et impuritate ipsum officio dejecit, denique urbe et agro ejecit.' In his reply of 4 December, Beza expressed surprise that so much was being made of the dialogue on polygamy when the entire work was riddled with 'foedis erroribus' (ibid., no. 298). Never one to shirk a confrontation, however, he later undertook a detailed refutation of the arguments for polygamy contained in dialogue 21 (*Tractatio de polygamia, in qua et Ochini apostatae pro polygamia, et Montanistarum ac aliorum adversus repetitas nuptias argumenta refutantur* [Geneva, 1567]).

211 In the *Spongia*, the Zurichers also responded to the allegations made against Bullinger in the *Dialogo della prudenza humana*, a copy of which was procured for them by Johannes Fabricius and the Bergamasco exile Francesco Bellinchetti (Fabricius to Bullinger, 20 March 1564 [StAZ E II 376, 112; Schiess, II, no. 593; Bainton, *Ochino*, p. 196]). Returning the dialogue on 7 April, Bullinger commented: 'Vere illi boni viri dixerunt, serpentem nos in sinu et hypocritam mirificum fovere' (StAZ E II, 373, 507; Schiess, II, no. 596; Bainton, *Ochino*, p. 197).

212 For the report, see StAZ E II 367, 271–9, published in Bainton, *Ochino*, pp. 183–8; copy in StAZ E II 445a, 967–74. For the notes, see StAZ E II 367, 298–332. The work appears to have been shared out as follows: dialogues 7, 10, 12, 13, 22, 27 (Bullinger); dialogues 2–6 (Gwalther); dialogues 7–9 (unidentified); dialogues 18, 26 and 28 (Wolf); dialogues 19–20 (Simler).

investigation, Bullinger and his colleagues came to believe that in the *Dialogi* they were being confronted not with minor, isolated instances of dissent, but with an attack on the very foundations of Reformed doctrine. Thus when Martino Muralto visited Bullinger on 30 November in a final effort to have the sentence against Ochino rescinded, he was told that Ochino would be best advised to leave Zurich before the three weeks allotted to him by the council had passed, 'because the longer things go on, the worse his case appears ('dann sin sach ye lenger ye böser sich finde').[213] The *Antistes* also sought to rally support for the Zurich authorities' actions by sending copies of incriminating passages from the *Dialogi* to leading churchmen in Basle (Wolfgang Wyssenburg) and Berne (Johannes Haller).[214] On hearing that there were plans to secure a refuge for Ochino in the Italian-speaking territories of the Rhaetian Freestate, Bullinger urged Johannes Fabricius to take steps 'to prevent Rhaetia from becoming a hiding place and an asylum for those expelled from the orthodox churches on account of their perverse doctrine'.[215]

In their comments on the *Dialogi XXX*, the Zurich divines reiterated their earlier criticisms of Ochino's mode of argument. The author's inability or unwillingness to present a clear case in favour of orthodoxy testified, they argued, to his underlying malign intent. In dialogue 27, they noted Ochinus' failure to offer a satisfactory response to the charges levelled against the Reformed by his adversary Eusebius, concluding from this 'that it must be clear to anyone that he is cunningly disseminating his unfounded teachings in the churches under another person's name'.[216] The Zurichers were similarly sceptical of Ochino's formal defence of monogamy in dialogue 21:

> If one examines the dialogue truly and in detail, it becomes clear
> that he presents and adorns the arguments of his opponent with
> much greater fidelity, zeal, conviction, diversity and strength than
> the case for the one true Christian marriage. He does not put
> forward the counter-arguments with the faithfulness or skill that is
> required. And although he occasionally offers a riposte, he delivers

---

[213] ZB Ms. F 15, fol. 445ᵛ; Meyer, *Locarnergemeinde*, II, pp. 176–7. In the event, Ochino left Zurich for Basle on 2 December (see Bullinger to Fabricius, 3 December 1563 [StAZ E II 373, 391; Schiess, II, no. 559; Bainton, *Ochino*, p. 190]).

[214] See Wyssenburg to Bullinger, 6 December 1563 (Bainton, *Ochino*, p. 191), and Haller to Bullinger, 16 December 1563 (ibid., p. 192).

[215] Letter of 27 December 1563 (StAZ E II 373, 479; Schiess, II, no. 566; Bainton, *Ochino*, p. 194). Similar warnings were sent to Friedrich von Salis and to Count Ulisse Martinengo in Chiavenna (Martinengo to Bullinger, 27 December 1563 (StAZ E II 365, 268; Schiess, II, no. 568; Bainton, *Ochino*, p. 195); Bullinger to Beza, 6 January 1564 [*Correspondance*, V, no. 303]).

[216] Bainton, *Ochino*, p. 183.

it in a cold or lukewarm manner that suggests that he is not serious. Indeed, with his answers he always gives his opponent the opportunity to pour forth and disgorge much more of his mischief and impure chatter.[217]

The 'academic' rhetoric of the *Dialogi* could not be reconciled with the Zurichers' pastorally orientated approach to theology, as exemplified by Bullinger's own *Summa Christenlicher Religion*. In the *Summa*, Bullinger expresses his distaste for 'abstruse questions' ('seltzamen fragen'), which serve only to sow confusion and to undermine faith. The theologian's task is to steer his reader away from such matters, back to the simple and enduring truths of Christ's teaching.[218] In their comments on the *Dialogi*, Bullinger and his colleagues suggest that Ochino's work was likely to have the diametrically opposite effect: 'Any God-fearing person can imagine what indignation and rebuke such things will provoke from both believers and unbelievers.'[219] In the later *Spongia*, they argue that if Ochino had wanted to use the medium of the dialogue for the purpose of refuting heresy he ought to have modelled himself on the orthodox writers of the early church, Athanasius, Jerome and Theodoret of Cyrrhus: 'For they expounded the arguments of their heretical adversaries faithfully but briefly, while refuting them at much greater length and much more faithfully and powerfully. In Bernardino's dialogue, the opposite appears to be the case.'[220] In support of their claim that Ochino's intention in the *Dialogi* was to subvert orthodoxy by covert means, they cite several passages in which Ochinus himself expresses support for doctrinal positions otherwise associated with his fictional antagonists.[221]

---

[217] Ibid., p. 187. Simler argues that Ochinus' function in dialogue 19 is essentially that of a foil for his interlocutor Spiritus: 'Verum primum se suspectum facit quod ipse testimonia multa ad probandam trinitatem adducit, contra quae Spiritus novas scripturarum explicationes, instantias et argumenta profert, quae Ochinus neque replicat neque confutat, ita ut videatur ideo tamen nostra argumenta proferre ut contra ea Spiritus ille virus suum posset effundere' (StAZ E II 367, 304).

[218] Bullinger, *Summa*, sigs aii[v]–iii[r].

[219] Bainton, *Ochino*, p. 185.

[220] *Spongia*, p. 488: 'Nam hos adversariorum vel Haereticorum argumenta fideliter exposuisse, sed strictim: at longe copiosius et fidelius validiusque illa confutasse. Contraria vero omnia apparere et reperiri in Bernhardini Dialogo.' The Zurichers are referring specifically to dialogue 21.

[221] Bullinger notes that in dialogue 27 Ochinus concurs with views expressed by Jacobus Judaeus in dialogue 13 (Jacobus had argued that the love of God above all creatures amounted to full obedience to the Law). See StAZ E II 367, 313–14, 319, 321; Bainton, *Ochino*, pp. 184–5; *Spongia*, p. 484. Compare Gwalther's negative assessment of Ochinus' views on original sin in *Dialogi XXX*, I, p. 259: 'Ochinus ipse: Si quis puer ante adultam aetatem mortuus regnum coeleste non adipiscitur, id ideo fit, quia ea natura

Turning to the theological content of the *Dialogi*, the Zurich divines identify several areas where Ochino departs from official teaching. In dialogue 27 he is accused of failing to offer a cogent defence of infant baptism, of advocating 'spiritual colloquies, in which even the unlearned are given an opportunity to speak', and of defending the Anabaptist doctrine of the community of goods. Dialogues 26 and 28, with their denunciation of the use of force in the defence of religion against the twin enemies of persecution and heresy, are also heavily censured.[222]

But Bullinger and his colleagues reserve their most potent criticisms for Ochino's teaching on justification and the atonement, the issues which dominate the first volume of the *Dialogi* and which provide the clearest evidence of the Sienese exile's divergence from Reformed orthodoxy.[223] The Zurichers' completed report includes a strong statement of the doctrines of justification through the imputation of Christ's merits to believers ('the most fundamental teaching of the holy Christian church'), and of the dual status of the elect in this life, in whom remains 'a certain weakness ('blödikeit') and inclination to sin'.[224] Against those teachings, they argue, Ochino posits a 'Jewish' doctrine of works righteousness, failing to distinguish adequately between the extrinsic process of justification and its attendant consequence, sanctification; he also plays down unacceptably the significance of Christ's vicarious sacrifice. In his notes on dialogue 13, Bullinger underlines Jacobus Judaeus' assertion that the elect are justified 'not by imputation, but by participation' ('non imputatione, sed participatione').[225] According to Gwalther, by questioning the Anselmian

---

dignus non est, non quia in eo insit ullum peccatum' (StAZ E II 367, 308). Simler claims that in dialogue 19 both Spiritus and Ochinus describe Christ as God by participation rather than by nature (ibid., 305).

[222] Bainton, *Ochino*, pp. 187–8; StAZ E II 367, 314, 329–30; *Spongia*, p. 489. Such criticisms touched a raw nerve with the Zurich divines because of the violent circumstances of Zwingli's death.

[223] In the *Dialogo della prudenza humana* Ochino insisted that his criticisms of Reformed soteriology were the real reason for his dismissal (BL Additional Ms. 28568, fol. 20v). But as has been noted, the preliminary investigation which prompted the sentence of 22 November was confined to dialogue 21, although the ministers were aware that unspecified allegations had been made against other parts of the *Dialogi XXX*.

[224] Bainton, *Ochino*, p. 183. Their position is restated in the *Spongia* in response to the savage criticisms of the Reformed understanding of predestination, justification and concupiscence contained in the *Dialogo della prudenza humana* (*Spongia*, p. 508).

[225] StAZ E II 367, 319. Bullinger had already polemicized against the Anabaptists on the question of 'essential' righteousness (*Widertöuffer*, fols 23v–4v; see M. Burrows, '"Christus intra nos vivens": The peculiar genius of Bullinger's doctrine of sanctification', *Zeitschrift für Kirchengeschichte*, 98 (1987), pp. 48–69). In the *Summa Christenlicher Religion* he writes: 'Alle die zů gnaden von Gott in Christo durch den glouben und durch die widergeburt angenommen sind / legend das fleisch nit so gantz und gar dahin / das sy

doctrine of the substitutionary atonement, '[Ochino] takes away our principal consolation, namely, that our salvation is dependent no less on God's justice than on his mercy'.[226] Gwalther also claims that Ochino sets up an artificial contradiction between election by mere grace and the mediatorial office of Christ, effectively reducing the latter to a bit-player in the drama of salvation.[227]

The Ochino affair forced the Zurichers to re-evaluate their attitude towards the Italian exiles. Previously, Bullinger had been less inclined than some other Reformed leaders (notably Calvin and Beza) to assume the worst of those Italians suspected of heresy; as we saw in the case of Lelio Sozzini, he was often prepared to accept public conformity as sufficient demonstration of an individual's orthodox credentials. After 1563, his attitude seems to have become a good deal less trusting. In a letter to the Nuremberg jurist Christoph Herdesian of September 1571, Bullinger excepted only Peter Martyr Vermigli from a blanket condemnation of the Italian exiles:

> I have often been amazed by the fact that although [Vermigli] was from the Florentine aristocracy and from Italy, he had none of the characteristics that we associate with Italians. He was endowed with a simple and sincere faith and was most averse to argument and curiosity; he was a pious, humane and unfailingly cheerful man. How often did I overhear him severely chiding Lelio Sozzini and his Italian and Polish companions, who daily directed astonishing and most curious questions against the simplicity of the faith![228]

In his preface to Josias Simler's *De aeterno Dei filio*, published in August 1568, Bullinger singled out Ochino's conduct for special criticism, accusing him of failing to honour his oath to uphold the doctrines of the church he served, and of showing ingratitude both to God and to his benefactors in Zurich: 'from a friend he turned into an enemy, and from a herald of the truth he turned into a secret and Academic proponent and teacher of many profane heresies and errors'.[229] The episode also

---

keiner anfächtungen mee empfindend oder sich schwärer fälen nit mee zů besorgen habind. Dann die sündig art blybt in uns / biß jn unser grab' (*Summa*, fol. 116ʳ). Compare *Commentarii*, pp. 57, 65–7, 395, 466–7; *Decades*, fol. 174ʳ.

226 '[Ochinus] praecipuam consolationem tollit, quae est, quod salus nostra non minus Dei iustitia quam misericordia nititur'. The statement is reminiscent of Zwingli in the *Fidei expositio* (Z, VI/5, 64).

227 StAZ E II 367, 308.

228 Cited in Rotondò, 'Sulla diffusione', p. 88; L. Lavater, *Vom läben und tod deß Eerwirdigen und Hochgeleerten Herrn / Heinrychen Bullingers / dieners der Kyrchen zů Zürych / kurtze einfalte und warhaffte erzellung* (Zurich, 1576), fol. 21ᵛ. Shortly before his death Konrad Gesner pronounced a similarly negative judgment on the Italian national character (cited in Serrai, *Gesner*, pp. 355–6, n. 473).

229 *De aeterno Dei filio domino et servatore nostro Iesu Christo, et de Spiritu sancto,*

affected Bullinger's relations with Zurich's wider Italian-speaking community, at least in the short term: when, at the beginning of December 1563, the Zurich council turned down a petition from the Locarnesi to appoint a new Italian preacher in Ochino's stead, Bullinger chose not to intervene on their behalf, having already expressed fears that the disgraced minister's flock might have become 'contaminated' by his errors.[230]

The Ochino affair was still very much in Bullinger's mind when he was asked to give his opinion on the case of Antonio Mario Besozzi (December 1564). In a draft *Fürtrag*, subsequently amplified by Gwalther, Bullinger suggested that Besozzi had derived his heresies from the *Dialogi XXX* ('Bernhardini des weltschen Predicanten Buch').[231] In support of this claim, the *Antistes* noted that, like Ochino (Jacobus Judaeus) in the *Dialogi*, Besozzi had cited Zacharias as an example of justification via the Law; he also ascribed Besozzi's alleged antitrinitarianism to the influence of his former pastor.[232] Moreover, Bullinger indicated that he was no longer prepared to assume the good faith of those charged with heresy, or to make any distinction, in practice, between the public and private profession of unorthodox views. The members of the Zurich council could choose to accept Besozzi's protestations of innocence, but

---

adversus veteres et novos Antitrinitarios, id est Arianos, Tritheitas, Samosatenianos, et Pneumatomachos, libri quatuor (Zurich, 1568), sig. α6ʳ): '... ex amico inimicus, et ex praecone veritatis syncerae, prophanarum haeresum errorumque multorum subdolus adeoque Academicus assertor et doctor factus sit.' In the *Spongia* the Zurichers note, with a combination of mockery and outrage, the contrast between Ochino's unquestioning public support for the teachings of the Zurich church prior to his expulsion and his subsequent self-portrayal as an aspiring reformer of that church (*Spongia*, pp. 503–5).

230 Bullinger to Beza, 4 December 1563 (*Correspondance*, IV, no. 297): 'Quid futurum sit cum Locarnensi ecclesia vehementer dubio. Dissipavit hanc vereor, infelix ille senex.'

231 Autograph in StAZ E II 367, 289–92. Gwalther's revision of the *Fürtrag* is published in Meyer, *Locarnergemeinde*, II, pp. 395–8 (for details, see Bächtold, *Bullinger*, p. 85, n. 138).

232 'Zů unsern ziten hatt ein Hispanier Michael Servetus disen jrrthumm ernüweret / und sind jezund ettliche Italiäner in Poland / die mit glichem irrthumm grosse unrůw und iamer anrichtend. H. Bernardin disputiert ouch in sinem verworffnen 18 [sic] Gespräch das Christus wol sye und gnempt werde ein Sun Gottes / er sye aber nit Gott / sunder ein creatur / der erstgeboren aller creaturen / aber nitt von eewikeit. Darinn verduncklet und verkeert er alle Zügnußen in alltem und nüwem testament die da heyeter kundtschafft gäbend der eewigen waren Gottheit unsers herren Christi.' In their report on the *Dialogi*, the Zurich theologians drew back from openly accusing Ochino of antitrinitarianism. Privately, Bullinger was less restrained. Writing to Fabricius on 3 December 1563, he remarked, 'Dialogi de Trinitate scripti duo sunt pestilentissimi et penitus proculcandi' (StAZ E II 373, 391; Schiess, II, no. 559; Bainton, *Ochino*, p. 190).

we will not conceal from them that the Servetians, Davidians [followers of David Joris] and other such sects, which in our times have caused great confusion and trouble in many churches, believe and teach among other things that one is not obliged to confess one's faith publicly, but that each person may accommodate himself to the will and opinion of those under whose protection he lives. Yet at the same time they continue in secret to pour out their poison, thereby gaining a following for themselves ... .[233]

Bullinger had ceased to believe that it was possible to confine or channel heresy in such a way as to prevent it from causing harm to the wider community. Doctrinal error was by its nature contagious, and must be eradicated at source.

In Chapter 2, I argued that Zurich acquired increasing importance as a centre of the Italian exile diaspora during the late 1550s. This can be put down primarily to the establishment there of Italian-language worship following the decision to receive the Locarnese evangelicals, and the appointment of the highly respected Ochino as Zurich's Italian minister. Ochino's expulsion, and the Zurich council's refusal to consider installing a successor, made it far less likely that Zurich would continue to attract Italian exiles from elsewhere. Without the obvious focus that Ochino had provided as its pastor, the core Locarnese community itself began to dwindle. A survey carried out after Besozzi's banishment listed 149 exiles resident in Zurich, divided among 27 households;[234] by 1576 the number had fallen to 104, in 24 households, despite a significant rate of natural increase and the arrival of more evangelicals from Locarno (Ambrosio Portio and Francesco Riva).[235] The economic activities of the remaining exiles continued to meet with opposition from the guilds: a council mandate of April 1568 restricted their involvement in silk manufacturing, for instance.[236] Still more problematic was the continued exclusion of most Locarnese residents of Zurich from citizenship. Although the physician Giovanni Muralto was made a citizen in January 1566 in recognition of his services during an outbreak of the plague, it took another 25 years for this honour to be extended to many of his compatriots (Francesco and Giovanni Melchiore Orelli, and Giangiacomo and Giorgio Pebbia). Even then the exiles and their

---

233 Meyer, *Locarnergemeinde*, II, p. 397.

234 StAZ A 350.1; published in Meyer, *Locarnergemeinde*, II, pp. 393–4. This total included 21 servants who may or may not have been Locarnesi.

235 Published in Meyer, *Locarnergemeinde*, II, pp. 414–15. The figure does not include the family of Giovanni Muralto, which had acquired citizenship by this time.

236 This *Samtweberordung* is published in Meyer, *Locarnergemeinde*, II, pp. 411–13; and Schnyder, *Quellen*, I, pp. 329–31.

descendants did not enjoy the privileges of full citizens, but were excluded from government office.[237]

Ironically, the hostility that it faced from the host population may have helped the community to hold together in difficult circumstances. In the years following Ochino's expulsion, its institutions seemed in disarray: the common chest was rapidly becoming exhausted, and minutes for the meetings of the elders and congregation were no longer kept after January 1567.[238] However, from the early 1570s there were signs of a revival, with the common chest again being used for the benefit of both poorer Locarnesi and visiting foreigners; a new weekly collection was even instituted in 1595.[239] Much of the credit for this must go to Taddeo Duno, who appears to have rebuilt relations between the community and its erstwhile protectors in the Zurich church. Duno was on excellent terms with Bullinger,[240] Gwalther,[241] and their younger colleague Josias Simler, to whose much-reprinted work on the Swiss Confederation, *De Helvetiorum Republica*, he contributed a description of Locarno.[242] Duno's abilities were also held in high regard by later generations of Zurich churchmen, from Johann Wilhelm Stucki to Johann Jakob Breitinger, who drew up and witnessed his will.[243] Under Duno's tutelage, the Locarnesi remained a cohesive community, its identity reinforced by a tendency towards endogamy[244] and by

---

[237] As late as the 1590s, feeling against the Locarnesi continued to run high in some quarters, if the bitter criticisms of the decision to admit the Pebbia and Orelli to citizenship contained in ZB Ms. B 251, fols 44–5, are anything to go by.

[238] By 1567, total assets had fallen to just over 668 scudi (FA Orelli, 8.2, fols 90ᵛ–91ʳ).

[239] Ibid., fol. 115ʳ; Meyer, *Locarnergemeinde*, II, p. 346.

[240] When Duno submitted a Latin petition to the Zurich council in October 1567 requesting citizenship and an official salary, Bullinger translated it into German (StAZ E II 378, 1925ʳ–6ᵛ; Meyer, *Locarnergemeinde*, II, pp. 324–5). Josias Simler's life of Bullinger contains a tribute to the dead *Antistes* from Duno on behalf of the Locarnesi (*Narratio*, fol. 84ʳ).

[241] In December 1576, Duno sought and obtained Gwalther's opinion on questions arising from a divorce case referred to him by an Italian friend resident in Basle (StAZ E II 340, 361–2).

[242] J. Simler, *De Helvetiorum Republica* (Paris, 1577), fol. 189ᵛ.

[243] StAZ B VI 325, fol. 163ʳ. With his *De peregrinatione filiorum Israel in Aegypto, Tractatus chronologicus* (Zurich, 1595), Duno published letters from several Zurich professors (including Stucki, Rudolf Hospinian and Raphael Egli) endorsing his solution to this obscure exegetical problem (*De peregrinatione*, fols 2ᵛ–3ʳ). He also cultivated links with the Basle university rector Theodor Zwinger (in part through their mutual friend Francesco Betti) and with the Basle *Antistes* Johann Jakob Grynaeus.

[244] Of Martino Muralto's daughters, for instance, two married fellow Locarnesi (Cornelio Toma and Giovanni Melchiore Orelli) and one another Italian-speaking immigrant from Chiavenna, Gianantonio Pestalozzi (H. Schulthess, *Bilder aus der Vergangenheit der Familie Von Muralt in Zürich* (Zurich, 1944), p. 38).

continuing business ties (such as the trading company that Ludovico Ronco set up with Francesco Michele Appiano in 1576).[245] By the end of the 16th century the exiles were becoming more integrated into Zurich society – intermarriage was now common, and the Locarnesi enjoyed close relations with the Ziegler and Werdmüller families in particular – but only with Duno's death in 1613 can one begin to speak of the community's disappearance as a distinct entity.[246]

The consequences of Ochino's dismissal for those heterodox thinkers who had attached themselves to the Locarnese community were more immediate. The 1560s saw the departure from Zurich of Francesco Betti (in 1565), Guarnerio Castiglione (in 1567),[247] and Dario Scala and Camillo Sozzini (both around the time of the Ochino affair).[248] Zurich was no longer perceived as a secure location for their activities, or as sympathetic to their aspirations. Niccolò Camogli, a Genoese exile who received Ochino in Basle in early December 1563 and hoped to find a refuge for him in Graubünden, spoke of Ochino's oppressors as 'novi Pharisaei': similar language had been used of Calvin by Castellio, Matteo Gribaldi and others critical of Servetus' execution.[249]

The Ochino affair had, in fact, brought home to Bullinger and his colleagues how far some Italian exiles had drifted from the conservative and catholic vision of the Reformation that they espoused. Their previous encounters with 'heresy', in Poland and Rhaetia, had been more or less indirect; Ochino, by contrast, was a trusted colleague, a spokesman and representative of the Zurich church. His disgrace placed

---

[245] FA Orelli, 8.4, fol. 11ᵛ.

[246] The baptismal records of the three Zurich city churches (Stadtarchiv Zürich VIII, C.2; C.15; C.19) indicate that members of the Werdmüller and Ziegler families often served as godparents to Locarnese children.

[247] Weisz claims that Castiglione left Zurich as early as 1563 ('Tessiner', p. 392), but he was in fact present at the last documented meeting of the Locarnese heads of household on 1 January 1567 (FA Orelli, 8.2, fol. 20ʳ). Castiglione also received the sum of 6 scudi from the common chest on 1 October that year (ibid., fol. 105ʳ).

[248] The circumstances of Camillo's departure are described in Cantimori, Eretici, p. 306. Cantimori's source is a letter from Gwalther to Scipione Lentolo of 9 March 1571, cited in Lentolo's Commentarii, fols 24ᵛ–5ʳ. The letter describes how, after the Zurichers got wind of Camillo's antitrinitarianism, they instructed the Locarnese elders 'ne eum foverent, sed et dimitterent, neque invidia ipsis conflaretur'. Camillo then left Zurich before Bullinger and Gwalther could denounce him to the city authorities.

[249] Lentolo, Commentarii, fols 47ʳ–8ᵛ; Bainton, Ochino, pp. 189–90. For some time, Zurich's Italian-speaking community may have continued to harbour elements sympathetic to the ideas of Ochino, Besozzi and other radicals. Johann von Muralt, a descendant of the original exiles who entered the service of the Transylvanian prince Sigmund Báthory, was forced to defend himself against allegations of antitrinitarianism from Simone Simoni (L. Weisz, 'Johann von Muralt, der siebenbürgische Hofarzt', Neue Zürcher Zeitung, 14, 15 and 16 August 1929).

a question-mark against the Zurichers' own orthodoxy: the point could be made (and was) that Zurich had nurtured and abetted the development of a notorious heretic. The increasing involvement of the Zurich divines in the anti-heretical campaign being waged by Europe's Reformed churches during the 1560s was in part an attempt to lay those suspicions to rest.

CHAPTER FOUR

Defining and Defending Orthodoxy: the Zurich Church's Response to Italian Religious Radicalism in Eastern Europe

The middle decades of the 16th century saw the consolidation of Reformed Protestantism as a mature theological system. Bullinger's *Decades*, the Heidelberg catechism, the Second Helvetic Confession: all appeared during this period, and all testify to the growing preoccupation of the 'second generation' of Reformed churchmen with precise doctrinal definition. This process did not take place in isolation, but in the context of polemical debate with theological opponents. As is well known, the evolution of Reformed Christology proceeded against the backdrop of the ongoing Eucharistic schism with the Lutherans. In the same way, from the late 1550s confrontation with various Italian radical thinkers over the doctrines of the Trinity and the two natures of Christ forced the Zurich divines to undertake a reconsideration of those questions. In the course of that exchange, Bullinger and his colleagues reiterated their commitment to Nicene orthodoxy, along with their conviction that the Reformation entailed not a radical break with Christian tradition, but the resumption of the church's natural development, interrupted by the rise of the papacy. It was to the early church creeds, the ecumenical councils and the orthodox Fathers that the Zurichers invariably turned when detailed responses to the radicals' arguments were required. Just as previous polemical exchanges with Catholics and Lutherans had helped define where the Reformed churches stood in relation to more conservative opponents, so the conflict with the Italian 'heretics' and their followers in eastern Europe set the limits to Zwinglian radicalism. The episode clarified what the Zurich divines understood by reform: an attack on 'a limited spectrum of doctrinal and practical abuses with the intention of reaffirming the values of the historical church catholic'.[1] It reaffirmed their sense of solidarity with the Constantinian and post-Constantinian church

---

[1] R. Muller, *Post-Reformation Reformed Dogmatics: Volume 1, Prolegomena to Theology* (Grand Rapids, 1987), p. 63.

(Reformed polemicists identified closely with the Fathers in *their* conflicts with ancient antitrinitarians) and buttressed their claim to catholicity, and therefore to exemption from the penalties for heretics prescribed by the Theodosian code.

i. The Stancarist controversy and the Reformed doctrine of the mediator

Events in eastern Europe explain the Zurich church's growing preoccupation with issues of Christology and triadology from the late 1550s onwards. During this period, fundamental divisions over doctrine opened up within the nascent Reformed church of Little Poland, culminating in a schism between orthodox Nicenes (henceforth known as the *ecclesia maior*) and antitrinitarian radicals (who formed the *ecclesia minor* or Polish Brethren). The Zurich church was at the forefront of efforts to check the spread of heterodox ideas among Polish Protestants and thereby to safeguard the prospects for the Reformation in the kingdom. In the process, Bullinger and his colleagues were obliged to make explicit Zurich's position on the complex doctrinal questions under discussion.

The Reformation was slow to make an impact within the vast Polish-Lithuanian commonwealth.[2] A Lutheran state church had been established in neighbouring ducal Prussia as early as 1525, but under the Jagiellon king Sigismund I the Old stringent and at times draconian measures were taken to prevent the spread of Protestantism into Poland proper.[3] However, following the accession of his son Sigismund II in April 1548 this regime was relaxed considerably, and the Reformation began to win adherents among the Polish nobility. In 1553, it registered a particularly notable success with the conversion of the powerful Lithuanian magnate Mikołaj Radziwiłł, who controlled a vast fiefdom around Vilna. Outside royal Prussia and Great Poland, with their large German-speaking populations, Reformed Protestantism of the Swiss type quickly came to predominate. The return to Poland in December

---

[2] On the Reformation in Poland, see L. Hein, *Italienische Protestanten und ihr Einfluß auf die Reformation in Polen während der beiden Jahrzehnte vor dem Sandomirer Konsens (1570)* (Leiden, 1974); T. Wotschke, *Geschichte der Reformation in Polen* (Leipzig, 1911); Williams, *Radical Reformation*, pp. 991–1036.

[3] In 1523, for example, the introduction, reading and distribution of Protestant writings was prohibited on pain of death. A later decree applied the death penalty to those who sent their children abroad to be educated in Protestant schools (A. Kawecka-Gryczowa and J. Tazbir, 'The book and the Reformation in Poland', in Gilmont, *The Reformation and the Book*, pp. 410–31 [422–3]).

1556 of Jan Łaski, formerly the superintendent of the Strangers Church in London, led to a further strengthening of ties between the Polish Reformed and the Swiss churches.[4]

Bullinger was quick to take advantage of these developments. On 12 November 1555, he wrote to Sigismund II urging him to reform his realm after the example of that archetypal godly magistrate, the Old Testament king Josiah.[5] He also initiated a correspondence with Radziwiłł, in the hope that the latter might use his influence to bring about the conversion of other members of the Polish nobility, and perhaps even of the king himself.[6] However, the Zurichers' principal point of contact in Poland was Francesco Lismanini, a Greco-Italian from Corfu who had formerly served as confessor to Sigismund I's wife Bona Sforza.[7] Long sympathetic to Protestantism, Lismanini had embraced the Reformed faith openly after a visit to Zurich in autumn 1554, in the course of which he forged strong links with Bullinger, Johannes Wolf and the leaders of Zurich's Italian community.[8] On returning to Poland in March 1556, Lismanini established himself as an influential figure within the kingdom's emerging Reformed church. Indeed, his regular letters became the Zurich divines' principal source of information on the progress of the Reformation in Poland.

Until the very end of the 1550s, the Reformed of Little Poland were more or less united over doctrine. Peter Gonesius (Piotr z Goniądza), a Pole who came under the influence of Matteo Gribaldi while studying in Padua, caused a minor stir when in January 1556 he presented the Polish synod with a confession in which the full divinity of Christ was denied and the Athanasian creed dismissed as contrary to scripture; however, he failed to garner any significant support for his views.[9] Over

---

[4] G. Williams, 'The Polish-Lithuanian Calvin during the "Superintendency" of John Laski, 1556–60', in B.A. Gerrish and R. Benedetto (eds), *Reformatio Perennis: Essays on Calvin and the Reformation in honor of Ford Lewis Battles* (Pittsburgh, 1981), pp. 129–58.

[5] L. Hein, 'Heinrich Bullinger und sein Einfluß auf die reformierten Gemeinden in Kleinpolen', *Kyrios*, 4 (1964), pp. 91–107 (93); Mühling, *Bullinger*, p. 235.

[6] Mühling, *Bullinger*, pp. 236; 325–7.

[7] See Hein, *Italienische Protestanten*, pp. 27–65.

[8] Ibid., p. 37. Lismanini formed a particularly close association with Ochino. The latter dedicated his *Dialogo del Purgatorio* to Lismanini, who in turn arranged the publication of two of Ochino's works in Polish (see B. Nicolini, 'Bernardino Ochino e la Polonia', in Nicolini, *Ideali e passioni nell'Italia del Cinquecento* (Bologna, 1962), pp. 117–26). Lismanini was also in correspondence with Lelio Sozzini and Guarnerio Castiglione (Wotschke, nos 83; 96). In a letter to Johannes Wolf dated 16 August 1562, he sent greetings to Martino Muralto and 'li signori locarnesi' (ibid., no. 252).

[9] For Gonesius' condemnation, see M. Sipayłło, *Acta synodalia ecclesiarum Poloniae reformatorum* (3 vols, Warsaw, 1966–83), I, p. 47; Williams, *Radical Reformation*, pp. 1009–10.

the next three years, the doctrinal issues which Gonesius had raised retreated into the background, as Łaski and the other leaders of the Polish Reformed concentrated on building a viable organizational and disciplinary framework for the church, and on negotiations for union with the Bohemian Brethren, who had settled in Great Poland in large numbers. In the former task they were ably supported by Bullinger, who through correspondence sought to persuade various prominent Lutheran and Catholic nobles to switch their allegiance to the Reformed camp.[10] Although not particularly successful in these endeavours, the *Antistes* had every reason to be confident about the long-term prospects for the Reformation in Poland, particularly given the heavy Protestant presence within the ranks of the Polish nobility (*szlachta*), which at the Diet of Piotrków in May 1555 had won effective autonomy from the crown in religious matters.[11]

But just when it seemed on the verge of a breakthrough, the Polish Reformed church was plunged into an internal crisis from which it did not emerge for close to a decade. The catalyst for this change was the arrival in Poland in May 1559 of Francesco Stancaro, whose early contacts with the Zurich church were discussed in Chapter 1.[12] Stancaro was already a familiar figure on the eastern European Protestant scene. Nearly ten years earlier, he had been instrumental in organizing the first Polish Reformed synod, held at Pińczów in October 1550. Shortly after this, he composed a statement on doctrine and discipline for the new church, the *Canones reformationis ecclesiarum polonicarum*, which was later translated into Polish and formally adopted by the Polish synod.[13] After being expelled from Poland (December 1550), Stancaro settled first in Königsberg and then in Frankfurt an der Oder, where his distinctive views on the mediatorial office of Christ brought him into conflict with Andreas Osiander, Andreas Musculus and, eventually, Philipp Melanchthon himself. Moving on to Hungary, where he spent the years 1553–59, Stancaro continued to court controversy, this time clashing with the local Lutheran superintendent Francis Dávid.

Stancaro's theology of the mediator, which served as the catalyst for debate about the doctrine of the Trinity among the Polish Reformed,

---

[10] Mühling, *Bullinger*, pp. 244–5.

[11] Williams, *Radical Reformation*, pp. 1004–5.

[12] The principal study of Stancaro's career to date is F. Ruffini, 'Francesco Stancaro: contributo alla storia della Riforma in Italia', in Ruffini, *Studi sui riformatori italiani* (Turin, 1955), pp. 165–406. See also Hein, *Italienische Protestanten*, pp. 66–118.

[13] Hein, *Italienische Protestanten*, pp. 70–72. This was the basis for Stancaro's later claim to have founded the Polish Reformed church, made in the preface to his *De Trinitate et Mediatore nostro Iesu Christo* (Cracow, 1562), sigs Aii^r–Bvii^v.

may be briefly summarized.[14] Taking his cue from Peter Lombard, the Mantuan exile argued that the mediatorial office of Christ was restricted to his human nature. A mediator, he pointed out, is inferior to the one with whom he intercedes. Consequently, any attempt to involve Christ's divinity in the work of mediation entails his subordination to the Father. The orthodox doctrine of co-equality between the persons of the Godhead can be safeguarded only by the rigorous exclusion of the Son's divine nature from the mediatorial office: anything else would incur the charge of Arianism.

Stancaro's critics feared that his doctrine of the mediator, with its stress on the utter separateness of the divine and human natures within the incarnate Christ, undermined the notion of the *communicatio idiomatum* and lent credence to the charge of Nestorianism levelled against the Reformed by Lutherans. Even more seriously, his assertion that the man Christ mediated not with the Father, but with the Godhead as a whole, appeared to compromise the distinction of persons within the Trinity, leaving God an undifferentiated monad, a 'Deus trinitas' alien to scripture. The problem was compounded by the Mantuan's use (and vigorous defence) of scholastic terminology.

Stancaro's insistence on making a shibboleth of what many considered an arcane doctrine, and his habit of denouncing opponents in the most extreme terms imaginable, soon brought him into conflict with Łaski, Lismanini and the other leaders of the Polish Reformed church. Shortly after his return to Poland, Stancaro published a provocative work comparing statements by the Hungarian Lutherans Dávid, Kaspar Heltai and Matthias Hebler, as well as Melanchthon, with the teachings of the arch-heretic Arius.[15] The Polish synod reacted by formally condemning the book at a meeting in Włodzisław in June 1559. Two months later Stancaro appeared before another meeting of the synod, this time in Pińczów, to defend his position, but after a furious altercation with Łaski he was convicted of Nestorianism and excommunicated.[16] The same assembly issued its own confession on the mediator, a copy of which was sent to Zurich with an accompanying letter from Lismanini and a copy of Stancaro's work.[17] But Stancaro had a powerful patron in the lord of Dubiecko, Stanisław Stadnicki, from

---

[14] For a more detailed discussion of Stancaro's views, see Hein, *Italienische Protestanten*, pp. 89–97.

[15] *Collatio doctrinae Arii et Philippi Melanchthonis et sequacium* (Pińczów, 1559).

[16] Hein, *Italienische Protestanten*, pp. 98–9; Sipayłło, *Acta synodalia*, I, pp. 310–12; Williams, *Radical Reformation*, pp. 1028–9.

[17] Lismanini to the Zurich ministers, 1 September 1559 (Wotschke, no. 174). For the text of the Pińczów confession, see ibid., no. 172.

whose estates in Ruthenia he continued to hurl anathemas against his theological opponents. To combat this threat, Łaski's successor as leader of the Polish Reformed, Felix Cruciger, solicited the public approval of the Zurichers (and of their colleagues in Geneva, Basle and Strasbourg) for the confession issued by the synod of Pińczów.[18] The united condemnation of Europe's leading Reformed churches would, it was hoped, bring Stancaro to heel.

The Stancaro affair raised particular difficulties for the Zurich church. In their defence of the Reformed doctrine of the Eucharist against the Lutherans, Zwinglian churchmen had developed a Christology which, while formally consistent with the position laid down by the councils of Ephesus (431) and Chalcedon (451), emphasized the distinction of Christ's two natures within the unity of his person. As a result, they had frequently been obliged to fend off accusations of Nestorianism, most recently from the reformer of Württemberg, Johannes Brenz. In Stancaro, one might say, Bullinger and his colleagues were confronted with the extreme logic of their own anti-ubiquitarian position. However, that did not prevent them coming out firmly on the side of the Polish Reformed leadership in its dispute with Stancaro. One of the principal authors of the Zurichers' response to Cruciger's request, Peter Martyr Vermigli, had already made clear his objections to Stancaro's doctrine of the mediator in a letter to the Polish church dated 14 February 1556. Replying to one of four questions put to him by Lismanini, Vermigli insisted that the efficacy of Christ's mission depended on the participation of both natures in the mediatorial office. If salvation could have been won for humanity through the efforts of Christ's human nature alone, he maintained, there would have been no reason for the incarnation to take place, as a man such as Moses could have interceded with God on our behalf.[19] In a joint letter to the Poles dated 27 May 1560, the Zurichers argued along similar lines, continuing to stress the distinction of natures within the incarnate Christ,[20] but resisting the consequences that Stancaro sought to draw from this. Mediation, they argued, has several aspects, some of which (suffering, dying etc.) are proper to the human nature of Christ, others of which (such as the sanctification of believers) are attributable solely

---

[18] Cruciger to the Zurich ministers, 17 March 1560 (Wotschke, no. 184). Lismanini had already asked the Zurichers to clarify their position in the letter of 1 September 1559 cited above.

[19] Vermigli, *Loci communes*, p. 1113.

[20] *Epistolae duae, ad ecclesias polonicas* ... (Zurich, 1561), p. 3: 'duarum naturarum, quae in Christo sunt, proprietates distinctas, integras et impermixtas conservare oportet, ita ut nullo pacto confundantur.'

to his divinity. The text repeatedly cited by Stancaro, 1 Timothy 2:5 ('There is one God, and one mediator between God and man, the man Jesus Christ') does not exclude Christ's divine nature from the office of mediator: 'When Paul called Christ a man, he did not at the same time deny that he was God. Neither did he exclude this by adding the particle "only".'[21]

But this relatively brief letter (it runs to only 10 pages) left many of the questions raised by Stancaro unanswered; in particular, it did not provide a satisfactory explanation of how the involvement of Christ's divine nature in the process of mediation could be squared with the orthodox doctrine of the co-equality and co-essentiality of the three divine persons. On a practical level, too, the letter failed to silence the Stancarists, who argued that it and the statements received from the other Reformed churches were forgeries.[22] At another turbulent meeting of the synod held at Książ in September 1560, supporters of Stancaro, led by the nobleman Jerome Ossoliński, forced the Reformed leadership to submit his case to Calvin, Beza, Bullinger and Vermigli for further consideration. Once again, Lismanini turned to Bullinger for assistance, requesting that the Zurich divines issue a second public statement condemning Stancaro's doctrine of the mediator.[23] By this time, the Zurichers were fully aware of the seriousness of the challenge that Stancaro posed to the unity and (just as important in the long run) the reputation of the Reformed church in Poland. Stancaro's tendency to condemn those who disagreed with him as 'Arians' and 'tritheists' was of particular concern to them, as Bullinger and his colleagues understood that any association with Arianism, the archetypal heresy, could deter otherwise sympathetic magistrates from embracing the Reformed cause, as well as providing ammunition for Catholic polemicists.

The Zurichers' second letter to the Poles – published in March 1561, together with their earlier statement, as the *Epistolae duae ad ecclesias polonicas* – is dominated by this concern.[24] First the charge of tritheism is repudiated:

---

[21] Ibid., p. 8: 'Dum hominem Paulus appelavit Christum, eundem simul Deum esse non negavit. Neque apposuit TANTUM, particulam exclusivam.'

[22] Wotschke, *Reformation in Polen*, p. 185.

[23] See his letter of 20 October / 3 November 1560 (Wotschke, no. 203): 'Vestrum erit, mi Bullingere, succurrere hoc tempore nobis non certe privatis literis, sed scripto aliquo istae ecclesiae digno. Utinam et pater meus Bernardinus Ochinus lingua italica scribat adversus hunc miserum Iudaeum.' Lismanini enclosed several works by supporters and opponents of Stancaro for the Zurichers' perusal.

[24] See the letter from Wolf to Lismanini of 29 September 1561 (ibid., no. 229): 'Ac velim, Lismanine reverende, nostras ad vos epistolas non alia de causa in lucem editas

> We believe, preach, teach and write that there are three divine persons, the Father, the Son and the Holy Spirit, who are consubstantial, equal and of the same essence, having one will and one operation by virtue of their common nature. However, we wish this doctrine to be accepted in such a way that the distinctiveness of the persons is preserved intact. Thus the Son does not generate, as the Father does, the Father is not sent, as the Son is, and the Father and the Holy Spirit have not assumed human flesh, as the Son did.[25]

Next the Zurichers set out their Christology, placing themselves firmly within the Chalcedonian mainstream and rejecting the opposing alternatives of Nestorianism and Eutychianism, together with the related monothelite heresy.[26] Throughout the letter, their priority is to demonstrate that the Reformed doctrine of the mediator conforms fully to the historical teaching of the church catholic. To that end, they affirm the authority of the first six ecumenical councils,[27] and quote at length from a litany of early church writers: Irenaeus, Chrysostom, Theophylact, Ambrose, Epiphanius, Theodoret, Cyril, John Damascene and Augustine.[28]

Elsewhere, the Zurichers take issue with Stancaro's central premise: namely, that the doctrine of consubstantiality depends on restricting the office of mediator to Christ's human nature. The assumption of this function by the Logos, they argue, is an example of the *diversitas*

---

putes, quam ut arianae haereseos crimen, a quo semper abhorruimus semperque alienissimi fuimus, a nobis depelleremus totique orbi potius quam Stancaro soli, quid ad vos perscripsissemus, innotesceret.'

[25] *Epistolae duae*, p. 12: 'Nos enim ut sentimus, ita praedicamus, docemus et scribimus, tres esse divinas personas, Patrem, Filium, et Spiritum sanctum, consubstantiales, aequales, et eiusdem essentiae, utque sunt eiusdem naturae, ita etiam unam voluntatem habent, et operationem, quod tamen accipi volumus incolumi personarum proprietate: non enim Filius generat, ut Pater, neque Pater mittitur ut Filius, neque Pater et Spiritus sanctus, instar Filii carnem humanam sumpserunt.'

[26] Ibid., pp. 14–15.

[27] Ibid., pp. 15–16: 'Recipimus item concilium Nicenum, Constantinopolitanum, Ephesinum prius, et Chalcedonense, nec non quintam et sextam Synodum, quatenus de beatissima Trinitate, incarnatione Filii dei, ac redemptione humani generis per ipsum parta decreverunt, quod nobis compertum sit, nihil ibi vel definitum vel constitutum, quod a scripturis divinitus revelatis non doceatur.'

[28] Most of the authorities cited in fact argue for the full divinity and humanity of Christ (which was not in dispute) rather than for the involvement of Christ's divine nature in the office of mediator. Stancaro noted this in his reply to the work: 'Praemissae falsae sunt, quia illae Sanctorum Patrum authoritates, quas pro se allegant, excludunt naturam Divinam ab officio Mediatoris, sed non a persona Mediatoris. Falsa ergo est conclusio, quod Christus sit Mediator secundum Divinam naturam' (*De Trinitate et Mediatore*, sig. Kiii^r). The Zurichers themselves seem to have been aware that they were on shaky patristic ground (see their rather unconvincing attempt to explain away those passages in the Fathers which appeared to support Stancaro's position in *Epistolae duae*, pp. 46–7).

proprietatum which exists between the persons of the Trinity within the divine economy and is most clearly manifested in the incarnation (which, of course, pertained to the Son alone). 'Things that are characterized by different actions are not separated in perpetuity from the same essence', Bullinger and his colleagues insist.[29] Like Vermigli in his earlier letter to the Poles, they also draw attention to the negative soteriological implications of Stancaro's views. According to the Zurich divines, Christ's created human nature – for all its perfection – was incapable of bringing about a reconciliation between sinful humankind and God; rather, the efficacy of the atonement depends on the participation of the Son's divinity in the work of mediation.[30] Stancaro, the Zurichers imply, is depriving the incarnation of its rationale and thereby opening the way to those who would deny Christ's divinity altogether.

The publication of the *Epistolae duae* pleased Stancaro's Polish adversaries, but it did not put an end to the controversy over the mediator. The following year Stancaro issued a new work entitled *De Trinitate et Mediatore Domino nostro Iesu Christo*, which included a typically forthright attack on the Zurichers. Comparing his treatment by the Polish Reformed to the persecution suffered by Athanasius at the hands of the heretical Emperor Constantius, Stancaro argued that the Zurich church's public support for his 'Arian' and 'Eutychian' opponents belied its claims to catholicity. As if to underline this, he repeatedly accused the Zurichers of defending positions anathematized by the third council of Constantinople (notably the characterization of the mediatorial office as 'theandric')[31] and of compromising the unity of the Godhead by their teaching, which he did not hesitate to condemn as tritheism.[32] He even turned the charge of Nestorianism back on his opponents, contending that by involving Christ's Godhead in the office

---

[29] *Epistolae duae*, p. 29: 'Neque quod assumitur, verum esse in universum, Diversas esse naturas, quarum opera diversa fuerint, quoniam filius mittitur, pater autem non mittitur, sed mittit. Filius carnem assumit, cuius pater et spiritus sanctus expertes manent. Non itaque illa perpetuo separantur ab eadem essentia, quae variis actionibus ornantur.'

[30] Ibid., p. 20: 'Ad reconciliationem generis humani cum deo, non satis erat Christum laborare, fatigari, pati et mori, sed oportuit haec eius opera tam praeclara, excellentia, eximia, et gratiosa esse, quo deus illa suo beneplacito complecteretur, et quemadmodum scriptura loquitur, ceu suavissime olentia odoraretur: tanta vero dignitas a natura humana praeberi non poterat, nisi divinitas eam suppeditasset.' This argument had a long pedigree in the Zurich church. In his Berne sermon on the creed of 1528, Zwingli had used similar reasoning to explain the need for the incarnation (see W.P. Stephens, *The Theology of Huldrych Zwingli* (Oxford, 1986), p. 111; Z, VI/1, p. 463).

[31] *De Trinitate et Mediatore*, sigs Iiiiv–iiiir.

[32] Ibid., sigs Aiiv–iiir: 'Faciunt … unum Deum incarnatum, orantem, supplicantem, et ad pedes patris alterius Dei prostratum intercedentem, gementem, lachrimantem.'

of mediator they introduced, in effect, two divine Sons, one of whom mediates with the other on behalf of humanity.[33] Stancaro also accused the Reformed of inconsistency, arguing that until recently they had expressed themselves in full agreement with his doctrine of the mediator. In support of this claim he cited Christological statements contained in earlier published works by Bullinger and Vermigli, among others.[34]

By the time the Zurichers received a copy of this work (late 1562), the Stancarist controversy was no longer the burning issue that it had once been. However, the allegations contained in *De Trinitate et Mediatore* were sufficiently great to warrant a public response from Bullinger and his colleagues.[35] The task was undertaken by Josias Simler, who had succeeded to Vermigli's chair of Old Testament following the latter's death in November 1562. Simler's *Responsio ad maledicum Francisci Stancari Mantuani librum* (published in March 1563) is divided into four sections, corresponding to those parts of *De Trinitate et Mediatore* that were directed against the Zurichers. In the first of these, he replies to Stancaro's main charges, in particular his claim that the doctrine of the *diversitas proprietatum* proposed in the Zurichers' second letter to the Poles compromised the unity of substance within the Godhead. Like Stancaro's Polish critics, Simler retorts that the Mantuan's position is reminiscent of ancient Sabellianism, with its negation of any real distinction between the persons of the Trinity. Simler also objects to the suggestion that the Zurichers constitute two Christs, one the incarnate mediator, the other the God with whom he intercedes; rather, it is Stancaro's insistence on positing a purely human mediator that has the effect of dividing Christ's person.[36] Neither can the Zurichers be accused of Eutychianism, as they carefully preserve the distinction of natures *within* the office of mediator.[37]

Elsewhere in the *Responsio*, Simler defends Bullinger and his late predecessor, Peter Martyr, against the charge of doctrinal innovation,

---

[33] Ibid., sig. Bviii[v].

[34] Ibid., sigs Dvii[v]–E[v]; also Iiiii[r].

[35] Ibid., sig. Aiii[r]: 'Tigurini et Genevenses, Arrianam, Eutychianam, Apollinaristarum, Timotheianarum, Accephalorum, Theodosianorum, Gaianitorum et Macarianorum, haereses, pro fide catholica ad vos miserunt, ut demonstrative in hoc libro videbitis et manibus vestris contrectabitis.'

[36] *Responsio ad maledicum Francisci Stancari Mantuani librum adversus Tigurinae ecclesiae ministros, de Trinitate et Mediatore Domino nostro Iesu Christo, auctore Iosia Simlero Tigurino* (Zurich, 1563), fol. 14[r]: 'Potius dicendum esset, eos facere duos Filios qui naturam divinam prorsus a Mediatione removent, ut sit secundum illos unus Filius homo Mediator, et alius Filius Deus, apud quem fiat mediatio: sed nos cum haec aliter mitigari possint, nolumus adversarios imitari et omnia detorquere calumniose.'

[37] Ibid., fols 14[v]–15[v].

citing Zwingli's early *Exposition of the Articles* (1523) to demonstrate the consistency of the Zurich church's position with regard to the mediator.[38] The Zurichers' interpretation of the patristic passages cited in the second of the *Epistolae duae* – which Stancaro claimed had been misapplied to the office, as opposed to the person, of the mediator – is also upheld:

> When the Fathers discuss the person of the mediator, they do not only teach that our mediator is both God and man, but show that no one could perform this function unless he were both God and man. If [mediation] is the work of [Christ's] humanity alone, without the involvement of his divine nature, I do not see how their argument can be justified.[39]

Like the authors of the *Epistolae duae*, Simler highlights the grave soteriological implications of Stancaro's doctrine of the mediator, insisting that the efficacy of Christ's mission depends on the participation of his divine nature in the mediatorial office. What had been implied in the earlier work – namely, that Stancaro's position makes the incarnation superfluous – is here made explicit. Echoing an argument first outlined by Vermigli in his letter to the Poles of February 1556, Simler asks, 'What was the point of this union [of human and divine natures in Christ], if the deity does not operate differently through the flesh that it has assumed than through Moses and Aaron, or any other holy man?'[40]

In his *Responsio*, Simler provided the Zurich church with a precise and closely argued statement of its position on the relationship between the two natures of Christ in the context of salvation, in the course of which he also sought to iron out some apparent discrepancies between Bullinger's and Calvin's doctrine of the mediator that Stancaro had highlighted.[41] For all the turmoil that it created, the Stancarist

---

38 Ibid., fol. 24r–v; compare Z, II, pp. 158–62.

39 Ibid., fol. 33v: 'Cum de Mediatoris persona Patres disputant, non tantum docent Mediatorem nostrum esse Deum et hominem, sed ostendunt neminem posse fungi hoc officio nisi sit Deus et homo: quod si humanitas omnia efficit, et nullae hic sunt partes divinae naturae, nescio qua recte hoc ab illis statuatur.'

40 Ibid., fol. 28v: 'Quid enim hac coniunctione opus erat, si deitas non aliter per carnem assumptam operatur quam per Mosem et Aaronem, aut quemvis alium sanctum hominem.'

41 In two short works against Stancaro dated June 1560 and March 1561, Calvin had argued that Christ exercised the office of mediator 'ab initio creationis' (CO, IX, 337–42; 349–58). The Zurichers, by contrast, preferred to designate the pre-incarnate Logos as mediator only by anticipation, i.e. in the sense that he was predestined to take flesh and die for humanity's sins (*Epistolae duae*, p. 19). In *De Trinitate et Mediatore*, Stancaro seized on this as evidence of his opponents' disunity, but Simler explained it as simply a difference of emphasis. The Zurichers, he maintained, did not exclude Christ absolutely

controversy could in one sense be regarded as beneficial, as it presented the Zurich Reformed with an opportunity to clear themselves once and for all of the accusation of Nestorianism. Whereas in dialogue with the Lutherans they were continually obliged to emphasize the distinction between Christ's two natures, against Stancaro they were able to make plain their acceptance of the other side of the Chalcedonian equation, the unity of the Saviour's person. The exchange was also in many ways a conventional one, relating as it did to the correct interpretation of traditional doctrinal formulas: at no point was the continued relevance of such doctrines as the Trinity and the two natures of Christ called into question. If anything, Stancaro may be regarded as more conservative than the Zurichers, because of his reliance on scholastic (Peter Lombard's) as well as patristic authority.

The controversy did, however, force the Zurichers to give detailed consideration to some technical aspects of doctrine which they had in the past preferred to gloss over: for example, the distinction between Christ considered as incarnate mediator and as God, and the relationship between the persons of the Trinity within the economy of salvation. It deepened their knowledge of patristic Christology, already quite extensive as a result of the ubiquitarian controversy, and impressed on them further the importance of catholicity as a defining characteristic of the Reformation. Stancaro, by raising the spectre of Arianism, threatened the future progress of reform in eastern Europe. Unfortunately for the Zurichers, the increasingly heterodox positions adopted by Polish Protestants in reaction to Stancaro's views lent credence to his claim that the Reformed doctrine of the mediator was at variance with Nicene orthodoxy. Over the next decade, Zurich's churchmen were repeatedly obliged to fend off the allegation that their teachings were responsible for the emergence of organized antitrinitarianism.

---

from the office of mediator prior to the incarnation, while Calvin did not designate the pre-existent Christ as mediator without qualification, 'sed dispensationis ordine' (*Responsio*, fol. 26ʳ). Simler's argument is not entirely convincing in doctrinal terms, as Calvin does seem to attribute a 'cosmological' as well as a soteriological role to Christ as mediator, but he did at least succeed in establishing a formal equivalence between the positions of the two churches. On Calvin's doctrine of the mediator, see G. Williams, 'Strains in the Christology of the Emerging Polish Brethren', in S. Fiszman (ed.), *The Polish Reformation in its European Context* (Bloomington, 1984), pp. 61–95; J. Tylenda, 'Christ the Mediator: Calvin versus Stancaro', *CTJ*, 8 (1973), pp. 5–16; and 'The Controversy on Christ the Mediator: Calvin's second reply to Stancaro', *CTJ*, 8 (1973), pp. 131–57.

ii. Giorgio Biandrata and the Polish Reformed schism

By the end of 1561, Bullinger and his colleagues had ceased to regard Stancaro as the principal threat to the unity and orthodoxy of the Polish Reformed church. That dubious distinction had passed to the Piedmontese exile Giorgio Biandrata.

Biandrata was born in the marquisate of Saluzzo, south-west of Turin, around 1516.[42] After studying medicine in Montpellier, Pavia and Bologna, he was appointed personal physician first to the Polish queen Bona Sforza (1540) and then to her daughter Isabella, the widow of the Transylvanian prince John Zápolya. In 1552 he returned to Italy, eventually settling in Pavia, but four years later he emigrated to Geneva, where he was elected an elder of the city's Italian church. Within a few months of his arrival he came under suspicion of heresy, after questioning the biblical foundations for the doctrine of the Trinity first with the Italian pastor Celso Martinengo and then with Calvin himself.[43] Rather than subscribe to the orthodox confession proposed by Martinengo's successor Lattanzio Ragnoni, Biandrata fled Geneva in mid-May 1558, to be followed some days later by his fellow antitrinitarian Giovanni Paolo Alciati.

After failing to find a haven in Berne or Zurich, Biandrata resolved to return to Poland, where he quickly entered into contact with Lismanini. Although Calvin advised both Lismanini and the rector of the Reformed school in Pińczów, Peter Statorius, not to have any dealings with the Piedmontese physician, his warnings fell on deaf ears. In the months following his arrival in Poland, Biandrata succeeded not only in allaying concerns about his orthodoxy, but in securing the patronage of the most powerful Reformed nobleman in the kingdom, Mikołaj Radziwiłł. When, in the revised preface to the second edition of his commentary on the Acts of the Apostles, Calvin denounced Biandrata as a follower of Servetus – 'worse than Stancaro' – the leaders of the Polish Reformed did all in their power to convince the Genevan reformer that his judgment was at fault.[44] At a meeting of the synod at Pińczów in January 1561, Lismanini, Cruciger and others professed themselves satisfied of Biandrata's orthodoxy, after he publicly declared his faith in the deity of Christ and the Holy Spirit, in a single indivisible divine essence and in

---

[42] For much of what follows, see *DBI*, X, 257–64, and J.N. Tylenda, 'The Warning that Went Unheeded: John Calvin on Giorgio Biandrata', *CTJ*, 12 (1977), pp. 24–62 .

[43] See the *quaestiones* of Biandrata in CO, XVII, 169–71, and Calvin's response in ibid., IX, 325–32. English translations of both texts appear in Tylenda, 'Biandrata', pp. 52–61.

[44] CO, XVIII, no. 3232 (1 August 1560). The work was dedicated to Radziwiłł.

the existence of three distinct divine hypostases (while being careful not to specify the precise nature of the relationship between the persons of the Trinity).[45] A final pronouncement on the issue was delayed so that further attempts could be made to reconcile Biandrata with Calvin,[46] but in December the synod declared Biandrata wholly innocent of the charge of Servetianism.[47]

A detailed reconstruction of Biandrata's activities in Poland is beyond the scope of this study; the conflicting statements of contemporaries make it difficult, in any case, to unravel precisely what was happening behind the scenes in the Polish church. However, the general consensus is that Biandrata took advantage of the turmoil created by the controversy over the mediator to propose a radical reassessment of the received doctrine of the Trinity and, in particular, of the *homoousion*, on the basis of scripture and the Apostles' creed. Some leading figures within the Polish Reformed church, frustrated by Stancaro's intransigence and by their own inability to match his mastery of the relevant patristic and scholastic arguments, seized on this as a way of changing the terms of debate and thereby neutralizing the troublesome Mantuan. Many Polish ministers, Lismanini among them, had been repelled by Stancaro's penchant for scholastic and non-scriptural formulations, which in their eyes smacked of 'popery': it was to this constituency that Biandrata was able to address his appeal.[48]

Bullinger was quick to express misgivings about the welcome that had been afforded Biandrata by the Polish Reformed. In a letter to the reform-minded Catholic bishop Jacob Uchański dated 27 May 1560, he warned:

> You will need to be on your guard in these parts not just against Stancaro, but against all those who with Arius and Servetus deny the divinity of Christ the saviour. I hear that in your region a certain Biandrata, who practises medicine, has been infecting not a few with the Servetian poison. If it is the same person who was in Geneva and left because Calvin, the most vigilant pastor of that church, pressed him hard and wanted to make him confess the

---

[45] Sipayłło, *Acta synodalia*, II, pp. 84–6; Cruciger to Radziwiłł, 13 March 1561 (CO, XVII, no. 3359).

[46] Radziwiłł to Calvin, 14 July 1561 (CO, XVIII, no. 3443); the ministers of Vilna to Calvin, 23 July 1561 (ibid., no. 3453). For Calvin's rejection of these overtures, see ibid., nos 3559; 3561; 3562; 3564; 3565.

[47] The Polish synod to Calvin, 13 December 1561 (CO, XIX, no. 3648).

[48] The Polish Reformed aversion to non-scriptural language and precise doctrinal definition had already been evident in the context of Łaski's attempts to reach an agreement with the Lutherans and Bohemian Brethren over the Eucharist. Hein comments: 'Das Pochen auf das "satis est" in der Theologie Laskis hat später die antitrinitarischen Umtriebe in Polen ungewollt gefördert' (*Italienische Protestanten*, p. 60).

sincere and true faith, and who then in Zurich began to dispute with us about matters of which we entirely disapproved, we seriously admonish you to be on your guard. For we consider that we ought to preserve unsullied the mystery of the worshipful Trinity. But we judge that Servetians, as plagues of the church, are to be expelled and not listened to, seeing that they utter nothing but blasphemies. May the Lord protect his church from evil.[49]

Stancaro, who until the publication of the *Epistolae duae* had not given up hope of regaining the Zurichers' support, skilfully played on these fears. In a letter dated 4 December 1560, he informed the Swiss that his opponents in Poland were misusing their authority in order to propagate a form of tritheism.[50] In fact, prompted by Biandrata, a number of Polish ministers were coming to accept what Stancaro had long been saying were the logical consequences of involving Christ's divine nature in the office of the mediator: the subordination of the Son to the Father and the effective abandonment of the doctrine of consubstantiality. Increasingly, the *homoousion* was taken to signify commonality rather than identity of essence.

As news of these developments filtered back to them, Bullinger and his colleagues became alarmed by the unexpectedly radical turn that the anti-Stancarist reaction in Poland was taking. Their concerns are evident from the second of the *Epistolae duae*, in which they instructed their Polish counterparts not to be duped by those – meaning Biandrata and his proselytes – who were taking advantage of the controversy over the mediator to lead the church into heresy:

> Because they are cunning men, they pretend to be on the same side as right-thinking brethren, by boasting that they embrace fully a belief in Christ as mediator according to both natures. However, on the other hand they agree with Stancaro, from which it is to be inferred that the Son is inferior to the Father. Although they do not say this publicly, to their co-conspirators and to the simple, whom they strive to corrupt, they continually pour it forth, as if they have conquered.[51]

Privately, too, Johannes Wolf was critical of the strategy being pursued by the Polish church leadership. Writing to Lismanini on 5 March 1561, he warned his correspondent to take care 'lest those who call you heretics are

---

49 Wotschke, no. 189.

50 CO, XVIII, no. 3288.

51 *Epistolae duae*, pp. 51–2: 'Ii, ut sunt astuti homines, cum fratribus nostris recte sentientibus facere se assimulant, iactando se ambabus ulnis amplecti Christum quoad utranque naturam esse mediatorem, sed ex altera parte cum Stancaro sentiant, inde concludi Filium esse minorem Patre, quod etsi publice non dicunt, suis tamen coniuratis, et simplicioribus quos corrumpere student, id perpetuo ingerunt, quasi vicerint.'

able to detect heresies in your opinions': Stancaro's comments had clearly hit home.[52] However, Lismanini resisted attempts to drive a wedge between himself and Biandrata, of whose fundamental orthodoxy he remained convinced; in his reply to Wolf, dated 15 May, he even came close to reproaching the Zurichers for their earlier dismissive treatment of his compatriot.[53] To make matters worse, Bullinger and his colleagues were starting to have their suspicions confirmed from other sources. In September Stanisław Sarnicki, a Reformed pastor in Cracow, confided to the *Antistes* that he had doubts about the orthodoxy of a confession of faith submitted by Lismanini to the recent synod of Włodzisław, which could be interpreted as teaching 'a pagan belief in three gods and Arianism, to the dishonour of the son of God'.[54] Shortly afterwards, Bullinger cautioned Cruciger and the leaders of the Polish Reformed against giving credence to the assurances of those 'who simulate piety but who, being crammed with most impious dogmas, breathe only the destruction of true religion'.[55]

In a letter to Lismanini written around the same time, Wolf tried a more conciliatory approach. Unlike Calvin, and even Bullinger, he was prepared to accept the possibility that Biandrata might have retracted his earlier heterodox views. At the same time, he made clear that Biandrata's rehabilitation was conditional on his accepting the doctrine of consubstantiality, the Athanasian and Nicene creeds, and the writings of the orthodox Fathers on the Trinity.[56] By this stage, however, the radical drift of the Polish Reformed church had acquired a seemingly unstoppable momentum. Under Biandrata's influence, Lismanini himself began to waver in his commitment to Nicene orthodoxy: writing to Wolf towards the end of December, he admitted that the Stancarist controversy had forced him to reconsider his position on the Trinity, and described how he had embarked on an ambitious programme of reading, including works by Erasmus and most of the major Greek and Latin Fathers, in order to help him clarify his views.[57] At meetings in

---

[52] Wotschke, no. 217.

[53] Ibid., no. 221a : 'Si duole non poco de qualch'uno di vostri, per non haverlo uddito quando passo per Tiguro.' In the same letter, Lismanini argued that in his criticism of scholastic theology and 'le chimere de' sophisti' Biandrata was merely following the example set by Luther.

[54] Ibid., no. 228. Compare Sipayłło, *Acta*, II, pp. 119–23.

[55] Bullinger to Cruciger, 30 September 1561 (*CO*, XVIII, no. 3540).

[56] Wotschke, no. 229.

[57] Ibid., no. 246. The fruits of Lismanini's reading are apparent in a letter to the Polish nobleman Ivan Karniński dated 10 September 1561, in which, following Biandrata, he argues for the supremacy of the Father within the Godhead (S. Lubieniecki, *History of the Polish Reformation and Nine Related Documents*, trans. G. Williams (Minneapolis, 1995), pp. 177–83).

Książ and Pińczów the following spring, the Polish synod placed a moratorium on the use of non-biblical language in relation to the Godhead, highlighting the growing split between doctrinal conservatives such as Sarnicki, who resisted the decision, and the radicals clustered around Biandrata.[58] The ascendancy of the Biandratists was confirmed at a subsequent meeting of the synod in Pińczów on 18–20 August. The confession issued by this assembly, which Sarnicki boycotted, endorsed the Nicene creed and repudiated Arianism, but voiced only qualified acceptance of the *Quicunque vult* (a particular bugbear of the radicals on account of its 'scholastic' vocabulary and alleged Sabellian tendencies).[59]

Some of Biandrata's supporters were prepared to go further. In a letter to the Zurich church of November 1562, the Lublin ministers Stanisław Paklepka and Martin Krowicki, along with the superintendent of Chełm, Mikołaj Żytno, denounced the Athanasian creed as an invention of the 'scholae papanae' and the source for later errors concerning justification, the mediation of Christ and the intercession of saints. In sum, they argued that the Reformed establishment's fidelity to the received doctrine of the Trinity was inconsistent with the founding principles of the Reformation:

> It is wrong to believe concerning the papacy that this one article of the Trinity remained intact, when from the rest of its structure it is easy to identify the firm foundation on which so many monstrosities were built – even though, for the sake of the elect, God by his singular goodness left intact beneath the impurities the form of baptism.[60]

By this stage a formal schism within the Polish church was imminent. On 14 November, Sarnicki convened a breakaway synod in Cracow at which he and his allies affirmed their adherence to the conciliar creeds and to a series of Reformed confessional statements on

---

58 Lubieniecki, *History*, pp. 186–8; Williams, *Radical Reformation*, pp. 1041–2; Hein, *Italienische Protestanten*, pp. 160–61. This measure had first been proposed by Biandrata (with Lismanini's support) at the synod of Cracow the previous December (Lubieniecki, *History*, pp. 184–6).

59 Sipayłło, *Acta*, II, p. 323: 'Tamen nec symbolum, quod dicitur Athanasii reicimus, quo unitas naturae divinae in Patre, Filio, et Spiritu S. contra Arium demonstratur, modo ne quis illo Apostolici symboli puritatem et veritatem inconcussam inficere tentet, quales Sabellianos esse nunc novimus, tum ut iuxta mentem ipsius Athanasii praecipue in expositione fidei, quae continetur in *Epistola ad Epictetum*, interpretatio eius constet.' See also Wotschke, no. 254.

60 Wotschke, no. 264. Compare Paklepka to Vermigli, 18 August 1562 (ibid., no. 253): 'Reliqui omnes articuli magna vi ex faucibus tartarei huius Cerberi erepti, hic unus, in quo est vitae aeternae colophon, integer relinquetur?' Bullinger responded to the Polish ministers' arguments in a letter to Lismanini dated 29 April 1563 (ibid., no. 280).

the Trinity.[61] Shortly afterwards, the Cracow superintendent and fervent Biandratist Gregory Paul (Grzegorz Paweł) published his *Tabula de Trinitate*, in which he rejected the doctrine of consubstantiality as traditionally understood. Although this work does not survive, a subsequent letter from Paul to the Zurichers provides some indication of its contents.[62] Here Paul argues that the persons of the Trinity are distinct beings whose unity consists merely in sharing a single divine nature. The 'one God' of scripture is not some incomprehensible 'Deus essentia', but the Father, from whose substance the Son is generated. Paul purports to uphold the Nicene creed – its description of the Son as 'God from God' is cited at several points in the letter – but rejects the intrinsic authority of the church Fathers and councils.[63]

The Zurichers would have detected in Paul's letter the unmistakable influence of the Italian 'tritheists' Giovanni Paolo Alciati and Valentino Gentile, both of whom were in Poland by late 1562.[64] The close ties between Paul and Gentile – who, unlike Biandrata, made no secret of his differences with the Reformed establishment – alarmed even Lismanini, who in letters to Wolf dated 28 April and 24 May 1563 distanced himself from Paul's views and sought to re-establish his orthodox credentials.[65] By this time, however, he was in no position to influence events. Although Biandrata left Poland for Transylvania during the summer of 1563, under the leadership of Paul and his fellow anti-Nicene Stanisław Lutomirski the majority of Polish ministers continued to move in an antitrinitarian direction. Paul's victory – and the break-up of the Polish Reformed church – was sealed in September that year, when the synod adopted a confession condemning the orthodox doctrine of consubstantiality as Sabellian. The same confession boldly asserted the sole authority of scripture in matters of faith: 'The elect are to give reverence to the divine word alone ...

---

[61] See Sarnicki to Christopher Thretius, October 1562 (CO, XIX, no. 3875). Bullinger was sent a copy of this letter.

[62] The letter is dated 20 July 1563 (Wotschke, no. 297). Compare Paul to the Zurich ministers, 17 November 1562 [CO, XIX, no. 3877]).

[63] 'Cavete vobis a Gabaonitis, qui imponebant populo dei laceris vestibus mucido pane, etiam sub nomine dei nostri se venire dicebant et imponebant populo dei. Non imponant nobis patres, vetustas, concilia etc. Unus Christus sit magister, in aliis articulis nihil valebant patres et concilia. Sunt etiam hic plerique Gabaonitae, qui vobis se amicos profitentur et nihil aliud quam ad Aegyptum reducere conantur populum dei confessione Augustana. Patefaciet vobis eos postea dominus.'

[64] Gentile attended a meeting of the synod at Pińczów in November that year (Lubieniecki, *History*, p. 167; Wotschke, p. 155, n. 1).

[65] Wotschke, nos 277 and 292.

believing that it should be neither added to nor diminished in any way'.[66]

The programme of doctrinal reform devised by Biandrata and his supporters represented a much more fundamental challenge to Reformed orthodoxy than Stancaro's doctrine of the mediator. The tritheists' demand for a return to the simple language of scripture and the Apostles' creed – a persistent refrain, as we have seen, of Italian dissenters from Renato onwards – placed a question-mark against the traditional formulations which enshrined the Nicene doctrine of the Trinity. It also put the onus on the Zurich divines to demonstrate that their retention of extra-biblical terminology was consistent with the principle of *sola scriptura*.

This was a problem to which Bullinger had given some consideration even prior to the Polish trinitarian controversy. In an early work, the *Assertio utriusque in Christo naturae*, he explains the introduction of such terms as *homoousios* as an attempt to preserve the true meaning of scripture against the 'curiosity of certain profane men' ('curiositas prophanorum quorundam hominum').[67] In support of his argument that apparently subordinationist passages within scripture are to be understood with reference to Christ's human nature alone, he cites a variety of ancient writers, including some quite obscure ones (Hippolytus, Amphilochius, Eustathius of Sebaste, Antiochus of Ptolemais, Tertullian and Chrysostom).[68] Similarly, when challenged by the Catholic polemicist Johannes Cochlaeus on how the Reformed were able to reconcile their continued faith in the Trinity, as defined by the doctors of the early church, with their belief in the all-sufficiency of the Bible, Bullinger again insisted on the primacy of the sense over the letter of scripture:

> For who does not know that good men do not clash about words when there is proper agreement about issues of substance? And what, I ask, prohibits us from expressing things in clearer words, so long as those are faithful to the truth of scripture and reflect its meaning, especially when we are dealing with intricate and obscure matters? The pastors of the church have been forced, in response to quarrels about vicious teachings, with careful precision to devise

---

[66] *CO*, XX, no. 4125. The divine origin of the term Trinity had already been rejected by the Lithuanian Reformed at a synod meeting in Mordy on 6 June (Sipayłło, *Acta*, p. 152; Lubieniecki, *History*, pp. 218–19; Williams, *Radical Reformation*, p. 1046).

[67] *Utriusque in Christo naturae tam divinae quam humanae, contra varias haereses, pro confessione Christi catholica, Assertio orthodoxa, per Heinrychum Bullingerum* (Zurich, 1534), fols 15ᵛ–18ʳ. The *Assertio* was directed against the Savoyard antitrinitarian Claude d'Aliod (*HBBW*, IV, p. 336, n. 2).

[68] Ibid., fols 57ʳ–60ᵛ.

terms for certain things that explain what is meant by them and leave quarrelsome persons with nowhere left to hide. But those who reject such terms, and those who continually abuse them – thereby detracting from the absolute perfection of the scriptures – would seem to be equally foolish.[69]

These points are developed at greater length in the Zurich divines' responses to Biandrata and other antitrinitarians. In correspondence with Lismanini, for example, Wolf argued that Biandrata's protestations of orthodoxy did not ring true, as in the same breath he rejected the creeds and the Fathers:

> Those who believe in and are convinced of that which scripture teaches about our Lord Jesus Christ the only-begotten son of God – if not in the same language that the Fathers used, then with the same meaning as those words convey – do not repudiate the Athanasian or Nicene creeds or the writings of the doctors [of the church] on the holy Trinity.[70]

Wolf could not resist comparing Biandrata's stance with the tactics employed by the fourth-century heresiarch Arius, who also cloaked his heresies with fine words so as to be able to disseminate them more effectively; for that reason alone, the Poles should be wary of taking Biandrata's protestations at face value.[71] The history of the early church

---

[69] *Ad Ioannis Cochlei de canonicae scripturae et Catholicae ecclesiae authoritate libellum, pro solida Scripturae canonicae authoritate, tum et absoluta eius perfectione, veraque Catholicae ecclesiae dignitate, Heinrychi Bullingeri orthodoxa Responsio* (Zurich, 1544), fol. 14v: 'Quis enim nesciat bonos viros de verbis non digladiari, ubi probe convenit de rebus? An quid vetat, obsecro, quo minus liceat quae perplexa et obscura sunt, planioribus enunciare verbis, quae tamen serviant veritate scripturae, et quae nihil aliud significent, quam quod scripturis consignatum est? Coacti sunt ecclesiarum pastores, pravorum dogmatum certaminibus exagitati, exquisita perspicuitate vocabula aliquot rebus apposita invenire, quibus quid sentirent explicarent, caverentque ne obliqua subterfugia relinquerent rixatoribus. Atqui ex aequo desipere videntur qui illas voces repudiare, vel ipsis in derogationem absolutae scripturarum perfectionis abuti perrexerint.' Bullinger's aim in the *Responsio* was to provide evidence for the catholicity of the Reformed and to demonstrate that, despite their differences with Rome, they ought not to be subject to the imperial penalties for heresy (ibid., fol. 52r). See further Hollweg, *Heinrich Bullingers Hausbuch*, pp. 200–2.

[70] Wotschke, no. 229.

[71] Ibid.: 'Manet alta profecto mente mihi repositum, quod ecclesiasticae historiae de Arrii moribus et ingenio referunt, qui potuerit et consueverit pro eo, ac res tempusque ferrent, simulare ac dissimulare.' See also Wolf to Calvin, 28 September 1561 (CO, XVIII, no. 3537): 'Vereor ... ne quid ille vocum ab ecclesia prisca receptarum horror et praetextus alienarum a sacris literis argutiarum, et quae in eo genere hominum alia video, aliquid mali maioris tegant, quam in praesentia scire velint. Laudat [Biandrata] symbolum apostolicum: Athanasiano et Niceno minime esse opus existimat. Hic suspicor latere anguem in herba et vereor ne qui isthac blandi rati se pateretur excipi, ultra pontum Euxinum vel in Aegyptiam illam Alexandriam veheretur. Neque enim nescio quam

generally testified to the need for precise statements of doctrine which the heretics, for all their cunning, would be unable to circumvent. Writing to Radziwiłł in early 1565, the Zurichers contrasted times of doctrinal unity, when adherence to the 'purity' and 'simplicity' of the Apostles' creed was enough to define a believer, with periods such as their own, when the church was threatened by dissent from within its ranks. In such situations, they argued, a more aggressively confessional approach was called for:

> In the ancient church, when the Arians, Macedonians, Nestorians and other plagues confessed the words of the Apostles' creed, but violated the substance of it with their doctrines, the pious doctors were forced to produce other confessions of faith. We have come to the conclusion that we must do likewise.[72]

The defence of non-scriptural language, both as a practical tool for safeguarding the church against heresy and as a legitimate exegetical device, is a central feature of the *Responsio ministrorum Tigurinae ecclesiae ad argumenta Antitrinitariorum Italopolonorum*, a short work written in early 1563 at the request of Sarnicki and the pro-Nicene faction within the Polish Reformed church.[73] Here the Zurichers attack the 'tritheism' and subordinationism of Biandrata, Gentile and Paul, arguing for the co-essentiality of the Father, Son and Holy Spirit. With Calvin, and against the radicals, Bullinger and his colleagues insist that, wherever scripture refers to God without qualification, all three persons are to be understood, rather than the Father alone.[74] They also repudiate

---

callidem et versutum fuerit ipsius Arrii ingenium quamque facile sit Satanae artes cum dogmate simul omnes posterorum animis inserere.' The tendency to equate Biandrata with Arius was fostered by a theological mindset and an accompanying polemical vocabulary which had the effect of erasing the distinctions between contemporary 'heresy' and its ancient prototype. Whether accurate or not, the parallel was constantly in the Zurichers' minds when they considered developments in Poland.

[72] Wotschke, no. 332.

[73] StAZ E II 371, 931–5. The title and marginal notes to the tract are in Bullinger's hand. Sarnicki had asked Bullinger for a statement condemning the radicals in a letter dated 23 January 1563 (Wotschke, no. 268). Sarnicki's ally Christopher Thretius brought the *Responsio* with him when he returned to Poland from Switzerland in June that year (T. Wotschke, 'Christoph Thretius: Ein Beitrag zur Geschichte des Kampfes der reformierten Kirche gegen den Antitrinitarismus in Polen', *Altpreussische Monatsschrift*, NF 44 (1907), pp. 1–42; 151–210 [21–3]).

[74] StAZ E II 371, 933ʳ: 'De tribus his, inquiunt, semper distincte loquuntur scripturae neque usquam tres in unum conflantur, neque unus esse dicuntur, sed cum unus Deus dicitur, aut nomen Dei absolute ponitur, Deus Pater intelligitur. Scripturas loqui distincte de Patre, Filio et Spiritu sancto nos non negamus, qui realem distinctionem personarum docemus, non tamen semper ita distincte loquuntur, ut non etiam unam ostendant in singulis essentiam, quod vos conflare in unum appellatis.' Compare CO, IX, 633–38; 645–50.

the suggestion that the orthodox doctrine of the Trinity actually amounts to a quaternity of three persons and one essence.[75] The doctrine of consubstantiality, the Zurichers argue, is no papal invention, but a faithful exposition of the facts of scripture: namely, that God is one, and that the Father, Son and Holy Spirit are each truly divine.[76] The extra-biblical terms Trinity, essence, person and relation – unlike the scholastic vocabulary deployed by Catholics and Lutherans in support of their teaching on the Eucharist – are neither sophistic nor pagan in origin, but sanctified by time-honoured usage within the church. Here we see articulated Bullinger's essentially conservative understanding of the scope and nature of religious reform. Whereas the radicals maintain that whatever is not specifically taught in scripture ought to be repudiated, the Zurichers turn this argument on its head: whatever cannot be shown to contradict scripture is to be retained by the church, even if the Bible does not explicitly prescribe it. The burden of proof is thus shifted from the Reformed establishment on to its challengers:

> Either … they should show that there is fault and error in these confessions and confute them, or if they cannot demonstrate anything of the sort, they should admit that they are quarrelsome and arrogant, refusing to approve things that they cannot, however, rebut or confute.[77]

The same conservatism informs another unpublished work by Bullinger from this period, the *Trinitas Dei, et patris filiique in*

---

[75] StAZ E II 371, 932ʳ: 'Tertio accusant nos, qui unitatem essentiae divinae et personarum trinitatem docemus, quod habeamus fidem sophisticam imo Mahometicam ex Alcorano desumptam. Statuere enim nos non trinitatem sed quaternitatem, nempe unum Deum essentiae, Deum patrem, Deum filium, et Deum spiritum sanctum. Sed in his et aliis accusationibus, nobis manifestam iniuriam faciunt, et nostram doctrinam aut non intelligunt, vel malitiose et improbe corrumpunt. Nos enim neque personas ex essentia derivamus, nec ut ipsi fingunt, essentiam a personis separamus, sed unam in tribus personis essentiam seu deitatem agnoscimus, quae tota ex integro sit in singulis personis.' This charge was central to Gentile's critique of Reformed triadology. See his Genevan confession of June 1558, published in T. Beza, *Valentini Gentilis impietatum … brevis explicatio* (Geneva, 1567), pp. 3–14, and the reply of the Genevan divines in ibid., pp. 14–24.

[76] StAZ E II 371, 931ᵛ: 'Quod si dicant ea tantum reiicienda esse, quae sub Papatu conventa et conficta fuerunt, facilis nobis est responsio: Doctrina enim de trinitate personarum, et unitate essentiae divinae non est in Papatu conficta et excogitata, sed ex sacris literis desumpta, quae et unum Deum praedicant et patrem Deum et filium Deum et spiritum sanctum Deum nobis tradunt.'

[77] Ibid., 931ᵛ–2ʳ: 'Aut … ostendant vitium et errorem in his confessionibus et eas confutent, aut si nihil tale ostendere possunt, fateantur se contentiosos et arrogantes esse, qui ea probare nolint, quae tamen reprehendere et confutare non possunt.' The Zurichers note that one of the technical terms whose use is most contested, 'hypostasis', actually appears in scripture (Hebrews 1:3).

substantia coaequalitas.[78] As its title suggests, the *Trinitas Dei* is directed principally against the arguments of the Italian 'tritheists'; indeed, it is prefaced by short biographical sketches of Gentile and Biandrata, as well as of the arch-heretic Servetus. More generally, the work provides evidence of how the Polish schism had reinforced Bullinger's confessionalism. With some reluctance, the *Antistes* indicates, he has come to the conclusion that subscription to the Apostles' creed alone is insufficient to protect the church against infiltration by heretics, who have learnt to twist its meaning to support their errors. He continues:

> On account of such pests, the ministers of the churches have been forced to draw up brief formulas of faith, by which they may profess the received and apostolic teaching, and exclude and refute strange teaching. For that reason, certain terms have been included that reveal the true opinion of confessors, depending on whether they accept or reject them, and many creeds – the Nicene creed, the Constantinopolitan creed, the creed of Chalcedon and others – have been added.[79]

In a by-now familiar refrain, the *Antistes* defends the non-scriptural terms Trinity, person, essence and consubstantial as compatible with the scripture principle, on the grounds that the Word of God contains 'what is expressed by those words' ('quod istis vocibus exprimitur').[80] In focusing so exclusively on the letter (*verbum*) of scripture, Bullinger implies, the antitrinitarians have lost sight of its import (*res*). The doctrinal statements of the early church, on the other hand, exemplify the principle articulated in his own Second Helvetic Confession: 'praedicatio verbi Dei est verbum Dei'.

iii. 'Malleus haereticorum': the anti-heretical writings of Josias Simler

During the early 1560s, Zurich's theologians became caught up in the complex doctrinal debates raging within the Polish Reformed church.

---

[78] ZB Ms. Car XV 20, pp. 109–74. It is difficult to date this work with any certainty. However, the *terminus a quo* is the promulgation of the edict of Parczów (August 1564) expelling foreign heretics from Poland, as Bullinger refers to Valentino Gentile as active in both Poland and Transylvania. The *Trinitas Dei* also presumably predates Gentile's execution by the Bernese authorities in September 1566, as that is not mentioned.

[79] Ibid., p. 117: 'Propter huiusmodi pestes ministri ecclesiarum coacti sunt, breves fidei formulas conscribere, quibus receptam et apostolicam profiterentur doctrinam, et excluderent refutarentque peregrinam. Eo consilio posita sunt aliqua vocabula in quibus vel recipiendis, vel reiiciendis confitentes suum aperirent animum. Hoc consilio addita sunt symbola plurima Nicenum, Constantinopolitanum, Chalcedonense et alia.'

[80] Ibid., p. 125.

Although deeply averse to the metaphysical speculation that discussion of the Trinity tended to involve,[81] the Zurichers were aware that failure to mount a cogent defence of this core doctrine would seriously undermine their claim to be an authentically 'catholic' church. The rapid evolution of eastern European antitrinitarianism under the intellectual leadership of Biandrata and other Italian exiles during the later 1560s and 1570s only emphasized the urgency of this task, the greater part of which was assigned to Bullinger's talented younger colleague Josias Simler. In his anti-heretical works – *De aeterno Dei filio* (1568), the *Scripta veterum latina de una persona et duabus naturis Christi* (1571), and the *Assertio orthodoxae doctrinae de duabus naturis Christi* (1575) – Simler sought to provide a historically and theologically convincing explanation for the (re)-emergence of antitrinitarianism in recent times, and to draw together the arguments for the Nicene doctrine of the Trinity, both patristic and contemporary, in a single comprehensive synthesis.

Simler was born on 6 November 1530, the son of the former prior of Kappel and Reformed convert Peter Simler.[82] In 1544 he moved to Zurich, where Bullinger (his godfather and later father-in-law) took personal charge of his education. Between 1546 and 1549 he attended the university of Basle and the Protestant academy in Strasbourg, before returning to Zurich for ordination. In 1551 he was appointed professor of New Testament at the *Carolinum*, coupling his teaching duties with service as pastor in Zollikon (1551–57) and deacon at St Peter (1557–60). In 1563 he succeeded to Vermigli's chair of Old Testament, a post which he held until his death in July 1576. Besides his anti-heretical works, Simler wrote the earliest biographies of Bullinger, Gesner and Vermigli, and a defence of the Reformed doctrine of the Eucharist against Andreas Musculus.[83] In 1555 he published two supplementary volumes to Gesner's *Bibliotheca universalis*, the *Epitome* and the *Appendix*, which were followed in 1574 by a revised and updated edition of the entire work. To these must be added a commentary on Exodus, published posthumously, an edition of the

---

[81] See Wolf to Lismanini, 15 March 1563 (Wotschke, no. 270): 'Censeo, sacrosanctum hoc de trinitate mysterium potius adorandum quam curiose excutiendum'.

[82] In the absence of a full-length modern study of Simler's career, see J.W. Stucki, *Vita clarissimi viri D. Iosiae Simleri Tigurini sanctae theologiae in Schola Tigurina Professoris fidelissimi* (Zurich, 1577); G. von Wyss, 'Josias Simler', *XVII Neujahrsblatt zum Besten des Waisenhauses in Zürich für 1855*, pp. 1–24; H.U. Bächtold, 'Simler, Josias', in F.W. Bautz (ed.), *Biographisch-Bibliographisches Kirchenlexikon* (Hamm, 1970–), XV, 1298–1303 (with accompanying bibliography).

[83] *De vera Iesu Christi Domini et servatoris nostri secundum humanam naturam in his terris praesentia, orthodoxa et brevis expositio* (Zurich, 1574).

Cosmographia of Aethicus, and an early work on astronomy.[84] In co-operation with the Glarner humanist Aegidius Tschudi, Simler also planned to write a history of the Swiss Confederation from the earliest times. Although this ambitious project was never brought to fruition, before his death Simler was able to publish two works arising from it, the *Descriptio Vallesiae* (which included a topography of the Alps) and *De Helvetiorum Republica*, which Hans Ulrich Bächtold describes as 'a real best seller' (the work was translated into German, French and Dutch, and went through as many as 25 editions during the 16th, 17th and 18th centuries).

Throughout his career Simler had extensive contact with Italian religious exiles. As a student in Basle he attended Curione's lectures on rhetoric, while in 1553 he accompanied Vergerio on his journey to Württemberg to take up the post of counsellor to Duke Christoph.[85] In later years Simler corresponded with Italian exiles of widely differing religious persuasions, from the staunchly orthodox (Scipione Lentolo, Giovanni Battista Rota, Girolamo Zanchi, Francesco Porto) to the radical (Simone Simoni, Marcello Squarcialupi).[86]

More important still was his friendship with Peter Martyr Vermigli.[87] Reference has already been made to Simler's biography of Vermigli; after Vermigli's death, he also co-ordinated plans for an edition of the Florentine's complete works. Simler himself edited his predecessor's commentary on Samuel (*In Samuelis prophetae libros duos commentarii*) and *Preces sacrae de Psalmis Davidis desumptae*, both of which first appeared in 1564. Later he planned to publish Vermigli's correspondence and to produce an expanded edition of the *Loci communes* first compiled by Robert Masson.[88] Vermigli's thought

---

[84] *Exodus. In Exodum vel secundum librum Mosis ... commentarii* (Zurich, 1584); *Aethici cosmographia. Antonii Augusti itinerarium provinciarum. Ex bibliotheca P. Pithoei* (Basle, 1575); *De principiis astronomiae libri duo* (Zurich, 1555). Fragments of a commentary on Deuteronomy also survive (ZB Ms. B 239, fols 1r–140v; ZB Ms. S 342, fos 74r–246v).

[85] See Simler to Bullinger, 23 January [1547?] (ZB Ms. F 62, 478); 4 June 1553 (ZB Ms. F 40, 441).

[86] Simler's correspondence is still largely unexplored territory. Around 500 letters (most of them unpublished) are held at the Zurich Zentralbibliothek alone.

[87] In a letter to Zanchi dated 16 December 1562, Bullinger observed that '[Simlerum] mirum in modum Martyr noster amavit, et cum [eo] in summa concordia vixit' (Zanchi, *Epistolae*, I, 126).

[88] K. Rüetschi, 'Gwalther, Wolf und Simler als Herausgeber von Vermigli-Werken', in Campi, *Peter Martyr Vermigli*, pp. 251–74; C. Schmidt, *Peter Martyr Vermigli: Leben und ausgewählte Schriften* (Elberfeld, 1858), pp. 293–6; *Correspondance*, XVI, p. 61, n. 6; ibid., XVII, pp. 111–12, n. 6; G.B. Rota to Simler, 25 March and 22 April 1576 (ZB Ms. F 61, 81; 80). Work on the new edition of the *Loci*, incorporating what could be assembled

influenced many aspects of Simler's theology, notably his views on predestination: the projected new edition of the *Loci* was to include an oration on free will delivered by Peter Martyr at the time of his dispute with Bibliander.[89] More generally, Simler was impressed by Vermigli's unimpeachable orthodoxy regarding the doctrines of God and Christ, which could be offered as an alternative, positive, model to the radicalism of so many of his compatriots. In his preface to the *Commentary on 1 and 2 Samuel* (dedicated, significantly, to the Lithuanian and future antitrinitarian John Kiszka) Simler emphasized Peter Martyr's doctrinal rectitude:

> There is nothing in these writings that conflicts with holy religion. For in respect of doctrine Martyr was not only pure, but simple and clear. He hated arguments and the cunning sophistries that we see in some people. If there were many teachers like him in the church, perhaps many of the controversies by which the church of Christ is now sadly afflicted, giving offence to our weak adversaries and making us an object of ridicule to others, could be resolved.[90]

Zurich's other senior Italian churchman, Bernardino Ochino, left a very different impression on Simler, who was a member of the team of theologians that examined the *Dialogi XXX* in November 1563. Without doubt, the revelation of Ochino's heterodox views influenced Simler's subsequent approach to dealing with the problem of heresy. In particular, it brought home to him the link between dissent and dissimulation, and the corresponding need for the churches to guard against subversion by radicals within their ranks. This is evident from Simler's preface to the *Scripta veterum latina*, in which he reflected

---

of Vermigli's correspondence, was completed by Rudolf Gwalther after Simler's death. See Gwalther's preface to the volume, addressed to candidates for the ministry in Zurich, which extols the benefits of the 'loci' method of scriptural exposition (*Loci communes*, sigs aiiiʳ–viʳ).

[89] Simler to Beza, 10 May 1576 (*Correspondance*, XVII, no. 1199). As has already been noted, Vermigli played a key role in breaking down the Zurichers' traditional resistance to the 'Calvinist' doctrine of double predestination. The culmination of this process was the endorsement by the Zurich church of the strongly predestinarian theses of the Bernese theologian Abraham Musculus in 1588 (G. Adam, *Der Streit um die Prädestination im ausgehenden 16. Jahrhundert: Eine Untersuchung zu den Entwürfen von Samuel Huber und Aegidius Hunnius* (Neukirchen, 1970), pp. 74–5). For Simler's views on predestination, see *Exodus*, fol. 34ʳ⁻ᵛ.

[90] *In Samuelis prophetae libros duos*, sig. aa5ᵛ: 'Nihil enim in his scriptis occurret quod cum sacra religione pugnet: fuit enim Martyr in dogmatibus non modo purus, sed etiam simplex et perspicuus, et plurimum a contentionibus et argutis nonnullorum sophismatibus abhorruit: cui si multi similes essent in Ecclesia doctores, multae forte controversiae componi possent, quibus nunc alioqui misere ecclesia Christi laceretur, ita ut adversariis nostris infirmis quidem offensioni, aliis vero ludibrio simus.' Compare Bullinger's remarks in Chapter 3:iv above.

bitterly on the Ochino affair and on the 'betrayal' of the Zurich church
by a man whom he had previously regarded as a friend:

> What shall I say about Ochino? I saw him and knew him, and was
> at one time counted among his friends. He was called to Zurich by
> our supreme magistrate to teach the Italian church that had recently
> been established here. When, at a full meeting of ministers of the
> church, he was asked whether he subscribed to the doctrine that we
> hold and to our order of ecclesiastical discipline, he replied that he
> endorsed them wholeheartedly and spoke at length on certain
> articles, in order to show that he did not share the mad ideas of the
> Anabaptists. Afterwards, according to the custom of our church, he
> promised and swore an oath not to propose any new dogma at odds
> with our teaching, either publicly or privately, without first bringing
> it before the public synod, which usually meets twice a year. The
> *Laberinti*, his academic *Dialogues* and his other published works
> make clear how faithful and true he was to his oath and promises.
> When we later asked him to account for his actions, we were unable
> to persuade him to defend what he had written in a public
> disputation or to explain his position publicly in writing. And an
> injury is to supposed to have been done to this man – a perjurer
> who, contrary to an oath that he had made and a promise that he
> had given, spread mad ideas and blasphemies among the rabble, for
> which he himself later did not dare to claim responsibility.[91]

Simler's involvement in the Stancarist controversy has already been
discussed. However, from his preface to the *Responsio ad maledicum
Francisci Stancari Mantuani librum* it is clear that by the time this work
appeared he was preoccupied more with the threat to church unity
posed by the activities of Biandrata and other 'tritheists' than with the
fading challenge of Stancaro's Nestorianism. This shift in priorities
manifested itself in a shift in historical perspective. In Simler's account
of the dispute over the mediator, the order of events as they are known
to have occurred is reversed. Stancaro ceases to be characterized as the
instigator of the dispute; instead, his Nestorianism is seen as an extreme
reaction to the subordinationism of other Italian exiles:

> Just as once Dionysius, bishop of Alexandria, when arguing too
> passionately against Sabellius, wrote some things from which later
> Arius was able to derive his error, so Stancaro, when attacking those
> whom he calls new Arians, at times writes and teaches things from
> which many conclude that he himself supports the ancient errors of
> Sabellius and Nestorius.[92]

---

[91] *Scripta veterum*, fol. *5ʳ; also cited in Firpo, *Antitrinitari*, pp. 7–8, n. 22. Compare
Wolf to Dudith, 26 August 1570 (A. Dudith, *Epistulae* (Budapest, 1992–), ed. L. Szczucki
and T. Szepessy, II, no. 255 [pp. 202–4]).

[92] *Responsio*, fol. 3ʳ: 'Ut olim Dionysius Alexandriae episcopus nimio ardore
disputandi contra Sabellium, quaedam scripsit ex quibus deinde suum errorem Arius

Simler goes on to attack the arguments contained in Paul's *Tabula*, a copy of which the Zurichers had received from Sarnicki.[93] On the one hand, he seeks to demonstrate the incompatibility of Paul's position with the monotheism of the Bible. On the other, he argues that by making Christ's divinity dependent on that of the Father – who alone is described by Paul, following Gentile, as *autotheos* – the radicals effectively reduce him to the status of a creature.[94] In Simler's view, 'tritheism' is nothing more than a revival of the ancient Arian heresy, albeit in concealed form.[95]

The schism within the Polish church continued to preoccupy Simler and his colleagues throughout the mid-1560s. In March 1565, an attempt to reunify the orthodox Reformed with Paul's anti-Nicene party at the Diet of Piotrków merely exposed the widening doctrinal gulf between the two sides, which thereafter went their separate ways. Just as worrying for the Zurichers was the spread of antitrinitarianism in neighbouring Transylvania, where the Reformed superintendent Francis Dávid was being wooed by Biandrata.[96] After a compromise formula committing the radicals and their orthodox opponent, Peter Melius, to renounce non-biblical language broke down towards the end of 1566, the slide towards schism quickly became irreversible. The ensuing polemical exchange between Dávid and Melius revealed an important theological shift within antitrinitarianism – away from Gentile's 'tritheism' and towards a more radical unitarianism involving the denial of Christ's pre-existence, the primary inspiration for which was Lelio Sozzini's *Brevis explicatio in primum Iohannis caput*.[97] News of this development was swiftly passed on to the Zurichers and other Swiss Reformed theologians by their

---

hausit, ita Stancarus dum novos Arianos, ut ait, impugnat, aliquando ea scribit et docet ex quibus plerique existimant ipsum veteres Sabellii et Nestorii errores fovere.' Interestingly, where this image of the two extremes – and specifically, the comparison with Dionysius of Alexandria – is used elsewhere by the Zurichers, the priority of the 'Sabellian' Stancaro is maintained, in an exact reflection of the ancient paradigm. Compare StAZ E II 371, 931[r], where the Zurich divines cite Basil's judgment on Dionysius (*PG*, XXXII, 269–70); and Wolf to Lismanini, 15 March 1563 (Wotschke, no. 270): 'Verebamur enim, ne quid iam aggressos esse eos accepimus, ea via adversus Stancarum procedendum iudicarent, qua in Arii Servetique diverticula simplices et incautos seducerent. At Sabellium ita fugere, ut divertas ad Arium, quid est aliud, quam dum Charybdim vitare studes, in Scyllam incidere?'

[93] *CO*, XIX, 636.

[94] *Responsio*, fol. *6[r–v].

[95] Ibid., fol. *7[r].

[96] See M. Balázs, *Early Transylvanian Antitrinitarianism (1566–1571): From Servet to Palaeologus* (Baden-Baden, 1996).

[97] Antonio Rotondò summarizes the evidence for Lelio's authorship of this text in Sozzini, *Opere*, pp. 344–71.

correspondents in Poland and Transylvania. In his preface to the collaborative volume *Valentini Gentilis impietatum et triplicis perfidiae ac periurii ... brevis explicatio* (Geneva, 1567), which was published following Gentile's execution in Berne,[98] Theodore Beza noted the increasing diversity of antitrinitarian opinions; significantly, he reserved his fiercest condemnation for the views of the 'new Samosatenes' who had embraced Sozzini's Christology.[99]

The publication of the Gentile anthology, which included texts by Beza, Calvin, Andreas Hyperius, Johannes Wigand and Alexander Alesius as well as Simler's preface to the *Responsio*,[100] was the first move in a sustained and co-ordinated polemical campaign against the antitrinitarians (on this issue at least, Lutheran and Reformed theologians were able to unite).[101] The volume's principal weakness was that – Beza's preface aside – it failed to address the specific issues raised by the more radical forms of antitrinitarianism that were gaining ground in Poland and Transylvania. *De aeterno Dei filio*, which appeared the following year, was intended to make good that deficiency.

Like the Zurichers' earlier interventions in eastern European triadological disputes, *De aeterno* was written in response to an appeal for assistance from the orthodox Polish Reformed. In summer 1567 the rector of the Reformed college in Cracow, Christopher Thretius, was sent to Zurich, Berne and Geneva with instructions to recruit a senior Swiss theologian to write against the Samosatenes.[102] By Simler's own

---

[98] Geneva and the Swiss churches had co-operated closely in the lead-up to Gentile's trial. On receiving news of the Italian's arrest, Beza urged Bullinger to use his influence with the Bernese authorities to ensure that Gentile did not escape the death sentence, as he had done previously in Geneva (*Correspondance*, VII, no. 476). Bullinger replied to say that he had written to his colleagues in Berne to that effect ('hortans ut faciant quod in re tanta decet' [ibid., no. 481]). Johannes Haller kept the Zurich *Antistes* informed of developments in the case until Gentile's execution on 10 September 1566, which Bullinger greeted with satisfaction (Bullinger to Zanchi, 6 January 1567 [Zanchi, *Epistolae*, II, 131; Schiess, III, no. 6]).

[99] *Correspondance*, VIII, p. 242; the preface is discussed in more detail by A. Dufour, 'L'histoire des hérétiques et Théodore de Bèze', in *Pour une histoire qualitative: Etudes offertes à Sven Stelling-Michaud* (Geneva, 1975), pp. 35–44. On the term Samosatene, see Firpo, *Antitrinitari*, pp. 202–6.

[100] Appended to the work was a *Valentini Gentilis iusto capitis supplicio ... brevis historia* by the Bernese professor of theology Benedikt Aretius, which contains a detailed refutation of Gentile's now-lost *Antidota*. See T.R. Castiglione, 'La <<impietas Valentini Gentilis>> e il corrucio di Calvino', in *Ginevra e l'Italia*, pp. 149–76 [164–5]).

[101] See Simler's approving reference to the Gnesio-Lutheran Wigand in *De aeterno*, fol. 250r, which is coupled with an exhortation to Wigand and his colleagues 'ut hanc normam qua hic utuntur retineant in aliis controversiis, et in ea praecipue quae est in Coena Domini'.

[102] Wotschke, 'Thretius', pp. 163–7.

account, he was initially reluctant to accept this charge, on the grounds that Beza, Zanchi and Zacharias Ursinus were all said to be planning works against the antitrinitarians. However, the persistence of Thretius and his Polish colleagues Jan Łasicki, Sarnicki and Paul Gilowski eventually persuaded him to rethink his position.[103] In a letter to Beza dated 7 June 1568, Bullinger expressed the hope that the resulting work, arranged in four parts, would be ready for sale at the forthcoming Frankfurt book fair.[104] Before the end of August, Simler was able to send the Genevan churchman a copy of his finished text.[105]

In *De aeterno Dei filio*, Simler's primary objective was to offer an authoritative rejoinder to the arguments of the Italian and eastern European 'Samosatenes': for that reason, a good deal of book 1 is taken up with refuting Lelio Sozzini's commentary on the Johannine prologue.[106] But this was only part of a much grander project. In scale and conception, *De aeterno Dei filio* may be compared to Bullinger's *Der Widertöufferen ursprung*, which Simler had previously translated into Latin. Of course Simler's focus was narrower: whereas Bullinger had ranged over the entire spectrum of Anabaptist views, his younger colleague confined himself to the single issue of the Trinity. Within those limits, however, he strove to achieve the same degree of comprehensiveness in his coverage of heretical opinion. The specific arguments with which Simler takes issue are culled from a wide array of texts (often without acknowledgement), most notably Ochino's *Dialogi XXX* and the *Sylvae* of Andrzej Frycz Modrzewski (Thretius had procured the original manuscript of the *Sylvae* from the Basle printer Johannes Oporinus, who was planning to publish it).[107] Also cited are a number of works by Gentile (the *Protheses*, the *Antidota*, the *Annotationes in Calvini Institutiones* and the 1561 *Confessio*);[108] Matteo

---

[103] *De aeterno*, sig. δ7r–v. Beza, too, encouraged Simler to accede to the Poles' request (see Beza to Bullinger, 6 July 1567 (*Correspondance*, VIII, no. 560); and 13 April 1568 [ibid., IX, no. 600]). His own promised response to the antitrinitarians failed in the end to materialize, although see the preface to his edition of the dialogues of Athanasius in ibid., XI, pp. 319–30.

[104] Ibid., IX, no. 610.

[105] Simler to Beza, August 1568 (ibid., no. 629).

[106] For references, see Sozzini, *Opere*, p. 348, n. 95.

[107] For the citations from the *Dialogi XXX*, see *De aeterno*, fols 78r; 79v; 81r–v; 85v–6r; 86v; 94r–v; 116r–v; 117r; 117r–v; 121r–v; 122r; 131r–v; 139r–v; 140r; 304r; 305r; 309r; 313v–14r. For the *Sylvae*, see ibid., fols 29v; 80v; 81v–2r; 83r; 84r–v; 85v; 94v–5r; 101r; 102r; 102v; 123r–4r; 136r; 141r–2r; 194r–v; 202r; 203v–4r; 206r; 207v–8r; 228r; 229v–30v; 232r–v; 262v; 268r; 268v–9r; 326r; 327v–8r; 329r; 329v; 334r–v.

[108] For the *Protheses*, see *De aeterno*, fols 104v, 105r–v, 277r, 277v, 278r; for the *Antidota*, see ibid., fols 220r, 251r, 277r, 281r, 281v; for the *Annotationes*, see ibid., fols 277v, 278r–v; for the *Confessio*, see ibid., fols 175r–v, 177v, 182v.

Gribaldi's *Epistola de Deo et Dei Filio;*[109] Jan Kazanowski's reply to Calvin's letters to the Poles;[110] Paul's *Tabula de Trinitate;*[111] a letter from Mikołaj Radziwiłł to Calvin dated 6 July 1564;[112] and Servetus' *De Trinitatis erroribus* and *Christianismi restitutio.*[113] Furthermore, at the time of publication of *De aeterno Dei filio* Simler is known to have possessed a copy of the *Brevis enarratio disputationis Albanae de Deo trino et Christo duplici* (the antitrinitarian account of the second disputation of Alba Julia in March 1568),[114] and of Stephen Csázmai's *De horrendis simulachris Deum trinum et unum adumbrantibus,* another Transylvanian radical work.[115]

Simler was the first Reformed theologian to attempt a systematic classification of the antitrinitarian movement, hence the division of *De aeterno Dei filio* into four books dealing in turn with the Samosatenes, Arians, tritheists and 'Pneumatomachi'. Of course, this scheme is to some extent merely a convenient polemical device. Book 4, for example, brings together several contrasting heresies relating to the divinity of the Holy Spirit, and includes a defence of the *filioque* clause in the western version of the Nicene creed against the Greek church.[116] Similarly, the 'Arians' whose views are refuted in Book 2 are less a real contemporary grouping than a sect constructed by Simler on the basis of statements by Ochino's fictional interlocutor in dialogues 19 and 20 of the *Dialogi XXX, Spiritus.*[117] The distinction between 'Arians' and 'tritheists' is also

---

109 Ibid., fols 265v–6r; 281v–2r.

110 Ibid., fols 197v–8r; 199v–200r; 201r–v; 203r–v; 220r; 225r; 265r; 267v. The Zurichers received a copy of this work from Mikołaj Radziwiłł in October 1564 (Wotschke, no. 329) and responded to it early the following year (ibid., no. 332). On Kazanowski, see *Correspondance,* XI, p. 326, n. 5.

111 Ibid., fol. 251r.

112 Ibid., fols 248v; 271r–2v.

113 Ibid., fols 16r–17r; 19r; 76v–7r.

114 Simler to Beza, August 1568 (*Correspondance,* IX, no. 629).

115 Bullinger had been sent a Hungarian edition of *De horrendis simulachris* by Matthias Thury (*De aeterno,* sig. δ5v; *Miscellanea Tigurina* (3 vols, Zurich, 1722–24), II, pp. 207–13). While the *De aeterno* was in press, Simler received a further batch of antitrinitarian writings from Thretius, including Francis Dávid's *Refutatio scripti Petri Melii* and an 'interpretationem anonymam primi capitis Ioannis Evangelistae, cuius partem ante manu descriptam vir bonus ad me miserat' (*De aeterno,* sig. δ8v; Thretius to Bullinger, 15 July 1568 [Wotschke, no. 386]). The second text is probably to be identified with the *Explicatio primae partis primi capitis Iohannis,* published in late 1568 and usually attributed to Fausto Sozzini (the case for and against Fausto's authorship is summarized in Balázs, *Early Transylvanian Antitrinitarianism,* pp. 78–94).

116 Even before the schism between the major and minor churches in Poland–Lithuania had been formalized, some Lithuanian radicals had begun to call for the abandonment of the *filioque.* See Szymon Budny to Bullinger, 18 April 1563 (Wotschke, no. 273).

117 It is possible, however, that Simler had in mind the faction known as 'ditheists' or

rather loosely observed: for example, some of the *Protheses* of Valentino Gentile, designated elsewhere as the founder of the tritheist sect, are refuted in the course of Book 2.[118] The subordinationist aspect of tritheism, in particular the refusal of Gentile and his followers to identify the Son with the 'one God' of scripture, was seen by Simler as tantamount to Arianism in any case.[119]

The individual sections of *De aeterno Dei filio* are arranged to support a carefully constructed historical account of the origins and development of contemporary antitrinitarianism. According to Simler, all of the sects described in his work may be traced back to Servetus, the second Simon Magus, whose ideas served as the point of departure for both the later Arians and the 'Samosatenes'.[120] However, the transformation of antitrinitarianism into an organized movement is seen as the achievement not of Servetus himself, but of the Spaniard's Italian disciples. In his preface to *De aeterno Dei filio*, Simler reflects on earlier events in Poland, identifying Biandrata, Gentile and (to a lesser extent) Lismanini as those responsible for the schism within the Polish Reformed church. Following what had by now become the standard Reformed account of these developments, he describes how the Italians succeeded in popularizing their tritheistic and subordinationist views under the guise of combating Stancaro.[121] The fragmentation and doctrinal radicalization of eastern European antitrinitarianism after 1563 was, again, the work of Italian exiles. Simler identifies the arrival of Ochino in Poland, following his expulsion from Zurich, as a key moment in this process. It was under Ochino's influence, Simler claims,

---

Farnovians, after their leader Stanisław Farnowski. This grouping continued to insist on the pre-existence of Christ and opposed attempts by Paul, Szymon Budny and Georg Schomann during the later 1560s to move the minor church towards a more explicitly unitarian position. Eventually the Farnovians split from the Pińczowians, forming an independent sect based at Nowy Sącz near the Polish border with Hungary (see Williams, *Radical Reformation*, pp. 1088–90; 1158).

[118] *De aeterno*, fols 104v–5r.

[119] Ibid., fol. 188v.

[120] *De aeterno*, fol. 1r. For the Arians, see ibid., fols 76v–7r; for the Samosatenes, fols 3v, 43r–v. Most antitrinitarians (with the significant exception of Fausto Sozzini) continued to number Servetus among the founding fathers of their movement, even after they themselves had gravitated to more radical positions (see Pirnát, *De falsa et vera*, p. 43).

[121] *De aeterno*, sig. δ4r–v: 'Hi primum simulabant se nihil aliud agere quam ut Stancari delirium una nobiscum refellerent, interea tamen sensim et clam animis multorum instillabant, Christum qua Deus est Patre minorem esse, ideoque secundum eam naturam pro nobis intercedere, neque Patrem, et Filium, atque Spiritum Sanctum esse unum Deum, sed esse horum perpetuam quasi divisionem, et tres prorsus spiritus esse, e quibus solus Pater sit ἀγένητος et unus Deus, Filium vero et Spiritum Sanctum duos esse Spiritus a summo illo uno Deo Patre essentiatos, et ab eo dependentes.'

that many Polish radicals eventually rejected adult baptism and the deity of the Holy Spirit: the *Dialogi XXX* became the founding text of a neo-Arian sect which openly asserted the creatureliness of the Logos and confirmed the antitrinitarians' repudiation of Christian orthodoxy.[122] Around the same time another fundamental split was taking place, between tritheists loyal to the ideas of Valentino Gentile and others who, like the third-century heretic Paul of Samosata, had come to doubt the pre-existence of Christ;[123] this new Samosatene party was led by Gregory Paul in Poland, and by Giorgio Biandrata and Francis Dávid in Transylvania.[124] In his final anti-heretical work, the *Assertio orthodoxae doctrinae de duabus naturis Christi*, Simler summarized these three phases in the development of antitrinitarianism as follows:

> On abandoning the papacy, [the antitrinitarians] first joined our churches. Then, dissenting from [us] in the most important article of doctrine, the knowledge of God, they first confessed that Christ existed before the incarnation, but made him an essentiated God – eternal, but in both person and essence distinct from the Father and inferior to him [tritheism]. Soon they invented a Christ created before all creatures, who assumed his flesh from a virgin [Arianism]. At last they simply asserted that he did not exist before his birth from a virgin.[125]

Nor, Simler argued, was the evolution of heresy likely to stop there. In

---

[122] Ibid., fols 3ʳ; 73ʳ⁻ᵛ. Compare Simler, *Narratio*, fol. 40ʳ. Others shared Simler's assessment of Ochino's importance for Polish antitrinitarianism. Writing to Beza on 21 May 1565, Łasicki observed: 'Habent [the radicals] ingenio pollentem Ochinum, qui eis novas opiniones et excogitabit et suppeditabit, cujus Dialogos a nostris studiose legi audio, adeo quidam sunt natura rerum novarum studiosi, porro ubi imperiti se esse peritos in animum induxerunt suum, infinitos errores parere solent, fit enim ut error errorem secum trahat' (*Correspondance*, VI, no. 396).

[123] Like Beza in his preface to the Gentile collection, Simler identified the *Brevis explicatio* as the source for this error. But unlike his Genevan colleague, he repeatedly sought to dissociate Lelio Sozzini from the movement to which his ideas were said to have given rise. See *De aeterno*, sig. δ5ʳ; *Assertio orthodoxae doctrinae*, fol. 4ʳ⁻ᵛ; *Bibliotheca*, p. 443: 'De singulis fere dogmatibus religionis semper disputavit, et scripsit, nihil tamen ipse in publicum edidit: at Samosateniani nostrae aetatis eum inter principes suae haereseos nominant, ac dicitur illius esse, impia interpretatio in primum caput Ioannis absque nomine authoris ab illis edita.' Rotondò suggests that Simler was reluctant to acknowledge Sozzini's authorship of the *Brevis explicatio* as to do so would raise questions about the Zurich church's failure to take action against him while he was still alive ('Sulla diffusione', p. 108; Sozzini, *Opere*, pp. 352–3). It is also possible that Simler was misled by the existence of another commentary on the Johannine prologue – that of Fausto – which could not be ascribed to Lelio on stylistic grounds.

[124] *De aeterno*, sig. δ5ʳ⁻ᵛ.

[125] *Assertio orthodoxae doctrinae*, fol. 4ᵛ: 'De aliis quid dicemus? Qui primum Papatu relicto nostris ecclesiis se coniunxerunt, postea in summo capite doctrinae, in cognitione Dei a vobis [sic] dissentientes, primum Christum ante carnem extitisse fassi sunt, sed eum

his anti-heretical works, he characterizes the antitrinitarian movement as in a state of continual flux, the consequence of its departure from the sure and constant teaching of the church.[126] Ultimately, he predicts, the radicals will abandon even those trappings of Christianity which they have thus far retained.

Simler, like Wolf earlier, explains such 'gradualism' as a deliberate tactic of the antitrinitarian leadership, designed to facilitate the transition of potential converts from orthodoxy to heresy and to divert suspicion from themselves. In his preface to the *Responsio ad maledicum Francisci Stancari Mantuani librum*, he warns: 'The defenders of this error do not reveal their impiety at once, but start by abandoning traditional teaching in little things, while they worm their way into men's souls little by little. Only then do they pour forth their impiety freely.'[127] As the above passage illustrates, in the course of their dealings with Lelio Sozzini, Ochino and Biandrata, Simler and his colleagues had become convinced of the link between heresy and dissimulation. The subtle 'academic' mode of proceeding, exemplified by Ochino's *Dialogi XXX*, would, they believed, give way to the open profession of heresy as soon as circumstances permitted. In support of this point Simler cites the example of Gentile:

> Among his own the leader of this faction [Gentile] teaches openly that there are two Gods and says many impious things about the incarnation of God that thus far, perhaps, his disciples have hardly dared to mutter. Truly, given the right place and time, you will in the end see them preach Arianism openly.[128]

Deum quendam essentiatum fecerunt, aeternum quidem, verum et persona sic essentia quoque a Patre distinctum et illo inferiorem: mox spiritum quendam creatum ante omnes alias creaturas confinxerunt, qui carnem ex virgine assumpserit: tandem eum ante nativitatem ex virgine reipsa prorsus non extitisse affirmarunt.' The *Assertio* was Simler's response to a work by Szymon Budny, in which Budny set out to refute the arguments for Christ's divinity contained in the first chapter of *De aeterno Dei filio*. This tract, which Simler received from Thretius in April 1575 (Wotschke, no. 470), is published in Firpo, *Antitrinitari*, pp. 289–328.

[126] See *De aeterno*, sig. ε[r]: '... ut Astrologi singulis annis novas quasdam praedicationes edunt, et novas Ephemerides syderum cudunt, ita nostri illi adversarii quotannis novas quasdam et prioribus contrarias fidei confessiones edunt.'

[127] *Responsio*, fol. *8[r]: 'Huius erroris patroni suam impietatem non statim produnt, sed initio in paucis ab usitata doctrina recedunt, donec se in animos hominum penitus insinuarint: tum enim demum libere suam impietatem effundunt.' Compare *De aeterno*, fol. 58[r–v].

[128] *Responsio*, fol. *8[r]: 'Huius factionis princeps inter suos aperte docet duos esse Deos, et multa impie de incarnatione Dei nugatur, quae eius discipuli apud vos forte adhuc vix mussitare nunc audent: verum si locum nanciscantur et tempus idoneum, tum demum aperte Arrianismum eos praedicare videbitis.'

In a barely veiled reference to Biandrata, Simler warns the Poles that there is more to be feared from the feigned friendship of those who purport to be allies of the Reformed in their dispute with Stancaro than from the latter's open hostility.[129]

Earlier in the chapter, I noted how the Zurichers seized on the practice of dissimulation as evidence for the similarity between contemporary radicals and the heretics of the early church. This dual perspective is deeply embedded in the structure of Simler's anti-heretical works – Gentile, for example, is accused of summoning up the Anomoeans Aetius and Eunomius 'ab inferis'.[130] It is perhaps most apparent in the *Scripta veterum latina*, which includes a detailed account of Christological debates within the early church from Nestorius to Mohammed, followed by a brief description of the revival of ancient errors in recent times.[131] The history of the early church also provided Simler and other Reformed polemicists with an explanation for the reappearance of heresy in their own times. In the *Assertio*, Simler (following Gregory of Nyssa) argues that the overthrow of 'crassa idololatria', first by the apostles and their successors, and now by the Reformation, has prompted Satan to revise his strategy for undermining the church and to raise up heretics bent on introducing a more subtle brand of idolatry, the worship of a unipersonal God.[132]

According to Simler, the development of ancient heresy from the Arian controversy onwards offers a clear pointer to the ultimate destiny of its modern counterpart, if allowed to proceed unchecked. In both *De aeterno Dei filio* and the *Scripta veterum latina*, the Zurich professor describes Islam as the summation of the various Christological and triadological heresies which plagued the early church, and predicts the

---

129 Ibid.: 'Turbavit aliquandiu ecclesias vestras Stancarus, sed mihi credite plus est periculi ab his qui se amicos nobis in eo impugnando simulant, quam ab eius aperta maledicentia.'

130 *De aeterno*, fol. 176ᵛ.

131 For the circumstances of this work's composition, see Chapter 5 below. In the *Scripta veterum* Simler's principal target was the 'Eutychianism' of the Anabaptists, Kaspar Schwenckfeld and Johannes Brenz. However, the patristic texts edited there were also intended for use against the Samosatenes (*Scripta veterum*, fol. *2ᵛ*).

132 *Assertio orthodoxae doctrinae*, fols 58ᵛ–9ᵛ. In the *Assertio utriusque in Christo naturae*, Bullinger draws a direct comparison between the situations of the ancient and contemporary church in this regard: 'Diu ille [Satan] veterem ecclesiam quassavit persecutionibus tyrannorum, postea et haeresibus prophanorum quorundam hominum concussit. Idem videmus illum et moliri et agere nostro etiam saeculo' (fol. 6ᵛ). See also Beza's introduction to the Gentile anthology, in which he explains antitrinitarianism as Satan's response to his failure to suppress the Gospel by force of arms (*Correspondance*, VIII, p. 240).

same fate for contemporary antitrinitarianism.[133] Simler observes that it
was precisely those areas of eastern Christendom most affected by the
Arian, Nestorian and Eutychian controversies which later succumbed to
the armies of Mohammed; in the same way, failure to deal with
antitrinitarian activity in Poland and Transylvania is likely to facilitate
the Ottoman advance into eastern Europe. The new sect of Samosatenes,
with its emphasis on the humanity of Christ, poses a particularly sinister
threat from this point of view: 'Anyone who truly believes with the
Samosatenes that Christ is just a man will not consider himself to be
failing Christ when he hears that Mohammed writes so excellently of
him, attributing more to him than the Samosatenes themselves do.'[134]
The discovery in Heidelberg, in spring 1570, of a group of
antitrinitarian sympathizers that was allegedly seeking to make contact
with both Biandrata and the Turkish Sultan supported that assertion,
which was made still more credible by the conversion to the Muslim
faith of Adam Neuser, a Heidelberg radical who had taught briefly at the
Transylvanian Unitarian college in Cluj.[135] With such events in mind,

---

[133] *Scripta veterum*, fol. 206ᵛ. The association between antitrinitarianism, Judaism and
Islam was a Reformed commonplace. In a letter to Radziwiłł dated 30 September 1561,
Bullinger argued that the Christian faith stands or falls on the question of Christ's full
divinity: if the Messiah is not truly God 'vicerunt ... Iudaei et Turcae et praestat fides
eorum, christiana fides inanis erit' (*CO*, XVIII, no. 3539). By the mid 17th century, Simler
was being cited as an authority on the issue: see J.J. Crugotius, *Parallela Socino-
Muhammedica: Sive luculentissimus Socianismi et Muhammedismi consensus* (Heidelberg,
1657), sig. Aᵛ (the passage quoted is from *De aeterno*, fols 282ᵛ–3ʳ).

[134] *De aeterno*, fol. 283ᵛ: 'Qui vero Christum tantum hominum credit cum
Samosatenianis, is non existimabit se a Christo defuere si audiat Mahometum tam
praeclare de Christo scribere ut plus illi ipsis Samosatenianis tribuat.' In his preface to the
same work, Simler notes the proximity of Transylvania to the Ottoman empire and warns
his readers there to beware 'ne Samosateniana doctrina Mahumetanae aditus paretur, cum
tanta sit utriusque affinitas' (ibid., sig. ε3ᵛ). According to Simler, this 'affinitas' is
explained by the fact that Mohammed derived his teachings from the monk Sergius, who
combined the heresies of Nestorius and Paul of Samosata. See *Scripta veterum*, fol. 179ʳ;
De aeterno, fol. 283ʳ⁻ᵛ: 'Credendum est complures huiusmodi errorum contagiis infectos,
apud quos Christi deitas ante in dubium vocata erat, avidius Muhameti deliria arripuisse:
praesertim cum Sergii monachi et Iudaeorum quorundam consilio, ea delecta essent, et
Alcorano a Muhameto comprehensa, quae in tanta opinionum varietate maxime
videbantur popularia.' In his characterization of Islam as a Christian heresy, Simler follows
a well-established medieval tradition previously affirmed by his fellow Zurichers Bullinger
and Bibliander. Both reproduce the legend of the monk Sergius (Bahira), who was said to
have planted in Mohammed's mind the seeds of the religion that became Islam. This story
was propounded in its classic form by the ninth-century writer Theophanes (V. Segesvary,
*L'Islam et la Réforme: Etude sur l'attitude des réformateurs zurichois envers l'Islam
(1510–1550)* (Lausanne, 1978), p. 108).

[135] On these controversies see C. Burchill, *The Heidelberg Antitrinitarians* (Baden-
Baden, 1989).

Simler was able to describe Islam as the 'end goal ... of this new teaching' ('finis ... novae huius doctrinae').[136]

As we have seen, conflicting interpretations of the scripture principle were at the heart of the debate between the orthodox Reformed and Italian 'heretics'. The radicalization of antitrinitarianism during the mid to late 1560s led to an even sharper polarization of opinion over this issue. For all their biblicist rhetoric, the Italian and Polish 'tritheists' of the early 1560s were selective in their rejection of traditional doctrinal authority. Although they tended to repudiate the later Fathers (Augustine, the Cappadocians), they continued to cite works by earlier writers (especially Justin Martyr's *Dialogue with Trypho*, Tertullian's *Adversus Praxeam* and Hilary's *De synodis*) which they interpreted as offering support for their views. Initially they also retained the Nicene creed, in the belief that it enshrined the distinction between the divinity of the Father (ingenerate) and that of the Son (generate). Reformed polemicists lost no time in pointing out this inconsistency. Gentile, in particular, was frequently pilloried for employing terms alien to scripture, such as the designation of the Father as *essentiator*. In the preface to his *Responsio*, Simler remarks: 'I am amazed that some [of the heretics] criticize us for using expressions that are not found in scripture, when the terms God the essentiator and God the essentiated, which they certainly did not receive from the prophets or the apostles, are constantly on their lips.'[137]

The later Samosatenes, by contrast, were far more consistent in their opposition to extra-biblical authority and terminology.[138] The author of

---

[136] *Assertio orthodoxae doctrinae*, fol. 59ᵛ. Elsewhere in the work Simler notes the defection of some antitrinitarians to Islam and Judaism (fols 5ʳ⁻ᵛ; 53ʳ). Compare *Scripta veterum*, fol. *5ʳ. The radicals sought to turn such accusations to their advantage, arguing that their simplification of Christian doctrine would encourage the conversion to Christianity of Jews and Turks, 'qui portentosis istis opinionibus, quae Christianae fidei axiomata esse creduntur, ab ea amplectenda semper sunt deterriti' (F. Sozzini, *Explicatio primae partis primi capitis Iohannis*, in *Opera*, I, p. 75; compare *De falsa et vera*, pp. 37–8).

[137] *Responsio*, fol. *3ᵛ: 'Miror esse aliquos ex his qui nobis obiiciant nomina a nobis usurpari quae in scripturis non habeantur, cum illis subinde in ore sint nomina Dei essentiatoris et essentiati, quae certe non a prophetis aut apostolis acceperunt.' Compare *De aeterno*, fol. 249ᵛ: 'Postremo reprehendendi nobis sunt adversarii qui illas voces quas ecclesia publico consensu recepit, et mox ab Apostolorum aetate in usu habuit, repudiant ut alienas a scriptura, et interim suas locutiones novas et peregrinas sacris literis nobis obtrudunt, Deum essentiatorem et Deum essentiatum, αὐτόθεον, Deus Apostolicus, Solidus ille unus Deus et Pater, Deus emphaticus et articulatus, Deus author et Deus executor et alias huius generis phrases complures.'

[138] On the biblicism of Lelio Sozzini and his followers, see Rotondò, 'Calvino', p. 777; and Firpo, *Antitrinitari*, pp. 23–5.

the preface to the antitrinitarian anthology *De falsa et vera unius Dei Patris, Filii et Spiritus Sancti cognitione* (probably Biandrata) asserted: 'Where there are arguments about the fundamentals, and about the knowledge of the one God, we say that we should be most careful not to use foreign terms or to depart in any respect from the most holy words of God, because it is dangerous to try to say anything true about God by going beyond his word, and it is anathema to seek anything outside it'.[139] An unidentified Samosatene work cited in *De aeterno Dei filio* denounces even the ante-Nicene writers Irenaeus, Justin and Ignatius for failing to acknowledge the true humanity of Christ, prompting Simler to observe that on this score the Samosatenes have outdone even their master Servetus, 'who attempted to bolster his [opinions] with false and badly distorted testimonies from the Fathers'.[140]

The radicals' appeal to the scripture principle represented nothing less than a challenge to the hermeneutical basis of Reformed theology. Against Catholic opponents, Bullinger and other Reformed writers insisted on the all-sufficiency of scripture and decried the Roman church for its reliance on tradition. Now their own weapons were being turned against them. Worse still, Catholic and Lutheran polemicists were able to point to antitrinitarianism as the logical outcome of the Reformed rejection of extra-biblical authority. This argument was made most forcefully in an anonymous *Iudicium et censura ministrorum Tigurinorum et Heidelbergensium de dogmata contra adorandam Trinitatem in Polonia nuper sparso*, published in Cologne in 1565. Citing the work most likely to cause the Zurichers embarrassment, Ochino's *Dialogi XXX*, the author of the *Iudicium* asserted that the charges levelled against the Reformed leadership by the radicals were the same as those which mainstream Protestants had historically directed against the papacy.[141]

---

[139] *De falsa et vera*, pp. 5-6: '... ubi de fundamento controvertitur, et de uno Deo agnoscendo disputatur, dicimus summopere cavendum esse, ne exoticis utamur vocibus, vel aliquo pacto a sacrosanctis Dei phrasibus discedamus, cum praesertim de Deo vera etiam dicere extra verbum, periculosum sit, et quicquid extra quaeritur, anathema.' For the evidence of Biandrata's authorship of the preface, see ibid., pp. lii–liii.

[140] *De aeterno*, fol. 69ᵛ: 'Papistarum tyrannis non est ferenda, qui Patrum nomine quasvis naenias nobis obtrudere conantur: sed non minus intolerabilis est horum ἀναρχία qui absque exceptione omnem vetustatem damnant, Irenaeum, Iustinum, Tertullianum, Ambrosium, Augustinum, Hieronymum, Athanasium, Basilium, Nazianzenum, Epiphanium et reliquos omnes ne uno quidem excepto: hac quidem in re impudentia Servetum suum superantes, qui etiam ementitis et male detortis Patrum testimoniis sua stabilire conatus est.'

[141] *Iudicium et censura*, pp. 43–5; 68; 75–7.

At Thretius' request, Bullinger composed a lengthy refutation of this work, which appeared as a preface to *De aeterno Dei filio*.[142] Here the *Antistes* again draws a sharp distinction between the principle of *sola scriptura* as understood by the Reformed and the biblical literalism of the radicals. Quoting at times word for word from his earlier reply to Cochlaeus, Bullinger argues that the limits to theological enquiry and exposition ought to be set by the content, but not the language, of scripture. All doctrinal statements, regardless of the vocabulary used, are legitimate provided that they substantially express what is contained in God's word. For example the Bible describes Christ as a true man free from sin: from this we may deduce that he possesses human flesh and a rational soul, even though neither of those terms appears there.[143] In the same way, the traditional trinitarian formulations clearly articulate the biblical understanding of God's nature.[144]

Simler's treatment of the problem of extra-biblical language proceeds along much the same lines. The Zurich professor recognized the superficial attractiveness of the radicals' biblicism. In the preface to his *Responsio*, he even declared himself willing to dispense with certain technical terms, provided that the substance of doctrine remained intact. Almost immediately, however, Simler withdrew this concession, arguing that the traditional language ought to be retained in situations where orthodoxy was under threat.[145] Similarly, in *De aeterno Dei filio* he suggested that those who professed themselves to be orthodox but rejected such formulations were either naive or – more probably – secret heretics.[146] Like Bullinger, Simler stresses the distinction between the

---

[142] See Thretius to Bullinger, 3 October 1565 (Wotschke, no. 344). Thretius identifies Cardinal Stanislas Hosius as the author of the *Iudicium et censura*.

[143] *De aeterno*, sigs α7v–8r. The same point is made in almost identical form in *De canonicae scripturae et Catholicae ecclesiae authoritate libellum* (see fol. 14r).

[144] Ibid., sig. α8v: '... cum scriptura Deum hunc verum et unum, diserte nuncupet Patrem, Filium, et Spiritum sanctum, singulisque suam tribuat proprietatem, nec inter se confundat, ut cum manifeste angelus Dei ad virginem Mariam dicit, Spiritus sanctus superveniet in te, et virtus Altissimi obumbrabit tibi: et quod nascetur sanctum, vocabitur filius Dei: Sicuti et in baptismo Christi, auditur vox patris delata super Filium, et cernitur specie columbae Spiritus sanctus: ut et alias Dominus ipse baptizare iubet in nomen Patris et Filii et Spiritus sancti: cumque apertissime ipse Dominus Iesus alibi etiam dicat, Ego et Pater unum sumus, quem posthac offendet vocabulum vel Trinitatis vel Personae? Quibus nihil aliud significatur quam quod de ipsis rebus manifestissime commemoratis docetur testimoniis, unum videlicet esse Deum, tribus distinctum personis, ut hae tamen unitatem Dei non discindant aut lacerent.'

[145] *Responsio*, fol. *3v: 'Ubi vero in rebus ipsis dissensio est, suspecta nobis et periculosa videtur omnis receptorum nominum immutatio.'

[146] *De aeterno*, sig. δ8r: 'Illi vero qui de rebus nobiscum se consentire profitentur, et tamen usitatas Ecclesiae locutiones repudiant, nimium certe delicati sunt, et parum

word and substance of scripture, contending that the principle of *sola scriptura* applies only to the latter. For Simler, this is closely bound up with the Zwinglian notion of the pastor as prophet, which inspired the exegetical endeavours of the Zurich *Lectorium* and of Reformed biblical scholarship in general. Such an understanding of the office of minister is wholly at odds with the radicals' insistence on the letter of scripture:

> For God has given the church the gift of prophecy and of interpreting the scriptures, which would be completely abolished by this rule. It is the task of interpreters to explain those things that we find perplexing and difficult to understand in other, clearer words which are, however, scrupulously faithful to the truth of scripture.[147]

Following Bullinger and Calvin, Simler defends the received ways of speaking about the Godhead as fully consistent with the meaning of scripture.[148] In what might be construed as an attempt to steal the heretics' clothes, he asserts that his opponents' much-vaunted fidelity to the *verbum* disguises a lack of regard for the plain and logical sense of biblical texts. As an example of this tendency, Simler cites Lelio Sozzini's reinterpretation of the 'in principio', which in the *Assertio orthodoxae doctrinae* he attributes to Biandrata.[149] The radicals' misuse of scripture in order to defend their doctrinal innovations is, he argues, comparable with that of the papists.[150]

The dispute over non-scriptural language was symptomatic of a more fundamental difference of opinion between the Reformed and their antitrinitarian critics concerning the authority and value of church tradition. This was already apparent from the exchanges of the early 1560s, in which the Zurichers took issue with the radical assertion that *all* doctrine inherited from the papacy ought to be jettisoned as corrupt. In his anti-heretical works Simler develops this line of thought, accusing the heretics of failing to grasp that vestiges of true Christianity

---

exercitati in his certaminibus cum hominibus fraudulentis, quorum summa est sapientia verborum ambiguitate in gravissimis quaestionibus bonis et piis viris illudere. Verum plerunque qui ab usitatis locutionibus abhorrent, ne de rebus quidem ipsis nobiscum consentiunt, sed clam aliquid monstri alunt.'

[147] Ibid., fol. 249r: '... dedit enim Deus ecclesiae donum prophetiae seu interpretandi scripturas, quod hac regula prorsus aboleretur: id enim est interpretum munus ut ea quae captui nostro perplexa impeditaque sunt, explicent aliis et planioribus verbis, quae tamen religiose et fideliter ipsius scripturae veritati serviant.'

[148] Simler commends Calvin's justification of extra-biblical language in *Institutes* 1:13 as the definitive statement on the matter (ibid., fol. 248v). Compare ibid., fols 159r–v; 240v–1r.

[149] *Assertio orthodoxae doctrinae*, fol. 9r: '... non tantum a veterum sententia, verum etiam a perspicuo simplici et genuino verborum sensu recedat.' Compare ibid., fols 16v; 39r; 41r.

[150] Ibid., fol. 11r–v.

(scripture, the Apostles' and Nicene creeds, the essentials of baptism) remained even amid the errors of the medieval church: 'They hate papistical doctrine, but they fail to distinguish between that which is papistical – things that have been thought up by the popes without the sanction of God's word and transmitted to the church – and that which is Christian and in agreement with the word of God.'[151] Indeed, he suggests, if his opponents' argument is taken to its logical conclusion then the authority of scripture itself must be in doubt.[152]

In *De falsa et vera unius Dei cognitione*, Biandrata and Dávid argued that the antichristian captivity of the church was to be attributed first and foremost to its abandonment of the Christian *fundamentum*, biblical monotheism; in their view, the rise of the papacy was merely a corollary of that initial lapse.[153] The orthodox Reformed, by contrast, preferred to see the fall of the church as a direct consequence of the papal 'usurpation'. On the basis of that very different interpretation of Christian history, Simler was able to steer a middle course between the radicals' outright rejection of tradition and the 'second source' approach of the post-Tridentine Catholic church.

This is reflected in his statements concerning the Fathers. Like the earlier Stancarist controversy, the triadological disputes of the 1560s and 1570s acted as a powerful stimulus to patristic study in Zurich. In the *Responsio ad argumenta Antitrinitariorum Italopolonorum*, one of the Zurichers' principal aims was to quash attempts by their radical opponents to gain legitimacy by arguing that passages in the writings of certain Fathers (Irenaeus, Justin, Tertullian, Athanasius, Hilary) lent themselves to a 'tritheistic' or subordinationist interpretation. Thus, they point out, Irenaeus' intention in emphasizing the unique deity of the Father is not to exclude the Son from the Godhead, but to demonstrate the continuity of revelation in the Old and New Testaments; similarly,

---

[151] Ibid., fol. 5[r]: 'Abhorrent a Papistica doctrina, sed non discernunt quid Papisticum sit ab ipsis Papis extra Dei verbum excogitatum et ecclesiae traditum, et quid Christianum sit et verbo Deo consentaneum.' Compare *De aeterno*, fols 250[v]–1[r].

[152] *De aeterno*, fol. 67[r]. The same point is made in StAZ E II 371, 911[v].

[153] See the genealogy of the papacy given in *De falsa et vera*, pp. 20–21: 'Fictus ille Christus est regni Antichristi vita, et omnium eius blasphemiarum caput. Fictus enim iste aeternus Deus Christus alium et secundum Deum introduxit (cum tantus sit unus Deus pater): Pluralitas vero Deorum unam Essentiam peperit: Essentia autem una plures personas, vel Trinitatem genuit: Persona genuit naturas: Natura incarnationem, et hypostaticam unionem: haec autem sibi opposita Idiomatum communicationem pepererunt, sequuta tandem hanc meretricem Babylonicam alia scorta, ut Missa, Monstrantia, Monstrosam enim matrem monstrosas filias edere oportuit, ut sit conformis partus suae genetrici.' The Italian radicals had a tendency to link reform of the 'sophistic' and 'idolatrous' doctrines of the Trinity and the Mass: see the remarks of Ochino's interlocutor Spiritus in *Dialogi XXX*, II, p. 49; and StAZ E II 371, 931[v].

Tertullian's teaching on the distinction of the persons is accompanied by an equally strong affirmation of their unity of substance.[154] In his *Trinitas Dei*, Bullinger also makes considerable use of the Fathers (especially Augustine's writings against the Arians) to refute the teachings of Gentile and others.[155]

In the first book of *De aeterno Dei filio*, Simler operates under something of a self-denying ordinance with regard to the Fathers, his aim being to challenge the Samosatene claim that the orthodox doctrine of God has no foundation in scripture.[156] However, he is by no means consistent in his application of this rule, and both ante-Nicene and post-Nicene Fathers are cited at various points in the book (the use of the former is justified specifically on the grounds of their antiquity). In the later sections of *De aeterno Dei filio*, Simler continues to quote liberally from the Fathers, especially Hilary, whose anti-Sabellian stance had made him a particular favourite of the 'tritheist' party.[157] Indeed, more radical antitrinitarians subsequently condemned Simler's work precisely because of its reliance on extra-biblical support.[158]

Simler's conception of patristic authority is spelled out most clearly in the *Scripta veterum latina*, an anthology of orthodox responses to the Christological heresies of the fifth and sixth centuries.[159] In his preface to

---

[154] StAZ E II 371, 934ᵛ: 'Tertullianus adversus Praxeam totus in hoc est et si tres sint, pater, et filius et spiritus sanctus, non tamen ideo esse tres deos, neque distinctione personarum monarchiam tolli, aut unitatem lacerari, et hic non alio respicit, quam ad essentiae unitatem, nam inter alia sic scribit. Quasi non sic quoque unus sit omnia dum ex uno omnia, per substantiae scilicet unitatem, et nihilominus custodiatur economiae sacramentum quae unitatem in trinitatem disponit.' For the text cited, see *PL*, II, 157.

[155] ZB Ms. Car XV 20, pp. 161–74.

[156] *De aeterno*, fol. 4ʳ: 'Utemur ... in horum confutatione, paucissimis Patrum testimoniis, non quod ea desint nobis, sed ut adversariis morem geramus, hi enim nos ad scripturas provocant.'

[157] See his defence of Hilary's orthodoxy in *De aeterno*, fols 186ʳ–8ᵛ; 272ᵛ–7ʳ: '... ubi urget distinctionem Patris et Filii et uterque inquit unum sunt, et duo non sunt unus: et cum subinde repetit Filium esse Deum ex Deo, Spiritum ex Spiritu, lumen de lumine, item cum sacrilegium inquit esse Patrem et Filium singularem Deum praedicare: non essentias distinguit, sed adversus Sabellium personarum distinctionem urget: singularis enim Deus illi est Deus unus persona, una hypostasis' (fol. 273ᵛ). Simler is believed to have been working on an edition of Hilary in the months before his death (*Correspondance*, XVI, no. 1152).

[158] Matthias Vehe claimed that Simler's work had proved ineffective against the heretics 'aus ursach, das er ire argumenta allein aus götlichem wort genomen, nit hat umbgestoßen und kein andere argumenta wider sie hat bringen, dan der patrum consilia und erclärung, die nit gegründet sein in göttlichem wort in ursprünglicher sprachen' (Dán, *Matthias Vehe-Glirius*, p. 280).

[159] The texts are: Justinian, *Edictum ... rectae fidei confessionem continens et refutationem haeresium quae adversantur Catholicae Ecclesiae* (E. Schwartz (ed.), *Drei*

this work, Simler stakes out the Reformed 'middle position' on the correct use of the Fathers, in opposition to the rival extremes of Tridentine Catholicism and religious radicalism. According to Simler, the Zurich church does not attribute to the Fathers an authority equal to that of scripture, and asserts the right to criticize statements in their works that do not accord with biblical truth. At the same time, it rejects the pretensions of the Anabaptists and Samosatenes, who condemn the Fathers without exception as 'accomplices of Antichrist' and 'defenders of a three-personed God', and deny that any true church has existed between the time of the apostles and their own appearance. As in *De aeterno Dei filio*, Simler insists that it is possible to defend Reformed orthodoxy and to refute heretical error on the basis of the Bible alone; in theory at least, he resists any attempt to dilute the basic Protestant tenet that scripture is its own interpreter.[160] On the other hand, he accords the Fathers a certain confirmatory authority, as witnesses to the consistency down the centuries of the Catholic church's teaching on the core doctrines of the Trinity and the two natures of Christ, and thus to that *consensus ecclesiae* with which he is seeking to align the Zurich Reformation.[161]

---

dogmatische Schriften Justinians (2nd edn, Milan, 1973), pp. 129–69); Boethius, *Liber de persona et duabus naturis contra Eutychen et Nestorium* (*PL*, LXIV, 1338–54); John Cassian, *De incarnatione Christi contra Nestorium haereticum* (*PL*, L, 9–272); Maxentius Joannes, *Libellus fidei* (*PG*, LXXXVI(1), 75–86; *CCSL*, LXXXV A, pp. 3–25); *Capitula ... contra Nestorianos et Pelagianos* (*PG*, LXXXVI(1), 87–8; *CCSL*, LXXXV A, pp. 27–30); *Professio brevissima catholicae fidei* (*PG*, LXXXVI(1), 89–90; *CCSL*, LXXXV A, pp. 31–6); *Brevissima adunationis ratio verbi Dei, ad propriam carnem* (*PG*, LXXXVI(1), 89–92; *CCSL*, LXXXV A, pp. 37–40); *Responsio ad Acephalos* (*PG*, LXXXVI(1), 111–16; *CCSL*, LXXXV A, pp. 41–7); *Dialogi duo contra Nestorianos* (*PG*, LXXXVI(1), 115–58; *CCSL*, LXXXV A, pp. 49–110); *Responsio ad epistolam, quae dicitur esse Papae Hormisdae* (*PG*, LXXXVI(1), 91–112; *CCSL*, LXXXV A, pp. 115–53); Pope Leo I the Great, letter to Flavian, Patriarch of Constantinople (*PL*, LIV, 755–82); letter to Emperor Leo I (ibid., 1155–90); Pope Gelasius, *Tractatus de duabus naturis in Christo adversus Eutychem et Nestorium* (*PL* S, III, 763–87); Vigilius of Thapsus (wrongly identified by Simler as Vigilius of Trent), *Libri quinque contra Eutychetem* (*PL*, LXII, 65–154); Fulgentius of Ruspe, *Libri tres ad Thrasimundum Vandalorum regem* (*PL*, LXV, 223–304; *CCSL*, XLI, pp. 95–195); Rusticus, *Contra Acephalos disputatio* (*PL*, LXVII, 1167–1254).

160 *Assertio orthodoxae doctrinae*, fols 8ᵛ–9ʳ: 'Lectionem veterum non ita commendamus quod eorum auctoritate velimus confirmare dogmata fidei, ut falso nos calumniantur Adversarii, sed cum iudicio eorum scripta legi volumus, et ad normam sacrarum literarum examinari, neque enim aliter sua scripserunt, et dogmata non nuda proponunt, sed scripturis singula confirmant.' Compare Bullinger in *De aeterno*, sigs α6ʳ–7ʳ.

161 *Scripta veterum*, fol. *2ᵛ: 'Nos enim Patrum scripta non ideo edemus, quod illis eam tribuamus authoritatem, quam Canonicis scripturis, memores illius quod a D. Augustino scriptum est, neque quorumlibet disputationes, quamvis Canonicorum et

The confrontation with the Italian antitrinitarians and their eastern European followers did not trigger any fundamental changes in the doctrinal position of the Zurich church. The doctrines of the Trinity and the full divinity of Christ had been affirmed in all of the principal Zwinglian statements of faith, from the *Commentarius de vera et falsa religione* through to the Second Helvetic Confession. However, the triadological controversies of the 1560s and 1570s forced the Zurichers to give more detailed consideration to those questions and to confront the formidable array of objections to Nicene orthodoxy raised first by the 'tritheists' and then by the Samosatenes. Despite the highly technical nature of the arguments involved, at its core this dispute was about the Zurich church's doctrinally conservative understanding of the Reformation enterprise. Catholic and Lutheran polemicists had long argued that Helvetic Protestantism was merely the respectable face of religious radicalism, a charge to which the emergence of antitrinitarianism from within the Reformed churches of Switzerland and eastern Europe appeared to lend credence. Conversely, the Polish and Hungarian schisms presented Bullinger, Simler and other Reformed theologians with an opportunity to place the catholicity of the Swiss churches beyond dispute. The excesses, as they saw them, of the antitrinitarians exemplified for the Zurichers the dangers of a wholesale rejection of catholic tradition, and their anti-heretical works were intended to make clear to conservative as well as radical opponents the Reformed churches' continued acceptance of that tradition's core elements – the doctrines of God and Christ. The redefinition of the scripture principle to permit the use of extra-biblical vocabulary was an important element in this process of harmonizing the central tenets of the Reformation with the historical teachings of the western church. Institutionally, it meant the consolidation in Switzerland, Poland and

---

laudatorum hominum, veluti Canonicas scripturas habere debemus, ut nobis non liceat salva honorificentia quae illis debetur hominibus, aliquid in eorum scripturis improbare, si forte invenerimus quod aliter senserint quam veritas habet divino adiutorio vel ab aliis intellecta vel a nobis. Rursus Anabaptistarum et Samosatenianorum sententiam improbamus, qui veterum lectionem prorsus aspernantur, et non verentur omnes qui ab Apostolorum usque aetate fuerunt sanctos Patres, Graecos simul atque Latinos damnare, et Antichristi satellites et tripersonati Dei defensores vocare, cumque neque Patres probant, et eos etiam contra quos illi scripsere Samosatenum, Sabellianum, Photinum, Arrium se probare negent, nulla iuxta illos prorsus fuerunt Ecclesia, scilicet ut ipsi soli verae Ecclesiae nomine gaudere possint. At vero nobis sufficit quidem Apostolorum doctrina, et ex ea abunde haurimus quicquid ad tuendam pietatem et errores confutandos necessarium est, tamen nihilominus lectis veterum coniuncta scripturarum cognitioni, magnam affert confirmationem, cum animadvertimus eorum fidem et dexteritatem in citandis et exponendis scripturis, et perpetuum quendam consensum in praecipuis fidei dogmatibus.'

elsewhere of confessionally defined Reformed churches, rather than the sort of 'open' churches, hedged around with minimal doctrinal requirements, to which many Italian exiles aspired. In Chapter 5, I shall consider the impact of this development on the Italian Protestant communities of the Rhaetian Freestate.

CHAPTER FIVE

The Zurich Church and the Confrontation with the Italian 'Heretics' of Rhaetia, 1561–72

During the 1540s and 1550s, the Zurich church helped create the conditions for the establishment of Protestant congregations throughout the Italian-speaking southern communes of Graubünden and the Rhaetian subject lands. At first, it seemed possible that Rhaetia's Italian churches might become for Italy what Geneva was becoming for France: a refuge for the persecuted faithful and the springboard for a sustained Protestant missionary assault. However, by 1560 few northern Protestants still clung to the hope that one or more of the Italian states could be captured for the Reformation. Although the Zurich divines retained a lively interest in the affairs of Graubünden's Italian-speaking congregations, increasingly their concerns centred on the activities of dissident elements within those communities. Already Bullinger's intervention in the Chiavenna sacramentarian controversy of the late 1540s, whose main protagonists were Camillo Renato and Agostino Mainardi, has been noted. I now wish to turn to further disputes of this type from the 1560s and early 1570s, which pitted conservative reformers in the mould of Mainardi against opponents of confessionally defined Reformed orthodoxy. Both sides looked to the Zurich church to authenticate their understanding of the Reformation, sometimes competing actively for the support of Bullinger and his colleagues. However, following the Ochino affair and the series of dramatic schisms in the Reformed churches of Poland and Transylvania, the distinction between 'orthodoxy' and 'heresy' had become much more clear-cut in the minds of Zurich's theologians. The Zurichers offered firm backing to the Rhaetian Reformed leadership in its campaign against the radicals, helping to ensure that Reformed orthodoxy prevailed in Protestant Graubünden. In the process, they demonstrated their new-found determination to root out dissent from within the Italian exile community.

i. From Mainardi to Lentolo: conflicts within the Italian churches of Graubünden, 1561–67

Between 1547 and 1551, the theological and personal differences between Agostino Mainardi and Camillo Renato threatened to split the Reformed church of Chiavenna, the largest of the Italian-speaking congregations in the Rhaetian subject lands. Renato's departure from Chiavenna towards the end of 1551 put Mainardi in a position to reimpose his authority on the town's Reformed congregation, but elsewhere in Italian Graubünden radical ideas continued to attract support. Renato himself returned to his old haven, Caspano, where he remained until the early 1570s under the protection of the Paravicini family.[1] Besides orthodox stalwarts such as Mainardi and Giulio da Milano, the Reformed pastorate of the Valbregaglia, Poschiavo and the subject lands harboured a number of known radical sympathizers – antitrinitarians, antipedobaptists and 'libertines' who asserted the futility of good works in the light of predestination.[2] Indeed, it was to combat their errors that Comander and Gallicius introduced the Rhaetic Confession in April 1553.

Even after the confession's endorsement by the Bündner synod, the leadership of the Rhaetian Reformed church continued to view resident Italians as a potential source of heretical contamination. For example, in November 1557 Comander's successor as senior minister in Chur, Johannes Fabricius, counselled Bullinger against responding to some doctrinal questions put to him by Ludovicus Arcadius of Mantua. Arcadius, who purported to be a pastor serving in Graubünden, had asked the *Antistes* whether ministers should be obliged to affirm the Athanasian creed, whether communion should be dispensed privately to the sick, and whether the synod should hear accusations against ministers in their absence.[3] Fabricius' response was dismissive: 'Among

---

[1] U. Campell, *Raetiae alpestris topographica descriptio*, ed. C.J. Kind (Basle, 1884), p. 427; Renato, *Opere*, p. 265.

[2] 'Libertinism' is associated particularly with two Italian exiles active in the Engadine during the first half of the 1540s, Francesco Calabrese and Girolamo Milanese. Calabrese defended his ideas against a mixed delegation of Catholic and Protestant clerics in a disputation at Susch in the Engadine in 1544 (Campell, *Historia Raetica*, pp. 297–307; Cantimori, *Eretici*, pp. 63–4; E. Morse Wilbur, *A History of Unitarianism: Socinianism and its Antecedents* (Cambridge, 1946), pp. 99–101). As late as the 1570s, Ulrich Campell continued to face opposition from libertines in the Engadine (Campell, *Historia Raetica*, pp. 614–47; *De divina Providentia simul atque Praedestinatione fidei confessio* [StAG, B 143]).

[3] See Bullinger to Fabricius, 29 October 1557 (StAZ E II 373, 19; Schiess, II, no. 37.2). It is worth noting that private communion for the sick was advocated by Ochino, among others, in opposition to usual Reformed practice (Ochino, *Catechismo*, pp. 294–6; *Dialogi XXX*, II, pp. 360–63).

us there are to be found many men of this sort, curious and exceedingly keen on novelties. Generally the more uneducated they are, the more confidently they strive after new things.'[4]

It was only a matter of time before a new confrontation between the conservative and radical factions in the Italian churches erupted. The conflict was triggered by the decision of the church of Chiavenna in January 1560 to require new members to subscribe to an elaborate confession of faith that Mainardi had drawn up in opposition to Renato's teaching on the sacraments, the atonement, and the fate of the soul after death. For some of Mainardi's less hardline colleagues in the Italian pastorate, the imposition of subscription on the laity amounted to an unacceptable extension of discipline into the realm of private conscience. Particularly fierce in his criticism of the measure was Michelangelo Florio, formerly minister to the Italian congregation in London under Edward VI and now pastor at Soglio in the Valbregaglia.[5] In early 1561, Florio and five other ministers (Girolamo Turriani of Piuro and Hieronymus Tryphernas of Mese in the Valchiavenna; Francesco Cellario of Morbegno and Augustinus a Crema of Tirano in the Valtellina; and Giorgio Stefano of Casaccia in the Valbregaglia) put their names to a list of 25 *quaestiones* that implicitly condemned Mainardi's approach to dealing with 'heresy'.[6] The dissenting pastors objected in particular to the suggestion that all church members should be required to make an explicit declaration of faith in the Trinity, as defined by the Nicene and Athanasian creeds and the creed of Pope Damasus. In question 20, for example, they asked whether an individual whose beliefs and lifestyle were otherwise beyond reproach, and who had shown great charity towards the poor (here one detects an echo of Ochino's emphasis on the exercise of Christian virtue, as opposed to correct doctrine) ought to be excommunicated solely on account of error with regard to the Trinity, 'a most holy mystery that even the angels can barely understand'.[7] Elsewhere, Florio and his supporters suggested that verbal acceptance of the church's doctrines ought to be regarded as

---

[4] StAZ E II 373, 507; Schiess, II, no. 39.

[5] On Florio, see F. Yates, *John Florio: The Life of an Italian in Shakespeare's England* (Cambridge, 1934), pp. 1–26; L. Firpo, 'Giorgio Agricola e Michelangelo Florio', in Firpo, *Scritti sulla Riforma in Italia* (Naples, 1996), pp. 245–59; and L. Vischer, 'Michelangelo Florio tra Italia, Inghilterra e Val Bregaglia', in Campi and La Torre, *Il protestantesimo*, pp. 77–88.

[6] For the original text of the *quaestiones*, see StAZ A 248.1. A copy (in which the questions number 26 rather than 25) is held in Berne and published in Trechsel, *Antitrinitarier*, II, pp. 417–19. The *quaestiones* are also discussed in Rotondò, 'Esuli', pp. 784–5; and Cantimori, *Eretici*, pp. 282–3.

[7] Trechsel, *Antitrinitarier*, II, p. 419.

sufficient proof of orthodoxy, and voiced doubts as to whether 'idiotae' and 'simplices' could justly be compelled to assent to propositions that they were unable to understand and that were framed in non-scriptural language.

In May 1561, shortly before a meeting of the Rhaetian synod that was due to discuss the dispute, Florio presented Bullinger with a copy of the *quaestiones*: in effect, the Zurich church was being asked to act as an arbiter in the conflict, as it had during the Chiavenna sacramentarian controversy 13 years earlier. But if Florio hoped that Bullinger would intervene to moderate Mainardi's demands, he misjudged the situation badly. Over the previous decade, Bullinger had maintained the links forged between Mainardi and the Zurich church at the time of the former's dispute with Renato: two of Mainardi's works, the *Trattato dell'unica, et perfetta satisfattione di Christo* and the *Pia et utile sermone della gratia di Dio*, were published in Zurich in 1552,[8] while reference has already been made to Mainardi's correspondence with Bullinger on behalf of the evangelical Locarnesi. More importantly, Bullinger approached the *quaestiones* in the light of his cumulative experience of Italian religious radicalism, most recently in eastern Europe. In Florio's opposition to subscription, he probably saw an echo of Biandrata's demands for a return to 'scriptural simplicity' – soon to be revealed as code for the abandonment of Nicene orthodoxy. Writing to Mainardi on 11 May, the *Antistes* brushed aside Florio's reservations about demanding adherence from the laity to anything more than the Apostles' creed, as a well-tried tactic of heretics anxious to escape detection:

> Those who receive the Apostles' creed genuinely and in truth do not shrink from the Nicene, Constantinopolitan and Athanasian creeds, as things in agreement with it. Those who decline to acknowledge them have monstrous opinions.[9]

After inspecting the *quaestiones*, Bullinger told Johannes Fabricius that they would leave the church helpless against antitrinitarianism, and

---

[8] The *Trattato* has been read as a defence of the orthodox Reformed doctrine of Christ's merits against radical criticisms of the Protestant teaching on satisfaction, of the sort made by Ochino, Lelio Sozzini and, by all accounts, Renato (Armand Hugon, *Mainardo*, p. 94). However, the work's main target is clearly the Catholic understanding of redemption, in particular the distinction between the 'guilt' and the 'penalty' for sin.

[9] Schiess, II, no. 340. Bullinger clearly made the connection between concurrent developments in Poland and Rhaetia: with the letter he sent Mainardi a copy of the *Epistolae duae ad ecclesias polonicas*, in order to clarify the Zurich church's teaching on the Trinity.

warned his Rhaetian counterpart to be vigilant: 'Those Italian minds are restless minds.'[10]

In his official response to Florio's queries, dated 24 May, Bullinger mounts a vigorous defence of the use of credal language in the service of the church, using arguments that he had already rehearsed in the *Assertio utriusque in Christo naturae, De canonicae scripturae et catholicae ecclesiae authoritate* and the *Decades*, and was shortly to deploy again in the context of the Polish trinitarian controversies.[11] There is no harm, Bullinger maintains, in ministers resorting to extra-biblical terminology, 'so long as that does not involve changing in any way what is recorded in scripture, but making it clearer and protecting the simplicity of truth against the evil deceit of men'.[12] He illustrates this point with an example from the history of the early church:

> At one time the sectarians, and the Arians in particular, complained that the words *Trinity, person, consubstantial* and other similar terms were not found explicitly in holy scripture. Accordingly, they saw it as unfair to require the faithful to confess more than a belief in one God, the Father, the Son and the Holy Spirit. But the vigilant pastors of the churches, sensing that this concealed a heretical snake in the grass, strictly insisted on those terms, as expressing more clearly the orthodox truth and excluding heretical corruption.[13]

On the authority of Athanasius, Bullinger argues that the church has the right to react to changing situations – and the emergence of new forms of heresy – by formulating doctrinal statements suited to dealing with them. Again he sets up an implicit comparison between the problems facing the contemporary church and those which had confronted its ancient forerunner: in the early church, too, misuse of the Apostles' creed by heretics had necessitated the introduction of more elaborate confessions of faith. Bullinger concludes that the Nicene, Constantinopolitan and Athanasian creeds do not add to, but merely make explicit, what is taught in scripture concerning the Trinity. Refusal to accept them is therefore tantamount to a rejection of scripture itself.[14]

---

[10] Bullinger to Fabricius, 16 May 1561 (StAZ E II 373, 267; Schiess, II, no. 343). Bullinger also wrote to friends in Basle (which Florio intended to visit next) to advise them against giving succour to the dissidents. Again he criticized the 'ingenium Italicum' that had prompted Florio to attempt to bypass the Rhaetian Reformed authorities by seeking support from outside Graubünden (StAZ E II 373, 279; Schiess, II, no. 345).

[11] *Tigurinorum Consilium ad Synodum Curiae* (StAZ A 248.1; published in Trechsel, *Antitrinitarier*, II, pp. 419–28).

[12] Trechsel, *Antitrinitarier*, II, p. 421.

[13] Ibid., p. 422.

[14] Ibid., p. 424: 'Qui amplectitur ea, quae tradita sunt in scripturis sanctis de Trinitate deque incarnationis Filii mysterio et de Spiritu Sancto non potest non eadem ratione eadem extra scripturas in Symbolis illis comprehensa atque tradita. Ergo qui Symbola haec

The Zurichers' comments on the *quaestiones* were addressed to the Rhaetian synod, which duly gave its backing to Mainardi when it met in June 1561. As proof of its orthodox credentials, the synod reissued Gallicius's Rhaetic Confession and upheld the sentences of excommunication passed by the consistory of Chiavenna against two dissident members of the congregation, Ludovico Fieri and Pietro Leone; an attack on Mainardi which Leone had published in collaboration with Michelangelo Florio was also formally condemned.[15] But despite these measures, the synod of 1561 failed to provide a permanent solution to the 'problem' of heresy in the Italian churches. Critically, subscription was not made a general precondition of church membership, although it was encouraged; individual congregations and ministers, rather than the Rhaetian Reformed church as a whole, remained responsible for ensuring that doctrinal uniformity was maintained.[16] As a result, the practice of church discipline continued to vary considerably across the Valbregaglia and the subject lands during the 1560s, with the strict regime presided over by Mainardi in Chiavenna only one of several possible models.

For proof of this, one need only turn to the neighbouring congregation of Piuro, whose pastor was the Cremonese exile Girolamo Turriani, one of the signatories to Florio's 25 *quaestiones*.[17] Indeed, the association between the two men predated this episode by some years: Florio's *Apologia* (1557) includes a prefatory epistle by Turriani, who at that time was serving as minister in Bondo.[18] Turriani was judged

---

respuunt, non videmus, quomodo sincere credant et sensu incorrupto retineant aut custodiant, quae in scripturis sanctis de illis ipsis capitibus sunt exposita aut comprehensa.' In the *Consilium* Bullinger also mounts a spirited defence of the creed of Pope Damasus, which Mainardi's critics found especially objectionable (not least because of its supposed pontifical authorship). Significantly, this creed, with its precise definitions of orthodox teaching on the Trinity and the two natures of Christ, was later included in the preface to the Second Helvetic Confession.

[15] This work no longer survives. On Leone, see Lentolo, *Commentarii*, fols 3ᵛ–4ʳ; Bonorand, *Reformatorische Emigration*, pp. 169–71.

[16] See the *Acta synodi* published in Trechsel, *Antitrinitarier*, II, pp. 429–30, which state: 'Ne tamen quis in posterum eam, quae totius est ecclesiae, confessionem possit Clavennensem aut Maynardicam appellare, nos unanimi consensu eam confessionem confecimus, quae a vestra nihil discrepat, quod ad religionis capita attinet, quae posthac tamen non Clavennensis sed Rhaetica dicetur, *ad cuius subscriptionem neminem cogendum quidem censemus ad tollendas occasiones rixarum*, sed oretenus tamen a ministris et senioribus sunt examinandi, quotquot ecclesiis accenseri et inscribi cupiunt. Si quis tamen volens minime coactus subscribere velit, id neutiquam improbamus. *Quod autem ad examen attinet, singulis ecclesiis suum ius permittimus integrum et ponimus in potestate ministrorum et totius ecclesiae, qui sufficientem aut minus sufficientem edant confessionem*'. The emphasis is my own.

[17] For biographical details, see Bonorand, *Reformatorische Emigration*, pp. 176–7.

[18] *Apologia di M. Michelagnolo Fiorentino, ne la quale si tratta de la vera e falsa chiesa* (Camogask, 1557), sigs A8ʳ–B3ᵛ.

theologically unreliable by the Rhaetian church leadership at an early stage. In a letter to Bullinger dated 4 September 1564, Johannes Fabricius described him as 'a man of perverse understanding and intellect'.[19]

Turriani and his ally Florio were in contact with other Italian radicals resident in Basle and Zurich. In September 1563 the Genoese merchant Niccolò Camogli (whom we encountered briefly in Chapter 3) wrote to the two ministers from Basle to urge them to continue to resist the introduction of the death penalty for heresy in Rhaetia. In the same letter, he praised Ochino's recently published *Dialogi XXX*, promising to send Florio and Turriani a copy of the work via Camillo Sozzini, whom he commended as a 'fine youth' much persecuted by the 'new Pharisees'. With the Zurich authorities increasingly on their guard against heretical activity, it would seem that the group of Italian exiles associated with Ochino and Lelio Sozzini had begun to look for an alternative haven: Camogli went on to explain that Camillo would soon be visiting Piuro with a view to settling there permanently, possibly with his nephew Fausto.[20] In a subsequent letter, he indicated that there were also plans for Dario Scala to move to Graubünden.[21] Had news of Camogli's efforts to arrange for Ochino's reception in either Soglio or Piuro following his expulsion from Zurich not reached the ears of Bullinger, who raised the alarm with Fabricius in Chur, the 'secta senensis' might have been able to relocate to Rhaetia in its entirety.[22] In the event, both Camillo Sozzini and Camogli took up residence in Piuro during the course of 1564; the latter was even appointed an elder in the town's Reformed church.

Recent work on the Archiv Salis-Planta, much of which is now held at the Staatsarchiv Graubünden in Chur, has added considerably to our knowledge of the Piuro radicals' activities during the 1560s. In particular, a number of letters addressed to Camillo Sozzini have been rediscovered and published.[23] These letters reveal that, from Piuro,

---

[19] Fabricius to Bullinger, 4 September 1564 (StAZ E II 375, 747; Schiess, II, no. 634).

[20] Lentolo, *Commentarii*, fols 48ᵛ–9ʳ; part-published in Bainton, *Ochino*, p. 180. Fausto Sozzini advised his uncle Camillo to leave Zurich in a letter dated 3 November 1563: 'Lo star dove eravate non fa per la sanità né della persona né della borsa' (Marchetti and Zucchini, *Aggiunte*, p. 91).

[21] Camogli to Florio and Turriani, 29 December 1563 (*Commentarii*, fols 50ᵛ–51ʳ). Camogli dispatched a copy of Scala's confession of faith to the two ministers for their approval. A good deal of subterfuge seems to have been involved in this transaction: Camogli writes, 'ut tutiora sint omnia, rogo alterum ex vobis ut in mei gratiam eius exemplum excribat sine Darii nomine, et cui opus erit, eam ostendat'.

[22] See Chapter 3:iv above.

[23] Marchetti and Zucchini, *Aggiunte*; Zucchini, *Celso e Camillo Sozzini*.

Camillo remained in communication with other, possibly 'heretical', Italians who were or had been resident in Zurich, notably Guarnerio Castiglione and Francesco Betti.[24] Camogli and Turriani participated indirectly in this network of contacts: writing to Camillo on 14 April 1565, Castiglione asked the latter to pass on his greetings to Camogli, 'whom I love in the Lord', and 'to our reverend Turriani, whose greetings I was delighted to receive and whose sermons I envy you'.[25] Camillo was also in correspondence with his nephew Fausto, who had returned to Siena from Switzerland in late 1563 after depositing Lelio's papers with Betti. While in Basle, Fausto had made the acquaintance of Camogli, whom he describes in one letter as 'vero bruodero mio'.[26]

In Piuro, the radicals' activities appear to have encountered little interference, although Fausto Sozzini was still keen to restrain his uncle Camillo from embarking on too open a proselytizing campaign. Their presence in Piuro also had implications for neighbouring Chiavenna: with only a few miles separating the two towns, the hawkish Reformed leadership in Chiavenna was left fighting an uphill battle to prevent radical influence spilling over into its own community.[27] The shakiness of the orthodox ascendancy locally was underlined in June 1563, when the Rhaetian Diet imposed a sentence of death on Pietro Leone after it was reported that he had returned to Chiavenna to disseminate his heresies. Informing Bullinger of the Diet's decision, Fabricius indicated that he had not sought Leone's execution; on the other hand, the severity of the Rhaetian magistrates might at least preserve the churches of Rhaetia from the fate of their Polish counterparts, now locked in internecine strife because of failure to take decisive action against Stancaro some years before.[28] Mainardi's death at the end of July was a major blow to the efforts of Fabricius and his colleagues to repel the challenge that dissidents such as Leone posed to their authority. On hearing the news, Bullinger expressed the hope that a successor of like

---

24 See the letters from Betti to Camillo Sozzini of 30 March 1565 (*Aggiunte*, pp. 117–18); April/May 1565 (ibid., pp. 120–21); 21 February 1568 (ibid., p. 136); 26 June 1569 (ibid., pp. 145–6); 30 June 1570 (ibid., pp. 150–52); and Castiglione's letter to Camillo Sozzini of 14 April 1565 (ibid., pp. 118–20).

25 *Aggiunte*, p. 119.

26 Ibid., p. 98.

27 Welti describes 1560s Piuro as a 'Bollwerk der <<Heresie>> gegen das orthodoxe Chiavenna' (*Kleine Geschichte*, p. 94).

28 Fabricius to Bullinger, 14 June 1563 (StAZ E II 376, 90r–91v; Schiess, II, no. 519): 'Malim aliquid durius in Stancarum primo in Polonia constitutum quam nunc tot ecclesias inter se commissas.' Leone seems to have fled Graubünden before the death sentence could be carried out.

mind could be found, so that Chiavenna did not become a haven for sectarians.[29]

From Bullinger's perspective, the congregation's choice of his long-time correspondent Girolamo Zanchi could not have been more apposite. Although on some issues, notably predestination, Zanchi took his cue more from Geneva than from Zurich,[30] the Zurich church had offered Zanchi particularly vocal support during the latter stages of his conflict with the Lutheran Johann Marbach in Strasbourg.[31] In December 1561, Bullinger and his colleagues issued a favourable judgment on 14 theses summarizing Zanchi's understanding of eschatology, predestination and perseverance, despite their strongly Calvinist overtones.[32] The following year, the Zurich divines offered Zanchi the chair of Old Testament at the *Carolinum* formerly held by his compatriot Vermigli, although the plan foundered on resistance by the Zurich council to the appointment of another foreigner to its academy.[33] Despite this setback, in a letter to Friedrich von Salis dated 22 October 1563, Bullinger made clear that he continued to hold Zanchi's talents in high regard.[34]

The *Antistes* was in regular correspondence with Zanchi throughout the latter's period of service in Chiavenna and never questioned his commitment to Reformed orthodoxy. Neither have most modern scholars: the Thomist Zanchi is best known as a formative influence on Reformed 'scholasticism' and as the author of *De tribus Elohim* (1572), a systematic defence of the doctrine of the Trinity.[35] From Strasbourg, Zanchi had

---

[29] Bullinger to Fabricius, 13 August 1563 (StAZ E II 373, 395r; Schiess, II, no. 530).

[30] For example, during the late 1550s Zanchi supported attempts by Calvin, Beza and Farel to reopen dialogue between the Swiss Reformed and the German churches – an enterprise viewed with scepticism, if not outright hostility, by the Zurichers (see Zanchi to Bullinger, 8 March 1558 [StAZ E II 356, 573–5; 848–50]).

[31] See J. Kittelson, 'Marbach vs. Zanchi: The Resolution of Controversy in Late Reformation Strasbourg', *SCJ*, 8 (1977), pp. 31–44.

[32] The judgment was written by Vermigli and signed by nine Zurich ministers. It is published in Hottinger, *Historia ecclesiastica*, VIII, pp. 39–58. Walser challenges the traditional interpretation of the judgement, as signalling a fundamental shift in Bullinger's theology, towards acceptance of double predestination. In his view, the *Antistes*' support for Zanchi was motivated as much by political as by theological considerations (Walser, *Prädestination*, pp. 181–93).

[33] See Gesner to Zanchi, 15 December 1562 (Zanchi, *Epistolae*, II, 132); Bullinger to Zanchi, 16 December 1562 (ibid., 126); Wolfgang Haller to Zanchi (ibid., 131–2).

[34] Schiess, II, no. 549.

[35] The work is organized as follows: book 1 – defence of the technical terms used to describe the Godhead; book 2 – proofs of Christ's divinity from the Old Testament; books 3, 4 and 5 – proofs of Christ's divinity from the New Testament and the Fathers; book 6 – defence of the orthodox interpretation of the Johannine prologue against Servetus, Arius, the tritheists and Fausto Sozzini; book 7 – scriptural proofs of the deity of the Holy Spirit

urged the leaders of the Polish Reformed to resist the drift away from Nicene orthodoxy,[36] and there is no suggestion that he underwent a change of heart in Chiavenna. In August 1565, he informed Bullinger that a local cobbler, Antonio of Padua, had been excommunicated for denying the divinity of Christ and the Holy Spirit. Bewailing the spread of Servetus' errors among his compatriots, Zanchi endorsed the prevalent conception of Italians as untrustworthy in theological matters. It was inadvisable, he told Bullinger, to provide 'our Italians' with testimonies of sound doctrine 'unless you have ascertained fully what they believe about God, original sin, the baptism of infants etc.'[37]

Zanchi could therefore hardly be accused of turning a blind eye to heresy.[38] Despite that, some of the Piuro radicals took encouragement from his appointment. Zanchi was linked by marriage to Basle's heterodox Italian community, through his first wife Violanthis Curione. Furthermore, when he passed through Basle en route to Chiavenna in late November 1563 Zanchi lodged with Camogli, his visit coinciding with the latter's attempts to arrange a safe haven for Ochino in Graubünden. In letters to Florio and Turriani, Camogli noted that Zanchi had expressed sympathy for Ochino's plight, and claimed that the Bergamasco had pledged himself to a policy of conciliation *vis-à-vis* Chiavenna's own 'heretics'; apparently, Camogli believed that Zanchi might act as a counterweight to Mainardi's assistant Simone Fiorillo, who had recently blocked a move to readmit Camillo Renato to Reformed worship.[39] In the event, Zanchi's association with Camogli,

---

and defence of the *filioque*; book 8 – on the unity of the three divine persons; book 9 – consideration of the causes of antitrinitarian heresy; book 10 – refutation of Socinian and Sabellian objections to the orthodox doctrine of the Trinity; book 11 – response to heretics' arguments for the creatureliness of the Son; book 12 – response to objections to the deity of the Holy Spirit; book 13 – response to objections to the homoousion and to the claim by Spiritus in Ochino's *Dialogi XXX* that belief in the Trinity is not essential for salvation.

[36] For Zanchi's involvement in the doctrinal controversies affecting the Polish church, see the letters published in Zanchi, *Epistolae*, I, 36–41.

[37] Zanchi to Bullinger, 19 August 1565 (StAZ E II 356, 805ᵛ; Schiess, II, no. 715).

[38] The 'D. Hieronymus' denounced by the church of Chiavenna in September 1571 for failing to heed repeated warnings to break off contact with heretics is not Zanchi, as Giampaolo Zucchini suggests, but Turriani (Lentolo, *Commentarii*, fols 1ᵛ–2ᵛ; G. Zucchini, *Riforma e società nei Grigioni: G. Zanchi, S. Florillo, S. Lentolo e i conflitti dottrinari e socio-politici a Chiavenna (1563–1567)* (Chur, 1989), pp. 20–21).

[39] See Camogli's letters of 20 September, 1 and 3 December 1563 (Lentolo, *Commentarii*, fols 48ᵛ–9ᵛ; 46ᵛ–7ʳ; 47ʳ–8ᵛ). However, after reading the *Dialogo della prudenza humana* Zanchi condemned the work's contents and endorsed the action taken by the Zurich church with respect to Ochino (Zanchi to Bullinger, 29 March 1564 (StAZ E II 346, 518–19; Schiess, II, no. 595; Bainton, *Ochino*, p. 196).

together with the fact that his second wife was a member of the powerful Lumaga merchant family, which operated out of Piuro, seems to have deterred him from taking a hard line in his dealings with the Piuro radicals. There is even evidence of good relations between himself and Turriani. When the Piuro minister deserted his post during an outbreak of the plague in 1564, for example, Zanchi rallied to Turriani's support, to the annoyance of Johannes Fabricius in Chur.[40] Incidents of this kind demonstrate that, although events such as Ochino's expulsion from Zurich had brought the theological differences between radical and orthodox thinkers in the Italian exile community into sharper relief, there was as yet no permanent rift: Zanchi later admitted to having cultivated a friendship with Lelio Sozzini, which ended only when Sozzini, abandoning his customary discretion, sought to win Zanchi over to antitrinitarianism.[41]

In any case, Zanchi's attention was fully occupied by a challenge to his authority from within the church of Chiavenna, orchestrated by his deputy Fiorillo.[42] The conflict between Zanchi and Fiorillo has been examined in detail by Giampaolo Zucchini, so there is no need for me to do more than summarize it here. Fiorillo, it would seem, exploited tensions between native Chiavennaschi and Italian exiles who had settled in the town in order to destabilize Zanchi's position. In February 1567, at Fiorillo's instigation, the church of Chiavenna decided that henceforth only natives (*terrieri*) should be eligible for election as elders – a move that was directed principally against Zanchi's close ally and fellow Bergamasco Francesco Bellinchetti.[43] When Zanchi refused to recognize the decision, accusing its authors of fomenting schism, the congregation suspended him from preaching; significantly, the offences with which he was charged included conspiracy with the church of Piuro to bring about Fiorillo's dismissal.[44] Zanchi responded by attempting to drum up support for his case in the Valbregaglia, Zurich and Geneva, and from Italian pastors in the Engadine (Pietro Parisotto and Giovanni Antonio Cortese), but that was not enough to prevent the church of Chiavenna from voting to dismiss him on 18 May. After failing to have the decision overturned by the church authorities in Chur, Zanchi

---

[40] Fabricius to Bullinger, 27 November 1564 (Schiess, II, no. 643). Fabricius was moved to remark on this occasion, 'Italia nonnisi habuit unum Martyrem'. Zanchi's support for Turriani was not entirely altruistic: he himself had fled to the mountains around Piuro to escape infection (Zanchi, *Opera*, VII, 36–7).

[41] *De tribus Elohim*, fol. ii^v, in Zanchi, *Opera*, I.

[42] Fiorillo's biography is reconstructed in Zucchini, *Riforma*, pp. 10–12.

[43] Ibid., p. 42.

[44] Ibid., p. 65.

admitted defeat and accepted the offer of a professorship in Heidelberg.[45]

From Heidelberg, Zanchi continued to correspond with the Zurichers, particularly Bullinger and Simler. Although he and the Zurich divines were on opposite sides in the Heidelberg disciplinarian controversy of the late 1560s,[46] they were able to make common cause in the polemical struggle against antitrinitarianism. In a letter to Bullinger dated 24 August 1568, for instance, Zanchi welcomed the imminent publication of Simler's *De aeterno Dei filio*, noting that the work was likely to prove especially useful to his fellow Italians.[47] Simler, for his part, provided Zanchi with a copy of the antitrinitarian account of the disputation of Alba Julia (*Brevis enarratio disputationis Albanae de Deo trino et Christo duplici*) for use in the latter's *De tribus Elohim*,[48] a work which he later described as 'most useful for blunting the impious undertakings of our adversaries'.[49]

Many of Zanchi's difficulties in Chiavenna can be put down to his lack of pastoral experience and consequent inability to manage the conflicts of interest that inevitably arose within the congregation. As an established theologian with ties to Europe's leading Reformed churchmen, he may also have found it difficult to adapt to a much smaller stage: certainly Zanchi's opponents in Chiavenna believed that he was guilty of high-handedness, and accused him 'of wanting to usurp the office of superintendent over everyone else' and of failing to act in consultation with the college of elders or his colleague Fiorillo.[50] Zanchi's period as minister in Chiavenna stands out as a time during which still-unresolved theological differences took second place to personal or social rivalries: between the minister and his assistant, and between exiles and natives. Significantly, both the radical and orthodox camps were divided in their opinion of Zanchi. While it is likely that Zanchi enjoyed the support of Camogli and Turriani, his accusers in the

---

[45] Ibid., pp. 50–56.

[46] Zanchi was one of the leading advocates of the introduction of Calvinist-style church government to the Palatinate, while the Zurichers favoured the anti-disciplinarian stance of Thomas Erastus (see Zanchi to Wolf, n.d. [*Epistolae*, I, 63–4]).

[47] StAZ E II 356a, 833–5; *Epistolae*, II, 128–9.

[48] *Correspondance*, IX, no. 629; Zanchi, *Opera*, I, fol. *iiiiiᵛ.

[49] Ludwig Lavater to Zanchi, 19 December 1572 (*Epistolae*, II, 186): 'Quanquam ego adversariorum nostrorum scripta non legerim, ideoque minus de hac caussa iudicare possim: tamen ex Simlero nostro, qui in hac diligenter multumque versatus est, intellexi, tuum hoc scriptum dilucidum esse, ideoque se non dubitare, quin ad retundendum adversariorum nefarios conatus utilissimum futurum sit.' Compare Simler, *Bibliotheca*, p. 300.

[50] Zucchini, *Riforma*, pp. 63–4.

church of Chiavenna included some who later came under suspicion of heresy, such as Giovanni Battista Bovio of Bologna.[51] In a letter dated 30 March 1565, Francesco Betti informed Camillo Sozzini that he would be unable to visit Chiavenna 'until the calumny that has been spread about me among certain gentlemen of that church by Messer Girolamo Zanchi has been withdrawn': Zanchi had apparently referred to Betti as a liar, slanderer and evil spirit ('maligno').[52]

Bullinger was saddened to learn of Zanchi's dismissal. Writing to Fabricius' successor as senior minister in Chur, Tobias Egli, he observed regretfully, 'Rhaetia does not have many Zanchis'.[53] Yet such comments could not obscure Zanchi's failure to tackle what the Reformed leadership regarded as the most urgent problem facing the Italian congregations of Rhaetia: heresy. That task was left to his successor, the Neapolitan Scipione Lentolo.

ii. Scipione Lentolo and the anti-heresy edict of June 1570

Lentolo was a former Franciscan who fled to Geneva in 1558 after having been imprisoned by the Inquisition in Naples and Rome.[54] Unlike Zanchi, he came to the post of minister in the troubled church of Chiavenna with considerable pastoral experience. Prior to his appointment, Lentolo had spent five years as minister to the Waldenses (at Angrogna, Ciabàs and Prali), followed by a brief spell at Monte di Sondrio in the Valtellina. His uncompromising disciplinarianism had not endeared him to congregations in either area,[55] but it proved the key to tackling the problem of heresy in Chiavenna. Whereas Zanchi had managed to alienate the elders and deacons of the church of Chiavenna, Lentolo worked in harness with them in order to marginalize and

---

[51] Ibid., p. 66.

[52] *Aggiunte*, p. 117.

[53] Schiess, III, no. 22.

[54] Lentolo is best known for his history of the Waldensian persecutions, first published in 1906 by Teofilo Gay (see J.-F. Gilmont, 'L'<<Historia delle grandi e crudeli persecutioni>> de Scipione Lentolo', *BSSV*, 151 (1982), pp. 51–68). Recent contributions to the study of his later career include E. Balmas, 'Un inedito di Scipione Lentolo', *BSSV*, 152 (1983), pp. 31–56; G. Zucchini, '<<In coërcendis haereticis>>: L'esilio di Scipione Lentolo in Svizzera e il suo inedito epistolario (1567–1599)', in S. Rota Ghibaudi and F. Barcia (eds), *Studi politici in onore di Luigi Firpo* (2 vols, Milan, 1990), I, pp. 525–43; and 'Scipione Lentolo pastore a Chiavenna: notizie del suo inedito epistolario (1567–1599)', in Pastore, *Riforma e società*, pp. 109–27. Lentolo is also the subject of a doctoral thesis by Emanuele Fiume of the University of Zurich.

[55] E. Cameron, *The Reformation of the Heretics: The Waldenses of the Alps, 1480–1580* (Oxford, 1984), pp. 193–6; Zucchini, *Riforma*, pp. 105–7.

exclude his theological opponents. He also managed to engineer the dismissal of Simone Fiorillo, who had proved such a thorn in Zanchi's side.[56] Finally, he was able to enlist orthodox colleagues from across the Valbregaglia and the subject lands in support of his campaign against heresy. They included Guido Zonca of Mese, Giulio da Milano of Tirano, Paolo Gaddi of Teglio and Armenio Guliotta of Bondo.[57]

As we have seen, shortly before his death Agostino Mainardi had succeeded in having subscription accepted as a condition of church membership by the Reformed community of Chiavenna. However, because of his differences with the Chiavenna college of elders Zanchi was unable to sustain this strict disciplinary regime, leading to the infiltration (as the orthodox saw it) of the church of Chiavenna by a small but articulate group of radicals.

Following his appointment as Zanchi's successor, Lentolo embarked on a concerted campaign to rid the congregation of these dissidents. In a letter to Johannes Wolf dated October 1569, he claimed that he was engaged in almost daily conflicts with fellow Italians 'to whom no religion is pleasing once they begin to be dissatisfied with popery'. Nevertheless, Lentolo was confident that with the support of 'pious and prudent men' – meaning the members of the Chiavenna college of elders and his orthodox allies within the Italian pastorate – the heretical challenge could be overcome.[58]

A more detailed account of these clashes is provided in an unpublished work written by Lentolo in the immediate aftermath of the events that it describes, entitled *Commentarii conventus synodalis de excommunicatione Hieronymi Turriani, Nicolai Camulii et Camilli Sozzini*. In the *Commentarii*, particular attention is devoted to the case of one Johannes Mutinensis, identified by Rotondò with the Modenese exile Giovanni Bergomozzi.[59] On 21 May 1568, Bergomozzi was

---

[56] Lentolo informs Bullinger of Fiorillo's dismissal in a letter of 31 October 1568, but does not provide any explanation of the circumstances which had led to it (StAZ E II 365, 318; Schiess, III, no. 127).

[57] On the Neapolitan exile Guliotta (or Bugliotta), who later served as minister in Mese, Poschiavo and Grosotto, see Bonorand, *Italienische Exulanten*, p. 88. Gaddi's orthodox orientation is evident from his correspondence with Calvin, in which he noted with concern the popularity of Servetus' ideas in Italy and besought the Genevan reformer to write against them (CO, XIV, no. 1763; Pastore, *Valtellina*, p. 98, n. 31).

[58] ZB Ms. F 60, 309[v]: 'Mihi vero, ut aliquid de rebus huius Ecclesiae, cui servio, tibi communicem, mihi inquam fere quotidie est quasi confligendum cum hominibus Italicis, quod tamen et ipse Italus quum sim, minime me pudebit dicere, quibus nulla religio placet, quando Papistica eis incipit displicere: sed Dei beneficio sunt hic pii et cordati viri qui una mecum fortiter resistant, neque ullo modo permittant Satanum praevalere.'

[59] Between 1543 and 1567, the merchant Bergomozzi was a leading figure within the evangelical community of Modena, one member of which termed him 'uno Santo Paulo' for his rhetorical ability and tireless efforts on behalf of the Gospel (*DBI*, IX, pp. 96–8).

summoned before the Chiavenna college of elders to respond to the charge that he had taught the sinlessness of the regenerate. When the Modenese exile failed to give straightforward answers to 20 doctrinal questions put to him at this meeting, he was asked to provide the college with a written statement of his position, which was not, however, forthcoming. Further attempts to secure Bergomozzi's abjuration were also unsuccessful, resulting in his temporary suspension from the Lord's Supper on 10 December. In February 1569, the college instructed members of the church of Chiavenna to avoid Bergomozzi's company, on the grounds that he had been seen associating with known heretics; formal excommunication followed a month later.[60]

During the course of 1569, proceedings were initiated against several other suspected heretics. On 4 March, the college instructed Lentolo and the elder Gianandrea Pellizari to follow up reports that Francesco Vacca, an exile from Bagnacavallo in the Romagna, had questioned the doctrine of the Trinity. Under examination the accused openly denied the true divinity of Christ and refused to receive correction, a stance that led to his excommunication on 20 March.[61] The same fate befell Giovanni Battista Bovio, who (like Bergomozzi) proclaimed the sinlessness of the regenerate, while dismissing the doctrines of the Trinity and the incarnation as 'instruction for children and milk for princes' ('puerorum catechesim et lac procerum').[62]

Another radical to come under investigation was a local man known as Solomon of Piuro. Lentolo reports that Solomon had been excommunicated by Mainardi in August 1560 for denying the divinity of Christ, but had continued to reside in Chiavenna, where he made no secret of his heterodox views. In March 1569, Lentolo reopened proceedings against the heretic, who was given a solemn warning to renounce his errors. In response, Solomon agreed to sign the Rhaetic Confession, but only as an act of obedience to the magistrate. When a month later the college of elders demanded that he acknowledge the confession as pious, Christian and consistent with the word of God, Solomon refused, with the result that he remained excluded from the sacraments. According to Lentolo, he subsequently continued to associate with other dissidents and to question the divinity of Christ.[63]

Lentolo's *Commentarii* are our main source for the doctrinal views of the Chiavenna radicals, although given their provenance they obviously

---

[60] Lentolo, *Commentarii*, fols 5r–9v.

[61] Ibid., fols 22r–4r.

[62] Ibid., fols 25v–31r.

[63] Ibid., fols 39v–43r.

need to be approached with caution.[64] Opposition to the orthodox doctrine of the Trinity was cited in most, though not all, cases (Francesco Vacca, Giovanni Battista Bovio, Solomon of Piuro). That opposition does not appear to have been particularly coherent: while Vacca, influenced perhaps by the advanced antitrinitarianism of Lelio Sozzini, denied the divinity of Christ, a certain Jacobus Venetus was accused of reviving the ancient Sabellian heresy.[65] A clearer picture emerges in respect of the radicals' soteriology. From the *Commentarii*, it is apparent that Bergomozzi, Bovio, Solomon of Piuro and others processed by the Chiavenna college of elders rejected the orthodox Protestant distinction between imputed and essential righteousness, arguing instead for the perfection of the regenerate. In some cases, there is evidence of exposure to the teachings of the executed Benedictine Giorgio Siculo, whose 'Pelagianism' had earlier been refuted by Calvin. In others, the influence of Ochino – whose works are known to have enjoyed wide circulation in Italian-speaking Rhaetia – seems to have been decisive.[66] Lentolo himself detected parallels with Ochino's thought in the radicals' conception of the mediatorial office of Christ. Noting Bovio's refusal to accept that Christ had made satisfaction for sin by his death, the Neapolitan observed:

---

[64] See also Lentolo, *Responsio orthodoxa* (Geneva, 1592), pp. 187–8.

[65] On 9 March 1569, Jacobus was summoned before the elders to explain why he kept the company of excommunicated heretics such as Solomon of Piuro and Francesco Vacca. Jacobus denied that he shared their views and claimed to believe everything contained in the three ancient creeds. However, he also expressed dissatisfaction with the Athanasian creed's stress on the distinction of persons within the Godhead (*Commentarii*, fols 34ᵛ–5ʳ). Jacobus' Sabellianism is reminiscent of views said to have been held years earlier by Gianandrea Paravicini and by Renato (see Chapter 1:iii above).

[66] On 22 August 1568, one Camillo Carrara was summoned before the presbytery of Chiavenna and charged with reading Ochino's works (*Commentarii*, fol. 35ʳ). Later Giovanni Cortese, pastor at Sils in the Engadine, was investigated by the Rhaetian synod for possessing works by Ochino (Zucchini, 'Lentolo', p. 120). Further evidence of Ochino's importance for the Italian-speaking Reformed communities of Graubünden is provided by Scipione Calandrini in his *Trattato dell'origine delle heresie*. Calandrini writes: 'Io lascio passar per brevità molti altri heretici heresiarchi, et huomini seditiosi, per non esser tedioso, et in spetiale alcuni della natione nostra italiana, tra quali uno è stato Bernardino Occhino, che prima essendo stato instrumento assai giovevole all'Evangelio, nondimeno poi per isdegno conceputo contra la chiesa di Geneva, e per ambitione comincio a macchinare una setta a parte et a metter innanzi cose nuove sotto una certa forma accademica, onde i cervelli de semplici, o d'altri inclinati per natura pur troppo al male, son messi a partito, o indotti, o confermati nel male, si come ha ben dato a conoscere in questi stessi paesi uno che era stato suo disciepolo, il quale havendo una moglie in Italia che era donna nobile et honesta, e veramente christiana, non lasciò perciò di torne un'altra in questo paese, senza la licenza del magistrato, e senza causa legittima di poter cosí fare, e nondimeno la memoria e del maestro e del discepolo è anchora pretiosa appresso di molti, che vogliono esser tenuti buoni christiani' (*Trattato*, pp. 56–7).

In this matter he showed himself not at all obscurely to concur with that impure scoundrel Ochino, who argued that Christ is our saviour not because he made satisfaction for us to the Father – if that were the case, our salvation would not be a free gift from God – but because as a prophet he revealed God's will to us and fulfilled it faithfully, to the extent of being willing to suffer death. As if Christ's merit conflicted with divine grace, rather than adorning and highlighting it! For God so loved the world that he did not fear to give his only begotten, that those who believe in him might have eternal life.[67]

Similar views were professed by Camillo Sozzini, who is reported to have said that Christ's death was of no more benefit to humanity than that of the martyr Cyprian.[68] On this evidence at least, it would seem that during the course of the 1560s the criticisms directed against the traditional understanding of the atonement by Ochino and Lelio Sozzini had been appropriated and elaborated by the radicals of Piuro and Chiavenna.

Within months of his appointment, Lentolo had succeeded in placing his opponents on the back foot. Writing to Camillo Sozzini on 21 February 1568, Francesco Betti lamented the demise of 'Christian liberty' in Rhaetia:

As someone who loves and desires true Christian freedom, both for myself and for others, I rejoice to see it advocated and established, and am saddened to see it not only buried, but replaced by tyranny through the actions of those who would like to be considered pillars of Christianity. And yet? These things are not new. In my judgment, we experience such evils on account of our sins, which is why we should turn back to God and, abasing ourselves before him, seek his mercy and help so that not only we but all who fear him and wish to follow his ways may serve him in every place and at every time.[69]

Some radicals, such as Giovanni Battista Bovio and Francesco Vacca, thought it advisable to leave Graubünden for the safer climes of Poland and Transylvania.[70] Most, however, remained, aware that Lentolo's writ

---

[67] Lentolo, *Commentarii*, fol. 28r–v: 'Qua ... in re haud obscure ostendebat, se cum Ochino impuro illo nebulone sentire: qui negat Christum esse servatorem nostrum, quatenus pro nobis Patri satisfecerit, sed quatenus ut Propheta nobis divinam voluntatem explicuerit, ac, ut fideliter praestaret, ne mortem quidem subire recusaverit: alioquin salus nostra non esse gratuitum Dei donum. Quasi vero Christi meritum cum divina gratia pugnaret ac non potius illam extolleret, et commendaret: quum Deus sic mundum dilexerit, ut non sit veritus unigenitum dare, quo credentes vitam consequerentur aeternam.'

[68] Ibid., fol. 25r.

[69] Marchetti and Zucchini, *Aggiunte*, p. 136.

[70] The accounts of the Locarnese community for 25 September 1569 record the payment of a subvention to 'Ms. Gio. Batta de Bovi Bolognese che venendo di Chiavenna

did not run beyond Chiavenna. In the *Commentarii*, Lentolo complains that the sanctions imposed by the church of Chiavenna were rendered ineffective by the fact that the 'heretics' could always turn to Turriani in the expectation of support: he notes, for instance, that those accused of heresy by the Chiavenna college of elders habitually requested time to reply in writing to the charges levelled against them, during which they visited Piuro to receive instructions from their 'teacher or teachers' ('magistrum sive magistros').[71] Lentolo goes so far as to ascribe the resurgence of religious radicalism in Chiavenna to the influence of Turriani and his associates. Thus, according to the *Commentarii*, Francesco Vacca's errors were the product of a stay of several months with Camogli in Piuro, prior to which his views had been orthodox.[72] Given the nature of the source (the *Commentarii* were written as a vindication of Lentolo's role in subsequent proceedings against the Piuro radicals, and tend therefore to emphasize Turriani's subversive influence) it would be dangerous to accept such claims at face value. Vacca, for example, could have been exposed to heterodox ideas prior to his exile, as these are known to have been current in the Modenese 'comunità di fratelli' with which he (along with several others investigated by the church of Chiavenna) had been associated.[73] On the other hand, there is no reason to doubt Lentolo's assertion that Turriani was prepared to receive excommunicates from Chiavenna into his church.[74] By doing so, he would merely have been implementing a suggestion first made in the 25 *quaestiones* of 1561, which mooted the possibility of ministers disregarding sentences of excommunication that they considered to have been unjustly imposed by other churches.[75]

---

era per andare in Eidelberga per speciale ordine della Chiesa computa la spesa del'hosteria et la condutta de la carretta fin'Basilea' (FA Orelli, 8.2, fol. 105ᵛ). On Bovio's subsequent activities in Poland, see V. Marchetti, 'Una polemica di Scipione Lentolo con l'antitrinitario Fabrizio Pestalozzi (1581)', *Il pensiero politico*, 5 (1972), pp. 284–301 (291). In a letter dated November 1569, Francesco Vacca chided Camillo Sozzini for his reluctance to abandon Piuro: 'Sciebam te non esse relicturum dulcia tuguria pluriensia ut eo venires ubi multo melius et animo et corpore esses' (*Aggiunte*, p. 146).

[71] Lentolo, *Commentarii*, fol. 5ʳ.

[72] Ibid., fols 22ʳ; 24ʳ.

[73] See C. Bianco, 'La comunità di <<fratelli>> nel movimento ereticale modenese del '500', *RSI*, 92 (1980), pp. 621–79.

[74] See Lentolo, *Commentarii*, fols 1ʳ, 2ʳ, 25ʳ (Camillo Sozzini); fol. 30ʳ⁻ᵛ (Giovanni Battista Bovio); fols 32ᵛ, 34ᵛ (Giovanni Fratino); fol. 35ʳ (Jacobus Venetus); fol. 35ᵛ (Camillo Carrara); fols 36ʳ, 38ᵛ (Petrus Romanus).

[75] Trechsel, *Antitrinitarier*, II, p. 419 (question 24): 'An alicuius Ecclesiae minister videns aliquem pium fratrem inique, et violenter ab alio quopiam ministro excommunicatum, ecclesiaeque prorsus explosum, illum recipere possit, eique sacram Dei coenam exhibere?'

By late 1569, it had become apparent to Lentolo that heresy could be effectively tackled in Chiavenna only as part of a general assault on the problem throughout the Italian Reformed churches of Graubünden. Campaigns centred on a single church had proved ineffective, as 'heretics' expelled from one congregation could always find refuge elsewhere so long as no common approach to discipline existed across the region. Already Lentolo had established close ties with several other local ministers who shared his opposition to the radicals: in May 1570, for instance, the Chiavenna college of elders proceeded to the formal excommunication of Giovanni Fratino after consultation with Guido Zonca and Scipione Calandrini, preachers in Mese and Morbegno respectively.[76] Together, Lentolo and his orthodox allies in the Italian-speaking pastorate now began to put pressure on the secular authorities to intervene on their behalf. On 7 November 1569, the church of Chiavenna asked the Reformed leadership in Chur to petition the Diet for the expulsion of all religious dissidents from Graubünden.[77] In a second letter, dated May the following year, it made a point of emphasizing that heresy was a problem not limited to Chiavenna: the churches of the Valtellina, too, were infested with Arians and Anabaptists.[78] In effect, Lentolo was seeking universal subscription for those professing membership of the Rhaetian Reformed church, the goal that had eluded Mainardi in 1561.

Lentolo's timing was fortunate, in that his demand for magisterial action against the heretics coincided with the outbreak of a conflict between orthodox and dissenting ministers in Chur itself. There Johannes Gantner, the pastor of St Regula, had condemned as a violation of Rhaetian liberty the banishment by the city council of a local bookseller, Georg Frell, for disseminating Schwenckfeldian and Anabaptist literature. The ensuing controversy persuaded Gantner's colleague Tobias Egli – already concerned by the reports of heretical activity that he was receiving from Chiavenna – to throw his weight behind the punitive measures suggested by Lentolo.[79] On 27 June 1570,

---

[76] Lentolo, *Commentarii*, fol. 34r.

[77] *Responsio orthodoxa*, pp. 38–46.

[78] Ibid., pp. 47–9. The churches of the Valtellina had become involved in Lentolo's campaign against the Chiavenna radicals in response to the activities of one Petrus Romanus, said to be a member of the 'setta giorgiana' (followers of Giorgio Siculo). In November 1570, the Chiavenna college of elders opened proceedings against Romanus on the basis of information received from Giulio da Milano. See Lentolo, *Commentarii*, fols 35v–6v; Cantimori, *Eretici*, pp. 308–9.

[79] Egli, like his predecessor Fabricius, was a protegé of Bullinger. Originally from the Thurgau but educated in Zurich, he served as minister in Weiach, Frauenfeld, Davos and Russikon before taking over as preacher at the church of St Martin in Chur (Schiess, III,

those measures received the formal endorsement of the Rhaetian Diet, through the promulgation of an edict instructing all inhabitants of the Freestate to adhere, on pain of banishment, to one of Graubünden's two recognized faiths: Catholicism, or Reformed Protestantism as defined by the Rhaetic and Second Helvetic Confessions.[80]

Lentolo was quick to take advantage of the new statute's provisions. On 15 September, Solomon of Piuro was denounced to the *commissario* of Chiavenna, Christian Hartmann, as a heretic under the terms of the edict.[81] Two months later another radical, Jacobus Venetus, suffered the same fate. However, persuading Hartmann and other Bündner governing officials to implement the penalties laid down by the edict proved more difficult than securing it in the first place. When no action was forthcoming against Solomon of Piuro, for example, the Chiavenna college of elders resorted to asking Hartmann to attend a meeting at which the alleged heretic was due to answer the charges against him, so that there could be no doubt that he had received a fair hearing.[82] To complicate matters, Lentolo now found himself the subject of criticism by orthodox members of his congregation who were unable to endorse his hardline approach to dealing with religious radicalism. The death of Giovanni Bergomozzi, in early 1571, provided a focus for their discontent. Lentolo was determined that the excommunicate should be interred without religious rites, but another Modenese exile, Giulio Sadoleto, arranged for Turriani to conduct the funeral, which was attended by several members of the church of Chiavenna in defiance of their pastor's interdict.[83] When admonished, Bergomozzi's mourners refused to accept that they were at fault and absented themselves from the Lord's Supper for a whole year in protest. To bring the situation under control, Lentolo was forced to seek the assistance of his fellow pastors Zonca, Guliotta, Gaddi and Giulio da Milano.[84]

Outside Chiavenna, too, the edict encountered considerable

---

pp. ix–xix). On the clash between Egli and Gantner, see E. Wenneker, 'Heinrich Bullinger und der Gantnerhandel in Chur (1570–1574)', *Zwa*, 24 (1997), pp. 95–115; S. Rageth and O. Vasella, 'Die Autobiographie des Täufers Georg Frell von Chur', *Zwa*, 7/7 (1942/1), pp. 444–69. In a letter to Bullinger dated 5 June 1570, Egli signalled his awareness of the threat represented by the Italian heretics, arguing that by means of the proposed edict 'via praecludetur Haereticis et Arrianismo, qui Clavennae suppullulare videbatur' (StAZ E II 377, 2477r; Schiess, III, no. 204).

80 Text in Lentolo, *Responsio orthodoxa*, pp. 52–4.

81 Lentolo, *Commentarii*, fol. 41r.

82 Ibid., fol. 42v.

83 On Giulio Sadoleto and, especially, his links with Camogli, see Pastore, *Valtellina*, pp. 114–15; and Rotondò, 'Esuli', pp. 776–82. Like Bergomozzi, Sadoleto was formerly a prominent member of Modena's 'comunità di fratelli'.

84 Lentolo, *Commentarii*, fols 11r–21v.

opposition. If Tobias Egli is to be believed, even Scipione Calandrini, who had earlier approved Lentolo's excommunication of Giovanni Fratino, appears to have expressed reservations about the measure.[85] But the edict's most vocal critic was Bartolomeo Silvio, an exile from Cremona who, after spells as minister at Pontresina, in the Engadine, and Casaccia, in the Valbregaglia, had taken charge of Lentolo's former parish of Monte di Sondrio.[86] Shortly after the promulgation of the edict, Silvio wrote a short tract fiercely criticizing the new anti-heresy measures.[87] Like Florio before him, Silvio had grave reservations about both the wisdom and the propriety of requiring subscription of church members. By demanding that prospective members assent to a series of complex doctrinal formulas, he argued, the Reformed churches were likely to drive potential converts back into the arms of the Catholic church;[88] given the evangelicals' minority status in the Valtellina in particular, this was a luxury they could ill afford. Silvio maintained that Rome, rather than internal dissidents, ought to be the principal target of the Reformed leadership. In this respect his position recalls that of Ochino and Aconcio, who had also sought to make anti-papalism the basis of Protestant unity.

In his tract Silvio echoes the concern expressed by Florio in his earlier *quaestiones* for those persons 'weak in faith' who are as yet unable to

---

[85] Egli to Simler, 28 May 1571 (ZB Ms. F 59, 410–12): 'Scipio ille Calandrinus multis antequam hinc discederet eadem de re mecum egit, sed in faciem meam non omnino male de isto decreto sentire voluit: imo D. Commissariorum (inter quos fuit et D. Willius noster) sedulam et diligentem operam in decreto eiusmodi explicando, et declarando, mire praedicavit, quam declarationem grato animo omnes susceperint, et mentes denique Legislatorum exacte cognoverint. Non hoc decretum sicuti Itali conqueruntur, infirmis quicquam incomodat, neminem etiam vi quadam sive ad pontificiam sive Evangelicam professionem rapit. Sed praefractis pacis publicae turbatoribus modum et terminum statuit, qui cum neque nostrae ecclesiae sese adiungant, neque etiam sordibus Pontificiis delectari videri volunt, nescio quid tertium et singulare penes se fovent, ecclesias turbant, exotica apud promiscum vulgus evomunt, Confessioni piae et orthodoxae nostrae, eiusque assertoribus ministris, sese opponunt, nihilque non speciatim et clanculum factitant, modo separatione et alienatione ab ecclesia, cuius membra tamen esse volunt, magni et caeteris scientiores esse videantur. Quae autem haec est impudentia, ne quid durius dicam, istius Calandrini, qui post decreti illius sensum explicatum et approbatum a dominis et ministris, imo ab illo ipso, nihilominus praesertim apud vos impugnat?'

[86] G. Zucchini, 'Notizie su Bartolomeo Silvio nei Grigioni', *Clavenna*, 19 (1980), pp. 61–9. Silvio's only known published work is a Zwinglian-sounding attack on the worship of Christ in the elements of the Mass, *De Eucharistia Tractatulus D. Barptolomei Sylvii Cremonensis, Verbi Dei apud D. Rhaetos concionatoris* (n.p., 1551). Copies are located in Cambridge University Library, C.*.14.84 and in the Bodleian Library, Oxford, 8 delta 58(3) BS.

[87] ZB Ms. F 61, 343r–8r. Silvio's text also appears, with some significant textual variations, in Lentolo's *Responsio orthodoxa*.

[88] ZB Ms. F 61, 344r.

embrace the full theological package of Swiss Reform.[89] Again like
Florio, he argues that all who accept the Apostles' creed are to be
considered brethren in Christ, and dismisses subscription as an
unbiblical practice, with its roots in the papacy:

> Against the papacy we have all shouted ourselves hoarse for the
> simplicity of the holy scriptures, saying with Paul that holy writ can
> bring us (ministers included) to salvation in Christ, so that the man
> of God may be perfect and capable of every good work. Now,
> however, as if forgetful of this, we wish to multiply the number of
> creeds, laws and ordinances. Reading and hearing that, what will
> the papists not be able to say against us?[90]

For Silvio, subscription represents an attack on evangelical liberty and a
violation of Christian charity. Thus he warns his fellow ministers: 'Let
us beware lest we fall into a papist frenzy, not wanting to allow anyone
to criticize us, even if we end up dragging down hosts of souls to hell.'[91]
According to Silvio, it is also contrary to the established practice of the
Rhaetian synod, which in the past continued to regard as 'fratres' those
who refused to put their names to the Athanasian creed, while excluding
them from the ministry.[92] Silvio accepts that the Christian magistrate has
a duty to maintain order within the church and to punish those who
offend outwardly against God's law. That power does not, however,

---

[89] Ibid., 345ʳ⁻ᵛ; *Responsio orthodoxa*, pp. 179–80: 'Volunt itidem, ut si quis sese
simpliciter religioni, ordini et statutis Curiensis Synodi subscribere noluerit, is pro
haeretico per magistratum plectatur exilio perpetuo, et severius pro ipsius magistratus
arbitrio, quod si fiat, ubi erit in ecclesia membrorum differentia, infirmorum scilicet et
fortiorum? Ubi imbecillium tolerantia? Alicubi apostolorum aetate mixtae erant ecclesiae
ex iudaeis et gentibus. Ex iudaeis infirmi plerique nondum adducti ut omnino ceremoniis
valedicerent, diu in illis assueti. Gentes noverant se ad illas non teneri, sed ad illarum
corpus et veritatem. Aliqui doctiores ea in diversitate rixas movebant, et infirmos
contemnebant et iudicabant quasi Deus in scientia illos potentiores fecisset ut infirmos
fatigarent, opprimerent et perderent, ad renunciandum religionem vel ad faciendum contra
proprias sui conscientias adductos. Euismodi mandat Paulus infirmum in fide suscipere,
non ad contendendum in quaestionibus, non contemnere, nec servum iudicare non suum,
sed alienum.'

[90] ZB Ms. F 61, 344ʳ; *Responsio orthodoxa*, p. 105: 'Omnes adversus papatum ad
ravim clamavimus pro sanctarum scripturarum simplicitate, cum Paulo dicentes: Sacras
literas posse nos (etiam ministros), ad salutem instruere per fidem in Christo, et ut
perfectus sit homo Dei ad omne opus bonum formatus. Nunc autem veluti immemores,
symbola multiplicari volumus, leges et ordinationes. Quid papani adversum nos non
possunt isthaec legentes et audientes?'

[91] ZB Ms. F 61, 345ʳ; *Responsio orthodoxa*, pp. 170–71: 'Caveamus ne in papanam
phrenesim cadamus, volentes non posse quenquam nos arguere, etiamsi animas turmatim
ad inferna trahamus'. Silvio's language here is reminiscent of Ochino in his preface to
dialogue 26 of the *Dialogi XXX* (see Chapter 3:ii above).

[92] ZB Ms. F 61, 344ʳ; *Responsio orthodoxa*, p. 100.

extend to policing private consciences, where the individual is answerable to God alone.[93]

According to Lentolo, Silvio's tract was disseminated and discussed in Chiavenna, 'first in corners, then openly in public places and taverns' ('primum in angulis, denique palam in triviis et tabernis').[94] That would imply widespread support for his views, not only from religious radicals but also from moderates (like those who had attended Bergomozzi's funeral), who saw the edict as an affront to Rhaetia's traditions of religious liberty. Faced with such opposition, the orthodox pastorate had no choice but to issue a defence of its position on the treatment of heretics. At the request of Giulio da Milano and Paolo Gaddi, Lentolo produced a lengthy response to Silvio's work, the *Responsio orthodoxa pro edicto illustrissimorum D.D. trium foederum Rhaetiae*.

In its final version, Lentolo's *Responsio orthodoxa* consists of two prefaces – the first addressed to the Rhaetian Diet, the second to the Christian reader – followed by a section-by-section rebuttal of Silvio's work. There is nothing original about the arguments that Lentolo deploys in support of the magistrate's right to punish deviation from orthodoxy, most of which had been well rehearsed in such works as Beza's *De haereticis a civili Magistratu puniendis Libellus* and Bullinger's *Decades*. Like Beza, Lentolo equates support for the toleration of heretics with support for their errors, arguing that Silvio's real aim is to create space within the church for those who are intent on its destruction: thus Silvio and his followers oppose the use of force against dissidents

> not because you deny that heretics are to be punished, but because you do not believe that those currently being censured by the true Christian magistrate – namely Arians, Anabaptists and followers of Giorgio Siculo, together with other fanatics of that sort – are actually heretics, but rather good men. Nor do you believe that they are to be tolerated or supported as simple and uneducated persons, but rather that they are far more versed in the knowledge of matters divine than we are.[95]

---

[93] ZB Ms. F 61, 346ᵛ; *Responsio orthodoxa*, pp. 262–3: 'Magistratus autem domino serviens, et ecclesiae nutritius iudex erit in iram ei qui male agit, non autem inquit qui male credit. Nam externorum iudex est, non cordium et mentium. Adulteria externa, non cordium concupiscentias, punire debet; et homicidia, non iram et odia cordium: sic seductorem et ecclesiarum turbatorem, ac dissecatorem, sacrorum externum contemptorem, ac verbi ac veritatis blasphemum, etc, non eum discipulum docilem se exhibentem, qui necdum evangelica mysteria doctus est, vel percipere valuit, consentire et cum conscientia confiteri, profiteri, et sese illis subscribere.'

[94] *Responsio orthodoxa*, p. 51.

[95] Ibid., p. 178: 'Sed adversamini certe huic doctrinae, non quod haereticos negetis puniendos, verum quia in quos hodie Magistratus vere Christianus animadvertit, nempe Arianos, Anabaptistas, Georgianos, aliosque id genus fanaticos, non credetis esse

Silvio is being disingenuous when he accuses the edict of targeting the 'weak in faith'. In reality, it is aimed at incorrigible heretics who despise the most basic tenets of Christianity.

Lentolo also dismisses his opponent's appeal to charity: ministers, he insists, have a sacred duty to protect their flock against false prophets, to combine the simplicity of doves with the cunning of serpents. Charity does not entail standing by while enemies devastate Christ's sheepfold. If Silvio's prescription were followed, Lentolo argues, the church would be powerless to act against sinners.[96] Discipline must be exercised with especial rigour in the case of heresy, because it is not a private matter but rather a contagion which, left unchecked, will spread inexorably through the body of the Christian community. 'What is to be expected of a man of this sort', he asks, 'but that he will corrupt others?'[97] Neither is Lentolo impressed by Silvio's suggestion that efforts to impose conformity on Reformed believers will detract from the ongoing struggle with the Roman church: in his view, doctrinal unity among Protestants is the precondition for any successful challenge to Catholic hegemony.[98] It is more difficult for Lentolo to brush aside his adversary's claim that by endorsing the edict, which confirms the legal parity of Catholicism and Reformed Protestantism in the Rhaetian Freestate, the Reformed leadership has recognized idolatry as a legitimate form of worship. He resolves this problem by, in effect, replacing the traditional polarity of Catholics and evangelicals with one of 'orthodox' (both Catholic and Protestant) and 'heretics'. Catholicism, Lentolo implies, is to be preferred to the heterodox Protestantism of his opponents because it at least pays lip-service to the historical witness of the church, as set out in the ancient creeds.[99] Although the edict is not without its flaws – Lentolo acknowledges with regret that he and his colleagues have hitherto failed to convince the Rhaetian magistrates of their duty to promote a single, biblically based form of worship – it is to be commended for its positive features: the recognition of the Reformed faith on an equal footing with Catholicism, and the proscription of heresy.[100]

---

haereticos, sed potius bonos viros, et qui sint ut simplices et rudes ferendi, immo fovendi: vel potius quod multo quam nos rerum divinarum cognitione sint instructiores.'

[96] Ibid., p. 240.

[97] Ibid., p. 297: 'Quid enim ab huiusmodi homine expectandum erit, nisi ut alios corrumpat?' Compare ibid., p. 296: 'Quis sibi persuadebit, nisi omnino fuerit rerum imperitus, fore ut huiusmodi homines sensim facti moderatiores ita sese contineant, quin tandem, sicuti soliti sunt, furiosissime coelum terrae misciant?'

[98] Ibid., p. 94: 'Si tibi non placet ista Papismi toleratio: primum iube caeteras etiam haereses exterminari, et optime tunc inter nos conveniet.'

[99] Lentolo notes that the heresies outlawed by name in the edict (Anabaptism and Arianism) are condemned by both evangelicals and papists (ibid., p. 85).

[100] Ibid, p. 93.

iii. The Zurichers' intervention and the triumph of Reformed orthodoxy in Rhaetia

Although Lentolo's formative years as a Protestant had been spent either in or in close contact with Geneva, he was also well acquainted with the Zurich divines. Passing through Zurich in spring 1567, the Neapolitan had met both Bullinger and Johannes Wolf, with whom he subsequently remained in correspondence.[101] In a letter to the Zurich *Antistes* dated 8 September 1567, he also passed on greetings to Gwalther and Simler.[102]

Yet it was Lentolo's adversary Silvio who first drew Zurich into the controversy surrounding the anti-heresy edict. In September 1570, Silvio wrote to Bullinger to make known his concerns about the new decree, enclosing a Latin translation of the tract analysed above.[103] It is worth pausing for a moment to reflect on why Silvio should have wanted to involve Bullinger in his dispute with the Rhaetian Reformed leadership. There are parallels with Florio's mission to Zurich almost a decade earlier: both Florio and Silvio were Italian exile ministers uncomfortable with the sort of confessional orthodoxy that was being promoted by the church of Chiavenna, and both perceived in Bullinger a readiness to respond positively to their criticisms. Memories of Zurich's relatively conciliatory stance towards the Italian radicals prior to the early 1560s may well have played some part in that. In his tract Silvio warns his fellow ministers against excessive suspicion of others' orthodoxy, which he considers incompatible with Christian charity as described by the apostle Paul in 1 Corinthians 13:6–7.[104] In July 1555, Bullinger had offered Giulio da Milano similar advice with respect to Lelio Sozzini.[105]

It is likely that Silvio was also attracted by Zurich's approach to the question of discipline, which differed in several crucial respects from that of Geneva. Both Bullinger and Gwalther opposed the use of excommunication as a disciplinary sanction, arguing that it contradicted the purpose of the Lord's Supper as a sign of the inclusiveness of God's kingdom and the unity of believers. More generally, the Zurichers were suspicious of attempts to separate out ecclesiastical from magisterial

---

[101] In a letter to Wolf dated 15 March 1568, Lentolo praises the Zurich minister as a 'chiara stella' of the church and asks to be accepted by his correspondent as 'vostro familiare, et così intimo, che non lasciamo passare nessuna occasione di scriverci, e farci l'un l'altro servitio' (ZB Ms. F 39, 601).

[102] StAZ E II 365, 326–7; Schiess, III, no. 31.

[103] ZB Ms. F 61, 343r; Schiess, III, no. 220.

[104] ZB Ms. F 61, 346r; *Responsio orthodoxa*, p. 228: 'Charitas ... non cogitat malum, omnia credit, omnia sperat, omnia suffert ...'.

[105] Schiess, I, no. 290: 'Fratres enim sumus, qui mutuam invicem charitatem debemus; suspicationes autem numerat Paulus inter opera carnis.'

discipline, which they feared could lead to a revival of the sort of clerical tyranny for which Protestants had traditionally condemned Rome.[106] As we have seen, those sentiments were shared by Italian exiles such as Aconcio and Ochino, whose warnings against the emergence of a new papacy within the Reformed churches struck a chord with many of their compatriots, including those settled in Rhaetia. Significantly, in the 25 *quaestiones* of 1561 Florio and his colleagues had questioned the (Calvinist) practice of examining communicants before admitting them to the Eucharist.[107]

At issue in the controversy over the edict was not simply the question of the magistrate's right to punish heretics, but how and by whom discipline should be exercised in Graubünden's Italian churches. In Silvio's work the main target of criticism was not in fact the Rhaetian magistracy, but the local Reformed clergy, whose desire to impose absolute conformity to their views was identified as the inspiration for the recent crackdown.[108] Some of the Chiavenna radicals explicitly voiced a preference for magisterial over ecclesiastical discipline. Giovanni Fratino, for example, insisted that he was not subject to the jurisdiction of the Chiavenna college of elders, but only to that of the 'Rhaetian lords'; others summoned before the college likened it to a 'papal' or 'Spanish' inquisition.[109] In an anonymous letter to the pastor of Geneva's Italian church, Niccolò Balbani, a supporter of Turriani compared the Genevan system of church government unfavourably with the statist model that had evolved in the Swiss churches.[110] This

---

[106] J. Wayne Baker, 'In defense of magisterial discipline: Bullinger's "Tractatus de excommunicatione" of 1568', in Gäbler and Herkenrath, *Bullinger*, I, pp. 141–59.

[107] Trechsel, *Antitrinitarier*, II, p. 419. Gwalther criticized such examinations in the context of the Heidelberg controversy over church discipline. See his letter to Beza of 2 August 1570: 'Ista certe, quae infinitis exemplis tam Veteris quam Novi Testamenti probari poterant, nos movent, ut privatim illud examen, quo quisque se ipsum probat, secundum Pauli praeceptum sufficere putemus iis qui ad Domini mensam volunt accedere' (*Correspondance*, XI, no. 798). In the Palatinate, as in Rhaetia, religious radicals and antitrinitarians were prominent among those opposed to the introduction of Calvinist-style discipline (see Burchill, *Heidelberg Antitrinitarians*).

[108] ZB Ms. F 61, 343r: 'En in quadam ditione Illustrissimorum Dominorum Rhetorum, ubi satis numerosa evangelicorum ecclesia, papanorum tamen aliquanto numerosior, haec proclamatio prodiit: quam non veluti magistratus mentem, sed tanquam evangelicae ecclesiae seu eius ministrorum voluntatem examinatam mihi displicuisse non diffiteor, et ardore quodam ... impulsus reprehendi scripto, censurae tamen et iudicio cuiusdam illustrissimi et excellentissimi ll. doctoris illius ecclesiae praecipui membri submisso'.

[109] Lentolo, *Commentarii*, fol. 33v. Compare ibid., fols 5v (Bergomozzi); 29r (Bovio). Fratino was disciplined for expressing Anabaptist opinions on the sacraments and for keeping company with known heretics such as Giovanni Bergomozzi.

[110] M. Celsi, *In haereticis coërcendis quatenus progredi liceat* (Naples, 1982), ed. P. Bietenholz, pp. 638–44.

argument was taken a stage further by the Sienese exile Mino Celsi in his response to the edict, entitled *In haereticis coёrcendis*. There, quoting selectively from Zwingli and Bullinger, Celsi asserted that the Zurich church had consistently opposed the punishment of heresy.[111]

But the Zurichers did not approach the Rhaetian dispute as a battle between rival 'Swiss' and 'Genevan' forms of church discipline of the kind that was currently under way in Heidelberg. To do so would have been to ignore the fact that the immediate object of contention was not an ecclesiastical but a magisterial measure, the edict of June 1570. 'Calvinists' – like Lentolo – and 'Zwinglians' – like Bullinger and Gwalther – were in complete agreement on this issue. By the same token, Silvio's call for the church to refrain from the use of force, and his indifference to the finer points of doctrine, were positions that Bullinger and his colleagues had come to associate with religious radicalism, and especially with the so-called 'academici': Castellio, Ochino and their followers.[112] Silvio, the Zurichers believed, was questioning the magistrate's *cura religionis*, as Castellio had done in the wake of Servetus' execution. That, and the conviction that behind Silvio's protest lurked the familiar spectre of Italian heresy, explains the vigour with which they took up the cudgels on Lentolo's behalf.

The opening salvo in this campaign was fired by Rudolf Gwalther. In early 1571, the Zuricher published his *Six sermons on the Incarnation of the Son of God*, dedicated to the *Bürgermeister* of Chur, Stefan Willy.[113] In his preface to the work, dated 1 December 1570, Gwalther argues that the dual nature of Christ, divine and human, is the central teaching of the Christian faith, the foundation of all others. This

---

[111] Ibid., pp. 50–51; 120–21; 218; 228–39. On Celsi, see P. Bietenholz, 'Questioni su Mino Celsi da Siena', *BSSV*, 132 (1972), pp. 69–76; and 'Mino Celsi and the Toleration Controversy of the Sixteenth Century', *BHR*, 34 (1972), pp. 31–47. Writing to Beza on 13 October 1569, another Italian exile, Simone Simoni, also invoked the Zurichers when contesting the legitimacy of consistorial discipline (*Correspondance*, X, no. 713). In subsequent letters to Josias Simler, Simoni distinguished sharply between the Zurich church and 'sanguinarii illi Lemanici' (11 October 1573 and 12 May 1574 [ZB Ms. F 61, 317–22]). Simler responded by emphasizing Geneva's positive services to the Protestant cause: its hospitality towards exiles, the many excellent books published there, and the ministers that it had supplied to France (17 March 1574 [ZB Ms. S 129, 134]).

[112] The term 'academicus' was coined by Theodore Beza to describe those opposed to the treatment of heresy as a civil crime (principally Sebastian Castellio). It was applied to Ochino by both Bullinger and Josias Simler (see Chapters 3:iv and 4:iii above).

[113] *Die Menschwerdung deß waarenn ewigen und eingebornen Suns Gottes unsers Herren Jesu Christi erklärt und ußgelegt in sechs predigen / diser zyt allerley Secten nützlich zůläsen: durch Růdolffen Walther diener der kirchen Zürych* (Zurich, 1571). Of the six sermons, three had been published previously in Gwalther's *Die Geburt und Menschwerdung unsers Herrn Jesu Christi* (Zurich, 1553) and three were new.

doctrine has come under attack from two fronts: first, from those who deny Christ's godhead; and secondly, from those who compromise his humanity through monophysitism. Both groups, it may be inferred, are to be found in Rhaetia, in the form of the Italian radicals and the Schwenckfeldian bookseller Frell respectively. Next Gwalther addresses Silvio's criticisms of the June edict, accusing the statute's opponents of seeking to turn the church into 'a stable of Circe ... in which, just as in a zoo, all sorts of sectarian, confused minds mingle, introducing all kinds of contradictory and conflicting teachings or opinions, and in which ... each person is allowed to utter his own warblings and screechings, and every day to make up something new to which the others are opposed'.[114] Like Bullinger and Zwingli before him, Gwalther concedes that only God can bring the individual to an acceptance of the truth, but insists that this does not absolve the magistrate of the responsibility for ensuring that orthodoxy is publicly upheld and that their subjects are not corrupted by evil example.[115] He ridicules the suggestion that magistrates have no business in the cure of souls:

> Who is so brutish and lacking in reason as not to be able to grasp that if lords and rulers are responsible for protecting individuals' bodies and properties, they are all the more obliged to do their best to ensure that no one is robbed of his soul and suffers damage to it?[116]

Following Beza and Bullinger, Gwalther defends the application of the Mosaic laws against blasphemy and false prophecy in Leviticus

---

114 Ibid., fol. 4ᵛ: 'Weliches alles sy endtlich dahin ziehend / daß sie die Christenliche kirchen zů einem stabulo Circaeo machen / darinnen glych wie in einem Thiergarten / allerley sectische verworrne köpff durchein anderen lauffind / die auch allerley widerwertiger unnd strytiger leeren oder meinungen ynfürind / und in summa einem yeden gestattet werde sin gesang oder geschrey ußzelassen / unnd täglich nach sinem kopff etwas nüws unnd das den anderen zů wider sye / anzůrichten.'

115 Ibid., fols 5ᵛ–6ʳ: 'Hienebend wirdt nieman löugnen können / daß man die lüt wol umb so vil dämmen und in saum halten kan / daß sie mit dem das sy in jren hertzen gefaßt und fürgenommen habend / nit ußbrächind / oder wider Gottes wort falsche und irrige meinungen offentlichen ynfürind. Es kan zwar ein Oberkeit dem kein anders hertz gäben / der von natur zornmütig oder rachgirig / oder von ardt diebisch und räubisch ist: sy kan aber mit strengen Mandaten und gebürlicher straaf wol weeren / daß dise nit nach jren anfächtungen etwas thetlich handlind / ist auch schuldig die selbigen / so sy etwas wider das gemein rächt und alle billickeit thůnd / nach jrem verdienen zestraffen / darmitt fromme lüt vor jnen sicher syend / unnd nit auch andere durch jr byspil verböseret werdind.'

116 Ibid., fol. 6ʳ⁻ᵛ: 'Wer ist aber so grob unnd unverstendig / daß er nit könne die rechnung machen / Diewyl die fürgesetzten und Regenten einen yeden lyb und gůt schirmen söllend / sy vil mer schuldig syend so vil jnen müglich zůverhüten / daß nieman siner seel halben verfürt werde / und an der selben schaden empfahe?'

24:14–16 and Deuteronomy 13:1–11 to contemporary heresy.[117] During the time of the apostles, he argues, the secular authorities were hostile to Christianity, but with Constantine's conversion the responsibility of maintaining 'unity in doctrine and in faith' ('einigkeit in der leer und im glauben') reverted to the magistrate.[118] Gwalther repudiates Sebastian Castellio's interpretation of the parable of the wheat and the weeds, a key text for all 16th-century advocates of religious toleration. According to Bullinger's deputy, the parable is simply a warning against excessive zeal in the pursuit of wrongdoing, which may lead to the conviction of the innocent: where the weeds may be safely destroyed without harming the wheat, that task should be carried out. Gwalther continues:

> One should be even more prepared to resist weeds when they harm the good seed, so that it is unable to grow – that is to say, when the true faith is restricted by misleading teachings and sects that have established themselves, and when the whole church is troubled and torn apart.[119]

The magistrate has a duty to be especially vigilant when the church is threatened, as now, by heretics who cast doubt on 'the true fundamentals of the Christian religion, which even the papist teachers left untouched', that is to say the orthodox doctrines of the Trinity and the two natures of Christ.[120]

Gwalther's contribution to the debate was warmly welcomed by

---

117 Ibid., fol. 6ᵛ: 'Wie kan aber sin [God's] Namm mer geschmächt werden / dann wenn man den selben mißbrucht zů der falschen leer / und under sinem schyn die einfaltigen lüt von Gott und dem wäg deß ewigen hails abfüret? Es sind auch yetzgemelte gebott Gottes im Nüwen Testament so wenig abgethon / als andere / die zů abstellung der sünden und offentlich lasteren geordnet und gäben sind: diewyl der Herr Christus selbs sagt / Er sye nit kommen das gsatz ufzelösen / sonder zů erfüllen.'

118 Ibid., fols 6ᵛ–7ᵛ.

119 Ibid., fols 8ᵛ–9ʳ: 'Noch vil mer aber sol man dem unkrut weeren / wenn es dem gůten samen schaden thůt / also / daß der selbig darvor nit mag ufwachsen / das ist / wenn der waar glaub durch die verfürisch leer und angerichte secten verhinderet / dar zů die gantze kirch betrübet unnd zerissen wirdt.' For Bullinger, the parable expresses the reality of the church as a *corpus permixtum*, and indicates the futility of attempts to construct a church of the elect prior to Christ's return (*Widertöuffer*, fols 166ᵛ–7ʳ). Beza, in keeping with his greater emphasis on ecclesiastical discipline, interprets the field in the parable not as the church, but as the world, and the weeds as all evildoers, rather than simply heretics (*De haereticis a civili Magistratu puniendis Libellus, adversus Martini Bellii farraginem, et novorum Academicorum sectam* (Geneva, 1554), pp. 139–55).

120 *Die Menschwerdung*, fol. 10ʳ: 'Diß ist nun zů unseren zyten wol zů bedencken / diewyl die alten secten allenthalben ynbrächend / und ettliche so unverschampt und frässen sind / daß sy deß Herren Jesu Christi selbs nit verschonend und die rechten gründ der Christenlichen Religion / die doch die Papistischen leerer unverruckt habend lassen blyben / understond umbzekeeren / diewyl sy (wie obgemelt) deß selbigen ewige Gottheit / oder sin angenomne menschheit antasten.'

Lentolo. In a letter of 12 February 1571, he predicted that it would strengthen the leaders of the Rhaetian church in their determination to resist the 'enemies of Christ'. More importantly, it would impress on them the seriousness of the threat posed by heresy in the subject lands, and make them more inclined to provide much-needed assistance to Lentolo and his colleagues in their continuing battle to suppress dissent.[121] In the same letter, Lentolo informed his correspondent that he had sent a copy of the *Responsio orthodoxa* to Chur to be corrected by Egli, his fellow pastor Ulrich Campell, and Johannes Pontisella, the rector of the Chur Latin school, who in turn were under instructions to forward the work to Zurich for assessment alongside Silvio's text. Lentolo implied that the orthodox cause in the Italian churches would receive a much-needed boost if the Zurichers gave the *Responsio* their public approval.[122] As if to underline his need for outside support, he reported that the radicals congregated around Turriani in Piuro were continuing to defy the edict. Camillo Sozzini, for example, had refused to subscribe to either of the two recognized faiths, publicly declaring himself to be a follower of the 'novi academici'. Neither was Camillo's disruptive influence confined to Piuro: Lentolo describes him as 'always running to and fro, and ingratiating himself with the unwary through a show of honesty and uprightness, so that I am not easily able to persuade my [flock] to avoid his company'.[123]

---

[121] StAZ E II 377, 2469r: 'Tua cohortatio fratribus Curiensibus adeo opportune se obtulit, ut nihil unquam opportunius, nihilque magis in tempore videatur esse factum. Non quod ipsi diligentissimi non sint atque strenui ad resistendum Christi hostibus sed vel fortissimi, quum congrediendum est indigent cohortatione aliqua praesertim, eorum, qui et virtute et autoritate prae caeteris valent. Exercuit enim eos his diebus Satan, sed nec exercere desinet, quanvis nunc indutias concedere videatur. Verum is est praecipuus illius tuae cohortationis fructus, quod ea inducis optimos illos commilitones, ut, dum ipsi, non ita praemuntur, nos respiciant, nobisque suppetias ferant, qui propemodum semper sub armis et in excubiis, esse cogimur, imo quibus in singula prope momenta cum hostibus manus conserere necesse est.' Although the letter is dated 1570, this is clearly an error since Lentolo refers to the edict as already in force and assumes familiarity on Gwalther's part with Bartolomeo Silvio's polemic, which the Zurichers did not receive until September that year.

[122] StAZ E II 377, 2469v: 'Ego respondi, ita iubentibus bonis piisque symmistis aliquot, et inter alios D. Iulio Mediolanensi ac D. Paulo Gadio, quos prae aliis honoris causa nomino, mittoque meam responsionem D. Thobiae nostro, ut ipse una cum D. Huldrico Campello ac D. Pontisella viris piis ac doctis corrigant eam ac emendent, tandem ad te mittant, quandoquidem audax ille non est veritus scriptum suum ad vos mittere, ut de utroque iudicium feratis vos, qui et doctrina et pietate merito estis percelebres, ac eo modo siquid respondi, quod vestram approbationem mereatur, ego possim postea illud magis tuto maioreque cum fructu in publicum emittere.'

[123] Ibid., 2471r: 'Et quoniam ob vicinitatem multa mala Ecclesiae, cui servio, infert, huc illuc semper excurrens, ac se incautis insinuans lenocinio nescio cuius simulatae honestatis et probitatis, ut non ita facile possim meos ab eius consuetudine amovere.'

By the end of 1570 Bullinger, too, had begun to take an active interest in the conflict that was unfolding in Graubünden. In November, he sent Egli a copy of Beza's *De haereticis*, in order that his Rhaetian colleague might be better placed to refute the arguments against the punishment of heretics put forward by Johannes Gantner, who the previous month had been dismissed from his post in Chur.[124] In March 1571 Gantner's replacement, Ulrich Campell, went so far as to suggest that one of the senior Zurich churchmen – either Bullinger himself, Gwalther, Wolf or Ludwig Lavater – should attend the forthcoming meeting of the Rhaetian Reformed synod (scheduled for June), at which the cases of Gantner, Silvio and the Piuro radicals were due to be discussed.[125] In the event, Bullinger declined this invitation, for fear of being seen to undermine the independent authority of the Rhaetian church leadership.[126] However, he did advise Egli on how to proceed against the 'heretics' at the synod, emphasizing that they should be prevented from turning the assembly into a platform for their heterodox views.[127] In particular, Egli was to avoid allowing himself to be drawn into debating the Trinity or the divinity of Christ ('it is unworthy that we should place in doubt things that are absolutely certain'). Typically, Bullinger refers back to one of the defining moments in the history of the early church, the Arian controversy, to illustrate the dangers of parleying with heretics: 'As his letters in Eusebius still testify, the great Constantine was most displeased that Alexander [the bishop of Alexandria and Arius' great opponent] and Arius should have descended into the arena and confused articles of the faith with arguments.'[128]

After the synod had met, Egli sent Bullinger an extended account of its proceedings.[129] According to Egli, the first two days of the meeting

---

[124] Egli to Bullinger, 27 November 1570 (StAZ E II 376, 183; Schiess, III, no. 230).

[125] Campell to Bullinger, 24 April 1571 (StAZ E II 375, 859; Schiess, III, no. 246).

[126] Bullinger to Egli, 1 June 1571 (StAZ E II 342a, 630ʳ; Schiess, III, no. 251): 'Prodesse et vobis ministris et ecclesiae vestrae videtur, quod nulli ex nostris ad vos evocantur, ne forte domini vestri et populus vester suspicetur vos non esse instructos satis etc. sicque vestrae decedat authoritati.'

[127] Bullinger to Egli, 27 April 1571 (StAZ E II 342a, 628; Schiess, III, no. 248).

[128] Bullinger to Egli, 25 May 1571 (StAZ E II 342a, 629; Schiess, III, no. 249): 'Magnus ille Constantinus indignissime ferebat, ut eius adhuc epistolae apud Eusebium testantur, quod Alexander et Arius in hanc descendissent arenam, et articulos fidei contentionibus miscuissent.' In his letter of 1 June Bullinger writes: 'Sitis autem constantes et simplices, in omnibus nostrae confessioni inhaerentes nec alio sinentes vos ad aliena abstrahi.'

[129] *Acta Synodi Curiensis Mense Iunio 1571* (StAZ E II 381, 1270ʳ–82ʳ), published in Rosius de Porta, *Historia Reformationis*, I:2, pp. 517–53. See also Schiess, III, no. 252. Ulrich Campell's account of the synod focuses on the dispute between Gantner and Egli, leaving aside the proceedings against Turriani and his associates (Campell, *Historia Raetica*, II, pp. 474–90).

were taken up with an exchange of views between himself and Gantner, which eventually resulted in the latter's condemnation by the ministers present.[130] Then attention switched to the question of the Italian dissidents. Turriani was accused of receiving heretics excommunicated by the church of Chiavenna and of defending 'that academic dogma' (religious toleration), while Camogli was charged with offering asylum to convicted heretics. Egli implies that the synod was initially reluctant to take punitive action against the radicals, but swung behind Lentolo following an intervention by the latter's ally Giulio da Milano, who urged his fellow ministers to give a clear sign of their determination to protect the Italian churches from the 'emissaries of Antichrist'.[131] Giulio also produced the orthodox faction's trump card: Camogli's letters to Florio and Turriani of late 1563, in which the possibility of settling Ochino in Rhaetia was mooted.[132] His evidence was supplemented by Lentolo's own testimony, 'in which he provided sufficient proof that [Turriani] was not a pastor or minister, but a protector of wolves'. Camogli did not help his case by remarking, under examination, that 'he knew as much about the Holy Trinity as his shoe'.[133] The synod eventually suspended Turriani and Silvio from the ministry, pending further investigation, and excommunicated Camogli and Camillo Sozzini.[134]

Bullinger was pleased by the outcome of the meeting, and urged Egli now to press for the comprehensive implementation of the edict.[135] Achieving that was less straightforward than one might imagine, as the Piuro radicals – especially Camogli – had powerful allies within the Rhaetian aristocracy. Soon Egli was reporting magisterial indifference, even hostility, to his calls for better enforcement of the anti-heresy

---

130 During the course of this debate Gantner produced a book (probably Castellio's *De haereticis an sint persequendi*) containing passages from ancient and contemporary authors arguing against the use of force to suppress heresy. Egli responded by citing Beza's rejoinder to Castellio's work.

131 StAZ E II 381, 1275ᵛ; Rosius de Porta, *Historia Reformationis*, I:2, p. 545.

132 The letters seem to have been intercepted by the ever-watchful Giulio; Lentolo had translated them into Latin.

133 StAZ E II 381, 1275ʳ; Rosius de Porta, *Historia Reformationis*, I:2, p. 544: 'His accedebant singularia quaedam quae D. Lentulus in Turrianum habuit, ex quibus omnibus satis constabat, illum non pastorem, ministrum, sed luporum protectorem esse. Camulius examinatus, respondit, er wüße als vil von der h. Trinitet, als sin schůch.'

134 AERSG B 3, p. 292.

135 'Camulius et eius similes indigni sunt quos terra ferat, non iam dico Rheti tolerent. Ad corvos!' (Bullinger to Egli, 27 July 1571 [StAZ E II 342a, 626ʳ; Schiess, III, 256]). Compare the *Antistes*' letter of 9 December 1571 (Schiess, III, no. 267): 'Dominum oro, ut magistratus spiritum excitet, quo semel bene statuta tueatur et non seducatur nebulonum fabulis atque ita conduplicentur novae vobis molestiae.'

measures. In a letter to Josias Simler of 20 August 1571, the Chur minister complained:

> Certain leading men [of this republic] who profess to be more religious and evangelical than others may now complain that we are being too rigid in subduing and driving off these fanatics. The Rhaetian lords unanimously approved our actions, but privately some of them now criticize that which they previously approved with good will, thus contradicting themselves.[136]

Members of Graubünden's Reformed elite appear to have been reluctant to endorse a crackdown on the radicals that might adversely affect the position of Protestantism as a whole in the Freestate, with the Catholic minority taking the opportunity to call for the general expulsion of all Italian exiles from Rhaetia, orthodox as well as 'heretics'.[137] The knowledge that some leading Rhaetian magnates shared their doubts about the approach favoured by Egli and Lentolo gave the edict's Italian opponents renewed heart. In letters to Bullinger and Simler, Egli reported that the church of Piuro had refused to elect a replacement for Turriani and was threatening to ask the Diet to overturn the sentence of suspension imposed by the synod. Ministers in the Valbregaglia had also called for Turriani to be reinstated.[138]

Aware of the difficulties faced by the Rhaetian church leadership, Zurich continued to offer what it could by way of support. In June 1571 Gwalther completed a Latin translation of his *Six Sermons*, which he hoped would prove a good antidote to heretical 'poisons' ('toxicis').[139] This was followed by publication two months later of the *Scripta veterum latina*, which Simler dedicated to the three Rhaetian Leagues.[140]

---

136 ZB Ms. F 59, 413r: 'Principes viri quidam [huius reipublicae], qui se prae caeteris religiosos ac evangelicos profitentur, de nobis nunc conquerantur ceu rigidioribus, in fanaticis istis revincendis ac deturbandis. Approbarunt Rheti Domini uno ore omnes nostras actiones: sed privatim nunc quidam repperiuntur, qui a seipsis dissidentes, id in nobis culpant, quod antea benevole confirmarunt.' Egli reports that Peter Guler, the *Ammann* of Davos, was unhappy about the suspension of Silvio, whom he knew from his time as *podestà* in Traona (Egli to Bullinger, 1 October 1571 [ZB Ms. S 125, 27]).

137 Egli to Simler, 28 May 1571 (ZB Ms. F 59, 410v).

138 Egli to Simler, 11 September 1571 (ZB Ms. F 59, 415r–17r); Egli to Bullinger, October 1571 (ZB Ms. S 125, 27).

139 Gwalther to Bullinger, 26 June 1571 (StAZ E II 340, 357). Earlier that month, Gwalther's fears about the threat posed by heresy to the stability of the Rhaetian church had been stoked by rumours that Giorgio Biandrata had acquired citizenship in Mesocco and would arrive in Graubünden shortly (Gwalther to Bullinger, 19 June 1571 (StAZ E II 340, 356); cited in Rotondò, 'Atteggiamenti', pp. 1009–10, n. 67).

140 Egli had suggested the dedication (see ZB Ms. F 59, 410v). Further evidence of Simler's involvement in the campaign against religious radicalism in Rhaetia is to be found in a letter of his to Bullinger dated 22 June (1571?). There Simler records that one of his

Like Gwalther in his *Sermons*, in the *Scripta veterum* Simler addresses the specific situation in which the Reformed church of Graubünden found itself.[141] First he emphasizes the peculiarity (and perilousness) of Rhaetia's geographical position: interposed between Germany and Italy, the Freestate is vulnerable to the spread of heresy from both quarters – in the one case Anabaptism and Schwenckfeldianism, in the other Samosatene antitrinitarianism.[142] This is a clear reference to the twin dangers posed by the 'Eutychians' Gantner and Frell, and the Italian radicals. Simler then embarks on an extended defence of the Rhaetian anti-heresy edict, reiterating many of the points made by Lentolo and Gwalther in their works on the same subject. The control of heresy, he insists, is one aspect of the magistrate's *cura religionis*; indeed, the edict has precedents in the actions of the Old Testament kings of Israel and Judah, and of the early Christian emperors. Like Gwalther, Simler argues that the intention behind such measures is not the coercion of consciences, but the maintenance of 'the external discipline of doctrine and manners' ('doctrinae et morum externam politiam').[143] The Zurich professor has no time for Silvio's objections to the 'dogmatism' of the confessional orthodoxy demanded by Lentolo of Reformed believers: all that is being called for, he maintains, is acceptance of the basic tenets of the Christian faith.[144] The advocates of religious toleration – to whom Simler applies the by-now familiar epithet 'academici' – would strip Christianity of all that is distinctive and essential to it, leaving believers

---

students, the Bregagliotto Johann Baptist Müller, has been offered the position of minister in Morbegno, and suggests that it would be useful to have a pastor of proven orthodoxy in the town to prevent misuse of the local printing-press by heretical elements (ZB Ms. F 40, 442; T. Schiess, 'Josias Simler und sein Schüler Johann Baptist Müller von Vicosoprano', *Zürcher Taschenbuch* (1903), pp. 223–53 [231–2]). In the *Commentarii conventus synodalis*, Lentolo refers to a letter that he received from Simler, dated 3 October 1571, informing him that Petrus Romanus had visited Zurich and spoken critically of the church of Chiavenna (*Commentarii*, fols 38ᵛ–9ʳ).

[141] There is a fine analysis of Simler's preface to the *Scripta veterum* in Firpo, *Antitrinitari*, pp. 1–8.

[142] *Scripta veterum*, fol. *2ᵛ.

[143] Ibid., fol. *3ʳ.

[144] It is likely that Simler had read Silvio's tract by this time. In a letter to Ambrosius Marti and Stefan Willy written shortly after the publication of the *Scripta veterum*, he describes the work as a response to complaints about the edict by persons claiming that it is 'ein große tyranny so iemants einicher confeßion zů underschriben genötiget werde', and notes that he has encountered such complaints both orally and in writing (ZB Ms. F 46, 348–51). Late the following year, Lentolo asked Bullinger to have Simler return his manuscript of the *Responsio orthodoxa*, in which, of course, Silvio's work was reproduced (StAZ E II 365, 332–4; Schiess, III, no. 336; Zucchini, 'Lentolo', p. 122; Zucchini, 'In coërcendis', p. 538). Simler mentions the *Responsio orthodoxa* (then still unpublished) under the entry for Lentolo in his *Bibliotheca* of 1574 (*Bibliotheca*, p. 618).

with only 'a certain general knowledge of Christ, shared with Mohammedanism'.[145] This last reference is significant: in Simler's heresiology, as we have seen, Islam represents the final destination of those who abandon the path of Nicene-Chalcedonian orthodoxy.[146]

The publication of the *Scripta veterum* earned Simler a letter of thanks from the council of Chur together with a goblet worth 60 Gulden from the Rhaetian Diet, awarded in recognition of his services to orthodoxy.[147] The Graubünden church leadership was equally appreciative: Egli described the *Scripta* to Bullinger as a true 'hammer of heretics',[148] and asked Simler to have the Zurich printers Froschauer and Gesner dispatch copies of the work to Chur for sale 'so that they may quickly also reach Italy, where there is great need of this remedy'.[149]

From the tone of his letters to the Zurichers, it would seem that Egli favoured the permanent exclusion of Silvio and the Piuro radicals from the Rhaetian Reformed church. Camogli's great wealth – estimated at 30,000 gold florins – combined with the notorious venality of the Rhaetian ruling elite, made that an unrealistic proposition.[150] Having secured Zurich's backing in such a public manner, however, the

---

[145] *Scripta veterum*, fol. *3ᵛ: 'O Sathanam vafrum artificem, qui cum tot annis laborarit in oppugnanda Christi religione, novis subinde erroribus per haereticos in publicum prolatis, nunc persuadere conatur, haec omnia adiaphora esse, de quibus absque iactura salutis liceat opinari quicquid cuique lubitum fuerit: interim pro Christianorum fide obtrudit generalem quandam Christi notitiam, cum Machometanismo communem.'

[146] In the letter cited in n. 144 above, Simler raises explicitly the spectre of a Turkish-heretical alliance, referring his correspondents to recent events in the Palatinate: 'Und wiewol ettlich gemeinden und gerichte der Roemischen oder wie sy sich nemmend der Catholischen religion sind hoff ich doch sy söllind dise min arbeit nitt für übel uffnemmen / dann dise secten glich wol inen alß auch unß widerig sind / so mag auch zů gemeiner frid und einigkeit nitt erhalten werden / ... dan mangklich weißt waß uffrürige artickel die teuffer wider die oberkeit habend / so sind auch der Servetaner gotteßlesterungen offenbar / und ist seer zů besorgen daß dem algemeinen fyend Christenlicher religion dem Türken durch sy der weg bereitet werde / da ia auch ettliche under inen schon erfunden sind die früntlich practic mitt den Turken gemacht habend / und daruff von dem Christenlichen dur[ch]lüchtigen Churfürsten und herren pfalzgraffen am Rin gefangklich inzogen sind'.

[147] *Bürgermeister* and council of Chur to Simler, 31 August 1571 (ZB Ms. F 57, 44); Schiess, III, p. 271, n. 1.

[148] Egli to Bullinger, 3 September 1571 (StAZ E II 376, 195ʳ; Schiess, III, no. 259). The same phrase is used by Johannes Pontisella in a letter to Simler, also dated 3 September (ZB Ms. F 61, 7).

[149] Egli to Simler, 11 September 1571 (ZB Ms. F 59, 415ᵛ): 'Necesse autem omnino erit ut D. Frosch. vel Gesnerus copiam exemplorum procurent, interque nostros vendendo distrahunt, quo mature in Italiam quoque deveniant, ubi hoc remedio valde indigent.'

[150] See Egli to Simler, 11 September 1571 (ZB Ms. F 59, 416ᵛ): 'Dives est Camulius, et plus valent sollicitationes, quam iustitiae leges et decreta.' Zucchini highlights the links between Camogli and the Rhaetian magnates Rudolf von Salis and Conradin Planta ('Di una lettera inedita di Niccolò Camogli (1581)', *BSSV*, 137 (1975), pp. 15–20).

orthodox party within the Rhaetian church was able to exact a heavy price from the dissidents for their eventual rehabilitation. At a meeting in Davos in February 1572, the synod agreed to lift the sentences on Camogli and Turriani, provided that each formally abjured his errors. The conditions attached to Turriani's rehabilitation left little room for calculated ambiguity of the sort which the Rhaetian church leadership and its allies in Zurich now associated with the Italian exiles. The Piuro minister was to subscribe to the Second Helvetic Confession and to promise to have no further contact with heretics, either verbally or in writing. Furthermore, he was to demonstrate the sincerity of his abjuration by preaching on the doctrinal issues in dispute – the unity and Trinity of the Godhead, the two natures of Christ, the perpetual virginity of Mary,[151] the judgment of the soul immediately after death, infant baptism and the magistrate's *cura religionis* – before a four-man commission that included his arch-rival Lentolo.[152] The following year Silvio was readmitted to the synod after he agreed to abjure his errors, both in writing and before the church of Sondrio.[153]

Since Cantimori, scholars of the Italian Reformation have tended to regard the events of 1570–72 as marking a decisive turning-point in the history of the Italian churches of Graubünden. In his study of the 16th-century Valtellina, Alessandro Pastore observes:

> Following these harsh measures heretical activity in the Valtellina ceased to be as important, and only a few of the more dissatisfied and courageous Anabaptists again took the road into exile in Poland and Transylvania. Most of them, exhausted and dejected from their past struggles, adopted Nicodemite practices, masking their true beliefs, or began to participate sincerely in the community of faithful followers of Swiss Reformed orthodoxy.[154]

Pastore's comments do not quite do justice to the complexity of the situation in the Italian churches after 1572. The fact that Silvio, Turriani

---

[151] Denial of the perpetual virginity of Mary (which had been upheld consistently by the Zurich church since Zwingli) was a long-standing feature of religious radicalism in the Rhaetian Freestate. In the early 1550s, Gianandrea Paravicini had scandalized Gallicius by teaching that Christ's mother did not remain a virgin *post partum* (see Chapter 1:iii). One of Gantner's followers, Johannes Möhr, was excluded from the synod for espousing the same error, which the Reformed leadership considered a revival of ancient Helvidianism.

[152] AERSG B 3, pp. 2–3; Lentolo, *Commentarii*, fols 51ᵛ–2ᵛ; Zucchini, '<<In coërcendis>>', p. 537; 'Lentolo', pp. 120–21.

[153] AERSG B 3, p. 5. Camillo Sozzini was less fortunate: the last we hear, he had fled Piuro after being accused of sodomizing a local youth (Egli to Simler, 20 August 1571 (ZB Ms. F 59, 414); Campell, *Descriptio*, pp. 412–13).

[154] Pastore, *Valtellina*, pp. 86–7.

and Camogli eventually secured their readmission to the Reformed fold in itself demonstrates that the victory of Lentolo and his allies was not in the first instance complete. The Reformed leadership also had every reason to doubt the sincerity of the former dissidents' abjurations, given the tendency of many Italian radicals to condone outward conformity and Nicodemism as legitimate responses to persecution. There is evidence that Silvio, for one, continued to wage a rearguard action against the terms of the edict, as in 1577 the Rhaetian synod admonished him for failing to place sufficient stress on the importance of subscription and for administering communion to non-subscribers.[155] No similar manifestations of dissent are attested for Turriani but, like other Italian exiles who shared his difficulties with Reformed orthodoxy (Simone Simoni and Francesco Pucci, for instance), he seems eventually to have returned to Catholicism.[156]

The records of the Rhaetian synod bear testimony to continuing radical activity – albeit at a lower level of intensity – in the Italian-speaking areas of Graubünden during the 1570s and early 1580s. At the annual meeting of the synod for 1575, Scipione Calandrini complained that Petrus Romanus, who had been excommunicated by the church of Chiavenna two years earlier, was continuing to disseminate his errors.[157] The same assembly excluded from its ranks the minister of Vicosoprano, Francesco Thrana, for remaining stubbornly opposed to the edict.[158] However, for its disciplinary sanctions to take effect the synod remained dependent on the co-operation of local congregations and magistrates – co-operation that was often difficult to secure. The case of Lorenzo Sonzini, pastor in Mello, illustrates well the problems faced by the orthodox authorities in this regard. In 1575 Sonzini was suspended from the ministry for associating with Petrus Romanus, but his congregation seems to have paid little heed to this decision: five years on, the synod was still appealing to the evangelicals of Mello to find themselves a new pastor. In 1581 Sonzini was readmitted to the synod, but the following

---

[155] AERSG B 3, p. 20: 'Bartolomaeus Sylvius acriter reprehensus est de eo, quod non satis pro officio suo auditores suos ad subscribendum synodali confessioni cohortatus sit, imo subscribere renuentibus Coenam Domini administrarit.' The last direct testimony that we have for Silvio is a letter to Johannes von Salis dated February 1577 (see Zucchini, 'Silvio', p. 69).

[156] Lentolo to J.W. Stucki, 10 April 1598 (StAZ E II 380, 385).

[157] AERSG B 3, p. 6.

[158] Ibid., p. 7. The following year the synod reaffirmed the sentence, on the grounds that Thrana was continuing to correspond with Gantner and to resist its authority. The disgraced pastor was informed that in order to be readmitted to the synod he would have to seek a pardon for his offences and agree to subscribe to either the Second Helvetic or the Rhaetic Confession (ibid., p. 12).

year he was again suspended after failing to provide evidence of a genuine change of heart. This sentence was finally lifted in June 1585, although doubts continued to be voiced about Sonzini's fitness for the ministry. Indeed, one imagines that the saga would have continued in similar vein had Sonzini not been abducted shortly afterwards, to suffer a martyr's death in Rome.[159]

That being said, the edict and the disciplinary measures subsequently taken by the synod did send out an important signal to the Italian radicals. The lines between Reformed orthodoxy and heresy had been clearly demarcated, and the principle of subscription conceded. Evidence of the changed climate in the Reformed churches of Italian Graubünden is provided by an unpublished catechism from Sondrio dated 1583, which requires belief in the distinctiveness and consubstantiality of the three divine persons, and in the dual procession of the Holy Spirit.[160] Although isolated instances of dissent continued to be recorded, concerted resistance to the imposition of orthodoxy collapsed after 1572. As we have seen, Lentolo's opponents in the Italian pastorate grudgingly came to terms with the new religious dispensation; prominent laypersons either did the same (Camogli, Giulio Sadoleto) or sought out a more secure base for their activities.[161] In a letter to the Zurich churchman Johann Wilhelm Stucki dated 21 April 1596, Lentolo felt able to pronounce the final demise of heresy in Italian Graubünden.[162]

The controversy over the edict was also significant in terms of its

---

[159] Ibid., pp. 46; 55; 76; 84. See also Bonorand, *Reformatorische Emigration*, pp. 71–2.

[160] *Catechismus Religionis Christianae ad usum Sondriensis Ecclesiae* (ZB Ms. D 157, fols 484–50), fol. 487r:

'I.: Cur dicis te credere in Deum Patrem, et in Iesum Christum, et in Spiritum Sanctum?
R. Propterea quod tres distinctae Personae sunt, ac una et eadem Essentia ab aeterno: Pater qui generavit ab aeterno Filium et Spiritus sanctus qui procedit ab ambobus inseparabiliter.'

I am indebted to Emanuele Fiume for bringing this text to my attention.

[161] Among the emigrants were Mino Celsi and Marcello Squarcialupi, both of whom left Piuro for Basle towards the end of 1571. On Squarcialupi, see C. Madonia, 'Marcello Squarcialupi tra Poschiavo e Alba Iulia: note biografiche', in Pastore, *Riforma e società*, pp. 89–108; and G. Zucchini, 'Per la ricostruzione dell'epistolario di Marcello Squarcialupi: alcune lettere inedite dai Grigioni (1556–1588)', in R. Dán and A. Pirnát (eds), *Antitrinitarianism in the second half of the 16th century* (Budapest, 1982), pp. 323–40. Zucchini notes Squarcialupi's connections with Betti, Castiglione and Taddeo Duno.

[162] StAZ E II 380, 345; cited by Rotondò in Renato, *Opere*, p. 331. The last known case of heresy dealt with by the church of Chiavenna concerned Fabrizio Pestalozzi, a local merchant who had come under the influence of Giovanni Battista Bovio while resident in Poland (see Marchetti, 'Una polemica').

effect on how the Zurich church was perceived by the more radical Italian exiles. The notion of Zurich as a moderate counterweight to Genevan severity was difficult to perpetuate after Bullinger, Gwalther and Simler had identified themselves so closely with the suppression of dissent. The Zurich church's treatment of Ochino had already drawn criticism from some quarters – at the synod of June 1571, Egli had been forced to defend the punishment meted out to him eight years before – and these attacks intensified after the Zurichers gave their blessing to the Rhaetian anti-heresy edict.[163] For example, in October 1571 Egli informed Bullinger that the minister of Vicosoprano (Francesco Thrana) had condemned Zwingli as a 'bloodthirsty man' ('virum sanguinarium') who had engineered the deaths of Anabaptists without just cause.[164]

Conversely, the affair strengthened relations between the orthodox Reformed pastorate of Italian-speaking Rhaetia and the Zurich church. Lentolo had earned the Zurichers' approbation by his tireless and ultimately successful pursuit of heresy, and over subsequent decades he established himself as their most important Italian correspondent in the region.[165] Lentolo's success in combating religious radicalism meant that Zurich's relationship with the Italian Reformed congregations of Rhaetia ceased to be dominated by the question of heresy: the focus of its attention now shifted to supporting their efforts to consolidate and sustain a Protestant presence in this important frontier region.

---

[163] StAZ E II 381, 1276ᵛ; Rosius de Porta, *Historia Reformationis*, I:2, p. 549: 'Historiam ac causas Ochiniani exilii ex praefatione tua quam libro Domini Simleri [*De aeterno Dei filio*] praefixisti, fratribus vere exposui, ne quid aliorum maledicentia sinistrius de quoquam iudicarent.'

[164] ZB Ms. S 125, 27.

[165] Zucchini ('In coërcendis', p. 538) suggests that Lentolo's eventual failure to have his *Responsio* published in Zurich as originally planned testifies to a lack of enthusiasm for the project on (in particular) Bullinger's part. Against this, see Lentolo to Egli, 22 January 1574 (StAZ E II 365, 363–4). When the *Responsio* did finally appear in Geneva in 1592, it included a warm letter of commendation from Bullinger, dated January 1574, along with some verses by Gwalther praising Lentolo for having purged the 'Augiae stabulum' of heresy (*Responsio*, pp. 348; 2).

CHAPTER SIX

From Heretics to Martyrs: Zurich and the Italian Churches of Graubünden, 1572–1620

'A holy anchor, and a secure refuge': that was how Vincenzo Paravicini described Zurich in the preface to his translation of Johann Jakob Breitinger's *Fundamental instruction as to whether a sect may endure more or less than 100 years*, published in 1622.[1] Paravicini, as minister to the congregation of Valtellinese exiles established in Zurich following the infamous 'sacro macello' of July 1620 – in which up to 600 Protestants perished at the hands of their Catholic neighbours – had more reason than most to be aware of the benefits that the Italian-speaking Reformed of the Valtellina and other parts of Graubünden had derived from their association with the Swiss city. During the early decades of these communities' existence, their relationship with Zurich was dogged by controversy over doctrine, as orthodox ministers like Mainardi and Lentolo struggled (with the assistance of the Zurichers) to subdue 'heretical' and other dissenting elements within the Italian churches. After 1572, religious radicalism was more or less a spent force in Graubünden: Lentolo and his allies in the Rhaetian pastorate would henceforth set the theological tenor for the Reformed churches of Chiavenna, the Valtellina and the Valbregaglia. Those churches remained in close contact with Zurich, but the latter now functioned more as a provider of practical assistance (in the form of education, books and advice) than as an arbiter in intra-community disputes. The relationship was, it must be stressed, one of mutual benefit: for their part, Rhaetia's Italian-speaking congregations offered the Zurich church a means of continued access to the world of Italian culture and scholarship at a time of hardening intellectual divisions between Catholic and Protestant Europe.

---

1 '... hà l'onnipotente Iddio scelta questa Nobilissima, è Christianissima Città di Zurigo, acciò ad essa come ad una sacrata Ancora, è sicura ritratta, havessero rifugio la maggior parte de sopradetti fedeli ...' (*Instruttione fondamentale se una setta duri più ò meno di cent'Anni. Similmente, qual sia l'antica è nuova fede, è dove avanti la Reformatione essa sia statta. ... Dal molto Rev. & Dottiss. Sig. Gio. Giacobo Breitingero, primario Pastore della Chiesa di Zurigo* (n.p. [Zurich], 1622), sig. A4ᵛ. On Paravicini, see E. Campi, 'Vincenzo Paravicino (1595–1678) tra la Valtellina e la Svizzera', in Campi and La Torre, *Il protestantesimo*, pp. 89–98.

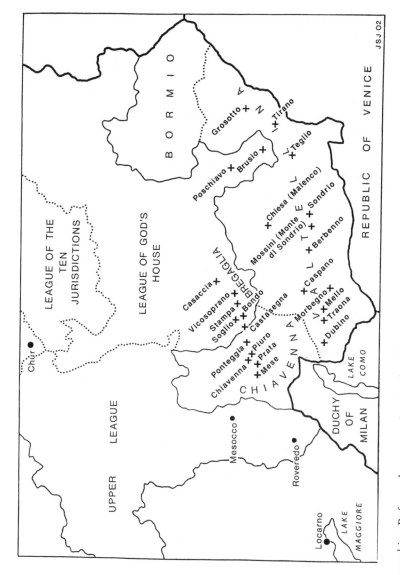

2 Italian-speaking Reformed congregations in the Rhaetian Freestate and its subject lands around 1600

Within the map:

LEAGUE OF THE TEN JURISDICTIONS

LEAGUE OF GOD'S HOUSE

UPPER LEAGUE

BORMIO

REPUBLIC OF VENICE

DUCHY OF MILAN

Chur

Mesocco

Roveredo

Locarno

LAKE MAGGIORE

LAKE COMO

VALTELLINA

BREGAGLIA

CHIAVENNA

Grosotto
Tirano
Teglio
Brusio
Poschiavo
Chiesa (Malenco)
Mossini (Monte di Sondrio)
Sondrio
Berbenno
Casaccia
Vicosoprano
Stampa
Soglio
Bondo
Castasegna
Caspano
Morbegno
Mello
Traona
Dubino
Ponteggia
Piuro
Prata
Chiavenna
Mese

JSJ 02

i. 'In his Antichristi faucibus': the situation of the Italian churches prior to the 'sacro macello'

In order to appreciate why links with Zurich came to assume such importance in the life of Graubünden's Italian-speaking churches during the closing decades of the 16th century, one needs to be aware of the context within which those congregations were operating. With the submission or emigration of religious radicals such as Niccolò Camogli and Camillo Sozzini, the internal threat to the unity and cohesiveness of Rhaetia's Italian Reformed communities had receded, but their situation remained precarious. Thanks to the efforts of Pier Paolo Vergerio, the Valbregaglia had been fully protestantized, but in Poschiavo and the subject lands Reformed believers were very much in the minority. On the basis of a report compiled by the marquis of Meregnano, Andreas Wendland has argued that in the late 16th and early 17th centuries the population of the subject lands exceeded that of Rhaetia proper, standing at somewhere in the region of 90–95,000.[2] Contemporary estimates of the size of the Protestant presence in the area vary, but all serve to highlight the overwhelmingly Catholic character of the subject lands. Broccardo Borrone, an evangelical exile from Padua who subsequently returned to the Catholic church, claimed in his *Relazione intorno alla Rezia* (1601) that there were no more than 800 Protestants in the Valchiavenna and 2,500 in the Valtellina,[3] while an anonymous report from 1619 placed the Reformed population of the Valchiavenna at 2,000 and that of the Valtellina at 5,000.[4] Wendland prefers the figure for the Valtellina given by Meregnano (just under 2,000) and suggests a total for the subject lands of approximately 4,000 Reformed.[5] Whatever the precise number, it is unlikely that Protestants constituted much more than 5 per cent of the population of the subject lands.

Some distinction should be made between the position of Protestantism in the Valchiavenna and in the much more populous Valtellina. The evangelical communities of Chiavenna and Piuro were large and wealthy, and included within their membership most of the leading citizens and merchant families of both towns.[6] In the Valtellina,

---

2 Wendland, *Pässe*, pp. 45–6. Of these around 10,000 lived in the county of Chiavenna, 6,000 in Bormio and the remainder in the Valtellina.

3 Rosius de Porta, *Historia Reformationis*, II:3, pp. 179–81. Borrone's figure for the total population of the subject lands is much lower than that given by Wendland.

4 A. Wendland, 'Republik und <<Untertanenlande>> vor dem Veltlineraufstand (1620)', *BM* (1990), pp. 182–213 (210).

5 Wendland, *Pässe*, p. 61.

6 Filippo Archinto, bishop of Como, noted during his visitation of 1614–15 that one third of the population of Chiavenna was Reformed, and that the town's Protestants were

by contrast, scores of parishes had been left virtually untouched by the Reformation. The Venetian envoy to Graubünden, Giovanni Battista Padavino, reported early in the 17th century that 'no place is held absolutely by heretics' and that Protestants did not form as much as 1 per cent of the local population.[7] Some Reformed communities, such as those of Cermeledo, Grania and Boalzo, were too small even to support their own preacher.

In those places where formally constituted Reformed churches did exist, Protestants still tended to be heavily outnumbered by their Catholic neighbours. According to the Catholic bishop of Como, Feliciano Ninguarda, who carried out a visitation in the Valtellina during the late 1580s with the specific intention of gathering information on the extent of the Protestant presence there, in Dubino only four out of 40 and in Caspano only 15 out of 200 households were Reformed.[8] The sole exception to this pattern was in the area around Sondrio, which had been a focus of Vergerio's missionary work back in the early 1550s; there Ninguarda reports that some villages were almost exclusively Protestant.[9] Otherwise the largest concentrations of Protestants were to be found in the urban centres of the Valtellina, especially Teglio, Tirano and Sondrio. Some authorities put the Protestant population of Sondrio at as high as 700 to 800.[10]

Evidence for the state of relations between the Catholic and Protestant communities is rather mixed. If an anonymous account written some time between 1584 and 1618 is to be believed, in the Valchiavenna at least they were surprisingly good. In this work

offering financial inducements to local Catholics to convert (U. Mazzone, '<<Consolare quei poveri cattolici>>: Visitatori ecclesiastici in Valtellina tra '500 e '600', in Pastore, *Riforma e società*, pp. 129–57 (148); G.B. Crollolanza, *Storia del contado di Chiavenna* (Milan, 1870), p. 238). For evidence of the strength of Protestantism in the Valchiavenna from an early date, see the letter of 12 May 1568 from the syndics of the Catholic church of San Lorenzo in Mese to Giovanni Antonio Volpe (K. Fry (ed.), *Giovanni Antonio Volpe Nunzius in der Schweiz: Band II: Die zweite und dritte Nunziatur 1565, 1573 (–1588)* (Stans, 1946), no. 842).

7 A. Giussani (ed.), 'Relatione del Segretario Padavino ritornato dal paese de' Signori Grisoni', *Periodico della Società storica per la Provincia e antica Diocesi di Como*, 15 (1903), pp. 161–212 (190).

8 Società storica comense (ed.), *Atti della visita pastorale diocesana di F. Feliciano Ninguarda Vescovo di Como (1589–1593)* (2 vols, Como, 1892–5), I, pp. 245; 249; 280.

9 In Mossini, only one of the 42 households continued to adhere to the old faith (Ninguarda, *Atti*, p. 305). Compare C. di Filippo Bareggi, 'Tra Sondrio e le Leghe grigie: la Valmalenco del tardo Cinquecento', *BSSV*, 178 (1995), pp. 109–40 (122–3).

10 Di Filippo Bareggi, 'Tra Sondrio e le Leghe grigie', p. 123, n. 78. Ninguarda identifies 39 out of 265 households in Teglio as Protestant (Ninguarda, *Atti*, I, p. 330). The town's Reformed community included a significant group of exiles from Cremona (Pastore, *Valtellina*, pp. 97–103).

Chiavenna's Protestants and Catholics are described as co-existing harmoniously – so harmoniously, in fact, that disputes over religion between the two groups were virtually unknown.[11] In addition, the practice of mixed marriage (which is attested in both Chiavenna and the Valtellina) had the effect of rendering confessional boundaries relatively fluid across the generations. From the records of Ninguarda's visitation, we know that children born as a result of such unions could be brought up in the religion of either parent, depending on the dynamics of the particular relationship.[12] In some cases a compromise solution prevailed, with fathers taking charge of the religious education of their sons while mothers did the same for their daughters.[13] The need for co-operation between the two religious communities was reinforced by the fact that in many places (Ponteggia, Dubino, Caspano, Chiesa and Lanzada in the Valmalenco) Protestants and Catholics worshipped in the same church building.[14]

However, by the early 17th century such arrangements were showing signs of strain. In 1609, for example, the Reformed community of Chiesa petitioned the Rhaetian Diet to be allowed their own church and cemetery; significantly, their request was supported by local Catholics anxious to 'liberate' the parish church of St James and St Philip from heretical use.[15] There was also conflict over ecclesiastical revenue, a proportion of which had been assigned to the Reformed by the Rhaetian Diet in 1558.[16] In 1602, the evangelicals of the church of San Pietro in Chiavenna complained that they had been forced to supplement their minister's salary out of their own pockets because the rival Catholic foundation of San Lorenzo was withholding the portion of church income due to them.[17]

For the Catholics of the Valtellina, the Rhaetian Diet's insistence that

---

[11] ZB Ms. A 12, fol. 327^{r-v}.

[12] Of particular interest in this connection are the examples that Ninguarda provides from Mello in the Valtellina (Ninguarda, *Atti*, pp. 251–2).

[13] Mazzone, 'Visitatori', p. 154.

[14] Church-sharing (the so-called *simultaneum*) was a feature of religious life in other bi-confessional areas, such as the Thurgau (H. Meyer, *Der zweite Kappeler Krieg: Die Krise der Schweizerischen Reformation* (Zurich, 1976), pp. 239–40). The author of the anonymous account of the Valchiavenna cited above describes briefly the arrangements for the shared use of the church of San Sebastiano in Ponteggia, where on Sundays the celebration of the Mass was followed by a Reformed service (ZB Ms. A 12, 331^r).

[15] Di Filippo Bareggi, 'Tra Sondrio e le Leghe grigie', pp. 136–7. For an example of the tensions that could arise over the use of church buildings, see ibid., pp. 123–4 and n. 80.

[16] F. Jecklin (ed.), *Materialien zur Standes- und Landesgeschichte Gem. III Bünde (Graubünden), 1464–1803* (2 vols, Basle, 1907/9), II, no. 285; Schiess, II, no. 125; Camenisch, *Reformation und Gegenreformation*, p. 44.

[17] StAG D II b 3.

they share church revenue and buildings with the Reformed was evidence not of their rulers' even-handedness, but of a systematic campaign to weaken their attachment to the old faith. This sense of grievance was fuelled by the Diet's persistent meddling in Catholic religious affairs, which often seemed designed specifically to frustrate attempts by the Catholic hierarchy to improve pastoral provision for the subject lands and to implement Tridentine reforms there.[18] At times the Rhaetian authorities even called into question the doctrinal authority of the church, twice declaring papal indulgences and jubilees invalid, and prohibiting the celebration of Catholic feast days according to the Gregorian calendar.[19] For their part – and not without reason – the Bündner magistrates suspected the Valtellinese Catholics of conspiring with neighbouring Milan to undermine Rhaetian control of the subject lands.[20] That pushed them into closer co-operation with the local Protestant minority, whose security and freedom to worship were in any case dependent on magisterial support (it is no coincidence that the largest Protestant communities were to be found in those towns where Rhaetian governing officials were based). Some Reformed churches, notably that of Chiavenna, owed their establishment to the patronage of Rhaetian magnates who had taken up residence in the subject lands, while leading Reformed families from the area, such as the Vertamate of Piuro and Pestalozzi of Chiavenna, demonstrated their loyalty to the Rhaetian state by acquiring citizenship in member communes of Graubünden proper.[21] Prominent Valtellinese Protestants also sought to forge direct links with the Rhaetian aristocracy: thus Hortensia, sister of the exiled Count Ulisse Martinengo di Barco, married into the powerful Salis clan.[22]

Such evidence of collusion with the hated Rhaetian overlords had the effect of intensifying the hostility felt by Valtellinese Catholics towards the Protestants dwelling in their midst. According to Wendland, the

---

[18] The Diet's hostility towards Catholic reform in the Valtellina was inspired in part by the fact that the area fell under the ecclesiastical jurisdiction not of the Rhaetian bishop of Chur, but of the Lombard bishop of Como.

[19] Wendland, *Pässe*, pp. 66–9.

[20] See the comments of Padavino: 'Per tutte queste cause di religione, et di disordinato governo, quei popoli, alienissimi con l'animo dal giogo de' Grisoni, et desiderosi di mutar fortuna inclinano grandemente alla Maestà Cattolica dalla quale per l'ampiezza delle forze, et perchè la memoria dell'antico dominio suol dar colore di nuova pretensione, et di attacco sopra li medesimi stati, benchè una volta ceduti, si promettteriano di essere sicuramente diffesi et rispettati' (Giussani, 'Padavino', p. 193).

[21] Wendland, *Pässe*, pp. 57; 71.

[22] G. Giorgetta, 'Documenti inediti sul conte Ulisse Martinengo', *Bollettino della società storica valtellinese*, 31 (1978), pp. 45–66 (48).

Reformed of the Valtellina came to be regarded as a foreign body in the region, the cutting edge of Rhaetian rule.[23] The community's alleged 'foreignness' was underlined by the prominence of exiles within it, both as ministers and as lay spokespersons like Martinengo. To some extent, the increasing polarization of the two confessions was also a product of differences in the socio-economic status of their adherents; most native converts to Protestantism in the subject lands were drawn either from aristocratic families (such as the Paravicini, Marlianici and Guicciardi) or from the mercantile elite (the Lumaga of Chiavenna and Piuro, for example), with the peasantry remaining almost exclusively Catholic.[24] The economic dominance of the Reformed was such that, while attempting to conduct a visitation of the Valtellina in 1578, Bishop Gianfrancesco Buonhomini of Como was forced to accept lodgings in Chiuro because all of the best inns in nearby Sondrio were owned by Protestants.[25]

The most visible consequence of deteriorating confessional relations in the Valtellina during the closing decades of the 16th century was an upsurge in religious violence and intimidation throughout the region. Protestants played their part in this with some highly provocative gestures. In February 1592, one Andreino Ferrari entered the parish church of Sondrio, seized the host from the tabernacle and ground it underfoot, while three years later an attempt was made to set fire to the town's Catholic presbytery.[26] However, the majority of violent acts emanated from the Catholic community and followed patterns similar to those that have been identified by historians working on other parts of Europe, notably France.[27] Church feast days, for example, were often the focus for attempts to force local Protestants to acknowledge the Catholic identity of the community as a whole. There are reports of this happening both in Morbegno (a notorious flashpoint) and in Sondrio,

---

23 Wendland, *Pässe*, pp. 71–2.

24 On the 'elitist' character of Protestantism in the subject lands, see Di Filippo Bareggi, 'Tra Sondrio e le Leghe grigie', p. 125, and L. Musselli, 'La riforma protestante in Valmalenco e il diritto ecclesiastico dei Grigioni', *Bollettino della società storica valtellinese*, 32 (1979), pp. 45–63 (48).

25 J.R. Truog, 'Aus der Geschichte der evangelischen Gemeinden in den bündnerischen Untertanenlanden: Ein Beitrag zur bündnerischen Synodalgeschichte', *BM* (1935), pp. 236–48; 257–85; 311–18 (245).

26 F. Palazzi Trivelli, 'Riformati, cattolici, reti, valtellini: baruffe in Sondrio a cavallo tra Cinque e Seicento', *Bollettino della società storica valtellinese*, 44 (1991), pp. 133–58 (135–6).

27 See the recent article by A. Pastore, 'Dalla notte di San Bartolomeo (1572) al Sacro macello di Valtellina (1620): forme e obiettivi della violenza religiosa', *BSSV*, 178 (1995), pp. 141–59. Taking his cue from the work of Natalie Zemon Davis on Lyon, Pastore emphasizes the ritualistic character of much religious violence in the Valtellina.

where members of the Reformed church were targeted for failing to hang out banners to commemorate Corpus Christi.[28] Another favoured tactic was desecration of the Protestants' sacred space, exemplified by the ringing of church bells during Reformed services and the smearing of Protestant churches with excrement. In 1608 the Catholics of Traona – supported, unusually, by the Bündner *podestà*, who was himself a Catholic – broke into the local Reformed church of Santa Trinità to bury an infant that had died prior to baptism.[29]

Reformed ministers, as the most energetic defenders of Protestantism in the subject lands and the perceived source of this heretical 'contamination', appear to have been singled out for special attention. Of particular interest is a letter from Scipione Calandrini to Tobias Egli dated 13 February 1572, in which Calandrini provides a graphic account of a failed assassination attempt on his colleague in Mello, Lorenzo Sonzini, and describes the daily humiliations to which he was subject as minister in Morbegno (Catholics taunted Calandrini that he would not last the year).[30] The proximity of the Valtellina to Catholic-ruled Milan also exposed pastors to the risk of abduction by hostile locals.[31] In the most celebrated incident of this kind, Calandrini's predecessor in Morbegno, Francesco Cellario, was seized while returning from a meeting of the synod in June 1568 and conveyed to Como, Milan and, finally, Rome (the abduction having been carried out on the personal instructions of Pius V). Despite frantic attempts by the Rhaetian Diet to secure his release, Cellario was subjected to an Inquisition trial, condemned and executed as an impenitent heretic.[32] As

---

[28] See the records of the Rhaetian synod for June 1608 (AERSG B 3, p. 198; also cited in Camenisch, *Reformation und Gegenreformation*, p. 151). Eight years earlier the synod made the following observations on the situation in Morbegno: 'Fratres singuli memores sint ut admoneant suos legatos ad proxima Comitia profecturos ut commendatam habeant causam fratrum ecclesiae Morbenniensis, quos contra decreta et libertatem Christianam volunt cogere ad observationem feriarum Papisticarum, nec sicut hactenus volunt nostris locare aedes, quo hac ratione discedere cogantur' (AERSG B 3, p. 155).

[29] AERSG B 3, p. 198: '... in specie conquesti sunt de Balthasare a Monte Praetore Trahonensi, qui infantem recens natum, quem Papaei propter baptismi privationem in suis sepulchris terrae mandare nolebant, vi praefractis templi Evangelicorum portis, in ipsorum sepulchris illum sepeliri curaverit.'

[30] ZB Ms. F 182, 162ʳ–3ᵛ; copy in Ms. S 125, 139: 'Non dico quas contumelias in me ipsum saepius viri, mulieres ac pueri evomuerint, ut lapides in me iecerint, imo etiam in templum ipsum inter concionandum Morbenii, seram quoque ianuae templi lapillis saepius obstruentes ne obserari posset. Taceo in me iactatum esse non annum me duraturum Morbenii, ac talia eiusmodi.' Morbegno was home to a Dominican monastery often cited in connection with anti-Protestant intrigues (see AERSG B 3, p. 1).

[31] The Rhaetian synod brought the problem of abductions to the attention of the Diet in 1588 (AERSG B 3, p. 96).

[32] *DBI*, XXIII, 430–33; Bonorand, *Reformatorische Emigration*, p. 70.

we have seen, the same fate later befell Lorenzo Sonzini.[33] Some Catholics were intent on purging their region not only of the troublemaking Reformed clergy, but of the Protestant presence as a whole. In 1584, Sondrio was abuzz with talk of an imminent 'Sicilian vespers', which would culminate in the slaughter of the heretics.

Reformed ministers were fully conscious of the dangers to which they and the congregations they served were exposed. In a letter to the Rhaetian magnate Johannes von Salis dated 22 October 1605, Niklaus Kesel, pastor in Monte di Sondrio, referred to his community as 'so many sheep destined for the slaughter ('tante pecore destinate al macello').[34] Kesel's colleague Antonius Andreoscha, minister in Tirano, described the predicament of the Valtellinese Reformed in almost identical terms: for him, they were 'like sheep in the midst of wolves' ('come pecore nel mezo dei lupi').[35] The pastors' response to this threat to their congregations' survival was not, however, to seek an accommodation with local Catholics, but to attempt to shore up Protestantism in the subject lands by drawing closer to the Rhaetian magistracy and to more established foreign Reformed churches, principally Zurich. In that way they hoped both to compensate for the minority status of the Reformed in the subject lands, and to reinforce their communities' distinct confessional identity.

ii. Zurich and Italian Graubünden: the channels of communication

The continuing relationship between the Zurich church and the Italian Reformed communities of Graubünden during the later 16th and early 17th centuries is amply documented in correspondence held at the Zurich Staatsarchiv and Zentralbibliothek. Until his death in 1599, Scipione Lentolo was a key figure in that relationship: by providing a counterweight to the long-standing perception of the Italian Reformed as doctrinally suspect, he was in large measure responsible for rehabilitating the scandal-prone churches of the Valbregaglia, Chiavenna and the Valtellina in the eyes of Protestant Europe. In Zurich, the Neapolitan's correspondents during the first half of the 1570s comprised Bullinger, Gwalther, Simler and Johannes Wolf. At times Lentolo appears almost reverential in his devotion to the Zurich divines. In a letter to Tobias Egli dated August 1574, he indicated his desire to

---

33 See Chapter 5:iii above. Scipione Calandrini was also the target of kidnap attempts, notably in July 1594.
34 StAG D II a 3 c.
35 Andreoscha to J. von Salis, 20 April 1607 (ibid.).

obtain portraits of Bullinger and, if possible, other Zurich ministers so that he might draw inspiration from their visible presence.[36] On another occasion, he called down God's blessings on the 'famous town, most learned school, and most celebrated and pious church' of Zurich.[37]

During the years immediately following the deaths of his established correspondents Wolf (1572), Bullinger (1575), and Simler (1576), Lentolo was in less frequent communication with Zurich; this development coincided with a general loosening of ties between the Reformed churches of Zurich and Graubünden during Gwalther's period as *Antistes* (1575–85).[38] From the early 1580s, however, contacts were resumed on a more intensive basis than before. Lentolo's principal correspondent during this period was Johann Wilhelm Stucki, who between 1571 and 1607 occupied the chair of Old Testament at the *Carolinum*;[39] more than 40 letters from Lentolo to the Zurich professor survive, covering the years 1587 to 1599. The association was a natural one, given Stucki's orthodox orientation (he represented Zurich at the Berne disputation of April 1588, where the doctrine of double predestination was reasserted against Samuel Huber) and humanist background. A key formative influence on Stucki was Lentolo's fellow Italian Peter Martyr Vermigli, whom Stucki accompanied to the colloquy of Poissy and with whose disciple Girolamo Zanchi he later corresponded.[40] Stucki's affinity with Italian culture is further evident from the fact that he knew Italian,[41] and had attended an Italian university (Padua) to study Hebrew during the late 1560s.[42]

Stucki's correspondents included several other figures of note within

---

[36] StAZ E II 365, 381.

[37] Lentolo to Stucki, 26 June 1591 (StAZ E II 380, 170–73): 'Dispeream, nisi vos omnes loco habeam cognatorum, et consanguineorum. Ita me Deus semper bene amet, ut Tigurinorum nomen mihi adeo est carum, adeo iucundum, ut carius, iucundiusve sit nihil. Deus semper optime fortunet istam inclytam Urbem, istam eruditissimam Scholam, istam denique celeberrimam maximeque piam Ecclesiam.'

[38] C. Bonorand, *Die Entwicklung des reformierten Bildungswesens in Graubünden zur Zeit der Reformation und Gegenreformation* (Thusis, 1949), p. 54.

[39] See K. Waser, *De vita et obitu Reverendi, nobilis et clarissimi Viri Domini Ioh. Guilielmi Stuckii sacrarum literarum professoris in Schola Tigurina, oratio historica* (Zurich, 1608); *ADB*, XXXVI, pp. 717–20.

[40] See Zanchi, *Epistolae*, I, 71–3; II, 201–2.

[41] See especially the letter from Ulisse Martinengo to Stucki dated 5 March 1600 (StAZ E II 380, 434): 'Prendo ardire di scrivere a VS. in lingua Italiana, poiche ho vedute due lettere da lei in Italiano bene, et politamente scritte, al signor Horatio Paravicino.' Compare Martinengo to Stucki, 17 February 1601 and 11 October 1604 (ibid., 490–91; 508–9).

[42] See Stucki to Gwalther, 18 December 1567 (StAZ E II 380, 4), and StAZ E I 13, 104v–5r. I am grateful to Dr Karin Maag for the latter reference.

the Italian Reformed churches of the subject lands. The most prominent of these, after Lentolo, was Scipione Calandrini, a former pupil of Aonio Paleario and member of a Lucchese patrician family that contributed many distinguished converts to Protestantism.[43] For around a decade, Calandrini was based in Geneva, where he assisted the city's Italian pastor, Niccolò Balbani, and taught rhetoric and dialectics at the academy. In 1568 he moved to the Valtellina, where he was elected Francesco Cellario's successor as minister in Morbegno. Calandrini seems to have wavered temporarily in his support for the anti-heresy edict of June 1570, but any doubts about his orthodoxy were dispelled following the publication in February 1572 of his *Trattato dell'origine delle heresie*, in which he defended both the practice of excommunication and the magistrate's *cura religionis*.[44] Around 1577, Calandrini took charge of the Reformed church of Sondrio, the largest in the Valtellina, where his combative style – in evidence at two set-piece disputations held with the Catholic clergy of the subject lands in Tirano and Piuro during the 1590s – was particularly resented by local Catholics. Broccardo Borrone identified Calandrini as one of the most dangerous and committed of the Valtellinese ministers ('homo perniciosissimus'), and accused him of translating Reformed works from French and Latin for dissemination by friends in Italy.[45] In one such translation (of Philippe du Plessis-Mornay's *Traité de l'Eglise*), Calandrini confirmed that he did not see his mission-field as confined to the Valtellina, calling in a lengthy prefatory epistle on the rulers of Italy to follow the example of magistrates elsewhere (in Poland, Transylvania,

---

43 See the article by M. Luzzati in *DBI*, XVI, 458–63; Bonorand, *Reformatorische Emigration*, pp. 78–80.

44 For the background to the publication of the *Trattato*, see the letter from Calandrini to Tobias Egli of 13 February 1572 (Ms. F 182, fol. 163ᵛ): 'Haec raptim ad te scribo Posclavium contendens hortatu D. Iulii Mediolanensis et D. Pauli Gaddii, quo typis tradam opusculum quoddam, quod ante paucos menses adversus haereses exaravi.' Luzzati regards this work as a highly significant contribution to the process of restoring the tarnished image of the Italian Reformed: 'Lo scritto di un italiano, in lingua italiana, contro eretici in massima parte italiani, doveva in certo modo fornir la prova dell'ortodossia di quella nazione italiana che i padri della Riforma svizzera sospettavano in blocco d'esser la pecora nera del gregge evangelico' (*DBI*, XVI, 462). In the *Trattato* Calandrini argues that the aim of those who oppose the exercise of discipline in doctrinal matters is to acquire for themselves 'una sfrenata licentia di spargere il lor veleno, e di mettere sempre a campo cose nuove' (*Trattato*, p. 3). The 'charity' which they invoke would leave the Church defenceless against its enemies: 'Qual charità sarebbe del pastore il lasciare distruggere il gregge dal lupo, o rubbarlo dal ladro? o il lasciare infettare tutto il gregge da una pecora marcia et appestata? Qual charità et amore sarà del padre che lascia vivere in casa sua uno scelerato, il quale seduca la moglie et le figliuole inducendole a fornicare?' (ibid., p. 151).

45 Rosius de Porta, *Historia Reformationis*, II:3, p. 188.

Rhaetia and the Swiss Confederation) by extending toleration to orthodox Protestantism.[46]

Calandrini's links with the Zurichers were of long standing. Passing through Zurich in December 1558, after fleeing Lucca, he entered his name in Gesner's *liber amicorum*.[47] Just over three years later he visited Zurich again, this time as a spokesman for Geneva's Lucchese community, which was seeking support for its campaign to persuade the authorities in Lucca to rescind a punitive decree that they had issued against Protestant citizens living abroad.[48] Apart from Stucki, Calandrini's Zurich correspondents included Gwalther, Heinrich Wolf and Heinrich Bullinger, grandson of the *Antistes*.[49]

Closely associated with Calandrini in Sondrio was a figure whom I have already mentioned in passing, Ulisse Martinengo of Brescia. A number of recent studies have highlighted the leading role played by Martinengo within the Reformed community of the Valtellina.[50] The same point is made by contemporary observers such as Raphael Egli, who praised Martinengo for the support that he had given to those

---

[46] See S. Adorni-Braccesi, 'Religious Refugees from Lucca in the Sixteenth Century: Political Strategies and Religious Proselytism', *ARG*, 88 (1997), pp. 338–79 (375–8). In his last known published work, the *Confutatione delle calunnie et delle maledicentie* (Geneva, 1596), Calandrini seeks to counter Catholic attempts to associate the Reformed with those genuine 'heretics' (Anabaptists and 'Trinitarii') whom he had denounced in his earlier *Trattato* (see pp. 7–8; 12–15). I am grateful to Emanuele Fiume for allowing me to consult his copy of this extremely rare text.

[47] Serrai, *Gesner*, p. 363.

[48] Letter from the Italian church in Geneva to the Zurich council, 11 March 1562 (StAZ A 241.1; copy in ZB Ms. S 103, 166): 'Cum his litteris mittimus ad vos D. Scipionem Calandrinum gentilem nostrum, his mandatis, ut Dominationibus vestris nonnulla exponat, atque ab illis exoret, quae ad Christi Redemptoris causam, nostrum fratrumque commodum pertinere arbitramur. Rogamus igitur vos cum omni (ut decet) humilitate, ut ei fidem indubiam habeatis in omnibus, quae nostro nomine narraverit, aut petierit; votisque nostris pro Dei gloria, quam vobis ante oculos semper proponitis pro vestri Imperii dignitate, generis nobilitate, pietateque ac solita erga omnes oppressos atque afflictos humanitate, annuere dignemini.' The letter is signed by Niccolò Balbani and other prominent Lucchese exiles. On the edict in question, see S. Adorni-Braccesi, 'Le <<Nazioni>> lucchesi nell'Europa della Riforma', *Critica storica*, 28 (1991), pp. 363-426 (369-73; 381-83). Calandrini's petition received strong backing from Bullinger, who commended him to Fabricius in Chur (Schiess, II, no. 421).

[49] Heinrich, son of Johannes Wolf, was professor of New Testament and Hebrew at the *Carolinum* (U. Ernst, *Geschichte des Zürcherischen Schulwesens bis gegen das Ende des sechzehnten Jahrhunderts* (Winterthur, 1879), p. 112). From 1592 until his death two years later he held the post of preacher at the Fraumünster (Dejung and Wuhrmann, *Zürcher Pfarrerbuch 1519-1952*, p. 633). On Heinrich Bullinger (III), see ibid., pp. 229-30.

[50] See Giorgetta, 'Martinengo'; Pastore, *Valtellina*, pp. 107–11; Bundi, *Frühe Beziehungen*, pp. 152–4; Bonorand, *Reformatorische Emigration*, pp. 80–84.

exiled on account of the Gospel, and identified him as the principal benefactor of the Italian Reformed churches.[51] In a letter to Carlo Borromeo dated 2 March 1584, the Barnabite Domenico Boveri, who had been sent to preach in Poschiavo, provided further examples of Martinengo's activism, noting his itinerant lifestyle and his sponsorship of efforts to train local youths as ministers.[52] In identifying the count as Catholicism's most dangerous opponent in the subject lands ('fa peggio di tutti gli altri contro la religion catholica'), Boveri reflected a general feeling among Valtellinese Catholics, who had not forgiven Martinengo for his role in persuading the Rhaetian authorities to curtail Gianfrancesco Buonhomini's visitation of their region in 1578.[53] During the 1580s several attempts were made on Martinengo's life, but like his friend Calandrini he came through all of them unscathed. Also like Calandrini, Martinengo was in regular correspondence with Johann Wilhelm Stucki. We possess around 30 of his letters to the Zurich professor, beginning in 1594 and continuing until shortly before Stucki's death in 1607.

Besides Stucki, the Italian churches' most important correspondent in Zurich around the turn of the 16th century was Kaspar Waser, successively professor of Hebrew, Greek and theology at the *Carolinum*. Waser, who according to his biographer Jodocus Kvosen knew 11 languages including Italian, probably ranks as Zurich's foremost intellectual during this period (he is best known for his work on oriental languages, which included grammars of Hebrew, Chaldaean and Syriac).[54] Like Stucki, Waser had a strong attachment to Italian culture. In the early 1590s, prior to his ordination, he had accompanied the Augsburg nobleman Johann Peter Hainzel von Degerstein on an extended tour of Italy, in the course of which he made the acquaintance of Scipione Lentolo.[55] Later he built on these contacts through correspondence first with Lentolo and then with the Neapolitan's successor Ottaviano Mei, who as pastor in Teglio had already forged links with Zurich through Stucki.[56] During the years immediately prior

---

51   Egli to Gwalther, 16 May 1584 (ZB Ms. S 142, 16): 'Qui ... fratres ob Evangelium exules illo arctius et maiore caritate complectatur nemo est, nec qui plus consilio et re ipsa his Ecclesiis profuerit, ac prodesse possit, quam ipse.'

52   Cited in Pastore, *Valtellina*, p. 110.

53   Mazzone, 'Visitatori', p. 139.

54   J. Kvosen, *De vita et obitu reverendi et clarissimi viri, Domini Caspari Waseri* (Basle, [1626]); *ADB*, XLI, pp. 227–8. In a letter of 1597, Lentolo refers specifically to Waser's (and Stucki's) knowledge of Italian (ZB Ms. S 152, 93.1).

55   Lentolo to Stucki, 26 June 1593 (StAZ E II 380, 272). See also Paolo Lentolo to Jakob Zwinger, 15 July 1593 (Basel UB Fr. Gr. Ms. II 4, 152).

56   Mei, who served as minister in Teglio from 1581, and as pastor in Chiavenna from

to the 'sacro macello', Waser also corresponded with the Engadiners Johann Peter Danz and Caspar Alexius, ministers in Teglio and Sondrio respectively.

In fact, the correspondence now held at the Zurich Staatsarchiv and Zentralbibliothek comprises only a fraction of the total number of letters that passed between Zurich and the Italian churches of the subject lands during this period. At various points, Lentolo indicates that he was also in correspondence with Felix Trüb, one-time professor of New Testament and Hebrew at the Zurich academy;[57] with Gabriel Gerber, a former Catholic canon from Lucerne who converted to Protestantism in 1589 and was subsequently appointed minister in the Zurich town of Bülach;[58] with Huldrych Zwingli, grandson of the reformer and professor of New Testament at the *Lectorium* from 1585 to 1591;[59] and with Raphael, son of Tobias Egli.[60] Egli's association with Lentolo dated back to the 1570s, when the Neapolitan had acted as his tutor in Chiavenna. By 1598, however, they were barely on speaking terms, following the revelation of Egli's involvement in a massive financial scandal and several dubious alchemical projects.[61] The episode cast a shadow over Lentolo's old age, particularly when he learned that Egli had accused him of showing insufficient charity towards the Sicilian exile Giulio Cesare Pascali during a visit by the latter to Chiavenna, and of owing large sums of money to Egli's disgraced aristocratic patrons, Johann Heinrich and Ludwig Hainzel von Degerstein. In correspondence with Stucki, Lentolo professed himself bitterly disappointed by the conduct of his former protegé.[62]

1599 until his death in 1619, was another product of Geneva's Lucchese community (for biographical details, see G. Giorgetta, 'Un codicillo di Ottaviano Mei', *Clavenna*, 17 (1978), pp. 24–8; Bonorand, *Reformatorische Emigration*, pp. 52–5). Like Calandrini, he was a vocal defender of Reformed doctrine against the Catholic clergy of the subject lands and took part in the disputation of Tirano. Stucki's papers contain a copy of six theses by Mei, dated 19 April 1593, condemning the Mass, purgatory, auricular confession, papal primacy and a string of Catholic devotional practices as without scriptural foundation (StAZ E II 358a, 571ʳ).

[57] See Lentolo to Stucki, 7 July 1589 (StAZ E II 380, 93).

[58] Ibid. On Gerber, see Dejung and Wuhrmann, *Zürcher Pfarrerbuch*, p. 293; G. Busino, 'Prime ricerche su Broccardo Borrone', *BHR*, 24 (1962), pp. 130–67 (149).

[59] Lentolo to Stucki, 26 June 1593 (StAZ E II 380, 273).

[60] Lentolo to Stucki, 3 November 1588 (ibid., 75).

[61] H. Hotson, *Johann Heinrich Alsted 1588–1638: Between Renaissance, Reformation and Universal Reform* (Oxford, 2000), pp. 60–62. Egli's interest in alchemy and other forms of esoteric knowledge was stimulated by contact with Giordano Bruno, who passed through Zurich in 1591. On this relationship, see J. Gerber, 'Giordano Bruno und Raphael Egli: Begegnungen im Zwielicht von Alchemie und Theologie', *Sudhoffs Archiv*, 76 (1992), pp. 133–63; and G. Schmidlin, 'Giordano Bruno im Kreis der Zürcher Alchemisten und Paracelsisten', *Nova acta paracelsica*, 8 (1994), pp. 57–86.

[62] Letter of 13 September 1598 (StAZ E II 380, 392–5).

The final element in the network of contacts between Zurich and the Italian churches of Graubünden was the Zurich Locarnesi.[63] In Chapter 2, I discussed the early links between the Locarnese exiles and Reformed congregations in the Rhaetian Freestate. Evidence that their relationship survived the dissolution of Zurich's Italian church in December 1563 is provided by the accounts of the Locarnese community, which record grants to a son of the minister of Stampa in the Valbregaglia (21 March 1585);[64] to Daniele, son of Bartolomeo Chiesa, minister in Malenco (10 February 1589);[65] to Salvatore Madera, a Portuguese exile and former schoolmaster in Sondrio (20 March and 5 August 1595);[66] and to 'un povero garzone di Chiavenna' (12 March 1599).[67]

Direct contacts between Scipione Lentolo and Taddeo Duno, the *eminence grise* of the Locarnese community, are also documented. During Bullinger's final illness, Duno provided Lentolo with reports on the deteriorating condition of the *Antistes*, which were subsequently relayed to Paolo Gaddi and Giulio da Milano in the Valtellina.[68] On other occasions, Duno appears to have acted as an intermediary between Lentolo and the Zurich divines, whose respect for his abilities has already been noted. When Niccolò Marini (also known as Niccolò da Eremo), a former minister of Casaccia who had settled in England, complained to his new hosts of mistreatment at the hands of Lentolo and the church of Chiavenna,[69] Lentolo sent an extended refutation of

---

63 Compare Bonorand, *Bildungswesen*, p. 73.

64 FA Orelli, 8.2, fol. 108ᵛ.

65 Ibid., fol. 109ʳ.

66 Ibid., fol. 115ʳ⁻ᵛ. While in Sondrio, Madera caused a scandal by entering a Catholic church naked and profaning the host (supposedly during a bout of insanity). Local Catholics demanded the schoolmaster's execution, but at the request of the Rhaetian synod he was released and handed over to the Zurichers (AERSG B 3, pp. 126; 129–31). Calandrini provided Stucki with a detailed account of the episode in a letter dated 15 July 1595 (StAZ E II 358a, 607). Taddeo Duno's *De peregrinatione filiorum Israel in Aegypto*, published in August that year, was prefaced by some laudatory verses from Madera's pen (*De peregrinatione*, fol. 4ʳ).

67 FA Orelli, 8.2, fol. 116ᵛ.

68 Lentolo to Bullinger, 6 April 1575 (StAZ E II 365, 404; Schiess, III, no. 450).

69 On 16 February 1591, the *coetus* of the London stranger churches wrote to the Rhaetian synod to request confirmation of Marini's credentials (StAZ E II 380, 158–9 (copy in Lentolo's hand); AERSG B 3, pp. 109–11). On 12 June, the synod replied that Marini's conduct as minister in Casaccia had been satisfactory, but censured him for his ingratitude towards Lentolo and the church of Chiavenna. It also repeated the charge (first made by Lentolo) that Marini was unsound on the question of predestination (StAZ E II 380, 168–9 [copy in Lentolo's hand]). See also J.H. Hessels, *Ecclesiae Londino-Bataviae Archivium: Epistulae et Tractatus cum Reformationis tum Ecclesiae Londino-Bataviae Illustrantes* (4 vols in 3 pts, Cambridge, 1887–97), III:1, nos 1063; 1096; 1121; 1150; 1176; 1190; 1191; 1192; 1212; 1216. Lentolo wrote personally to the Italian minister in

this charge to Duno, with the request that he read it and pass it on to Stucki.[70] The favour was repaid shortly afterwards, when Lentolo helped to ensure that the will of a local evangelical, Paolo Beccaria, who had left part of his fortune to Zurich's Locarnese community, was upheld against a challenge by Catholics from the Mesolcina.[71] Lentolo was among those to whom Duno appealed for support after his revised chronology of the Exodus, *De peregrinatione filiorum Israel in Aegypto*, attracted criticism from Matthias Dresser, professor of classics and history at Leipzig. Whereas senior Reformed figures such as Beza cautiously withheld their approval (while not condemning the work outright), Lentolo was impressed by Duno's reading of the Old Testament texts in question. Replying to the Locarnese exile on 15 October 1596, he enthused:

> Please believe me – for I am telling you exactly what I think, without a trace of flattery – when I say that I do not recall reading anything on this matter that has been more truly, knowledgeably and intelligently thought out, and more conclusively demonstrated. I have read and re-read the book, and the more I read it, the more it pleases, teaches and persuades me.[72]

Lentolo was sufficiently impressed to ask Duno to send him copies of other works, both theological and medical, that he had published.[73]

Martinengo, too, was in correspondence with members of

---

[70] Lentolo to Stucki, 29 June 1591 (StAZ E II 380, 170–73). Another copy of Lentolo's defence (for which see StAZ E II 380, 162–7) was sent to Jacques Couet, minister of the French church in Basle, to be forwarded to England.

[71] StAZ E II 380, 172–3. See also Lentolo to Stucki, 6 October 1591 (StAZ E II 380, 3). The legal expenses incurred by the Zurich Locarnesi in the course of this dispute are recorded in the community's accounts (FA Orelli, 8.2, fol. 109r).

[72] ZB Ms. Car. C. 40, fol. 64r–v: 'Crede quaeso mihi, loquor quod plane sentio, et prorsus omni amota adulatione, me hactenus nequaquam meminisse legere in eo argumento quod visum mihi sit verius, eruditius, acutius excogitatum, atque probatum solidius. Legi, relegi librum, ac quo magis lego, eo magis delectat, docet, persuadet.' The manuscript volume in which the letter appears contains a revised and expanded version of *De peregrinatione*, along with related correspondence that Duno had copied out with a view to subsequent publication (see Duno to J.J. Grynaeus, 24 January 1597; 1, 14 and 23 August 1600 (Basel UB G II 4, fols 100–103); Duno to Jakob Zwinger, 18 February 1603 [Basel UB Fr. Gr. Ms. II 23, no. 176]).

[73] More than two decades earlier, Duno had sought Lentolo's opinion on a work entitled *Two treatises on ecclesiastical discipline*. Although the current whereabouts of this text are uncertain, the autograph manuscript is known to have included appendices containing Lentolo's judgment on the treatises and Duno's response to the latter's 'obiectiones' (see the summary in ZB Ms. S 125, 88).

London, Giovanni Battista Aureli, to warn him against Marini, who quickly came into conflict with both Aureli and the *coetus*. See Boersma and Jelsma, *Unity in Multiformity*, pp. 89–105, 202–3; Boersma, *Vluchtig Voorbeeld*, p. 99.

Zurich's Locarnese community. In March 1596, after becoming involved in a dispute with Johann Heinrich Hainzel over unpaid debts, the count wrote to both Duno and Ludovico Ronco requesting that they inform Stucki of the background to the case.[74] Two years later, Martinengo was pleased to learn via a letter from Duno that the Zurich authorities had agreed to refund the money owing to him out of Hainzel's property.[75] There are no references to Duno in the correspondence of Martinengo's close friend Scipione Calandrini, but he is known to have made use of passing Locarnese merchants such as Ludwig Orelli (1576–1632) as couriers for his letters to Stucki.[76]

The emergence in the later 16th century of Bergamo as a hub of transalpine trade reinforced the links between the Zurich Locarnesi and Reformed communities in the Valtellina and Valchiavenna – a natural port of call for those travelling from Chur to the Veneto via the Splügen pass.[77] The subject lands were home to important merchant families such as the Lumaga and Scandolera of Piuro, both of which featured among the trading partners of Ludovico Ronco during the 1570s and 1580s. On 5 October 1578, for example, Ronco received a bale of 'stami di strusi di Verona' from Bartolomeo Scandolera, while his accounts for February the following year record the payment of a loan of 800 scudi to Lorenzo Lumaga on behalf of the Venetian Paolo Fanzago.[78] During the early 17th century another Locarnese exile, Giorgio Pebbia,[79] acted as a courier for letters from Kaspar Waser to his numerous acquaintances in the subject lands: one of Waser's correspondents, Giovanni Battista Calandrini, specifically advised the Zuricher to entrust his replies to Pebbia, who would ensure that they were safely delivered to Calandrini

---

[74] Martinengo to Stucki, 31 March 1596 (StAZ E II 380, 357): 'Excellens Doctor D. Thadeus Dunus, et D. Roncus quid in hac causa egerint adhuc ignoro, scripsi tamen ad illos ut tibi communicarent quid hactenus factum sit.'

[75] Martinengo to Stucki, 1 May 1598 (StAZ E II 380, 402): 'Ex epistola Excellentissimi Domini Doctoris Duni cognovi ab integerrimis Tigurinis Iudicibus decretam mihi fuisse solutionem ex bonis Domini Enzellii pro summa mihi debita.'

[76] Calandrini to Stucki, 10 October 1599 (ZB Ms. F 80, 337). Orelli inherited the cloth export company founded by his father Giovanni Melchiore. See Weisz, 'Tessiner', pp. 437–8; H. Schulthess, *Die von Orelli von Locarno und Zürich: Ihre Geschichte und Genealogie* (Zurich, 1941), pp. 82–3.

[77] See D. Fretz, *Die Frühbeziehungen zwischen Zürich und Bergamo 1568–1618* (Zurich, 1940).

[78] FA Orelli, 8.4, fols 16ᵛ; 18ᵛ.

[79] StAZ E II 383, 709. Pebbia was involved in trade with Lyon, Milan and Bergamo. Initially he worked in concert with his brother Giangiacomo, but their company had to be wound up after it ran into difficulties in the late 1590s (Weisz, 'Tessiner', pp. 433–5; StAZ A 369.3).

in Sondrio via the Chiavenna merchant Giacomo Curtabate.[80] In the
light of those ties, it comes as no surprise to discover that the Locarnese
brothers Martin, Ludwig and Johann Jakob Orelli were among the main
contributors to the relief fund established for survivors of the 'sacro
macello' who sought refuge in Zurich.[81]

iii. Areas of co-operation

During the late 16th and early 17th centuries, the Italian Reformed
communities of Graubünden saw themselves as an integral part of the
'Calvinist international' that some historians have postulated for this
period. Although they were not exile congregations in the formal sense
– the bulk of their membership consisted of local converts, rather than
incomers – the role of exiles in defining their sense of identity was
crucial. Men such as Lentolo and Martinengo came to Rhaetia
deracinated, having by their conversions renounced traditional
allegiances to home, family and Catholic society: henceforth, the main
focus of their loyalties was the wider fellowship of Reformed believers
with which they had chosen to align themselves. Under the exiles'
influence, and in response to deteriorating relations between Catholics
and Protestants in the subject lands, cosmopolitanism became a general
feature of Graubünden's Italian-speaking Reformed communities.
Protestants in Chiavenna and the Valtellina developed into keen
observers of the European political scene, instinctively drawing parallels
between their own embattled situation and the difficulties faced by
fellow believers abroad. Among the documents held at the Staatsarchiv
Graubünden (Archiv Salis-Planta) is an anonymous anti-Nicodemite
work which warns French Protestants against the 'dangerous and fatal
illusion(s)' ('periculose e funeste illusioni') that it is possible to believe in
Christ without confessing his name publicly.[82] The accession to the
French throne of Henry IV sent a wave of optimism through the Italian-
speaking Reformed community, prompting Ottaviano Mei to compose

---

[80] G.B. Calandrini to Waser, 10 March 1611 (ZB Ms. S 162, 154.1). In all likelihood,
this is the same Giovanni Battista Calandrini who was ordained minister of Dubino in
1604 (J.R. Truog, *Die Pfarrer der evangelischen Gemeinden in Graubünden und seinen
ehemaligen Untertanenlanden* (Chur, 1934–35), p. 264; Bonorand, *Reformatorische
Emigration*, p. 73; AERSG B 3, pp. 177, 182). For confirmation that he was a son of
Scipione Calandrini, see S. Calandrini to Johannes von Salis, 24 January 1606 (StAG D II
a 3 c).

[81] StAZ E II 279, 5.

[82] *Lettera pastorale alli Protestanti di Francia caduti per forza de tormenti* (StAG D II
b 3).

verses in honour of the Huguenot prince. Such hopes were dampened by Henry's apostasy in July 1593, but even after that date Lentolo clung to the conviction that his return to the Catholic fold would prove temporary.[83] In numerical terms, the Italian Reformed of Graubünden may have been insignificant players on the European stage, but they made up for that with fervent commitment to the international 'Protestant cause': the churches of Brusio, Poschiavo, Tirano, Teglio, Sondrio, Berbenno, Chiavenna, Piuro and the Valbregaglia all contributed to the relief fund for Geneva that was set up following the *Escalade* of 1602.[84] As the sole representatives of Protestantism in Italian-speaking lands – the Italian identity of the Waldenses was a much later development – they seem to have been in a position to punch above their weight.

Yet there were barriers to the full participation of Rhaetia's Italian churches in the cultural and intellectual life of Reformed Europe. The most formidable of those was geography. Southern Graubünden and the Rhaetian subject lands were on the periphery of the Protestant world, separated by two or three days' journey even from Chur, the nearest Reformed centre of any significance. The physical isolation of the Italian Reformed conferred added importance on their links with Zurich: in practice, the Zurich church acted as a mediator between these communities and Protestant northern Europe, facilitating the passage of individuals, books and correspondence across the Alpine barrier. As will become clear, it also assisted local pastors in their efforts to consolidate the gains that the Reformation had made in Italian Graubünden since the 1540s.

Before 1572, the major obstacle to such co-operation had been the Italian churches' reputation for doctrinal instability, and for some years the attitudes of older Zurich churchmen continued to be shaped by their experience of 'heresy'. This is best illustrated by an exchange from 1576 between Rudolf Gwalther and the church of Chiavenna. In February that year, Chiavenna's Reformed community asked Gwalther to support its campaign for relaxation of the prohibited degrees in the subject lands, on the basis that consanguineous marriages were preferable to unions with 'unbelievers'; in an accompanying submission, Scipione Lentolo suggested that such unions were responsible for leading members of his church into idolatry.[85] However, Lentolo's arguments

---

[83] StAZ E II 358a, 531r; Lentolo to Stucki, 6 June 1595 (StAZ E II 380, 325–6).

[84] *RCP*, VIII, p. 234, n. 60. The security of Geneva was a major preoccupation of the Italian Reformed at this time. Shortly before his death, Lentolo told Stucki that he feared for the city's future at the hands of the Savoyards (StAZ E II 380, 420–21).

[85] StAZ E II 377, 2656, published in *RCP*, IV, 231–3; StAZ E II 365a, 681–5.

failed to impress the new Zurich *Antistes*, who urged the Chiavennaschi to continue to observe the prohibited degrees lest their conduct give occasion for scandal. In a thinly veiled allusion to the history of doctrinal aberrations within the Italian Reformed community, he observed:

> What pains me most is that among the professors of the Gospel there have arisen some who, inventing new Christs and fashioning new heavens, start arguments unknown to learned antiquity about other articles, tearing the church apart and causing most dangerous schisms.[86]

In a letter to Beza, whose opinion had also been solicited, Gwalther indicated that he remained deeply suspicious – 'not without good reason' – of 'Italorum ingenia'. In this case, he feared that the Chiavennaschi were seeking sanction for licentiousness under cover of evangelical liberty.[87]

However, by the time Gwalther made these comments the threat posed by Italian religious radicalism was fast receding. The mid-1570s saw a temporary resurgence of heretical activity in Basle, where Pietro Perna and Fausto Sozzini oversaw the publication of Castellio's *Dialogi IV*,[88] but by the end of that decade Basle had joined the other Swiss churches in embracing Reformed orthodoxy. For the generation that succeeded Gwalther, the theological and polemical exchanges of the 1550s and 1560s were no more than a distant memory; lacking direct experience of the campaign against heresy, ministers such as Stucki and Waser were far less inclined than their predecessors to associate the Italian Reformed with heterodox belief. Indeed, it was to the Zurichers that the Protestants of the subject lands invariably turned when they felt that their orthodoxy or morals had been impugned. In December 1590,

---

[86] StAZ E II 381, 1407ᵛ: 'Quod maxime dolendum inter Evangelii professores exorti sunt, qui dum novos Christos fingunt, coelos item novos fabricant, deque aliis articulis disputationes eruditae vetustati plane incognitas instituunt, Ecclesiam in partes distrahunt, et periculosissimorum scismatum sunt authores.' In a letter dated 12 September 1576, Lentolo reported the church of Chiavenna's acceptance of Gwalther's judgment (StAZ E II 377, 2657). For Gwalther's conservatism on the question of the prohibited degrees, see further his letter to Kaspar Hubenschmid of 27 November 1579 (StAZ E II 382, 968).

[87] *Correspondance*, XVII, no. 1185.

[88] A. Rotondò, 'Pietro Perna e la vita culturale e religiosa di Basilea fra il 1570 e il 1580', in Rotondò, *Studi e ricerche*, pp. 273–391; H.R. Guggisberg, 'Pietro Perna, Fausto Sozzini und die Dialogi quatuor Sebastian Castellios', in *Studia bibliographia in honorem Herman de la Fontaine Verwey* (Amsterdam, 1967), pp. 171–201; Gilly, 'Zensur'. It is worth noting that in late 1577 and early 1578 Sozzini visited Zurich to receive treatment at the hands of an 'amici Medici' (Taddeo Duno?). While there, he penned his *Copiosa refutatio* of the universalist theses of Francesco Pucci (L. Firpo, 'Francesco Pucci a Basilea', in Firpo, *Scritti*, pp. 67–96; Sozzini, *Opera*, II, p. 119).

for example, Lentolo wrote to Stucki to deny rumours that he and his son Paolo were the prime movers behind a recent edition of Thomas Erastus' anti-disciplinarian *Explicatio gravissimae quaestionis*. Lentolo reported that, far from sponsoring the work, he had turned down a request from the London-based exile Giacomo Castelvetro to arrange for its publication in Poschiavo.[89] Later, he had refused to distribute copies of the *Explicatio* sent to him by Castelvetro, on the grounds that Erastus' teachings would turn the church into a 'stable of Circe' ('stabulum Circaeum').[90] Lentolo concluded his letter by urging Stucki to write to the churches of Geneva and Basle to set the record straight – a task that the Zurich professor seems to have been more than happy to perform. Stucki also gave Lentolo unstinting support in his efforts to counter the charges of Niccolò da Eremo, unlike some of Lentolo's own colleagues in the Rhaetian Reformed synod.[91]

Perhaps the clearest evidence of Zurich's enhanced commitment to the Italian churches after 1572 is to be found in the sphere of education. Most of the major population centres in the subject lands – Chiavenna, Sondrio, Teglio, Tirano – were able to offer local boys a basic Reformed education, provided either by the minister himself or by schoolmasters employed by the Protestant community.[92] However, for more advanced

---

89 Lentolo to Stucki, 1 December 1590 (StAZ E II 380, 121). Although published in London, Castelvetro's edition of the *Explicatio* bore the false imprint of Poschiavo (see Bornatico, *L'arte tipografica*, pp. 44–5; A.W. Pollard, G.R. Redgrave et al. (eds), *A Short-Title Catalogue of Books printed in England, Scotland, and Ireland and of English Books printed abroad 1475–1640* (3 vols, London, 1976–91), no. 10511). According to Lentolo, the Spanish exile Antonio del Corro ('quendam Doctorem Corunum Hispanum impurae religionis suspectum') had assisted Castelvetro with the production of the work.

90 Compare Gwalther's use of the same image to condemn opponents of the anti-heresy edict of June 1570 (cited in Chapter 5:iii above). Interestingly, Lentolo assumes that Geneva and Zurich are united in their condemnation of Erastus and support for Calvinist-style discipline: 'Semper, dei summo beneficio, ego et filius toto pectore abhorruerimus ab ea doctrina, quae diversa sit ab ea quae fideliter et pura iuxta praescriptum Divini verbi praecipue docetur, *et istic, et Genevae*' [my emphasis].

91 See Lentolo to Stucki, 30 August 1591 (StAZ E II 380, 174–7): 'De illo viro autem, qui non ea prudentia et constantia se gessit in illo suo responso ad prudentes et cordatos Ministros exterarum, quae Londini sunt, Ecclesiarum, sicut tu vere et scite eos vocas: doleo mirum in modum cum eius caussa, tum Synhodi ipsius, cui prae est. Quod vel pueri, nedum viri sapientes, cognoscere possunt, parum sibi in re praesertim gravi, vel minime, ut deceret, constare. Sivit bonus vir se velut abripi ab auctoritate quorumdam, qui nebuloni illi faverunt, decepti cum illius pollicitationibus tum sua ipsorum levitate, ac etiam cupiditate ditescendi, ac suae cuticulae consulendi, ne dicam ventri, quippe cui, ut multis argumentis apparet, longe magis serviunt, pro dolor et pudor, quam Deo.' The target of Lentolo's criticisms appears to be the president of the synod, Johannes Contius Bisaz.

92 See Bonorand, *Bildungswesen*, pp. 40–50.

study the Italian Reformed were obliged to look further afield. Students from the Valbregaglia, Poschiavo and the subject lands were attending Zurich's Latin schools and the *Lectorium* as early as 1534, but their numbers rose appreciably from the end of the 1570s. Italian-speakers formed a high proportion of the Rhaetian contingent of students in Zurich, which itself constituted the largest single foreign element: according to Conradin Bonorand, of the 18 Bündner whose names appear in the Zurich *Album* of students for the years 1578–79, 11 were from the Italian-speaking communes of southern Rhaetia or from the subject lands.[93] Zurich remained the most popular centre of higher education for boys from these areas up until the 'sacro macello', with more than 50 Italian-speaking Bündner known to have studied in the city between 1590 and 1620.[94]

Unsurprisingly, many of the students were relatives of the Zurichers' Italian correspondents. They included Lentolo's son Paolo, along with several members of the Marlianici family, to which Scipione Calandrini was related by marriage.[95] In some cases, financial assistance was offered to Italian-speaking students. In June 1606, for example, the Rhaetian synod sent Paolo Gaffori, the son of a former minister in Poschiavo, to Zurich with the request that he be offered a scholarship.[96] Six years later Josua Resta, the minister of Caspano, wrote to Waser on behalf of one Bartolomeo (identified by Bonorand as Bartolomeo Paravicini), who was returning to Zurich to resume his studies at the *Carolinum*. Could Waser do his best, Resta asked, to ensure that the boy continued to receive financial support?[97]

Sometimes ministers and professors took personal responsibility for the welfare of Italian students during their stay in Zurich. The best-documented case is that of Azzo Guicciardi, from Teglio, who spent the years 1610–11 as a house-guest of Kaspar Waser. While in Zurich the

---

[93] Ibid., p. 72; *Reformatorische Emigration*, p. 217.

[94] See the list in C. Bonorand, 'Bündner Studierende an höhern Schulen der Schweiz und des Auslandes im Zeitalter der Reformation und Gegenreformation', *JHGG* (1949), pp. 91–174 (100–30).

[95] Lentolo to Bullinger, 3 June 1575 (StAZ E II 365, 409; Schiess, III, no. 454). Paolo went on to study in Geneva and Basle, where he obtained a doctorate in medicine. After spending several years at the court of Elizabeth I, he was appointed city doctor in Berne (J. Picot, 'La famiglia di Scipione Lentolo', *BSSV*, 100 (1956), pp. 66–7; Busino, 'Italiani', p. 516). On the Marlianici, see Bonorand, 'Bündner Studierende', pp. 111–12; StAZ E II 358a, 642ᵛ.

[96] AERSG B 3, p. 186. Paolo's brother Cesare later trod the same path (see J.B. Paravicini to the Zurich professors, 16 August 1609 [StAZ E II 459, 365]). The records of the Grossmünsterstift's *Studentenamt* record a grant of 16 s to a 'Gafforo' (presumably Cesare) in 1609 (StAZ G II 39.12).

[97] ZB Ms. S 162, 139; Bonorand, 'Bündner Studierende', p. 115.

boy improved his command of Latin and learnt German, receiving instruction from his host in 'buone lettere' and 'buoni costumi'; in a letter to Azzo's mother Juditta dated 12 July 1611, Waser described the young man as a model pupil.[98] Of course, such arrangements did not always turn out to the satisfaction of both parties. Massimiliano Piatti, a companion of Guicciardi's who also lodged with Waser, fell in with bad company and ended up storming out of the professor's house after a row with one of his sons.[99] Following this incident, Piatti rebuffed attempts by Waser to persuade him to return or to accept alternative lodgings with another minister, ceasing to attend school and embarking on a love affair with a local girl. Eventually, the Zuricher had no choice but to send his errant pupil home.[100]

The single most important function of the Zurich academy was to provide trained pastors for service in the state's rural subject territories. As its output of graduates increased, the *Lectorium* was also able to supply ministers to other parts of eastern Switzerland – including German-speaking Graubünden – which suffered from a shortage of adequately trained clergy.[101]

Because of the difference in language, Zurich was not equipped to offer similar assistance to Italian or Romantsch-speaking congregations in the Freestate. Instead, those communities were forced to make use of the services of Italian evangelical exiles, often recent converts from Catholicism whose doctrinal probity could not be guaranteed. Although by the 1580s religious radicalism had been more or less eliminated from the Italian Reformed churches, the records of the Rhaetian synod show that exile pastors continued to fall short of the Reformed ideal in other ways. Most were repeatedly fined for failing to attend the annual meetings of the synod,[102] while some were accused of favouring Catholic doctrines or of being too intimate with Catholic clergy. There are several documented cases of ministers reverting to the old faith.[103] At the same

---

[98] StAZ E II 383, 721; compare Gianandrea Paravicini to J. Guicciardi, 12 January 1611 (StAZ E II 383, 713).

[99] Waser to Pietro Pozzi, 1 December 1610 (ibid., 705); Waser to Niccolò Guicciardi, 10 December 1610 (ibid., 707).

[100] See Waser to Cecilia Piatti, 19 January and 10 March 1611 (ibid., 715; 718). After arriving back in Teglio, Massimiliano wrote to Waser to apologize for his misdemeanours (ibid., 789).

[101] Bonorand, *Bildungswesen*, p. 35.

[102] See, for example, AERSG B 3, pp. 13; 88; 104. Eventually the synod was forced to allow ministers from Chiavenna, the Valbregaglia and the Valtellina to transact business in separate 'colloquies' (ibid., pp. 141; 153).

[103] In 1608 the Neapolitan Ferdinandus Carresius, minister in Bondo, was suspended on suspicion of apostasy: 'Ferdinandus minister ecclesiae Bondiensis (quoniam compertum est ipsum Mediolani fuisse apud Cardinalem) indignus nostro consortio iudicatur, et a

time, the synod had little option but to go on approving such appointments, faced as it was with a chronic shortage of candidates. The gravity of the situation was highlighted by Niklaus Kesel, minister in Monte di Sondrio, who in March 1606 declined an invitation to exchange his post for one in German-speaking Graubünden on the grounds that four Valtellina churches were already without pastors.[104]

Given the personal danger to which Reformed clerics in the subject lands were exposed, it is hardly surprising that the region's churches had difficulty attracting suitably qualified ministers. A further deterrent was the poor remuneration attached to such posts: in May 1597 the Rhaetian synod noted that ministers in the Valtellina were finding it hard to maintain their households on their current stipends, and resolved to lobby the Diet for an increase in salary levels.[105] Lentolo also drew attention to the poverty of himself and his colleagues, at one point grumbling, 'The Italian nation hardly feeds its ministers, never mind enriching them'.[106] More than two decades later, the situation had not changed a great deal. In a letter to J.J. Breitinger dated 24 July 1620 the Neapolitan exile Michele Terenzio, minister in Soglio, emphasized the difficulty he was having supporting a large family on the salary from his current post, which he was keen to exchange for a teaching position at the Zurich academy. Terenzio claimed that in desperation he had even considered a return to Catholicism ('ad vomitum Paternae meae domus').[107]

---

synodo excluditur, idque iniungitur Domino Ministro, ut ecclesiam de exclusione hac moneat, et ad ipsum dimittendum exhortetur' (AERSG B 3, pp. 194–5). See also the cases of Giovanni Battista Thei (ibid., p. 95), Martino Ponchieri (ibid., pp. 114; 116–17) and Michael Capuanus (ibid., p. 146).

[104] Kesel to J. von Salis, 13 and 21 March 1606 (StAG D II a 3 c). In the second of these letters, Kesel alludes to the recent death of Scipione Calandrini.

[105] AERSG B 3, p. 141: 'Propositum fuit V. Synodo, plerosque Volturenae fratres propter exigua salaria sese cum familiariis alere non posse. Ideoque in proximis comitiis proponendum esse a Dominis supplicandum iudicat, ut sua autem salaria statuantur honesta a Comitatibus solvenda, quo fratres pauperes Ecclesiarum minus graventur, et Ecclesiae pauperes Ministros sustinere [?] possint.' Two years later the Valtellinese ministers informed the synod that their salaries were still not being paid on time (ibid., p. 150).

[106] Lentolo to Stucki, 7 January 1599 (StAZ 380, 420): 'Italica natio vix alit suos ministros, nedum ditet.'

[107] StAZ E II 390, 457. Breitinger advised Terenzio not to desert his congregation, but sought to ease his hardship by arranging an apprenticeship for his son in Zurich (ibid., 461; 453; 454a; 463–4; 449–50). Other members of the family also settled in Zurich: a list of refugee children compiled after the 'sacro macello' includes references to two daughters of a 'Michael Terentius', Lucrezia and Maria (StAZ E II 279, 80, 85; compare K. Schultheß, 'Glaubensflüchtlinge aus Chiavenna und dem Veltlin in Zürcher Kirchenbüchern 1620–1700', Der Schweizer Familienforscher, 36 (1969), pp. 1–38 [30–1]).

One solution to the staffing crisis was to appoint Romantsch-speaking Rhaetians to Italian parishes: at the time of the 'sacro macello', five of the 17 Reformed congregations in the subject lands, both churches in Poschiavo, and Bondo and Casaccia in the Valbregaglia were in the care of ministers from the Engadine. A more satisfactory approach was to make good the shortfall with Italian-speakers native to Graubünden.[108] When Pietro Menghino of Poschiavo came to Zurich in June 1593, Lentolo singled him out to Stucki as a potential future minister: 'For we hope that at some point he will prove useful to the Italian churches of this region, which suffer from a great shortage of good pastors.'[109] In the event, Menghino returned to Rhaetia as a schoolmaster rather than as a minister, but among the Italian Bündner who studied in Zurich were several who later underwent ordination: Bartolomeo Paravicini (Dubino, Soglio), Vincenzo Paravicini (Bondo, Casaccia), Giovanni Battista Calandrini (Dubino), and Simone Pellizari (Piuro). Most of the Engadiners who served as ministers in the Italian lands were also Zurich-trained.[110]

The Zurich church's interest in improving educational opportunites for the Italian Reformed was most apparent in its support for attempts to set up a Latin school for the subject lands in Sondrio.[111] This had long been a cherished project of the Rhaetian Reformed leadership: as early as October 1563, Zanchi informed Pierre Viret that the creation of 'some sort of academy in the Valtellina' ('Academiam aliquam in valle Telina') had been mooted.[112] In May 1581 proposals for the

---

108 The appointment of Romantsch-speakers to Italian parishes appears to have been regarded as less than ideal by the synod. See G. Baserga, 'Il movimento per la Riforma in Valtellina e le sue relazioni con Ginevra', *Periodico della Società storica della Provincia e antica Diocesi di Como*, 21 (1914), pp. 97–128; ibid., 22 (1915), pp. 51–35 (20): 'In illis locis desunt nobis candelabra, desunt φωσφοροι, desunt pastores; alii enim propter linguam, alii propter aetatem, alii propter nationem alii propter alia minus idonei.'

109 Lentolo to Stucki, 23 August 1594 (StAZ E II 380, 314): 'Speramus namque eum futurum huius regionis Italicis Ecclesiis aliquando utilem: quippe quae maxima laborant penuria bonorum Pastorum.' See also Lentolo to Stucki, 3 June and 31 December 1593 (ibid., 286–9; 314–16).

110 For example, Caspar Alexius (Sondrio), Antonius Andreoscha (Brusio, Tirano), Samuel Andreoscha (Mello), Johann Peter Danz (Teglio), Jörg Jenatsch (Berbenno) and Gaudentius Tack (Brusio, Malenco). My information is derived from Truog, *Pfarrer*; 'Die Pfarrer der evangelischen Gemeinden in Graubünden und seinen ehemaligen Untertanenlanden (Ergänzungen und Berichtigungen)', *JHGG*, 75 (1945), pp. 113–47; and Bonorand, 'Bündner Studierende'.

111 The standard account of this episode is C. Camenisch, *Carlo Borromeo und die Gegenreformation im Veltlin mit besonderer Berücksichtigung der Landesschule von Sondrio* (Chur, 1901), pp. 140–233. See also Bonorand, *Bildungswesen*, pp. 55–9; *Reformatorische Emigration*, pp. 212–16.

112 Zanchi, *Epistolae*, II, 174.

establishment of such a school were put to the Rhaetian Diet by Johannes Contius Bisaz, the president of the synod, and later that year the measure was approved by the communes.[113] Inevitably, it was to Zurich that the Rhaetians turned in search of someone qualified to head the new institution, the bulk of whose funding was to come from the proceeds of the dissolved Humiliati foundation of St Ursula and St Margaret in Teglio. Lentolo suggested his former pupil Raphael Egli, who had recently been ordained in Zurich, and in October 1582 wrote to Gwalther to request Egli's release.[114] The *Antistes* gave his blessing to the enterprise, informing the Zurich council 'that the said Raphael Egli is fit and suitable for such a post, and that our school is able to spare his services at this time'.[115] As a further indication of Zurich's support, Egli was offered an annual grant from the Grossmünsterstift to supplement the salary of 60 Kronen assigned him by the Bündner.[116]

After arriving in the Valtellina, the new rector published a school order setting out his vision for the college, entitled *Via ac ratio scholae illustrium dominorum D.D Rhaetorum qui nomine Trium Foederum nuncupantur.*[117] In this work, Egli drew heavily on existing Zurich models, particularly Bullinger's own *Schulordnung* of 1532.[118] Although the Rhaetian Diet had expected due weight to be given to the teaching of Italian and other practical skills, the curriculum that Egli proposed was entirely dominated by study of the classics. Like its counterparts in Zurich, the Sondrio school was to consist of three classes, each with its own teacher. Authors to be studied in the second class included 'Cato' (*Disticha*), Cicero and Ovid, while pupils in the third class were required to master Sallust, Terence, Virgil and Horace, along with the rudiments of Greek from the New Testament. Egli attached particular importance to students' acquiring fluency in spoken as well as written Latin: the school order stipulates that in the third class anyone guilty of using the vernacular or of speaking Latin 'incongrue' or 'barbare' should be derided as a blockhead ('asinus'). Each December, pupils attending the school were to be subject to a public examination, the result of which would determine whether they progressed to the next class.

---

[113] Camenisch, *Borromeo*, p. 143.

[114] Letter published in Camenisch, *Borromeo*, pp. 250–51.

[115] For the full text of Gwalther's address, see ibid., pp. 147–8. Gwalther may have been only too pleased to be rid of Egli, who while studying in Geneva had come under the influence of the heterodox Calabrese exile Agostino Doni (see Gwalther to Beza, 10 March 1581 [*Correspondance*, XXII, no. 1467]).

[116] StAZ G II 39.7, entries for 17 November 1582, 28 September 1583 and 6 July 1584. Compare Calandrini to Gwalther, 12 February 1583 (ZB Ms. A 49, 222–3).

[117] Published in Camenisch, *Borromeo*, pp. 253–61. See also ibid., pp. 156–7.

[118] Summarized in Ernst, *Geschichte des Zürcherischen Schulwesens*, pp. 88–93.

However, by the time the *Via ac ratio* appeared (April 1584) the school had run into serious difficulties. Local Catholics were inclined to regard it as little more than an instrument for the dissemination of Protestantism in the subject lands, even though religious instruction was specifically excluded from its curriculum and at least one of its three teachers was required to be a Catholic. The appointment of Egli, with his Zurich connections, appeared to give substance to claims that the long-term goal of Graubünden's Protestant majority was to bring about the Reformation of the Valtellina by stealth. In March 1584 the archpriest of Sondrio, Giangiacomo Pusterla, denounced the proposed school as a Protestant seminary; a visiting Franciscan preacher, Francesco of Balerna, went further by calling on Catholic women to withhold sex from their unbelieving husbands. When the *Landeshauptmann*, Rudolf von Schauenstein, instructed Pusterla to dismiss Francesco, he responded by leading an armed demonstration of 200 Catholics through the streets of Sondrio, who administered beatings to any Protestants unfortunate enough to cross their path. Guards also had to be posted around the town's Reformed church to protect it from attack.[119]

Calandrini, at the centre of the storm, urged Gwalther in Zurich to intervene to stiffen the resolve of the Rhaetian magistracy, and for a time the school's prospects did indeed seem to be improving.[120] At the end of June, the Diet appointed a 15-strong commission to investigate the Sondrio disturbances and punish those responsible. While in Sondrio, the commission also decided to purchase a building to house the school, to increase Egli's salary to 80 Kronen, and to provide him with the resources needed to recruit the other two teachers envisaged in the original plan.[121] However, the respite proved to be temporary. With the support of Carlo Borromeo and Pope Gregory XIII, the Swiss Catholic states put pressure on Graubünden to close the school, threatening to abrogate their alliance with the Freestate if defied.[122] Zurich, Berne and

---

119 Camenisch, *Borromeo*, pp. 167–70.

120 Calandrini and the church of Sondrio to Gwalther, 5 April 1584 (StAZ E II 382, 1049; part-published in Camenisch, *Borromeo*, pp. 269–70): 'Quia ... res in proxima Synodo Ministrorum Rhaetiae circa tempus Comitiorum tractabitur, non dubitamus pastores omnes rem corde habituros. Gravium vero virorum exhortatio, quales tu, vir praestantissime, cum Collegis tuis estis, non inutilis eis futura esset.'

121 Camenisch, *Borromeo*, pp. 177–81. In September the previous year, the ministers and elders of the Reformed church in Sondrio had informed Gwalther that progress towards establishing the school was being hampered by a lack of funds and suitable accommodation (ZB Ms. A 49, 281–9). At their request, the Zurich council wrote to the Rhaetian Leagues to demand that these problems be addressed (Camenisch, *Borromeo*, pp. 261–3) .

122 Camenisch, *Borromeo*, pp. 182–3.

Basle also began to advise postponement of the project, given the strength of Catholic opposition to it.[123] By November, Egli was heartily sick of the whole saga and asked the Zurich council to secure his release, which he obtained the following January.[124] Eventually the Sondrio college was transferred to Chur, where it was amalgamated with the existing *Nikolaischule*.[125]

Hopes of establishing a public school in the subject lands had not been extinguished completely. In an undated letter written shortly after Egli's return to Zurich, Gwalther pledged his continuing support, assuring the Protestants of the Valtellina that the same God who had preserved 'schools of prophets' under the impious Israelite kings Joram, Ahaziah and Ahab would stand by them in their hour of need.[126] However, the Rhaetian synod was forced to wait until 1616 before attempting to revive the scheme, which again received the blessing of the Protestant-dominated Diet.[127] The synod proposed that Caspar Alexius, a Bündner who had been teaching in Geneva for the past decade, should be appointed rector of the new institution.[128] Once again, the Zurich church emerged as a key sponsor of the school project: when the Genevan scholarchs refused to agree to Alexius' release, claiming that their academy was chronically short of staff and could not afford to dispense with his services,[129] the Zurichers urged them to reconsider. In a letter dated 13 February 1618, Breitinger, Waser and Rudolf Hospinian argued that Alexius' presence in the Valtellina would be of benefit to local churches, and that the school, once established, would assist the progress of the Reformation in Rhaetia more generally.[130] This intervention, supported by a similarly worded request from Berne, was enough to persuade the Genevans to let Alexius go.

In the months following Alexius' appointment, significant progress was made towards realizing the school project. Perhaps the most notable

---

[123] See Calandrini to Gwalther, 28 November 1584 (StAZ E II 382, 1050); Camenisch, *Borromeo*, pp. 186–7.

[124] R. Egli to Gwalther, 20 November 1584 (ZB Ms. S 142, 51); address by Gwalther to the Zurich council, 12 December 1584 (StAZ A 248.3); Rhaetian Diet to Zurich, 18 January 1585 (ibid.).

[125] Bonorand, *Bildungswesen*, pp. 59–70.

[126] ZB Ms. F 41, 141–2.

[127] A. Pfister, *Jörg Jenatsch: Sein Leben und seine Zeit* (5th edn, Chur, 1991), pp. 55–6. For much of what follows, see Bonorand, *Bildungswesen*, pp. 87–92; *Reformatorische Emigration*, pp. 233–8.

[128] *RCP*, XII, pp. 411–13; 430–33.

[129] Ibid., XII, pp. 217, 220–21, 437–8, 440–41; Baserga, 'Il Movimento', pp. 116–23, 16–18.

[130] StAZ E II 384, 421–2; Baserga, 'Il Movimento', pp. 21–3.

development was the publication of a school order, which proposed a structure and curriculum similar to those outlined in Egli's *Via ac ratio* 30 years earlier. If anything, the refounded school was more ambitiously conceived than its predecessor: it was to have four classes, rather than three, and provision was to be made for public lectures on philology, history and philosophy. As in Zurich the fourth class was originally the *Lectorium* itself, it is hard to escape the conclusion that Alexius' ultimate aim was the establishment of a Reformed-style academy on Rhaetian soil.[131] This ambition was never realistic, given the confessional make-up of the subject lands and the unwillingness of Valtellinese Catholics to sanction the establishment of any school whose dominant ethos was Reformed. By early 1619 a combination of local Catholic opposition and political instability in Graubünden as a whole had fatally undermined the scheme, although attempts to revive it continued to be made right up to the eve of the 'sacro macello'.[132] For our purposes, the episode is important primarily because it illustrates the Zurichers' consistent support for initiatives aimed at bolstering the Reformed presence in the subject lands. Indeed, in the matter of Alexius' appointment Zurich showed itself to be more 'internationalist' even than Geneva, which on this occasion was inclined to put parochial concerns first.[133]

The Zurichers had reasons of their own for wanting to see the school project come to fruition. For years, young men from the city had been taking advantage of the links that existed between Zurich and the Italian churches to spend extended periods in Graubünden's subject lands studying with local ministers and schoolmasters, many of whom had impeccable humanist credentials. Gradually what amounted to an informal 'exchange scheme' took shape. As early as August 1570, Lentolo sought to interest Johannes Wolf in such an arrangement, which would have seen one of Wolf's sons travel to Chiavenna to receive tuition while Paolo Lentolo studied in Zurich.[134] In the late 1590s, Calandrini successfully brokered an exchange between a Valtellinese youth named Francesco Paravicini and Stucki's son Johannes, who attended the school run by the former Zurich student Pietro Menghino

---

[131] Bonorand, *Bildungswesen*, pp. 89–90; *Reformatorische Emigration*, p. 236.

[132] In a letter to J.H. Waser dated 10 June 1620, Johann Peter Danz outlined plans to relocate the school to Teglio (ZB Ms. B 65, 244–5); Bonorand, *Bildungswesen*, p. 83; *Reformatorische Emigration*, pp. 228–9.

[133] In a letter to the company of pastors dated 28 September 1616, the Rhaetian synod dared to reproach the Genevans for their neglect of the Italian churches: 'Dedistis Galliae doctores innumeros, cur non etiam Italiae?' (*RCP*, XII, p. 431; Baserga, 'Il Movimento', p. 115).

[134] ZB Ms. F 39, 605.

in Sondrio.[135] During his stay in the Valtellina, Johannes received support from both Calandrini and Ulisse Martinengo, who provided Stucki with regular updates on the boy's progress. In a letter dated 27 December 1598, Martinengo observed admiringly, 'He speaks Italian so well that from his pronunciation you would no longer know that he was German';[136] the following February he reported that Johannes had come as far as was possible in the study of Greek with Menghino and that 'he now knows Italian so thoroughly that, if when he is back home he spends some time practising it to preserve what he has learned, that should be enough to ensure satisfactory progress in the language'.[137] The fact that Stucki later sought to persuade Francesco Paravicini's father Orazio to agree to a further exchange (this time between their younger sons) provides some indication of the value that he perceived in such arrangements.[138] Stucki's view was shared by Kaspar Waser, whose sons Johann Heinrich (a future *Bürgermeister* of Zurich) and Johann Kaspar were dispatched to Teglio and Sondrio respectively.[139] Correspondence relating to Johann Heinrich's stay in the Valtellina provides us with a glimpse of the intricate and multilayered relationships that had been built up between families in Zurich and Italian Graubünden by the early 17th century. Passing through Chiavenna, the young Zuricher met Ottaviano Mei, who advised him on how to go about learning Italian. Later he was able to call on a former schoolfriend from Zurich days, Azzo Guicciardi, while on arrival in Teglio he took lodgings with Ascanio Gatti, whose brother Lelio was studying under Waser in

---

[135] Calandrini to Stucki, 28 November 1597 (StAZ E II 358a, 642ᵛ): '... nobilis quidam Ecclesiae nostrae Horatius Paravicinus nomine, homo dives, et perhumanus, cupit filium suum primogenitum annorum tredecim isthuc mittere, et nobilem aliquem adolescentem vestratem eiusdem aetatis vel circiter eius loco in aedes suas recipere, qui munde, et liberaliter tractaretur, quem etiam in studiis literarum a Menghino nostro institui suis ipsius sumptibus curaret. Quare me rogavit ut de ea re tecum per literas agerem, teque rogarem ut pro tua singulari humanitate eius desyderio satisfieri curares.' Calandrini himself acted as tutor to a number of Zurich youngsters (for details, see Bonorand, *Bildungswesen*, p. 85; *Reformatorische Emigration*, p. 230).

[136] StAZ E II 380, 418: 'Italice ita loqui ut non amplius pro Germano ex pronuntiatione dignosci posset.'

[137] Ibid., 422: 'Italici vero sermonis est iam ita penitus, ut si isthic aliquando stilum exerceat ad conservationem eius quod didicit, satis et ample in hoc idiomate nobis profecisse videatur.'

[138] O. Paravicini to Stucki, 28 October 1600 (StAZ E II 380, 22). Paravicini turned down the offer on this occasion as he did not believe that his son Cesare was ready to leave home. However, the exchange may have occurred at a later date: in a letter to Stucki dated 20 March 1605, Martinengo discusses arrangements for the return to Zurich of one of his correspondent's sons, who had been staying with a 'dominus Paravicinus' (StAZ E II 380, 518). See also Bonorand, *Bildungswesen*, p. 86; *Reformierte Emigration*, p. 231.

[139] Bonorand, *Bildungswesen*, p. 83; *Reformierte Emigration*, p. 228.

Zurich.[140] The experience of another Zurich student, Johannes Bräm, was similar: when Bräm visited Sondrio in January 1615, he stayed with one Cesare Paravicini, whose father had played host to his own many years earlier.[141]

It is easy to grasp the attraction for the Zurichers of the exchange scheme, which provided some of the city's most promising young men with an opportunity to round off their education by learning Italian in a Reformed setting. In a letter to Waser dated 20 June 1616, Ottaviano Mei spoke encouragingly of the progress made in this regard by a group of Zurich students, now returning home, during their time in Chiavenna: 'In my view, the efforts that they have made to learn our mother tongue have not been in vain, as they seem to able to converse easily enough in the language of this region'.[142] The role played by the Italian churches and schools of Graubünden in relation to Zurich is comparable (albeit on a smaller scale) with that of the Genevan academy, to which Zurich youths were sent with the primary aim of learning French.[143] Many of the Italian ministers and schoolmasters were accomplished teachers of their native tongue: Lentolo was the author of a highly regarded Italian grammar that went through nearly 20 editions between 1567 and 1650, and was translated into French, English and German.[144] For young Zurichers, time spent learning Italian in Chiavenna or the Valtellina could serve as valuable preparation for study at an Italian institution of higher education. This is best illustrated by the case of Johann Ulrich Grebel, who was resident in Teglio between August 1582 and the summer of the following year. While there, he received instruction in Italian and Justinian's *Institutes* from the local schoolmaster, Annibale Guicciardi – himself a former pupil of Josias Simler in Zurich – before going on to Padua to read law.[145] Johann

---

140   Mei to Waser, 21 March 1616 (ZB Ms. S 166, 9); J.H. Waser to K. Waser, 14 March 1616 (ZB Ms. B 42, 94r–5r); A. Gatti to K. Waser, 19 February 1619 (ZB Ms. F 172 d, 157r).

141   StAZ E II 387, 100. This may well be the same Cesare Paravicini mentioned in n. 138 above. For further evidence of Zurichers' studying in Sondrio at this time, see Johann Jakob Ulrich to Breitinger, 8 November 1615 (StAZ E II 387, 163).

142   ZB Ms. S 166, 19: 'Eos non arbitror inutilem omnino operam vernaculae linguae nostrae impendisse: satis enim expedite vernaculo huius regionis idiomate videntur fabulari.'

143   K. Maag, *Seminary or University?: The Genevan Academy and Reformed Higher Education, 1560–1620* (Aldershot, 1995), pp. 152–3.

144   P. Buzzoni, *I praecepta di Scipione Lentulo e l'adattamento inglese di Henry Grantham* (Florence, 1979), pp. 105–6.

145   See StAZ E II 380, 36–65; Bonorand, *Bildungswesen*, p. 82; *Reformatorische Emigration*, p. 227. In a letter to Stucki dated 18 August 1582, Grebel reported that he had received a copy of Lentolo's grammar from the author (ibid., 37). For Guicciardi's relations with Simler, see ZB Ms. F 61, 19.

Heinrich Waser also studied at the university of Padua, as part of a tour of Italy undertaken in 1617.[146] By making it easier for Zurichers to attend Italian universities, the frontier churches of Italian Graubünden helped in a small way to bridge the divide between the cultures of Catholic and Reformed Europe.

A two-way traffic was also established in books. The surviving correspondence details numerous instances of Zurich ministers supplying their Italian contacts with theological literature, especially their own works. In a letter to Simler dated 12 May 1574, for instance, Lentolo thanked the Zuricher for sending him his latest polemic against the ubiquitarians, *De vera Iesu Christi ... secundum humanam naturam in his terris praesentia, orthodoxa ... expositio* (Zurich, 1574).[147] Later Lentolo was presented with a copy of Stucki's *Helvetica gratulatio ad Galliam de Henrico huius nominis iv Galliarum et Navarrae rege Christianissimo*;[148] Calandrini received the same author's *De angelis angelicoque hominum praesidio atque custodia meditatio*, which he read 'most avidly, and with the greatest pleasure' ('maxima cum animi voluptate, atque aviditate') and described as a source of consolation in troubled times.[149] The relationship continued under Waser, who sent Ottaviano Mei a copy of his *Analysis Psalmi CX* (Zurich, 1612).[150] At times the Zurichers' Italian correspondents sought their help in acquiring specific works. Lentolo, for example, was keen to lay hands on Simler's life of Peter Martyr,[151] as well as the Latin original of Ludwig Lavater's

---

[146] *Johannis Henrici Waseri de vita sua* (ZB Ms. A 132), pp. 86–7.

[147] ZB Ms. F 60, 306. Compare Bullinger to Egli, 2 April 1574 (Schiess, III, no. 416); and Egli to Bullinger, 18 May 1574 (ibid., no. 423).

[148] Lentolo to Stucki, 8 December 1591 (StAZ E II 380, 187). Stucki's work was the main source for an unpublished *Discorso della vera successione d'Arrigo Quarto*, dated 1592 and held at the Zurich Zentralbibliothek (Ms. B 239). This text may have been written by Calandrini: the preface, dedicated 'All'Italia', is signed S.C.R., while the hand resembles that of Calandrini in his letters. The author of the *Discorso* also argues for the possibility of co-existence between rival confessions in a single state, as Calandrini had done in his recently published translation of the *Traité de l'Eglise*.

[149] Calandrini to Stucki, 15 July 1595 (StAZ E II 358a, 607[r]). Lentolo also read the *De angelis* – see his letter to Stucki of 30 March 1596 (StAZ E II 380, 342) – along with two works by Stucki's colleague Rudolf Hospinian, *De origine, progressu, usu et abusu templorum ac rerum omnium ad templa pertinentium, libri v* (Zurich, 1587), and *De origine et progressu monachatus libri v* (Zurich, 1588). See Lentolo to Stucki, 29 May 1590 (StAZ E II 380, 129).

[150] Mei to Waser, 18 January 1613 (ZB Ms. S 164, 10).

[151] ZB Ms. F 60, 306. Simler replied that his oration was no longer available in the original separate printing, so Lentolo instead requested a copy of the work – presumably the 1569 Zurich edition of Vermigli's *Commentary on Genesis* – to which it was prefaced (see Lentolo to Simler, 15 September 1574 [ZB Ms. F 60, 307]).

De spectris, lemuribus atque insolidis fragoribus, which he hoped to translate into Italian.[152] Similarly, on 30 January 1589 Calandrini wrote to Heinrich Bullinger, the grandson of the *Antistes*, on behalf of a certain 'Signor Marc'antonio', whose attempts to acquire a copy of 'il ... libro della Tragedia' (probably Francesco Negri's *Tragedia del libero arbitrio*) had thus far come to nothing 'because in these parts [copies] are not to be had for money'.[153] In January 1600, Orazio Paravicini asked Stucki to procure some volumes for the minister of Berbenno in the Valtellina.[154]

In return for such material, the Reformed of the subject lands provided the Zurichers with books, verses and other publications circulating in Italy. In the letter just cited, Calandrini thanked Bullinger for sending him a recent work by Rudolf Hospinian and promised to match this gift 'with some other fine book that may come into my hands, which I think you will appreciate' ('con qualche altro bel libro che mi venga alle mani, quale io giudichi doverai esser grato').[155] On another occasion, Lentolo asked Stucki to have Gabriel Gerber supply him with a list of books that Gerber wished to have purchased in Venice;[156] Waser received Italian-language works from both Lentolo and Giovanni Battista Calandrini (in the latter case, a manuscript of Tommaso Campanella's *Monarchia di Spagna*).[157]

The Zurichers' Italian correspondents also occupied an important niche in their information-gathering network. During the early 1570s, Lentolo sent regular 'schedulae' or news-bulletins to Tobias Egli, which were then passed on to Bullinger. After Egli's death in 1575, Lentolo expressed the hope that the arrangement might continue under his successor as senior minister in Chur, Kaspar Hubenschmid. Whether it did so for long is unclear,[158] but by the late 1580s Lentolo was again sending such reports to Stucki on a weekly basis, via a merchant in Chur (Calandrini assumed the same responsibility for the Valtellina).[159] In

---

[152] Lentolo to Simler, 13 September 1575 (ZB Ms. F 60, 295). Lentolo had already received a copy of the work in French from Johann Baptist Müller.

[153] StAZ E II 365a, 789: 'Il Signor Marc'antonio aspetta con desiderio il suo libro della Tragedia perche in questi paesi non sene trovano per denari'.

[154] StAZ E II 385, 1a[r].

[155] StAZ E II 365a, 788.

[156] Letter of 19 March 1593 (StAZ E II 380, 268).

[157] Lentolo to Waser, 1 February 1598 (ZB Ms. S 152, 93.3); 15 March 1598 (ZB Ms. S 153, 14b); 11 April 1598 (ibid., 14a); G.B. Calandrini to Waser, 17 June 1612 (ZB Ms. S 162, 140).

[158] Lentolo to Bullinger, 11 February 1575 (StAZ E II 365, 401; Schiess, III, no. 448). See also Lentolo to Simler, 13 September 1575 (ZB Ms. F 60, 295).

[159] Lentolo to Stucki, 20 June 1589 (StAZ E II 380, 92); Martinengo to Stucki, 11 August 1598 (StAZ E II 380, 412). 'Schedulae' addressed to Stucki are preserved in StAZ E II 380, 472–89.

return, the Zurichers dispatched news of developments elsewhere in Europe, which Lentolo and Calandrini then forwarded to their fellow ministers.[160] Stucki and his colleagues also facilitated communication between Rhaetia's Italian communities and other Reformed churches, on one occasion passing on books from Lentolo to Antoine Sadeel and Antoine de La Faye in Geneva.[161] Many of the Italian-speakers who attended the Zurich academy used it as a stepping-stone to study at other, more internationally prestigious, Reformed centres of higher education (Basle, Geneva, Marburg and Heidelberg).[162]

Throughout the late 16th and early 17th centuries, the Italian churches and their ministers were able to call on Zurich for assistance in various matters of practical concern. In December 1568, for example, Lentolo asked Bullinger to mediate in a family quarrel involving one of the deacons of his church, whose son was refusing to return home from Zurich after the failure of a business venture in Germany.[163] On another occasion he asked the *Antistes* to put in a word with the Zurich council on behalf of the Rhaetian magnate Hercules von Salis, who was hoping to acquire Zurich citizenship.[164] Lentolo was not above using his Zurich contacts to benefit members of his own family. In a letter to Stucki dated 5 February 1589, he outlined the predicament of a relative who had been recruited as a 'passemains' by the Werdmüller family but given insufficient work to support his dependents; Lentolo hinted that Stucki's

---

160 See Martinengo to Stucki, 29 January 1593 (StAZ E II 380, 294): 'De bello Argentinensi quae scripsisti statim communicavi Reverendo D. Calandrino nostro, qui sibi iamdiu hoc muneris suscepit, et scribendi, et accipiendi ceterisque communicandi novas res quae afferuntur, maxime cuiusmodi hae sunt ad communem pietatis causam pertinentes'.

161 See Lentolo to Stucki, 1 December 1590 (StAZ E II 380, 119). Lentolo's theology was Genevan in orientation. Euan Cameron maintains that, under his guidance, the Waldenses of Piedmont adopted 'a distinctively Calvinist set of articles of faith and church discipline' (Cameron, *Reformation of the Heretics*, p. 213), while in the *Responsio orthodoxa* Lentolo defines the sacraments in unmistakably Calvinist terms against the 'Zwinglian' Bartolomeo Silvio: 'Sacramenta non modo externa sunt quaedam instituti Christiani signa: sed illis adhibitis dantur quoque nobis, a quibus illa cum fide participantur, res ipsae quae per illa significantur' (*Responsio orthodoxa*, pp. 135–6). The influence of the Genevan model of church government on Lentolo is obvious from his willingness, during the confrontation with the radicals, to resort to excommunication as a disciplinary sanction once other options had been exhausted. Calandrini and Mei also favoured the use of excommunication (see part 3 of the former's *Trattato*, and Mei to the ministers of the Upper Engadine, 2 December 1617 [StAG D II b 3]).

162 See the lists in Bonorand, 'Bündner Studierende'. In 1573 the Chiavenna exile Andrea Pizzarda left 12 scudi 'ali studenti ittaliani dimandati li stippendiati, quali studiano in theologia nella città di Geneva' (G. Giorgetta, 'Andrea Pizzarda di Pallanza a Chiavenna', *Clavenna*, 27 (1988), pp. 67–75 [73]).

163 StAZ E II 365, 332–3; Schiess, III, no. 137.

164 Lentolo to Bullinger, 23 October 1572 (StAZ E II 365, 332–3; Schiess, III, no. 336).

intervention on the man's behalf would be appreciated.[165] The Zurich professors Stucki, Trüb and Egli may also have had a hand in Paolo Lentolo's appointment as city doctor in Berne four years later.[166]

Commendations of Italian religious exiles (usually converted Catholic clergymen who were passing through Chiavenna and Zurich en route to Geneva) are another regular feature of Lentolo's correspondence. In a letter to Bullinger dated June 1573, Lentolo praised Alessandro Maranta, a renegade Dominican from Bisceglie in Puglia, as a 'learned man, well versed both in the writings of the scholastics and in our Christian writings, and with experience of teaching and preaching in the most famous places in Italy',[167] while in February 1597 he asked the Zurich church to contribute to the expenses of Niccolò Calvo, a Milanese exile and the son of a distinguished professor of medicine at the university of Pavia, who was planning to study in Geneva.[168] The financial records of the Grossmünsterstift's *Studentenamt* indicate that the Zurichers responded positively to requests of this sort: they contain numerous entries for donations made to Italian exiles carrying letters of recommendation from the churches of Chiavenna, Sondrio and Tirano.[169]

During the final quarter of the 16th century, Rhaetia's Italian Reformed pastorate was faced with a major new challenge: fending off the assaults of an increasingly militant Catholic church and population. Some of the literature requested from Zurich was clearly intended for use in polemical exchanges with the local Catholic clergy, which had begun to be reinforced by graduates of Borromeo's *Collegium Helveticum* in Milan. In September 1587, for instance, Lentolo asked

---

[165] StAZ E II 380, 82.

[166] See Lentolo to Stucki, 3 June 1593 (StAZ E II 380, 270–71). Later Stucki helped Lentolo to arrange the transfer to Berne of a loan that the Neapolitan had procured for his son (see his letters of 3 September 1593 (ibid., 278); and 3 October 1593 [ibid., 284]). Correspondence between the two Lentoli was also channelled through Stucki (see Scipione's letters of 30 July 1594 (ibid., 312); and 8 August 1598 [ibid., 388]).

[167] StAZ E II 365, 339; Schiess, III, no. 373. On this occasion Lentolo's judgment was well wide of the mark: within a few months of arriving in Geneva, Maranta was expelled from the city after clashing with Beza (Bullinger to Egli, 18 December 1573 (Schiess, III, no. 404); *RCP*, III, pp. 110, 118). On his subsequent fate, see Ambrosini, *Storie di patrizi*, pp. 201–2.

[168] StAZ E II 380, 369-70. For a similar request, see Lentolo to R. Egli, 27 June 1596 (ZB Ms. F 81, 119). Calvo was received into the Rhaetian synod in 1598 and later served alongside Mei in Chiavenna (Busino, 'Borrone', p. 147; AERSG B 3, p. 175).

[169] Maranta was given 4 lb on the basis of Lentolo's commendation (StAZ G II 39.5). On 15 June 1599 the Spanish exile Juan Herrera, commended to the Zurichers by the church of Sondrio, received 8 lb 16 s from the *Studentenamt* along with a smaller sum from the Locarnese common chest (StAZ G II 39.10; FA Orelli, 8.2, fol. 117r).

Stucki to send him several copies of a recent work by Heinrich Wolf attacking the papal reforms of the calendar (probably the *Chronologia* of 1585), which the Protestant majority in the Rhaetian Diet had rejected despite demands from the Catholics of the Valtellina that it implement them.[170] Calandrini also received a copy of Wolf's book, which he promised to circulate among his colleagues throughout the Valtellina.[171]

In the late 1590s, formal disputations between Catholic and Protestant clergymen took place in Tirano (October 1595–November 1596) and Piuro (March 1597). For the first of these there is evidence of indirect Zurich involvement on the side of the Reformed delegation, made up of Scipione Calandrini, Ottaviano Mei, Niklaus Kesel, Cesare Gaffori and Antonius Andreoscha. The disputation had been triggered by the curate of Tirano, Simone Cabasso, who attempted to equate Calvin's doctrine of the mediator with subordinationism; at issue was whether Christ mediated with God in both natures (as the Reformed maintained) or in his human nature alone (as the Catholics present, following Robert Bellarmine, contended).[172] In a letter to Stucki dated 28 November 1595, Calandrini reported that he and his colleagues had managed to hold their own at the first colloquy, but emphasized the urgent need for reinforcement in the form of Protestant works controverting the views of Bellarmine.[173] It is unclear whether such works were ever sent, but later Calandrini wrote to thank Stucki for endorsing the stance adopted by the Valtellinese ministers at Tirano.[174]

---

170 Lentolo to Stucki, 21 September 1587 (StAZ E II 380, 67). On the Rhaetian Diet's decision to retain the Julian calendar, see Rosius de Porta, *Historia Reformationis*, II:3, p. 75; and F. Maissen, 'Der Kalenderstreit in Graubünden (1582–1812)', *BM* (1960), pp. 253–72. The issue acquired symbolic importance in the light of the growing confessional tensions in the subject lands: one of the first acts of the rebel Catholic administration that seized power after the 'sacro macello' was to introduce the Gregorian calendar (*Vera relatione della vittoria et libertà ottenuta da Cattolici, contro gli Heretici, nella Valtellina* (Pavia, 1620), sig. A4r).

171 Calandrini to H. Wolf, 12 November 1588 (ZB Ms. F 38, 221).

172 The position of the Catholic disputants was close to that of Francesco Stancaro (see Chapter 4:i above). Their Reformed adversaries were not slow to make this connection (see *Disputationis tiranensis inter pontificios et ministros verbi Dei in Rhaetia, anno 1595 et 1596 habitu partes IV* (Basle, 1602), pp. 37; 168–70).

173 StAZ E II 358a, 611. Calandrini was interested specifically in Antoine de La Faye's *Theses de verbo Dei*. In the letter he acknowledges having already received a work by David Pareus defending Calvin against the charge of Arianism, probably *Calvinus orthodoxus de Sacrosancta Trinitate et de aeterna Christi Divinitate*, first published in Neustadt in 1595 (*Verzeichnis der im deutschen Sprachbereich erschienenen Drucke des XVI. Jahrhunderts* (24 vols, Stuttgart, 1983–97), XXI, p. 269, W 32).

174 Letter of 18 July 1597 (StAZ E II 358a, 642). The Zurichers had been sent a work entitled *Sacrificulorum vulturenorum liber adversus Pastores Rhaetiae Evangelicos,*

When the official Protestant account of the disputation was eventually published in 1602, a copy of the work was presented to Stucki by Calandrini on behalf of his colleagues.[175]

As religious tensions in the subject lands increased, ministers from the area turned increasingly to Zurich for moral and political support. In October 1590 Calandrini informed Stucki that at a forthcoming meeting of the Rhaetian Diet the mainly Catholic Upper League intended to propose that the majoritarian principle which determined confessional allegiance in the communes of the Freestate proper should be extended to the subject lands, as a way of preventing further Protestant expansion in the area; Calandrini wanted Stucki to persuade the Zurich council to use its influence with the Diet to block this measure.[176] Some years later Antonius Andreoscha appealed to the Zurich divines, in the name of their common faith, to come to the aid of the embattled Valtellinese churches:

> We want to inform you of the danger that faces the Reformed churches of the Valtellina because of storms whipped up by Spanish sympathizers in our own Rhaetia, for two reasons: first, so that you may include us in your pious prayers; secondly, so that both publicly and privately you may urge your most worthy magistrate to provide us with help and advice in all things, given that we are all members of the body of Christ, and in the same boat.[177]

Andreoscha's reference to Spanish sympathizers ('hispanizantes') is

---

together with the responses of Mei, Calandrini and Gaffori (StAZ E II 382, 1120r–1273r). See StAZ E II 365, 207r–61r for another copy of Calandrini's contribution. Further material generated by the Tirano disputation is to be found in StAZ E II 449.

[175] See Mei to Stucki, 3 March 1603 (StAZ E II 385, 75).

[176] ZB Ms S 147, 84. Calandrini would have preferred to see the religion of the subject lands determined by the (Protestant) majority of the ruling Bündner communes, following the precedent set by the Swiss Confederation in its dealings with its own subject territories. Earlier Ulrich Campell had expressed similar views on behalf of the Rhaetian synod (see AERSG B 3, pp. 27–35; R. Head, 'Rhaetian Ministers, from Shepherds to Citizens: Calvinism and Democracy in the Republic of the Three Leagues 1550–1620', in W.F. Graham, *Later Calvinism: International Perspectives* (Kirksville, Mo., 1994), pp. 55–69 [62–3]).

[177] StAZ E II 381, 1791r: 'Quanto in periculo versantur Ecclesiae reformatae in Vulturena propter turbulentias excitatas ab Hispanizantibus in Rhetia nostra, vobis indicare volumus: idque propter duas praesertim causas; prima est, ut nostri memores esse dignemini in vestris piis precibus, altera ut publice et privatim amplissimum vestrum Magistratum admoneatis ut nobis in omnibus et auxilio, et consilio esse velit, cum simus omnes membra corporis Christi, et in eadem navi' (letter dated 8 April 1607). In a letter to the Zurich ministers and professors of 15 June, the churches of the Ten Jurisdictions lent their support to Andreoscha's analysis, arguing that Protestantism in Graubünden, 'sonderlich der welschen kilchen in den grentzen Italiens', was under severe threat (StAZ A 248.6).

significant: by 1600, the Protestant cause in the Rhaetian subject lands had become bound up with the broader factional struggle in Graubünden between proponents of an alliance with Spain and those whose loyalities lay with either France or, more especially, Venice.[178] Reformed ministers based in the subject lands were among the most uncompromising opponents of a Spanish alliance, which they regarded as a Trojan horse for the recatholicization of Graubünden. That concern is reflected in their correspondence with the Zurich churchmen. In a letter to Stucki dated 30 March 1596, for example, Lentolo reported that although many of the leading men of the republic inclined towards accepting Spain's overtures out of greed (the corruptibility of the Rhaetian aristocracy was notorious), others were prepared to resist them for the sake of piety and freedom; Lentolo expressed himself confident that the patriotic faction would carry the day.[179] In November 1600, Martinengo informed Stucki that Spain was attempting to secure the Rhaetian Leagues' consent to an alliance by underhand means: 'it does not put its request to the communes openly – for fear of refusal, I believe – but deals only with the principal and leading men.'[180] With the letter Martinengo enclosed two drafts of the terms proposed by the Spanish. Later he also provided Stucki with reports on the construction of a fortress at the approaches to the Valtellina by the Count of Fuentes, governor of Milan.[181] Relations with Spain were an equally pressing concern for Ottaviano Mei, who in 1604 sent Stucki a copy of an oration he had delivered to an assembly of Rhaetian officials the previous year, advising them to reject a new offer of a treaty from Fuentes.[182] It was with some regret that, in January 1613, Mei informed Waser of the Diet's decision not to renew the alliance that it had concluded with Venice ten years earlier.[183]

The second half of the 1610s was characterized by an intensification of confessional and factional conflict within the Rhaetian Freestate,

---

[178] On the unstable political situation in the Freestate during this period, see Head, *Grisons*, pp. 168–98; Pfister, *Jenatsch*, pp. 36–52.

[179] StAZ E II 380, 341–2.

[180] Ibid., 438–9: 'Il Re di Spagna per mezo d'un Capitano Gabriele cerca lega con li signori nostri Grigioni; ma non la dimanda apertamente alle Comunità, credo per timore di ripulsa, ma solamente la prattica con li principali, et primati.'

[181] See Martinengo's letters of 11 October 1604 (ibid., 508–9) and 28 February 1605 (ibid., 516).

[182] StAZ E II 385, 71. Compare Mei to Stucki, 22 September 1604 and 25 April 1605 (ibid., 98; 108a)

[183] ZB Ms. S 164, 10. Waser was kept informed of the negotiations surrounding the possible renewal of this alliance by Giovanni Battista Calandrini (ZB Ms. S 162, 154.7; 154.11).

which at times threatened to descend into outright civil war. Tensions were stoked by the arrival on the scene of a new generation of Reformed ministers bent on eliminating 'hispanizantes' from the Rhaetian body politic. This faction – which included a number of ministers attached to churches in the subject lands – made no secret of its desire to complete the stalled Reformation of the Valtellina. The revival of the Sondrio school project was the prelude to a renewed proselytizing offensive in the region, spearheaded by Jörg Jenatsch and Blasius Alexander, ministers in Berbenno and Traona respectively, and supported by Caspar Alexius. The approach adopted by Jenatsch and Alexander was openly confrontational. In Boalzo, for example, they encouraged Protestants to demand a share in parish revenues and use of the local church, to the fury of the Catholic inhabitants.[184] More dramatically, they masterminded the abduction from Sondrio of Niccolò Rusca, the spiritual leader of Valtellinese Catholicism, who was afterwards sentenced to death by a *Strafgericht* in Thusis (September 1618).[185] In this fervid atmosphere, some Rhaetian Protestants began to dream of reviving the spent evangelical movement in Italy proper: one reason they gave for wanting Caspar Alexius to head the proposed school in Sondrio was that Alexius' writings and preaching would help to spread 'the seed of the teaching of the son of God even in Italy, where Jesus Christ is profaned with idolatry, by giving a spiritual refuge to those who continually leave behind the darkness of the papacy.'[186]

The anti-Spanish fervour of the Bündner ministers was shared by Kaspar Waser, who in a letter to Johann Peter Danz dated 20 May 1617 welcomed the Rhaetian Diet's recent rejection of yet another offer of a pact with Milan and urged continued opposition to the intrigues of the 'hispanizantes'.[187] Two years earlier, Waser had been instrumental in persuading the Zurich council to enter into a three-cornered alliance with Berne and Venice. Whereas other Zurich ministers, including the *Antistes* Breitinger, opposed entry into any agreement with a Catholic state on confessional grounds, Waser adopted a position more akin to that of his Rhaetian correspondents: like them, he saw the Venetian alliance as the vehicle for a renewed attempt to establish Protestantism in Italy.[188]

---

[184] Pfister, *Jenatsch*, pp. 79–80; Wendland, *Pässe*, p. 104.

[185] Ibid., pp. 68–70. One of the reasons given for Rusca's condemnation was his alleged involvement in earlier attempts to kidnap Scipione Calandrini.

[186] The church of Sondrio to the Genevan company of pastors, 8 June 1617 (Baserga, 'Il Movimento', p. 124).

[187] Waser to Danz, 20 May 1617 (ZB Ms. S 166, 57).

[188] In a letter written following the establishment of the alliance, Waser declared: 'Dieu la veille prosperer, qu'elle regarde un jour aussi bien le fait de la religion, come l'estat. Car

But the politicization of the Rhaetian Reformed clergy was to have disastrous consequences for the Protestants of the subject lands. Instead of hastening the triumph of the Reformation in the Valtellina, the activities of Alexius, Jenatsch and others elicited the sort of Catholic backlash that the Bündner authorities in the region had long feared.

In the early hours of 19 July 1620 a carefully planned uprising, led by members of the Valtellinese Catholic aristocracy and supported by Spain, took place in Tirano.[189] The rebels' chief target was the local Reformed minority, around 60 of whose members were killed. From Tirano, the revolt spread to Teglio, whose Reformed community was surprised at worship and massacred, and Sondrio, where a sizeable number of Protestants – led by Alexius and Jenatsch – put up fierce resistance and were able to negotiate safe passage to the Upper Engadine. The casualty toll was lower in the western half of the Valtellina, as most of the Reformed population had fled by the time the rebels arrived in the area. For the time being Chiavenna was spared attack, but in 1621 Spanish forces occupied the town and suppressed Reformed worship there. Over the next decade or so of 'Bündner Wirren', Protestantism also came under severe pressure in the Valbregaglia and Poschiavo.

After the dust had settled, the Zurichers resumed their correspondence with ministers serving those Italian-speaking Reformed communities that survived (largely in the Valbregaglia), but following the disappearance of so many congregations the relationship was never able to recapture its former intensity. Of greater significance was the role played by Zurich in co-ordinating assistance to refugees from the 'sacro macello', around 250 of whom were received in the city. Two collections were taken up in Zurich's churches on their behalf, and a relief fund was set up which continued to operate for years to come.[190] Given that he had lost a number of close personal friends and correspondents in the violence,[191] it was to be expected that Kaspar Waser should take a special interest in the fate of the Valtellinese exiles, many of whom wrote to him

---

le te[m]ps n'est pas encor d'en parler à ceste heure' (H. Gmür, *Das Bündnis zwischen Zürich / Bern und Venedig 1615/18* (Zurich, 1945), p. 121).

[189] For a full discussion of the uprising, see Wendland, *Pässe*, pp. 105–16.

[190] The first collection (on 20 August 1620) raised 1620 lb 21 s 4 h; the second (on 1 January 1621) raised 2225 lb 20 s (StAZ E II 279, 133–4). Money was also contributed by Berne (StAZ A 248.11), Schaffhausen (ibid.), the Dutch and Italian stranger churches in London (ibid.), and the churches of Middelburg, Amsterdam and Emden (StAZ E II 279, 2ʳ).

[191] Among the victims of the 'sacro macello' were the former Zurich students Samuel Andreoscha (minister in Mello), Johann Peter Danz, Josua Gatti and Azzo Guicciardi; Guicciardi's tutor Pietro Pozzi; and Cesare Paravicini, a nephew of Ulisse Martinengo.

personally or were commended to him by Bündner ministers.[192] Waser's biographer Kvosen also credits him with authorship of the best-known account of the events of July 1620, entitled *Außführliche / umbstendtliche und warhaffte Beschreibung deß grausamen und unmenschlichen Mordts / so in dem land Veltlyn / ... ist geübt worden.*[193] In the tradition of Reformed martyrography, the *Beschreibung* is packed with edifying tales of heroism and steadfastness: among several noteworthy examples are the stories of Paula Baretta, who resisted demands to invoke the mother of God and the saints while continuing to confess the orthodox Zwinglian doctrine of Mary's perpetual virginity; and of Waser's former student Giovan Abondio Nova, whose recovery of faith and martyrdom after a temporary lapse are compared to the fate of the apostle Peter.[194] When Waser himself died in September 1625, his funeral was attended by a considerable number of exiles who, according to Kvosen, saw themselves as 'having lost a protector, or rather a father' ('se patrono, imo patre orbatos esse').[195] These sentiments were echoed in sonnets by the minister to the newly established Italian congregation in Zurich, Vincenzo Paravicino, who praised Waser for his 'learned piety' ('dotta pietà') and 'pious love' ('amor pio'), and berated death for depriving the refugees of their surest support.[196]

During the half-century between the Rhaetian anti-heresy edict of June 1570 and the 'sacro macello', the relationship between the Zurich church and the Italian Reformed entered a new phase. The doctrinal conflicts of earlier years receded into the background, to be replaced by close co-operation between the Zurich divines and an Italian pastorate eager to affirm its orthodox credentials. The Italian churches of

---

192 StAZ A 248.11. See, for example, the letter from Jakob Ramp, pastor in Poschiavo, on behalf of Michael Montius of Brusio. Montius, a former minister of Traona whose son had been killed in the 'sacro macello', is praised as an energetic defender of the Protestant cause in the Valtellina.

193 Kvosen, *De vita*, p. 19. The work, which also exists in an Italian version, is sometimes attributed to Vincenzo Paravicini.

194 *Beschreibung*, pp. 42–5; 24–5. In June 1616, Waser had asked his son Josias to commend Nova and Vincenzo Paravicini to the teaching staff at Heidelberg, where they planned to continue their studies (ZB Ms. B 42, 35r).

195 Kvosen, *De vita*, p. 26.

196 Ibid., p. 58. Italian-language worship was reinstituted in Zurich in August 1620 (see the exiles' petition in StAZ E II 384, 572). Like the Locarnesi before them, the Valtellinese refugees encountered considerable hostility from native Zurichers, who decried them as 'Wälsche Bättelvögl' (StAZ 279, 125). In July 1625 the Zurich council ordered all able-bodied refugees to return home; most eventually settled in southern Germany (Schultheß, 'Glaubensflüchtlinge', p. 3).

Graubünden were less directly under Zurich's sway than those of eastern Switzerland (for example, in the Thurgau and Appenzell Ausserrhoden), and the Zurichers were unable to prevent the majority of them falling victim to the confessional politics of the 30 Years War.[197] However, in the late 16th and early 17th centuries the Zurich church did more than any other to connect these embattled congregations with the culture of Reformed Europe, providing them with a point of entry to social networks that spanned the continent. A relationship which began as an amicable correspondence between ministers gradually took on a wider significance, as the exchanges between well-to-do families in Zurich and the subject lands demonstrate. Given the extent of those contacts, it is worth considering whether Zurich after Bullinger has been too easily dismissed as a second-rank Reformed centre, with little to contribute either theologically or politically to the development of European Protestantism. For the Italian correspondents of Stucki and Waser, in particular, the Zurich church remained an important player on the international stage.

---

[197] Zurich did, however, contribute forces to a failed attempt by the Rhaetian Freestate to reconquer the Valtellina in August–September 1620 (Pfister, *Jenatsch*, pp. 98–9).

Conclusion

When the first Italian evangelical exiles arrived in Switzerland around 1540, a new area of international involvement opened up for the Zurich church. However, hopes of establishing a mutually beneficial relationship were soon compromised by theological differences – differences that became more apparent in the light of attempts by the Reformed leadership to consolidate and systematize Zwinglian doctrine. A series of controversies ensued, during which the Zurich church was forced to revise its estimation of the Italian evangelicals and to spell out its understanding of orthodoxy with unprecedented clarity. But throughout this difficult period the Zurichers maintained their association with the Italian Reformed, forming alliances with exiles, such as Scipione Lentolo, who shared their opposition to 'heresy'. After 1572, those alliances provided the basis for improved relations between the Zurich church and Italian-speaking congregations in Graubünden. Although circumscribed by a city council suspicious of foreign entanglements, Bullinger and his successors remained committed to the international Protestant cause. Their relationship with the Italian exiles, both 'orthodox' and 'heretical', and with other Italian-speaking converts to the Reformation, bears witness to that engagement.

The middle decades of the 16th century saw a steady exodus of evangelical sympathizers from the Italian cities to Geneva, the Rhaetian Freestate and parts of the Swiss Confederation. Although this emigration was on a far smaller scale than the mass movements of religious refugees from France and the Netherlands which took place around the same time, its impact was considerable. The Italian exiles and their descendants brought with them new skills – in trade, in finance and in manufacture – and an intellectual vigour born out of the late Italian Renaissance. As John Tedeschi and others have demonstrated, they played a key role in transmitting the works of Machiavelli, Guicciardini, Pietro Bembo and others to a northern European readership.[1]

Because of its position of leadership among the Swiss Reformed, its strong traditions of biblical and humanist scholarship (centred on the

---

[1] J. Tedeschi, 'The Cultural Contributions of Italian Protestant Reformers in the Late Renaissance', *Schifanoia*, 1 (1986), 127–51.

Lectorium) and, above all, the personality of Heinrich Bullinger, the Zurich church held a special attraction for the Italian exiles. During the 1540s and early 1550s, their most prominent representatives came to feature among the correspondents of Bullinger and other senior Zurich churchmen (Rudolf Gwalther, Konrad Pellikan and Konrad Gesner). The welfare of the exiles – and, by extension, the cause of the Gospel in Italy – became part of the international remit of the Zurich church.

Compared with the missionary efforts sponsored by Geneva in France and the Waldensian valleys, Zurich's support for its Italian co-religionists might seem modest: distance, the linguistic barrier, and the experience of the Second Kappel War – which the Zurich council was determined not to see repeated – restricted Bullinger's ability to promote the Reformation in the Italian-speaking regions on the fringes of the Swiss Confederation. But through its contacts with evangelical sympathizers in those territories and with exiles who had settled there (such as Vergerio, Negri and Mainardi), the Zurich church was able to ensure that the Reformed faith gained a foothold in Italian Graubünden and in Locarno. Although the support of Bullinger and his colleagues proved insufficient to protect the Reformed minority in Locarno against a concerted campaign by the Catholic Swiss states to enforce the terms of Kappel, it was enough to ensure that the Zurich council resisted pressure from the *Fünf Orte* to co-operate in that community's suppression. On Bullinger's recommendation, the Locarnese exiles were also permitted to form a semi-autonomous Italian-speaking congregation in Zurich.

Even with the backing of the Zurich church leadership, the Italian exiles experienced difficulties in adapting to their new circumstances. In Zurich, the Locarnesi had to confront not only poverty and culturally unfamiliar surroundings, but a conservative guild establishment jealous of its monopoly control of the city's economic life, a xenophobic population, and a council keen to see them move on elsewhere as soon as possible. The Italian exiles as a whole had to adjust their (often highly idealized) perceptions of the Reformed churches to match the reality they encountered north of the Alps. Differences of approach between the leaderships of the host churches and a minority of more radical exiles (Cantimori's 'heretics') quickly manifested themselves. Arguments over specific questions of doctrine – the interpretation of the sacraments, the Trinity, and the relationship between justification and sanctification – were symptomatic of a more basic disagreement about the scope, nature and objectives of religious reform. Such dissent was not a phenomenon unique to the Italian exiles: the French and, especially, the Dutch stranger churches of London also contained a heterodox element. But 'heresy' was proportionately more common among the Italian exiles because of the peculiarly ill-defined and doctrinally eclectic character of the Italian evangelical movement through which most of them had first encountered Protestantism. It is hardly surprising that when the products of that movement came face to face with the confessional systems that were evolving north of the Alps, conflict was the result.

Bullinger was a leading representative of one such system. Besides the Protestant shibboleths of *sola fide* and *sola scriptura*, his theology was predicated on the notion of catholicity: a commitment to the historical tradition of the western church, as embodied in the writings of the Fathers and the credal statements of the earliest councils. Bullinger's emphasis on catholicity was a crucial plank in the Zurich church's campaign to distance itself from sectarian Anabaptism and to legitimize the Reformation – often in a literal sense, because by affirming kinship with the Constantinian church the Zurichers were excluding themselves from the definition of heresy enshrined in imperial law. The priorities of the Italian 'heretics' were very different. Seeking a radical break with the papist past, they devised an uncompromising, literalist interpretation of the scripture principle which led them to question doctrines that the Reformed establishment continued to hold sacrosanct: above all, the Trinity and the full divinity of Christ. They thereby threatened to undermine the efforts of Bullinger and others to demonstrate the basic orthodoxy and respectability of the Reformed creed.

Unlike Calvin, who was quick to grasp the seriousness of the challenge embodied in such views and to take steps to suppress them, Bullinger preferred to proceed through dialogue. This difference in approach may be accounted for in part by a difference in temperament between the two reformers, but also by differences between the intellectual and theological traditions of the Genevan and Zurich churches. The Zurich church continued to draw inspiration from Erasmus, as well as Zwingli: the emphasis of its theology was pastoral, rather than dogmatic. By the standards of Geneva, Zurich was slow to develop a systematic theology in some areas. As late as the 1550s, the doctrinal consensus within the church was broad enough to accommodate differences of opinion about some quite significant theological matters (for evidence of this, one need look no further than Bibliander's idiosyncratic views on predestination). Initially, at least, Bullinger appears to have felt that room could also be found for the views of Italian dissidents such as Lelio Sozzini: as 'bishop' of Zurich, his duty was to keep the church as inclusive as possible.

The heretics, for their part, saw in the Zurichers potential allies against the 'rigidity' and 'intolerance' of Geneva: Bullinger's and

Gwalther's opposition to the use of excommunication as a disciplinary sanction was repeatedly invoked by anti-Calvinist Italians.[2] The radicals were also able to cite Zwingli's rejection of the real presence as a precedent for (and the precursor to) their own criticisms of traditional doctrine.[3] As they were aware, the Zwinglian tradition was open to both radical and conservative readings.

During the 1540s, 1550s and 1560s that putative alliance unravelled, as a series of doctrinal controversies revealed to Bullinger the extent of his differences with the radicals, and the misguidedness of his attempts to reach an accommodation with them. Like Calvin and such theologically conservative exiles as Giulio da Milano, Bullinger came to believe that the radicals' activities represented a genuine threat to the integrity of the Reformed churches. He also became convinced that this threat could be effectively countered only by insisting on subscription to detailed and explicit confessions of faith, which even the heretics' notorious rhetorical ingenuity would be unable to circumvent. The danger of settling for anything less was illustrated for Bullinger by Bernardino Ochino's *Dialogi XXX*, which he interpreted as a covert but systematic attack on the fundamentals of Reformed teaching. By the early 1560s, the Zurich church was fully engaged in the defence of orthodoxy (especially trinitarian orthodoxy) against the attempts of dissident exiles to subvert it, and in efforts to impose doctrinal conformity on the region with the largest concentration of Italian Reformed churches: Graubünden and its subject lands.

Bullinger's changing relationship with the Italian radicals offers insights into the evolution of Reformed orthodoxy more generally during this crucial period. In the early 1540s, when the first wave of Italian exiles arrived in Switzerland, Reformed doctrine was still comparatively unsystematized; no single theological tendency had yet achieved dominance, as the struggles between 'Zwinglians' and 'Calvinists' in the Pays de Vaud around this time demonstrate.[4] By 1570, that diversity had become much less pronounced, as an agreed Reformed line emerged on

---

[2] See Chapter 5:iii above.

[3] As late as 1590, Fausto Sozzini argued that his purely memorialist interpretation of the Eucharist was authentically representative of Zwingli's position, which the Zurich church had abandoned under the influence of Bucer and Calvin (*Opera*, I, pp. 423; 433; 701; 770). In the *Disputatio scholastica* of Jacobus Palaeologus, which pits Catholic and orthodox Protestant theologians against the representatives of Italian and eastern European antitrinitarianism, 'Zwingli' is one of the first to be persuaded of the veracity of the radicals' arguments (Firpo, *Antitrinitari*, p. 243).

[4] C.B. Hundeshagen, *Die Conflikte des Zwinglianismus, Lutherthums und Calvinismus in der Bernischen Landeskirche von 1532–1558* (Berne, 1842).

the main doctrinal issues that had once divided Geneva and the Swiss; Bullinger's Second Helvetic Confession may be seen as the culmination of this process. The Italian radicals, who had earlier benefited from the lack of an agreed definition of orthodoxy, found themselves squeezed to the margins and, finally, excluded from the Reformed fold altogether. Advocates of an inclusive, loosely defined Protestantism, such as Aconcio, Ochino and Bartolomeo Silvio, lost out to proponents of a new Reformed confessionalism, epitomized by the Rhaetian anti-heresy edict of June 1570.

In a perceptive recent study, Ben Kaplan has charted the unfolding of a similar process in the Protestant northern Netherlands.[5] In Utrecht, a powerful local faction, derided by their Calvinist opponents as libertines, preached a broad-based evangelical settlement. Like the Italian radicals, the libertines were averse to the imposition of confessions of faith, the concentration of power in the hands of the clergy, and the application of ecclesiastical discipline, in which they detected the seeds of a 'new papacy'.[6] On a doctrinal level, they had reservations about the doctrines of double predestination and imputed justification (like Ochino and some of the Chiavenna radicals who fell foul of Lentolo).[7] In the Reformed churches of both the Netherlands and the Swiss states, confessionalism prevailed after a protracted struggle. However, whereas in Switzerland the upshot of its triumph was religious uniformity, in the Netherlands the Reformed church failed to project its vision of orthodoxy on to society at large, leaving the libertines and their successors free to opt out of formal church membership altogether.

The gradual disappearance of radical elements from within the Italian exile community allowed for the emergence of a new relationship – or perhaps more accurately, a return to the sort of relationship that had originally been envisaged – between the Zurich church and the Italian Reformed. Before 1570, Zurich's commitment to the fragile Italian-speaking Reformed congregations that it had helped establish in the Rhaetian Freestate was undermined by fears that those churches were becoming breeding-grounds for the most pernicious kind of heresy. Once this threat had receded, the Zurichers were able to give more wholehearted support to the efforts of local pastors to consolidate the Protestant presence in the region. The rebuilding of relations may have been facilitated by the emergence of a new generation of Zurich churchmen, such as Johann Wilhelm Stucki and Kaspar Waser, who

---

[5] B. Kaplan, *Calvinists and Libertines: Confession and Community in Utrecht 1578–1620* (Oxford, 1995).

[6] Ibid., p. 27.

[7] Ibid., pp. 88–9.

associated the Italian reformers not with religious radicalism or antitrinitarianism, but with the impeccable orthodoxy of Scipione Lentolo and Scipione Calandrini.

In the decades prior to the 'sacro macello', the Zurich church acted as a bridge between Italian-speaking congregations in Graubünden and the international community of Reformed believers, with which they were only too anxious to engage. Waser's hagiographic account of the massacre, with its litanies of the slaughtered and tributes to individual acts of heroism, confirmed the rehabilitation of Italian-speaking Protestantism – ironically, in the wake of events that had seen it virtually destroyed. From Reformed orthodoxy's most persistent critics, the Italian evangelicals had undergone a remarkable transformation: into some of the faith's most exemplary confessors.

Bibliography

Primary Sources – Manuscript

Staatsarchiv Zürich

A 71.1	Bürgerrecht 1342–1670
A 248.1–248.11	Valtellina
A 350.1	Locarno
A 369.1	Fremde Personen c.1445–1565
A 369.3	Handbuch der Gebrüder Pebbia von Zürich 1595–98
B II	Ratsmanuale
B II 1080	Ratschläge 1553–60
B IV	Ratsmissiven
B V	Ratsurkunden
B VI 259	Rats- und Richtbücher 1561–68
B VI 312–30	Gemächtsbücher 1532–1675
B VI 337–43	Schirmbücher 1553–1615
E I 4	letters of 22 and 24 November 1563
E II 279–449	Antistitialarchiv (correspondence, manuscript tracts etc.)
G II 39.3–39.13	Grossmünsterstift Studentenamtsrechnungen 1552–1622
W 20.72	Familienarchiv von Muralt
YY 1.21	Ehegerichtsprotokoll 1557–58

Zentralbibliothek Zürich

A 12	Kopienband zur Graubündner und Veltliner Geschichte
A 52	Briefband, Kaspar Waser
A 70, no. 48	Schriftstücke betreffend die Vertreibung der evangelischen Locarner 1554
A 132	Johannes Heinrich Waser, *De vita sua*, vol. 1
A 157	*Descritione d'un viaggio da Zurigho a Napoli*
B 31	Daniel Orelli von Gemsberg, *Locarnische Verfolgung*

B 42	Briefband, Johann Heinrich Waser
B 65	Kopienband, Kaspar und Josias Waser
B 80	Kopienband zur schweizerischen Reformationsgeschichte
B 239	*Discorso della vera successione d'Arrigo Quarto*
B 251	Sammelband zur Geschichte und Kirchengeschichte des 16. und 17. Jahrhunderts
C 50a	Sammelband (Briefe von und an Konrad Gesner)
D 75	Sammelband (Fest- und Trauergedichte)
D 157	Miszellaneenband theologischen Inhaltes
D 236	Sammelband theologischen Inhaltes
E 15	Sammlung allerhand Geschichten, Begebenheiten und Merkwürdigkeiten
F 12–35	Johann Jakob Wick, Sammlung von Nachrichten zur Zeitgeschichte
F 36–87	Thesaurus Hottingerianus
F 154	Sammelband
F 172d	Epistolae virorum clarorum ad Dominum Casparum Waserum Theologum
F 182	Sammelband (Bündner Unruhen der Jahre 1571–73)
G 21	Sammelband zur Zürcher Geschichte des 14.–17. Jahrhunderts
J 255	Miscellanea Helvetiae, 1525–1741
J 287	Bernhard Sprüngli, Annalen über zürcherische und eidgenössische Begebenheiten der Jahre 1538–1567
S 1–266	Simlersche Briefsammlung, Kirchengeschichte des 16.–18. Jahrhunderts
Car C.40	Taddeo Duno, *De quadringentinaria Israelitarum peregrinatione in Aegypto tractatus*
Car XV 20	Sammelband (Theologische Schriften)

Stadtarchiv Zürich

III.A.2	Bürgerbuch B der Stadt Zürich 1545–1723
VIII.C.2	Tauf- und Ehenbuch der Kirchgemeinde Grossmünster 1546–1600
VIII.C.15	Tauf-, Ehen- und Totenbuch Fraumünster 1528 bis 1730
VIII.C.19	Taufbuch St Peter 1553–1690
VIII.C.24a	Ehenbuch St Peter 1554–1802
VIII.C.48	Bullingers Totenbuch 1549 bis 1574

Familienarchiv von Orelli (Zurich)

4.300	Akten betr. Bürgerrecht der Familien von Muralt und Pestalozzi 1566–1673
7.3	Briefe, Briefentwürfe, Schuldscheine, Testamente aus dem Besitz verschiedener Glieder der Familie von Orelli 1563–1830
8.2	Protokolle, Briefe, Rechnungen der Kirche der Locarner in Zürich 1555–1600
8.4	Geschäftsbuch des Ludovico Ronco 1571–84
8.7	Sammelband mit Dokumenten zur Geschichte der Locarnischen Verfolgung 1554–1680

Staatsarchiv Graubünden

AB IV 8 a 3	Veltlin: Akten, Urkunden und Missiven 1380–1599
B 143	Ulrich Campell, *De divina Providentia simul atque Praedestinatione fidei confessio*
B 721	*Acta synodalia rhetorum evangelicorum concionatorum 1572–1608* *Breve Ragguaglio dello Stato delle Chiese Evangeliche nel Contado di Chiavenna*
D II a 1	Archiv Salis-Planta Samaden
D II a 3 a	Archiv Salis-Planta Samaden
D II a 3 b	Archiv Salis-Planta Samaden
D II a 3 c	Archiv Salis-Planta Samaden
D II a 5	Archiv Salis-Planta Samaden
D II a 6	Archiv Salis-Planta Samaden
D II a 7	Archiv Salis-Planta Samaden
D II a 111	Archiv Salis-Planta Samaden
D II b 3	Archiv Salis-Planta Samaden
D II c	Archiv Salis-Planta Samaden

Archiv der Evangelisch-Rhätischen Synode Graubündens

B3	Synodal-Protokoll, 1572–1608
B4	Acta synodi 1608–41

Universitätsbibliothek Basel

C VI a 35[1]	correspondence

Fr. Gr. Ms. I, 12	correspondence
Fr. Gr. Ms. I, 13	correspondence
Fr. Gr. Ms. II, 1	correspondence
Fr. Gr. Ms. II, 4	correspondence
Fr. Gr. Ms. II, 5	correspondence
Fr. Gr. Ms. II, 5a	correspondence
Fr. Gr. Ms. II, 18[1]	correspondence
Fr. Gr. Ms. II, 23	correspondence
G[2] I, 3	correspondence
G[2] I, 5	correspondence
G[2] I, 20b	correspondence
G I, 66	correspondence
G II, 4	correspondence
G II, 31[3]	correspondence

Bürgerbibliothek Bern

A 93, 4 — Disputatio inter Camillo Sorrino [sic] et Augustino del battismo et cena sancta

A 93, 7 — Commentarii conventus synodalis convocati mense Iulii 1571 in oppido Chiavenna de excommunicatione Hieronymi Turriani, ecclesiae Pluriensis ministri, Nicolai Camulii et Camilli Sozzini

British Library

Add. Ms. 28568 — Bernardino Ochino, dialogues

Primary Sources – 16th and 17th-Century Printed Works

Adamo, Antonio di, *Annotomia della Messa, la qual scuopre gli enormi errori, et gli infiniti abusi, dal volgo non conosciuti, si della Messa, quanto del Messale ... Con un Sermone della Eucharistia nel fine, il qual dimostra se Christo e corporalmente nel Sacramento, ò non.* (n.p. [Zurich: A. Gesner and R. Wyssenbach?], 1552)

Aretius, Benedikt, *Valentini Gentilis iusto capitis supplicio Bernae affecti brevis historia: et contra eiusdem blasphemias orthodoxa defensio articuli de sancta Trinitate* (Geneva: F. Perrinus, 1567)

Betti, Francesco, *Lettera di Francesco Betti Romano, all'Illustrissimo et*

Eccelentissimo S. Marchese di Pescara suo padrone, ne la quale da conta à sua Eccellenza de la cagione perche licentiato si sia dal suo servigio (n.p., 1557)

Beza, Theodore, *De haereticis a civili Magistratu puniendis Libellus, adversus Martini Bellii farraginem, et novorum Academicorum sectam, Theodoro Beza Vezelio auctore* (Geneva: R. Etienne, 1554)

———— *Valentini Gentilis teterrimi haeretici impietatum ac triplicis perfidiae et periuriae, brevis explicatio, ex actis publicis Senatus Genevensis optima fide descripta* (Geneva: F. Perrinus, 1567)

———— *Tractatio de polygamia, in qua et Ochini apostatae pro polygamia, et Montanistarum ac aliorum adversus repetitas nuptias argumenta refutantur: addita veterum Canonum et quarundam Civilium legum ad normam verbi divini examine* ... (Geneva: J. Crespin, 1568)

Bibliander, Theodor, *De summa trinitate et fide catholica* ... (Basle: J. Oporinus, 1555)

Breitinger, Johann Jakob, *Instruttione fondamentale se una setta duri più ò meno di cent'Anni. Similmente, qual sia l'antica è nuova fede, è dove avanti la Reformatione essa sia statta* ..., trans. Vincenzo Paravicini (n.p. [Zurich], 1622)

Bucer, Martin, *Martini Buceri Scripta Anglicana fere omnia ... a Conrado Huberto ad explicandas sedendasque religionis cum alias, tum praesertim Eucharistias controversias, singulari fide collecta* (Basle: P. Perna, 1577)

Bullinger, Heinrich, *Utriusque in Christo naturae tam divinae quam humanae, contra varias haereses, pro confessione Christi catholica, Assertio orthodoxa* ... (Zurich: C. Froschauer, 1533)

———— *In sacrosanctum Iesu Christi Domini nostri Evangelium secundum Matthaeum, Commentariorum libri XII* ... (Zurich: C. Froschauer, 1542)

———— *De scripturae sanctae authoritate, certitudine, firmitate et absoluta perfectione, deque Episcoporum, qui verbi dei ministri sunt, institutione et functione ... Accessit authoris Responsio ad Ioannis Cochlaei de canonicae scripturae et Catholicae ecclesiae authoritate libellum* ... (Zurich: C. Froschauer, 1544)

———— *Warhaffte Bekanntnuß der dieneren der kilchen zu Zürych / was sy uß Gottes wort / mit der heyligen allgemeinen Christenlichen Kilchen gloubind und leerind / in sonderheit aber von dem Nachtmal unsers herren Jesu Christi* ... (Zurich: C. Froschauer, 1545)

———— *In omnes apostolicas epistolas, divi videlicet Pauli xiii. et vii. canonicas, commentarii* ... (Zurich: C. Froschauer, 1549)

———— *Das die Evangelischen Kilchen weder kätzerische noch*

abtrünnige / sunder gantz rechtglöubige und allgemeine Jesu Christi kilchen syend / grundtliche erwysung ... (Zurich: A. Gesner and R. Wyssenbach, 1552)

—— *Summa Christenlicher Religion. Darinn uß dem wort Gottes / one alles zancken und schälten / richtig und kurtz / anzeigt wirt / was einem yetlichen Christen notwendig sye zů wüssen / zů glouben / zů thůn / und zů lassen / ouch zů lyden / und säligklich abzůsterben* ... (Zurich: C. Froschauer, 1556)

—— *Catechesis pro adultioribus scripta* ... (Zurich: C. Froschauer, 1559)

—— *Der Widertöufferen ursprung / fürgang / Secten / wäsen / fürnemen und gemeine jrer leer Artickel / ouch jre gründ / und warumm sy sich absünderind / unnd ein eigne kirchen anrichtend / mit widerlegung und antwort uff alle und yede jre gründ und artickel* ... (Zurich: C. Froschauer, 1561)

—— *De conciliis* ... (Zurich: C. Froschauer, 1561)

—— *Sermonum Decades quinque, de potissimis Christianae religionis capitibus, in tres tomos digestae* ... (Zurich: C. Froschauer, 1577)

Calandrini, Scipione, *Trattato dell'origine delle heresie et delle schisme, che sono nate, o che possono nascere nella chiesa di Dio, et de rimedii che si devono usare contra di quelle, cio è, della scommunica, et della potestà del magistrato civile* (Poschiavo: C. Landolfi, 1572)

—— *Trattato della chiesa. Nel quale sono dichiarate le principali controversie nate a nostri tempi intorno a questa materia* ... (n.p. [Geneva: J.A and S. De Tournes], 1591)

—— *Confutatione delle calunnie, et delle maledicentie, le quali da gli avversari della verita sogliono esser date alle chiese Evangeliche, et allor Pastori, e Ministri di Dio* (Geneva: n. pub., 1596)

Castellio, Sebastian, *Sebastiani Castellionis Defensio suarum translationum Bibliorum, et maxime Novi foederis* (Basle: J. Oporinus, 1562)

—— *Contra Libellum Calvini in quo ostendere conatur Haereticos jure gladij coercendos esse* ... (n.p. [Amsterdam(?)], 1612)

—— *Sebastiani Castellionis Dialogi IV* (Gouda: C. Tournaeus, 1613)

Corradi, Alfonso, *In Apocalypsim D. Ioan. Apostoli commentarius* ... (Basle: P. Perna, 1560)

Crugotius, Johann Jakob, *Parallela Socino-Muhammedica: Sive luculentissimus Socianismi et Muhammedismi consensus* ... (Heidelberg: A. Walter, 1657)

Curione, Celio Secundo, *Coelii Secundi Curionis Araneus, seu de Providentia Dei libellus vere aureus, cum aliis nonnullis eiusdem Opusculis* ... (Basle: J. Oporinus, 1544)

———— *Coelii Secundi Curionis, pro vera et antiqua Ecclesiae Christi autoritate, in Antonium Florebellum Mutinensem, Oratio* ... (Basle, n.d. [1547?])

———— *Una familiare et paterna institutione della Christiana religione, di M. Celio Secundo Curione, piu copiosa, et piu chiara che la latina del medesimo* ... (Basle: n. pub., n.d. [1551])

———— *Caelii Secundi Curionis selectarum epistolarum Libri duo* (Basle: J. Oporinus, 1553)

———— *Coelii Secundi Curionis de amplitudine beati regni Dei, dialogi sive libri duo* ... (n.p. [Poschiavo: D. Landolfi], 1554])

Della Rovere, Giulio, *Esortatione al martirio, di Giulio da Milano, riveduta, et ampliata* ... (n.p. [Poschiavo: D. Landolfi], 1552)

Duno, Taddeo, *In laudem ornatissimi praesulis, viri praetorii doctissimi, Ioachym Beldi Glaronensis* ἐγκώμιον (Basle: n. pub., 1555)

———— *Muliebrium morborum omnis generis Remedia* (Strasbourg: J. Rihelius, 1565)

———— *Thaddaei Duni Locarnensis medici, epistolae medicinales locis multis auctae* ... (Zurich: J. Wolf, 1592)

———— *Thaddaei Duni Locarnensis, medicinae doctoris et Christi exulis: de peregrinatione filiorum Israel in Aegypto, Tractatus chronologicus* ... (Zurich: J. Wolf, 1595)

———— *Thaddaei Duno Locarnensis medicinae doctoris et Christi exulis: Ad graves calumnias et sophisticas disceptationes, Danielis Angelocratoris Corbachiensis, de tempore peregrinationis Israelitarum in Aegypto, Responsum Apologeticum* (Zurich: n. pub., 1603)

Epistolae duae, ad ecclesias Polonicas, Iesu Christi Evangelium amplexas, scriptae a Tigurinae ecclesiae ministris, de negotio Stancariano, et mediatore dei et hominum Iesu Christo, an hic secundum humanam naturam duntaxat, an secundum utranque mediator sit (Zurich: C. Froschauer, 1561)

Florio, Michelangelo, *Apologia di M. Michelagnolo Fiorentino ne la quale si tratta de la vera e falsa chiesa* (Camogask: G. Catani, 1557)

Francisci Spierae, qui quod susceptam semel Evangelicae veritatis professionem abnegasset, damnassetque, in horrendam incidit desperationem, historia ... (Basle: n. pub. [J. Oporinus?], 1550)

Gaffori, Cesare, Scipione Calandrini and Ottaviano Mei, *Disputationis Tiranensis inter pontificios et ministros verbi Dei in Rhaetia, anno 1595, et 1596 habitu partes IV* (Basle: K. Waldkirch, 1602)

Gesner, Konrad, *Bibliotheca universalis, sive Catalogus omnium scriptorum locupletissimus, in tribus linguis, Latina, Graeca, et Hebraica* ... (Zurich: C. Froschauer, 1545)

Gwalther, Rudolf, *Rudolfi Gualtheri Tigurini ad Catholicam Ecclesiam omnemque fidelium posteritatem, pro D. Huld. Zuinglio et Operum eius aeditione Apologia* (Zurich: C. Froschauer, 1545)

—— *L'Antichristo di M. Ridolfo Gualtero, ministro della Chiesa Tigurina* ..., trans. Giacomo Susio (n.p. [Basle: J. Oporinus], n.d. [1550])

—— *Die Menschwerdung deß waarenn ewigen und eingebornen Suns Gottes / unsers Herren Jesu Christi erklärt und ußgelegt in sechs predigen / diser zyt wider allerley Secten nutzlich zů läsen: durch Růdolffen Walther diener der kirchen Zürych* (Zurich: C. Froschauer, 1571)

[Hosius, Stanislas], *Catholici cuiusdam et orthodoxi iudicium et censura, de iudicio et censura ministrorum Tygurinorum et Heydelbergensium, de dogmate contra adorandam Trinitatem in Polonia nuper sparso* (Cologne: M. Cholinus, 1565)

Hottinger, Johannes Heinrich, *Historiae ecclesiasticae novi Testamenti*, 9 vols (Zurich: Schaufenberg, 1667)

Il nuovo ed eterno testamento di Giesu Christo. Nuovamente da l'original fonte Greca, con ogni diligenza in Toscano tradotto. Per Massimo Theofilo Fiorentino (Lyon: [J. Frellon], 1551)

Kvosen, Jodocus, *De vita et obitu reverendi et clarissimi viri, domini Caspari Waseri* ... (Basle: J. Schroeder, 1626)

Lavater, Ludwig, *Historia de origine et progressu Controversiae Sacramentariae de Coena Domini, ab anno nativitatis Christi M.D. XXIIII usque ad annum M.D. LXIII deducta* ... (Zurich: C. Froschauer, 1563)

—— *Vom läben und tod deß Eerwirdigen und Hochgeleerten Herrn / Heinrychen Bullingers / dieners der Kyrchen zu Zürych / kurtze einfalte und warhaffte erzellung* ... (Zurich: C. Froschauer, 1576)

Lening, Johannes, *Dialogus / das ist ein freundtlich Gesprech zweyer personen / Da von / Ob es Göttlichem / Natürlichem / Keyserlichem und Geystlichem Rechte gemesse oder entgegen sei / mehr dann eyn Eeweib zugleich zuhaben. Unnd wo yemant zu diser zeit solchs fürnehme ob er als eyn unchrist zuverwerffen unnd zuverdammen sei oder nit* (n.p., 1541)

Lentolo, Scipione, *Responsio orthodoxa pro edicto illustrissimorum D.D. trium foederum Rhaetiae, adversus haereticos et alios Ecclesiarum Rhaeticarum perturbatores promulgata: in qua de Magistratus auctoritate et officio in coërcendis haereticis ex Dei verbo disputatur* (Geneva: J. le Preux, 1592)

Mainardi, Agostino, *Trattato dell'unica, et perfetta satisfattione di Christo, nel qual si dichiara, et manifestamente per la parola di Dio si pruova, che sol Christo ha satisfatto per gli peccati del mondo, ne quanto à Dio cè altra satisfattione che la sua, o sia per la colpa, o sia per la pena, composto per M. Agostino Mainardo Piamontese* (n.p. [Zurich: A. Gesner and R. Wyssenbach], 1551)

———— *Una pia et utile sermone della gratia di Dio, contra li meriti humani* (published with the above text)

Negri, Francesco, *In dominicam precationem Meditatiuncula, per Franciscum Nigrum Bassianatem* ... (Zurich: C. Froschauer, n.d. [1560?])

———— *Della tragedia di M. Francesco Negro Bassanese, intitolata libero arbitrio, Editione seconda, Con accrescimento* (n.p. [Basle: J. Oporinus], 1550 [1551])

———— *De Fanini Faventini, ac Dominici Bassanensis morte, Qui nuper ob Christum in Italia Rom. Pon. iussu impie occisi sunt, Brevis Historia* ... (n.p. [Poschiavo: D. Landolfi], 1550)

Ochino, Bernardino, *Bernhardini Ochini Senensis expositio Epistolae divi Pauli ad Romanos, de Italico in latinum translata* (Augsburg: P. Ulhart, 1545)

———— *Espositione di Messer Bernardino Ochino sopra la Epistola di Paulo à i Galati* (n.p., 1546)

———— *La seconda parte delle Prediche, di Meß Bernardino Ochino Senese, accuratamente castigate* ... (n.p. [Basle: M. Isengrin], n.d.)

———— *La terza parte delle Prediche di M. Bernardino Occhino, non mai piu stampate, nella quale si tratta, della Fede, Speranza et Carità* ... (n.p. [Basle: M. Isengrin], n.d.)

———— *La quarta parte delle Prediche di M. Bernardino Occhino* ... (n.p. [Basle: M. Isengrin], n.d.)

———— *Dialogo del Purgatorio di Messer Bernardino Occhino di Siena, Pastore della Chiesa de Locarnesi, in Zuricho* ... (n.p. [Zurich: A. Gesner and H.J. Gesner], 1556)

———— *Bernardini Ochini senensis viri doctissimi, De Purgatorio dialogus* (Zurich: [A. Gesner and H.J. Gesner], n.d [1556])

———— *Syncerae et verae doctrinae de Coena Domini defensio, per Bernardinum Ochinum Locarnensium Ecclesiae Pastorem: contra Libros tres Ioachim VVestphali, Hamburgensis Ecclesiae praedicatoris* (Zurich: [A. Gesner and H.J. Gesner], 1556)

———— *Prediche di M. Bernardino Ochino Senese, nomate Laberinti del libero, o ver servo Arbitrio, Prescienza, Predestinatione, et Libertà divina, et del modo per uscirne* ... (Basle: P. Perna, n.d. [1560])

———— *Il catechismo, o vero institutione christiana di M. Bernardino Ochino da Siena, in forma di Dialogo. Interlocutori, il Ministro, et Illuminato* ... (Basle: [P. Perna], 1561)

—— *Disputa di M. Bernardino Ochino da Siena intorno alla presenza del corpo di Giesu Christo nel Sacramento della Cena. Non mai per l'adietro stampata* (Basle: [P. Perna], 1561)

—— *La quinta parte delle Prediche di M. Bernardino Ochino, non mai prima stampate* ... (Basle: [P. Perna?], 1562)

—— *Bernardini Ochini Senensis Dialogi XXX. In duos libros divisi, quorum primus est de Messia, continetque dialogos xvii. Secundus est, cum de rebus variis, tum potissimum de Trinitate* ... (Basle: P. Perna, 1563)

[Paravicini, Vincenzo], *Vera narratione del massacro degli evangelici fatto da' papisti rebelli nella maggior parte della Valtellina, nell'anno M.DC.XX addì ix. Luglio, e giorni seguenti, stilo vecchio* (n.p. [Zurich?], 1621)

Servetus, Michael, *De Trinitatis erroribus libri septem* (n.p. [Hagenau: J. Secerius], 1531)

[Servetus, Michael], *Christianismi restitutio* (n.p. [Vienne: B. Arnoullet and G. Geroult], 1553)

Silvio, Bartolomeo, *De eucharistia tractatulus D. Barptolomaei Sylvii Cremonensis, Verbi Dei apud D. Rhaetos concionatoris* (n.p., 1551)

Simler, Josias, *Responsio ad maledicum Francisci Stancari Mantuani librum adversus Tigurinae ecclesiae ministros, de Trinitate et Mediatore nostro Iesu Christo* ... (Zurich: C. Froschauer, 1563)

—— *Oratio de vita et obitu viri optimi, praestantissimi Theologi D. Petri Martyris Vermilii, Sacrarum literarum in Schola Tigurina Professoris* (Zurich: C. Froschauer, 1563)

—— *Vita clarissimi philosophi et medici excellentissimi Conradi Gesneri Tigurini* ... (Zurich: C. Froschauer, 1566)

—— *De aeterno Dei filio domino et servatore nostro Iesu Christo, et de Spiritu sancto, adversus veteres et novos Antitrinitarios, id est Arianos, Tritheitas, Samosatenianos, et Pneumatomachos, libri quatuor* (Zurich: C. Froschauer, 1568)

—— *Scripta veterum latina, de una persona et duabus naturis Domini et Servatoris nostri Iesu Christi, adversus Nestorium, Eutychen et Accephalos olim aedita* (Zurich: C. Froschauer, 1571)

—— *Bibliotheca instituta et collecta primum a Conrado Gesnero. Deinde in Epitomen redacta et novorum librorum accessione locupletata, imo vero postremo recognita, et in duplicem post priores editiones aucta, per Iosiam Simlerum Tigurinum* (Zurich: C. Froschauer, 1574)

—— *Narratio de ortu, vita, et obitu reverendi viri D. Henrici Bullingeri, Tigurinae Ecclesiae pastoris* ... (Zurich: C. Froschauer, 1575)

―――― *Assertio orthodoxae doctrinae de duabus naturis Christi Servatoris nostri, opposita blasphemiis et sophismatibus Simonis Budnaei nuper ab ipso in Lituania evulgatis* ... (Zurich: C. Froschauer, 1575)

―――― *Iosiae Simleri Tigurini de Helvetiorum Republica, Pagis, Foederatis, Stipendiariis, Oppidis, Praefecturis, Foederibus tum domesticis, eorumque origine ac legibus, tum externis, Pagorumque singulorum privata Reipublicae ratione, libri duo* (Paris: J. du Puys, 1577)

―――― *Exodus. In Exodum vel secundum librum Mosis, Iosiae Simleri Professoris Divinarum literarum in Schola Tigurina Commentarii* ... (Zurich: C. Froschauer, 1584)

Sozzini, Fausto, *Fausti Socini Senensis opera omnia in Duos Tomos distincta* (Amsterdam: n. pub., 1656)

Stancaro, Francesco, *Ispositione de la Epistola canonica di S. Giacobo Vescovo di Gierusaleme, pia, dotta et diligente: ornata de molti luoghi comuni a utilita grande de la chiesa catholica, et massime de presenti tempi* ... (Basle: n. pub., 1547)

―――― *Explanatio divi Iacobi, et Conciliationes quorundam locorum Scripturae* ..., trans. Taddeo Duno (Basle: J. Parcus, 1547)

―――― *Opera nuova di Francesco Stancaro Mantoano della Riformatione, si della dottrina Christiana, come della vera intelligentia de i sacramenti* ... (Basle: n. pub., 1547)

―――― *Franciscus Stancarus Mantuanus de Trinitate et Mediatore Domino nostro Iesu Christo, adversus Henricum Bullingerum, Petrum Martyrem, et Ioannem Calvinum, et reliquos Tigurinae ac Genevensis ecclesiae Ministros, ecclesiae Dei perturbatores* (Cracow: Scharfenberg, 1562)

Stucki, Johann Wilhelm, *Vita clarissimi viri D. Iosiae Simleri Tigurini, S. Theologiae in schola Tigurina Professoris fidelissimi* ... (Zurich: C. Froschauer, 1577)

Vera relatione della vittoria et libertà ottenuta da Cattolici, contro gli Heretici, nella Valtellina. ... (Pavia, Cremona and Bologna: Moscatelli, 1620)

Vergerio, Pier Paolo, *Del battesmo et de fiumi che nascono ne paesi de signori Grisoni* (n.p. n.d.)

―――― *Epistola del Vergerio, nella quale sono descritte molte cose della Città, e della Chiesa di Geneva* (Geneva: C. Badius, 1550)

Vermigli, Pietro Martire, *Loci communes D. Petri Martyris Vermilii, Florentini, sacrarum literarum in schola Tigurina Professoris* ... (London: T. Vautrollerius, 1583)

―――― *In Samuelis prophetae libros duos D.D. Petri Martyris Vermilii*

Florentini, S. Theologiae in Schola Tigurina professoris, Commentarii doctissimi ... (Zurich: J. Wolf, 1595)

Waser, Kaspar, *De vita et obitu Reverendi, nobilis et clarissimi Viri Domini Ioh. Guilielmi Stuckii, sacrarum litterarum professoris in Schola Tigurina, Oratio historica, habita publice et edita a Casparo Wasero, Tigurino* (Zurich: J. Wolf, 1608)

[————], *Außführliche / umbstendliche und warhaffte Beschreibung deß grausamen und unmenschlichen Mordts / so in dem land Veltlyn gemeinen dreyen Pündten gehörig / Anno M. DC. XX den IX. Jul. unnd folgende tag / alten Calenders / an den Evangelischen einwohneren daselbst / durch etlich verzweifelte Bößwicht / Rebellen und Banditen / gantz barbarischer weise ist geübt worden* (Zurich: J.R. Wolf, 1620)

Zanchi, Girolamo, *Clarissimi viri D. Hie. Zanchii omnium operum theologicorum Tomi octo* (Geneva: S. Crespin, 1619)

Primary Sources Published Post-1700

Aconcio, Giacomo, *Stratagematum Satanae libri VIII*, ed. Giorgio Radetti (Florence: Vallecchi Editore, 1946)

———— *De Methodo e opuscoli religiosi e filosofici*, ed. Giorgio Radetti (Florence: Vallecchi Editore, 1944)

Arbentz, Emil and Hermann Wartmann (eds) *Die Vadianische Briefsammlung der Stadtbibliothek St Gallen*, 7 vols (St Gallen: Huber, 1890–1913)

Beza, Theodore, *Correspondance de Théodore de Bèze*, ed. Fernand Aubert et al. (Geneva: Librairie E. Droz, 1960–)

Boersma, Owe, and Auke Jelsma (eds), *Unity in Multiformity: The minutes of the coetus of London, 1575 and the consistory minutes of the Italian Church in London, 1570–1591* (London and Amsterdam: Huguenot Society and Editions de la Bibliothèque Wallonne, 1997)

Bullinger, Heinrich, *The Decades of Henry Bullinger, Minister of the Church of Zurich*, ed. T. Harding, 4 vols (Cambridge: Cambridge University Press, 1849–52)

———— 'Confessio et expositio simplex orthodoxae fidei', in Wilhelm Niesel (ed.), *Bekenntnisschriften und Kirchenordnungen der nach Gottes Wort reformierten Kirche* (Zurich: Theologische Buchhandlung, 1985), pp. 219–75

———— *Heinrich Bullinger Briefwechsel*, ed. Ulrich Gäbler et al. (Zurich: Theologischer Verlag, 1973–)

Burlamacchi, Vincenzo, *Libro di ricordi degnissimi delle nostre famiglie,*

ed. Simonetta Adorni-Braccesi (Rome: Istituto storico italiano per
    l'età moderna e contemporanea, 1993)
Calendar of State Papers, Foreign, 23 vols (London: HMSO,
    1863–1950)
Calvin, John, *Ioannis Calvini opera quae supersunt omnia*, ed. Wilhelm
    Baum, Eduard Cunitz, Eduard Reuss et al., 59 vols (*Corpus
    Reformatorum*, vols XXIX–LXXXVII) (Braunschweig: Schwetschke,
    1863–1900)
——— *Institutes of the Christian Religion*, ed. John T. McNeill, 2 vols
    (Philadelphia: The Westminster Press, 1960)
Campell, Ulrich, *Ulrici Campelli Raetiae alpestris topographica
    descriptio*, ed. C.J. Kind (Basle: Verlag von Felix Schneider, 1884)
——— *Ulrici Campelli Historia Raetica*, ed. Plac. Plattner, 2 vols (Basle:
    Verlag von Adolf Geering, 1890)
Castellio, Sebastian, *Conseil à la France désolée*, ed. with an
    introduction and notes by Marius Valkhoff (Geneva: Librairie E.
    Droz, 1967)
——— *De l'impunité des hérétiques / De haereticis non puniendis*, ed.
    Bruno Becker and Marius Valkhoff (Geneva: Librairie E. Droz, 1971)
——— *De arte dubitandi et confidendi ignorandi et sciendi*, ed. with an
    introduction and notes by Elisabeth Feist Hirsch (Leiden: E.J. Brill, 1981)
Celsi, Mino, *In haereticis coërcendis quatenus progredi liceat. Poems –
    Correspondence*, ed. Peter G. Bietenholz (Naples and Chicago: Prismi
    Editrice and the Newberry Library, 1982)
Corpus Christianorum: Series Latina (Turnhout: Brepols, 1954–)
De Bujanda, J.M. (ed.), *Index des livres interdits III: Index de Venise
    1549; Venise et Milan 1554* (Geneva: Librairie E. Droz, 1987)
*De falsa et vera unius Dei Patris, Filii et Spiritus Sancti cognitione libri
    duo* (Alba Julia: [Hoffhalter], 1568), facsimile edition with an
    introduction by Antal Pirnát (Budapest: Akadémiai Kiadó, 1988)
Dudith, Andreas, *Epistulae*, ed. Lech Szczucki and Tibor Szepessy
    (Budapest: Akadémiai Kiadó, 1992–)
Egli, Emil (ed.), *Heinrich Bullinger Diarium (Annales vitae) der Jahre
    1504–1574* (Basle: Basler Buch- und Antiquariatshandlung, 1904)
Enzinas, Francisco de, *Epistolario*, ed. Ignacio J. García Pinilla (Geneva:
    Librairie E. Droz, 1995)
*Epistolae Tigurinae de rebus potissimum ad Ecclesiae Anglicanae
    Reformationem pertinentibus conscriptae 1531–1558* (Cambridge:
    Parker Society, 1848)
Firpo, Massimo and Dario Marcatto (eds), *Il processo inquisitoriale del
    cardinal Giovanni Morone*, 6 vols (Rome: Istituto storico italiano per
    l'età moderna e contemporanea, 1981–95)

Fry, Karl (ed.), *Giovanni Antonio Volpe Nunzius in der Schweiz: Dokumente: Band 1: Die erste Nunziatur 1560–1565* (Florence: Olschki, 1935)

—— (ed.), *Giovanni Antonio Volpe Nunzius in der Schweiz: Band II: Die zweite und dritte Nunziatur 1565 (–1588)* (Stans and Milan: Verlag Josef von Matt and Ambrosiana, 1946)

Ginzburg, Carlo (ed.), *I costituti di don Pietro Manelfi* (Florence and Chicago: Sansoni and the Newberry Library, 1970)

Giussani, A. (ed.), 'Relatione del Segretario Padavino ritornato dal paese de' Signori Grisoni presentata nell' Ecc.^mo Collegio a' 20 Agosto 1605', *Periodico della Società storica per la Provincia e antica Diocesi di Como*, 15 (1903), pp. 161–212

Hartmann, Alfred (ed.), *Die Amerbachkorrespondenz* (Basle: Universität Basel, 1942–)

Hessels, J.H., *Ecclesiae Londino-Bataviae Archivium: Epistulae et Tractatus cum Reformationis tum Ecclesiae Londino-Bataviae illustrantes*, 3 pts in 4 vols (Cambridge: n. pub., 1887–97)

Jecklin, Fritz (ed.), *Materialien zur Standes- und Landesgeschichte Gem. III Bünde (Graubünden), 1464–1803*, 2 vols (Basle: Basler Buch- und Antiquariatshandlung, 1907/9)

Kingdon, R.M., J.-F. Bergier et al. (eds), *Registre de la Compagnie des Pasteurs de Genève* (Geneva: Librairie E. Droz, 1964–)

Lubieniecki, Stanislas, *History of the Polish Reformation and Nine Related Documents*, trans. George Huntston Williams (Minneapolis: Fortress Press, 1995)

Luther, Martin, *D. Martin Luthers Briefwechsel*, 11 vols (Weimar: Hermann Böhlaus Nachfolger, 1930–48)

Marchetti, Valerio, and Giampaolo Zucchini (eds), *Aggiunte all'Epistolario di Fausto Sozzini 1561–1568* (Warsaw and Łódź: PWN, 1982)

Migne, Jacques Paul (ed.), *Patrologiae cursus completus … Series Graeca …* (Paris: J.P. Migne, 1857–87)

Migne, Jacques Paul (ed.), *Patrologiae cursus completus [Series Latina] …* (Paris: J.P. Migne, 1844–55)

Miscellanea Tigurina, 3 vols (Zurich: Bodmer, 1722–24)

Modrzewski, Andrzej Frycz, *Sylvae*, ed. Kasimierz Kumaniecki (Warsaw: Państwowy Instytut Wydawniczy, 1960)

Ochino, Bernardino, *I 'dialogi sette' e altri scritti del tempo della fuga*, ed. Ugo Rozzo (Turin: Claudiana, 1985)

Renato, Camillo, *Opere, documenti e testimonianze*, ed. Antonio Rotondò (Florence and Chicago: Sansoni and the Newberry Library, 1968)

Riggenbach, Bernhard (ed.), *Das Chronicon des Konrad Pellikan* (Basle: Bahnmeier's Verlag, 1877)

Rott, Jean (ed.), *Correspondance de Martin Bucer* (Leiden: Brill, 1979–)

Schiess, Traugott (ed.), *Bullingers Korrespondenz mit den Graubündnern*, 3 vols (Basle: Verlag der Basler Buch- und Antiquariatshandlung, 1904–06)

Schnyder, Werner (ed.), *Quellen zur Zürcher Wirtschaftsgeschichte*, 2 vols (Zurich and Leipzig: Rascher Verlag, 1937)

Sipayłło, Maria (ed.), *Acta synodorum ecclesiarum Poloniae reformatorum/Akta synodów różnowierczych w Polsce*, 3 vols (Warsaw: Wydawnictwa Universytetu Warszawskiego, 1966–83)

Società storica comense (ed.), *Atti della visita pastorale di F. Feliciano Ninguarda Vescovo di Como (1589–1593)*, 2 vols (Como: Tipografia provinciale F. Ostinelli d. C.A., 1892/5)

Sozzini, Lelio, *Opere*, ed. Antonio Rotondò (Florence: Olschki, 1986)

Valdés, Juan de, *Alfabeto cristiano*, ed. with an introduction by Massimo Firpo (Turin: Einaudi, 1994)

Von Kausler, Eduard, and Theodor Schott (eds), *Briefwechsel zwischen Christoph Herzog von Württemberg, und Petrus Paulus Vergerius* (Tübingen: H. Laupp, 1875)

Von Segesser, Anton Philipp, et al., *Amtliche Sammlung der ältern eidgenössischen Abschiede, 1245–1798*, 8 pts (Lucerne and Berne, 1839–78)

Wotschke, Theodor (ed.), *Der Briefwechsel der Schweizer mit den Polen* (Leipzig: M. Heinsius, 1908)

Zucchini, Giampaolo (ed.), *Celso e Camillo Sozzini nel gruppo ereticale familiare: Nuovi documenti in Svizzera (1561–1570)* (Bologna: Centro Stampa 'Lo Scarabeo', 1981)

The Zurich Letters, ed. Hastings Robinson, 2 vols (Cambridge: Parker Society, 1842/5)

Zwingli, Huldrych, *Huldreich Zwinglis sämtliche Werke*, ed. Walther Köhler et al. (*Corpus Reformatorum* vols LXVIII–) (Leipzig: M. Heinsius, 1905–)

Secondary Sources

Adam, Gottfried, *Der Streit um die Prädestination im ausgehenden 16. Jahrhundert: Eine Untersuchung zu den Entwürfen von Samuel Huber und Aegidius Hunnius* (Neukirchen: Neukirchener Verlag, 1970)

Adorni-Braccesi, Simonetta, 'Le "Nazioni" lucchesi nell'Europa della Riforma', *Critica storica*, 28 (1991), pp. 363–426

────── 'Una città infetta': La repubblica di Lucca nella crisi religiosa del Cinquecento (Florence: Olschki, 1994)

────── 'Religious Refugees from Lucca in the Sixteenth Century: Political Strategies and Religious Proselytism', ARG, 88 (1997), pp. 338–79

Ambrosini, Federica, Storie di patrizi e di eresia nella Venezia del '500 (Milan: FrancoAngeli, 1999)

Anderson, Marvin Walter, Peter Martyr: A Reformer in Exile (1542–1562): A chronology of biblical writings in England and Europe (Nieuwkoop: De Graaf, 1975)

────── 'Vista Tigurina: Peter Martyr and European Reform (1556–1562)', Harvard Theological Review, 83 (1990), pp. 181–206

Armand Hugon, Augusto, Agostino Mainardo: Contributo alla storia della Riforma in Italia (Torre Pellice: Società di Studi Valdesi, n.d. [1943])

Aureggi, Olimpia, 'I Lumaga di Piuro e di Chiavenna', Archivio storico lombardo, 89 (1962), pp. 222–89

Backus, Irene, 'Randbemerkungen Zwinglis in den Werken von Giovanni Pico della Mirandola', Zwa, 18/4 (1990/2), pp. 291–309

Bächtold, Hans Ulrich, 'Heinrich Bullinger und die Krise der schweizerischen Reformation', in Gäbler and Herkenrath, Bullinger, I, pp. 269–89

────── Heinrich Bullinger vor dem Rat: Zur Gestaltung und Verwaltung des Zürcher Staatswesens in den Jahren 1531 bis 1575 (Berne and Frankfurt: Peter Lang, 1982)

────── (ed.), Schola Tigurina: Die Züricher Hohe Schule und ihre Gelehrten um 1550 (Zurich: Pano, 2000)

Bänziger, Paul, Beiträge zur Geschichte der Spätscholastik und des Frühhumanismus in der Schweiz (Zurich: Verlag AG. Gebr. Leemann & Co., 1945)

Bainton, Roland H., Bernardino Ochino, esule e riformatore senese del Cinquecento, trans. E. Gianturco (Florence: Sansoni, 1940)

Baker, J. Wayne, 'Christian Discipline, Church and State, and Toleration: Bullinger, Calvin, and Basel 1530–1555', in Oberman, Das Reformierte Erbe, 2 vols (Zurich: Theologischer Verlag, 1992), I, pp. 35–48

────── 'In defense of magisterial discipline: Bullinger's "Tractatus de excommunicatione" of 1568', in Gäbler and Herkenrath, Bullinger, I, pp. 141–59

Balázs, Mihály, Early Transylvanian Antitrinitarianism (1566–1571): From Servet to Palaeologus (Baden-Baden and Bouxwiller: Editions Valentin Koerner, 1996)

Balma, T., *Il pensiero religioso di C.S. Curione* (Rome: Edizioni di 'Religio', 1935)

Balmas, Enea, 'Un inedito di Scipione Lentolo', *BSSV*, 152 (1983), pp. 31–56

Barbieri, Edoardo, *Le Bibbie italiane del Quattrocento e del Cinquecento: Storia e bibliografia ragionata delle edizioni in lingua italiana dal 1471 al 1600*, 2 vols (Milan: Editrice Bibliografica, 1992)

Baserga, Giovanni, 'Il movimento per la Riforma in Valtellina e le suoi relazioni con Ginevra', *Periodico della Società storica della Provincia e antica Diocesi di Como*, 21 (1914), pp. 97–128; 22 (1915), pp. 5–36

Bassetti, Aldo, 'I riformati locarnesi in Zurigo alla luce di nuovi documenti', *Bollettino storico della Svizzera italiana* (1941/3), pp. 1–10

Baumann, Michael, 'Petrus Martyr Vermigli: Doctor, Lehrer der Heiligen Schrift und Zürcher', in Campi, *Peter Martyr Vermigli*, pp. 214–24

Becker, Bruno (ed.), *Autour de Michel Servet et de Sébastien Castellion* (Haarlem: H.D. Tjeenck, Willink & Zoon N.V., 1953)

Benrath, Karl, *Bernardino Ochino of Siena: A Contribution towards the History of the Reformation*, 1st edition, trans. Helen Zimmern (London: James Nisbet & Co., 1876)

——— *Bernardino Ochino von Siena*, 2nd edn (Braunschweig: Schwetschke, 1892)

Beretta, Francesco, 'L'archivio della Congregazione del Sant'Ufficio: bilancio provvisorio della storia e natura dei fondi d'antico regime', *Rivista di Storia e Letteratura Religiosa*, 37 (2001), pp. 29–58

Bertrand-Barraud, Daniel, *Les idées philosophiques de Bernardin Ochin, de Sienne* (Paris: Librairie Philosophique J. Vrin, 1924)

Besta, Enrico, *Storia della Valtellina e della Val Chiavenna*, 2 vols (Milan: Dott. A. Giuffrè Editore, 1955/64)

Bianco, Cesare, 'La comunità di "fratelli" nel movimento ereticale modenese del '500', *RSI*, 92 (1980), pp. 621–79

Biel, Pamela, *Doorkeepers at the House of Righteousness: Heinrich Bullinger and the Zurich Clergy 1535–1575* (Berne: Peter Lang, 1991)

Bietenholz, Peter G., *Der italienische Humanismus und die Blütezeit des Buchdrucks in Basel: Die Basler Drucke italienischer Autoren von 1530 bis zum Ende des 16. Jahrhunderts* (Basle: Verlag von Helbing und Lichtenhahn, 1959)

——— 'Questioni su Mino Celsi da Siena', *BSSV*, 132 (1972), pp. 69–74

——— 'Mino Celsi and the Toleration Controversy of the Sixteenth Century', *BHR*, 34 (1972), pp. 31–47

Biondi, Albano, 'La giustificazione della simulazione nel Cinquecento', in *Eresia e riforma*, pp. 5–68

Bodmer, Walter, *Der Einfluß der Refugianteneinwanderung von 1550–1700 auf die schweizerische Wirtschaft: Ein Beitrag zur Geschichte des Frühkapitalismus und der Textilindustrie* (Zurich: AG Gebr. Leemann & Co., 1946)

Boersma, Owe, *Vluchtig Voorbeeld: de Nederlandse, Franse en Italiaanse Vluchtelingenkerken in Londen, 1568–1585* (n.p. [Kampen], 1994)

Boesch, Paul, 'Julius Terentianus: Faktotum des Petrus Martyr Vermilius und Korrektor der Offizin Froschauer', *Zwa* 8/10 (1948/2), pp. 587–601

—————— 'Die englischen Flüchtlinge in Zürich unter Königin Elisabeth I', *Zwa* 9/9 (1953/1), pp. 531–5

Bonorand, Conradin, *Die Entwicklung des reformierten Bildungswesens in Graubünden zur Zeit der Reformation und Gegenreformation* (Thusis: Buchdruckerei Rott & Co., 1949)

—————— 'Bündner Studierende an höhern Schulen der Schweiz und des Auslandes im Zeitalter der Reformation und Gegenreformation', *JHGG* (1949), pp. 91–174

—————— 'Le relazioni culturali tra i protestanti di Valtellina e i protestanti della Svizzera tedesca', *Archivio storico lombardo*, serie 9, 5/6 (1966–67), pp. 1–9

—————— 'Humanismus und Reformation in Südbünden im Lichte der Korrespondenz der Churer Prediger mit Joachim Vadian und Konrad Gesner', in *Festschrift 600 Jahre Gotteshausbund* (Chur, 1967), pp. 439–88

—————— 'Dolfin Landolfi von Poschiavo: Der erste Bündner Buchdrucker der Reformationszeit', in Martin Haas and René Hauswirth (eds), *Festgabe Leonhard von Muralt* (Zurich: Verlag Berichthaus, 1970), pp. 228–44

—————— 'Stand und Probleme der Forschung über die Bündner Geschichte der frühen Neuzeit seit 1945, mit besonderer Berücksichtigung Südbündens, einschliesslich der ehemaligen Bündner Untertanenländer und der auf diese Gebiete sich beziehenden Sachbereiche: Allgemeine Kulturgeschichte, Religionsexulanten, konfessionelle Auseinandersetzungen, Bündner Wirren, Personal- und Familienforschung, Pass- und Verkehrsgeschichte', *JHGG* (1979), pp. 85–130

—————— 'Mitteleuropäische Studenten in Pavia zur Zeit der Kriege in Italien (ca.1500 bis ca.1550)', *Pluteus*, 4–5 (1986–87), pp. 295–357

—————— *Die Engadiner Reformatoren Philipp Gallicius, Jachim Tütschett*

Bifrun, Durich Chiampell: Voraussetzungen und Möglichkeiten ihres Wirkens aus der Perspektive der Reformation im allgemeinen (Chur: Evangelischer Kirchenrat Graubünden, 1987)

—— *Vadian und Graubünden: Aspekte der Personen- und Kommunikationsgeschichte im Zeitalter des Humanismus und der Reformation* (Chur: Terra Grischuna Verlag, 1991)

—— 'Attuale situazione delle ricerche sulla Riforma e sulla Contrariforma in Valtellina e in Valchiavenna', *Quaderni grigioni italiani* (1991), pp. 91–9

—— *Reformatorische Emigration aus Italien in die Drei Bünde: Ihre Auswirkungen auf die kirchlichen Verhältnisse – ein Literaturbericht* (Chur: Verein für Bündner Kulturforschung, 2000)

Bornatico, Remo, *L'arte tipografica nelle Tre Leghe (1549–1803)* (Chur: Gasser & Eggerling AG, 1971)

Bouvier, André, *Henri Bullinger, réformateur et conseiller oecuménique, le successeur de Zwingli, d'après sa correspondance avec les réformés et les humanistes de langue française* (Neuchâtel and Paris: Delachaux & Niestlé S.A. and Droz, 1940)

Brassel, Thomas, 'Drei umstrittene Traktate Peter Martyr Vermiglis', *Zwa* 11/7 (1962/1), p. 476

Brown, Horatio F., 'The Valtelline', in A.W. Ward, G.W. Prothero and Stanley Leathes (eds), *Cambridge Modern History, Volume 4: The Thirty Years' War* (Cambridge: Cambridge University Press, 1906), pp. 35–63

Büsser, Fritz, 'Die Überlieferung von Heinrich Bullingers Briefwechsel', in Büsser, *Wurzeln der Reformation in Zürich: Zum 500. Geburtstag des Reformators Huldrych Zwingli* (Leiden: E.J. Brill, 1985), pp. 125–42

—— 'Josias Simmlers Gedenkrede auf Petrus Martyr 1563: Vermigli in Zürich', in Alfred Cattani, Michael Kotrba and Agnes Rutz (eds), *Zentralbibliothek Zürich: Alte und neue Schätze* (Zurich: Verlag NZZ, 1993), pp. 74–7

Buisson, Ferdinand, *Sébastien Castellion: Sa vie et son oeuvre: Etude sur les origines du Protestantisme libéral français*, 2 vols (Paris: Hachette, 1892)

Bundi, Martin, *Frühe Beziehungen zwischen Graubünden und Venedig (15./16. Jahrhundert)* (Chur: Gasser AG Druck und Verlag, 1988)

Burchill, Christopher J., *The Heidelberg Antitrinitarians* (Baden-Baden and Bouxwiller: Editions Valentin Koerner, 1989)

—— 'Girolamo Zanchi: Portrait of a Reformed Theologian and His Work', *SCJ*, 15 (1984), pp. 185–207

Burnett, Amy Nelson, 'Simon Sulzer and the Consequences of the 1563 Strasbourg Consensus in Switzerland', *ARG*, 83 (1992), pp. 154–79

Burrows, Mark S., '"Christus intra nos Vivens": The Peculiar Genius of Bullinger's Doctrine of Sanctification', *Zeitschrift für Kirchengeschichte*, 98 (1987), pp. 48–69

Busino, Giovanni, 'Italiani all'università di Basilea dal 1460 al 1601', *BHR*, 20 (1958), pp. 497–526

────── 'Prime ricerche su Broccardo Borrone', *BHR*, 24 (1962), pp. 130–67

────── 'Di Broccardo Borrone e del suo "Ritratto della Rezia"', *Bollettino della società storica valtellinese*, 16 (1962), pp. 25–60

Buzzoni, Paola, *I Praecepta di Scipione Lentulo e l'adattamento inglese di Henry Grantham* (Florence: Valmartina Editore, 1979)

Caccamo, Domenico, *Eretici italiani in Moravia, Polonia, Transilvania (1558–1611): Studi e documenti* (Florence: Sansoni, 1970)

Calvani, Simona, 'Camillo Renato', in André Séguenny (ed.), *Bibliotheca Dissidentium: Répertoire des non-conformistes réligieux des seizième et dix-septième siècles, 4* (Baden-Baden: Editions Valentin Koerner, 1984), pp. 155–90

────── 'Note sul carteggio di Celio Secundo Curione dal 1535 al 1553', *BSSV*, 159 (1986), pp. 35–40

Camenisch, Carl, *Carlo Borromeo und die Gegenreformation im Veltlin mit besonderer Berücksichtigung der Landesschule von Sondrio* (Chur: Kommissionsverlag der Hitz'schen Buchhandlung, 1901)

Camenisch, Emil, 'Die Confessio Raetica: Ein Beitrag zur bündnerischen Reformationsgeschichte', *JHGG* (1913), pp. 223–60

────── *Bündnerische Reformationsgeschichte* (Chur: Bischofberger & Hotzenkocherle, 1920)

────── *Geschichte der Reformation und Gegenreformation in den italienischen Südtälern Graubündens und den ehemaligen Untertanenlanden Chiavenna, Veltlin und Bormio* (Chur: Bischofberger & Co., 1950)

────── 'Broccardo Borrone: Ein des bündnerischen Asylrechts unwürdiger Flüchtling aus Oberitalien', *BM* (1954), pp. 145–74

Cameron, Euan, *The Reformation of the Heretics: The Waldenses of the Alps, 1480–1580* (Oxford: Clarendon Press, 1984)

Cameron, James, 'The British Itinerary of Johann Peter Hainzel von Degerstein by Caspar Waser', *Zwa* 15/3–4 (1980/1–2), pp. 259–95

Campi, Emidio, ' "Conciliatione de dispareri": Bernardino Ochino e la seconda disputa sacramentale', in Oberman, *Das Reformierte Erbe*, I, pp. 77–92

────── *Michelangelo e Vittoria Colonna: Un dialogo artistico-teologico ispirato da Bernardino Ochino, e altri saggi di storia della Riforma* (Turin: Claudiana Editrice, 1994)

———— 'Remarques sur l'histoire de la Réforme en Italie', *BHR*, 56 (1994), pp. 495–507

———— 'Petrus Martyr Vermigli (1499–1562): Europäische Wirkungsfelder eines italienischen Reformators', *Zwa*, 27 (2000), pp. 29–46

———— and Giuseppe La Torre (eds), *Il protestantesimo di lingua italiana nella Svizzera: Figure e movimenti tra Cinquecento e Ottocento* (Turin: Claudiana Editrice, 2000)

———— 'Vincenzo Paravicino (1595–1678) tra la Valtellina e la Svizzera', in Campi and La Torre, *Il protestantesimo*, pp. 89–98

———— 'Pier Paolo Vergerio ed il suo epistolario con Heinrich Bullinger', in Rozzo, *Vergerio*, pp. 277–94

———— (ed.), *Peter Martyr Vermigli: Humanism, Republicanism, Reformation/Petrus Martyr Vermigli: Humanismus, Republikanismus, Reformation* (Geneva: Librarie Droz, 2002)

Cantimori, Delio, *Bernardino Ochino: uomo del Rinascimento e riformatore*, in *Annali della R. Scuola Normale Superiore di Pisa, Classe di Lettere e Filosofia*, 30 (Pisa: Tipografia Editrice Pacini Mariotti, 1929)

———— *Italiani a Basilea e a Zurigo nel Cinquecento* (Rome and Bellinzona: Cremonese Editore and Ist. Edit. Ticinese S.A., 1947)

———— *Eretici italiani del Cinquecento e altri scritti*, ed. Adriano Prosperi (Turin: Giulio Einaudi Editore, 1992)

———— *Umanesimo e religione nel Rinascimento* (Turin: Giulio Einaudi Editore, 1975)

———— and Elisabeth Feist, *Per la storia degli eretici italiani del secolo XVI in Europa* (Rome: G. Bardi, 1937)

———— et al. (eds), *Ginevra e l'Italia: Raccolta di studi promossa dalla Faccoltà di Teologia di Roma* (Florence: Sansoni, 1959)

Caponetto, Salvatore, *Aonio Paleario (1503–1570) e la Riforma protestante in Toscana* (Turin: Claudiana Editrice, 1979)

———— 'Una sconosciuta predica fiorentina del minorita Benedetto Locarno', in Caponetto, *Studi sulla Riforma in Italia* (Florence: Università degli Studi di Firenze, 1987), pp. 205–18

———— *La Riforma protestante nell'Italia del Cinquecento* (Turin: Claudiana Editrice, 1992)

Castiglione, T.R., 'Valentino contro Calvino: Il processo del "secondo Serveto" nel 1558, a Ginevra', in Ludwik Chmaj (ed.), *Studia nad arianizmem* (Warsaw: PWN, 1959), pp. 49–71

———— 'La "impietas Valentini Gentilis" e il corrucio di Calvino', in Cantimori, *Ginevra e l'Italia*, pp. 148–76

Cavazza, Silvano, 'Libri in volgare e propaganda eterodossa: Venezia

1543–1547', in Adriano Prosperi and Albano Biondi (eds), *Libri, idee e sentimenti religiosi nel Cinquecento italiano* (Modena: Panini, 1987), pp. 9–28

—— 'Pier Paolo Vergerio nei Grigioni e in Valtellina (1549–1553): attività editoriale e polemica religiosa', in Pastore, *Riforma e società*, pp. 33–62

—— 'La censura ingannata: polemiche antiromane e usi della propaganda in Pier Paolo Vergerio', in U. Rozzo (ed.), *La censura libraria nell'Europa del secolo XVI* (Udine: Forum, 1997), pp. 273–95

Chabod, Federico, *Per la storia religiosa dello stato di Milano durante il dominio di Carlo V: Note e documenti*, ed. Ernesto Sestan (Rome: Istituto storico italiano per l'età moderna et contemporanea, 1962)

Chenou, Albert, 'Taddeo Duno (1523–1613)', *BSSV*, 120 (1966), pp. 55–61

—— 'Taddeo Duno et la Réforme à Locarno', *Archivio storico ticinese*, 12 (1971), pp. 237–94

Church, Frederic C., *The Italian Reformers 1534–1564* (New York: Columbia University Press, 1932)

Collett, Barry, *Italian Benedictine Scholars and the Reformation: The Congregation of Santa Giustina of Padua* (Oxford: Clarendon Press, 1985)

Corda, Salvatore, *Veritas Sacramenti: A Study of Vermigli's Doctrine of the Lord's Supper* (Zurich: Theologischer Verlag, 1975)

Cox, Virginia, *The Renaissance dialogue: Literary dialogue in its social and political contexts, Castiglione to Galileo* (Cambridge: Cambridge University Press, 1992)

Crollolanza, G.B., *Storia del contado di Chiavenna* (Milan: Presse Serafino Muggiani e comp. Librai editori, 1870)

Dändliker, Karl, 'Zürcher Volksanfragen von 1521 bis 1718', *Jahrbuch für Schweizerische Geschichte*, 23 (1898), pp. 149–225

Dalbert, Peter, *Die Reformation in den italienischen Talschaften Graubündens nach dem Briefwechsel Bullingers: Ein Beitrag zur Geschichte der Reformation in der Schweiz* (Zurich: Dissertationsdruckerei Leemann AG, 1948)

Dall'Olio, Guido, *Eretici e Inquisitori nella Bologna del Cinquecento* (Bologna: Istituto per la Storia di Bologna, 1999)

Dán, Robert, *Matthias Vehe-Glirius: Life and Work of a radical antitrinitarian with his collected writings* (Budapest and Leiden: Akadémiai Kiadó and E.J. Brill, 1982)

D'Ascia, Luca, 'Celio Secundo Curione, erasmista o antierasmista?', in Achille Olivieri (ed.), *Erasmo Venezia e la cultura padana nel '500* (Rovigo: Associazione Culturale Minelliana, 1995), pp. 209–23

———— 'Tra platonismo e riforma: Curione, Zwingli e Francesco Zorzi', *BHR*, 61 (1999), pp. 673–99

Del Col, Andrea, 'Il Nuovo Testamento tradotto da Massimo Teofilo e altre opere stampate a Lione nel 1551', *Critica storica*, 15 (1978), pp. 642–75

Denis, Philippe, *Les églises d'étrangers en pays rhénans (1538–1564)* (Paris: Société d'Edition 'Les Belles Lettres', 1984)

Denzler, Alice, *Geschichte des Armenwesens im Kanton Zürich im 16. und 17. Jahrhundert* (Zurich: Buchdruckerei J. Rüegg, 1920)

Di Filippo Bareggi, Claudia, 'Tra Sondrio e le Leghe grigie: la Valmalenco del tardo Cinquecento', *BSSV*, 178 (1995), pp. 109–40

Donnelly, John Patrick, *Calvinism and Scholasticism in Vermigli's Doctrine of Man and Grace* (Leiden: E.J. Brill, 1976)

———— 'Italian Influences on the Development of Calvinist Scholasticism', *SCJ*, 7 (1976), pp. 81–101

———— 'Three disputed Vermigli tracts', in Sergio Bertelli and Gloria Ramakus (eds), *Essays presented to Myron P. Gilmore*, 2 vols (Florence: La Nuova Italia Editrice, 1978), I, pp. 37–46

Dufour, Alain, 'L'histoire des hérétiques et Théodore de Bèze', in *Pour une Histoire Qualitative: Etudes offertes à Sven Stelling-Michaud* (Geneva: Presses Universitaires Romandes, 1975), pp. 35–44

Dufour, Alain, 'Simonius entre le Catholicisme et le Protestantisme', in Marc Lienhard (ed.), *Les Dissidents du XVIᵉ siècle entre l'Humanisme et le Catholicisme* (Baden-Baden: Editions Valentin Koerner, 1983), pp. 155–61

Egli, Emil, 'Biblianders Leben und Schriften', in Egli, *Analecta Reformatoria II: Biographien* (Zurich: Druck und Verlag von Zürcher & Furrer, 1901), pp. 1–144

Eresia e riforma nell'Italia del Cinquecento: Miscellanea I del Corpus Reformatorum Italicorum (Florence and Chicago: Sansoni and the Newberry Library, 1974)

Ernst, Fritz, 'Taddeo Dunos Bericht über die Auswanderung der protestantischen Locarner nach Zürich', *Zwa* 9/2 (1949/2), pp. 89–104

Ernst, Ulrich, *Geschichte des Zürcherischen Schulwesens bis gegen das Ende des sechzehnten Jahrhunderts* (Winterthur: Druck und Verlag von Bleuler-Hausheer & Cie, 1879)

Fast, Heinold, *Heinrich Bullinger und die Täufer: Ein Beitrag zur Historiographie und Theologie im 16. Jahrhundert* (Weierhof: Mennonitischer Geschichtsverein e.V., 1959)

Febvre, Lucien, 'Une question mal posée: Les origines de la réforme française et le problème des causes de la réforme', in Febvre, *Au coeur religieux du XVIᵉ siècle* (Paris: Sevpen, 1957), pp. 3–70

Firpo, Luigi, 'La chiesa italiana di Londra nel Cinquecento e i suoi rapporti con Ginevra', in Cantimori, *Ginevra e l'Italia*, pp. 307–412

—— *Scritti sulla Riforma in Italia* (Naples: Prismi, 1996)

—— 'Francesco Pucci a Basilea', in Firpo, *Scritti*, pp. 67–96

—— 'Giorgio Agricola e Michelangelo Florio', in Firpo, *Scritti*, pp. 245–59

Firpo, Massimo, 'Sui movimenti ereticali in Italia e in Polonia nei secoli XVI–XVII', *RSI*, 86 (1974), pp. 344–71

—— *Antitrinitari nell'Europa orientale del '500: Nuovi testi di Szymon Budny, Niccolò Paruta e Iacopo Paleologo* (Florence: La Nuova Italia Editrice, 1977)

—— *Tra Alumbrados e 'Spirituali': Studi su Juan de Valdés e il Valdesianismo nella crisi religiosa del '500 italiano* (Florence: Olschki, 1990)

—— *Riforma protestante ed eresie nell'Italia del Cinquecento: Un profilo storico* (Rome and Bari: Laterza, 1993)

Fiume, Emanuele, 'La Chiavenna di Mainardo, Zanchi e Lentolo', in Campi and La Torre, *Il protestantesimo*, pp. 77–88

Flüeler, Niklaus and Marianne Flüeler-Grauwiler (eds), *Geschichte des Kantons Zürich: Band 2: Frühe Neuzeit – 16. bis 18. Jahrhundert* (Zurich: WerdVerlag, 1996)

Fretz, Diethelm, *Die Frühbeziehungen zwischen Zürich und Bergamo 1568–1618* (Zurich: Seeverlag Zollikon, 1940)

Gäbler, Ulrich, 'Zu: Bizzarri und Bullingers Briefwechsel', *BHR*, 37 (1975), pp. 99–100

—— and Erhard Herkenrath (eds), *Heinrich Bullinger 1504–1575: Gesammelte Aufsätze zum 400. Todestag*, 2 vols (Zurich: Theologischer Verlag, 1975)

Gastaldi, Ugo, *Storia dell'anabattismo*, 2 vols (Turin: Claudiana Editrice, 1972/81)

Gay, Teofilo, 'Scipione Lentolo', *Bulletin de la société d'histoire vaudoise*, 23 (1906), pp. 104–7

Geering, Traugott, *Handel und Industrie der Stadt Basel: Zunftwesen und Wirtschaftsgeschichte bis zum Ende des XVI Jahrhunderts* (Basle: Druck und Verlag von Felix Schneider, 1886)

Gerber, Johannes, 'Giordano Bruno und Raphael Egli: Begegnungen im Zwielicht von Alchemie und Theologie', *Sudhoffs Archiv*, 76 (1992), pp. 133–63

Gilly, Carlos, *Spanien und der Basler Buchdruck bis 1600: Ein Querschnitt durch die spanische Geistesgeschichte aus der Sicht einer europäischen Buchdruckerstadt* (Basle and Frankfurt: Verlag Helbing & Lichtenhahn, 1985)

—— 'Das Sprichwort "Die Gelehrten die Verkehrten" in der Toleranzliteratur des 16. Jahrhunderts', in Jean-Georges Roth and Simon L. Verhaus (eds), *Anabaptistes et dissidents au XVIe siècle, tenu à l'occasion de la XIe Conférence Mennonite mondiale à Strasbourg* (Baden-Baden and Bouxwiller: Editions Valentin Koerner, 1987), pp. 159–72

—— 'Das Sprichwort "Die Gelehrten die Verkehrten" oder der Verrat der Intellektuellen im Zeitalter der Glaubensspaltung', in Rotondò, *Forme e destinazione*, pp. 229–375

—— 'Die Zensur von Castellios *Dialogi quatuor* durch die Basler Theologen (1578)', in Michael Erbe et al. (eds), *Querdenken: Dissens und Toleranz im Wandel der Geschichte: Festschrift zum 65. Geburtstag von Hans R. Guggisberg* (Mannheim: J & J Verlag, 1996), pp. 169–92

Gilmont, Jean-François, 'L' "Historia delle grandi e crudeli persecutioni" di Scipione Lentulo', *BSSV*, 151 (1982), pp. 51–68

—— (ed.), *The Reformation and the Book* (Aldershot: Ashgate, 1998), trans. Karin Maag

Ginzburg, Carlo, *Il nicodemismo: Simulazione e dissimulazione religiosa nell'Europa del '500* (Turin: Giulio Einaudi Editore, 1970)

—— and Adriano Prosperi, *Giochi di pazienza: Un seminario sul 'Beneficio di Cristo'* (Turin: Giulio Einaudi Editore, 1975)

Giorgetta, Giovanni, 'Dissidi tra cattolici ed evangelici in Villa di Chiavenna', *Clavenna*, 3 (1964), pp. 75–120

—— 'Francesco Negri a Chiavenna: Note inedite', *Clavenna*, 14 (1975), pp. 38–46

—— 'Un codicillo di Ottaviano Mei', *Clavenna*, 17 (1978), pp. 24–8

—— 'Documenti inediti sul conte Ulisse Martinengo', *Bollettino della società storica valtellinese*, 31 (1978), pp. 45–66

—— 'Andrea Pizzarda di Pallanza a Chiavenna', *Clavenna*, 27 (1988), pp. 67–75

Giovanoli, Gaudenzio, 'Erinnerungen an hervorragende Pfarrer in Soglio', *BM* (1932), pp. 51–6

Giussani, Antonio, *La rivoluzione valtellinese del 19 luglio 1620* (Milan: Dott. A. Giuffrè Editore, 1940)

Gmür, Helen, *Das Bündnis zwischen Zürich / Bern und Venedig 1615/18* (Zurich: Verlag AG Gebr. Leemann & Co., 1945)

Gordon, Bruce, *Clerical Discipline and the Reformation: The Synod in Zürich, 1532–1580* (Berne: Peter Lang, 1992)

Graf, Werner, 'Evangelische Kirchenordnung im Freistaat Gemeiner Drei Bünde', *Zwa* 11/10 (1963/2), pp. 624–48

Grebel, Hans Rudolf von, *Antistes Johann Jakob Breitinger 1575–1665* (Zurich: Kommissionsverlag Beer & Co., 1964)

Grell, Ole Peter, *Dutch Calvinists in Early Stuart London: The Dutch Church in Austin Friars 1603–1642* (Leiden: E.J. Brill, 1989)

—— 'Merchants and ministers: the foundations of international Calvinism', in A. Pettegree, A. Duke and G. Lewis (eds), *Calvinism in Europe, 1540–1620* (Cambridge: Cambridge University Press, 1994), pp. 254–73

—— *Calvinist Exiles in Tudor and Stuart England* (Aldershot: Scolar Press, 1996)

Grendler, Paul, *The Roman Inquisition and the Venetian Press, 1540–1605* (Princeton: Princeton University Press, 1977)

Guggisberg, Hans R., 'Pietro Perna, Fausto Sozzini und die Dialogi quatuor Sebastian Castellios', in S. van der Woude, *Studia bibliographica in honorem Herman de la Fontaine Verwey* (Amsterdam: Menno Hertzberger & Co., 1967), pp. 171–201

—— 'Sebastian Castellio und der Ausbruch der Religionskriege in Frankreich: Einige Betrachtungen zum *Conseil à la France désolée*', *ARG*, 68 (1977), pp. 253–67

—— *Basel in the Sixteenth Century: Aspects of the City Republic before, during and after the Reformation* (St Louis, Mo.: Center for Reformation Research, 1982)

—— '"Ich hasse die Ketzer". Der Ketzerbegriff Sebastian Castellios und seine Situation im Basler Exil', in Silvana Seidel Menchi, Hans R. Guggisberg and B. Moeller (eds), *Ketzerverfolgung im 16. und frühen 17. Jahrhundert* (Wiesbaden: Otto Harrassowitz, 1992), pp. 249–65

—— 'Das lutheranisierende Basel: ein Diskussionsbeitrag', in Hans-Christoph Rublack (ed.), *Die lutherische Konfessionalisierung in Deutschland* (Gütersloh: Gerd Mohn, 1992), pp. 199–201

—— 'Tolerance and intolerance in sixteenth-century Basel', in Ole Peter Grell and Bob Scribner (eds), *Tolerance and intolerance in the European Reformation* (Cambridge: Cambridge University Press, 1996), pp. 145–63

—— *Sebastian Castellio 1515–1563: Humanist und Verteidiger der religiösen Toleranz im konfessionellen Zeitalter* (Göttingen: Vandenhoeck & Ruprecht, 1997)

Hassinger, Erich, *Studien zu Jacobus Acontius* (Berlin Grünewald: Verlag für Staatswissenschaften und Geschichte, 1934)

Hauser, Angelika, *Pietro Paolo Vergerios protestantische Zeit* (Tübingen: Fa. H.-J. Köhler, 1980)

Head, Randolph C., 'Rhaetian Ministers, from Shepherds to Citizens: Calvinism and Democracy in the Republic of the Three Leagues 1550–1620', in W. Fred Graham (ed.), *Later Calvinism: International*

Perspectives (Kirksville, Mo.: Sixteenth Century Journal Publishers, 1994)

———— *Early Modern Democracy in the Grisons: Social Order and Political Language in a Swiss Mountain Canton, 1470–1620* (Cambridge: Cambridge University Press, 1995)

Hein, Lorenz, 'Heinrich Bullinger und sein Einfluß auf die reformierten Gemeinden in Kleinpolen', *Kyrios*, 4 (1964), pp. 91–107

———— *Italienische Protestanten und ihr Einfluß auf die Reformation in Polen während der beiden Jahrzehnte vor dem Sandomirer Konsens (1570)* (Leiden: E.J. Brill, 1974)

Hendrix, Scott H., 'Deparentifying the Fathers: the Reformers and Patristic Authority', in Lief Grane et al. (eds), *Auctoritas Patrum: Zur Rezeption der Kirchenväter im 15. und 16. Jahrhundert / Contributions on the Reception of the Church Fathers in the 15th and 16th century* (Mainz: Verlag Philipp von Zabern, 1993), pp. 55–68

Hollweg, Walter, *Heinrich Bullingers Hausbuch: Eine Untersuchung über die Anfänge der reformierten Predigtliteratur* (Neukirchen: Verlag der Buchhandlung des Erziehungsvereins Neukirchen Kreis Moers, 1956)

Holtrop, Philip C., *The Bolsec Controversy on Predestination, from 1551 to 1555: The Statements of Jerome Bolsec, and the Responses of John Calvin, Theodore Beza, and Other Reformed Theologians* (Lewiston, NY, Queenston, Ont., and Lampeter: Edwin Mellen Press, 1993)

Hotson, Howard, *Johann Heinrich Alsted 1588–1638: Between Renaissance, Reformation and Universal Reform* (Oxford: Clarendon Press, 2000)

Hubert, Friedrich, *Vergerios publizistische Thätigkeit nebst einer bibliographischen Übersicht* (Göttingen: Vandenhoeck & Ruprecht, 1893)

Hulme, Edward M., 'Lelio Sozzini's Confession of Faith', in *Persecution and Liberty: Essays in Honor of George Lincoln Burr* (New York: The Century Co., 1931), pp. 211–25

Hundeshagen, C.B., *Die Conflikte des Zwinglianismus, Lutherthums und Calvinismus in der Bernischen Landeskirche von 1532–1558* (Berne: C.N. Zaini, 1842)

Jacobi, Verena, *Bern und Zürich und die Vertreibung der Evangelischen aus Locarno* (Zurich: Leemann AG, 1967)

James, Frank A. III, *Peter Martyr Vermigli and Predestination: The Augustinian Inheritance of an Italian Reformer* (Oxford: Clarendon Press, 1998)

Jecklin, Fritz, 'Die Amtsleute in den Bündnerischen Unterthanenlanden', *JHGG*, 20 (1891), pp. 29–40

—— 'Bündnerischer Beitagsbeschluß betreffend der lebenslänglichen Pensionierung des Prädikanten Scipio Lentulus in Clefen 1596', *BM* (1925), pp. 121–3

Jenny, Beat Rudolf, 'Jakob Clausers unvollendetes Porträt des italienischen Refugianten Vincenzo Maggi (ca. 1488–1564) im Amerbach Kabinett: Veranlasst es eine Korrektur im Personenkommentar zum Opus epistolarum Erasmi?', *Basler Zeitschrift für Geschichte und Altertumskunde*, 91 (1991), pp. 59–68

Jenny, Wilhelm, *Johannes Comander: Lebensgeschichte des Reformators der Stadt Chur*, 2 vols (Zurich: Zwingli-Verlag, 1969/70)

Jung, Eva-Maria, 'On the Nature of Evangelism in Sixteenth-Century Italy', *Journal of the History of Ideas*, 14 (1953), pp. 511–27

Kaplan, Benjamin J., *Calvinists and Libertines: Confession and Community in Utrecht 1578–1620* (Oxford: Clarendon Press, 1995)

Kawecka-Gryczowa, Alodia and Janusz Tazbir, 'The book and the Reformation in Poland', in Gilmont, *The Reformation and the Book*, pp. 410–31

Kind, Christian Immanuel, *Die Reformation in den Bisthümern Chur und Como* (Chur: Verlag der Grubenmann'schen Buchhandlung, 1858)

Kittelson, James M., 'Marbach vs. Zanchi: The Resolution of Controversy in Late Reformation Strasbourg', *SCJ*, 8 (1977), pp. 31–44

Klaniczay, Tibor (ed.), *Rapporti veneto-ungheresi all'epoca del Rinascimento* (Budapest: Akadémiai Kiadó, 1975)

Köhler, Walther, 'Zwingli und Italien', in *Festschrift zum 60. Geburtstag von Paul Wernle: Aus fünf Jahrhunderten schweizerischer Kirchengeschichte* (Basle: Verlag von Helbing & Lichtenhahn, 1932), pp. 22–38

Körner, Martin, 'Profughi italiani in Svizzera durante il XVI secolo: aspetti sociali, economici, religiosi e culturali', in Marino Berengo et al. (eds), *Città italiane del '500 tra Riforma e Controriforma: Atti del Convegno Internazionale di Studi Lucca, 13–15 ottobre 1983* (Lucca: Maria Paccini Fazzi Editore, 1988), pp. 1–22

Kutter, Markus, *Celio Secondo Curione: Sein Leben und sein Werk (1503–1569)* (Basle: Verlag von Helbing & Lichtenhahn, 1955)

Lecler, Joseph, *Toleration and the Reformation*, trans. T.L. Westour (New York and London: Association Press and Longmans, 1960)

Leemann-van Elck, Paul, *Die Offizin Froschauer, Zürichs berühmte*

Druckerei im 16. Jahrhundert: Ein Beitrag zur Geschichte der Buchdruckerkunst anläßlich der Halbjahrtausendfeier ihrer Erfindung (Zurich: Orell Füssli, 1940)

———— *Druck, Verlag, Buchhandel im Kanton Zürich von den Anfängen bis um 1850* (Zurich: Druck Leemann AG, 1950)

Liebenau, T. von, 'Della chiamata a Locarno di Bernardino Ochino', *Bollettino storico della Svizzera italiana*, 12 (1890), p. 30

Locher, Gottfried W., 'Bullinger und Calvin: Probleme des Vergleichs ihrer Theologien', in Gäbler and Herkenrath, *Bullinger*, I, pp. 1–33

———— 'The Theology of Exile: Faith and the Fate of the Refugee', in Miriam Chrisman and Otto Gründler (eds), *Social Groups and Religious Ideas in the Sixteenth Century* (Kalamazoo: Medieval Institute, 1978), pp. 85–92

Maag, Karin, *Seminary or University?: The Genevan Academy and Reformed Higher Education, 1560–1620* (Aldershot: Scolar Press, 1995)

McNair, Philip, *Peter Martyr in Italy: An Anatomy of Apostasy* (Oxford: Clarendon Press, 1967)

———— 'Ochino's Apology: Three Gods or Three Wives?', *History*, 60 (1975), pp. 353–73

———— 'Bernardino Ochino in Inghilterra', *RSI*, 103 (1991), pp. 231–42

Madonia, Claudio, 'Simone Simoni da Lucca', *Rinascimento*, 20 (1980), pp. 161–97

———— 'Bernardino Ochino e il radicalismo religioso europeo', *Bollettino senese di storia patria*, 98 (1991), pp. 110–29

Maissen, Felix, 'Der Kalenderstreit in Graubünden (1582–1812)', *BM* (1960), pp. 253–73

Maliniak, J., *Die Entstehung der Exportindustrie und des Unternehmerstandes in Zürich im XVI. und XVII. Jahrhundert* (Zurich and Leipzig: Rascher & Cie., 1913)

Marchetti, Valerio, 'Sull'origine e la dispersione del gruppo ereticale dei Sozzini a Siena (1557–1560)', *RSI*, 81 (1969), pp. 131–73

———— 'Una polemica di Scipione Lentulo con l'antitrinitario Fabrizio Pestalozzi (1581)', *Il pensiero politico*, 5 (1972), pp. 284–301

———— *Gruppi ereticali senesi del Cinquecento* (Florence: 'La Nuova Italia' Editrice, 1975)

———— 'Le "Explicationes" giovanee dei Sozzini e l'antitrinitarismo transilvano del Cinquecento', in Klaniczay, *Rapporti veneto-ungheresi*, pp. 347–59

———— 'La rottura ermeneutica sociniana: ricerca sulla struttura delle prefazioni alle "Explicationes" di Lelio e Fausto Sozzini', in Vittore Branca and Sante Graciotti (eds), *Italia Venezia e Polonia tra medio evo e età moderna* (Florence: Olschki, 1980), pp. 113–36

Martin, John, *Venice's Hidden Enemies: Italian Heretics in a Renaissance City* (Berkeley: University of California Press, 1993)

Mazzali, Ettore and Giulio Spini, *Storia della Valtellina e della Valchiavenna*, 2 vols (Sondrio: Editore Bissoni, 1968/9)

Mazzone, Umberto, '"Consolare quei poveri cattolici": Visitatori ecclesiastici in Valtellina tra '500 e '600', in Pastore, *Riforma e società*, pp. 129–57

Meyer, Ferdinand, *Die evangelische Gemeinde in Locarno, ihre Auswanderung und ihre weitern Schicksale: Ein Beitrag zur Geschichte der Schweiz im sechszehnten Jahrhundert*, 2 vols (Zurich: S. Höhr, 1836)

Meyer, Karl, *Die Capitanei von Locarno im Mittelalter* (Zurich: Druck der Buchdruckerei Berichthaus, 1916)

Meyer, Helmut, *Der zweite Kappeler Krieg: Die Krise der Schweizerischen Reformation* (Zurich: Verlag Hans Rohr, 1976)

Mikat, Paul, *Die Polygamiefrage in der frühen Neuzeit* (Opladen: Westdeutscher Verlag, 1988)

Monter, E. William, 'The Italians in Geneva, 1550–1600: A New Look', in Luc Monnier (ed.), *Genève et l'Italie: Etudes publiées à l'occasion du 50ᵉ anniversaire de la Société genevoise d'études italiennes* (Geneva: Librarie E. Droz, 1969), pp. 53–77

Mörikofer, J.C., *J.J. Breitinger und Zürich: Ein Kulturbild aus der Zeit des dreißigjährigen Krieges* (Leipzig: Verlag von S. Hirzel, 1874)

——— *Geschichte der evangelischen Flüchtlinge in der Schweiz* (Leipzig: Verlag von S. Hirzel, 1876)

Mottu-Weber, Liliane, *Economie et refuge à Genève au siècle de la Réforme: la draperie et la soierie (1540–1620)* (Geneva: Librairie E. Droz, 1987)

Mühling, Andreas, 'Lelio Sozzini: Bemerkungen zum Umgang Heinrich Bullingers mit "Häretikern"', in Athina Lexutt and Vicco von Bülow (eds), *Kaum zu glauben: Von der Häresie und dem Umgang mit ihr* (Rheinbach: CMZ-Verlag, 1998), pp. 162–70

——— *Heinrich Bullingers europäische Kirchenpolitik* (Berne: Peter Lang, 2001)

Muller, Richard A., *Post-Reformation Reformed Dogmatics: Volume 1: Prolegomena to Theology* (Grand Rapids: Baker Book House, 1987)

——— *Post-Reformation Reformed Dogmatics: Volume 2: Holy Scripture: The Cognitive Foundation of Theology* (Grand Rapids: Baker Books, 1993)

Muralt, Leonhard von, 'Zum Gedächtnis an die Übersiedlung evangelischer Locarner nach Zürich 1555', *Zwa* 10/3 (1955/1), pp. 145–60

――――― 'Renaissance und Reformation', in *Handbuch der Schweizer Geschichte: Band I* (Zurich: Buchverlag Berichthaus, 1980), pp. 389–570

Musselli, Luciano, 'La riforma protestante in Valmalenco e il diritto ecclesiastico dei Grigioni', *Bollettino della società storica valtellinese*, 32 (1979), pp. 45–63

Nabholz, Hans, 'Zürichs Höhere Schulen von der Reformation bis zur Gründung der Universität, 1525–1833', in Ernst Gagliardi, Hans Nabholz and Jean Strohl, *Die Universität Zürich 1833–1933 und ihre Vorläufer*, pp. 1–164 (Zurich: Verlag der Erziehungsdirektion, 1938)

Neuser, Wilhelm Heinrich, 'Calvins Kritik an den Basler, Berner und Zürcher Prädikanten in der Schrift "De praedestinatione" 1552', in Oberman, *Das Reformierte Erbe*, II, pp. 237–43

Niccoli, Ottavia, 'Il mostro di Sassonia: Conoscenza e non conoscenza di Lutero in Italia nel Cinquecento (1520–1530 ca.)', in Lorenzo Perrone (ed.), *Lutero in Italia: Studi storici nel V centenario della nascita* (Casale Monferrato: Marietti 1983), pp. 3–25

Nicolini, Benedetto, 'Il pensiero di Bernardino Ochino', *Atti della Reale Accademia Pontaniana di scienze morali e politiche*, 95 (1938), pp. 171–268

――――― *Ideali e passioni nell'Italia religiosa del Cinquecento* (Bologna: Libreria Antiquaria Palmaverde, 1962)

――――― *Aspetti della vita religiosa, politica e letteraria del Cinquecento* (Bologna: Tamari Editori, 1963)

Oberman, Heiko, et al. (eds), *Das Reformierte Erbe: Festschrift für Gottfried W. Locher*, 2 vols (Zurich: Theologischer Verlag, 1992)

Olivieri, Achille, 'Alessandro Trissino e il movimento calvinista vicentino del Cinquecento', *Rivista di storia della Chiesa in Italia*, 21 (1967), pp. 54–117

――――― 'Il "Catechismo" e la "Fidei et doctrinae … ratio" di Bartolomeo Fonzio, eretico veneziano del Cinquecento', *Studi veneziani*, 9 (1967), pp. 339–452

――――― *Riforma ed eresia a Vicenza nel Cinquecento* (Rome: Herder Editrice e libreria, 1992)

O' Malley, Charles Donald, *Jacopo Aconcio* (Rome: Edizioni di storia e letteratura, 1955)

Palazzi Trivelli, Francesco, 'Riformati, cattolici, reti, valtellini: baruffe in Sondrio a cavallo tra Cinque e Seicento', *Bollettino della società storica valtellinese*, 44 (1991), pp. 133–58

Pascal, Arturo, 'La colonia piemontese a Ginevra nel secolo XVI', in Cantimori, *Ginevra e l'Italia*, pp. 65–133

Pastore, Alessandro, *Nella Valtellina del tardo Cinquecento: fede, cultura, società* (Milan: SugarCo Edizioni, 1975)

——— (ed.), *Riforma e società nei Grigioni: Valtellina e Valchiavenna tra '500 e '600* (Milan: FrancoAngeli, 1991)

——— 'Domanda e offerta di cambiamento religioso in un'area di frontiera: la Valtellina fra Cinquecento e Seicento', *Archivio storico ticinese*, 115 (1994), pp. 17–28

——— 'Dalla notte di San Bartolomeo (1572) al Sacro macello di Valtellina (1620): forme e obiettive della violenza religiosa', *BSSV*, 178 (1995), pp. 141–59

Peer, Florian, *L'église de Rhétie au XVIme et XVIIme siècles* (Geneva: Imprimerie Rivera et Dubois, 1888)

Perini, Leandro, 'Note e documenti su Pietro Perna libraio-tipografo a Basilea', *NRS*, 50 (1966), pp. 145–200

——— 'Ancora sul libraio-tipografo Pietro Perna e su alcune figure di eretici italiani in rapporto con lui negli anni 1549–1555', *NRS*, 51 (1967), pp. 363–404

——— 'Gli eretici italiani del '500 e Machiavelli', *Studi storici*, 4 (1969), pp. 877–915

——— 'Note sulla famiglia di Pietro Perna e sul suo apprendistato tipografico', in Lech Szczucki (ed.), *Magia, Astrologia e religione nel Rinascimento* (Warsaw: Wydawnictwo Polskiej Akademii Nauk, 1974), pp. 163–209

——— 'Amoenitates Typographicae', in Rota Ghibaudi and Barcia, *Studi politici*, I, pp. 873–971

Pestalozzi Keyser, Hans, *Geschichte der Familie Pestalozzi* (Zurich: NZZ, 1958)

Pettegree, Andrew, *Foreign Protestant Communities in Sixteenth-Century London* (Oxford: Clarendon Press, 1986)

——— '"Thirty years on": progress towards integration amongst the immigrant population of Elizabethan London', in John Chartres and David Hey (eds), *English Rural Society, 1500–1800* (Cambridge: Cambridge University Press, 1990), pp. 297–312

Peyer, Hans Conrad, *Vom Handel und Bank im alten Zürich* (Zurich: Verlag Berichthaus, 1968)

Peyronel Rambaldi, Susanna, *Speranze e crisi nel Cinquecento modenese: Tensioni religiose e vita cittadina ai tempi di Giovanni Morone* (Milan: FrancoAngeli, 1979)

——— *Dai Paesi Bassi all'Italia: 'Il sommario della sacra scrittura': Un libro proibito nella società italiana del Cinquecento* (Florence: Olschki, 1997)

Pfister, Alexander, *Jörg Jenatsch: Sein Leben und seine Zeit*, 5th edn (Chur: Verlag Bündner Monatsblatt, 1991)

Pfister, Rudolf, *Die Seligkeit erwählter Heiden bei Zwingli: Eine*

Untersuchung zu seiner Theologie (Zollikon-Zurich: Evangelischer Verlag, 1952)

―――― *Um des Glaubens Willen: Die evangelischen Flüchtlinge von Locarno und ihre Aufnahme zu Zurich im Jahre 1555* (Zollikon-Zurich: Evangelischer Verlag AG., 1955)

―――― 'Die Reformationsgemeinde Locarno, 1540–1555', *Zwa* 10/3 (1955/1), pp. 161–81

―――― 'Reformation, Türken und Islam', *Zwa* 10/6 (1956/2), pp. 345–75

Pfister, Ulrich, *Die Zürcher Fabriques: Protoindustrielles Wachstum vom 16. zum 18. Jahrhundert* (Zurich: Chronos Verlag, 1992)

―――― 'Reformierte Sittenzucht zwischen kommunaler und territorialer Organisation; Graubünden, 16.–18. Jahrhundert', *ARG*, 87 (1996), pp. 287–333

Picot, Jacques, 'La famiglia di Scipione Lentolo', *BSSV*, 100 (1956), pp. 66–7

Pierce, Robert Archer, 'Agostino Mainardi, Pier Paolo Vergerio, and the *Anatomia Missae*', *BHR*, 55 (1993), pp. 25–42

Pirnát, Antal, *Die Ideologie der Siebenbürger Antitrinitarier in den 1570er Jahren* (Budapest: Akadémiai Kiadó, 1961)

―――― 'L'Italia e gli antitrinitari transilvani', in Vittore Branca (ed.), *Venezia e Ungheria nel Rinascimento* (Florence: Olschki, 1973), pp. 429–47

―――― 'Per una nuova interpretazione dell'attività di Giorgio Biandrata', in Klaniczay, *Rapporti veneto-ungheresi*, pp. 361–71

Plath, Uwe, *Calvin und Basel in den Jahren 1552–1556* (Zurich: Theologischer Verlag, 1974)

―――― 'Der Streit um C.S. Curiones "De amplitudine beati regni Dei" im Jahre 1554 in Basel', in *Eresia e Riforma*, pp. 271–81

―――― 'Sebastiani Castellionis annotationes ad Johannis Calvini Institutiones Christianae Religionis anno 1553 excusas', *BHR*, 37 (1975), pp. 87–98

Pollet, J.V., *Martin Bucer: Etudes sur la correspondance avec de nombreux textes inédits* (Paris: Presses universitaires de France, 1958/62)

Potter, G.R., 'The Renaissance in Switzerland', *Journal of Medieval History*, 2 (1976), pp. 365–82

'Predicanti italiani in Valtellina e nei Grigioni', *Archivio storico lombardo*, 29 (1902), pp. 469–70

Prosperi, Adriano, 'Un gruppo-ereticale italo-spagnolo: La setta di Giorgio Siculo (secondo nuovi documenti)', *Critica Storica*, 19 (1982), pp. 335–51

Rageth, Simon and Oskar Vasella, 'Die Autobiographie des Täufers Georg Frell von Chur', *Zwa* 7/7 (1942/1), pp. 444–69

Ricca, Paolo, 'Zwingli tra i Valdesi', *Zwa* 16/3 (1984/1), pp. 247–63

Rosius de Porta, Petrus Dominicus, *Dissertatio Historico Ecclesiastica qua ecclesiarum colloquio vallis Praegalliae et comitatus Clavennae olim comprehensarum reformatio et status, ex documentis authenticis maximam partem anecdotis exponitur* (Chur: Jakob Otto, 1787)

———— *Historia Reformationis ecclesiarum Raeticarum*, 2 vols in 4 pts (Chur / Chur and Lindau, 1771/77)

Rossi, Paolo, *Giacomo Aconcio* (Milan: Fratelli Bocca Editori, 1952)

Rota Ghibaudi, Silvia, and Franco Barcia (eds), *Studi politici in onore di Luigi Firpo*, 2 vols (Milan: FrancoAngeli, 1990)

Rotondò, Antonio, 'Per la storia dell'eresia a Bologna nel secolo XVI', *Rinascimento*, 13 (1962), pp. 107–54

———— 'I movimenti ereticali nell'Europa del Cinquecento', *RSI*, 68 (1966), pp. 103–39, republished in Rotondò, *Studi e ricerche*, pp. 5–56

———— 'Atteggiamenti della vita morale italiana del Cinquecento: La pratica Nicodemitica', *RSI*, 79 (1967), pp. 991–1030

———— 'Calvino e gli antitrinitari italiani', *RSI*, 80 (1968), pp. 759–84, republished in Rotondò, *Studi e ricerche*, pp. 57–86

———— *Studi e ricerche di storia ereticale italiana del Cinquecento 1* (Turin: Edizioni Giappichelli, 1974)

———— 'Sulla diffusione clandestina delle dottrine di Lelio Sozzini 1560–1568 (Risposta a Jerome Friedman)', in Rotondò, *Studi e ricerche*, pp. 87–116

———— 'Pietro Perna e la vita culturale e religiosa di Basilea fra il 1570 e il 1580', in Rotondò, *Studi e ricerche*, pp. 273–391

———— 'Esuli italiani in Valtellina nel Cinquecento', *RSI*, 88 (1976), pp. 756–91

———— (ed.), *Forme e destinazione del messaggio religioso: Aspetti della propaganda religiosa nel Cinquecento* (Florence: Olschki, 1991)

———— 'Anticristo e Chiesa romana: Diffusione e metamorfosi d'un libello antiromano del Cinquecento', in Rotondò, *Forme e destinazione*, pp. 19–164

Rozzo, Ugo, 'Sugli scritti di Giulio da Milano', *BSSV*, 134 (1973), pp. 69–85

———— 'Nuovi contributi su Bernardino Ochino', *BSSV*, 146 (1979), pp. 51–83

———— 'L'"Esortazione al martirio" di Giulio da Milano', in Pastore, *Riforma e società*, pp. 63–88

—— 'Editori e tipografi italiani operanti all'estero "religionis causa"', in M. Santoro (ed.), *La stampa in Italia nel Cinquecento* (Rome: Bulzoni Editore, 1992), pp. 89–118

—— 'Edizioni protestanti di Poschiavo alla metà del Cinquecento (e qualche aggiunta ginevrina)', in Campi and La Torre, *Il protestantesimo*, pp. 17–46

—— (ed.), *Pier Paolo Vergerio il Giovane, un polemista attraverso l'Europa del Cinquecento* (Udine: Forum, 2000)

—— and Silvana Seidel Menchi, 'The book and the Reformation in Italy', in Gilmont, *The Reformation and the Book*, pp. 319–67

Rüetschi, Kurt, 'Rudolf Gwalthers Kontakte zu Engländern und Schotten', in Schindler and Stickelberger, *Zürcher Reformation*, pp. 351–73

—— 'Gwalther, Wolf und Simler als Herausgeber von Vermigli Werken', in Campi, *Peter Martyr Vermigli*, pp. 251–74

Ruffini, Francesco, 'Francesco Stancaro: contributo alla storia della Riforma in Italia', in Ruffini, *Studi sui riformatori italiani* (Turin: Edizioni Ramella, 1955), pp. 165–406

Sanders, Paul, 'Heinrich Bullinger et le "zwinglianisme tardif" aux lendemains du "Consensus Tigurinus"', in Oberman, *Das Reformierte Erbe*, I, pp. 307–23

Schelhorn, Johann Georg, *Ergötzlichkeiten aus der Kirchenhistorie und Literatur*, 3 vols (Ulm and Leipzig: Bartholomäische Handlung, 1764)

Schiess, Traugott, 'Bullingers Beziehungen zur Familie Salis', *Zürcher Taschenbuch* (1901), pp. 116–53

—— (ed.), *Rhetia: Eine Dichtung aus dem sechzehnten Jahrhundert von Franciscus Niger aus Bassano* (Chur: Manatschal Ebner, 1897)

—— 'Die Beziehungen Graubündens zur Eidgenossenschaft, besonders zu Zürich, im XVI. Jahrhundert', *Jahrbuch für Schweizerische Geschichte*, 27 (1902), pp. 29–183

—— 'Josias Simler und sein Schüler Johann Baptist Müller von Vicosoprano', *Zürcher Taschenbuch* (1903), pp. 223–53

—— 'Briefe aus der Fremde von einem Zürcher Studenten der Medizin (Dr. Georg Keller)', *Neujahrsblatt herausgegeben von der Stadtbibliothek Zürich*, 262 (1906), pp. 1–38

Schilling, Heinz, *Niederländische Exulanten im 16. Jahrhundert: Ihre Stellung im Sozialgefüge und im religiösen Leben deutscher und englischer Städte* (Gütersloh: Verlagshaus Gerd Mohn, 1972)

Schindler, Alfred, 'Zwinglis Randbemerkungen in den Büchern seiner Bibliothek: Ein Zwischenbericht über editorische Probleme', *Zwa*, 18/1 (1989/1), pp. 1–11

────── 'Huldrych Zwingli e Giovanni Pico della Mirandola', in *Dall'accademia neoplatonica fiorentina alla Riforma: Celebrazione del V centenario della morte di Lorenzo il Magnifico* (Florence: Olschki, 1996), pp. 51–65

────── and Hans Stickelberger (eds), *Die Zürcher Reformation: Ausstrahlungen und Rückwirkungen* (Berne: Peter Lang, 2001)

Schmidlin, Guido, 'Giordano Bruno im Kreis der Zürcher Alchemisten und Paracelsisten', *Nova acta paracelsica*, 8 (1994), pp. 57–86

Schmidt, C., *Peter Martyr Vermigli: Leben und ausgewählte Schriften* (Elberfeld: Verlag von R.L. Friderichs, 1858)

Schnyder, Werner, *Aus der Geschichte des Zürcher Seidenhandels* (Zurich: Buchdruckerei a.d. Sihl AG, 1944)

────── *Handel und Verkehr über die Bündner Pässe im Mittelalter zwischen Deutschland, der Schweiz und Oberitalien*, 2 vols (Zurich: Schulthess Polygraphischer Verlag, 1973/5)

Schucan, Luzi, 'Der Brief Antonio Besozzis an Theodor Zwinger I: Ein Nachtrag', *Basler Zeitschrift für Geschichte und Altertumskunde*, 72 (1972), pp. 319–22

Schulthess, Hans, *Die von Orelli von Locarno und Zürich: Ihre Geschichte und Genealogie* (Zurich: Schulthess & Co., 1941)

────── *Bilder aus der Vergangenheit der Familie von Muralt in Zürich* (Zurich: Buchdruckerei Schulthess & Co. AG, 1944)

Schultheß, Konrad, 'Glaubensflüchtlinge aus Chiavenna und dem Veltlin in Zürcher Kirchenbüchern 1620–1700', *Der Schweizer Familienforscher*, 36 (1969), pp. 1–38

Schutte, Anne Jacobson, 'Periodization of Sixteenth-Century Italian Religious History: The Post-Cantimori Paradigm Shift', *Journal of Modern History*, 61 (1989), pp. 269–84

Schwarz, Brigitte, 'Ferdinand Meyer e la Riforma a Locarno', *BSSV*, 178 (1995), pp. 172–81

────── 'La diffusione della Riforma nei baliaggi italiani dei cantoni svizzeri nel Cinquecento', in Campi and La Torre, *Il protestantesimo*, pp. 53–66

Segesvary, Victor, *L'Islam et la Réforme: Etude sur l'attitude des réformateurs zurichois envers l'Islam (1510–1550)* (Lausanne: Editions l'Age d'Homme S.A., 1978)

Seidel Menchi, Silvana, 'Le traduzioni italiane di Lutero nella prima metà del Cinquecento', *Rinascimento*, 17 (1977), pp. 31–108

────── *Erasmo in Italia: 1520–1580* (Turin: Bollati Boringhieri Editore, 1987)

────── 'Les relations de Martin Bucer avec l'Italie', in Christian Krieger and Marc Lienhard (eds), *Martin Bucer and Sixteenth-Century Europe*, 2 vols (Leiden: Brill, 1993), pp. 557–69

—— *Erasmus als Ketzer: Reformation und Inquisition im Italien des 16. Jahrhunderts* (Leiden: E.J. Brill, 1993)

—— 'Chi fu Ortensio Lando?', *RSI*, 106 (1994), pp. 501–64

Serrai, Alfredo, *Conrad Gesner* (Rome: Bulzoni Editore, 1990)

Sieber, Marc, *Die Universität Basel und die Eidgenossenschaft 1460 bis 1529* (Basle: Verlag von Helbing & Lichtenhahn, 1960)

Simoncelli, Paolo, 'Inquisizione romana e Riforma in Italia', *RSI*, 100 (1988), pp. 5–125

Spicer, Andrew, 'Poor relief and the exile communities', in Beat Kümin (ed.), *Reformations Old and New: Essays in the Socio-Economic Impact of Religious Change c.1470–1630* (Aldershot: Scolar Press, 1996), pp. 237–55

—— *The French-speaking Reformed Community and their Church in Southampton, 1567–c.1620* (Stroud: Sutton Publishing, 1997)

Staedtke, Joachim, 'Der Zürcher Prädestinationsstreit von 1560', *Zwa* 9/10 (1953/2), pp. 536–46

—— 'Das Glaubensbekenntnis der christlichen Gemeinde zu Locarno vom 9. Juli 1554', *Zwa* 10/3 (1955/1), pp. 181–93

—— *Die Theologie des jungen Bullinger* (Zurich: Zwingli Verlag, 1962)

—— 'Drei umstrittene Traktate Peter Martyr Vermiglis', *Zwa* 11/8 (1962/2), pp. 553–4

—— (ed.), *Glauben und Bekennen: Vierhundert Jahre Confessio Helvetica Posterior: Beiträge zu ihrer Geschichte und Theologie* (Zurich: Zwingli Verlag, 1966)

Steinmetz, David, *Calvin in Context* (Oxford: Oxford University Press, 1995)

Stelling-Michaud, Sven, 'La Suisse et les universités européennes du 13ème au 16ème siècle: Essai d'une statistique de fréquentation', *Revue universitaire suisse* (September 1938), pp. 148–60

Stella, Aldo, 'Utopie e velleità insurrezionali dei filoprotestanti italiani (1545–1547)', *BHR*, 27 (1965), pp. 133–82

—— *Dall'anabattismo al socinianesimo nel Cinquecento veneto: Ricerche storiche* (Padua: Liviana Editrice, 1967)

—— *Anabattismo e antitrinitarismo in Italia nel XVI secolo: Nuove ricerche storiche* (Padua: Liviana Editrice, 1969)

Stephens, W.P., *The Theology of Huldrych Zwingli* (Oxford: Clarendon Press, 1986)

Stucki, Heinzpeter, '"Ergo legitima decernitur": Ein komplizierter Fall vor dem Zürcher Ehegericht, 1534', in Oberman et al. (eds), *Das Reformierte Erbe*, I, pp. 419–26

Subilia, Vittorio, 'Libertà e dogma secondo Calvino e secondo i riformatori italiani', in Cantimori, *Ginevra e l'Italia*, pp. 191–214

Szczucki, Lech, 'La prima edizione dell' "Explicatio" di Fausto Sozzini', *Rinascimento*, 7 (1967), pp. 319–27

Tedeschi, John (ed.), *Italian Reformation Studies in Honor of Laelius Socinus* (Florence: Le Monnier, 1965)

——— 'The Cultural Contributions of Italian Protestant Reformers in the Late Renaissance', *Schifanoia*, 1 (1986), pp. 127–51

——— 'Northern Books and Counter-Reformation Italy', in Tedeschi, *The Prosecution of Heresy: Collected Studies on the Inquisition in Early Modern Italy* (Binghampton, NY: Medieval and Renaissance Texts and Studies, 1991), pp. 335–53

Trechsel, F., *Die Protestantischen Antitrinitarier vor Faustus Socin*, 2 vols (Heidelberg: Universitätsbuchhandlung von Karl Winter, 1839/44)

Truog, Jakob Rudolf, *Die Bündner Prädikanten 1555–1901 nach den Matrikelbüchern der Synode* (Chur: Buchdruckerei Sprecher und Valer, 1902)

——— 'Aus der Geschichte der evangelischen Gemeinden in den bündnerischen Untertanenlanden: Ein Beitrag zur bündnerischen Synodalgeschichte', *BM* (1935), pp. 236–48; 257–85; 311–18

——— *Die Pfarrer der evangelischen Gemeinden in Graubünden und seinen ehemaligen Untertanenlanden* (Chur: Druck von Sprecher, Eggerling & Co., [1935])

——— 'Die Pfarrer der evangelischen Gemeinden in Graubünden und seinen ehemaligen Untertanenlanden (Ergänzungen und Berichtigungen)', *JHGG*, 75 (1945), pp. 113–47

——— *Aus der Geschichte der evangelisch-rätischen Synode 1537–1937* (Chur: Manatschal Ebner & Cie. AG, 1937)

——— 'Das Religionsgespräch von Plurs 1597', *Zwa* 9/5 (1951/1), pp. 317–23

Tylenda, Joseph N., 'Christ the Mediator: Calvin versus Stancaro', *CTJ*, 8 (1973), pp. 5–16

——— 'The Controversy on Christ the Mediator: Calvin's Second Reply to Stancaro', *CTJ*, 8 (1973), pp. 131–57

——— 'The Warning that Went Unheeded: John Calvin on Giorgio Biandrata', *CTJ*, 12 (1977), pp. 24–62

Urban, Wacław, *Der Antitrinitarismus in den Böhmischen Ländern und in der Slowakei im 16. und im 17. Jahrhundert* (Baden-Baden: Editions Valentin Koerner, 1986)

Vehlour, Katya, 'The Swiss Reformers Zwingli, Bullinger and Bibliander and their Attitude to Islam (1520–1560)', *Islam and Christian-Muslim Relations*, 6 (1995), pp. 229–54

Venema, Cornelis P., 'Heinrich Bullinger's Correspondence on

Calvin's Doctrine of Predestination 1551–1553', *SCJ*, 17 (1986), pp. 435–50

Vischer, Lukas, 'Girolamo Zanchi, reformierter Prediger in Chiavenna', *BM* (1951), pp. 289–301

—— 'Friedrich von Salis', *BM* (1952), pp. 329–57

—— 'Eine italienische Abhandlung über den "Antichristen" von Scipio Lentulus', *Zwa* 9/8 (1952/2), pp. 483–6

—— 'Die Abendmahlsschwierigkeiten in Chiavenna', *BM* (1956), pp. 268–78

—— 'Michelangelo Florio tra Italia, Inghilterra e Val Bregaglia', in Campi and La Torre, *Il protestantesimo*, pp. 77–88

Walder, Ernst, 'Pier Paolo Vergerio und das Veltlin 1550', *Schweizer Beiträge zur allgemeinen Geschichte*, 3 (1945), pp. 229–46

—— *Der Condottiere Walter Roll von Uri und die Beziehungen zwischen der Innerschweiz und Italien in der Wende zur Gegenreformation 1551–1561* (Berne: Buchdruckerei H. Möschler, 1948)

Walser, Peter, *Die Prädestination bei Heinrich Bullinger im Zusammenhang mit seiner Gotteslehre* (Zurich: Zwingli-Verlag, 1957)

Weisz, Leo, 'Johann von Muralt, der siebenbürgische Hofarzt', *Neue Zürcher Zeitung* (14, 15 and 16 August 1929)

—— 'Bernardino Ochino in Zürich', *Neue Zürcher Zeitung* (14 and 15 March 1935)

—— *Die Zürcherische Exportindustrie: Ihre Entstehung und Entwicklung*, 2nd edn (Zurich: Verlag der NZZ, 1937)

—— *Die Werdmüller: Schicksale eines alten Zürcher Geschlechtes*, 3 vols (Zurich: Schultheß & Co. AG, 1949)

—— 'Ein Lehrgedicht über die Locarner aus dem Jahre 1592', *Zwa*, 10/3 (1955/1), pp. 193–8

—— 'Die wirtschaftliche Bedeutung der Tessiner Glaubensflüchtlinge für die deutsche Schweiz', *Zwa* 10/4 (1955/2), pp. 228–48; *Zwa* 10/5 (1956/1), pp. 297–339; *Zwa* 10/6 (1956/2), pp. 376–98; *Zwa* 10/7 (1957/1), pp. 428–66; *Zwa* 10/8 (1957/2), pp. 506–36

Welti, Manfred E., 'Le grand animateur de la Renaissance tardive à Bâle: Pierre Perna, éditeur, imprimeur et libraire', in *L'Humanisme Allemand (1480–1540): XVIIIe Colloque international de Tours* (Munich and Paris: Fink Verlag and Librairie J. Vrin, 1979), pp. 131–9

—— *Kleine Geschichte der italienischen Reformation* (Gütersloh: Verlagshaus Gerd Mohn, 1985)

—— 'Per le relazioni editoriali fra Francesco Betti e Pietro Perna', *La Bibliofilia*, 89 (1987), pp. 203–5

Wendland, Andreas, 'Republik und "Untertanenlande" vor dem Veltlineraufstand (1620)', *BM* (1990), pp. 182–213

——— *Der Nutzen der Pässe und die Gefährdung der Seelen: Spanien, Mailand und der Kampf ums Veltlin (1620–1641)* (Zurich: Chronos-Verlag, 1995)

Wenneker, Erich, 'Heinrich Bullinger und der Gantnerhandel in Chur (1570–1574)', *Zwa*, 24 (1997), pp. 95–115

Wielich, Gotthard, *Das Locarnese im Altertum und Mittelalter: Ein Beitrag zur Geschichte des Kantons Tessin* (Berne: Francke Verlag, 1970)

Wilbur, Earl Morse, *A History of Unitarianism: I. Socinianism and its Antecedents* (Cambridge, Mass.: Harvard University Press, 1946)

Williams, George Huntston, 'Camillo Renato (c.1500–?1575)', in Tedeschi, *Italian Reformation Studies*, pp. 103–83

——— 'The Polish-Lithuanian Calvin during the "Superintendency" of John Laski, 1556–60', in B.A. Gerrish and Robert Benedetto (eds), *Reformatio Perennis: Essays on Calvin and the Reformation in honour of Ford Lewis Battles* (Pittsburgh: The Pickwick Press, 1981), pp. 129–58

——— 'Strains in the Christology of the Emerging Polish Brethren', in Samuel Fiszman (ed.), *The Polish Reformation in its European Context* (Bloomington: Indiana University Press, 1984), pp. 61–95

——— *The Radical Reformation*, 3rd edn (Kirksville, Missouri: Sixteenth Century Journal Publishers, 1992)

Willis, David, 'The Influence of Laelius Socinus on Calvin's Doctrines of the Merits of Christ and the Assurance of Faith', in Tedeschi, *Italian Reformation Studies*, pp. 231–41

Wotschke, Theodor, 'Christoph Thretius: Ein Beitrag zur Geschichte des Kampfes der reformierten Kirche gegen den Antitrinitarismus in Polen', *Altpreussische Monatsschrift* NF, 44 (1907), pp. 1–42; 151–210

——— *Geschichte der Reformation in Polen* (Leipzig: Verein für Reformationsgeschichte durch Rudolf Haupt, 1911)

Wyss, G. von, 'Josias Simler', *XVII Neujahrsblatt zum Besten des Waisenhauses in Zürich* (1855), pp. 1–24

Yates, Frances, *John Florio: The Life of an Italian in Shakespeare's England* (Cambridge: Cambridge University Press, 1934)

Zahnd, Urs Martin, 'Lateinschule-Universität-Prophezey: Zu den Wandlungen im Schulwesen eidgenössischer Städte in der ersten Hälfte des 16. Jahrhunderts', in Harald Dickerhof (ed.), *Bildungs- und schulgeschichtliche Studien zu Spätmittelalter, Reformation und konfessionellem Zeitalter* (Wiesbaden: Dr. Ludwig Reichert Verlag, 1994), pp. 91–115

Zimmermann, Georg Rudolf, *Die Zürcher Kirche von der Reformation bis zum dritten Reformationsjubiläum (1519–1819) nach der Reihenfolge der Zürcherischen Antistes* (Zurich: S. Höhr, 1878)

Zucchini, Giampaolo, 'Contributi agli studi sulla giovinezza di Fausto Sozzini', *BSSV*, 130 (1971), pp. 35–41

—— 'Di una lettera inedita di Nicolò Camogli (1581)', *BSSV*, 137 (1975), pp. 15–20

—— *Riforma e società nei Grigioni: G. Zanchi, S. Fiorillo, S. Lentulo e i conflitti dottrinari e socio-politici a Chiavenna (1563–1567)* (Chur: Archivio di Stato/Biblioteca Cantonale dei Grigioni, 1978)

—— 'Francesco Negri a Chiavenna e in Polonia', *Clavenna*, 17 (1978), pp. 16–23

—— 'Notizie zu Bartolomeo Silvio nei Grigioni', *Clavenna*, 19 (1980), pp. 61–9

—— 'Per la ricostruzione dell'epistolario di Marcello Squarcialupi: alcune lettere inedite dai Grigioni (1586–1588)', in Robert Dán and Antal Pirnát (eds), *Antitrinitarianism in the Second Half of the Sixteenth Century* (Budapest and Leiden: Akadémiai Kiadó and E.J. Brill, 1982), pp. 323–40

—— '"In coërcendis haereticis": L'esilio di Scipione Lentolo in Svizzera e il suo inedito epistolario (1567–1599)', in Rota Ghibaudi and Barcia, *Studi politici*, I, pp. 525–42

—— 'Scipione Lentolo pastore a Chiavenna: Notizie dal suo inedito epistolario (1567–1599)', in Pastore, *Riforma e società*, pp. 109–27

Zürcher, Christoph, *Konrad Pellikans Wirken in Zürich 1526–1556* (Zurich: Theologischer Verlag, 1975)

Works of Reference

Allgemeine deutsche Biographie, 56 vols (Leipzig, 1875–1912)

Ammann, Hektor and Karl Schieb, *Historischer Atlas der Schweiz*, 2nd edn (Aarau: Verlag H.R. Sauerländer and Co., 1958)

Bautz, Friedrich Wilhelm (ed.), *Biographisch-bibliographisches Kirchenlexikon* (Hamm: Verlag Traugott Bautz, 1970–)

Cross, F.L. and E.A. Livingstone (eds), *The Oxford Dictionary of the Christian Church*, 2nd edn (Oxford: Oxford University Press, 1974)

Dejung, Emanuel, and Willy Wuhrmann (eds), *Zürcher Pfarrerbuch 1519–1952* (Zurich: Kommissionsverlag Schulthess & Co. AG, 1953)

Dizionario biografico degli italiani (Rome: Istituto della Enciclopedia italiana, 1960–)

Donnelly, John Patrick, and Robert M. Kingdon (eds), *A Bibliography of the Works of Peter Martyr Vermigli* (Kirksville, Mo.: Sixteenth Century Journal Publishers, 1990)

Dünki, Robert, *Pfarrbücher, Bürgerbücher und Genealogische Verzeichnisse im Stadtarchiv Zürich* (Zurich: Stadtarchiv Zürich, 1995)

Gagliardi, Ernst and Ludwig Förrer, *Katalog der Handschriften der Zentralbibliothek Zürich II: Neuere Handschriften seit 1500*, 5 vols (Zurich: Buchdruckerei Berichthaus, 1931–82)

Geisendorf, Paul-F., *Livre des habitants de Genève*, 2 vols (Geneva: Droz, 1957/63)

Historisch-biographisches Lexikon der Schweiz, 7 vols (Neuchâtel: Administration des historisch-biographischen Lexikons der Schweiz, 1921–34)

Jenny, Rudolf, *Staatsarchiv Graubünden: Gesamtarchivplan und Archivbücher-Inventare des Dreibündearchivs, des Helvetischen und des Kantonalarchivs* (Chur: Buch- und Offsetdruckerei Bündner Tagblatt AG, 1961)

—— *Handschriften aus Privatbesitz im Staatsarchiv Graubünden: Repertorium mit Regesten* (Chur: Calven-Verlag, 1974)

Kristeller, Paul Oskar, *Iter Italicum: A Finding List of Uncatalogued or Incompletely Catalogued Humanistic Manuscripts of the Renaissance in Italian and Other Libraries* (London and Leiden: The Warburg Institute and E.J. Brill, 1963–)

Leu, Hans Jacob, *Allgemeines Helvetisches / Eydgnößisches / Oder Schweizerisches Lexikon*, 20 vols (Zurich: Hans Ulrich Denzler, 1747–65)

Pollard, A.W., G.R. Redgrave et al. (eds), *A Short-Title Catalogue of Books printed in England, Scotland, and Ireland and of English Books printed abroad 1475–1640*, 3 vols (London: The Bibliographical Society, 1976–91)

Staedtke, Joachim, *Heinrich Bullinger Bibliographie: Beschreibendes Verzeichnis der gedruckten Werke von Heinrich Bullinger* (Zurich: Theologischer Verlag, 1972)

Stelling-Michaud, Sven (ed.), *Le livre du recteur de l'Académie de Genève (1559–1878)*, 6 vols (Geneva: Librairie E. Droz, 1959–80)

Tedeschi, John, *The Italian Reformation of the Sixteenth Century and the Diffusion of Renaissance Culture: A Bibliography of the Secondary Literature (Ca. 1750–1997)* (Ferrara and Modena: Istituto di Studi Rinascimentali and Franco Cosimo Panini Editore, 2000)

Theologische Realenzyklopädie (Berlin and New York: Walter de Gruyter, 1977–)

Verzeichnis der im deutschen Sprachbereich erschienenen Drucke des XVI. Jahrhunderts, 24 vols (Stuttgart: Anton Hiersemann, 1983–97)

Vischer, Manfred, *Bibliographie der Zürcher Druckschriften des 15. und 16. Jahrhunderts* (Baden-Baden: Verlag Valentin Koerner, 1991)

Wackernagel, Hans Georg, Marc Sieber and Hans Sutter (eds), *Die Matrikel der Universität Basel*, 3 vols (Basle: Verlag der Universitätsbibliothek, 1956)

Dissertations

Conradt, Nancy Marilyn, 'Jean Calvin, Theodore Beza and the Reformation in Poland' (unpublished doctoral dissertation, University of Wisconsin, 1974)

Dalbert, Peter, 'Bullinger und die Romanen italienischer Zunge' (unpublished thesis, University of Zurich, 1943)

Fiume, Emanuele, 'La vita e il pensiero teologico di Girolamo Zanchi e il "De religione christiana fides"' (unpublished thesis, Facoltà valdese di teologia, Rome, 1995–96)

Pierce, Robert Archer, 'Pier Paolo Vergerio the Propagandist' (unpublished doctoral dissertation, University of Virginia, 1996)

Riva, Nilde, 'Chiesa di Zurigo ed eretici italiani in Valtellina e in Valchiavenna (1542–1557): Il carteggio di C. Renato, A. Mainardi, F. Negri con Enrico Bullinger' (unpublished thesis, Università cattolica del sacro cuore, Milan, 1969–70)

Rivoir, Eugenio, 'La chiesa riformata di Chiavenna' (unpublished thesis, Facoltà valdese di teologia, Rome, 1964)

Sanders, Paul, 'Henri Bullinger et l'invention (1546–1551) avec Jean Calvin d'une théologie réformée de la cène: La gestion de l'héritage zwinglien lors de l'élaboration du "Consensus Tigurinus"(1549) et de la rédaction des "Decades" (1551)' (unpublished doctoral thesis, University of Lille, 1989)

Taplin, Mark, 'Bernardino Ochino and the Zurich Polygamy Controversy of 1563' (unpublished M.Litt thesis, University of St Andrews, 1995)

—— 'The Italian Reformers and the Zurich Church, c.1540–1620' (unpublished doctoral dissertation, University of St Andrews, 1999)

Valbusa, G. Pietro, 'Epistolario latino inedito di Scipione Lentulo' (unpublished thesis, Università degli Studi, Padua, 1972–73)

Walt, Hansueli, 'Der "Catechismo" von Bernardino Ochino: Eine Untersuchung zu dessen Herkunft, Stellung und Theologie'

(unpublished thesis, University of Zürich, 1996)

Williams, Glen Garfield, 'The Theology of Bernardino Ochino' (unpublished doctoral thesis, University of Tübingen, 1955)

Index